Native Listening

Native Listening

Language Experience and the Recognition of Spoken Words

Anne Cutler

The MIT Press
Cambridge, Massachusetts
London, England

MIT Press books may be purchased at special quantity discounts for business or sales promotional use. For information, please email special_sales@mitpress.mit.edu or write to Special Sales Department, The MIT Press, 55 Hayward Street, Cambridge, MA 02142.

This book was set in Times Roman by Toppan Best-set Premedia Limited. Printed and bound in the United States of America.

Library of Congress Cataloging-in-Publication Data

Cutler, Anne.
Native listening : language experience and the recognition of spoken words / Anne Cutler.
p. cm.
Includes bibliographical references and index.
ISBN 978-0-262-01756-5 (alk. paper)
1. Speech perception. 2. Listening. 3. Language and languages—Variation. 4. Speech processing systems. 5. Linguistic models. I. Title.
P37.5.S68C88 2012
401′.95—dc23
2011045431

10 9 8 7 6 5 4 3 2 1

To all those who made it possible, with a special salutation to those among them who are no longer here to read it, and foremost among the latter Betty O'Loghlen Cutler (1915–1994) and C. Ian Cutler (1920–2005), who involuntarily provided me with the cortical wherewithal to support a career in speech perception research (see chapter 8) and deliberately provided me with the confidence to pursue it.

Contents

Preface

Readers who reviewed my manuscript remarked that in some ways it is "personal." This is fair; the book recounts the development of psycholinguistic knowledge about how spoken words are recognized over the nearly four decades that this topic has been researched, and that makes it a personal story in that those decades are the ones I have spent as a psycholinguist. Inevitably (it seems to me), the book has turned out to center on my own work and that of the many colleagues and graduate students with whom I have been lucky enough to work, because whenever I wanted an example to illustrate a particular line of research, the rich archive of this long list of collaborations usually turned one up.

Most psycholinguists enter the field via linguistics or via psychology, rarely from a combination of the two. Although my background has more psychology in it than linguistics, it does have both. I trained as a language teacher and was at one time apparently set for an academic career teaching German in Australian universities, until I decided to abandon that and do a Ph.D. in psychology instead. What I took with me from the former line of work to the latter was suspicion as to whether conclusions drawn about one language could be expected to hold for another. This was reinforced by the choice of a dissertation topic in prosody, where language-specificity in structure is blindingly obvious. Some parts of this book's text are more narrative or more personal than others, and from those bits some more of the interplay of career and research choices can perhaps be gleaned. The central thread through the entire book, however, is the issue that has occupied me since soon after I came into psycholinguistics—namely, what is universal and what is language specific in the way we listen to spoken language.

This central thread delivered the book's title: listening to speech is a process of native listening because so much of it is exquisitely tailored to the requirements of the native language. The subtitle conveys the additional message that the story effectively stops at the point where listeners recognize words. How is it possible to fill a fat book with research on the perception of spoken language and only get the story as far as words? Partly this is because there has been explosive growth over recent years in our knowledge of how spoken-word recognition happens, but mainly it is because the spoken-word recognition story so beautifully forms a theater in which the whole story of language-specificity in listening plays out.

There is a tendency in all science for the majority of research, and certainly for the majority of highly cited research, to come from countries where English is the local language. In many branches of science this has no further consequences for the science itself, but in psycholinguistics it can have far-reaching implications for the research program and for the development of theory. As chapter 1 explains, this threat was indeed real in early psycholinguistics.

Psycholinguistics is lucky, however, in that a serious counterweight to the mass of English-based evidence has been added by the experiments of the Max Planck Institute for Psycholinguistics (where I have had the good fortune to work since 1993). This institute, in existence since the late 1970s, happens to be in Nijmegen, where the local language is Dutch. Dutch may not be that different from English, but in some respects it is certainly different enough to motivate interesting conclusions (see chapters 1 and 2). Quite a lot of the work discussed in this book was carried out on Dutch. I hope that one effect of this book is that evidence will be found from many more languages and wherever informative comparisons are to be made.

The Book and Its Audience

The book's introductory chapter lays out the necessity of a crosslinguistic approach to the study of listening to speech and illustrates it with two in-depth case studies. After this, the story of what speech is like, and how its structure determines every aspect of the spoken-word recognition process, is laid out in chapters 2–6. Chapters 11 and 12 then fill out the psychological picture—chapter 11 by addressing the flexibility of speech processing, and chapter 12 by drawing out further implications of the story for an overall view of the language processing system.

Whoops! What happened to chapters 7–10? They enrich the story with further indispensable detail: chapter 7 on the processing of prosodic structure, chapter 8 on infant speech perception, and chapters 9 and 10 on perception of speech in a second language.

The audience I had in mind while writing this book was, first of all, people like my own graduate students; the book contains what I would like young researchers to know as they survey the field in search of a productive area to work on. (My personal tip for readers falling into this category is that chapter 6 or chapter 11 could be exciting places to start right now—a lot of progress is happening there.)

My graduate students come from a variety of backgrounds, both disciplinary (psychology, linguistics, and adjacent fields) and theoretical. Theories, as we know, are the motors of science, with data being the fuel they run on. Surely, every single piece of research described in this book was motivated by a theoretical issue, and many were specifically prompted by particular models of spoken-word recognition. Although it is not hard to discern where my own theoretical preferences lie, this book is not aimed at pushing a particular approach. (Every theory, after all, is ultimately wrong in some way.) The data any theory have called into being will remain, however, and may serve as the foundation for new theories. So that research findings may be evaluated by everyone, regardless of their own preferences, the text mostly tries to concentrate on the implications of the findings for new theories, rather than on the particular motivations that brought them into being.

This has meant that many prominent theories in the field hardly appear in the text (although the data they have generated may appear). The focus of my investigation has not been a history of the field itself but the growth in our knowledge about how spoken-word recognition works and, in particular, the role of language structure in this process. Likewise, many important topics of debate are not discussed here if they do not directly generate lessons about how we understand words; this includes debates in the phonetic literature on the nature of speech sounds (i.e., not only does the spotlight not shine much above the word level, it doesn't shine much below it, either). A text has to stop somewhere, and unless a topic had serious influence in the psycholinguistic literature on recognizing words, I left it out. And finally, although I felt that chapters 7–10 were needed, I did not add further enriching chapters on, for instance, language impairment at the lexical level, the representation of words in the brain, children's representation of words, the role of spelling in spoken-word recognition, or many other topics that might have been added even without leaving the spoken/lexical level of focus or indeed without leaving the list of topics that have exercised me. Maybe these can be included in a future volume 2.

Thanks to All the Following

The book is dedicated "to all those who made it possible." The list of people in this category is far too long to enumerate on a dedication page. The list is so long because I have been so very lucky in my scientific life.

Best of all, I have enjoyed long-lasting collaborations. Experimental science is not a solitary undertaking; we all work in teams. But a long-term collaboration is like a bottomless treasure chest, always able to supply new gems of ideas and the riches of intellectual comradeship. For bringing such fortune into my life I am deeply grateful to Dennis Norris (35 years so far), James McQueen (25 years so far), Takashi Otake (21 years so far), and the co-makers of magical music with Dennis and me for more than a decade of the 1980s and early 1990s, Jacques Mehler and

Juan Segui. (What a lot of happy years all that adds up to!) Indeed I owe an enormous debt of gratitude to all the colleagues with whom I have worked productively and enjoyably, for however long that has been. This holds too for my students—thirty-three dissertation completions so far and more on the way; I am grateful not only for the joys of collaborative work but for all the times they made me rethink what I thought I knew. And while I am on that topic, let me also thank my scientific enemies (some of them from time to time good friends, too) for the same service. It is a mystery to me why any scientist would ever confuse theoretical disagreement with personal incompatibility. We should all cherish those who disagree with us; we would not progress half as quickly without them!

Now comes another enormous group to whom gratitude is owed. Throughout this book I describe experimental work in psycholinguistic laboratories. This work would be impossible without the enthusiastic participation (often for trivial monetary reward, or course credit, or no material reward at all) in those experiments by listeners who were willing to subject themselves to sometimes rather tedious tasks and only receive explanation of the purpose of the experiment after it is over. Their intelligent comments on the experiments and on their experience as subjects have frequently been of considerable help to the experimenters. The tasks to which they were subjected, however, were not designed by them nor did they know in advance the rationale of the study in which they participated. This allows me to get off my chest that it is entirely appropriate to refer to them under these circumstances as "subjects" and referring to them by this or any other term in no way signifies whether or not they were treated with respect.

For the past three decades these experiments have been carried out in some of the most supportive working environments any scientist could wish for; from 1982 to 1993 at the Medical Research Council's Applied Psychology Unit, from 1993 on at the Max Planck Institute for Psycholinguistics, and from 2006 on at MARCS Auditory Laboratories. Being privileged to work in such approximations to paradise is yet another way in which I have been inordinately fortunate, and I convey my thanks to all the colleagues who have contributed to making each place special.

Finally, I offer acknowledgments at the more specific level of the book itself. My life in science so far has made me aware that writing articles describing experimental work has become a natural exercise for me, but writing a book is highly unnatural; for advice on the art of completing a book manuscript, but even more for setting a magnificent example, I owe unending gratitude to Virginia Valian. To Bob Ladd, I offer heartfelt thanks for many years of patiently showing me how prosody works. Both of these also belong, with Ann Bradlow, Roger Wales, Elizabeth Johnson, Taehong Cho, Emmanuel Dupoux, the reading group of the MPI Comprehension Group, and Kate Stevens and the MSA Writing Group at MARCS, in the category of those who read and gave comments on all or part of the manuscript. I am awed and honored by their willingness to put so much of their time and effort into this task, and I am deeply grateful to them all. Roger Wales, especially, spent a month being the first manuscript's first reader; it was one of the last months in which he took good health for granted. I am but one of the many in psycholinguistics who wish that he could be a reader of the published version too, rather than one of its dedicatees.

At the manuscript preparation stage, a small army of MPI research assistants (I said this was one of the most supportive environments imaginable, didn't I?) has been involved in solving technical issues, including making figures. Thanks to all of them. Special thanks to Natasha Warner for lending her voice for many spectrograms, and to Bernadette Jansma, who (years ago!) drew the tasks in the panels. But by far the brunt of the manuscript work has been borne, as ever, by Rian Zondervan. The really essential people in one's life always figure right at the end of the acknowledgments! Rian's help with the work on the book has been without any doubt indispensable, and that has been true of her help on all counts for, now, nearly two decades. Last of all, so most essential of all, comes my husband, Bill Sloman, his years of patience with "The Book" now swelling the grand sea of all that I thank him for.

1 Listening and Native Language

This book is about listening to speech—specifically, how humans turn the sounds they hear into words they can recognize. The central argument of the book is that the way we listen is adapted by our experience with our native language, so that precisely how we listen differs from one language to another. The psycholinguist's task is to find out what parts of the process of listening are universal, what parts are language specific, and how they became that way. Two case studies in this chapter illuminate how the task needs to be approached. First, consider that listening is given a universal substrate by how speech is produced; this determines, for instance, the acoustic characteristics of vowels and consonants, which in turn determine how listeners perceive speech sounds. But although acoustic vowel-consonant differences are universal, studies of the perception of vowels and consonants, and of their role in word recognition, show that examining these issues in just one language is not enough. Only cross-language comparison allows the full picture to appear. Second, the same is true of a language-specific feature such as lexical stress. Comparisons across languages reveal its role in listening, and despite the language-specific nature of stress, its story further illuminates the universal account of listening. Listening must be studied crosslinguistically.

A book about listening should really be spoken. The recurring themes of this book are how naturally and effortlessly we understand speech in our native tongue and how different listening to a nonnative language can be from listening to the native tongue. Speech would do these themes greater justice than print. The final conclusion of the book is that listening to speech is so easy (when it is easy), or so hard (when it is hard), because it depends so much on our previous experience of listening to speech. A printed text leaves such experience untouched; a spoken text would augment it!

Using speech is one of humankind's favorite activities but also an outstanding achievement of the human mind. With such vital subject matter, psycholinguistics is an exceptionally rewarding discipline; speaking, listening, signing, reading, and writing are all cognitive operations of enormous complexity that have richly repaid investigation. Listening seems like the easiest of these operations; we cannot recall having had to learn to listen to speech, and under most circumstances we notice no difficulty in listening. Yet, as the following chapters will reveal, when we are listening we are carrying out a formidable range of mental tasks, all at once, with astonishing speed and accuracy. Listening involves evaluating the probabilities arising from the structure of the native vocabulary (see chapter 2), considering in parallel multiple hypotheses about the individual words making up the utterances we hear (see chapter 3), tracking information of many different kinds to locate the boundaries between these words (see chapters 4 and 5), paying attention to subtle variation in the way the words are pronounced (see chapter 6), and assessing not only information specifying the sounds of speech—vowels and consonants—but also, and at the same time, the prosodic information, such as stress and accent, that spans sequences of sounds (see chapter 7).

So listening is not really easy, though it undeniably seems easy. After those six chapters have laid out the complexities involved, chapter 8 discusses how listening to speech first begins and acquires its necessarily language-specific character, and chapters 9 and 10 detail the consequences of this language-specific specialization for listening to other languages. Chapter 11 elaborates on the flexibility and adaptability of listening (as long as we are listening in the native language), and chapter 12 draws some general conclusions about how language-specificity and universality fit together in our language processing system.

1. Psycholinguistic Experiments

The comprehension of spoken language is a mental operation, invisible to direct inspection. No techniques yet in existence allow us to observe the process of recognizing individual words across time. But psycholinguists have devised many ingenious ways of looking at the process indirectly (in the laboratory, mostly). These laboratory methods often involve measuring the speed with which a decision is made, or a target detected, or a verbal response issued (reaction time, or RT for short). Alternatively, the percentage of correct responses may be measured, or the percentage of responses of different types.

It is important to make sure that the task is reflecting what we want it to reflect—specifically, that there are no uncontrolled artifacts that might support alternative interpretations. Also it is important to relate the results of the highly controlled laboratory task to the natural processes we actually want to study. Some tasks that have been in use in the field for many years are now well understood and can provide quite subtle and detailed insights.

Ten of the most useful tasks—thus, the ones that are used in most of the research described in this book—will be illustrated and briefly described in panels in the first three chapters. Basic findings with most of these tasks are listed in Grosjean and Frauenfelder 1996. Panel 12 in chapter 12 gives some hints for deciding which task to use to test a particular hypothesis as well as how to construct a new task if none of the existing ones seems quite right for the job.

The rest of this introductory chapter explains why listening to speech should be studied, and understood, by comparing across languages. There are some ways in which languages are all much the same, and there are some ways in which they are wildly different, but whatever aspect is being considered, crosslinguistic comparison is vital for understanding it fully. Also, in this chapter, attention is given to how psycholinguists study listening. We know about the impressive number of cognitive operations so efficiently accomplished during listening because researchers have devised ingenious methods for distinguishing between these operations and assessing the course and outcome of each one in turn. These laboratory methods mostly involve simple tasks performed while listening to speech; panel 1 introduces this thread, which runs through this chapter and the two that follow.

1.1 How Universal Is Listening?

If psycholinguistics has one most fundamental premise, it is this: children learn the language of the environment. This concerns listening because of the vital role played by the language input that the little learner receives. Take a baby born of English-speaking parents, a baby born of Taiwanese-speaking parents, and a baby born of Igbo-speaking parents, place those children in the same monolingual Spanish environment, and they will all learn Spanish, in much the same way, and certainly without any differences that can be traced to the language spoken by their biological parents. Place them in a Tamil-speaking environment, and they will all acquire Tamil. Expose them to an environment where everyone is deaf and uses a sign language, and they will all acquire the sign language. The only thing that really matters for the learning outcome is the language input to which the child is exposed.

This leads us to conclude that the infant, not specialized for any particular language, is a sort of universal learning system. In line with this, the process of language acquisition runs its course in a very similar way for all languages. Not only that, there are structural similarities common to all natural languages. Acquisition of Spanish and acquisition of Taiwanese and acquisition of Igbo are not radically different achievements of the human mind, but in essence the same achievement.

This conclusion is important for psycholinguists because, as cognitive psychologists, they want to know how the mind works—the human mind. They want to know how the Spanish mind works, and the Taiwanese mind, and the mind of every language user in the world. Language is the core of the human mind and its operation. Psycholinguists thus seek to understand how language—any language—is spoken and understood. Since psycholinguistics began as a separate discipline in the mid-twentieth century, psycholinguists have had as their goal a universal model of language processing—that is, of the operations by which an intention to communicate becomes a produced utterance and a perceived message becomes understood communication. This universal model should account for language processing in any human mind. Universal commonalities in the acquisition of different languages are helpful in the pursuit of this goal.

However, languages do differ. The extent to which they differ can still only be guessed at. Many more languages have died out than are in existence today. The Ethnologue Web site (http://www.ethnologue.com) tells us that 94 percent of languages in existence today have fewer than a million speakers each, and together are spoken by only about 6 percent of the world's population. Those "smaller" languages are far less likely to have been fully described by linguists than the remaining 6 percent that comprise the "larger" languages with more than a million speakers each. This goes for psycholinguistic study too, needless to say; although in this book we will consider listening data from twenty or so different languages, they are all members of the top set of well-represented languages. Slovak (chapter 5) and Finnish (chapters 4 and 7), with around five million first-language speakers each, are as far toward "small" as the account in this book can go.

It might be tempting to think that the clearest view of a potentially universal model would be afforded by universal aspects of structure. Suppose that every language in the world indisputably evinces a particular feature. Surely, the processing of this feature will be the same in every language? By extension, it should then not matter in what language we study such processing—the result will always be the same. We can take one of the many tasks that psycholinguists have devised to examine language processing (see panel 1) and produce the same experimental outcome in any language. But, in fact, this will not work, as two detailed case studies in the middle section of this chapter will illustrate. One case study shows that understanding an aspect of language structure that is truly universal still requires attention to language-specific factors. We cannot assume that because something is universally present in languages, it will not matter what language we study it in—indeed, it does matter. The second case study shows that investigating an aspect of language structure that is unquestionably not universal, but definitely language specific, can still shed light on the way all humans process language. We cannot assume that because something is language specific, it will not be informative about universal characteristics of processing—it can be.

Much of this book, in fact, deals with the lines of research typified by these case studies. Crosslinguistic research has revealed an intricate interplay of language structure and the processes of spoken-language understanding. Even with the limited knowledge that we have of crosslinguistic diversity, and with the even more limited psycholinguistic data available, it has become clear that structural differences across languages have implications for how languages are understood and spoken. In other words, if there is a universal model of language processing, it cannot be one in which all the processes at every level of speaking and understanding are constant across languages. (We return to this issue in chapter 12.)

1.2 What Is Universal in Listening?

The question of what is universal across languages, or indeed whether anything is, has occupied much linguistic energy over the years (e.g., Greenberg 1963; Comrie 1989; and, as a recent installment, Evans and Levinson 2009, with the associated commentaries). Fortunately, there is an undisputed universal substrate to the task of listening to speech. Speech is spoken by humans; any aspect of speech that follows necessarily from the physiology of human speech production will be universal across languages. The nature of the task of recognizing words also has many unavoidable, and hence universal, characteristics, described in chapters 2 and 3. The separable sounds of speech, or phonemes, are universal constructs by definition: a phoneme is a minimal unit that distinguishes one word from another. Such a minimal unit can be a vowel (*bad* differs from *bed*), or it can be a consonant (*bad* differs from *sad* and from *bag*)—speech sounds come in these two varieties: vowels and consonants. This fundamental phonological difference is certainly determined by how we articulate speech and thus is certainly shared by all languages.

Consider that *mama* is a basic word in the vocabulary of many languages. This is not an accident: it is because it is so easy for an infant to say. If an infant expels air through the larynx, with the mouth otherwise in a relatively neutral position, the result is a vowel, probably one like [a].[1] If the infant then temporarily interrupts this production in the simplest way, by closing and reopening the mouth, the result is a syllable beginning with a bilabial consonant—*ma*, or if the closure is more abrupt, *ba* or *pa*. Assigning meaning to such simple early productions is apparently an irresistible option for language communities across the world.[2]

If we want to know how people understand spoken language, it makes good sense to begin with the speech sounds and their universal properties. Speech is produced by expelling air from the lungs through the vocal folds in the larynx to generate an auditory signal and then modulating this signal by adjusting the configuration of the reverberant chamber through which the sound passes—the mouth. This process creates the two different kinds of speech sounds. For the really, really full story, see Ladefoged and Disner 2012, but here is a brief summary: Vowels are sounds made without obstruction of the air passage—they differ according to the size and shape of the vocal cavity as they are uttered. This size and shape is controlled by where the speaker positions the tongue and whether the lips are protruded or spread. If there is constriction of the passage of air through the vocal tract, so that it is either entirely stopped for a moment, or it is modulated by being forced through a very narrow opening of the throat, teeth, or other articulators, the resulting sound is called a consonant. Consonants differ according to where the flow of air is obstructed (place of articulation), how it is obstructed (manner of articulation), and the timing of voiced phonation during the constriction (voicing). All languages make up their stock of communicative material on the basis of a small set of speech sounds—some vowels and some consonants.

Besides these phonetic (articulatory) differences between vowels and consonants, there are also phonological differences—that is, differences in the role that each may play in the sound patterns of language. Speech sounds are not uttered in isolation but as part of larger units; the unit where the phonological differences between vowels and consonants occur is the syllable. The syllable is also an articulatory unit in the sense that the smallest possible act of speech production is a syllable. In general, every word of every language must consist of at least one syllable, and every syllable must consist of at least a nucleus. The nucleus presents the primary vowel-consonant difference: all vowels can be the nucleus of a syllable, but most consonants cannot. In some languages, sonorous consonants such as [m] or [r] can function as a nucleus, and in a very tiny number of languages (some of which will turn up in chapter 5), other consonants can be a syllable nucleus, too. But in very many languages, only vowels can be the nucleus of a syllable.

Syllables may, but need not, also contain consonants accompanying the nucleus, either in the preceding (onset) or the following (coda) position. Vowels are near-obligatory and always central, consonants are permitted and near-universally peripheral: this is a general statement of syllable structure, although it covers a wide variation in legitimate syllable types (from languages where the only legal syllable structure is a single vowel preceded by a single consonant onset, to languages that allow syllables to be anything from a single short vowel to a long vowel preceded by a triconsonantal onset and followed by a triconsonantal coda—such as English *screeched* [skritʃt], which counts as a single syllable). Phonetic differences in articulation of vowels versus consonants apply in all languages, and so do vowel-consonant differences in phonological function within syllables.

What do these difference entail for the listener's task? For speakers, the articulatory differences between vowels and consonants are simple: either there is free flow in the vocal tract or there is constriction. Acoustically, however, and in consequence perceptually, the effects of the articulatory difference reach further. Phonetic information transmitted by an unobstructed airflow is continuous, and hence allows for greater durational range than information transmitted by a temporary obstruction. Vowels can vary from quite long to quite short, but a stop consonant such as [b] can only vary within a much more limited range. Similarly, the crucial portion of the speech signal of a vowel is a steady state, whereas the crucial portion of the signal for consonants can be a transition from one state to another. These differences have perceptual consequences. The longer a sound, and the more steady-state components it comprises, the more resistant it is to noise masking; so, for instance, vowels are sometimes perceived more accurately than are consonants against a noisy background (see, e.g., Cutler, Weber, et al. 2004), and slips of the ear are more likely to involve misperception of consonants than of vowels (see, e.g., Bond 1999).

When listeners are asked to decide which speech sound they are hearing—in other words, to perform phonetic categorization (see panel 2)—differences between vowels and consonants also arise. Typically, what listeners are presented with in phonetic categorization is a continuum of speech sounds that has been made by taking two sounds and gradually morphing the feature(s) distinguishing them. Thus the continuum runs from the value typical of one of the sounds to the value typical of the other. Then we can ask listeners to identify sounds along the

2. Phonetic Categorization

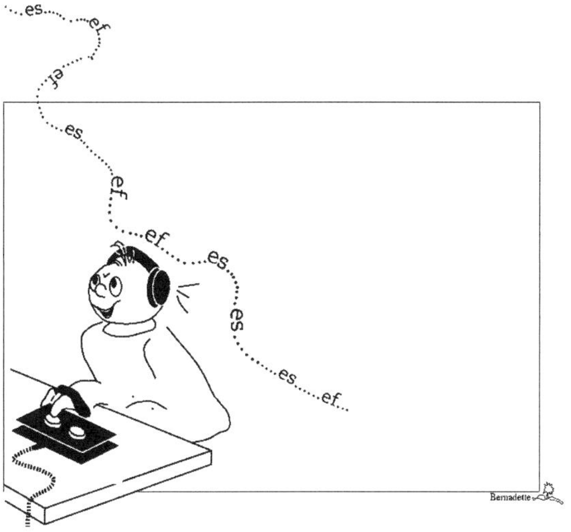

In normal speech, listeners hear speech sounds that are mostly reasonably good exemplars of their categories. But in phonetic categorization, listeners get to hear sounds that are not at all good category exemplars. It is possible to make an artificial continuum from one sound to another; the middle of this continuum then consists of sounds that the listeners presumably have never heard before. But they do not report hearing new sounds. They often report a sudden switch from tokens of one category to tokens of the other—"categorical perception" (see figure 1.1).

The phonetic categorization task was developed for phonetic research, but it has also proven useful in psycholinguistics. For instance, categorical functions can shift if one decision would make a word but the other would make a nonword. There is a lot more about research with this task in chapter 12.

continuum (is this [b] or [p]?); or we can ask them to discriminate pairs of sounds ([i], [ɪ]—same or different?). Even when the input is in fact ambiguous between two categories and corresponds to nothing in the listeners' prior perceptual experience, listeners find the task of identifying speech sounds as exemplars of one phoneme or another simple to do. It has long been known (Stevens et al. 1969; Pisoni 1973) that experiments of this kind produce different response patterns for vowels and consonants.

For consonants, the response function that usually appears reflects what is called "categorical perception"; only within a narrow range does each possible response receive substantial support, showing that listeners feel unsure only in that small portion of the continuum. Quite a lot of deviation from the typical value is tolerated before identification responses start to change from what the typical value itself receives. There is also a parallel effect in the discrimination responses; differences can only be well discriminated to the extent that they can be well identified. That is, although listeners can discriminate well between two exemplars of different categories, discrimination of exemplars within a category is poor.

For vowels, in contrast, the identification curves are less steep, which suggests that listeners perceive finer distinctions than they do with consonants. Most importantly, the discrimination function for vowels is not dependent on the identification function in the way it is for consonants. Within-category discrimination is at chance (i.e., 50%) for consonants but quite high for vowels. Listeners seem to be capable of discriminating small vowel differences even when no difference of category label is involved. Figure 1.1 depicts this difference in patterning, for one example vowel pair and one example consonant pair. The identification function shows a less steep crossover between categories for [i]-[ɪ] than for [b]-[p], whereas the discrimination function is always above 75 percent for [i]-[ɪ] but hovers around 50 percent for [b]-[p] except at the category boundary, where it shows a sudden peak.

Although these differences between vowels and consonants are striking, they are not really absolute. Vowels and consonants actually range along a continuum called the sonority hierarchy. On this continuum, vowels are at the most sonorous end, unvoiced stop consonants at the least sonorous or most consonantal end, and various continuant consonants range in between. Patterns of responses in categorization experiments differ with position along the sonority hierarchy. The patterns are even mirrored by our own experience as speakers—we can utter a continuous vowel sound and make it change gradually from any one vowel to another, but we would have enormous difficulty uttering sounds that we would accept perceptually as a sequence of intermediate steps along a continuum between most pairs of consonants. The articulatory reality of the vowel-consonant distinction, in other words, translates to a perceptual reality that causes strong category binding for consonants but a certain degree of category insecurity, or flexibility for vowels.

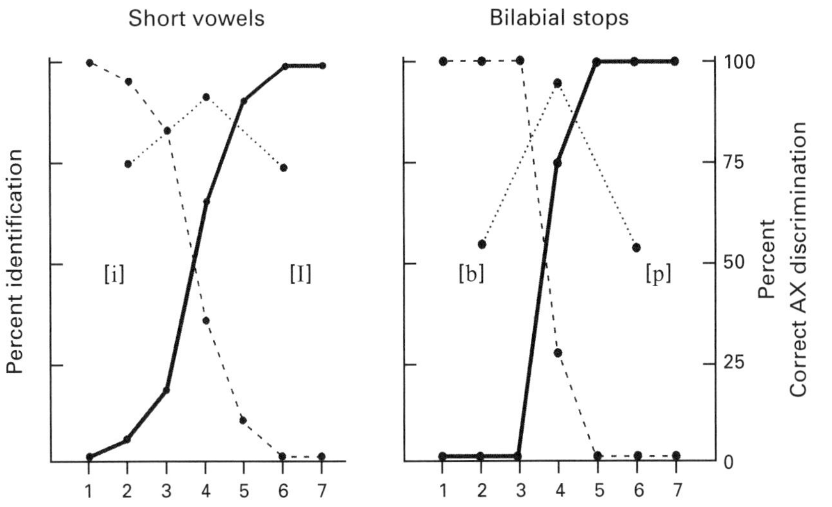

Figure 1.1
Identification functions for vowels varying from [i] to [ɪ], and for stops varying from [b] to [p], plus discrimination functions for the same continua. (Data from Pisoni 1973; reproduced with permission.) The identification functions show the percentage of choices in each case of the category of the endpoint at left (dotted line) and of the category of the endpoint at right (solid line). The discrimination functions show the percentage of correct discrimination between two differing tokens within a category (left and right points) versus across the category boundary (middle point).

Category insecurity for vowels may seem to conflict with the fact that vowels are more resistant to noise-masking. But in fact both effects follow from the continuous, steady-state nature of vowel sounds. Speech presents more acoustic evidence for vowels. This evidence gives listeners a better chance of recognizing a vowel against noise, but it also allows them to make a more fine-grained analysis of the acoustic support for one vowel rather than another. In a phonetic categorization experiment, where the acoustic evidence actually is mixed from two sources, listeners have a better chance of appreciating this ambiguity. The lesser amount of acoustic evidence for consonants, which renders them more likely to be misperceived (e.g., in noise), also makes it less likely that listeners will accurately interpret the ambiguous portion of a phonetic continuum. If external evidence (e.g., visual information about the speaker's lips) is on offer, listeners make more recourse to it in making decisions about consonants (Cohen and Massaro 1995) but base their decisions about vowels on the acoustic evidence. Thus the universal basis of the vowel-consonant difference surfaces, in speech perception, as a difference in how listeners make categorical decisions about the two types of speech sound.

1.3 What Is Language Specific in Listening?

Just about any aspect of language that is neither a consequence of the physiology or acoustics of speech nor a consequence of the nature of the word-recognition task can vary crosslinguistically. In fact, whole dimensions of phonological structure may be language specific, in that they feature in an account of some languages' phonology but are simply irrelevant for the description of other languages.

In contrast to the universal substrate of listening, which is really rather limited, the extent of language-specificity is certainly larger than we yet know. All different types of variation have consequences for the listener's task. Some of the language-specific phonological phenomena dealt with in this book are: tonal as well as segmental information to distinguish between words (chapter 3); harmonic restrictions on vowel patterns (chapter 4); constraints on the size of stand-alone words (chapter 5); linking phenomena across words, such as liaison in French (chapter 6); constraints on what phonemes may occur in sequence (chapters 4, 10, and 11); and there are many more. Chapter 7, which deals with prosodic structure, is probably all language specific.

Prosody provides notorious examples of the language-specificity of whole dimensions of structure. One case is stress. Stress can be accentuation of syllables within words, when it is called lexical stress (e.g., *LANGuage*; upper case marks the location of the stressed syllable, in this case the first one); or it can be accentuation of words within sentences, when it is called sentence stress (compare *What did the CAT eat?* with *What did the cat EAT?*). In languages with lexical stress, the syllables of a polysyllabic word are not created equal—some syllables may bear accentual prominence whereas others are prohibited from bearing prominence. English is a stress language, and it would be incorrect for prominence to fall on the second syllable of *language* in any English utterance. Perceptually, stressed syllables are more salient than unstressed syllables, and this alone makes stress a relevant aspect of spoken-word recognition in languages such as English.

However, lexical stress will not be at all relevant for an account of spoken-word recognition in Japanese, or Mandarin, or French, or many other languages. Words in those languages do not contrast stressed with unstressed syllables. Further, not all languages that do contrast stressed with unstressed syllables within a word do so in the same way. In some languages, such as Finnish or Polish, stress always falls at a particular position within the word ("fixed stress"). In other languages, such as English or Spanish, stress placement varies ("free stress"), so that some words have stress on an early syllable, others on a later syllable. There are at least as many fixed-stress as free-stress languages in the world (Goedemans 2003). We will see that stress provides some telling examples of how listening must sometimes be language specific (including the second case study in this chapter as well as more accounts in chapters 2, 4, and 7); but all of the language-specific phenomena that there are can similarly produce consequences for listening.

1.4 Case Study 1: The Role of a Universal Feature in Listening

Vowels and consonants differ in both their phonetic form and their phonological function, and these differences hold across languages. The vowel-consonant contrast is thus a universal part of listeners' experience. Does this mean that all listeners show exactly the same response patterns in listening experiments with vowels and with consonants, respectively? And do the differences between the two types of speech sound mean that they play different roles in the understanding of spoken language? For instance, do they differ in their contribution to understanding a word? We can use the psycholinguist's repertoire of tasks that provide insight into linguistic processing to ask whether listeners make different use of the two types of speech sound when they are recognizing spoken words. An appropriate task in this case is *word reconstruction* (see panel 3).

1.4.1 Vowels and Consonants in Word Recognition: Reconstructing Words

Does a *wemmen* remind you more of a *woman* or of a *lemon*? Each of the real nouns differs from *wemmen* by a single phoneme. But if listeners are given *wemmen* and asked to change a single phoneme to make this nonword into a real word, are they equally likely to produce either noun as a response? And if they are forced to change a vowel (i.e., respond with *woman*), is the task easier or harder than if they are forced to change a consonant (i.e., respond with *lemon*)? Word reconstruction, invented by Van Ooijen (1996), is quite a sensitive task because, as this summary suggests, it allows more than one view of what listeners will do with an input like *wemmen*.

When this task is carried out with Spanish listeners, we find that the two types of speech sound behave differently. Vowels are significantly easier to replace than consonants. Cutler et al. (2000) tried out all three types of condition: free choice of response, forced vowel replacement, and forced consonant replacement. Given a free choice, listeners were far more likely to replace vowels, thereby turning *pecto* into *pacto* 'pact' rather than into *recto* 'straight', or turning *cefra* into *cifra* 'number' rather than into *cebra* 'zebra'. When they had to replace vowels (i.e., the only correct responses were *pacto* and *cifra*), their reaction times (RTs) were faster than when they had to replace consonants (i.e., respond *recto*, *cebra*); in the latter condition they also made more intrusion errors in which vowels were accidentally replaced after all.

One thing we know about Spanish is that vowels and consonants are not equally represented in the phoneme inventory of the language. Spanish has a grossly unbal-

3. Word Reconstruction

Word reconstruction (WR) is a laboratory task in which listeners have to change a nonword into a real word by altering a single sound. The subject responds by pressing a response key as soon as a real word has been found, then speaks the word aloud (so that the experimenter can check the accuracy of the response). WR is one in a family of similar tasks (another member of the family is detection of mispronunciations). The input in WR partially corresponds to known words, and our natural response is to look for the nearest word. So the RT tells us how easy the nearest word is to find. Because this can be a relatively hard task, subjects sometimes fail to come up with a response within the available time window or their response is incorrect; so the success rate can also be informative. Results are typically reported in both forms: RTs and response rates. This task was used to look at the processing of vowels and consonants—which type of phoneme constrains word identity more strongly? If we hear *wemmen*, is the nearest word *woman*? Or *lemon*? It has also been used to look at units of prelexical representation (this research is described in chapter 12). Response patterns in WR tend to be similar across languages.

anced inventory, with five vowels and twenty consonants. So perhaps the asymmetric pattern of response in the word-reconstruction task is related to the asymmetric distribution of Spanish phonemes across the two major phoneme classes? For instance, given that Spanish listeners have only five vowels to choose from, trying out the five vowels might more easily yield the target word than trying out the twenty Spanish consonants.

In that case, we would have to expect a different pattern of results if we carried out the experiment in, say, Dutch. With a relatively balanced set of sixteen vowels and nineteen consonants, the makeup of the Dutch phoneme inventory differs significantly from the asymmetric Spanish situation. Cutler et al. (2000) indeed carried out the same experiment in Dutch. The pattern of results turned out to be exactly the same as in Spanish: vowels were easier to replace than consonants. Listeners found it easier to turn *hieet* into *hiaat* 'hiatus' than *dieet* 'diet', and easier to turn *komeel* into *kameel* 'camel' than *komeet* 'comet'. Again, the pattern was robust across the various conditions in the experiment.

Dutch is so close to having a balanced repertoire of vowels versus consonants that the vowel advantage here cannot be ascribed to an imbalance in the phonemic inventory. The vowel advantage also appears in English (*woman*, not *lemon*, is the preferred response to *wemmen*; *teeble* gives *table*, not *feeble*, and *eltimate* gives *ultimate*, not *estimate*; Van Ooijen 1996). Van Ooijen considered several reasons for the asymmetric results in her original study.

One suggestion was that English vowels might give rather unreliable information about word identity because they vary so much across dialects. Consider how the three words *look*, *luck*, and *Luke* are pronounced in American or standard southern British English. The three are different. But in Scottish English, *look* and *Luke* are pronounced the same, and they contrast with *luck*. In Yorkshire English, *look* and *luck* are pronounced the same, and they contrast with *Luke*. Nor do American and British vowels always run parallel. British English uses the same vowel in *pass* and *farce*—these words rhyme, and they contrast with *gas*. American English uses the same vowel in *pass* and *gas*, which contrasts with the vowel in *farce*.

On this explanation, English listeners would find it easier to change vowels because of their experience in adjusting between other dialects and their native dialect, whereby most of the adjustments involved vowels. The Dutch-Spanish study ruled this suggestion out, however. In Dutch, both vowels and consonants vary across dialects. In Spanish, the five vowels remain pretty much the same across the dialects of Peninsular Spain versus Latin America, but the consonants differ quite a lot, the most well known difference being seen in words like *gracias*, where the middle sound is spoken by Castilian speakers as [θ] (as at the end of English *path*) but by Latin American speakers as [s] (as in *pass*). So a dialectal explanation would predict equivalent word-reconstruction effects for vowels and consonants in Dutch, and a consonant advantage for Spanish. This was not what happened: Both languages showed a vowel advantage, as had English.

A second reason suggested by Van Ooijen (1996) was likewise language specific: Perhaps English just has too many vowels for listeners to be able to tell them apart reliably. Certainly British English, with seventeen vowels, does not make vowel discrimination easy for listeners. But because the pattern of results was essentially identical in English (seventeen vowels), Dutch (sixteen vowels), and Spanish (five vowels), we have to reject the vowel inventory size account, too.

Only the third explanation was based on articulatory and acoustic effects that occur in all languages and thus could correctly predict the universally consistent pattern observed. On this suggestion, vowels are intrinsically more likely than consonants to vary in different speech contexts. Change in the articulatory form of a vowel due to influence from surrounding consonants is more likely than change in a consonant due to influence of surrounding vowels. There are articulatory reasons for this: the articulation targets for consonants involve closures (of lips, tongue, etc.), whereas the articulation targets for vowels require that the vocal tract be open but in a certain shape or configuration. In speaking, the vocal tract configurations that produce vowels are notoriously approached and departed from at speed and with great variation induced by the closures surrounding them. This means that a vowel, especially a short vowel, can take quite different acoustic forms, depending on which consonants precede and follow it. Listeners should, as a result, have become used to the frequent experience of making an initial hypothesis about a vowel that turned out to be wrong. They have developed, in consequence, a certain facility in altering these initial hypotheses in the course of word recognition. This explanation in terms of universal properties of speech is the best account of the crosslinguistically consistent results.

1.4.2 Vowels and Consonants in Word Recognition: Initial Activation

The universal account of the word-reconstruction findings assumes that what matters to listeners is identifying words, as rapidly and efficiently as possible. There is a paradigm that allows us to test whether vowels and consonants contribute in the same or different ways to listeners' growing awareness of word identity as spoken words are heard. Suppose we hear *diff-*; it could be the beginning of *different*, or *difficult*, or *diffident*. If the next sound to arrive is [ə], then the word is more likely to be the first of these and not the second or third. If the next sound is not [ə] but [ɪ], then *different* is ruled out, but either *difficult* or *diffident* is still possible; the listener has to wait for another phoneme to come in, either the [k] of *difficult* or the [d] of *diffident*. In other words, sometimes vowel information distinguishes between alternative continuations; sometimes consonant information does. There are laboratory tasks for looking at how quickly phonemic information is processed in listening, and we can use them to compare the effect of vowel versus consonant distinctions. An appropriate technique for this is cross-modal fragment priming (see panel 4). If we speak or hear a word once, it is easier to speak or hear it once again shortly afterward; we call this effect "priming." (Priming is a useful phenomenon that helps make conversation easy. For instance, priming probably underlies the tendency of speakers to reuse their interlocutors' words and expressions in conversation; Schenkein 1980.) As the word "cross-modal" in panel 4 suggests, priming happens even if the word is processed once in one modality (e.g., it is heard) and once in another (e.g., it is read). And "fragment" priming refers to the fact that a part of a word will produce priming, too. So spoken *diff-* will prime written versions of all of *different*, *difficult*, and *diffident*, to a certain extent.

4. Cross-Modal Fragment Priming

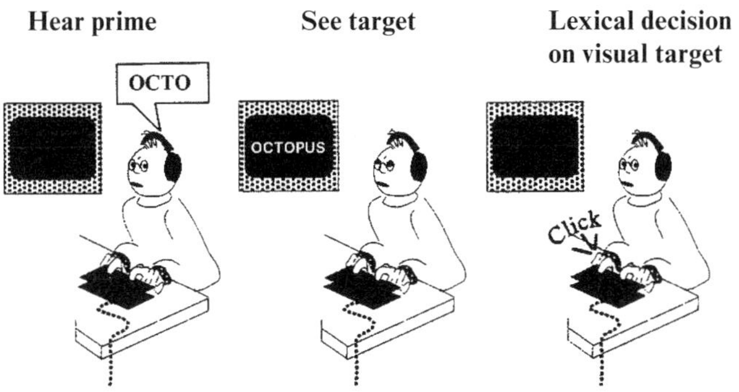

Cross-modal priming (CMP) is priming because it examines responses to one stimulus (the target) as a function of a preceding stimulus (the prime), and it is cross-modal because the prime is heard and the target is seen. Typically, the task is to decide whether the target is a real word or not. CMP is a way of investigating what words become available ("activated") when a listener hears speech. We measure the RT to make a lexical decision on the target; that is, to decide whether the target is a real word. If this RT varies when the spoken prime varies, then we have observed an effect of the prime. Related primes and targets may be identical (e.g., *give-GIVE*) or related in meaning (*take-GIVE*). The RT to accept the target word is expected to be faster after either of the related primes than after a control prime (*say-GIVE*). More information on the task can be found in Zwitserlood 1996 and in panel 7 (see chapter 2).

Cross-modal fragment priming (CMFP) is a version of CMP in which the prime is not fully presented. The initial fragment of a word may also be consistent with other words (e.g., *diff-* could become *difficult* or *different*; *oc-* of *octopus* could be the beginning of *octave* or *oxygen*). CMFP enables us to see, for example, whether all possible words beginning as the prime does are momentarily activated or whether factors such as the sentence context can rule some of them out. It can also be used (as in the examples in this chapter) to find out which types of mismatching information most strongly affect activation. CMFP has also been explored with ERPs, which are measures of the brain's electrophysiological responses to stimuli (e.g., Friedrich, Schild, and Röder 2009).

Soto-Faraco, Sebastián-Gallés, and Cutler (2001) compared vowels and consonants in this task. Their experiment was in Spanish. We have already seen that Spanish has a very asymmetric repertoire of vowels (few) and consonants (four times as many), and that Spanish listeners are sensitive to the realization of vowels and consonants in speech, as revealed in word reconstruction. In cross-modal priming, we can look more directly at word activation and compare vowel versus consonant cues to the right continuation. The vowel-consonant experiment compared pairs of words that began similarly, such as *protector* 'protector' and *proyectil* 'projectile', or *minoria* 'minority' and *mineria* 'mining'. The beginnings *pro-* and *min-* should prime both members of the respective pair. Then the next phoneme to come in will distinguish between the two words, further supporting one of the two but mismatching the other. Will there be any difference when this phoneme is a consonant (as in the *pro-* pair) versus a vowel (as in the *min-* pair)? Visual lexical decision responses (e.g., to PROTECTOR or MINORIA) were measured after primes like *prote-*, *proye-* or *mino-*, *mine-*, compared with control primes; the primes always occurred at the end of neutral (nonconstraining) sentences such as *Nadie supo leer la palabra proye-* 'Nobody knew how to read the word *proye-*'.

No vowel-consonant difference appeared. In both cases the effect of one mismatching phoneme was highly significant. Compared to the baseline of responses after hearing an unrelated fragment, listeners responded significantly faster when the fragment matched the word on the screen (*mino-* MINORIA, or *prote-* PROTECTOR) but responded significantly slower when a phoneme mismatched the visual word (*mine-* MINORIA or *proye-* PROTECTOR). It did not matter whether the mismatching phoneme was a vowel or a consonant. It also did not matter how close the phonemes were to one another—small differences (as in the fourth sounds of *concesion* 'concession' versus *confesion* 'confession', where only one phonological feature, place of articulation, distinguishes [θ] from [f]), or large differences (as in the [t] versus [j] of *protector-proyectil*), the effect was the same. In other words, what matters here is distinguishing between words. It does not matter whether the difference that effects the distinction is a big one or a small one, in terms of phonemic features. And it certainly does not matter whether the difference is in a vowel or a consonant. Both do the same job with the same efficiency in the same way.

1.4.3 Detecting Vowels or Consonants: Effects of Phonetic Context

So far, the universal vowel-consonant contrast has provided cleanly universal response patterns in all studies. Where the task is evaluating speech to distinguish between words, any relevant information, be it vocalic or consonantal, will always be seized on and used. Where the task is altering a sound to turn a nonword into a real word, vowel changes are always tried first because changing vowels is a more familiar experience to all. The latter results show that listeners are very sensitive to the way that phonemes in speech are influenced by the other phonemes that surround them. In general, across languages, vowels are influenced more. Consonants are less likely to be so altered that they are initially misidentified—at least, so those word-reconstruction results suggest.

Nonetheless, the more vowels there are in a language, the more variety there will be in their influence on adjacent consonants. Can we find a way of seeing whether this affects how the phonemes are processed?

The processing of individual phonemes can be examined with the phoneme detection task (see panel 5). This is one of the simplest tasks in psycholinguistics; all the listener has to do is press a button whenever a particular sound is heard. The speed with which this response can be made—the reaction time—is the measure of how difficult the task is at a given point.

5. Phoneme Detection and Fragment Detection

These detection tasks, in which subjects hearing speech listen for a target phoneme or fragment, are among the simplest of psycholinguistic tasks. RT is the dependent variable. Phoneme detection involves pressing a button whenever a particular sound is heard, such as the sound [a] in the example in the drawing. This is very easy to do and the speech input does not have to be understood for the task to be efficiently performed—the input can just as well be nonwords or words of a language unknown to the listener. The same goes for fragment detection—for example, responding to hearing the sequence *bal-*. These tasks have been around for over forty years and it was once thought that they could provide a direct measure of prelexical processing. Now their interpretation does not seem quite so simple (chapter 12 discusses this in more detail), but the tasks are still widely used. They can reflect how easy it is, at a given point, to extract sublexical information (i.e., information below the word level) from speech. Thus they can reflect segmentation, or how easy a preceding word or phoneme was to process, and so on.

Phoneme-detection times for different speech sounds can vary. For English listeners, it is often easier to detect consonants than vowels (Van Ooijen, Cutler, and Norris 1991; Cutler and Otake 1994). But this is not the case for listeners in all languages. In Cutler and Otake's study, for instance, Japanese listeners found detection of [n] in words like *inori*, *kinshi* and [o] in words like *tokage*, *taoru* equally easy, whereas English listeners presented with the same Japanese words (nonwords to the English) detected the [n] targets faster than the [o] targets, just as they also detected [n] in *canopy*, *candy* faster than [o] in *atomic*, *kiosk* in a further experiment in their native language.[3] There is certainly no systematic difference across languages in response times for vowels and consonants. Chapter 2 presents more discussion on the way language structure affects the processing of individual phonemes.

However, certain factors are known to make phoneme detection easier or harder in general. One of them is that the less uncertainty there is in the context, the easier the task becomes. Thus detection of [b] is faster in a string of nonsense syllables like *su*, *fu*, *tu*, *bu*, with a constant vowel, than in *si*, *fo*, *ta*, *bu*, with four varying vowels as context. It is slower still if the context can vary across eight vowels (Swinney and Prather 1980). So it is possible to compare the effect of vowel uncertainty on consonant detection, which Swinney and Prather discovered, with effects of consonant uncertainty on vowel detection. Is detection of [i] harder in *su*, *fo*, *ta*, *bi* than in *bu*, *bo*, *ba*, *bi*? If so, is the effect the same as the effect in consonant detection, or perhaps stronger, or weaker? And is the effect independent of the relative number of vowels and consonants in the language?

Costa, Cutler, and Sebastián-Gallés (1998) discovered that the effects indeed depended on which language the experiment was conducted in. They compared detection of vowels in varied versus fixed consonant contexts, and detection of consonants in varied versus fixed vowel contexts, in two languages. In Dutch, strong effects of consonant uncertainty were observed in vowel detection, and equally strong effects of vowel uncertainty were observed in consonant detection. So the two types of speech sound were equivalent as context for each other. But this was not the result that Costa et al. (1998) found in the other language in which they tested—namely, Spanish. In Spanish, the effect of consonant uncertainty on vowel detection was much stronger than the effect of vowel uncertainty on consonant detection.

Figure 1.2 shows Costa et al.'s (1998) results. Note that the actual number of varying phonemes in the experimental contexts in their study was held constant—at five vowels and five consonants—across the two languages. Thus there was no actual difference in the variability within the experiment—it was exactly the same for the Dutch and for the Spanish listeners. The nonsense syllables were also the same, and equally meaningless for each group. The difference in the result could therefore not

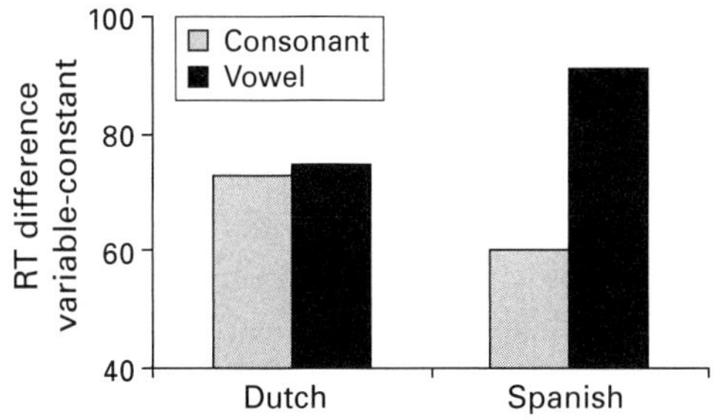

Figure 1.2
Inhibitory effect of variable context (variable-context RT minus constant-context RT) in detection of consonant and vowel targets. For Dutch listeners, variable consonant contexts threaten vowel perception about as much as vice versa. For Spanish listeners, variable consonant contexts threaten vowel detection much more than the reverse. (Data from Costa et al. 1998.)

be ascribed to anything in the experiment itself. Instead the difference had to be due to the languages in question—or, more precisely, to the language experience of the listeners who took part.

As we saw, Dutch and Spanish differ in the makeup of their phonemic inventories. Dutch has a relatively balanced set of vowels and consonants, whereas Spanish has four times as many consonants as vowels. All their lives, the Spanish listeners had heard vowels being affected by twenty different consonant contexts, and consonants being affected by only five different vowel contexts. Thus even though actual variability did not differ in this particular experiment, these listeners were well aware that the range of variability was greater in one direction than the other. The Dutch listeners, on the other hand, had heard vowels being affected by many different consonant contexts throughout their life, and consonants being affected by many different vowel contexts, so that in their experience the range of variability was pretty much equivalent. These expectations translated into equivalent uncertainty effects in each direction on the Dutch listeners' phoneme detections but significantly greater effects in one direction than in the other for the Spanish listeners.

1.4.4 A Universal Feature in Listening: Summary

All languages make up their words from a mixture of vowels and consonants. Speech sounds differ in how they are articulated, and this can be expressed as a continuum of sonority, with consequences for perception. Sounds at the vowel end of the continuum are realized with more acoustic evidence but, in turn, allow more room for influence of surrounding consonants. So their initial interpretation is easier, but changing that interpretation is often necessary, thus also easy. Sounds at the consonant end of the continuum are less acoustically present, so an initial interpretation can be harder, but they are less contextually variable so that the initial interpretation can be more secure.

Insofar as vowels and consonants perform the same function—distinguishing one word from another, for example—the way listeners process them seems to be much the same. Differences are attributable to acoustic realization rather than to language-specific structure. The cross-modal priming studies suggest that vowels and consonants equally effectively mismatch or match candidate words. The word-reconstruction studies show that listeners across different languages find it easier to change vowel hypotheses than consonant hypotheses, which we interpret as reflecting their experience of what happens to vowels in speech. Listeners are capable of discriminating the subtle changes that result from contextual influence on vowels, so they know that vowels are quite changeable as a function of the speech context surrounding them. Experience of altering decisions, from one vowel category to another, accrues as an inevitable consequence of the acoustic realization of vowels and its implications for perception. Just one cross-language difference was discussed, and it appeared not in a word-recognition task but in phoneme detection, where it reflected the influence of phoneme-inventory makeup on listeners' expectations of how target phonemes can vary. Listeners with a balanced vowel-consonant repertoire expected equivalent variation for vowel and consonant targets; listeners with an asymmetric repertoire expected asymmetric variation.

All the evidence suggests that speech perception is very sensitive to listener experience, especially the experience of speech acoustics. Speech signals are evaluated continuously, and any available information that is useful is exploited as soon as it arrives. Later chapters will bolster this claim with many more types of evidence (including evidence that the contextual influences of consonants on vowels actually provide listeners with valuable information about the consonants—see chapter 3). Vowels and consonants perform different functions in the structure of syllables, as we saw, but this does not seem to be relevant for speech perception. It may well be more important for speech production, given that producing speech requires compiling phoneme sequences into syllables in a prosodic structure (Levelt, Roelofs, and Meyer 1999). Clinical evidence from production indeed suggests a vowel-consonant dissociation: Caramazza et al. (2000) reported on an aphasia patient whose vowel production was disrupted but whose consonant production was unimpaired, and another patient with a differently located lesion and exactly the reverse pattern of impaired production. These patients had no impairments, and no differences in their response profiles, in word-recognition and perceptual-discrimination tasks. Perception studies in general show no vowel-consonant differences in the brain. For instance, PET scans made of listeners' brains while they were carrying out word reconstruction (Sharp et al. 2005) revealed the same location of brain activation during vowel versus consonant replacement. Only the amount of activation differed:

there was more for consonant replacement than for vowel replacement, as would be expected given that the former task is harder. When patients whose brains were being mapped prior to surgery made same-different judgments on simple syllables such as *pob*, *tob*, direct electrical stimulation of an area in the left hemisphere disrupted consonant processing but hardly affected vowel processing (Boatman et al. 1994; 1997). No region was found in which vowels were disrupted but consonants were not, however. Thus it does not seem that perception of consonants and vowels engages separate cortical systems, but rather that processing the two types of speech sound, with the differing types of acoustic evidence they provide, can cause differential activation within a single speech perception system.

Vowels and consonants are the phonetic building blocks of all languages. However, this case study shows that we could not have fully understood vowel-consonant differences without having looked at more than one language. Only the cross-language comparisons enabled us to interpret the word-reconstruction and phoneme-detection results.

The counterpart argument to this is that language-specificity does not rule out insight into universals of processing. This is the lesson of a second case study, which involves a structural feature that is unquestionably language specific: lexical stress.

1.5 Case Study 2: The Role of a Language-Specific Feature in Listening

Although stress is not a universal feature of languages, and free stress even less so, a comparison of spoken-word recognition in three free-stress languages (Spanish, Dutch, and English) nonetheless proves very informative about some universal characteristics of speech processing. The question at issue is whether stress differences between words play an important role in lexical activation. But the answer concerns not only languages with free stress, because it turns out to concern the vocabulary (and all languages have a vocabulary!).

The relation between stress and phonemes differs across these three languages. Phonemic distinctions, by definition, distinguish words from one another. Spanish *casa* and *capa* differ by a single phoneme, as do *casa* and *caso*, and English *case* and *cape*, or *cape* and *cope*. When listeners determine that they are hearing *casa* and not one of these other, minimally different, words, they are without question processing phonemic information.

In some languages, stress differences go hand in hand with phoneme differences. If this were taken to an extreme, so that the phonemes in stressed syllables always differed from those in unstressed syllables, listeners could extract stress information from words as a byproduct of processing phonemic information, which they need to do anyway to distinguish words. The relation between stress and phonemic segments is actually not so deterministic in any of the three languages discussed here.

There is quite a strong relation in English, as we shall see, and a somewhat less strong relation in Dutch. In Spanish, however, there is no necessary relation between stress and phonemes at all. The distinctions between stressed and unstressed syllables are solely suprasegmental (i.e., variations not at the level of phonemic segments but above it); the same phonemic segments are differently realized when they bear stress than when they do not. Thus *CAso* differs from *caSO* in the suprasegmental attributes fundamental frequency, duration, and amplitude. But the two words do not differ in vowel quality—they have the same vowels.

Spanish is therefore a good language in which to examine the role of stress in the recognition of spoken words, because the cues to stress are not mixed up with the cues to phonemes. If listeners extract stress information from the signal in order to recognize Spanish words, they are exploiting aspects of the signal that are not necessarily involved in phonemic discrimination.

1.5.1 Lexical Stress in Word Recognition: A Comparison with Vowels and Consonants

Consider the Spanish words *principe* 'prince' and *principio* 'principle'—they begin with the same initial string of seven phonemes. But it is not quite identical. This is because of stress. *Principe* is stressed on the first syllable and *principio* on the second. Can listeners use stress information to distinguish between words in the same way as they can use vowel and consonant information?

Yes, they can, as Soto-Faraco et al. (2001) discovered in the same study in which they compared pairs of words distinguished first by vowel differences or by consonant differences. Soto-Faraco et al.'s study also included pairs like *principe-principio* in which the first distinction was realized by stress. Compared with responses after a control fragment, the lexical decisions to the visually present words were significantly faster when fragment and word matched in stress (e.g., *PRINci-*, PRINCIPE or *prinCI-*, PRINCIPIO) but significantly slower when they mismatched (e.g., *prinCI-*, PRINCIPE or *PRINci-*, PRINCIPIO). Thus the stress information favored the matching word and disfavored the mismatching word in just the same way as the phonemic information had done in pairs like *protector-proyectil* and *minoria-mineria*.

We saw earlier that Spanish listeners and Dutch listeners differed in some aspects of their processing of vowels and consonants (they had language-specific expectations about the relative contextual variability of the two speech sound classes). Perhaps they also differ in their processing of stress—for instance, they may have language-specific expectations about permissible patterns of stress. Donselaar, Koster, and Cutler (2005) conducted a cross-modal fragment priming experiment in Dutch that closely resembled Soto-Faraco et al.'s (2001) stress study. They used pairs of Dutch words like *octopus* 'octopus' and *oktober* 'October'. Both words begin with the same first two syllables, *octo*, with the same vowels; but the first syllable is stressed in *octopus* and the second in *oktober*. The results of their experiment exactly paralleled the results found by Soto-Faraco et al. Responses were significantly faster after matching primes (*OCto-*, OCTOPUS or *okTO-*, OKTOBER) and significantly slower after mismatching primes (*OCto-*, OKTOBER or *okTO-*, OCTOPUS) than after a control prime.

Thus there is no difference in the use of stress information in Spanish and Dutch word recognition. Both Spanish and Dutch are stress languages, and in both languages listeners can use the stress information in a couple of syllables to reduce their set of lexical choices—including some phonemically matching candidates and excluding others.

1.5.2 Lexical Stress in Word Recognition: Language-Specificity

Now imagine (especially if you are an English native speaker) conducting the same experiment in English. Like Spanish and Dutch, English is a language in which stress distinctions can be the only difference between two unrelated words. Like *CAso* and *caSO*, or *BEbe* and *beBE* in Spanish, there are minimal pairs in English: *INsight* versus *inCITE*, or *FORbear* versus *forBEAR*, *FOREgoing* versus *forGOing*, *TRUSty* versus *trusTEE*. To be strictly correct, there are not that many more than these if the two members of the pair have to be unrelated in meaning—in all, there are maybe a little more than a dozen pairs in the language. But there are not that many minimal pairs in Spanish or Dutch, either. No stress language has many such unrelated minimal pairs, it turns out. The usefulness of stress in word recognition is not really in distinguishing minimal pairs but in distinguishing between whole sets of words beginning with stressed versus unstressed versions of the same syllable—*PRINci-* versus *prinCI-*, *OCto-* versus *okTO-*, and so on. This reduction of choices really helps.

So to do this experiment in English, we ideally need pairs of words beginning with the same two syllables, with the same vowels, where stress falls on the first syllable in one word and on the second syllable in the other—like the *PRINci-* versus *prinCI-* of *principe* and *principio*, or the *OCto-* versus *okTO-* of *octopus* versus *oktober*. The reader should now take a pause and generate pairs of such words in English.

The results are necessarily disappointing. Apart from the minimal pairs (and there aren't enough of them for a good experiment!) there are no such word pairs in English. The first syllables can often be matched (one stressed, one unstressed, otherwise phonemically identical) but then not the second. Consider English *October* versus *octopus*. These are quite similar to the cognate pair in Dutch. Both begin with *oc-*, and this syllable is stressed in *octopus* but unstressed in *October*. In the first syllables, the vowels are the same. But in the second syllables, the vowels in English are not the same (unlike the Dutch case). In English *October*, the stressed second syllable is *to*, pronounced [to]. In English *octopus*, however, the unstressed second syllable is not [to]. It is [tə]. An unstressed syllable that follows a stressed syllable in English, especially if the word is longer than two syllables, is nearly always going to be reduced. This makes for a phonemic difference between *octopus* and *October*, on top of the stress difference. As we discussed earlier, listeners always have to pay attention to phonemic differences; so if they have a phonemic difference to distinguish these two words, how can we tell whether they are attending to the stress difference or just to the phonemic difference? In order to tell whether they use stress, we have to find a case where the suprasegmental stress difference is all that can be used.

Well, there are such cases in English after all, and they are not completely different from the Spanish and Dutch pairs. Soto-Faraco et al. (2001) had some Spanish pairs that differed not in first versus second syllable stress, but in second versus third, such as *eSTAtua* 'statue' versus *estaTUto* 'statute'. Donselaar et al. (2005) likewise had pairs in Dutch like *paRAde* 'parade' versus *paraDIJS* 'paradise'. If one goes a step further and allows first-syllable stress to contrast with third-syllable stress, then English provides pairs in which the first two syllables differ only in stress. Indeed, Donselaar et al.'s Dutch materials even included some such pairs—for example, *DOminee* 'minister' versus *domiNANT* 'dominant'. Third-syllable stress in an English word necessarily means a secondary stress on the first syllable, because English does not allow a word to begin with two weak syllables in a row. (Again, this requirement is language specific—some free-stress languages, such as Dutch, do allow words in which the first and second syllables are both weak, such as the Dutch word *tegelijk*, 'simultaneously'.)

In English word pairs like *admiral* versus *admiration*, or *elephant* versus *elevation*, there is therefore a contrast between secondary versus primary stress on the first syllable. In both cases, the second syllable is reduced. The first syllable of both *admiral* and *admiration* is [æd] and the second syllable of each is [mə]; but *admiral* is stressed on the first syllable, whereas *admiration* is stressed on the third, which triggers secondary stress on *ad-*. This is the only kind of contrast that one can examine in an English experiment modeled on the Spanish and Dutch studies. Cooper, Cutler, and Wales (2002) conducted an English experiment just like the Spanish study of Soto-Faraco et al., using pairs like *admiral* and *admiration*, or *elephant* and *elevation*. The listeners (Australian students) heard fragments of these words at the end of nonconstraining sentences like *I can't believe he can't spell admi-*; their responses to a visual lexical decision target such as ADMIRAL or ADMIRATION were measured.

What they found was that English listeners could indeed make use of the stress information, but they appeared to rely on it to a lesser extent than Spanish or Dutch listeners did. Specifically, responses after a matching prime (e.g., *ADmi-*, ADMIRAL)

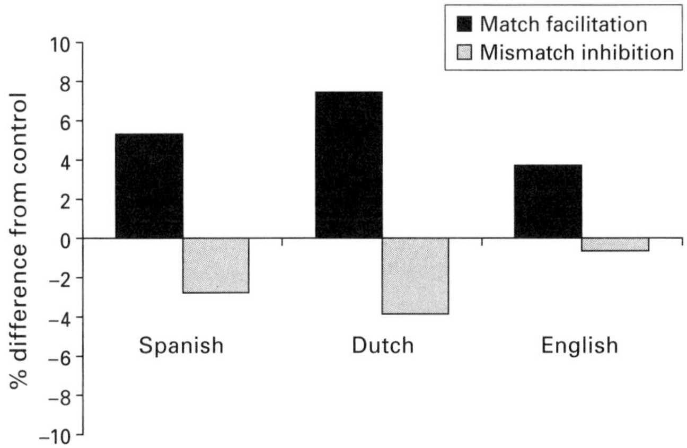

Figure 1.3
In comparable cross-modal fragment priming studies in Spanish, Dutch, and English, primes that match the target in stress pattern facilitate responses in all languages. Mismatching stress, however, produces inhibition in Spanish and Dutch but not in English. (The figure shows the difference between RT given matching or mismatching prime, and RT given control prime, expressed as percentage of control condition RT. Data from Soto-Faraco et al. 2001; Donselaar et al. 2005; Cooper et al. 2002.)

were significantly faster than after a control prime. But a mismatching prime (e.g., *admi-*, ADMIRAL) did not make responses slower than in the control condition. In other words, the English listeners could not use stress information as effectively to reject alternative interpretations of the input.

Figure 1.3 summarizes the facilitation due to stress match, and the inhibition due to stress mismatch, across the three experiments with comparable bisyllabic fragment primes. The English results resemble the results from other languages in the matching condition (although the amount of facilitation in English is less than in Dutch and Spanish), but they are really quite different in the mismatching condition (where the English effect is almost nonexistent). Thus all three languages have free stress, yet the degree to which listeners use the free-stress information in lexical activation differs across the three.

1.5.3 Stress in Word Recognition: The Source of Cross-language Variability

What is responsible for this crosslinguistic difference? Is it due to characteristics of the listener populations? Or to differences in the experiments? Or should we ascribe it to the languages themselves?

1. First, consider the listeners and how they activate words. Are English listeners simply less sensitive to mismatching information in word recognition? No, because

evidence from other experiments reveals that they have just as much sensitivity to mismatch as listeners in other languages. For instance, in a cross-modal fragment priming study in which English listeners responded to, say, DEAF after the prime *daff-* from *daffodil*, the vowel information was used rapidly and the potential competitor word was rapidly rejected. English listeners are apparently just as sensitive to mismatching segmental information as Soto-Faraco et al.'s Spanish listeners were when they inhibited *minoria* after hearing *mine-* from *mineria*.[4]

2. Then could differences in the experiments have played a role? The experimental design was closely matched across the three studies, but the materials could not be exactly the same. Recall that the type of stress contrast tested in the English experiment was primary versus secondary stress in *ad-* from *admiral* versus *admiration*, because pairs differing in primary stress versus no stress (as in *prin-* from *principe* versus *principio*) cannot be found in English. But pairs such as *admiral/admiration* also occurred in the Spanish and Dutch experiments, as we saw, and they showed stress effects no less than the pairs such as *principe/principio* or *octopus/oktober*. Donselaar et al. explicitly tested the type of stress contrast in their statistical analyses; pairs such as *DOMinee-domiNANT* contributed 45 milliseconds of facilitation and 30 milliseconds of inhibition. Post hoc analyses of Soto-Faraco et al.'s materials revealed that pairs such as *eSTAtua/estaTUto* likewise produced significant facilitation and inhibition effects.

3. Could the fault be with English speakers and the cues they provide to stress? Perhaps the information in the signal was simply not as useful in the English experiment as in the others. But, in fact, acoustic measurements reported later by Cutler et al. (2007) showed that the fragments in the Cooper et al. (2002) study differed significantly in all dimensions in which stress is cued (fundamental frequency, duration, and amplitude), with an effect size large enough to be extremely useful to perceivers.

4. Could the difference then arise from the use of stress as an interword distinction across languages—that is, from the rarity of stress-based minimal pairs such as *trusty/trustee* in English? No again, because such pairs are vanishingly rare in Spanish and Dutch, too.

5. Could English listeners' disregard of stress information then have arisen because English allows vowel reduction, so that stress covaries with vowel quality in words? No, again this alone cannot be the explanation, because Dutch has vowel reduction, too. Spanish does not, but as we saw, the effects of stress in word recognition were similar in Spanish and Dutch. It is only English that is different.

6. Thus a language-based difference between English on the one hand and Dutch and Spanish on the other is the most likely source of the asymmetric results pattern. Cooper et al. argued that the crucial difference was the rarity, in English, of unstressed syllables with full vowels. Unstressed English syllables nearly always have weak

(reduced) vowels. In Dutch, this is much less the case. Pairs of English and Dutch words with the same meaning and etymology (cognates) illustrate this point perfectly. In English, *cobra* has a weak second syllable; in Dutch, *cobra* has two strong syllables. English *cigar* has a weak first syllable; Dutch *sigaar* has two strong syllables. Cooper et al. suggested that these vowel patterns made pairs of English words more segmentally distinct. English listeners could rely to a much greater extent on segmental distinctions between words and had learned from experience that they need pay little attention to suprasegmental stress distinctions.

As is documented in chapter 2, such differences have far-reaching implications for the listener's task in translating speech into its component words. Cooper et al.'s explanation was resoundingly supported by vocabulary comparisons across the three languages: the profit that a listener has from using stress in word activation is significantly greater in Spanish and in Dutch than in English. Disregarding stress information is no more than sensible behavior for English listeners.

1.5.4 A Language-Specific Feature in Listening: Summary

Again, we could not have understood the role of this feature in listening by studying just one language. If we had only had the results from one of these free-stress languages, we would have been left with a misleading picture of the role of lexical stress in the initial activation of candidate words. Whether a feature of language is universal or language specific, its role in speech processing can best be understood by comparing across experiments in different languages.

Further, although stress is indubitably not universal, in that many languages do not distinguish between words in this way, considering the use of stress in word recognition has given us further insight into potentially universal characteristics of speech processing. It has highlighted once again the efficiency with which we listen. Many aspects of word phonology are represented by information in speech signals, but it is not the case that we as listeners necessarily take full account of all of the available information. The distinctions that are more useful to us are exploited; those that are less useful are not.

1.6 The Psycholinguistic Enterprise

The two detailed case studies have set the stage for the reviews of listening research in the chapters to come. From the studies of vowels and consonants, we see that most vowel-consonant processing differences have their roots in the articulatory phonetics of speech sound production. Consonants often change rapidly over time whereas vowels usually have a steady-state core; small differences between two vowel tokens are easier for the listener to discriminate than small differences between two consonant tokens, and vowel hypotheses are easier to alter than consonant hypotheses. Other effects, however, stem from the structure of the vocabulary. How easy it is to produce a rapid detection response for a phoneme target depends on one's language-specific experience with the potential for contextual variability.

From the stress studies, we see that a language-specific feature can vary because of a universal processing constraint. The roots of the crosslinguistic processing difference for Spanish, Dutch, and English stress lie in phonology; phonologically, all three languages are in the free-stress class, but the details of their stress realization are subtly different. In English, stress is realized in large part via segmental differences, whereas in Spanish it is realized fully via suprasegmental means. Dutch lies in between—on the one hand, there are segmental reflections of stress (i.e., vowel reduction occurs, but in unstressed syllables only); on the other hand, there are also many unstressed syllables with full vowels. Such syllables are much less common in English (as the English/Dutch comparisons such as *cobra* or *cigar/sigaar* illustrate). These differences force Spanish listeners to pay attention to suprasegmental structure in order to detect stress distinctions, encourage Dutch listeners to exploit suprasegmental cues to stress, but allow English listeners to get away with perceiving most stress distinctions without the need for any suprasegmental processing at all. Universally, each population is behaving with optimal efficiency for word recognition.

These case studies show how psycholinguists have to operate. Language processing is a universal set of procedures modulated by experience with a particular language. It is not enough to examine an aspect of language processing, even a universal one, in a single language and assume that the whole story is known. Psycholinguistics must always be comparative: we can only understand how listeners process language by establishing how listeners process languages.

1.6.1 When Psycholinguistics Acted as If There Were Only One Language

Psycholinguistics has, however, often been in some danger of assuming that there is really only one language (and not just because, as with so many scientific disciplines, most psycholinguists are speakers of English and the scientific output from English-speaking countries dominates the psycholinguistic literature). As already noted, the most significant fact about language acquisition is that the language a child acquires is the language that the environment makes available; the child's specific genetic endowment brings no leanings toward one language rather than another. The implied universality of the processing system underlying both language acquisition and later language use actually formed something of a danger to the psycholinguistic enterprise, because in the earlier decades of psycholinguistics—the 1960s and 1970s—it tended to be interpreted rather simplistically.

The task of psycholinguistics was seen as the discovery of the human language processing system. Precisely because of the fact that children acquire any language to which they are exposed, this system was assumed to have a universal basis. The consequences of crosslinguistic variation for language acquisition certainly played an important role in the early psycholinguistic program (see, for example, Slobin 1982); but the basic goal was an account of the universal system that dealt with these variable inputs. The aim of psycholinguistics could not be the study of language-specific phenomena, because a catalog of language-specific effects would never constitute an account of the universal underlying system. The effect of this credo was that early studies of adult processing were conceived as axiomatically independent of the language in which they happened to be carried out. It was entirely possible for an experiment carried out in one language to be followed up, supported, or countered by an experiment in another language, without any reference being made to whether the difference in language might play a role in the processes at issue.

An example is the history of the lexical ambiguity effect in phoneme detection. The inventor of this task, Foss (1970), reported that phonemes were detected less rapidly if the immediately preceding word was ambiguous (so detection of [b] was slower in *The punch barely affected the old man* than in *The cocktail barely affected the old man*). The word *cocktail* only invited one interpretation, but *punch* activated two potential interpretations; Foss suggested that in the second case more processing work was required, which slowed detection of the target phoneme at that point in the sentence. A minor industry arose in exploring this effect—for example, how long it lasted (Cairns and Kamerman 1975) and whether contextual cues could remove it (Foss and Jenkins 1973; Swinney and Hakes 1976). But the industry collapsed when Mehler, Segui, and Carey (1978) pointed out that there was a tendency in all studies of this ambiguity effect for the unambiguous words (such as *cocktail*) to be longer than the ambiguous words (such as *punch*). Mehler et al. showed that phoneme detection was slower after short words than after long words, and further that ambiguous words paired with unambiguous words of the same length did not differ in their effect on detection of a following phoneme. Mehler et al.'s interpretation of the length effect was that longer words require no more lexical processing than shorter words, but they occupy more input time, thus delaying the arrival of the next chunk of input to be processed. At the end of a long word, therefore, processing has progressed further than at the end of a short word, so that more processing capacity is available for detection of the target phoneme.

The four above studies reporting an ambiguity effect were conducted in English; Mehler et al.'s study was in French. No consequences were drawn from this difference, and the difference in language played no role at all in how the findings were interpreted.

It is not my intention here to postulate crosslinguistic differences in effects of word length or ambiguity in phoneme detection. Perhaps there are none. I record these old disputes only as an example of how far the possibility of cross-language processing differences was from the consciousness of leading psycholinguists in the early years of the discipline. Today, I assume that such a difference in the language in which listening experiments are carried out would never go unremarked. At the very least, researchers would feel bound to argue that the difference was irrelevant with respect to the theoretical question. This is because the last quarter century of psycholinguistic study has produced ample evidence of crosslinguistic processing asymmetries, as well as plenty of examples of fruitful comparison of results across languages of the type described in our two case studies.

As chapter 4 recounts, it was the study of the segmentation of continuous speech that really proved that language-specific processing formed a necessary part of adult listening. It should, however, have been obvious simply from a comparison of the listener's task given different languages. In chapter 2 we consider what spoken language is like and how language-specific structure can fundamentally alter the challenge that the listener faces in understanding speech. But first, let us consider the following question:

1.6.2 What Would Life Be Like If We Only Had One Language?

Figure 1.4 shows three views of Fouron-St.-Martin/St.-Martens-Voeren, a small village in northeast Belgium. The signpost at the entrance to the village has been

Figure 1.4
Signs in the village of Fouron-St-Martin/St-Martens-Voeren, September 2005 (photographs by the author).

defaced; someone tried to remove the Dutch name and leave only the French name. In the middle of the village, outside the village school, a cheery sign exhorting motorists to slow down near the school exit has also been disfigured; someone has spray-painted over the French text, leaving only the Dutch text legible. At the other end of the village, both parties must have attacked the village sign, for both the Dutch and the French names are blacked out. The village's identity is lost under the reciprocal display of hate.

Languages, and the fact that we do not all speak the same language, can cause a good deal of trouble. Seeing evidence of language conflict, as in this Belgian village and in many other places in the world, we have to ask: Surely life would be simpler if we all spoke the same language? In very many ways, of course it would. Certainly there would be no language conflicts, and thus no spray-painters in the night changing the language of signposts. There would be no need to select a lingua franca in international communication, with the disadvantages that brings for the scientists, international politicians, or business staff with a mother tongue other than the chosen medium. Many jobs would disappear: there would be no second-language teachers, translators, or interpreters (and certainly no comparative psycholinguists). But many would benefit—workers could more easily move to where the jobs are, refugees could more easily build up a new existence, and cross-cultural communication would face fewer barriers. Nevertheless, in countless ways life with only one known language would be the poorer. And there is no doubt that psycholinguistics would be poorer, for we would be permanently unable to understand language processing in the human mind.

Suppose that the one language we had were Spanish (or a language with all the characteristics of Spanish). We would conclude from our experiments that listeners use segmental and suprasegmental information in word recognition with equal readiness, and we would never suspect that it would be possible to ignore one of these information channels (almost) entirely. We would learn that in a simple phoneme detection task, vowels are more affected by uncertainty in consonantal context than vice versa, and that in word reconstruction, vowels are easier to replace than consonants, and we would have no way of finding out whether these patterns arose from intrinsic differences between vowels and consonants or from the asymmetry by which the one available language happened to have four times as many consonants as vowels.

If the one language we had were Dutch, we would conclude that suprasegmental information is used in word recognition, so the fact that stress also has segmental repercussions (via vowel reduction) has no effect on listeners' division of attention among the segmental and suprasegmental cues. We would also conclude that vowels and consonants are equally affected by contextual uncertainty in phoneme detection, but vowels are easier to replace than consonants in word reconstruction, so perhaps the latter result reflects a difference in the role of vowels and consonants in access to the lexicon.

And if the one language we had were English, we would conclude that stress produces a mixture of segmental and suprasegmental effects, and listeners can pretty much get by without the suprasegmental channel in word recognition. We would learn that vowels are easier to replace than consonants in word reconstruction, which might lead us to conclude that vowels play a lesser role than consonants in speech processing in general.

All of these conclusions differ from the more detailed picture we get by comparing across languages. Some of the conclusions are flat out wrong, some are half-truths, but all are inevitably dependent on the language-specificity that is only shown to exist by comparison. Vowels and consonants are the phonetic building blocks of all speech, but differences in the way they are processed by listeners can arise both as a result of their intrinsic properties and as a result of the structure of the language-specific phonemic repertoire. Stress occurs only in some of the world's languages, but the way it fits into language-specific phonology affects the way it is processed and hence tells us about the interdependence of phonology and processing. Thus even phenomena that are universal across languages cannot be properly evaluated with respect to their role in processing by looking in one language only, and even phenomena that are clearly not universal can tell us something about the universal processing model.

So, life might in many ways be simpler if we all spoke the same language. But for the psycholinguist, life would be harder, because the window onto language processing provided by cross-language comparison would be blocked.

2 What Is Spoken Language Like?

The ultimate determinant of how we listen to spoken language is what the spoken language itself is like. This chapter considers the nature of speech and shows how the makeup of phonemic inventories determines what vocabularies are like, which in turn determines what listeners have to learn. From the nature of speech it is inevitable that listeners have to process utterances that are fast, continuous, and variable, and from the relative size of phonemic repertoires versus vocabularies it is inevitable that words will resemble and overlap one another. Although these properties of spoken language are universal, languages differ in what kinds of words their vocabularies contain. Moreover, the ways in which languages express interword contrasts (segmental or suprasegmental) lead listeners to learn how words may be most efficiently distinguished in a particular vocabulary. Language processing is constrained, and made more language specific, by this learning. Finally, this chapter also discusses how growing knowledge of the structure of vocabularies shaped spoken-word recognition models, across the two distinguishable generations of such models so far.

What the listener has to do to understand speech is determined by the nature of the speech itself. Once we know what spoken language is like, much of what we need to know about what listening is like simply follows. There are four central properties of spoken utterances that are responsible for this, as section 2.1 lays out.

2.1 Fast, Continuous, Variable, and Nonunique

The first point to make about speech is that it is fast. Even slow speech is fast, because it presents a great deal of continually changing information. Figure 2.1 shows the rate at which information arrives in a ten-second excerpt from a monologue spoken at a comfortably slow rate by a native speaker of American English.[1] The top panel shows a waveform of the speech. The second panel divides the excerpt into its constituent propositions (there are four of these). In the third panel, the individual words are specified; depending on how filler syllables and repetitions are counted, there are not quite fifty of these—in any case, there are sixty-eight syllables. The bottom panel records the phonemes that were spoken in the ten seconds: all 175 of them. Given that this little excerpt is no trouble at all for a (native English)

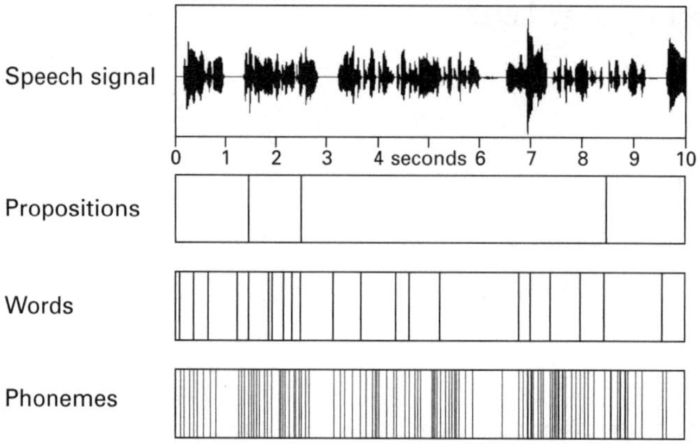

Figure 2.1
An American English speaker says, over 10 seconds, *Then once you have examined the city, you can get a, uh, nice contrast to the surrounding countryside, uh, a very unique countryside which contrasts the distinction between the, the mountains to the, uh, lowlands of the coastal regions where there is a lot more, uh, fishing.* The excerpt is taken from an experiment in which spontaneous speech was collected in the laboratory.

listener to understand, the listener obviously is not perturbed by having to process 6.8 words per second, involving 17.5 phonemic discriminations per second. At a fast rate of speech, much more is demanded, but listeners can easily cope with speech that is much faster than this. Dupoux and Green (1997) experimented with speech that was electronically compressed at different rates. They found that with (not very much) practice, listeners can understand speech that is presented at a rate faster than even the fastest speaker can possibly articulate.

The second important feature of speech is that it is continuous. An English utterance of six words (in fourteen syllables), spoken by a female native speaker, is shown as a spectrogram in figure 2.2. With a bit of effort, it is not too hard to find most of the syllables, by locating short portions that show what look like horizontal stripes. These stripes indicate a vowel (they are formants: resonances of the vocal tract during the period of unobstructed airflow as a vowel is uttered). But once we have counted the syllables, how should they be assigned to words? And where are the boundaries between the six words? (Look at the spectrogram before looking at the caption!)

In this sentence, there is a clear gap in the speech signal shortly after it begins. But this gap actually has nothing to do with a word boundary. It is due to a brief obstruction of the vocal tract in the course of producing one of the segments in the word *lexical*: the second [k] sound in this word. Many speech sounds involve such obstruction; lips must be closed to make a [b], the flow of air must be stopped by

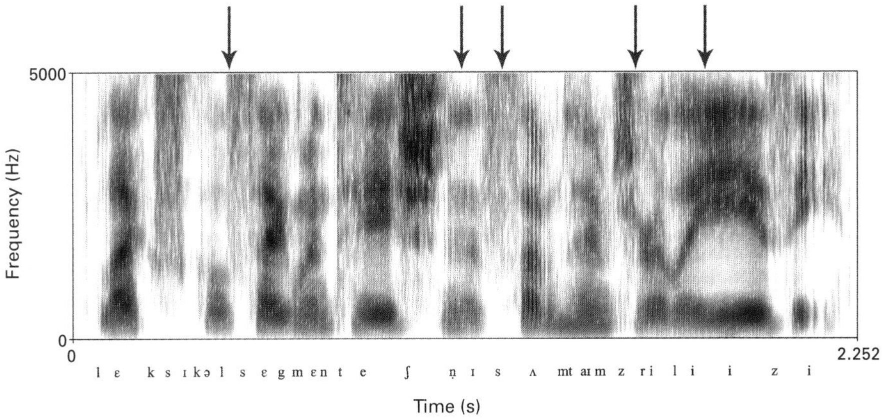

Figure 2.2
A spectrogram of the English utterance *Lexical segmentation is sometimes really easy*, uttered by a female speaker of American English. Spectrograms represent frequency on the vertical axis against time on the horizontal axis, with darker portions representing greater energy. If the vocal folds are vibrating, causing a voiced sound to be uttered, there is energy in the lowest regions of the spectrogram; voiceless sounds cause a gap in that region of the spectrogram. Fricatives have broadly distributed energy in the high-frequency regions, so they are easy to find; this utterance has seven of them (at the end of *lex*, - *is*, and *-times*, and at the beginning of *seg-*, *-tion*, *some-*, and *-sy*). Two of them (*is*, *some-*) have merged into one, so six can be seen, as fairly broad columns. Stripy-looking portions are vowels, where the vocal tract resonates at harmonics of the speaker's fundamental frequency (pitch of the voice) as the vowel goes on for a short period of time. What *cannot* be seen are clear divisions between words! The words run into one another without a gap. The arrows show where boundaries of words occur.

placing the tongue against the alveolar ridge behind the teeth to make a [t]. The result is a brief period in which nothing emanates from the vocal tract. Such silent periods are not there to divide the speech; they are just components of the information encoding segmental identity. Listeners extract phonemic information from the silence.

The boundaries are often not marked at all. One word just runs imperceptibly into the next. For instance, this utterance contains several fricatives, which can easily be seen because there is energy all the way up the frequency scale: the [s] in *lex-*, the [s] and [ʃ] of *segmentation*, and so on. One of these fricatives, just past the middle of the utterance, is longer than the others, and it is long because it is actually two phonemes—the final sound of *is* and the initial sound of *sometimes*. Where one of these ends and the next begins is really not possible to say. The same is true of the [i] at the end of *really* and the [i] that is the beginning of *easy*. It is not only when similar sounds abut that boundaries are hard to see in a spectrogram, either; the [l] at the end of *lexical* and the initial [s] of *segmentation* are quite different, so one can tell where the signal changes from one to the other, but they appear closer to one another in time than the [eɪ] and [ʃ] in *-ation*, which occur within the same word.

Speech in all languages is continuous, and this continuity has extensive implications for the listener's task. Chapters 4 and 5 are entirely devoted to research on segmenting speech into its component words. But spoken language has further features that the listener must deal with. For instance, it is variable. In figure 2.2, *lexical* has two instances of [k] (after *le-* and before *-al*), but they look very different. In figure 2.4, discussed below, there are three instances of [t], which are likewise different. Listeners cannot assume that speech will present each occurrence of a speech sound in exactly the same form. Chapter 6 is entirely devoted to research on the variability of speech and how listeners cope with it.

Again, this variability is a feature of speech in all languages, and it is not only caused by variation in the context (phonetic or lexical) in which a speech sound appears. The same sequence of sounds can convey more than one message. In English, for instance, we can say *I saw our cargo* or *I saw our car go*; the sequence of sounds is the same. This can happen in any language. Consider the two spectrograms of figure 2.3, which represent two Dutch utterances: *Voor mij is er geen luisteraar* 'There's no listener for me', and *Voor mij is er geen luis te raar* 'There's no louse too strange for me'. Like the *cargo/car go* sentences, these two utterances present the same sequence of speech sounds. The second utterance, though, contains two more word boundaries than the first, before each of the last two syllables, But as the spectrograms show, the last three syllables (from around 0.8 on the timescale) do not seem to differ very much across the two versions at all. In fact the overlapping earlier parts of the utterances—*Voor mij is er geen*, exactly the same five words in each sentence—differ at least as much, if not more, than the nonoverlapping later parts *luis te raar* versus *luisteraar*. In the later parts there is perhaps a longer closure for the [t] of *te* (the gap, at around 1.1) in utterance (b) *luis te raar*. But in the earlier parts, the word *voor* is notably longer (ending at 0.25) in (b) than in (a) (where it ends at 0.2), whereas the initial [x] sound of *geen* (the high-frequency energy visible just after 0.7) is clearly shorter in (b) *geen luis* than in (a) *geen luisteraar*.

Figure 2.3 and the next, figure 2.4, well illustrate the final important characteristic of speech: it is nonunique. Whenever we hear the word *luisteraar*, we also hear a string that could be the three words *luis te raar*. English is no better than Dutch in this respect. Whenever we hear the word *cargo*, we also hear a string that could be *car go*. The speaker in figure 2.4 intended there to be five words in the utterance, namely: *When do we start writing?*; but there are potentially many more. The speaker did not intend to say *wend*, *end*, *east*, *star*, *art*, *rye*, *try*, or *trite*, but these words were indeed said—or at least the sounds that would form these words were said, in the right order. The lower spectrograms in the figure show intended utterances of *wend*, *star*, and *trite*, spoken in isolation by the same speaker. They can be compared with

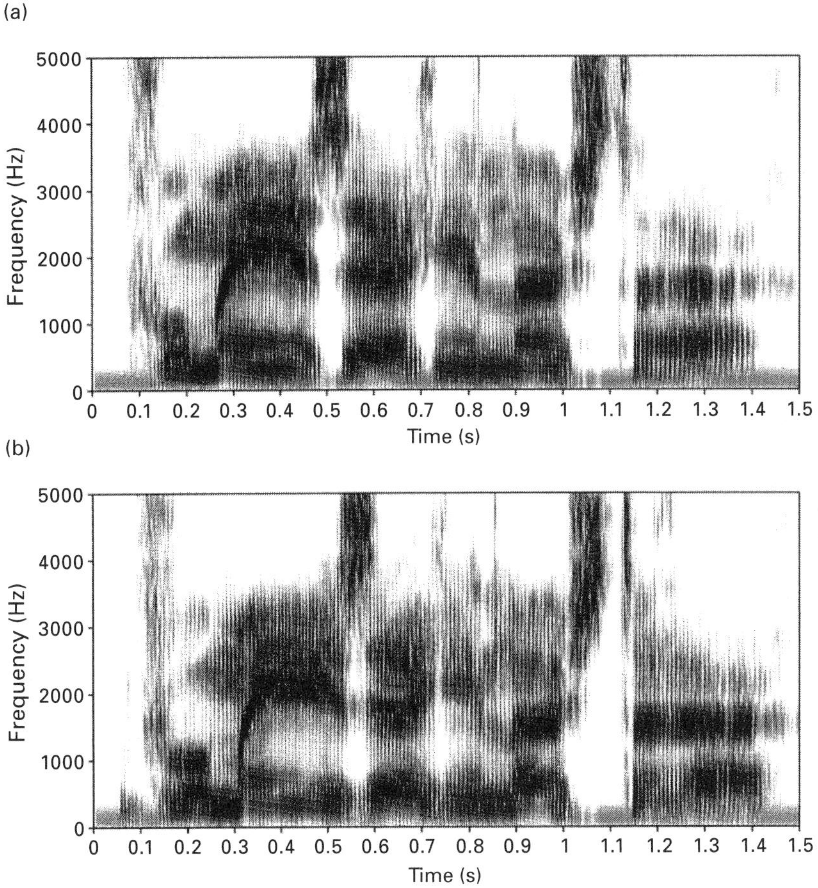

Figure 2.3
Spectrograms of an ambiguous sequence in Dutch. Above: *Voor mij is er geen luisteraar*; below: *Voor mij is er geen luis te raar*.

the corresponding portions of the upper figure 2.4. For the listener, then, processing an utterance like that in figure 2.4 involves contriving not to recognize those unintended words; recognizing the utterances in figures 2.3a and 2.3b likewise involves not getting mixed up with the other possible sequence of the same sounds. Chapter 3 and much of the rest of the present chapter deal with how listeners succeed in this task.

As will become clear (especially in chapter 6), the variability of speech sounds conveys a lot of information about position of sounds in words and in utterances. But it is important to realize that this does not necessarily remove the problem of nonuniqueness; it just means that the spuriously present words cannot necessarily

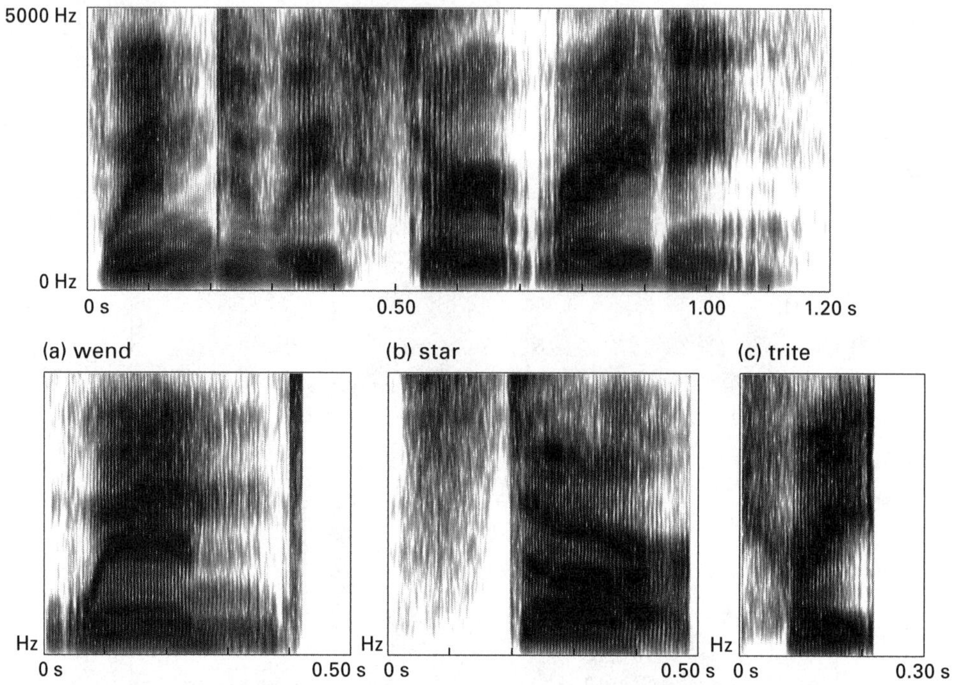

Figure 2.4
Upper panel: The utterance *When do we start writing?*, spoken by a female speaker of American English. There are three instances of [t], at 0.54, 0.72, and 0.92 on the time scale. All of them look different. Portions of the utterance could also be interpreted as other words; this is not only the case with words embedded in longer words (e.g., *star* in *start*) but also with sequences across two adjacent words (e.g., *wend* in *when do*; *trite* in *start writing*). Lower panels: The individual spectrograms (a-c) show the same speaker's utterances of the words *wend*, *star*, and *trite*, all spoken in isolation. They clearly resemble the renditions of the same phonetic sequences in the longer utterances: *wend* resembles the beginning portion of the sentence, up to about 0.21; *star* resembles the beginning of *start* (about 0.41 to 0.69); and *trite* resembles the portion following *star-*, up to about 0.91 in the upper panel.

be predicted from the citation forms of the actually present words. Depending on how *start* is said, it may contain an embedded *tart*, or *dart*. There may be no spurious utterance of *try* in *start writing* if the speaker deleted the final [t] of *start* (chapter 6 will show that this is quite likely); but the resulting string could then be compatible with *awry* instead. The statistics of lexical embedding, discussed in section 2.3, make it clear that however an utterance is realized, many more words are supported by the speech signal than the speaker actually intended.

Together with the continuity of speech, this presents the listener with a formidable selection problem. Nor is within-word embedding such as *luis* in *luisteraar* the whole

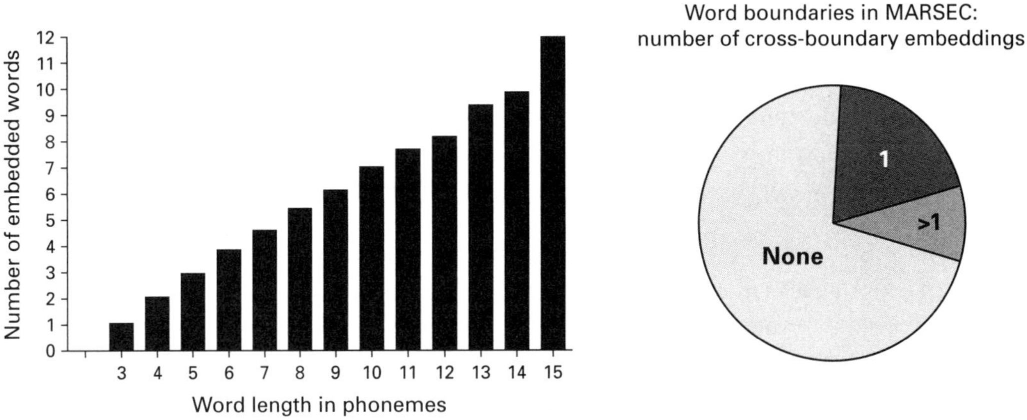

Figure 2.5
Lexical embedding in MARSEC (Machine-Readable Spoken English Corpus). Left: Mean number of embedded words within words, as a function of carrier word length in phonemes. Right: Proportion of word boundaries with no, one, or more than one cross-boundary embedding.

story. Many of the spuriously present words in figures 2.3 and 2.4 were not embedded in a single carrier word but were spread across adjacent words. The embedded word *end* combines material from *when* and *do*, *east* crosses the boundary of *we* and *start*, and so on. Some statistics from the Spoken English Corpus (SEC) are shown in figure 2.5. This is a small corpus by today's standards: about 50,000 words of spoken British English, collected in the 1980s (Roach et al. 1993). But it is good-quality speech, mostly taken from radio broadcasts; a lot of it might be termed semirehearsed, as it was spoken in panel discussions, interviews, and the like. Even in this not overly casual variety of speech, embedding within words is rife, as the figure shows. The longer the word, the more embeddings (an example from the right bar of the bar chart is *incompatibility*, with 15 phonemes and 11 embedded words: *ink*, *compatibility*, *pat*, *patter*, *at*, *to*, *a*, *bill*, *ill*, *ability*, *tea*). Further, nearly one-third of all word boundaries in this corpus have at least one word embedded across them (e.g., *swan* in *workforce wants*; *sting* in *against England*).

What speech is like, then, is: not immediately transparent for the listener. Speech is fast, continuous, variable, and nonunique. So now on to the rest of the story: how do listeners deal with this and actually manage to recognize what speakers say?

2.2 How Listeners Succeed in Recognizing Words in Speech

Much of this whole book is concerned with the consequences for the listener of the continuity of speech signals and the nonuniqueness of their mapping to words.

Before we go on here to explore the structure of the vocabulary in detail, we should note one important fact, perhaps the most basic fact of all, about spoken-word recognition; it is an active process of hypothesis construction. Listeners do not simply wait and understand utterances once they end. Nor do they even wait till the end of a word. Multiple word candidates, potentially consistent with the incoming speech, are considered concurrently. This has been established with a variety of laboratory techniques.

2.2.1 Ambiguous Onsets

As listeners, we are accustomed to using our eyes as well as our ears. If we are hearing a story, our eyes follow the speaker's concomitant gestures or move to mentioned participants or objects. This can be exploited in the laboratory by carefully tracking listeners' eye movements as they hear speech (see panel 6). Usually in such experiments there is a simple task involved: *click on the candle*, a listener might hear, while the computer screen presents a display of several objects, one of them a candle. Cooper (1974) first proposed the use of eye-tracking to study spoken-language processing, and Tanenhaus et al. (1995) brought the task into the armory of the modern spoken-word recognition researcher. In their version, eye movements were tracked with a head-mounted camera; later equipment is simpler, and tracks the pupils of the eye while the viewer's head stays more or less in the same place on a chin rest. Eye-tracking has become an invaluable tool for examining the time-course of word recognition and the availability of potential words as the speech signal unfolds. Suppose the display contains, besides a candle, a duck and a ladder and a picture of some candy. At the point at which listeners hear *click on the cand...*, they are as likely to be looking at the candy as at the candle. Listeners trying to understand speech do not wait until words are fully available; they consider multiple possible continuations in parallel. This includes words like *candy* and *candle* that begin in the same way, but also words that are embedded within other words and words that rhyme (i.e., end in the same way). Thus listeners might look at a ham when they were hearing about a hamster (Salverda, Dahan, and McQueen 2003), or at a speaker when they were hearing about a beaker (Allopenna, Magnuson, and Tanenhaus 1998).

The cross-modal fragment priming task described in chapter 1 is another good method for showing how listeners entertain multiple lexical hypotheses in parallel. The classic first demonstration of this is a study by Zwitserlood (1989) involving pairs of (Dutch) words like *kapitein* 'captain' and *kapitaal* 'capital'. In sentence (2.1a), both words may be considered equally likely. Swinney's (1979) original prime types were used here; that is, the targets were semantic associates of the prime words. An associate of *kapitaal* is GELD 'money', and an associate of *kapitein* is SCHIP 'ship'. Zwitserlood also carried out separate gating experiments (see panel 7) with

6. Eye-Tracking

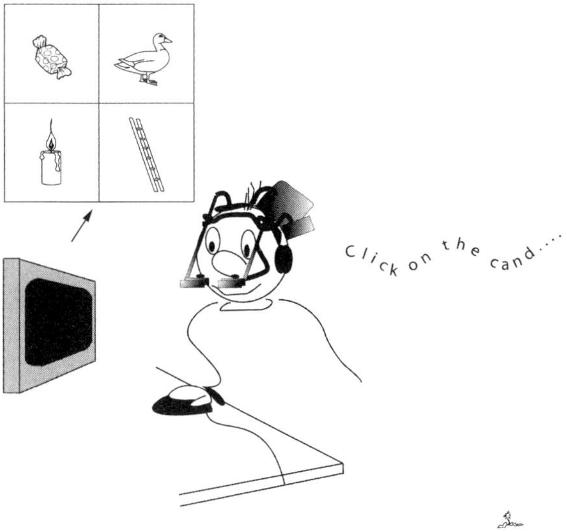

In an eye-tracking experiment in the domain of speech processing, cameras register the eye movements as the listener responds to spoken instructions. The first eye-tracking equipment was used mainly for reading research. Eye-tracking entered spoken-language research when miniature head-mounted cameras allowed eye movements to be monitored during tasks such as manipulation of objects in a computer display. The newest versions do not require cameras to be worn on the head.

Eye-tracking can be used to investigate the same kind of questions as CMP—activation of word candidates given a spoken input. Listeners who hear *click on the candle* may, at the point they hear . . . *the cand-*, be looking at the candy as much as at the candle, given that both are possible candidates. The added value of the eye-tracking technique is that it can give a continuous measure over time of listeners' evaluation of the incoming speech signal—for example, exactly when listeners are sure they are hearing *candle* and not *candy*. Usually, the results are presented as a continuously changing graph of the proportion of looks to alternative items in the display (the named target, the potential competitor, other distractors). Many eye-tracking studies use displays of pictures, but displays of printed words give the same kind of results (McQueen and Viebahn 2007).

7. Gating

In a gating experiment, listeners hear a word (or utterance) in fragments of increasing size, and after each presented fragment they produce a guess about what the input is—for example, *c-*, *ca-*, *cap-*, *capi-*, *capit-*.

The "gated" fragments can be of a constant size (e.g., 50 milliseconds, 100 milliseconds, 150 milliseconds), or they can systematically add more phonetic information (e.g., each fragment adds one more phoneme transition, so that fragment 1 runs to the middle of the first phoneme, fragment 2 to the middle of the second phoneme, fragment 3 to the middle of the third phoneme, etc.).

The gating task was launched into spoken-word recognition research by Grosjean (1980). It is not a very close approximation to natural word recognition, and it suffers from the problem that listeners sometimes stick with bad guesses. However, it can usefully tell us what information is available to be used at each point in the speech signal.

her materials and used the gating responses to determine the amount of the prime word that she presented in the CMFP experiment. At the point at which the gating study showed that listeners could come up with either *kapitein* or *kapitaal* on the basis of the fragmentary input, there was also, in priming, facilitation from the same input for lexical decision responses to both GELD and SCHIP (in comparison to a control target). This suggested that both possible words were available in parallel.

(2.1) a. Ze treurden om het verlies van hun kapit-
'They mourned the loss of their cap-'

b. In bedrukte stemming stonden de mannen rond het graf.
Ze treurden om het verlies van hun kapit-
'Downcast, the men stood round the grave.
They mourned the loss of their cap-. . .'

Another condition included biasing context, which made it clear that only one of the two words was an appropriate continuation. This is the context in (2.1b). In this condition, there was more facilitation for SCHIP (the associate of the contextually appropriate *kapitein*) than for GELD (associate of *kapitaal*, which is inappropriate in the context). This difference was only noticeable, though, when enough of the prime word was presented that listeners in the gating study had been able to identify it (thus, a portion of the final vowel of *kapitein*). Zwitserlood's findings motivate two main conclusions: first, that speech input activates any word that might be compatible with it, allowing multiple words to be concurrently available, irrespective of their contextual probability; and second, that contextual cues to selection are used very quickly, but only after the input has been processed anyway. Thus, context does not override processing of the incoming speech or render such processing unnecessary, and processing of incoming speech always requires consideration of multiple alternatives.

2.2.2 Within- and Cross-Word Embeddings

Cross-modal priming (in various versions, as described in panel 8), after Zwitserlood's pioneering study, became a standard means of displaying the effects of multiple activation. Words that are spuriously embedded within other words can also be activated; for instance, lexical decisions to RIB are facilitated after English listeners hear a sentence prime containing the word *trombone*, which by implication has primed RIB via activation of the embedded associate of RIB, namely *bone* (Shillcock 1990). Likewise, there is facilitation of HUID 'skin' after Dutch listeners hear *velg* 'rim', which contains the embedded word *vel* 'skin' (Vroomen and De Gelder 1997). Facilitation for FLOWER follows either of the prime sentences *She tried to put her tulips in a vase* or *She tried to put her two lips on his cheek*; apparently either the word *tulips* or the same speech sounds in the two-word sequence *two lips* can activate the concept of a flower (Gow and Gordon 1995). Ample evidence from the psycholinguistic laboratory thus shows that words that receive, even temporarily, support from the speech signal may be activated in the listener's mind. (Many comedians would be out of work if this were not true, of course!)

Even words that are embedded across two other words may become active. (Recall figure 2.5; a substantial proportion of boundaries in the Spoken English Corpus had some spuriously embedded word crossing them.) Tabossi, Burani, and Scott (1995) examined such cases in Italian, again with cross-modal priming. In (2.2a), the word *attimi* should produce facilitation for the associated target MOMENTI 'moments'—and indeed it did, compared with the control prime sentence (2.2c).

8. Cross-Modal Priming

As already described in panel 4, the listener in a cross-modal priming (CMP) experiment hears something (the prime) and then sees a target (word or nonword); the task is to decide: is that a real word? The fragment-prime version in panel 4 is especially appropriate for looking at the uptake of information and the consequent activation of candidate words. But the task has more variants. In the picture, the original form of the task is displayed: the participant hears a spoken sentence, during which at some point a visual word is presented.

If the prime and the target are identical (e.g., *give-GIVE*), we refer to identity priming. If the prime and the target are related by association (e.g., *give-TAKE*, as in the illustration) we call it associative priming. CMFP is more often a version of identity priming. But this is not always so (e.g., it was not the case in Zwitserlood's [1989] experiment described in the text). In either case, the reaction time to accept a target word is expected to be faster after a related prime than after a control prime (*say-GIVE* or *say-TAKE*). The two forms of priming do not tap into the same processing level (see chapter 3).

(2.2) a. Nella lettera Sandra parlava di attimi stupendi trascorsi con Carlo.
'In the letter Sandra talked about wonderful moments spent with Carlo.'
b. Nella lettera Sandra parlava di atti misteriosi compiuti da Carlo.
'In the letter Sandra talked about mysterious attitudes that Carlo adopted.'
c. Nella lettera Sandra parlava di gesti strani compiuti da Carlo.
'In the letter Sandra talked about odd gestures that Carlo made.'

But there was also facilitation for MOMENTI during the prime sentence (2.2b); this prime contains *attimi* only as a spurious embedding across the boundary between *atti* 'attitudes' and *misteriosi* 'mysterious'. This result again shows that (temporary) activation of words can involve many more forms than the speaker actually intended.

Chapter 3 presents the complete story of how listeners resolve the problem potentially caused by multiple parallel lexical hypotheses. But the brief results here already underline the importance of understanding the structure of the vocabulary. Spoken-word recognition is sensitive to whatever the speech signal brings in. It is essential to know what that is.

2.3 The Nested Vocabulary

So why does multiple availability of lexical hypotheses occur? Why don't languages ensure that words are unique, or at least minimally confusable? The fundamental reason, it turns out, is the size of the vocabulary. We know a huge number of words—tens of thousands, possibly hundreds of thousands. Vocabularies in all languages, even allowing for conceivable differences in the amount of variation that cultures need to capture in their language, are very large indeed.

Deciding on the exact size of any vocabulary requires a definition of what counts as the unit of vocabulary membership (see section 2.5 below). Dictionaries typically base their definitions on orthographic custom—entries are accorded to each form that may be written as a separate word. This results in some rather arbitrary cross-linguistic differences. The CELEX database (Baayen, Piepenbrock, and Van Rijn 1993) is a computer-readable lexical listing of the vocabularies of English, Dutch, and German, and so it enables us to make direct comparisons across these vocabularies. Even though these languages are really quite similar, remarkable asymmetries appear. For instance, the Dutch lexicon is about four times the size of the English lexicon: something over 280,000 words, compared to 70,000 words of English. This surely does not mean that the Dutch language is richer than English in the number of lexical concepts. Culturally, both languages are anchored in Western societies, both have been enriched by a past history of imperialism and colonial domination of cultures with very different languages, both are world languages spoken in several different societies, both have lively literary and intellectual traditions, and, most importantly, the two are very closely related. There is little doubt that the conceptual stock of the two languages is nigh on identical. The principal reason for the difference in CELEX vocabulary size is just an artifact of orthographic convention: compound concepts are written together as one form in Dutch but are written as two parts in English. The compound *can opener* in English and *blikopener* in Dutch are identical in meaning and structure; it is purely an accident of orthography that the Dutch form is written together (and thus adds one more word form to the CELEX total for Dutch), whereas the English form is written as separate units that are already listed in CELEX and hence need not be listed again.

An additional small part of the extra size comes from the richer morphology of Dutch (see section 2.5.1 below). CELEX contains a separate listing for each conventionally used separate form, so all inflected forms of a verb add to the total. The English verb *walk* has four forms: *walk*, *walks*, *walked*, and *walking*. Its Dutch equivalent, *lopen*, has seven: *lopen*, *loopt*, *loop*, *liep*, *liepen*, *lopend*, and *gelopen*. This too adds to the asymmetry between the two lists.

The orthographic differences between Dutch and English have practical significance for the makers of dictionaries, as well as for other specialist populations such as the solvers of crossword puzzles (consider that the clue for *false teeth* in a British crossword, including as customary the number of letters in its component words, might be *unnatural bite* (5,5); as an equivalent clue in Dutch, *onnatuurlijk bijten* (10) gives just a little less help for the puzzler to find *kunstgebit*). But the conventions governing how compound forms are written have no relevance at all to the listener's task. Nothing in the way *can opener*, *blikopener*, *false teeth*, or *kunstgebit* is said implies a difference in the way the compounds are lexically represented in the minds of users of these two languages.

Crucially, the hundreds of thousands of words we know are made up of only a handful of phonemes. Variability across languages in the number of phonemes is not very great at all. It can seem quite substantial—for instance, the phoneme inventory of British English is about twice the size of the inventory of Japanese. But considered in the light of the number of words that these phonemes make up, a difference between about two dozen versus not quite four dozen phonemes is relatively minor. In each case, the size of the phoneme inventory is just a tiny fraction of the size of the inventory of lexical forms. Maddieson (1984) compiled inventory-size statistics over a database of 317 languages; on current counts, this is only about five percent of the world's total stock of languages, but the sample was carefully chosen to be as representative as possible. Figure 2.6 plots, for this sample, the number of languages as a function of phonemic inventory size (in steps of three over the range that Maddieson observed). The average number of phonemes in the sample is around thirty, and the most commonly occurring number is twenty-five. Thus languages like Spanish or Mandarin, with twenty-five phonemes each, are most typical. There are relatively few

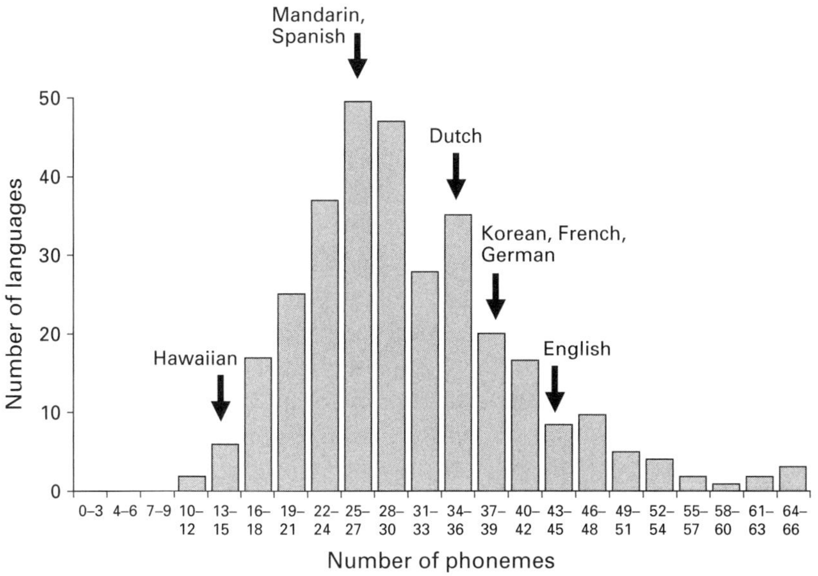

Figure 2.6
The number of languages having phoneme inventories of different sizes (the figure summarizes data of Maddieson 1984), with some example languages of various inventory sizes. The most typical phoneme inventory size is twenty-five; more languages have phoneme inventories of that size than any other size, and Mandarin Chinese and Spanish are just two such typically sized languages. As the graph shows, only very few languages (such as the Polynesian languages, of which Hawaiian is one) have less than sixteen phonemes; and few have more than forty-two. English (for which the count is for the British variety) is thus an atypical language. The range is so small that quite unrelated languages will inevitably happen to have the same inventory size (e.g., Korean and German); but it is also the case that related languages need not have phoneme inventories that are closely similar in size—German has fewer phonemes than English, and Dutch fewer again, whereas French has many more phonemes than its Romance relative, Spanish.

languages with more than forty phonemes (English is one, though), and there are no languages with many hundreds or thousands of phonemes.

In fact, the variation in phoneme inventory size is even less than Maddieson's count suggests. The count covers phonetic segments only, but languages can also use nonsegmental—suprasegmental—means of distinguishing between words. As noted in chapter 1, the term *suprasegmental* refers to variations "above" the segmental level but really describes variations in how segments are realized. These can be variations in the acoustic dimensions of fundamental frequency, duration, and amplitude (resulting in variations in the corresponding perceptual dimensions of pitch, length and timing, and loudness), and the structural effects they encode can pattern in a variety of ways. There is a discussion of the role of suprasegmental structure in lexical access in chapter 3, and the role of prosodic structure in listening is dealt with in chapter 7. The point here is that the languages with fewer phonemes are always free to capitalize on the option of distinguishing words suprasegmentally as well as segmentally. Thus we already saw in chapter 1 how the suprasegmentally cued stress distinctions between words are more useful to Spanish than to English listeners. Chinese languages use tone distinctions between words, and Japanese words can differ in pitch accent. Listeners efficiently exploit whatever structure in their language successfully distinguishes words, in whatever way that structure is reflected in speech. There is actually no general tendency in phonemic inventories for a trade-off in complexity across classes of phonetic segments or between segmental versus suprasegmental contrasts (Maddieson 1984, chap.1), and phoneme inventory size appears to correlate only with the size of the language community—more speakers, more phonemes (Hay and Bauer 2007).[2] But even the largest linguistic community shows the relative size mismatch; the relationship between number of phonemes (small) and number of words (very large) holds across all languages of the world. From the listener's point of view, it is this mismatch that is crucial. The quite trivial number of phonemes in any language's inventory, in comparison with the huge number of words in the language's vocabulary, leads to an inevitable consequence: rampant similarity. It is unavoidable that the words of any vocabulary resemble one another; further, they will often overlap or occur embedded within one another. Languages simply do not have enough phonemes to make words highly distinct.

2.3.1 Embedding Statistics

Lexical statistics support this conclusion. In a 24,279-word dictionary of English two- to six-syllable words, there are no fewer than 63,257 words embedded in longer words (McQueen and Cutler 1992). Thus each carrier word had on average 2.6 other words in it, even though in these calculations embeddings were only taken into account when their boundaries matched syllable boundaries in the carrier word (this meant, for example, that *scan* was counted in *scandal*, but *can* and *candle* were not). Only sixteen percent of English polysyllables are embedding-free (*heavy*, for example); eighty-four percent have other words embedded within them (McQueen et al. 1995; again, their analysis respected syllable boundaries). Embedding is similarly rife within the real-speech Spoken English Corpus; 92.3 percent of words in the corpus contain some embedded word, and 71.1 percent contain embedded words with syllable boundaries aligned with those of the carrier (the lower proportion than in the analyses above is due to the inclusion of monosyllabic carriers; Cutler et al. 1994).

Of course, even the small crosslinguistic variation that exists concerning number of phonemes does have some effect on the structure of the set of words built out of each phoneme set, including the patterns of embedding. A language with relatively few phonemes has two options to achieve the same coverage of lexical concepts as a language with more phonemes. Either it can choose more homophony—that is, more doubling up of forms across multiple conceptual interpretations—or it can go for longer word forms. Cutler, Norris, and Sebastián-Gallés (2004) undertook lexicostatistical analyses of British English (forty-four phonemes) and Spanish (twenty-five phonemes). They compared the English vocabulary in CELEX (Baayen et al. 1993) with the Spanish vocabulary of LEXESP (Sebastián-Gallés et al. 2000). The CELEX English list is approximately 60,000 word types, if homophones such as *sale* and *sail* are treated as single entries, and multiword lemmas such as *by and large* or *good morning* are excluded; LEXESP with the same constraints is a little over 70,000 word types. In each case, frequency statistics across large corpora were available, allowing generalization of the vocabulary statistics to estimates for natural language usage.

An initial computation concerned word length. This turned out, as expected, to be rather different across the two vocabularies. The mean word length in phonemes in the English vocabulary was 6.94, and in the Spanish vocabulary 8.3. Taking word frequency into account reduced the differences between the languages, because shorter words tend to have a higher frequency of occurrence than longer words.[3] But even when the vocabulary averages were combined with the frequency statistics to construct estimates of average word length in real speech, the cross-language difference remained: the average word length in English was 3.54 phonemes, and in Spanish it was 4.62 phonemes. Spanish words, therefore, tend to be longer than English words. They also tend to have more syllables—3.48 for Spanish versus 2.72 for English in the vocabulary, and 2.02 for Spanish versus 1.43 for English in the estimates of real speech. Spanish has therefore compensated for its smaller phoneme inventory by making longer words; or English has capitalized on its larger phoneme inventory by building up a larger set of short words.

This difference has implications for the listeners' task. Longer words have room in them for more embedded shorter words. Also, independently of word length, a language with fewer phonemes is likely to have more embedded words because the likelihood that any word-internal string is already a word will be higher. So Spanish is likely to have more embedded words than English. Indeed, when the extent of embedding in each vocabulary was calculated, Spanish turned out to have significantly more embedding than English. Figure 2.7 shows the proportion of words containing at least one other word. But many words contained more than one embedding. Averaged across words of different lengths, with embeddings beginning at different positions in the word, there were in fact 2.2 times as many embedded words in Spanish as in English. This is a shockingly large difference. It suggests that spoken-word recognition could be subject to a far greater degree of lexical competition in Spanish than in English—more than twice as much! The Spanish listener would seem to have to fight off many more alternative interpreta-

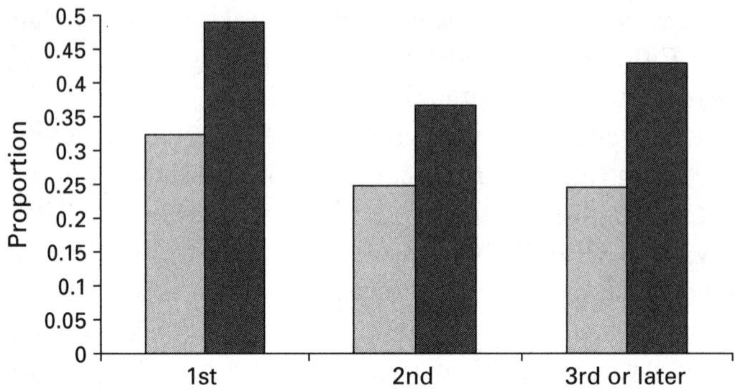

Figure 2.7
Embedding in words of two to five syllables in English (light bars) versus Spanish (dark bars). The figure displays the proportion of such words in each vocabulary with at least one embedded word beginning at the first syllable (English example: *cat* in *cattle* or *categorical*), at the second syllable (*come* in *succumb* or *accompaniment*), or at the third or later syllables (*tea* in *repartee*, *concertina*, *personality*). These counts include embedded words of one to four syllables; homophones (*sail*, *sale*) are treated as a single form, and syllable boundaries are respected (e.g., *cat* is not counted in *scatter* or *catchment*). Because stress marking is ignored, the embedding counts are much higher for Spanish than for English. However, if matching of stress level is taken into account (so in the English examples above, *cat* would no longer be counted in *categorical*, and *tea* would no longer be counted in *personality*, given that in each of these words the embedded form does not bear primary stress), the embedding counts for the two languages are much closer. The relative payoff, in terms of percent reduction in embedding, of including stress in the computations is 37% for English, but nearly 69% for Spanish; that is, the payoff is much greater for Spanish.

tions before arriving at the speaker's intended word sequence than the English listener does.

2.3.2 Lexical Statistics of Stress

Segmental structure is not the only feature one can analyze in the vocabulary, however. Both English and Spanish also have free stress, as we already saw. The lexical statistics of stress in English were computed by Cutler and Carter (1987). A markedly asymmetric picture emerges: words in the vocabulary overwhelmingly tend to have stress (primary or secondary) on the initial syllable. The vocabulary is not the whole story, of course, because many words do not occur very often in real speech. In a corpus of real speech, the London-Lund Corpus (Svartvik and Quirk 1980), Cutler and Carter found that there, too, lexical words (the open classes such as nouns and verbs; see section 2.5.2 below) were very likely to begin with strong syllables. Indeed, most strong syllables formed the beginning of a new lexical word. The statistics offered support for the proposal that English listeners make use of this distributional pattern in the vocabulary when they segment continuous speech into its component words; this will be discussed further in chapter 4.

Recall from chapter 1, however, that strong and weak syllables in English differ both segmentally and suprasegmentally. This is not the case in Spanish—there, stress is signaled by suprasegmental cues, but segmental structure does not vary (the vowels in *CAso* and *caSO* are the same). The evidence from cross-modal priming studies reported in chapter 1 showed that Spanish and English listeners differ significantly in the use of suprasegmental information in recognizing words. Spanish listeners make optimal use of such stress cues to distinguish between words—indeed, they use suprasegmental cues just as effectively as they use segmental cues—but English listeners do not. Cutler, Norris, et al. (2004) thus further examined the effect of taking stress into account in computing the amount of embedding in Spanish versus English. Their estimates described earlier and shown in Figure 2.7, indicating far more embedding in the Spanish vocabulary than in English, arose from computations in which stress differences between syllables were ignored.

If stress is taken into account, however, the picture changes radically. Ignoring stress, embeddings in English include, for instance, *awe* in *autumn* and *automatic*, and *tea* in *settee* and *hasty*. But taking stress into account leaves only the first of each pair in the embedded-word count. A monosyllabic word such as *awe* or *tea* counts as stressed (it cannot be spoken with a reduced vowel), and so there is a match with the first (stressed) syllable of *autumn* and the last (stressed) syllable of *settee*. But *automatic* is stressed on the third syllable, and *hasty* on the first; thus the syllables that match *awe* and *tea*, respectively, in terms of segments do not match them in terms of stress marking. By excluding such cases, the number of embedded words is drastically reduced. In English, the reduction is just over one-third: weighted by word frequency, carrier words of two to six syllables contain on average 0.94 embedded other words when stress is ignored, but only 0.59 when stress is taken into account.

The reduction in Spanish is significantly more substantial. Weighted by carrier-word frequency the asymmetry with the English count is even greater—2.32 embedded words on average if stress is ignored. But consideration of stress information reduces this by up to two-thirds—1.19 words if only content words are marked for stress, 0.73 words if all monosyllabic words, including function words, are considered to be stressed. In fact, the true value is probably somewhere between the latter two—somewhere just under one embedded word on average. Either way, the gain delivered by stress information is strikingly greater for Spanish than for English. For Spanish listeners, there is a clear payoff in reduction of alternative word candidates if attention is paid to syllable stress in word recognition. The payoff for English is very much smaller.

The cross-modal priming experiments described in chapter 1 suggested that English listeners do not bother taking much account of stress in word recognition. The amount of competition that they would be dealing with would accordingly be, on average, just under one spuriously activated word for every actually intended word. The experiments suggested that Spanish listeners, however, do take full account of stress. The amount of competition for them would therefore also average out at just under one spuriously activated word for every actually intended word. Thus the average embedding figures for the two languages are much closer when we assume the stress-adjusted figures for Spanish but the unadjusted figures for English. The reduction of embedding in Spanish by considering stress thus removes the cross-language asymmetry in probability of embedding. Perhaps that amount of competition—a little less than one spurious word per real word—is acceptable in spoken-word recognition.

2.3.3 The Lexical Statistics of Germanic Stress

English is a stress language, and its close relatives are, too. There are close parallels in stress patterning across Germanic languages (some startling variation in stress placement on cognates notwithstanding; compare, for example, English *CATalog*, stressed on the first syllable, with Dutch *caTAlogus*, stressed on the second syllable, and German *KataLOG*, stressed on the third, or a similar progression with even less segmental variation in *aCAdemy*, *akaDEmie*, and *AkadeMIE*). The distribution of lexical stress placement in the vocabularies of English, German, and Dutch is depicted in figure 2.8.

The informational value conveyed by phonetic segments in English is highest for vowels in stressed syllables (Altmann and Carter 1989). Vocabulary analyses show that stress information is helpful in narrowing lexical search in English (Huttenlocher and Zue 1984; Altmann and Carter 1989) and in Dutch (Van Heuven and Hagman 1988). Words in Dutch, for instance, could on average be identified after eighty percent of their phonemes (counting from word onset) had been considered, but when stress information was included, a forward search was successful given only sixty-six percent of the phonemes (Van Heuven and Hagman 1988). Nevertheless, the performance of listeners in word recognition experiments described in chapter 1 differed across the Germanic languages tested. Dutch listeners' performance resembled that of the Spanish more than that of English listeners.

The analyses that Cutler, Norris, et al. (2004) performed for English and Spanish were therefore extended to Dutch (Cutler and Pasveer 2006). The word recognition results motivate the prediction that the Dutch statistics, too, should look more like the Spanish than the English statistics. This is a fairly remarkable prediction, because in every other respect—historical, structural—Dutch is, of course, far closer to English than to Spanish. Nevertheless, if we wish to make the case that stress

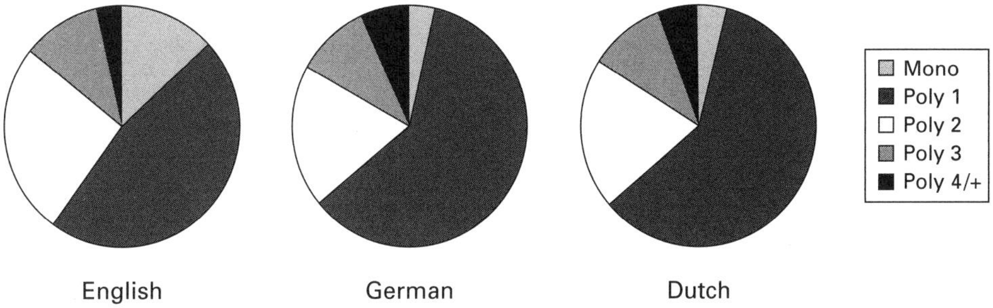

Figure 2.8
Distribution of lexical stress placement in English, German, and Dutch (based on figures from the CELEX lexical database; Baayen et al. 1993). The categories are monosyllabic words (Mono), and polysyllabic words with stress on the first (Poly1), second (Poly2), third (Poly3), or fourth or later syllable (Poly 4/+). The proportion of polysyllabic words is lower in English; as described, many compounds have their own listing in German and Dutch but not in English. The tendency to word-initial stress in all three languages can be further appreciated when statistics for secondary stress are taken into account. In English, about one-third of words with primary stress on the second syllable (7.7 percent in the 25.2 percent) and most words with primary stress on the third (10.7 percent in 10.9 percent) or later syllable (2.3 percent in 3.6 percent) have an initial syllable bearing secondary stress). In German and Dutch, much the same is true: German 15.4 percent in 19 percent, 6.2 percent in 10.1 percent, and 3.5 percent in 6.8 percent; Dutch 12.7 percent in 20.1 percent, 8.1 percent in 10.5 percent, and 4 percent in 5.6 percent. Adding together monosyllabic words, and words with either primary or secondary stress on the first syllable, reveals that 81 percent of the English lexicon and 89 percent of the German and Dutch lexicons is stress initial.

information is used in word recognition if and only if its use pays off in terms of competition reduction, then we have to predict that in Dutch, as in Spanish, the spurious activation count when stress is not taken into account will be above one per real word, and taking stress into account should reduce the count to below one.

That is indeed the pattern that analysis of the Dutch lexicon (using, as for the English analysis, the CELEX corpus) reveals. Weighted by word frequency, Dutch carrier words of two to six syllables contain on average 1.52 embedded other words when stress is ignored, but only 0.74 when stress is taken into account—consideration of stress here results in a reduction of just over one half in the spurious activation count. This count falls below the ratio of one per real word, and the payoff is thus substantial enough to motivate listeners to exploit stress information in word recognition.

Cutler and Pasveer (2006) also computed the corresponding CELEX statistics for German. Weighted by word frequency, German words contain on average 1.62 embedded other words when stress is ignored, but only 0.8 when stress is taken into account. Just as in Dutch, consideration of stress reduces the spurious activation count by just over one half. As will be discussed further in chapter 7, word-recognition studies directly comparable to the priming studies in Spanish, Dutch, and English have not been undertaken in German. The statistical analyses allow us to predict, however, that the results of such an experiment in German should parallel the results that Donselaar et al. (2005) found for Dutch.

As pointed out in chapter 1, the explanation for the observed differences in the use of stress information in word recognition is not to be found in differences among speakers of Spanish, English, and Dutch. Nor does it lie in the first instance in the differences we have now discovered between the Spanish, Dutch, and English vocabularies. Rather, it lies originally in phonology. We now see that in creating vocabulary, the language simply exploits what the phonology leads listeners to do—so Spanish is happy to allow embeddings that can be excluded when attention is paid to suprasegmental distinctions, because listeners are going to do this anyway. English avoids such embeddings to a greater extent, because they would cause problems for listeners who tend to ignore suprasegmental structure in word recognition. And Dutch, as the lexical statistics show, again falls in between, just as in the realization of stress Dutch falls between the purely suprasegmental stress realization of Spanish and the largely unavoidable segmental involvement in English. In each case, there seems to be a similar rough guideline for what counts as an acceptable amount of embedding. Multiple concurrent lexical hypotheses appear to be something that all listeners can handle as long as the spurious embedding count is below one per actual spoken word.

Nesting of words within other words is thus a universal feature of vocabularies, just as the continuity of the realization of words in speech is a feature of utterances in any language.

2.4 Categorizing Speech Input

If the embedding problem occurs in all languages, and speech in all languages is equivalently continuous, then the unavoidable consequence is that, in all languages, listening to speech will involve dealing with multiple concurrent lexical hypotheses. So, there will always be unwanted (temporary) intrusion of spuriously present word forms, such as *star* in *start*. Language-specific factors may affect precisely where such embeddings occur and what information listeners have to attend to in order to get rid of them. But the task for all listeners is the same: to evaluate the incoming input as rapidly as possible in order to discard the spurious forms and settle on the actually present ones. Given that the minimal difference between one word and another is, by definition, phonemic, this evaluation amounts to making categorical judgments. Accepting *start* and discarding *sky*, *stork*, or whatever else might have been briefly activated, is not logically different from evaluating the sound following [s] as a [t], not a [k], and the next sound as [a] not [ɔ], and so on. Note that how a given sound is realized differs as a function of such factors as position in word or the surrounding phonetic context. Chapter 6 shows that listeners attend to such subcategorical variation and make good use of it in word recognition. Thus viewing the evaluation of speech as involving categorical judgments does not imply that information is discarded. What is important to listeners is establishing what the words are, and thus they want to distinguish between two words at the earliest point at which a minimal—that is, phonemic—difference becomes apparent.

The phoneme inventory of a language constitutes the set of distinctions that matter for telling one spoken word in that language from another. Of course, the inventory is language specific; any of its distinctions may be irrelevant for other languages. In a language that distinguishes the sounds [r] and [l], *re* and *lea* are different words, but in a language that does not make this contrast, the two forms may be heard as pronunciation variants of the same word. Thus the categories that listeners distinguish are the categories that their language requires them to distinguish. Listeners are inordinately efficient at this categorization task (as chapter 8 will illustrate, it is one of the first elements of language-specific knowledge to emerge in infancy). Phoneme categorization as a listening task (see panel 2 in chapter 1) also provides a useful window onto the operations of phonemic processing and lexical access. The characteristic response function yielded by the task, known as categorical perception because listeners tend to agree in assigning the sounds to one or the other category, was described in chapter 1 (see figure 1.1).

2.4.1 Language-Specific Categorical Perception

Unsurprisingly, agreement about where category boundaries fall is only observed when listeners share a native language; the boundaries are defined by a language-specific phonetic repertoire and the way the phonemes included in the repertoire are realized. One of the earliest studies to demonstrate this was an experiment by Lotz et al. (1960). They compared English prevocalic stops that were voiced (e.g., [b] in *bill*), voiceless (e.g., [p] in *pill*), or postfricative (e.g., [p] in *spill*); the latter case is one where phonetic context alters the way a particular sound is realized. The differences between English syllable-initial [b] and [p] are that the lag until the voicing of a following vowel begins is longer for [p] than for [b], and [p] has aspiration. After [s], a [p] retains the long lag but loses the aspiration. If the [s] is removed from *spill*, English listeners tend to report the truncated word as *bill* not *pill*, as Lotz et al. confirmed. For Spanish-speaking listeners, however, this stimulus was clearly *pill*; Spanish does not have aspiration in syllable-initial [p]. Nor does Hungarian; and Hungarian listeners also reported the truncated *spill* as *pill*. The Thai phonemic system has a three-way opposition between voiced, unaspirated voiceless, and aspirated voiceless stops; the three English stimulus types were assigned to these three

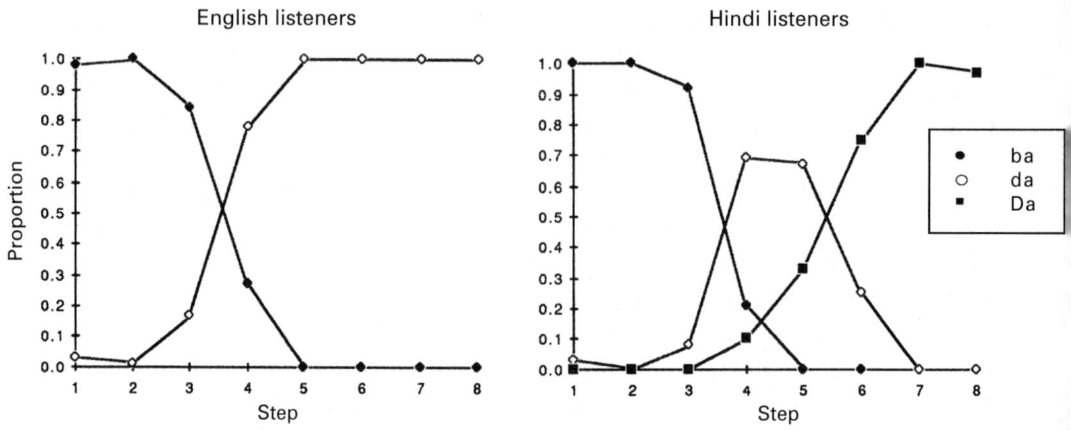

Figure 2.9
The same synthesized continuum is reliably categorized by English listeners in terms of their native categories [b] and [d], but by Hindi listeners as three categories: the bilabial [b], dental [d], and retroflex [D] of their native language. (Data from Werker and Lalonde 1988.)

categories in Thai listeners' responses (with, of course, the truncated *spill* being reported as the unaspirated voiceless stop it actually was).

This early study used natural stimuli excised from recordings; now, most phonetic categorization studies are conducted with synthesized or morphed speech stimuli. Figure 2.9 shows how category boundaries for synthesized stop consonant continua are different for speakers of different languages, in accord with their native language contrasts (Werker and Lalonde 1988). Such studies have also shown, for instance, that sounds on an [r]-[l] continuum are not reliably categorized by Japanese speakers but do produce typical categorical perception from English listeners (Goto 1971; Miyawaki et al. 1975; MacKain, Best, and Strange 1981).

Categorical curves are typically less steep for vowels than for consonants (as was shown in figure 1.1); this suggests that listeners perceive finer distinctions in vowels. Consistent with this is that adults can distinguish nonnative vowel contrasts more easily than nonnative consonant contrasts. English speakers tested by Werker and Polka (1993), for example, easily discriminated German contrasts between front and back rounded vowels ([u:] in *Buch* 'book' versus [y:] in *Bücher* 'books'), although English has no such phoneme contrast. Nevertheless, clear categorical effects can be observed with vowels, too. Hindi and Bengali have a distinction between oral and nasal vowels, but English does not, even though English vowels can in fact be spoken with nasality if they are followed by a nasal consonant such as [m] or [n]. Synthetic vowels varying in nasality are categorized into two classes by speakers of Hindi, but English listeners show no categorical perception with such stimuli

(Beddor and Strange 1982). Likewise, speakers of Bengali, when asked to guess the identity of a word truncated to its initial CV, guess words with nasal vowels if the V is nasal, even if the nasality is not phonemic but just the effect of a following nasal consonant on an oral vowel; speakers of English presented with similar stimuli (e.g., the initial CV of *ban*) use the vowel's nasality to derive information about the following consonant (Lahiri and Marslen-Wilson 1991, 1992).

In the phoneme detection task (see panel 5 in chapter 1), as in any other detection task, targets that have to be distinguished from among a large set of alternatives will be harder to detect than targets in a smaller set of alternatives. The task can thus reflect cross-language differences in phoneme inventory makeup. Wagner and Ernestus (2008) presented 120 nonsense words, in which stop consonants, fricatives, or vowels served as target sounds, to listeners from five different languages: English, Spanish, Dutch, Catalan, and Polish. The use of nonsense materials, the same for all listeners, meant that there was no need to control across the languages for lexical factors such as frequency that can affect responses. The five languages in this study hardly differ in the number of stop consonants they have, but they differ a lot in number of vowel categories (English and Dutch have many more than the other languages) and fricatives (Polish has the most). The pattern of responses in phoneme detection clearly reflected phoneme category size: the more vowels in the language, the slower the listeners' relative responses to vowels, and likewise the more fricatives in the language, the slower the listeners responded to fricatives. There was no cross-language difference in the stop-consonant detection. The likelihood of errors was also affected in the same way by category size. In other words, the makeup of the language, and the way experience with the language has trained listeners to approach a task such as speeded detection of a phoneme target, led to cross-language differences in the pattern of results in this simple task.

Not only does the phoneme inventory determine which distinctions are perceived, and how fast they can be perceived, it can also determine exactly how they are perceived. Sometimes listeners distinguish foreign phonemic contrasts that do not exist in their native inventory by attending to cues that are useful for their native contrasts—even though these are not the cues that are normally used for that particular contrast (Broersma 2005; Crowther and Mann 1992; Flege and Hillenbrand 1986; Flege 1989; Flege and Wang 1989). However, exactly the same contrast may be found in two languages but be perceived in a different way in each. Sometimes this can be because phonological constraints differ. Thus both Korean and Dutch have place of articulation distinctions among the stop consonants [p, t, k] in syllable-initial and syllable-final positions. Recall that stop consonants involve an obstruction of the airflow through the vocal tract; when this obstruction is released, the sudden resumption of airflow is called a burst. In syllable-initial position, the stops in both languages are released as the following sound begins, and listeners attend to the release burst in identifying the sounds. In syllable-final position, however, the languages differ in whether the stops are released. In Korean, released final stops are not legitimate. In Dutch, final stops should be released, at least when words are spoken in isolation. Cho and McQueen (2006) gave Korean and Dutch listeners a phoneme detection task, where the stimuli were VC nonsense syllables ending with stops in which the release burst either was intact or had been removed. The Korean listeners detected the stop targets without the burst more rapidly, whereas the Dutch listeners detected those with the burst more rapidly.

Unexpectedly, even the degree to which listeners make use of transitional information in identifying fricatives varies across languages as a function of differing makeup of the phonemic inventory. The transitional information here concerns cues in a vowel that indicate the place of articulation of a following consonant, and these cues are equivalently available for use in all the languages the authors tested. For English it had long been known that such transitional information was more valuable for identifying [f] than for identifying [s] (Harris 1958); but this could have arisen because high-frequency spectral information in [s] is so robust that it renders transitional cues redundant for identification. Wagner, Ernestus, and Cutler (2006) conducted a phoneme-detection experiment where the targets, fricatives in strings such as *tikufa* and *tikusa*, were cross-spliced among contexts. The results with this task for English replicated the previous findings that came from other tasks; listeners were not significantly slower detecting cross-spliced [s] tokens (compared with [s] tokens spliced from one [s] context into another [s] context so that the transitional information was still consistent). With [f] tokens, however, the same listeners' responses were slower when the tokens were cross-spliced. Cross-splicing, which disrupts transitional information, thus affected perception of [f] but not [s]. The same pattern appeared for (Castilian) Spanish listeners. However, a different pattern appeared with Dutch and German listeners; their responses were not significantly affected by any cross-splicing—that is, they were not relying on transitional cues for either [s] or [f].

Thus the response patterns were determined not by the acoustic robustness of [s] versus [f] but by differences in the constitution of the phonemic inventory across the four languages. In particular, the extra care (attention to transitional information) that English and Spanish listeners expended on [f] identification can be ascribed to the presence in both these phonemic repertoires of the dental fricative [θ], which is acoustically similar to [f]. This can be tested, of course, if there is a language with at least one fricative similar to [s] but none similar to [f]; in such a language the English pattern should reverse. Polish is such a language (in fact it has three fricatives that are potentially confusable with [s]). Indeed, when Wagner et al. (2006) carried out the same experiment with Polish listeners, the responses to [s] were significantly affected by mismatching transitional information, but the responses to [f] were not. The structure of the phoneme inventory thus determines what aspects of the speech signal are relevant for making phonemic distinctions, language by language.

2.4.2 Categories and Words

In chapter 1 we saw that listeners are exquisitely sensitive to all sorts of differences between vowels and consonants. But if a phonemic distinction is apprehended in an incoming utterance, and is put to work to winnow the set of concurrent lexical hypotheses, the rapidity with which this happens is not affected by whether the distinction is one between vowels or between consonants.

What necessarily will affect the rapidity with which a phonemic distinction is put to work is the number of alternatives needing to be evaluated. Categorical distinctions, as we have seen, can be influenced by the number and similarity of competing phonemic categories. Insofar as these categories produce lexical continuations to an equal extent, then the more possible phonemes there are, hence the more alternatives there will be for the listener to sort out. But, actually, phoneme categories differ in the number of words they appear in (some phonemes are rarer than others), and stretches of speech differ in how many words they are fully or partly compatible with (some words are unusual in structure). These are all part of language-specific vocabulary structure, and it turns out that listeners are sensitive to such factors, too.

The verbal transformation effect (Warren 1961) is the psycholinguists' name for the well-known phenomenon that hearing the same thing over and over again makes it sound as if it is not always the same thing after all. In experiments with this effect by Bashford, Warren, and Lenz (2006, 2008), listeners heard a repeating CV or VC syllable (e.g., *dee dee dee dee dee. . .*) and reported what it was at the start and what it changed to (though in reality it did not change at all, of course). The factor that most strongly determined the illusory changes that listeners reported was the lexical neighborhood of the syllable in question. Note that this task does not require word recognition. It induces revisions of categorization, however, and this is the same kind of categorization that word recognition requires. These categorical decisions then immediately reflect the population of available words.

Just about any actual spoken-word recognition task one can think of is similarly affected by the lexical neighborhood of the input. Explorations of the structure of the lexicon by Luce and colleagues have mapped this out in detail (Goldinger, Luce, and Pisoni 1989; Luce, Pisoni, and Goldinger 1990; Cluff and Luce 1990). The denser the neighborhood (i.e., the more words there are that sound like the input), the slower the word actually in the input is recognized. Also, the more similar the neighboring words are to the input (i.e., the more phonetic features the individual phonemes have in common), the slower recognition occurs. The same factors affect recognition of the individual phonemes within words, too (Benkí

2003). The spread of a word's neighborhood (i.e., the number of phonemes in the word that, if changed, produce another real word) also affects its recognition (Vitevitch 2007). Luce's neighborhood computations were first carried out for English CVCs, but other languages and longer words show the same effects (Vitevitch and Rodríguez 2005; Vitevitch, Stamer, and Sereno 2008). The population of available words, defined by the structure of the vocabulary, determines the course of word recognition.

Not only the structure of the native vocabulary is available to listeners but also abstraction of patterns within this structure. Consider, for example, that vocabularies tend to avoid having multiple occurrences of consonants within the same word (historical phonology describes a process, called dissimilation, by which sounds in words change precisely to avoid this situation). Then, one can see why *gandle* and *tandle* sound like better candidate words than *landle* (with repeated [l]) and *nandle* (with repeated [n]). Van de Weijer (2003, 2005) found that not only are words with repeated consonants very rare but listeners are slower at accepting strings with such repetitions as real words (if they are words) and faster at rejecting them (if they are not). The vocabulary of the native language and its internal structure and characteristic patterns determine the way listeners process all incoming sequences of sounds.

2.4.3 Vowel and Consonant Categories and Their Implications

The differences in how listeners treat consonants and vowels were laid out in section 1.4 of chapter 1. Listeners appreciate the patterning of vowels and consonants in the phoneme repertoire, and hence in the vocabulary, of their particular language; they know that vowels are more likely than consonants to vary as a function of the phonetic context they occur in; and they treat consonants as more constraining of lexical identity than vowels. These differences, and the differences in category security that they entail, have some interesting effects on the structure of vocabularies. Consider first a fact about lexical frameworks. There are languages in which families of morphologically related words share a consonant framework and differ in the vowels that are inserted into this framework (e.g., the Semitic languages, so in Hebrew, the words *write*, *writes*, *wrote*, *writer*, *letter* all share the root *ktb*). But there are apparently no languages in which families of morphologically related words share a vowel framework and differ in the consonants that are hung upon this framework. Consonants, as we saw, are more reliable indicators of lexical identity than vowels; thus they tend to form firm lexical frameworks.

Second, consider a fact about phonemic alterability: phonological processes that involve alteration of phonemes in general apply more to vowels than to consonants. Vowel harmony is a process common to many languages, by which all the vowels in a given word or prosodic unit must come from the same subset of the language's vowel repertoire (e.g., back vowels only, or front vowels only; so in Finnish, *maku* 'taste' has only the vowels [a, u], made in the back of the mouth, and *näkö* 'sight' has only [ɛ:, ø], made in the front of the mouth; *makö* and *näku*, with one vowel from each set, would not be permissible native words). Although vowel harmony of this kind is relatively common, consonant harmony is quite rare. Similarly, morphological processes commonly affect vowels more than consonants (consider the English process whereby the vowels in derived forms such as *serenity*, *divinity*, *appellate*, and *linear* differ systematically[4] from those in the underived forms *serene*, *divine*, *appeal*, and *line*; or consider the German Umlaut processes that relate singular and plural forms). Although there are also cases in which consonants take different forms in different morphological or syntactic environments (e.g., in Celtic languages such as Welsh), these are much less common than the vowel cases. Vowels, in short, are not only more mutable in the daily operations of speech processing, they are more mutable in the morphophonology of languages. Vowels, as we saw, are less secure indicators of lexical identity than consonants; thus they can fall into line with one another and alter their identity if required.

Language users are very sensitive to the asymmetry of patterns formed by vowels and consonants respectively, as is evidenced by a remarkable dissociation in response patterns in artificial language learning (ALL; see panel 9) experiments. Significant constraints on when subjects can learn an abstract template for what words have to be like, and when the subjects cannot, were revealed by a series of experiments in which they heard strings of syllables made up of "words" that all had the structure CVCVCV (Bonatti et al. 2005, 2007; Toro, Nespor, et al. 2008). Subjects could indeed learn that the first and third vowel in each CVCVCV must be the same, and also different from the second vowel. Thus participants in these experiments learned, from a training sequence incorporating this rule, that newly encountered items such as *penabe* and *kobado* satisfy the rule but *tipunu* does not. However, they could not learn the same dependency for consonants. Given a training sequence in which all items embody this C1C2C1 rule, the learners showed no sign of knowing that *banube* and *niteno* satisfy the rule but *pikeko* does not.

When it came to learning specific templates for a given vocabulary, however, the vowel and consonant success rates patterned the other way round. Given training on a vocabulary in which all the words contained either the consonants *tpn* in sequence, or *bdk*, learners readily displayed evidence of knowing that *tepane* and *bodeko* are permissible words and *katepa* is not; but given training on a vocabulary in which all words contained the vowel sequences *ieo* or *auɛ*, they showed no evidence of knowing that *niteno* and *banubɛ* are permissible words but *benoba* is not.

Thus the specific form of consonants was more salient than the specific form of vowels, whereas abstract patterns of vowels were more obvious than abstract patterns of consonants. The different results were not due to audibility differences

9. Artificial Language Learning (ALL)

In an auditory Artificial Language Learning (ALL) experiment, the spoken input consists of "words" of a made-up language. The first large set of studies using ALL addressed the learnability of grammatical structures; the derivation of the rules of a grammar from exposure to exemplars of the grammar output was held to exemplify *implicit learning* (Reber 1967). Some studies of this kind are described in chapter 3.

Recently, ALL has enjoyed a renaissance. The techniques have been used to look at how easily different phonological sequences can be segmented, the relative strength of different kinds of word-boundary cues, and whether listeners have expectations about what words will be like; see chapter 4 for an account of this more recent literature. The learning involved is now referred to as *statistical learning*; it is not clear (see Perruchet and Pacton 2006) that this is a different type of processing than what was earlier termed *implicit learning*, although it has been shown that statistical learning from speech does require attention and is hence not fully implicit (Toro, Sinnett, and Soto-Faraco 2005). ALL is particularly suited for cross linguistic comparisons, as the same strings of nonsense can be presented to (and be equally nonsensical for) speakers of different languages, who may be predicted to produce different patterns of results (again, see chapter 4). Suppose that listeners get to hear, for minutes on end, . . . *pabikutibudogolatudaropitibudopabikudaropigolatu* . . . and so on. The listeners' task is then to work out what the recurring "words" are (here, the artificial language has four words: *daropi*, *pabiku*, *golatu*, and *tibudo*). The listeners' learning is tested afterward,usually with two-alternative forced choice or yes-no questions (e.g., which is the real word: *golatu* or *dogola*?).

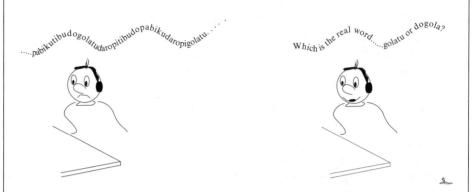

between the vowels and consonants presented, because the results did not change when audibility was artificially reversed (Toro, Shukla, et al. 2008). The asymmetry is exactly in accord with the patterning in languages—consonant patterns are specific and form secure lexical frameworks, whereas vowel patterns are more abstract and the specific form of vowels can be adapted to fit the pattern. The listeners' reactions to specific templates in these experiments are exactly in line with the data from word reconstruction—whereas the reconstruction task (in which frameworks have to be changed) makes the consonant condition hardest and the vowel condition easiest, the ALL task (in which frameworks have to be spotted as words) makes the consonant condition easiest and the vowel condition hardest. The listeners' reactions to abstract templates provide an interesting extension of the word-reconstruction results; they suggest that vowel mutability teaches listeners to look for patterns of vowels (i.e., a context within which the specific form of a given vowel is best interpreted), but comparable experience for abstract patterning of consonants is generally lacking.[5]

Bonatti et al. (2005; Toro, Nespor, et al. 2008) argued not only that consonants are better at constraining lexical access than vowels but also that vowels are more efficient encoders of abstract dependencies. (They referred to the latter as "syntax," using the term, apparently, for any type of dependency between nonadjacent elements). The different roles of vowels and consonants belonged, in their view, to different domains of language structure, with vowels contributing more to syntax by virtue of being carriers of prosody. Prosody, according to this argument, is a superordinate structure expressed over vowels; thus vowels are able to give information about higher levels of structure to a greater extent than consonants can.

This prosody claim is somewhat too strong; recent research has shown that prosodic structure is coded in consonantal patterns, too (Keating et al. 2003), and listeners are very sensitive to the consonantal patterning (see chapter 7 for more detail). But in fact invoking different levels of linguistic processing is unnecessary to explain the ALL results, because, as we have shown, listeners' experience of vowel and consonant patterning is quite capable of inducing differential attention to levels of patterning involving vowels and consonants, respectively. Vocabulary patterns alone should induce expectations that consonants will be more informative than vowels for lexical access. Not only do most phoneme repertoires have more consonants than vowels, and most words contain more consonants than vowels, but Keidel et al. (2007) computed that words specifically constructed in the same way as Bonatti et al.'s (2005) experimental items, CVCVCV, allow more options for the C-C-C- frame than for the -V-V-V frame. A lifetime of experience of consonants being more informative than vowels in such frames would have made listeners predisposed to attend more to consonants than to vowels in learning new CVCVCV words. In response to this, Bonatti et al. (2007; Toro, Shukla, et al. 2008) suggested that the causal relationship could just as well be the other way around; if language users are predisposed to look for larger units of structure primarily via vowels and to find words primarily via consonants, then languages would be most efficient if they conformed to these tendencies and made lexical identity more dependent on consonants.

The truth lies in between these proposals: consonants and vowels really do pattern differently in language, and the differences really do involve consonants in specific lexical patterns and vowels in mutable forms as a function of more abstract patterns. However, these differences of pattern participation are easily learnable from listeners' experience with the differences in discriminability across the two phoneme types, and the consequent category security and immutability of consonants, and category insecurity and mutability of vowels. A simple connectionist network given sounds in the form of a feature matrix will group them into two classes corresponding to vowels and consonants (Monaghan and Shillcock 2003).[6] In perception, as we have argued, the relative category security of phoneme types will cause different amounts of work in speech processing, but the demands of a constantly changing incoming speech signal require that speech be processed continuously as it arrives, without assignment of different phoneme types to different levels of linguistic processing.

2.5 Lexical Entries

So what is in the vocabulary, actually? It is already clear how the analyses of vocabulary structure that we have described capture listeners' knowledge of words; but there are also many questions that one can ask about vocabulary contents. First: what is a word? To psycholinguists the term is a sort of shorthand name for anything listed in the mental lexicon (which is itself another shorthand term, standing for a language user's mental representation of known words). In the spoken-word recognition literature, "words" are not orthographic forms, of course. But they are not just spoken equivalents of written words, either. The listener's lexicon is assumed to contain all elements with any independent function in language use, which means that any language has a huge stock of lexical entries, not all of which would necessarily fit other definitions of "word." In the case of English, the lexicon will contain words of the open classes, like nouns, verbs, and adjectives, but also words in closed classes, such as articles, conjunctions, and prepositions (see section 2.5.2); it will also contain compound forms (*false teeth*), multiword phrases with idiomatic use (*by and large*), and certain parts of words, such as productive affixes (e.g., *un-*, *re-*, *-ness*, or *-able*; how else would we understand the utterance *Is anything ungoogleable*?). Experimental evidence underlying these assumptions about lexical membership is described in chapter 3.

Languages differ widely in how they draw upon the range of possible independent elements. Some languages make extensive use of morphological structure (suffixes, prefixes, infixes, and morphological alternation in declension and conjugation), and other languages avoid it entirely. Similarly, some languages have many closed-class function words; other languages have none. Some languages have a majority of compound forms, but other languages use this option less. (As we have seen, orthographic representation of some of these elements also differs across languages, but this is not relevant to how the lexical forms are available to the listener.)

2.5.1 Morphological Structure

Morphology means internal structure. The word is also used in other disciplines, such as biology, where it refers to the internal structure of animals, plants, and their constituent cells, or in geology, where geomorphology concerns the structure of the earth and all its features. But linguistic morphology is a bit different from these other, somewhat more neutral, usages. In language, morphological structure is a level intermediate between phonology (which is in fact rather more closely analogous to the biological or geological use) and the lexicon. And importantly, languages differ in how much use they make of this structural level. That is why the term is less neutral than either phonology or the lexicon—because morphology varies so widely that whole levels of structure in some languages have no counterpart at all in others. In consequence, it makes sense to say that some languages require (or allow) processing operations that other languages render unnecessary. Morphological decomposition is an operation that has been postulated on the basis of experiments in Western languages, but it would have no processing counterpart for many Asian languages.

All logical possibilities for the use of this type of structure exist. In agglutinative languages like Turkish, effectively all words are complex, because utterances are made up of elements that largely cannot stand alone. In languages like Chinese, in contrast, all words are morphologically simple in that all elements can stand alone. In languages like English, some words are complex and others are simple. *Peace* and *purple* are simple words, given that they cannot be subdivided into smaller contributory elements, but *peas* and *herbal* are complex. Examples of typical English inflectional forms (*walks*, *walked*, *walking*) were given earlier; these can be subdivided, into a stem (*walk*) and affixes expressing tense and aspect. Besides these inflections on verbs, English also inflects for person on verbs (*I walk*, *she walks*) and number and possession on nouns (*one hawk*, *two hawks*, *the hawk's flight*). Derivational morphology allows many more possibilities because it can affect the class of words, turning nouns and adjectives into verbs (*personify*, *realize*), verbs and adjectives into nouns (*government*, *novelty*), and nouns and verbs into adjectives (*herbal*, *learnable*). Meaning can be reversed (*real*, *unreal*) or extended (*gain*, *regain*; *digestion*, *indigestion*). All of these effects can be stacked upon one another to create further forms (*count*, *countable*, *account*, *unaccountable*, *unaccountability*—and so on).

These examples of English derivational and inflectional morphology involve suffixes more often than prefixes, which is quite appropriate to affixes' distribution of occurrence. There are three possible relationships between a stem and an affix: stem first, affix second (suffixing); affix first, stem second (prefixing); or affix inserted into stem (infixing; presumably there is a fourth logical possibility, in which the affix is wrapped around the stem, but this, if it occurs, is treated as a prefix plus a suffix). There is a remarkable asymmetry in affixing across languages, though, which has been well known to linguists since Greenberg 1963. The three possibilities are far from equally preferred by the languages of the world. One of them is hugely preferred: suffixing.

An extensive survey by Hawkins and Gilligan (1988) showed that languages indeed overwhelmingly prefer stems to precede affixes. Especially, inflectional affixes tend to be suffixed. A processing explanation for the suffixing preference could invoke the salience of onsets for the listener plus evidence for separate processing of stems and affixes (Cutler, Hawkins, and Gilligan 1985). However, considering vocabulary statistics as we have throughout this chapter, the processing argument can also be formulated more concisely. Affixes are necessarily always the same, so that having them in onset position would increase the temporary ambiguity of the initial portion of the word; competing lexical hypotheses would proliferate. Computations for English prefixed words by Tyler et al. (1988) supported this suggestion.

Affixes are also prosodically weak (a side effect of their high frequency; see the next section). All the choices that languages make concerning morphology and other aspects of vocabulary structure have processing consequences. For instance, given the small size of phoneme repertoires it is impossible to avoid nonuniqueness (thus *peace* ends with [s] like inflected *walks*, *purple* ends with [əl] like suffixed *herbal*, and *Indian* begins in the same way as prefixed *indigestion*). Processing evidence on the internal structure of words can be found in chapters 3 and 5.

2.5.2 Open and Closed Lexical Classes

Word classes are often grouped into two super-classes: the open versus the closed class. English, like most European languages, indeed distinguishes these two major classes. The open class comprises "lexical" or "content" words like nouns, verbs, and adjectives, and it is open because new nouns (*modem*, *bling-bling*, *blog*), verbs (*to text*, *to Google*, *to download*), and adjectives (*streetwise*, *foxy*, *wired*) are being invented all the time. The remaining classes (articles, conjunctions, prepositions, pronouns, etc.) are "grammatical" or "function" words, which frame the open-class elements and express the syntactic functions and thematic roles in which they stand. These latter classes are said to be closed because new members are only very rarely added.[7]

This two-way classification has a reflection in frequency differences. There are overlaps in the distribution, from some very frequent open-class words (*man*, *go*, *good*) to some very infrequent closed-class words (*notwithstanding*, *albeit*), but in general the closed classes all consist nearly exclusively of highly frequent words, and the open classes are overwhelmingly populated by rare words. Conversely, frequency-ordered lists have exclusively closed-class words in their beginning portions but very few of them elsewhere.

The two-way classification also has a prosodic reflection. Zipf's Law says that frequent words tend to be shorter. This conspires with speakers' interests, as already forecast: the more often we say something, the easier we want it to be to say; short words are easier to remember and recall (Baddeley 1999), and even to start saying (Meyer, Roelofs, and Levelt 2003). There are limits on how short a word can be and still remain communicatively useful, of course, so, as pointed out indeed by Zipf (1949) himself, what is needed is a compromise between useful and effortless. The preference for shorter if frequent is also the reason why long personal names (*Sebastian*, *Alexandra*, *Emmanuel*, *Elizabeth*) tend among family and friends to give way to shorter forms (*Seb* or *Bas*, *Sandy* or *Alex*, *Manny*, *Liz*). The law applies within the open word classes—so high-frequency nouns, verbs, and adjectives like *girl*, *walk*, and *nice* tend to be shorter than low-frequency nouns like *hermaphrodite*, *perambulate*, and *accceptable*. But it also applies between classes. Thus open-class words all may be, and usually all are, prosodically strong, but closed-class words are usually prosodically weak. Chapter 7 explains in greater detail the difference between prosodically strong and weak elements in speech. Here it is enough to say that anything that bears stress must be prosodically strong, whereas anything that is prosodically weak cannot bear stress.

Most closed-class words, then, consist of a single weak syllable. Weak syllables are easier to say than strong; the easiest of all is a central vowel [ə] on its own, which happens indeed to be a function word in English, because it is the most frequent form of the indefinite article *a*. Zipf's Law makes it inevitable that if a language distinguishes the two super-classes at all, there will be a prosodic reflection of the distinction: closed-class words will, on the whole, be shorter and prosodically weaker than open-class words. In English, there are phonetic forms that can be either open- or closed-class words—*buy*/*by*, *just*, *may*, *hymn*/*him*, and so on. But a weak rendition of any of them can only be the closed-class member. Thus, *I loved 'm* can be *I loved him*, but *a loved 'm* cannot be *a loved hymn*.

Weak syllables are, in fact, extremely common in English speech. Cutler and Carter's (1987) analysis of the London-Lund corpus of spontaneous English speech (see section 2.3.2) found that weak syllables were in the majority (60.82 percent of all the syllables in the corpus) and indeed words consisting solely of one weak syllable were the most common of all word types (50.75 percent of all the words in the corpus). But these were nearly always the same words—*the*, *a*, *and*, *of*, *for*, *to*—that is, function words. On average, there are more function words than content words in English speech samples, and function words are usually monosyllabic and usually weak. They make up a very small (and prosodically atypical) fraction of the vocabulary but a large proportion of the actual input. Even in languages with very different structures from English, such as Mandarin and Turkish, lexical and functional elements are separated from one another prosodically, and in frequency, as they are in English (Shi, Morgan, and Allopenna 1998). These features ensure that the open/closed class distinction is eminently learnable (for more on this, see chapters 3 and 8).

Vocabulary structure is subject to a tension between signaling function effectively and economically, and maintaining maximal distinctiveness between lexical forms. A language's choice in any aspect of lexical structure inevitably has consequences for the listener's task. There are nevertheless more universal similarities than language-specific differences in the process of word recognition. In part this is because of the universal principles that constrain the spoken realization of lexical structure.

2.6 Frequency Effects

There is certainly universality in the frequency distributions found in vocabularies. As Baayen (2001) documents, the most important feature of vocabularies is that they are very highly skewed: they all contain relatively few common words and huge numbers of rare words. This property not only has significant consequences for vocabulary analyses involving frequency; consequences for listening also arise, because frequency can be shown to affect response speed or accuracy in any listening task.

Where there is room for response bias and guessing, frequency effects are particularly noticeable. Thus high-frequency words are recognized more accurately in noise than low-frequency words (Howes 1957; Luce et al. 1990; Savin 1963), but this effect is dependent on uncertainty in the response set; it goes away if listeners are choosing from a known response set (Pollack, Rubinstein, and Decker 1959). This is the sort of effect we can experience every day; *four* is a higher-frequency word than *ford*, but the latter may be much more likely in a conversation about cars. Similarly, the biggest effects of frequency in gating appear when only very little constraining input information is available (Grosjean and Itzler 1984; Tyler and Wessels 1983); and a high overall list frequency greatly increases the size of frequency effects in phonetic categorization (Connine, Titone, and Wang 1993).

Nonetheless, simple effects of frequency abound. In all the standard word-recognition tasks, words with higher frequency have an advantage over low-frequency words: in auditory lexical decision (Connine et al. 1990; Dupoux and Mehler 1990; Taft and Hambly 1986), in phonetic categorization (Connine 2004; Connine, Titone, et al., 1993), in phoneme detection (Foss and Blank 1980), rhyme monitoring (McQueen 1993), word spotting (Freedman 1992), cross-modal priming (Marslen-Wilson 1990), and eye-tracking (Dahan, Magnuson, and Tanenhaus 2001). The frequency of the words in the lexical neighborhood is a major part of the neighborhood's effects in recognition (Goldinger et al. 1989; Cluff and Luce 1990; Luce and Pisoni 1998; Vitevitch and Luce 1998; Bashford et al. 2008).

Because frequency effects are so subject to response bias, and because they are strong in tasks that tap lexical processing, but can be made to disappear entirely from tasks that can be performed on sublexical information alone (such as phoneme or fragment detection: Dupoux and Mehler 1990; Foss and Blank 1980), spoken-word recognition researchers have preferred to use frequency more as a diagnostic tool than as a component of their models. It proved useful as a diagnostic, in that presence or absence of effects of frequency on responses would locate the responses at a lexical or prelexical level of processing, respectively. The most recent models account well for frequency effects (see chapter 3), but frequency was hard to incorporate into the model structure brought into favor in the 1980s by a growing knowledge about vocabulary structure.

2.7 Conclusion: Vocabularies Guide How Spoken-Word Recognition Works

The study of spoken-word recognition by human listeners has a relatively short history, having only begun in earnest in the 1970s. Even since then, however, an important change has occurred whereby psychological models of language processing, which of course need to be primarily constrained by empirical data from laboratory studies of listening, have also come to be strongly influenced by computational analyses of the vocabulary and of real speech corpora. These analyses first provided the full picture of the properties of vocabularies, as described in this chapter. When these analyses became available they functioned as a "reality check" for spoken-word recognition modelers; they prompted the abandonment of some approaches in favor of others that promise better returns given the structure of speech input.

In the first generation of spoken-word recognition models (e.g., Cole and Jakimik 1978; Marslen-Wilson and Welsh 1978), the guiding insight was the temporal nature of speech. Previous word recognition models had initially been constructed to cope with written text; but whereas words in text can reach the reader's eye all at once, words in speech arrive at the listener's ear one after another. These early models were therefore specifically aimed at accounting for this sequentiality. They embodied the assumption that recognition of any one word yielded information about where recognition of the following word should commence, and this feature provided an inbuilt solution for the fact that speech is continuous so that word boundaries need to be discovered. The claims embodied in the sequential recognition assumption usefully stimulated a lot of empirical psycholinguistics that is described in more detail in chapter 3—for instance, research on whether word onsets enjoyed a special status in spoken-word recognition (e.g., Slowiaczek, Nusbaum, and Pisoni 1987), and on the notion of Uniqueness Point (the point at which an incoming word could only be continued with a unique completion; e.g., Taft and Hambly 1986).

However, the sequential recognition assumption was doomed; it is simply unrealistic in the light of the extensive nesting of words within other words, as laid out in section 2.3. The first word to arrive and meet criteria for recognition may not be the word intended by the speaker but just an inadvertently embedded shorter word. The advent of online dictionary resources made this consequence of the nested vocabulary obvious to all and signaled the end of sequentially based models. It was not until the early 1980s that such dictionary resources became available, and Luce (1986) first showed how they could be exploited to test the usefulness of theoretical models of spoken-word recognition. Luce analyzed a 20,000-word dictionary of English, in combination with frequency statistics, and established that a majority of words cannot be uniquely identified until at or after their ends. In particular, monosyllabic words are unlikely to be free of alternative interpretations until after their end. *Star*, for instance, as we saw, could continue as *start*, but also as *starch* or *stark* or *starling*; *start* too could continue as *startle* but also *star turn*; and so on. Once it was clear that reaching the end of a word in a speech input signal could never automatically entail that a new word's beginning would follow, the models based on this assumption fell into disuse.

The following generation of models was already in preparation, however, and these were models of a very different kind. Most of them used a connectionist architecture, with words of the vocabulary being viewed as nodes in a network. Input, received from prelexical levels, flowed to the lexicon and from there to higher levels of utterance processing, and connections also linked lexical nodes to one another. The prelexical signals resulting from apprehension of speech input caused multiple lexical candidates to be activated, possibly simultaneously, and the eventual parse of the input stream then resulted from competition between these concurrently activated words, whereby the competition could be instantiated by the flow of positive and negative signals between lexical nodes. The first such model was TRACE (McClelland and Elman 1986). Other second-generation models are, for instance, Shortlist (Norris 1994) and the Neighborhood Activation Model (NAM: Luce and Pisoni 1998) with its connectionist relative PARSYN (Luce et al. 2000).

These models were a direct, and an appropriate, response to the online dictionaries' revelations about the reality of vocabulary structure. By allowing words to become active whenever they are supported by the speech signal, and then to compete among themselves for recognition, these models naturally cope with the embedding problem. In the same way, they cope naturally with the absence of word boundaries in continuous speech. It does not matter that an utterance of *star charts* may also activate *starch* and *start* and *arch* and *art*; these spuriously embedded contenders will inevitably lose the competition to the combined activation of *star* and *charts*. In chapter 3, there is a figure showing an example of the activation of various candidates in such a model (Shortlist), and it can be seen how both the evidence in the signal, and the availability of alternative candidate words, affect the interpretation of the input simultaneously, which makes each individual word's relative probability rise or fall across time in response.

By far the most important fact about the second-generation models of spoken-word recognition was that they were computationally implemented. This enabled researchers to simulate the conditions of their experiments and compare the model's predictions with the outcome of laboratory studies. The computationally implemented models have been even more influential and empirically stimulating than their first-generation predecessors, and indeed, they can be said to have prompted the majority of the research described in this book. Since the advent of computational models, all spoken-word recognition modeling efforts have been of this kind; there is no longer a serious role for the first-generation models that preceded TRACE, or indeed for any models not implemented as computer programs and hence not allowing simulations of experimental findings. Implementation, as for example Norris (2005) has pointed out, is excellent for progress in the field, in that it fosters a continuous interplay between model and experiment; the models are built to capture existing data, but they can then be let loose on new situations for which they predict results, which in turn can be tested in experiments, which deliver new data, which can further constrain the models. Thus science marches on.

Needless to say, the architecture of the psychological processes in a model is not isomorphic with that of the brain in which the processes run their course. Modeling requires a good mastery of metaphor, always. The trick is to describe the postulated processes in terms that both capture the patterns of the experimental results and give the model an easily apprehended character. Since the beginning of word-recognition modeling, the dominant metaphor has been activation; the multiple lexical candidates among which the recognition system selects are viewed as activated elements of the vocabulary, bursting into temporary life in response to the incoming input. Of course, activation is a metaphor and should not be understood as a claim about neurally instantiated detectors for individual words. It has been variously understood as an absolute (i.e., on-off) property or as a gradient, and hence relative, property. It has featured in many different kinds of models—indeed, it was used in the first-generation models and even in their visual-recognition predecessors, as chapter 3 describes. Its greatest success may have come with incorporation into computational models; but basically the activation metaphor is successful because it transparently captures the notion of multiple simultaneous availability. As both vocabulary studies and experimental studies have shown, this notion is the basis of spoken-word recognition.

The spoken-word recognition models of the computational generation do a good job in accounting for how listeners cope with what all spoken communication is like: fast, continuous, variable, and nonunique. Note that the models are not at all language specific. This is reasonable, because the nature of the task is fundamentally just the same across languages. It is the precise realization of the listening task that is shaped by the vocabulary structure of a specific language. In other words, listening itself is language specific. It is always native listening. The task is to recognize words from a particular vocabulary, and features of the vocabulary itself determine what is the best way to achieve this. These features include: the size and nature of the phoneme repertoire drawn on to construct words; the degree to which the vocabulary incorporates suprasegmental distinctions between words; morphology and the closed class; and the characteristic shape of words. The end result is that listeners from different language backgrounds develop different ways of listening, propelled by differences in the native vocabulary structure.

Nonetheless, the differences are in the details, not in the general structure of the task. It remains the case that all vocabularies produce nonunique utterances, and speech in all languages is fast, variable, and continuous. Multiple concurrent evaluation of lexical hypotheses will be a good idea for all, therefore. Chapter 3 describes in more detail the evidence, collected over several decades and prompted in large part by spoken-word recognition models, of exactly how listeners succeed in recognizing words that they know from the not very transparent speech signals they receive.

3 Words: How They Are Recognized

This chapter summarizes evidence from all the laboratory methods for studying lexical activation, to compile a picture of the operations that efficiently turn a continuous speech input into a recognized string of words. First, multiple lexical candidates are considered concurrently. Simultaneously active candidates compete with one another, in the sense that evidence that favors one candidate also directly counts against its rivals. Words in the lexicon have separate representations of their phonological form and conceptual content. The interword competition process involves phonological representations only, but activation passes, where appropriate, as rapidly as possible to conceptual representations. Suprasegmental structure, morphological structure, word class, and gender can all also modify lexical activation. The chapter concludes with a comparison of how lexical activation is captured in different spoken-word recognition modeling architectures.

Speech contains more words than speakers intend it to, because words so often contain other words within them. Speech is continuous and word boundaries are frequently unclear, so the juxtaposition of words can create sequences that correspond to other words. As a result, the speech a listener is hearing may contain many spurious words that are just as well supported by the acoustic signal as the words that the speaker actually selected and uttered. This was the picture drawn in chapter 2. Now, we examine the consequences of this situation for the listener, as revealed in experimental evidence.

The vocabulary, as the population of all the words that might conceivably be part of an incoming speech signal, plays a central role. The speech signal presents continually more constraining evidence, so that only the relevant members of the vocabulary come into consideration—or are "active" in the recognition process, as we termed it. But the limited building material from which the vocabulary is constructed means that there are still far more active word candidates than real words in the incoming speech. The first three sections of this chapter describe how the activation of lexical candidates is tested and how the listener deals with the multiplicity of alternatives and uses it to settle on the correct set of words in the signal.

The following sections then consider the relation of form and meaning. What the listener wants to extract from the utterance is its meaning, but what is presented is, of course, its form. The role played in the spoken-word recognition process by the phonological versus the conceptual structure of words is thus the subject of sections 3.4 and 3.5.

Four further lines of evidence then help to fill out the picture of how considering multiple alternative word candidates in parallel leads to efficient spoken-word recognition. These four issues are motivated by research findings, most of which are already familiar to the reader from chapter 2. First, there is the need to consider not only the segmental but also the suprasegmental structure of words and to spell out the way in which these dimensions can codetermine activation (section 3.6). Second, there is morphological structure, in which substantial cross-language differences are to be found; internal structure of the representations of words in the lexicon and the relevance of this structure for lexical activation is considered in section 3.7. Third, there are the (semi-) arbitrary classes into which some languages group their vocabulary, using devices such as noun gender or classifiers; these classes can affect phonological representations and thus, potentially, lexical activation (section 3.8). Fourth, there is word class; for languages with stand-alone function words, word class tends to be reflected in word form, and this relationship is likewise relevant at the lexical activation stage (section 3.9).

3.1 Testing Activation

3.1.1 With Lexical Decision

Two methods for studying the multiple availability of lexical candidates in the laboratory have already been introduced: cross-modal priming (panels 4 and 8) and eye-tracking (panel 6). Another method is auditory lexical decision (see panel 10). Lexical decision with visual presentation is one of the most widely used tasks in psycholinguistics (it is an exceptionally tractable task: I once conceived a visual lexical decision experiment, devised and constructed the materials, tested twenty subjects, and analyzed the results, all in a single afternoon, and I doubt that this is a record). Auditory lexical decision takes a bit more work to set up, but it is still simpler in this respect than cross-modal priming or eye-tracking. There is an interesting point to make about how auditory lexical decision is used for assessing the activation of candidate words: Although it might seem more likely for the real words to be the most interesting items, and the nonwords merely fillers, in fact the nonwords are often what experimenters are really interested in, while the real words serve as fillers. The task in this form is excellently suited for looking at the time-course of processing mismatching information and thereby displaying effects of spurious activation. Figure 3.1 summarizes three examples of this.

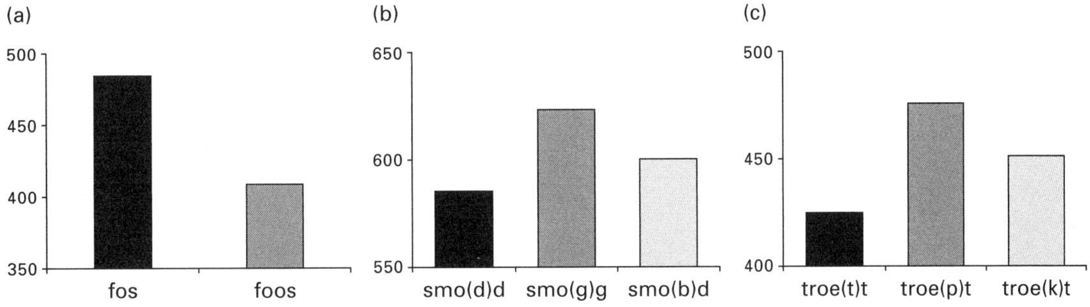

Figure 3.1
Rejecting nonwords in lexical decision is harder if a lexical candidate is available and offers (temporary) competition; summarized results from (a) Taft (1986); (b) Marslen-Wilson and Warren (1994); (c) McQueen et al. (1999). In (a), *fos* is slower because it could have become *fossil*; in (b) and (c), the *smod* and *troot* that are slower are the ones with vowels from *smog* and *troop*, respectively. The latter experiment was actually in Dutch; in Dutch, as in English, *troet* and *troek* are nonwords, whereas *troep*, pronounced like *troop*, is a real word (meaning 'stuff').

In the left panel of the figure is Taft's (1986) finding that spoken nonwords that could have continued to become words were rejected more slowly than nonwords that had reached their "nonword uniqueness point" (NUP)—the point at which they stopped overlapping with any real word. Listeners rejected *fos*, *krin*, and *kron* less rapidly than *foos* or *kren*; *fos* could have been the beginning of *fossil*, *krin* could still have become *cringe*, and *kron* could still have become *chronic*, but *foos* and *kren* could not be continued as words. Note that it did not matter here whether the nonword syllable was also a syllable in the word (*kron* in *chronic*) or not (*krin* in *cringe*); the only thing that mattered was whether the incoming speech signal still offered support to some existing word.

The other two panels in figure 3.1 show findings of Marslen-Wilson and Warren (1994) and McQueen, Norris, and Cutler (1999), from English and Dutch respectively. Both these experiments used cross-spliced versions of nonwords such as *smod* (in the English study) or *troot* (in the Dutch study; this is actually an English analog of the Dutch example because the example works for English too). In the cross-spliced versions, the onset and vowel either matched or mismatched the final consonant. So, there were versions in which the *smo-* or *troo-* part had been taken (a) from another utterance of the same nonword, (b) from a word starting in the same way but ending in a different sound (e.g., *smog*, *troop*), or (c) from another nonword ending with a different sound (e.g., *smob* or *trook*). In both the (b) and (c) cases, the coarticulatory information in the vowel mismatched the final consonant, and in both cases, as the figure shows, the nonword was rejected less rapidly than in the

10. Auditory Lexical Decision

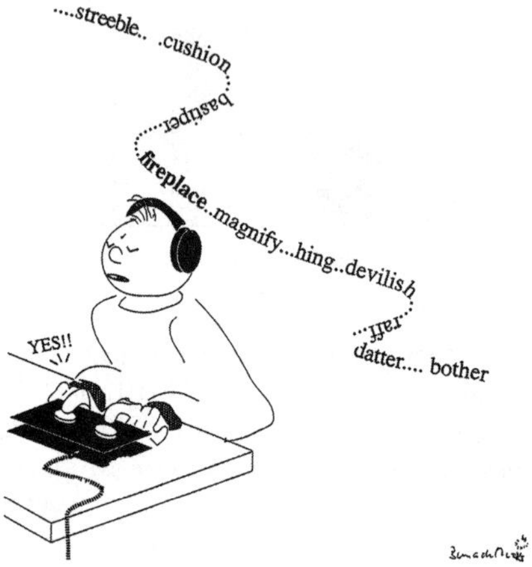

Lexical decision (LD) is arguably the simplest word-processing task. It is used both with visual or with auditory presentation; here, of course, it is the auditory version (ALD) that is relevant. The subjects hear words and nonwords and decide for each one: is that a real word, yes or no? ALD is dependent on word length—no response should be made until the end of each item, because the input could always become a nonword after all. Pressing YES on hearing *firepla-* (see picture) would be a wrong response if the input turned out to be *fireplape* and not *fireplace* after all. ALD can tell us, for instance, whether words can be recognized, or nonwords rejected, as soon as enough of them are heard that no other words are possible (the word or nonword uniqueness point).

The ALD situation may seem somewhat unrealistic, because in real life, people do not usually say nonwords to us. But exactly for that reason, ALD is a good measure; our natural tendency is always to try to interpret whatever we hear as a word. (The same mindset makes word reconstruction work; see panel 3.)

matching (a) case. But crucially, the (b) nonwords were even harder to reject than the (c) nonwords, because the coarticulatory information in the vowels in (b) was consistent with an existing word—*smog* or *troop*. This word was, until the final consonant arrived, more activated in the (b) case than in the (a) and (c) case, because in the (b) case the articulation of the vowel contained hints of the final consonant that would make the item a real word.

3.1.2 With Cross-modal Priming

Cross-modal priming has been around in psycholinguistics for nigh on three decades and probably now counts as one of the old workhorses of the field. Zwitserlood's

(1989) use of this task to demonstrate multiple concurrent consideration of lexical candidates has already been described, as have cross-modal priming studies of embedded-word activation. Connine, Blasko, and Wang (1994) extended Zwitserlood's approach, examining what happened when ambiguous speech input supported two possible words equally well. They found that both could become available. So a sound that could equally well be a [g] or a [k]—an artificially made sound, halfway along a continuum between a good [g] and a good [k]—was used as the beginning of a word; followed by [ɔ:z] it could make *gauze* or *cause*, followed by [o:st] it could make *ghost* or *coast*. Connine et al. found that these ambiguous forms led to facilitation for targets related to both possible interpretations—SPIRIT and BEACH related to *ghost* and *coast*; BANDAGE and REASON related to *gauze* and *cause*. When they presented the primes in a sentence context that rendered only one interpretation really acceptable (*She drove to the coast/ghost*; *He wrapped up the gauze/cause*), there was still facilitation for both associated words. Again, just as Zwitserlood had found in her study, the context did not prevent the multiple hypotheses that the speech signal motivated.

Cross-modal priming also offers a view of the time-course of activation build-up. How much support does a word form need before it becomes an active candidate? Zwitserlood and Schriefers (1995) compared fragments that had many versus few possible continuations—for instance, the Dutch fragment *kra-* could become any one of dozens of Dutch words (*krant*, *krap*, *krans*, *kracht*, *kras*, *krat*, and so on). But if the next phoneme is [n], as when the fragment is *kran-*, then there are exactly two ways in which one further phoneme makes a word: *krans* 'wreath' and *krant* 'newspaper'. BOEK 'book' is an associate of one of these, *krant*, and recognition of BOEK is certainly facilitated by prior presentation of the whole word *krant*. The fragment *kran-* also immediately primed BOEK, Zwitserlood and Schriefers found. Further, even the shorter fragment *kra-* primed BOEK, but this only happened if the presentation of the target BOEK was delayed so that it appeared at the same moment (measured from prime onset) after the short prime *kra-* as it did after the longer prime *kran-*. Zwitserlood and Schriefers concluded that activation of word candidates takes some time to build up but it happens automatically, given even relatively weak partial support for the candidate in the spoken signal. Later in this chapter, when the different types of representation that are involved in recognizing spoken words are examined, we will return to this issue and also see how the cross-modal priming task can provide more than one kind of view of the activation process.

3.1.3 With Eye-Tracking

Eye-tracking is a newer technique, as described in chapter 2 (see panel 6). At first, it was limited by the use of only picturable concepts as targets; however, comparable results were later found with a display containing printed words rather than pictures

(McQueen and Viebahn 2007). This made eye-tracking studies much easier to construct. The technique is widely used, especially because it offers a continuous view of the lexical activation process and how it changes over time. Cross-modal fragment priming can show that a fragment of speech activates one or more particular word candidates (e.g., *capt-* activates both *captive* and *captain*), but eye-tracking can also show what happens next (e.g., when only *capt-* has been heard, subjects' looks are divided between the words *captain* and *captive* in the display, but as soon as the next vowel is heard, the looks zero in on just one of these two words).

Researchers who use eye-tracking have been concerned to establish that it is a good measure of natural spoken-word recognition (and not just a measure of recognition among a fixed set of visually presented alternatives). Thus Dahan, Magnuson, Tanenhaus, et al. (2001) exploited the effects of mismatching coarticulatory information just described. They showed that listeners followed instructions to *click on the net* less rapidly when the *ne-* part of *net* came from the word *neck*, even though there was nothing in the visual display that this sequence could correspond to. Thus the speech signal was definitely causing activation of candidate words that were irrelevant to the visually available set of alternatives.

Magnuson et al. (2007) took this demonstration a step further by showing effects on activation of the number of available competitors in the vocabulary. In their study, a target picture (such as a horse) appeared together with three phonologically unrelated distractors (as it might be: a clock, a flag, and a table), so that nothing in the display itself offered a potentially competing activated word. Under these conditions, the time to respond to the target varied with the number of similarly beginning words in the lexicon. Given *horse* and *heart* as spoken input, the participants reliably clicked on the pictures of a horse or a heart, respectively. But their clicks were just a little less rapid on the heart than on the horse, even though the two words begin with the same consonant and are similar in frequency, rated familiarity, length, and phonological complexity, and even though everything else in the experiment, such as position on the screen and distractor pictures, was fully balanced across the conditions. Among the *h*-initial words of English, more share a vowel with *heart* than with *horse*, meaning that the number of potential alternatives beginning in the same way delays lexical selection just a bit more in the case of *heart*. Magnuson et al. argued that the eye-tracking task accurately reflects natural spoken-word recognition.

McMurray and colleagues (McMurray, Tanenhaus, and Aslin 2002, 2009; McMurray et al. 2008) and others (e.g., Salverda et al. 2003, as described in the preceding chapter) have also used eye-tracking to show how lexical activation is modulated by listeners' sensitivity to fine phonetic detail in spoken words (such as coarticulatory cues for upcoming sounds or syllable duration). Here, again, eye-tracking provides more information than previously existing methods for studying word activation. The auditory lexical decision (ALD) results in figure 3.1 also show that coarticulatory information has been used in deciding about a spoken word or nonword, but eye-tracking can provide a record of exactly when it is used.

3.2 Modeling Activation

3.2.1 Multiple Concurrent Alternatives

The simultaneous consideration of multiple lexical hypotheses is not a contentious notion. It is the basis of all spoken-word recognition models. Psycholinguistics is a relatively young branch of psychology; as pointed out in chapter 1, it grew into a separate subdiscipline only in the 1960s. In early research in this field, spoken language was not central. This was for practical reasons: researching written language is easier than researching spoken language (see the remarks on visual lexical decision experiments in the preceding section!), and tools for researching speech were not yet widely available. From the beginnings of research on spoken language, however, multiple activation has figured in the processing models that researchers constructed for this task.

The first psychological model of the recognition of spoken words was Morton's logogen model (1969, 1970). Based on Selfridge's (1959) pandemonium model of visual perception, the logogen model proposed lexical recognition units ("logogens") that would become active in response to any input that matched any part of their form. Essentially the same mechanisms were assumed to be involved in the recognition of visual and spoken words; the more the printed text being read, or the speech being heard, provided a match to the logogen's requirements, then the more response the logogen would deliver. The most active (best matched) logogen would triumph (i.e., attain the threshold for recognition) simply by having the highest response level. It is clear that the input would also partially match many unsuccessful logogens; in other words, the concept of multiple activation is intrinsic in this model.

The next generation of models was the first generation of real spoken-word recognition models already mentioned in chapter 2: the influential cohort model of Marslen-Wilson and Welsh (1978), and closely related suggestions by Cole and Jakimik (1978). The principal driving idea in each case was that spoken language differs from written text by its dependence on the temporal dimension. These models proposed that once any word has been recognized, a new lexical access attempt begins from the point in the continuous speech signal where the recognized word ends. Suppose that the next sound at that point is an [s]. In the cohort model, all words beginning with [s] would then become a little bit activated. If the following sound is [t], words beginning *st-* would be more activated, while other *s*-words would drop out of this initial "cohort" of candidates. Again, multiple activation is at the heart of the model. The concurrently activated set of candidate words is called the cohort, and this set is gradually whittled down by incoming speech information until—in the ideal case—only a single candidate remains (e.g., for this cohort, *strange*).

Such an emphasis on temporal order in the input has consequences for the relative importance of speech information. Not all information is equal. Word-initial segments have more impact in sorting out the cohort than word-final segments. Indeed, an important component of the cohort model was the notion of the uniqueness point (UP): the segment at which the word's cohort is reduced to a single member. To take an example from Marslen-Wilson (1980), the UP of the word *trespass* is the [p]. The cohort matching the first segment includes all [t]-initial words; [r] and [ɛ] reduce this to still substantial cohorts of all [tr]-initial words, then all [trɛ]-initial words; by the fourth segment, however, the cohort is tiny: *tress*, *trestle*, and *trespass*. The fifth segment then reduces the cohort to a single member. Segments after the UP no longer contribute to identification of the word. Correspondingly, if the cohort contains no members at all, then the input is not a word. Marslen-Wilson (1984), examining the responses to nonwords in ALD in the same way as in the experiments of figure 3.1, found that "NO" decision time was roughly constant if computed from the point at which the nonword could no longer be any real word.

The predictions of this first version of the cohort model motivated a great deal of research in the 1980s. The model predicted no activation of rhyming words, and though *honey* produced (cross-modal associate) priming for the target word BEE, *money* and *lunny* indeed did not (Marslen-Wilson and Zwitserlood 1989).[1] Tyler (1984) and Tyler and Wessels (1983) examined the makeup of cohorts; listeners' guesses about gated words, they found, showed effects of frequency only before the point at which phonetic information greatly narrowed the choice of words. Effects of syntactic and semantic information appeared only after that point. So when there is a large cohort, listeners guess among it on the basis of frequency, but the incoming speech information always controls the cohort membership. Higher-level context is most useful when there are only a few words to choose between.

As noted in chapter 2, the strictly sequential aspect of the model did not survive once the availability of online dictionaries made full analysis of cohorts feasible. Most real words, especially most frequently occurring words, do not have a word-internal uniqueness point. The UP concept seemed to be useful only with longer words (which are, by Zipf's Law, words less likely to be encountered anyway). However, three lines of experimental evidence also made it clear that word endings can also be important for recognition.

The first kind of evidence concerned what listeners can find out about words if they do not hear the beginnings. Slowiaczek et al. (1987) measured word recognition in noise as a function of prior primes. They found similar effects of primes that overlapped with either the beginning or the end of the target, whether in one phoneme (e.g., *flock* preceded by *fret* or by *steak*), two phonemes (*flap*, *stock*), or three (*flop*, *block*). Gated words, out of context, can likewise be reconstructed from either beginning or end information (Salasoo and Pisoni 1985; Nooteboom 1981; Nooteboom and Van der Vlugt 1988; Wingfield, Goodglass, and Lindfield 1997). Of course, lexical statistics ensure that the beginnings of words are more informative than the ends (consider: many words end with *-ics*, but few begin with *ling-*). In a meaningful context, less information is usually needed to correctly identify words from their beginnings than from their endings (Salasoo and Pisoni 1985).

The second type of evidence concerned how the later parts of words could influence activation. In the eye-tracking study of Allopenna et al. (1998) described in chapter 2, listeners clicked on a beaker less rapidly if the display contained a rhyme competitor (e.g., a speaker). This result suggests that final overlap causes competition. In a similar vein, auditory lexical decision studies by Taft and Hambly (1986) and by Goodman and Huttenlocher (1988) examined whether information after the uniqueness point could affect spoken-word recognition; in both cases, the crucial stimuli were again nonwords.

The nonwords in Taft and Hambly's study had the same nonword uniqueness point (NUP). For instance, *rhythlic* and *rhythlen* both become a nonword at the [l], so if everything after the NUP is irrelevant, the listener should be able to reject both at the same moment. But *rhythlic* also overlaps with *rhythmic* after this point, whereas *rhythlen* does not. Indeed, *rhythlic* turned out to be harder to reject, which suggests that this post-NUP information had temporarily weighed against classifying *rhythlic* as a nonword. Goodman and Huttenlocher did the opposite: they compared nonwords that differed in NUP, so that they should differ in when they could be rejected. Thus both *necomend* and *recolend* differ in exactly one phoneme from *recommend.* But the NUP of *necomend* is earlier (at the fourth phoneme, after which it can no longer be *neck* or *necromancy*), whereas the NUP of *recolend* is later (only at the last phoneme but one, where it becomes distinct from *recollect*). Thus *necomend* should be easier to reject than *recolend* because the NUP is reached earlier. But in fact *necomend* turned out to be harder, perhaps because it shares greater unbroken overlap with *recommend.* Again, the implication is that all parts of a spoken input, before or after a UP, are contributing to the evaluation of a lexical candidate. Taft and Hambly also compared real words with the same UP and the same number of post-UP phonemes, like *difficult* versus *diffident*; if this structure alone determined listeners' decision that these two were words, then response time to the two should be the same. But in fact the higher-frequency *difficult* was accepted more rapidly than the lower-frequency *diffident*; again, it seems that the lexical decision response was affected by post-UP segments.

The third type of evidence ran contrary to the prediction that reaching the UP should trigger word recognition. In gating studies by Grosjean (1985) and Bard, Shillcock, and Altmann (1988), a majority of word stimuli were not correctly identified until after their ends. Clearly, a strictly left-to-right model of spoken-word recognition could not accurately capture all of these experimental findings. It was then welcome news that the next generation of models, represented in the first instance by TRACE (McClelland and Elman 1986), allowed all parts of the word to be in principle relevant.

3.2.2 Competition between Alternatives

If left-to-right selection is not the way listeners convert the stream of incoming speech into a sequence of individual words, then there has to be some other mechanism by which multiple activation may be resolved. If *we start writing* could in principle activate *we*, *wee*, *east*, *star*, *start*, *tar*, *tart*, *art*, *try*, *rye*, *wry*, *write*, *right*, *eye*, *trite*, and *writing*, how can we sort out the correct string even in this short phrase, let alone in longer utterances? The solution offered by all spoken-word recognition models in the past couple of decades has been to allow concurrently active words to compete with one another for recognition.

Note that multiple activation does not in itself imply competition. Multiple activation could result in passive concurrent availability of many candidates without further adverse implications for the relative availability of any of them. Each word's activation would be independent of other words' activation. But this independence does not hold. Competition can, indeed, be thought of as a metaphor for interdependence among the population of words being considered for recognition; it is measured in the relative accessibility of members of the candidate population. In connectionist models of word recognition, competition ensures that active forms receive inhibition from other forms compatible with the same portion of input. Thus the different words potentially contained in *we start writing* are not only all simultaneously available, but *east* is specifically competing with *we* and *start*, *try* and *trite* are competing with *start* and *writing*, and so on.

This way of modeling competition, with inhibitory connections between alternative forms activated at the same processing level, was first proposed in the TRACE model (McClelland and Elman 1986) and also forms part of Shortlist (Norris 1994). Both of these are connectionist models, programmed using interactive activation techniques. Incoming speech causes word nodes to become active in proportion to the support they receive; input adds activation to words it matches, and subtracts activation from (inhibits) words it mismatches. The inhibitory links between word nodes, however, ensure that the more activation any node has, the more inhibition it can exercise on other nodes with claims on the same stretch of input. This models interword competition in a direct way. Other models incorporate competition differently. In the Neighborhood Activation Model (NAM) of Luce and Pisoni (1998), for instance, a decision rule controls the activity of active word units, but the overall activity in the system affects the decision process. In the Distributed Cohort Model (DCM) of Gaskell and Marslen-Wilson (1997), lexical representations supported by the input are simultaneously available, and the more of them there are, the more difficult it is for the model to compute an output. In Shortlist B (Norris and McQueen 2008), the probabilities of alternative outcomes overall sum to 1; it follows that higher probability for one candidate word means lower probability for another, so that the candidates' probabilities are interdependent. Some reflection of competition, like some form of multiple candidate availability, is now uncontroversially a component of spoken-word recognition modeling. (Chapter 12 returns to the similarities and differences between current models.)

Figure 3.2 shows how Shortlist would process the input *acoustics notwithstanding*. The beginning of *acoustics* presumably matches the beginning of *a coot*, *a coupon*, *a courier*, and *accoutrements*, but all of these are fatally mismatched when the first [s] arrives. After *acoustics* has been followed by *n-*, its activation remains stable and

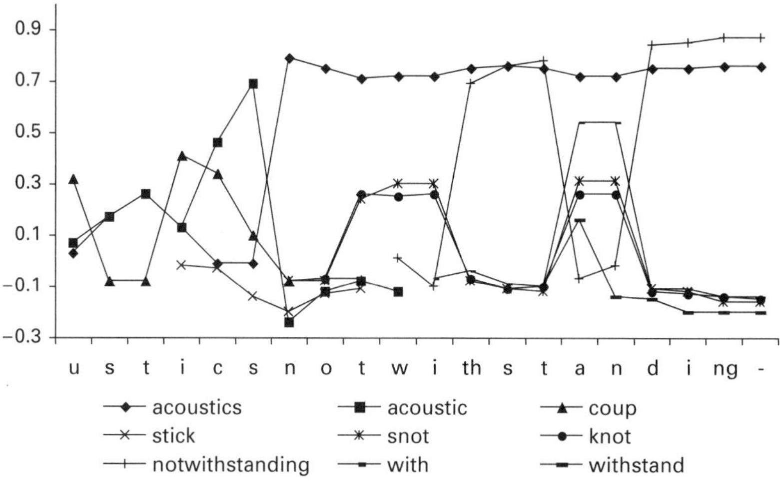

Figure 3.2
Shortlist processes *acoustics notwithstanding*. Only the most activated words are shown, and the very beginning of the input is not shown; by the third segment, however, there was already a dominant interpretation (*a coup*). As further input arrives, the interpretation is adjusted; for instance, *acoustic(s)* is more strongly activated than *coup* up to *acoust-*, but when the next vowel arrives, it is compatible with *stick*, which competes with *acoustic* and allows *coup* to become once again viable (*a coup stick*—meaning is not relevant here!). *Acoustics* becomes the best supported interpretation when its final phoneme arrives. *Notwithstanding*, in contrast, is the best supported interpretation even before its final syllable begins.

high, and all of its competitors (*acoustic*, *coup*, *stick*, etc.) have effectively dropped out. Thus the effects of the input (match and mismatch) on each word's activation level can be seen, and so can the effects of the other words. The activation of *notwithstanding*, for instance, takes a temporary hit as its third syllable is heard. This is not due to mismatch—the input continues to be fully consistent with it—but due to inhibition that has come from the temporary reactivation of *knot/not* and *snot*, which in turn has occurred because of the activation of *with* and *withstand*. The activation of any word depends in part on the activation of its competitors.

Shortlist (Norris 1994) is a useful model for showing simulations. First, it uses a realistic vocabulary—it draws on real online dictionaries containing tens of thousands of words. Second, it uses the full phoneme repertoire of any language it is simulating. Third, it has been programmed to work with several different language vocabularies. The CELEX vocabulary of English on which the simulation in figure 3.2 was run, for instance, contains 26,000 words; simulations of Dutch are also based on CELEX, with a vocabulary size of over 20,000 words. By comparison, simulations with TRACE typically require a handcrafted vocabulary of just a few hundred words and are limited to a subset of English phonemes, whereas simulations with NAM involve only a subset of the English lexicon (monosyllabic words). There are important theoretical differences between the models, to which chapter 12 will return, so that it is often desirable to do comparative simulations with alternative models. For illustrative purposes here, however, Shortlist is a good choice in that it reflects the real vocabulary, it can be run on multiple languages, and so it can capture the central point of this book: the importance in listening of the language-specific vocabulary.

Speech input is represented phoneme by phoneme in Shortlist, for lack (when the model was devised) of a computationally tractable way of representing speech more directly. Other computational models were similarly restricted. There is now a new version of Shortlist, called Shortlist B (Norris and McQueen 2008). In the new model, the input is expressed as relative probabilities of phonemes across time, whereby the probabilities are derived from responses in a giant experiment (Smits et al. 2003; Warner, Smits, et al. 2005) in which eighteen listeners categorized speech fragments representing all possible two-phoneme sequences of the Dutch language. There were over 2,000 such sequences, which were presented in fragments dividing each phoneme into three time slices. The response set produced in this study comprised nearly half a million phoneme categorizations (probably the largest speech perception database ever collected), which enabled Shortlist B to be armed with the actual probability that these listeners had been shown to entertain across time when given any phoneme in the context of any other phoneme. Thus the word *best* would be presented to the model as twelve time slices, three for [b] preceding [ɛ], three for [ɛ] following [b] and preceding [s], and so on, with the input coded in terms of the probability of the listeners' responses given the same input in the experiment. This coding thus not only represents the likelihood of a correct response but also the likelihood of every other response—for example, the degree to which the listeners responded to [s] with [z] or [ʃ] (19%; Smits et al. 2003, 567), as well as the fact that they never, ever called [s] a [k].

Shortlist B is a Bayesian model in which the conditional probability of candidate words arises from a combination of their prior probabilities, as well as the current evidence in favor of them. The relative probabilities in terms of which the input is expressed, being based on actual evidence from listening, make the modeling a significant step more realistic than any model in which the input is represented as a string of phonemes. However, because the experiment that delivered the probabilities was conducted in a specific language (Dutch), the relative probabilities pertain only to the phonemes of Dutch. A version of Shortlist B with built-in probabilities for English is under construction but was not ready in time for the simulations of the recognition of English words in this book; for them, we use the original version of Shortlist.

3.3 Testing Competition

The main reason why competition is uncontroversial is that it is now well supported by evidence from listening experiments. Evidence for competition would be provided, for instance, by interword inhibition as reflected in relative recognition success or in RTs: the more words that are active at any one time, the harder it becomes to recognize any one of them. The auditory lexical decision experiments with cross-spliced nonwords, described earlier (see figure 3.1), suggest that it would be possible to mislead listeners by cross-splicing real words—say, *job* and *jog*—in the same way. Indeed this is possible, and it has been shown in lexical decision (Streeter and Nigro 1979; Marslen-Wilson and Warren 1994), in phonetic decision (Whalen 1984), and in eye-tracking (Dahan, Magnuson, Tanenhaus, et al. 2001; see section 3.1.3).

The first direct evidence of inhibitory competition in recognition of unmodified words, however, came from a word-spotting experiment. The word-spotting task (see panel 11) is particularly suitable for looking at recognition of words as a function of the context that abuts or surrounds them. Take the two-syllable nonword string *nemes*, pronounced [nəmɛs]. Its second syllable is the same as the real word *mess*. Listeners in a word-spotting experiment would be expected to spot this embedded word; they should press the response button and report that they heard *mess*. The question is whether they would be faster with their response to *mess* in *nemes* than in, say, *domes-* (pronounced [dəmɛs]). The latter form is the beginning of *domestic* and should therefore activate *domestic* as well as *mess*. The former nonword, *nemes*, should activate no competitor. Once the nonword *domes-* ended without further

11. Word Spotting

In a word-spotting (WS) experiment, listeners hear nonwords and decide for each one whether they hear a real word in it somewhere. The task is especially designed to assess word recognition in context. The context, however, is reduced to a minimum—for example, just one phoneme or syllable abutted to the word! In the pictured example, the listener has just spotted *lunch* in *lunchef* and signals this by pressing the response key and saying "lunch" into the microphone. WS lets us look at the local effect of a context on how hard or easy it is to recognize a word. It was with WS that inhibitory effects of competition between simultaneously activated word candidates were first demonstrated (McQueen et al. 1994).

sounds, it would of course be clear that *domestic* was not being said, but a competition hypothesis would predict that the temporary availability of another potential interpretation of the input would conflict with recognition of the only embedded word actually present.

This prediction was supported. In the experiment (McQueen, Norris, and Cutler 1994), listeners found it significantly harder to spot *mess* in [dəmɛs] than in [nəmɛs]—they made more errors, and when they did find the embedded word, their responses were slower. Van der Lugt (1999) also replicated this competition effect in Dutch; *les* 'lesson' proved harder to spot if embedded at the end of *choles* (which could become *cholesterol*) than at the end of *boles* (which could not become a real Dutch word). In McQueen et al.'s study, words embedded at the beginning of nonwords were also harder to spot when there was a competitor—*sack* was harder to find in *sackrif* (the beginning of *sacrifice*) than in *sackrik*. Interestingly, though, these nonwords (where the word came first and the adjoined context second) produced differences in accuracy but not in RT. Successful detections of *sack* had apparently been made before the context became distinct. The beginning of both *sackrif* and *sackrik* would activate *sacrifice*, causing the same amount of competition in both and thus affecting detection equally in each. If a detection response had, however, not been made before the end of the nonword, then the arrival of [k] would reduce activation of *sacrifice* and make detection of *sack* more likely, whereas the arrival of [f] would increase activation of *sacrifice* and make detection of *sack* less likely—with the result being the observed significant difference in the proportion of correct detections.

Furthermore, the more competing forms that are activated, the more there is inhibition. Norris, McQueen, and Cutler (1995) compared detection of, for example, *mint* in *mintowf* versus *mintef*, and *mask* in *maskuk* versus *maskek*. The syllables *-ef* and *-ek* here are weak: [əf, ək]; the other second-syllable contexts are strong. Otherwise the items differed in how many competitors the vocabulary offered. Both second syllables beginning with *t* should activate relatively few competitors: *towel*, *town*, *tower*, and *tousle* (and their related forms) in the case of *-towf*, and words beginning with [tə] in the case of *-tef* (*today* and *tomorrow* are high-frequency examples here, but the rest of the cohort is words like *taboo* and *toboggan*). By contrast, both second syllables beginning *k* should activate large competitor sets: *cut*, *cup*, *couple*, *country*, *cutler*, *cuff*, *cull*, *come*, and many more in the case of *-kuk*, and in the case of *-kək* all the many words beginning with [kə] (e.g., all words beginning with unstressed *con-* or *com-*: *connect*, *conversion*, *compare*, *commission*, etc.).

Chapter 4 will present evidence of a difference between syllables that are strong (such as *-towf* and *-kuk*) and syllables that are weak (such as *-tef* and *-kek*). The former are assumed (in English and similar languages) to be probably word-initial; the latter are not. Thus the difference in the number of activated competitors would not be predicted to exercise any effect in the *maskek* and *mintef* cases, because listeners will not consider the weak second syllable to be word-initial. Where the second syllable is strong, however, it will be taken as word initial, and then it is of interest whether it makes a difference how many potential competitors begin in that way, and therefore are likely to come into action at that point. Norris et al. (1995) found that it did make a difference—more competitors led to a greater disadvantage for the strong-syllable over the weak-syllable context. The degree to which *mask* was harder to find in *maskuk* than in *maskek*, in other words, was significantly greater than the degree to which *mint* was harder to find in *mintowf* versus *mintef*. The extra disadvantage was explained as resulting from inhibition exercised, in the former case, by all the activated words like *cut*, *come*, and so on.

An analogous effect appeared in a cross-modal identity priming experiment in Dutch (Vroomen and De Gelder 1995). Embedded forms such as *melk* 'milk' were compared in *melkaam* (potentially activating a large cohort of Dutch words beginning with *ka-*) versus *melkeum* (where only a few words begin *keu-*). Visual targets (MELK, for instance) were less effectively primed (in comparison to a control) when there were more competitors for the second syllable (the *-kaam* case). The segmentation of Dutch, like the segmentation of English, is differentially sensitive to strong versus weak syllables, and so a weak continuation such as *melkem* resulted in more effective priming for MELK than either of the strong-syllable continuations (*-kaam*, *-keum*), which both initiate segmentation. In Japanese, segmentation is sensitive to moraic structure (see chapter 4), but in that language, too, a real word embedded in a nonsense context is easier to find if the context activates fewer competitors to it (Otake, McQueen, and Cutler 2010).

Just as all of the laboratory methods for testing activation have shown that multiple word candidates become simultaneously active, so can competition effects appear in all sorts of tasks. The eye-tracking studies of Magnuson et al. (2007), described in section 3.1.3, show competition. Verbal transformations show competitor effects (Bashford et al. 2008), as described in chapter 2. And in three tasks: auditory lexical decision, same-different judgment, and repetition, Vitevitch (2007) showed a competition effect dependent on how many different ways a word could have been another word. Compare, for instance, the words *fish* and *dish* used in his study. Both can become other words by changing their onsets (e.g., *wish*) or codas (*fit*, *dip*), but only *dish* can become another word (*dash*) by changing the vowel. Note that Vitevitch was not just testing a vowel-consonant difference here; there were also cases in which only the onset or only the coda of a word could not change (e.g., *league* can become *log* or *lease* but cannot change onset to become another word; *poise* can become *noise* or *pause* but cannot have any other single-consonant coda). In all those tasks, words with competitors at all points elicited significantly slower RTs (indicating more competition) than words with competitors at fewer points. This result demonstrates that overlap with competitors is relevant at any point in the word; this would not have been predicted by strictly sequential processing models but is, of course, predicted by models involving multiple overlapping activation and competition. Competition is an established component of human spoken-word recognition.

3.4 Phonological and Conceptual Representations

Incoming speech thus makes multiple lexical representations active, these compete with one another, and the process of competition assists the listener in reaching an interpretation of the sequence of words in the input. But what the listener needs, in reality, is to find out what message is being conveyed by the incoming speech. Does the multiple activation that we have documented entail multiple availability of all sorts of irrelevant word meanings?

We can translate this question into asking whether phonological and conceptual representations of lexical items are effectively one and the same or, if not the same, then necessarily linked such that activation of one implies activation of the other. There is an empirical tool that is suitable to answer this question. As panel 8 described, the primes and targets in cross-modal priming can display different kinds of relationships. Like Soto-Faraco et al. (2001), we can look at how a spoken word facilitates recognition of a visual representation of the same form (e.g., you hear *lease*, and you see LEASE); that is called identity priming or form priming, and it may be used, for example, to assess the effects of alterations in how a word is spoken. Alternatively, like Zwitserlood (1989), we can look at how a spoken word facilitates recognition of a semantic associate (e.g., you hear *lease*, and you see RENT); that is called associative priming, and it has been used to examine the time-course of sentence processing, among other topics.

These two variants make it possible to examine the activation of the same word's form and meaning, with other factors kept constant. Thus, one can present exactly the same auditory primes and examine the activation of representations corresponding to each prime's form and of representations associated with its meaning—given *lease*, for example, we can investigate the activations of LEASE and of RENT.

3.4.1 Separate Representations

The activation of form and meaning was teased apart in this way in experiments by Norris, Cutler, et al. (2006). First, as a baseline, spoken prime words were presented in isolation, with visual target words appearing as each single spoken word finished. The left panel in figure 3.3 shows the results, presented as the difference between the related trials (*lease*-LEASE or *lease*-RENT) versus control trials (*port*-LEASE or *port*-RENT). A big difference means a lot of priming. There was more priming with the form relationship than with the meaning relationship, but that is what one would expect, given that the second relationship is an indirect one. The important feature of the results is that there was significant priming in both cases; the related trials were always faster than the control trials.

Then they presented exactly the same visual target words preceded by exactly the same prime words spoken in a sentence context, for example:

(3.1) The residents complained about the lease on the premises.

Now, as the right panel in the figure shows, there was significant identity priming (although it was less than with isolated primes), but there was no associative priming to speak of. The very same associative prime-target pairs that had shown significant priming with isolated presentation seemed to produce no effect at all in context.

This pattern can be easily explained if phonological and conceptual representations are thought of as separate and (to a certain extent) independent components

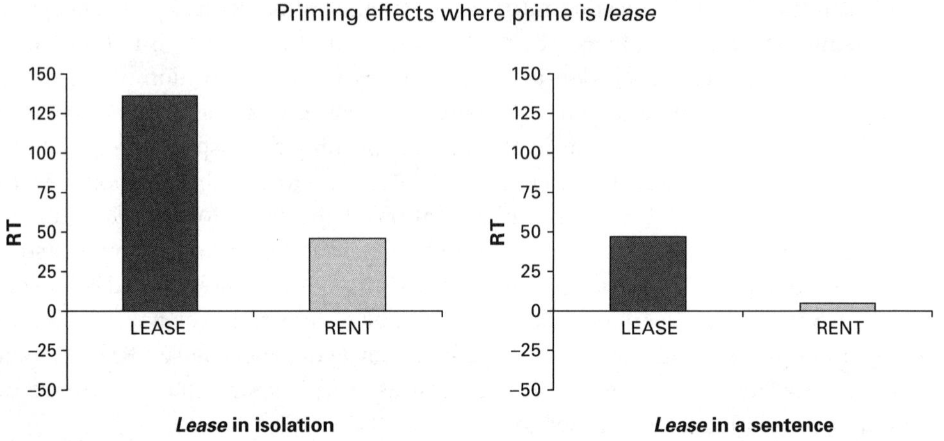

Figure 3.3
Cross-modal priming effects (lexical decision RT to target preceded by control prime minus RT to target preceded by related prime) of Norris, Cutler, et al. (2006). The left panel shows that there is facilitation for both identity and associate targets when primes are spoken in isolation. The right panel shows that there is facilitation for identity targets, but no significant facilitation for associate targets, when primes are spoken as part of a sentence.

of word recognition. Incoming speech activates phonological representations. These in turn activate the separate conceptual representations, which, put together, yield the meaning of the utterance as a whole.

These results show that activation of phonological representations does not automatically imply that the corresponding conceptual representations will be activated. *Lease* in a sentence can prime LEASE but not RENT; the activation of phonological information is separate from the activation of conceptual information. Norris, Cutler, et al. (2006) ran a number of follow-up studies to examine exactly when it was possible to obtain associative priming in sentences. With again the same recordings for which the results are shown in figure 3.3, they obtained significant priming for RENT if the sentence was truncated immediately after the prime:

(3.2) The residents complained about the lease—

In this case the word *lease* was effectively highlighted, perhaps somewhat like presenting it in isolation. This result showed that there was nothing in the acoustic form of the sentence preventing associative priming. They also found significant priming in sentences with contrastive accent:

(3.3) a. The manager arranged to LEASE both of the buildings.
b. The manager arranged to lease BOTH of the buildings.

Regardless of whether the accent fell on *lease* itself, or elsewhere in the sentence, responses to RENT were facilitated. This result showed that there was nothing about the word *lease* (and the other prime words they had used) that prevented associative priming in full sentences. Norris, Cutler, et al. argued that the activation of conceptual representations could vary with the amount of processing necessary. The effective context for priming could be just the word itself (if the word was uttered in isolation; or if the word was highlighted by the way the sentence was structured or the way it was spoken; or if the sentence was truncated such that the word was the last thing heard). This is the case in which conceptual representations are most likely to be activated. Alternatively, the effective context may be the sentence itself, or it may even be the wider context in which it occurs. In this case, conceptual representations may be most likely to be activated if they are related to the context and if they need to be activated for the sentence to be understood. If they are not necessary for understanding, they will not be activated. There is evidence that, in some cases, conceptual representations that do not correspond to the particular connotation that the word has in the sentence are indeed not primed. Thus, *chair* would normally be expected to prime TABLE, and *tree* would normally be expected to prime LEAVES, but Williams (1988) found no priming for TABLE after *chair* in (3.4a) and Tabossi (1988a) found no priming for LEAVES after *tree* in (3.5a).

(3.4) a. The man found that he could only reach the best apples by standing on a chair because they were all so high up.
b. The man entered the dining room and sat down on a chair in eager anticipation of a hearty meal.

(3.5) a. The woodsman worked hard to saw up the tree.
b. The sparrow hid in the thick foliage of the tree.

However, in (3.4b) and (3.5b), respectively, they each observed significant priming. In the (b) cases, the meanings of TABLE and LEAVES are relevant to the interpretation of the utterance, but in the (a) cases they are not. Thus these conceptual representations are activated in the (b) sentences because they effectively need to be activated for the sentence to be understood. There is no need for them in the (a) sentences: understanding a sentence about standing on a chair to reach apples does not require the concept of sitting at a table, and understanding a sentence about sawing wood does not require the concept of leaves on a living tree.

Conceptual representations can also be activated because the sentence as a whole, or the discourse context as a whole, encourages more extensive lexical processing. This was the likely source of the significant priming effects in example (3.3). The contrastive accent encouraged construction of a context that would warrant it.

In (3.3a), then, the situation calls up a contrast with an alternative scenario in which the manager might have decided not to lease the buildings but to buy or sell them instead, and (3.3b) likewise calls up a contrast with an alternative scenario in which the manager might have leased only one building rather than both of them. Such context construction, then, may encourage consideration of the full lexical meaning of all the words in the sentence. In this case, the activation of the conceptual representation follows not from integration of the word into the particular context but from the more extended semantic processing that, prompted by the contrastive accent, is undertaken to work out what the particular context must be.

The important lesson of this comparative study concerns not the precise determinants of conceptual activation, however, nor when priming does and does not occur. The important point is the separation of the two types of lexical representation. Phonological and conceptual representations are not irrevocably linked one with the other; they are independent. The participation of a phonological representation in the competition process does not automatically entail that the same word's conceptual representation will be activated and hence play a role in the same recognition operation.

3.4.2 Differences between Representations

In their comparison of identity and associative priming, Norris, Cutler, et al. (2006) further examined whether there is activation for embedded words that are accidentally present. For instance, *lease* is contained in *police*. They also tested for activation of *lease* and its associate *rent* when listeners heard *police*, either in isolation or in sentences such as:

(3.6) The residents complained about police on the premises.

This sentence is obviously matched to (3.1), which contains *lease*—indeed, it is even matched in rhythm so that the syllable [liːs] occurs at exactly the same point in the input stream. Figure 3.4 shows what happened. There was never any facilitation for either *lease* or *rent* when the prime was *police*. In contrast, there was actually inhibition for *lease*—both in isolation and, particularly strongly, when *police* was in a sentence.

The inhibition is an important finding. It shows that the phonological representations corresponding to embedded words, like *lease* in *police*, are momentarily activated but are inhibited by competition from the carrier words in which they are embedded.

There is no inhibition—and also no facilitation—for RENT given *police*. Responses to *rent* are not noticeably different from responses to the unrelated control words. So, the temporary activation of the phonological representation of *lease* has no implications for the conceptual representation of *lease*.

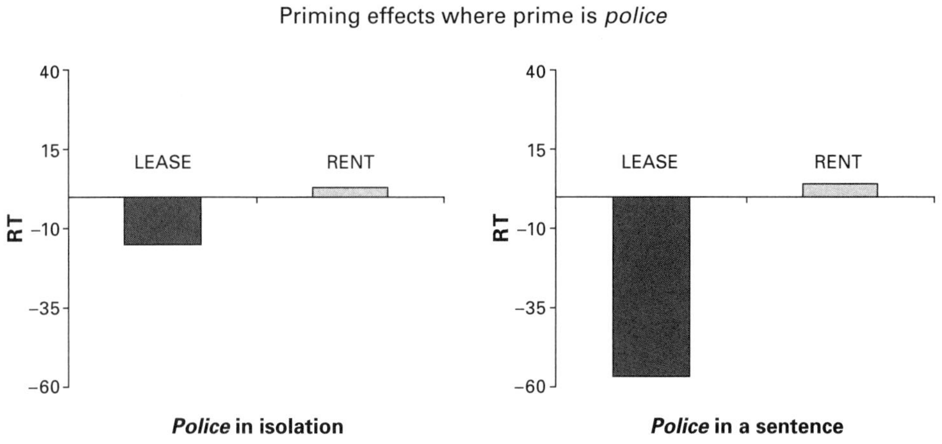

Figure 3.4
Cross-modal priming effects (lexical decision RT to target preceded by control prime minus RT to target preceded by related prime) of Norris, Cutler, et al. (2006). Both panels show that neither identity nor associate targets receive facilitation when the related prime (here, *lease*) occurs embedded in a longer word (*police*), whether spoken in isolation or in a sentence. The right panel shows that there is significant inhibition for identity targets following an embedded prime in a sentence.

This is also important. As we argued, the competition process initially involves phonological representations only. Phonological activation need not lead to conceptual activation. This simplifies the complexity that might have resulted from the enormous amount of embedding in words, and, particularly, in words in continuous speech. Embedding is a matter for the phonological representation level only. The input may indeed activate all compatible word phonological forms, but the competition process effectively gets rid of those that are only spuriously present. Their conceptual representations are unlikely to be troubled, so that the interpretation of the sentence is not further complicated by unnecessary and irrelevant conceptual activation.

Phonological representations that are doing well in the competition, in contrast, pass activation to their conceptual representations. This happens as soon as it can, and there is evidence that the operations (activation of phonological representations and activation of conceptual representations) are cascaded, not strictly sequential. That is to say: activation of a conceptual representation does not happen only after a unique winner has finally emerged from the phonological competition, but it happens continuously as a function of a leading position in the competition. If an embedded word then indeed fits well with the emerging interpretation of the context, its conceptual representation will, at least briefly, be considered. This was shown by Van Alphen and Van Berkum (2010), who constructed sentences in which an embedded word actually matched the context better than its carrier word did. For instance, the Dutch word *snorkel* (with the same meaning as in English, and with an embedded word *snor* 'moustache' as its first syllable) appeared in sentences about a man talking to a hairdresser or to a singer. Obviously, it is possible for such a conversation about a snorkel to occur in either case, but it is not very likely; in the hairdresser case, the conversation is far more likely to be about a moustache. This was an ERP experiment, and there is a well-known brain response (the N400—a negative-going waveform appearing roughly 400 ms into processing of a given input) that is observed when a sentence becomes implausible. Van Alphen and Van Berkum found that the N400 response was much bigger in the sentence about the singer than in the sentence about the hairdresser, which clearly suggested that the listeners did not experience so much implausibility in the latter case, where the embedded word *snor* offered a plausible conceptual representation in the context. The same thing happened with final embeddings (e.g., *meel* 'flour' in *kameel* 'camel' in sentences referring either to cooking or to buying clothes). Thus, a fully supported phonological representation (*snor*, *meel*) can rapidly activate its conceptual representation, and in an appropriate context the conceptual activation can be seen, even though the carrier word (*snorkel*, *kameel*) was clearly what the speaker in fact said.

The timing of the availability of different types of information was directly investigated by Huettig and McQueen (2007). It is a known effect in eye-tracking that listeners glance at pictures that share visual attributes with a named target—for instance, instructed to look at a snake, they may glance at a picture of a coiled-up rope (Cooper 1974; Dahan and Tanenhaus 2005). In Huettig and McQueen's study, listeners were instructed to look at targets that were not actually there; instead, the display contained a phonological competitor, a shape competitor, and a semantic competitor. If the named target was an arm, for instance, there would be no arm in the display, but there would be the three competitors: an artichoke (phonological, because *artichoke* begins like *arm*), a straw (shape, because a bent straw is shaped like a bent arm), and a nose (semantic, because like an arm it is a body part). They found that looks to the phonological competitor began first (unless listeners had not had time to retrieve the pictures' names, because the pictures appeared only as *arm* was being heard; in this case, the shape competitors received the earliest looks). If the display contained printed words instead of pictures, the phonological similarities were immediately obvious, and this difference due to timing went away; looks to the phonological competitor then began first, irrespective of when the display appeared. Huettig and McQueen interpreted this pattern of results in terms of the same account supported by the evidence reviewed above: phonological representations are activated first, but their activation cascades through to conceptual representations as quickly as it can. In this case, it was particularly revealing that the shape competitor was looked at first when there had not been enough time for the name of the phonologically related picture to be retrieved; the quick looks to a straw after hearing *arm* mean that some features of the conceptual representation of *arm* had been activated very rapidly indeed. Although the phonological and conceptual representations are separate, the flow of activation from sound to meaning is continuous and fast, in the interests of efficient word recognition.

3.5 One-to-Many Mappings of Phonological to Conceptual Representation

As discussed in chapter 2, there does not seem to be a high priority for uniqueness in phonological to conceptual mapping. Homophony is widespread in vocabularies, and language communities most often create new lexical entries by adding new meanings to old phonological forms, rather than by creating novel forms. The lexical activation and competition process, we have just argued, involves phonological forms only; meaning plays no part. This has an obvious consequence for the mapping from the phonological to the conceptual level where a phonological representation has more than one possible conceptual interpretation; a phonological form that triumphs in the initial competition process should pass activation to all conceptual representations associated with it. Unrelated words that happen to be pronounced in the same way, such as *pear* and *pair*, or *mussel* and *muscle*, would then provide a case in which unnecessary activation at the conceptual level might indeed occur.

Such spurious correspondences motivated the invention of the cross-modal priming task. As described in chapter 1, evidence from phoneme detection had seemed to show that recognizing phonological representations with more than one meaning is difficult, but this evidence had been called into doubt (Mehler et al. 1978). Swinney (1979) sought a better way of looking at activation of meanings. His combination of visual lexical decision with listening to speech was the result, and he first validated it with a series of studies showing that processing in the visual modality could indeed serve as a window onto processing in the auditory modality (Swinney et al. 1979). The first cross-modal priming study of homophones delivered precisely the result that he (and others) had previously thought to have demonstrated with phoneme detection: multiple interpretations of a homophone are activated even if the context makes it quite clear which meaning is intended. The context was sentences of the kind:

(3.7) The man was not surprised to find several bugs in his hotel room.

In this sentence, the word *bug* could refer to an insect or to a listening device (if these two meanings seem to differ in their intrinsic likelihood, consider that Swinney's experiment was run in the America of the 1970s, when the Watergate scandal elevated the probability of listening devices in the public consciousness). Obviously, associative priming is necessary to tell whether both these interpretations are active, and indeed, associative priming was the task's first instantiation. (Identity priming came along a decade or so later.) Swinney found that words associated to both the insect meaning of *bug* (e.g., ANT) and the listening device meaning (e.g., SPY) were accepted more rapidly than a matched control target word (e.g., SEW). This was true even if the sentence made it quite clear which meaning was intended:

(3.8) The man was not surprised to find several spiders, roaches, and other bugs in his hotel room.

In this case, both ANT and SPY were facilitated if they were presented right at the offset of the spoken word *bug* in the sentence. If they were presented 750 ms after *bug* had finished, however, only the contextually appropriate word—ANT—was facilitated, and SPY was not significantly different from SEW.

The appearance of associative priming in these sentences may mean that the effective context for priming was in these cases the word itself (as we argued earlier, this is the most likely situation for observing significant associative priming). If so, then when the lexical semantics are activated, all the possible conceptual representations that a word has will become active, even interpretations that turn out not to be useful for the context. The homophone case is the most obvious case for multiplicity of such representations. Multiple activation of homophone interpretations can occur even when one reading has higher frequency than the other (*scale* primes both WEIGHT and FISH; Onifer and Swinney 1981), and even when there are word-class differences and only one reading is viable in the syntactic context (*weak/week* primes both STRONG and MONTH; Lucas 1987).

Besides multiple unrelated meanings, the associate priming task has also been used to investigate the availability of multiple close connotations of words. Consider that a piano is always a musical instrument (so it should always prime MUSIC), and it is pretty much always a heavy thing (which might make it always prime HEAVY). Indeed, experiments with the task showed that multiple connotations can be activated, just like multiple meanings. But it became immediately clear that some aspects of meaning were more central—and thus more easily primed—than others. In the case of *piano*, the musical connotation is dominant: *piano* primes MUSIC regardless of whether the context concerns lifting the piano or playing it, but only in the former case, not in the latter, does it also prime HEAVY (Greenspan 1986; see also Whitney et al. 1985). Unsurprisingly, then, just as the dominant interpretation of *piano* (music) is more readily primed than a peripheral attribute (heavy), so is the more dominant interpretation of a homophone such as *scale* sometimes more likely to be activated (Tabossi 1988b; Tabossi, Colombo, and Job 1987).

However, in every case in which such conceptual activation has been observed, it must be assumed that one or other of the factors discussed earlier made the homophone the effective context for priming (for instance, there was prosodic variability, or abundant discourse context was available, or the primes were utterance final). Consistent with this, Blutner and Sommer (1988) discovered that multiple interpretations of homophones were activated when the prime word was in focus (where focus was determined by a preceding question, and prosody was constant) but not when focus fell elsewhere in the sentence. A delay between prime and target led to priming of the contextually appropriate associate of the homophone irrespective of focus location. The evidence discussed in section 3.4 provides a framework for understanding why, with homophones too, associative priming appears in some cases but not in others. The bottom line is that the activation and competition process involves, in the first instance, only phonological representations; activation spreads to the conceptual representations of the best-supported phonological representations. In certain circumstances, multiple conceptual representations become simultaneously active, but mostly, the conceptual activation involved in listening is the conceptual activation that the utterance warrants.

3.6 Dimensions of Activation: Segmental and Suprasegmental Structure

There is still more to be said about phonological representations and their makeup; as became clear in chapters 1 and 2, languages differ in choice of acoustic dimensions for distinguishing words from one another. Some languages use tonal distinctions between words, for example; others do not. Even when the same dimension is used by two languages, it may not be used to the same effect; the usefulness of stress in ruling out competition from embeddings is higher in Spanish than in Germanic languages, as we have seen, and within Germanic languages it is higher in Dutch and German than it is in English.

Activation will be affected by whatever aspects of the incoming signal serve usefully to identify the spoken word form. These may be the cues that distinguish one phoneme from another (and as will be shown in chapter 6, distinctions between phonemes can be communicated by very subtle aspects of the signal). The signal then provides essentially segmental information, indispensable for distinguishing between words in any language. But suprasegmental information can also be relevant. Suprasegmental, as we defined it in chapter 1, means any acoustic variation above the level of the segmental string. We used it there to characterize the pitch, amplitude, and duration variations that may realize stress differences.

These suprasegmental dimensions are clearly not optional. Speech is an acoustic signal, and these are the dimensions of acoustic form. Any fragment of speech, whether or not it corresponds to a linguistic entity such as phoneme, syllable, word, and so forth, necessarily has a certain duration, amplitude envelope, and fundamental frequency contour. For these dimensions to be critically involved in lexical activation, they have to vary in a distinctive fashion independently of segmental structure, not merely as a consequence of segmental variation. Languages differ in how they allow the suprasegmental dimensions to distinguish words, and thus in how they make these dimensions relevant for lexical activation.

There are essentially three possibilities with respect to activation. First, suprasegmental information may be quite irrelevant for distinguishing one word from another. There are many whole families of languages in which this is the case (e.g., the major languages of India). All languages with fixed stress fall into this category, obviously; if the position of stress is fixed, it cannot distinguish two otherwise identical words. This does not mean that suprasegmental information is not exploited in speech in all these languages; rather, it is likely to be useful for encoding syntactic structure, focus, and emphasis, for distinguishing sentence types (e.g., questions from statements), and for establishing discourse reference. But it does not determine word identity.

Second, suprasegmental information may encode prosodic structure at the lexical level, such as lexical stress (in Spanish, English, and so on) or pitch accent (as in Japanese or in Scandinavian languages). In this case the realization of lexical prosody depends in part on the prosodic utterance structure. We have already seen that the suprasegmental dimensions may play a varying role in the determination of word identity in stress languages. This story is fleshed out in chapter 7, which is all about the role of prosody in decoding speech.

Third, suprasegmental information may be an obligatory part of a word's identity. This is the case, for example, in lexical tone languages, in which words may be distinguished by the pitch height or contour of syllables. This kind of suprasegmental information thus functions in just the same way as segmental information to distinguish one word from another. Word recognition in tone languages is not yet widely studied, but there is sufficient evidence that tone plays a role in lexical activation, as the following section briefly summarizes.

3.6.1 Lexical Tone in Activation

The suprasegmental dimension of fundamental frequency (F0) is the primary signal of lexical tone. Thus the Cantonese word for *poem* is *si1* and for *time* is *si6*; the segmental string is the same in each case, [s] plus [i], but the two words have different tones (which the numbers indicate). Tone 1, in *si1*, is a high pitch contour, whereas tone 6, in *si6*, is a low contour. Cantonese has six tones (shown in figure 3.5), and all of them, as it happens, occur in combination with the syllable *si*. In contrast, *sa* only occurs with two of the six tones: tones 1 and 2 (*sa1* 'sand', *sa2* 'sprinkle'). The nonsense syllable *sa6* would mismatch each of the existing syllables *sa1* and *si6* in exactly one aspect: tone and vowel, respectively.

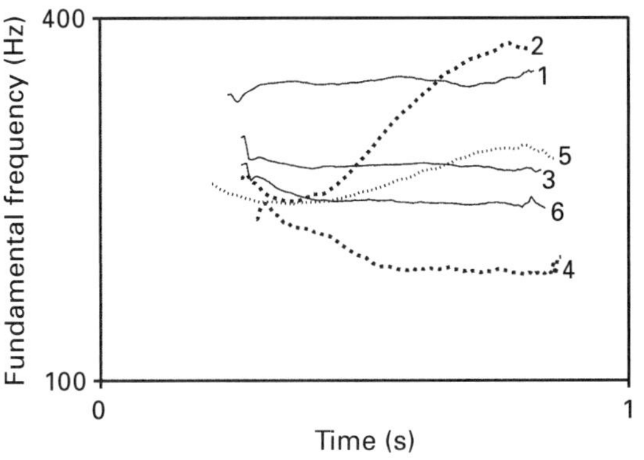

Figure 3.5
The six tones of Cantonese uttered on the syllable *si* by a female speaker. These syllables were spoken in isolation; see Fok (1974) for data on Cantonese tone realization in conversational context.

The F0 information coding tone can be highly informative even in the absence of segmental information; providing this information in the form of pulses synchronized with the talker's pitch greatly improves identification scores for lip-read Cantonese words, for instance (Ching 1988). Tones can be rapidly identified: Tseng (1990) found that only 25 percent of the vowel was enough for listeners to correctly identify the tone of Mandarin vowels pronounced in isolation; in later studies, even much shorter fragments of the beginning of the tone-bearing vowel proved sufficient to distinguish the same four Mandarin tones (Gottfried and Suiter 1997; Lee, Tao, and Bond 2008; Lee 2009—in this last study, the fragments were shorter than 50 ms). In fact, tones can often be identified solely from cues in surrounding segments (Gottfried and Suiter 1997; Lee et al. 2008). Note that this is also true of vowels (Strange, Jenkins, and Johnson 1983); that is, the way tones contribute to lexical activation is just like the way segmental information contributes.

Priming experiments in Cantonese also suggest that the role of a syllable's tone in word recognition is analogous to the role of the vowel; in auditory lexical decision, analogous effects are observed when a prime word overlaps with the target word either in tone or in vowel (Chen and Cutler 1997; Cutler and Chen 1995; Yip 2001).

For listeners without tone language experience, discrimination of tones is difficult in the same way as discrimination of phoneme contrasts that do not occur in the native language. It might seem that a contrast realized in F0 should be perceptually simple to process, in that it resembles the contrast between two musical notes. But English listeners discriminate musical tones significantly better than (Thai) speech tones, whereas Cantonese listeners discriminate the same speech and musical tones equally well; even though the tones were not those of their native language, the Cantonese were as accurate as native Thai listeners (Burnham et al. 1996; see also Gandour 1983). Cantonese and Mandarin listeners each perform better with their own than with the other language in same-different judgments on tone contrasts, but they also both do better than English listeners in both languages (Lee, Vakoch, and Wurm 1996). A set of artificial rising and falling tone continua presented as speech (i.e., realized on vowels) to Thai- and English-speaking listeners elicited from the Thais good discrimination and categorical response patterns. The English listeners did not show this pattern, however, and neither group showed it with exactly the same contours presented as music or as sine waves (Burnham and Jones 2002). So tones on vowels are not like music at all; they are speech, no less than segmental contrasts are.

Although the results described here suggest that the role of tone in word recognition is equivalent to the role of segmental information, tones may nonetheless constrain word recognition less surely than segments. Judging whether written characters in Mandarin or Cantonese sound the same is slower when the pronunciation of the two characters differs only in tone, as opposed to in the vowel (Taft and Chen 1992). This experiment involved no speech perception, only subjects' internal representation of how the words sounded; but Repp and Lin (1990), in a categorization experiment, found that Mandarin listeners categorized the tone of CV nonsense syllables less rapidly than either segment, and Tsang and Hoosain (1979) found that Cantonese subjects choosing between two transcriptions of sentences they had heard were more accurate at noticing vowel differences than tone differences.

Lesser accuracy in tone discrimination was also observed in an auditory lexical decision study in which, as in the experiments described early in this chapter, the crucial items were nonwords; Cantonese listeners were significantly more likely to erroneously accept a nonword as a real word if it differed from a real word only in tone than if it differed in a segment (Cutler and Chen 1997). In the same study, listeners were slower and less accurate in same-different judgments when two syllables differed only in tone, compared to when a segmental difference was present. Here the differential response was solely due to acoustic factors, given that nonnative (Dutch) listeners produced the same asymmetric pattern as the native listeners. Analogously asymmetric mismatch effects were observed in an identity priming task, again with Cantonese (Yip 2001), and in fragment detection, in Mandarin, where "NO" decisions were slower when the mismatch to the target was in a tone versus a vowel (Ye and Connine 1999). In both of Cutler and Chen's tasks, an error was most probable when the correct tone of the real word and the erroneous tone on the nonword began similarly; in other words, when the tone distinction was perceptually hard to make (tones 4 and 5 in figure 3.5, for example). Response times in the same-different discrimination were also faster, for nonnative as for native listeners, when the tones involved were discriminable right from the onset (tones 1 and 2 in the figure). Similar effects appear in the perception of Thai tones by English-speaking listeners: the order of difficulty of tone pairs in same-different judgment is determined by the starting pitch of the tones (Burnham et al. 1992). Analogously, Ye and Connine (1999) found that a mismatching similar Mandarin tone inhibited lexical access less effectively than a mismatching very different tone.

Although tone contrasts are realized in F0, they are realized upon vowels, and therefore they are processed together with the vowel information. Vowels themselves can be identified very early, such as from the transition into a vowel from a preceding consonant (Strange 1989; Strange et al. 1983), and tone identification also requires minimal information, as described earlier. On the basis of their results showing that preceding segments have analogous effects on identification of tones and vowels, Lee et al. (2008) argued that there is no processing asymmetry between the two. Schirmer et al. (2005) also found that Cantonese listeners' electrophysiological brain responses to semantic violations in highly predictable contexts were closely similar regardless of whether the violations resulted from tonal or segmental mismatch (unfortunately, however, they report nothing about the tone pairs involved, although, as we saw, pairs of Cantonese tones differ in how hard they are to discriminate). The evidence from speeded decision tasks reviewed above suggests that in cases where tones cannot be identified at their onset, subjects' responses may sometimes be made on the basis of vowel information, before the tone information has effectively been processed. The results from different lines of research appear not to be fully consistent, and systematic investigation of the strategic options available to listeners in each case seems called for.

What is also missing in this research area so far is a significant body of cross-language studies. Consider that the strongest evidence for slower tone than segment processing comes from Cantonese, which has six tones, some of which (as is clear from figure 3.5) begin very similarly. Much of the evidence for equivalence of tone and vowel processing, on the other hand, comes from Mandarin, with four tones that do not overlap initially to quite the same extent as tones do in Cantonese. More direct crosslinguistic comparisons would be welcome. Although tone information is indisputably necessary for distinguishing between words in tone languages, it may sometimes be the case that segmental information arrives more rapidly and thereby plays a more decisive role in initial lexical activation than tone information does.

3.6.2 Durational Structure (Quantity) in Lexical Activation

Chapters 6 and 7 describe how the fine detail of phonetic and prosodic structure can be continuously tracked by listeners, for instance to decide whether a syllable is a stand-alone monosyllabic word or part of a longer word. This discrimination is durational, as are many of the others described later. But many languages have so-called quantity distinctions, whereby the same vowel or the same consonant can occur in varying durational realizations. Otherwise identical minimal word pairs in these languages can then differ solely in segmental duration.[2] Several levels of use of such distinctions are possible. Some languages allow vowel duration differences only (in Dutch, for instance, *tak* 'branch' differs from *taak* 'task' in vowel length); some allow consonant differences only (Italian notably has geminate consonants; compare [l] in *allungo* 'spurt' versus *alunno* 'student'); and many languages have both (e.g., Japanese, where doubling of vowels or of intervocalic consonants occurs: *suu* 'inhale', *su* 'vinegar', *kako* 'past', *kakko* 'parenthesis'; or Finnish and Estonian, with their multiple levels of vowel and consonant quantity).

Listeners in such languages are, as might be expected, extremely sensitive to durational distinctions (see, e.g., Nooteboom and Doodeman 1980 for the Dutch *tak-taak* case; Pickett, Blumstein, and Burton 1999 for Italian geminates; Kakehi, Kato, and Kashino 1996 for Japanese; and Ylinen et al. 2005 for Finnish). Language experience conditions the sensitivity to durational contrasts, just as it does for tone contrasts. The cues listeners attend to differ across languages; so Spanish, German, Japanese, and Thai listeners produce similar vowel-length categorizations for a continuum that varies in duration only, but the judgments of the Japanese listeners (only) are affected by addition of F0 variation (Lehnert-LeHouillier 2010). There are numerous demonstrations that durational distinctions in a second language cause difficulty for learners whose native language has no such contrasts (many relevant references can be found in Ylinen et al. 2005, and the topic returns in chapter 9; chapter 8 also describes how infants learn what to use duration for in the language they are acquiring). A brain-imaging study by Gandour et al. (2002) compared detection of vowel quantity and consonant place of articulation distinctions in nonwords by Thai and English speakers; the consonant place of articulation task caused similar activation patterns in the brains of each listener group, and the Thai group showed the same pattern for the vowel duration task as well, but the English listeners did not. This too is as would be expected: quantity distinctions, like tonal distinctions, are speech. They are perceived, by listeners whose native language has such contrasts, in just the same way as segments.

As yet, few studies directly address the role of quantity distinctions in lexical activation. A cross-modal fragment priming study of Italian geminates by Tagliapietra and McQueen (2010) compared recognition of words with a geminate or a singleton consonant (e.g., *allungo*, *alunno*); recognition of *allungo* was faster after a matching fragment (*allu-*), whereas recognition of *alunno* was faster after a fragment with a singleton consonant (*alu-*). The Italian listeners were thus sensitive to the quantity distinction and used it to modulate lexical activation in just the way that segmental information is used, such as by Soto-Faraco et al.'s (2001) listeners.

Both tonal contrasts and duration contrasts, of course, are expressed in dimensions of the speech signal that are also used to express other aspects of the message. The same is true of stress contrasts, and all these are not in principle different from segmental contrasts, which are also expressed inter alia in the same dimensions and can also convey nonsegmental information—for example, in the clarity and force with which they are articulated. But it is still interesting to ask whether listeners keep the various streams of information apart while processing speech. One study, at least, suggests that duration contrasts may maintain their integrity more easily than tonal contrasts. In the dialects of Limburg, in the southeast of the Netherlands, there are word prosodic distinctions that are marked by duration and F0 in ways not used by Standard Dutch. Fournier et al. (2006) compared two such dialects: one in which the relevant contrast is realized in F0 alone, and another in which it is realized principally in duration. Listeners' ability to identify minimal pairs spoken in isolation, in various positions in sentences, and in focused versus unfocused position was in general very good. But only the listeners with the durational contrast maintained high performance across all types of context. The F0 dialect speakers discriminated accurately when the word in question was focused or was at the end of a sentence. They were far less accurate for words in isolation or in unfocused position midway in a sentence. For these listeners, at least, the lexical F0 distinctions were not being kept apart from the processing of sentence intonation and the semantic structure that it conveyed.

3.7 Morphological Structure in Lexical Activation

As we saw in chapter 2, the vocabulary structure of some languages requires (or encourages) processing operations that are unnecessary in other languages. Morphological decomposition as an operation is motivated by experiments in Western languages, but it would have no processing counterpart for many Asian languages. Morphology thus presents an interesting source of evidence for disentangling universal and language-specific processing. There are general asymmetries in morphological structure (everywhere, the most likely affix is a suffix), and these are, we saw, potentially explicable in processing terms. For lexical activation in spoken-language understanding, the issue is whether morphological structure plays any role at all.

Much of the research on morphology in processing has concerned reading, and much of the modeling has been based on the reading evidence (see McQueen and Cutler 1998 and Marslen-Wilson 2001, 2006 for reviews); but the ways in which written language and spoken language are different make it necessary to model visual and auditory processing of morphology separately. The issue of regularity versus irregularity in inflectional morphology has been particularly important in the modeling, but this issue has not often been tested with auditory experiments (though see Kempley and Morton 1982; Orsolini and Marslen-Wilson 1997; Clifton et al. 1999). Research on the processing of morphology in spoken words has, however, included analysis of the processing significance of contrasting morphological structures across languages; crosslinguistic experiments in Arabic, Polish, Chinese, French, and Italian (as well as English) have been carried out by Marslen-Wilson and colleagues.

The principal question for the present purposes is whether activated representations are unitary or decompositional, which has been operationalized as: what primes what? In the visual modality, repetition priming experiments by Stanners and colleagues (Stanners, Neiser, Hernon, et al. 1979; Stanners, Neiser, and Painton 1979) showed lexical decisions to base forms of verbs (e.g., *pour*) to be faster if an inflected form (e.g., *poured*) had occurred earlier in the list, whereas responses to morphologically complex words such as *progress* were unaffected by earlier occurrence of another word with the same stem (*regress*) or affix (*protect*). It has long been known that there is also auditory priming not only between words with the same stem (Kempley and Morton 1982) but also between words with the same affix (Emmorey 1989); in both cases, absence of priming between unrelated but similar words (*seen-seed*, *balloon-saloon*) again showed that the effects were not just due to phonological overlap. The most systematic auditory investigation is Marslen-Wilson et al.'s (1994) study of English prefixed and suffixed words using cross-modal form priming with one form of a word occurring as auditory prime and another form as visual target.

In different experiments, almost every possible comparison was carried out. Base forms were preceded or followed by derivationally suffixed or prefixed forms (e.g., *serene-serenity*, *friend-friendly*, *punish-punishment*, *sincere-insincere*, *fasten-unfasten*), so priming in each direction was investigated. Also, priming was studied between two derivatives of the same base form (e.g., *judgment-misjudge*, *confessor-confession*). Different types of morphological relationship led to different results. Suffixed forms (e.g., *friendly*) primed and were primed by their stems, but suffixed forms did not prime each other (e.g., *confession*, *confessor*). Derivationally prefixed forms (e.g., *unfasten*, *refasten*) primed and were primed by their stems, but, in contrast to suffixed forms, they also primed each other. Prefixed and suffixed forms sharing the same stem also primed each other (e.g., *distrust*, *trustful*). The bottom line, as revealed by these priming patterns, is that semantically transparent complex forms have their internal structure represented in the lexicon (hence the complex form and its components prime each other). Opaque complex forms (e.g., *casualty*) do not have their structure represented (and fail to prime). Some phonological variation between related forms (e.g., *sanity-sane*) does not reduce the amount of priming (Marslen-Wilson and Zhou 1999). Subsequent experiments in another language with a morphology much more complex than English but based on similar combinatorial principles, namely Polish, showed a similar pattern (Reid and Marslen-Wilson 2003).

Interestingly, evidence from reading, where suffixes are available at the same time as the beginning of a word, reveals a different picture; in reading, priming can be observed for opaque pseudocomplex forms (e.g., from *corner* to *corn*; see Marslen-Wilson 2006). This is the kind of effect that motivates separate modeling for visual and auditory processing. In speech, the beginning of a word is heard first; affixes are always the same, so having them in onset position would increase temporary ambiguity and thereby add competition. As described, this is possibly why languages prefer suffixing. Indeed, recognition of spoken prefixed words is sensitive to the competitor set defined by the full form (*reprint* competes with *reap* and *rebus* and *replay*) rather than to the set defined by the stem (e.g., for *reprint*, *prince* or *pretty*) or by the prefix alone, both in English (Tyler et al. 1988; Wurm 1997) and in French (Meunier and Segui 2002). However, the Marslen-Wilson et al. (1994) results make it clear that morphological structure plays a role in auditory recognition. Wurm and colleagues (Wurm and Ross 2001; Wurm and Aycock 2003) also found a decompositional effect with prefixes; *discredit* and *discretion* diverge from one another at the seventh phoneme, after [dɪskrɛ], but *discredit* is identified and repeated much more rapidly than *discretion*. This pattern appeared consistently for words in which the UP of the stem, given that prefix, was very early (i.e., *credit* is the only stand-alone form beginning *cr-* that combines with *dis-*). Spoken words with a single mispronunciation are easier to reconstruct if the mispronounced sound could occur in a morphologically related word (Ernestus and Baayen 2007; this experiment was in Dutch, but an analogous example from English would be that it should be easier to reconstruct *serene* from *serenn* than *ravine* from *ravenn*).

The evidence could imply that spoken-word recognition simultaneously involves both activation of full word forms and decomposition into their morphological components (Wurm 1997, 2000). A simpler model, however, would propose activation of all possible elements at once—full forms, stems, and affixes (Baayen, Dijkstra, and Schreuder 1997). The latter model was supported by data on auditory recognition of inflected plural nouns and verbs versus their singular forms (Baayen et al. 2003). Dutch plural forms were recognized less rapidly if the concept was singular-dominant (e.g., *soep* 'soup') but not if it was plural-dominant (e.g., *wolk* 'cloud'). The frequency of the individual form (rather than of all morphological relatives combined) was a stronger determinant of RTs for plurals than for singulars. This pattern can be explained neither by models in which only full word forms are activated (then the individual form frequency should be crucial both for plurals and singulars) nor by models in which all words are always decomposed (then the combined frequency should always be crucial). The Baayen et al. (1997) model is then supported by default. The forms in this model are held to be phonological representations that take part in the competition process; thus the proposal is compatible with competition-based recognition models. These studies also found durational differences between inflected and uninflected stems, which could cue the differing forms; Kemps and colleagues (Kemps, Ernestus, et al. 2005; Kemps, Wurm, et al. 2005) showed that listeners can use such durational differences in recognition. (There is much more in chapter 6 on the significant role of such interword differences in lexical processing.)

Languages that do not form words in such a complex manner nevertheless construct words out of combinations of other words; in Chinese, for example, compounding is ubiquitous. Zhou and Marslen-Wilson (1994, 1995) argue that the Chinese lexicon represents both full forms of compounded words and their component morphemes. They reached this conclusion on the basis of a long series of auditory lexical decision and cross-modal priming experiments, in which they observed (a) priming effects between words sharing a common morpheme, (b) effects in nonword decision of the morphemic status and frequency of component syllables, but (c) greater effects of the frequency of full forms than of the component morphemes. This model thus resembles the one proposed by Baayen et al. (1997) for Western languages; there may be no need to assume any language-specificity of morphological structure in lexical activation.

Marslen-Wilson (2001) pointed to three core properties of lexical processing, at least for languages like English: (a) constituent morphology is lexically represented; (b) morphology is combinatorial, so the stem in *clouded* and *cloudy* is the same *cloud-*, and the affix in *cloudy* and *fizzy* is the same *-y*; and (c) semantic transparency plays a crucial role in the representation of constituent morphology (*a tacky suggestion* does not activate the affix *-y*). McQueen and Cutler's (1998) review concluded with the suggestion that morphological decomposition is involved in lexical recognition not as a precursor of activation but more as a byproduct of it; this account still seems to be a good summary of the available evidence.

3.8 The Case of Gender

Expressed as morphological structure in some languages, but as a stand-alone element in others, there is also noun gender; an arbitrary classification, it can be used as a minimal distinguisher between otherwise identical word pairs (*die See* 'the ocean', *der See* 'the lake' in German; *le tour* 'the journey', *la tour* 'the tower' in French). There is evidence from several languages that matching gender is easier to process than mismatching.

In French, matching gender leads to earlier correct guesses of gated real words and faster lexical decision responses (Grosjean et al. 1994), and this result was replicated in German (Bölte and Connine 2004). In Italian, there was similar facilitation for matching gender in experiments in which subjects detected or repeated spoken words or verified whether an article-noun pair was correctly matched (Bates et al. 1996). The latter task was also used by Deutsch and Wijnen (1985) in Dutch. Dutch has two grammatical gender classes, with an asymmetric distribution: *de* nouns are far more numerous than *het* nouns. If gender-marked articles constrain lexical availability, this should work particularly in favor of the minority (i.e., *het* nouns) and result in faster responses to these words. However, responses to *de* nouns were faster. Gender thus cannot fully constrain lexical availability (ruling out everything with another gender); instead, Deutsch and Wijnen argued that any article will set up a noun-phrase schema into which the noun, once retrieved from the lexicon, can be slotted. The preponderance of *de* nouns in Dutch makes noun-phrase schemata with *de* the default option, and *de* the default response in article assignment, which results in the faster responses for the *de* items. The same asymmetry also leads to stronger gender mismatch effects for Dutch *de* nouns than *het* nouns (Johnson 2005a).

In eye-tracking, a gender-marked French article can inhibit looks to competitors for which it is not the appropriate article; for example, instructions to click on *le bouton* 'the button' did not produce looks to a bottle (*la bouteille*), although in a plural context, these competitors did get looks *(les boutons* where the plural of *bottle* would be *les bouteilles*; Dahan et al. 2000). This does not force the conclusion that the gender-marked article restricted the set of potential word candidates; instead, co-occurrence frequency of the correct article-noun combination (higher than the co-occurrence frequency of the incorrect combination) could be playing a role. In a subsequent experiment (D. Dahan, p.c.), the co-occurrence frequencies were neutralized by preceding the nouns with adjectives (*le joli bouton* 'the pretty button'); in this case, the competitor was activated, which suggests, in line with Deutsch and Wijnen's proposal, that gender does not directly constrain lexical availability. Finally, this was also the conclusion reached by Bölte and Connine (2004) on the basis of a failure to find effects of gender match in phoneme detection. In their experiment, detection of the final sound of *Referat* or *Mosaik* was faster than detection of the same sound in minimally different nonwords (*Veferat*; *Nosaik*), as had been found for English by Connine et al. (1997; to be discussed in more detail in chapter 12). However, it made no difference whether the words (or their nonword analogs) were preceded by appropriate versus inappropriate articles.

Gender, like morphology, has mainly been studied in the visual modality and, like morphology, then reveals more evidence of an early role for word-internal structure. For instance, explicit gender decisions—is this word masculine or feminine?—are influenced by the gender of embedded forms (Meunier, Seigneuric, and Spinelli 2008). Morphologically complex French words such as *citronnier* 'lemon tree' (masculine, derived from *citron* 'lemon', also masculine) were correctly decided on more rapidly than words such as *citronnade* 'lemonade' (feminine, but also derived from *citron*). The same effect appeared with pseudosuffixed words such as *baguette* (feminine, and *not* derived from the embedded form *bague 'ring'*, which is masculine). The conclusion drawn above for morphological structure, it seems, can hold for the arbitrary distinction gender, too: it is more a byproduct than a precursor of lexical activation.

3.9 Open versus Closed Classes in Lexical Activation

These results, which show that gender-marking on articles does not strongly constrain lexical activation of their companion nouns, lead us to the more general issue of whether the class of a word—for example, whether it is an article versus a noun—plays a role in activation. This issue has been predominantly addressed in English. Phoneme detection time is not sensitive to whether the target begins a word from the open class or the closed class; responses are faster for targets beginning stressed words than for targets beginning unstressed words, but when stress is held constant, there is no significant effect of word class (Cutler and Foss 1977). The same holds for word monitoring (which is like phoneme or fragment detection except that the target is a real word; Swinney, Zurif, and Cutler 1980). Repetition of a target word (cued by a voice switch) is less accurate for closed-class than for open-class versions of homophones in neutral context (*say by now*/*say buy now*) but not in appropriate context (*stand by me*/*can't buy me*; Herron and Bates 1997). Here, though, it is again the prosodic structure of the context that is responsible, because Herron and Bates found that this context facilitation for the closed class did not appear if the same context was provided visually.

All these results suggest that the spoken forms of open- and closed-class words are not different as a function of the word class they represent but rather as a function of the differing role they take in prosodic structure. Open-class words tend to be stressed; closed-class words are more likely not to be stressed. Consistent with this is evidence from speech production suggesting that open- and closed-class homophones have a unitary representation, because the combined frequency of homophone forms such as *buy*/*by* better predicts production latency than the individual sense frequency (Dell 1990; Jescheniak and Levelt 1994); and although speakers treat stressed and unstressed syllables differently when they try to make their speech clearer, it does not separately matter whether these syllables represent open- or closed-class words (Cutler and Butterfield 1990a).

There are a few findings that point to a word-class effect in activation. Nonwords beginning with real open-class English words (e.g., *thinage*) are significantly harder to reject than nonwords with no embedded word, but nonwords beginning with real closed-class words (e.g., *thanage*) exercise no such inhibition (Matthei and Kean

1989; another case of an auditory lexical decision task with nonwords as the crucial items). Some associative priming is found for Dutch open-class words embedded in other words (e.g., *bal* 'ball' in *balsem* 'balm') but not for closed-class embedded forms (e.g., *of* 'if' in *offer* 'sacrifice'); but recall that associative priming for embedded words is rarely found anyway. In short phrases, there is associative priming for both open- and closed-class words (e.g., *daar* 'there' was facilitated after *geef eens hier* 'give it here' as well as *goed* 'good' being facilitated after *toch niet slecht* 'not so bad'; all these results by Haveman 1997).

Do open- and closed-class homophones such as *buy/by* activate both meanings? Haveman could not find this (for Dutch homophones such as *hen* 'them; hen'). Nor could Shillcock and Bard (1993); in cross-modal priming, *would* did not prime TIMBER (an associate of its homophone *wood*). Shillcock and Bard did not test for closed-class priming (Haveman was the first to show this); however, their materials were of the sort that, according to the account in section 3.4, should be most likely to produce associative priming. Closed-class words may thus be integrated extremely rapidly into a sentence-level representation. The same conclusion arises from a German word-monitoring experiment (Friederici 1985). With certain verbs, a particular preposition is obligatory; for example, *Der Bauer hofft auf den Sommer* 'the farmer is looking forward to summer', can only have *auf*. Such obligatory prepositions attracted particularly fast responses and were responsible for an overall advantage for closed-class words in this study. Comparison of the materials sets used by Friederici and by Swinney et al. (1980), whose open-class words had been detected faster, revealed that the word class of the closed-class items was relatively more predictable in the former set, whereas the word class of the open-class items was relatively more predictable in the latter set. That is, the two major classes of words may not differ in initial activation except as determined by prosody, but they can differ in how rapidly they may be fitted into the understanding of what is being said.

The prosodic properties of open- and closed-class words also make the word class difference relevant for the segmentation of continuous speech (Grosjean and Gee 1987; Cutler and Carter 1987). Integration of closed-class words can be facilitated if the listener acts on the assumption that prosodically weak syllables (in English, at least) are likely to be such words. A post hoc analysis of mishearings collected by Cutler and Butterfield (1992; see chapter 4 for more about this study) showed strong links between word class and prosody when a word boundary that had not been present in the utterance was inserted in the misheard version (Cutler 1993). Boundaries inserted before strong syllables (e.g., *economists* misperceived as *the communists*) were more than eight times more likely to be followed by a reported open-class word (such as *communists*) than by anything else, whereas boundaries inserted before weak syllables (e.g., *dusty* misperceived as *thus he*) were more than three times more likely to be followed by a reported closed-class word (such as *he*).

Similar conclusions arise from the evidence concerning open- and closed-class words gleaned in studies of the learning of artificially constructed languages (ALL; see panel 9 in chapter 2). These techniques have proven extremely illuminating for examining word perception in continuous speech (see chapter 4), but they were first used to study the acquisition of syntax and, in particular, what kind of system is learnable and what is not.

These studies revealed that syntax learning is easier (for native speakers of English, anyway) if the grammar contains analogs of closed-class elements (Green 1979). To be useful, the closed-class analogs must have a high frequency of occurrence (Valian and Coulson 1988). These studies used very simple hierarchical grammars in which higher-level elements can be realized in terms of only a small set of lower-level elements. The grammar in example (3.9), for instance (one of Green's grammars), generates six possible types of string, in all of which terminal elements realizing an uppercase letter must be preceded by a terminal element realizing a lowercase letter. There are three or six possible terminal elements for each of A, B, C, and D, but only one each for a, b, c, and d; we can think of the former as open-class elements and the latter as closed-class elements. Typically—and fully in line with Zipf's Law—the former are generally longer than the latter; thus a cCaA string might be *alt puser erd fleam*. A grammar like this was really easy to learn, whereas a grammar with no closed-class analogs, or with inconsistent mappings of the closed-class items, proved almost unlearnable.

(3.9) S → P
S → P dD
P → aA cC
P → cC aA
P → aA bB cC
A → *lothog, stiny, tyan, pank, fleam, ling*
B → *batim, gort, skop*
C → *puser, rark, cumo, fengle, furd, stope*
D → *relo, doob, plack*
a → *erd*
b → *eth*
c → *alt*
d → *irp*

In most such grammar-learning studies, including Green's, the training input was presented visually. A few studies used auditory training (e.g., Morgan, Meier, and Newport 1987; Braine et al. 1990; Brooks et al. 1993; Valian and Levitt 1996). In these studies, phonological similarity within the artificial word classes proved helpful for learning, and so did explicit prosodic cues to class distinctions and syntactic structure. For instance, subjects in Morgan et al.'s study heard a series of grammatical spoken sentences of the language, each accompanied by visual presentation of a written version of the same sentence plus a graphic referent associated with each vocabulary item. They were then tested on pairing of referents and their "names," as well as on distinguishing grammatical from ungrammatical sentences of the language. When syntactic boundaries were consistently marked by prosodic cues, subjects were better at distinguishing grammar than when prosody and syntax were inconsistent. There was no such effect, however, on the test of referent-name pairing; in other words, consistency between prosodic and syntactic structure explicitly facilitated acquisition of the latter.

In Valian and Levitt's (1996) study, "sentences" such as *alt puser erd fleam* were spoken either grouped by prosody into two-word phrases or as a list of four separate words. In replication of Valian and Coulson's (1988) finding, the effect of closed-class element frequency was strongest. This effect was not modulated by the prosodic grouping manipulation. Prosody had most effect when the task was relatively hard (e.g., there was no visual referent linked to the sentences). Valian and Levitt suggested that prosodic grouping of the kind they provided can offer a crutch when no other cues to syntax are available.

As we saw earlier, however, the prosodic correlation of word class used by listeners in real life is: closed-class words tend to be weak, open-class words tend to be strong. Can consistent mapping between word class and this type of prosodic structure facilitate learning of an artificial language? In a study using Morgan et al.'s (1987) methodology, Stankler (1991) presented listeners with a version of grammar (3.9) in which the prosody/word-class relations were varied. All terminal elements were monosyllabic and could be "open class" (three or six possible realizations, hence lower frequency; cf. *A*, *B*, *C*, *D* in (3.9)) or "closed class" (a constant realization, hence higher frequency; cf. *a*, *b*, *c*, *d*). In one version of the language, all "closed class" elements were spoken as weak syllables, whereas "open class" elements were produced as strong syllables. This version of the language thus incorporated the mapping of prosody to word class that is found in English, so it should be easy for English listeners to learn. Another version was predicted to be hard to learn, because it contained no consistent mapping between prosody and word class at all: both word classes included some strong and some weak realizations. Two further versions of the language acted as controls: a reversal of the English mapping, to control for the possibility that any consistent mapping would be effective, and a version in which every element in both classes was realized as a strong syllable, to control for the possibility that simply having more vocabulary items realized as strong syllables could make language learning easier.

Again there were no effects of the prosody manipulation on the referent-name test. As figure 3.6 shows, however, the groups differed on the sentence structure test:

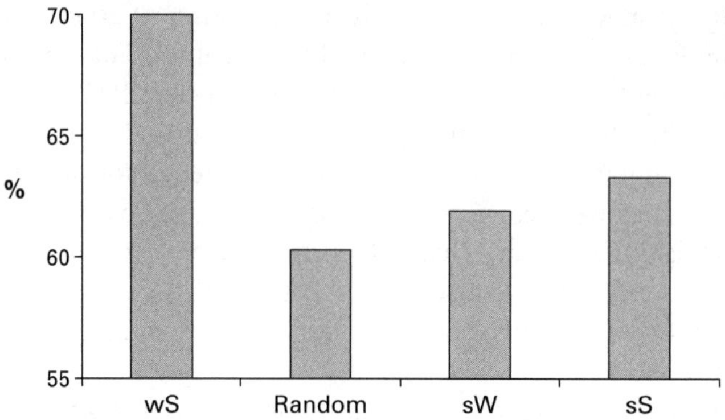

Figure 3.6
Percent correct in the sentence structure test of Stankler (1991), when the language embodied the grammar in example (3.9) and was realized in one of four ways: with the "closed class" elements of the grammar being weak syllables and the "open class" elements strong syllables (wS); with no consistent mapping of word class to prosody (Random); with a reversed mapping (closed-class strong, open-class weak: sW); or with an all-strong mapping (sS). The wS mapping, analogous to the pattern in English, was by far the easiest to learn.

the group given the English-like mapping performed significantly better than all the other three groups (which did not differ significantly from one another). When the language embodied a consistent mapping of prosody to word class, in the same direction as that found in English, it was easiest to learn. Thus Stankler's (1991) study indicates that listeners both know and can exploit correlations of word class and prosodic structure in the native vocabulary.

3.10 Conclusion

Spoken words are recognized by a process of concurrent consideration of multiple lexical candidates, with competition arising between their phonological representations but not necessarily involving their conceptual representations. Despite this separation of representations, activation passes rapidly in a cascaded fashion from the phonological to the conceptual level. The system thus deals with the structure of the vocabulary in an efficient (Norris and McQueen [2008] would say an optimal) way, exploiting incoming speech information to discard spuriously active competitors as fast as possible and discouraging spurious conceptual activation. Conceptual representations nonetheless receive activation as soon as this is warranted, thus enabling rapid integration into existing context.

The core concepts of multiple simultaneous activation, and of interword competition, are solidly established as a result of repeated experimental demonstration. All models of spoken-word recognition incorporate these concepts in one form or another. However, nontrivial problems arise in the precise relationship between models and experiment. Tanenhaus has called this the need for a linking hypothesis, and he has explored the issue for spoken-word recognition in general, for eye-tracking in particular, and for all procedures used to study sentence comprehension (Allopenna et al. 1998; McRae, Spivey-Knowlton, and Tanenhaus 1998; Tanenhaus et al. 2000).

Connectionist models are a case in point. Within these models, activation is the dependent variable in terms of which the model's operation is expressed. The degree to which a word node is activated at a particular point is crucially a relative concept. It does not matter what the absolute activation value is; what matters is whether that value is more or less than the values of potential competitor words, and how that pattern of relative activation changes across time.

But in this the models outstrip the listening data they need to simulate, because there is no laboratory (or neuropsychological) technique that can continuously reflect the relative degree of accessibility of a lexical candidate across time as connectionist models do. The models capture the results of experiments, in that the rankings they have assigned predict what the listener should be more or less likely to respond. But their account of the time-course of word recognition, and the rise and fall of individual node activations that it contains, are overpredictions with respect to what the experiments are capable of testing.

What does the term "activation" mean, then, when it occurs in accounts of studies such as those described at the beginning of this chapter—the eye-tracking experiments of Tanenhaus et al. (1995) or the cross-modal priming studies of Zwitserlood (1989) or Tabossi et al. (1995)? As noted in chapter 2, activation can be thought of as an absolute or as a relative notion. In these cases, the absolute reading seems to be called for. Hearing *cand-* makes both *candle* and *candy* active, and hence they are available word candidates. Hearing *kapit-* makes both *kapitein* and *kapitaal* active and available. Hearing *visi tediati* makes *visite* available. There is no real claim in these papers about how available, though. When these authors used the term "activation," they meant that a particular word form had become one of the lexical hypotheses under consideration.

Of course, it is possible to link model-generated predictions about likely responses with experimentally observed responses, while essentially ignoring the detail of the models' operation. It is even possible to test predictions about relative availability of a word as a function of the predicted availability of other words. The success of the computational models and the productivity of this field of psycholinguistics over the past two decades is adequate testimony to the operational viability of linking hypotheses. Nonetheless, it is important to realize that activation as demonstrated in eye-tracking, cross-modal priming, or other such experimental situations is in no sense a direct validation of the way the concept of activation is incorporated in these computational models.

A relative notion of word availability is most transparently captured by the recent model Shortlist B (Norris and McQueen 2008). Recall that this is a Bayesian model (hence the B in the name). Bayesian modeling computes the conditional probability of outputs (in this case, words) from a combination of their prior probabilities and the current evidence in favor of them. The listener is thus modeled in Shortlist B as a device evaluating, in a probabilistic manner, the set of words supported by the input. The relative probabilities in terms of which the input to a Shortlist B simulation is expressed have some claim to validity, in that they represent real listening data; Norris and McQueen argue that changes in the probability of a word candidate across time are likewise real in a sense that the connectionist models cannot match. The need for a linking hypothesis to experimental data is, in their view, pressing for connectionist models, where the activation in the model is a very indirect metaphor for probability of recognition by the listener, but it is less urgent for a Bayesian model, where the probabilities in the model should directly mirror the listener's probability of recognition.

Of course, the metaphors retain their force; the inclusion of a word form in the set of available words for which the relative probability is being evaluated, in Shortlist B, may again be viewed as activation of that word form in an absolute sense (in contrast to all the words in the vocabulary that are not activated because the input gives them no support at all). Further, it remains true that the experimental methods are just as incapable of tapping into minor fluctuations of relative probability across time, as produced by a Bayesian model, as into the relative fluctuations across time in the output of connectionist models.

The ability of the models to capture the overall pattern of activation and competition data, however, is almost indistinguishable. In their paper describing Shortlist B, Norris and McQueen (2008) present simulations showing that their model correctly accounts for the same range of data captured by Shortlist A (their name, by analogy, for Shortlist B's predecessor). Figure 3.7 shows how alike simulations with the two models appear, as relative activations and relative probabilities are computed across time. Where Shortlist A modeled the relative activations of candidate words, Shortlist B models the words' relative probabilities; but the underlying theoretical assumptions of the two versions of Shortlist are the same (more on these assumptions can be found in chapter 12).

This does not at all mean that the modeling enterprise is standing still. So far, there are no real-speech front ends that can support models of spoken-word recognition (a valiant attempt by Scharenborg et al. [2005] is still limited to a tiny vocabulary subset). This lack limits the models, because as a result of it, psycholinguists usually pretend that the initial stages of speech recognition are more orderly than

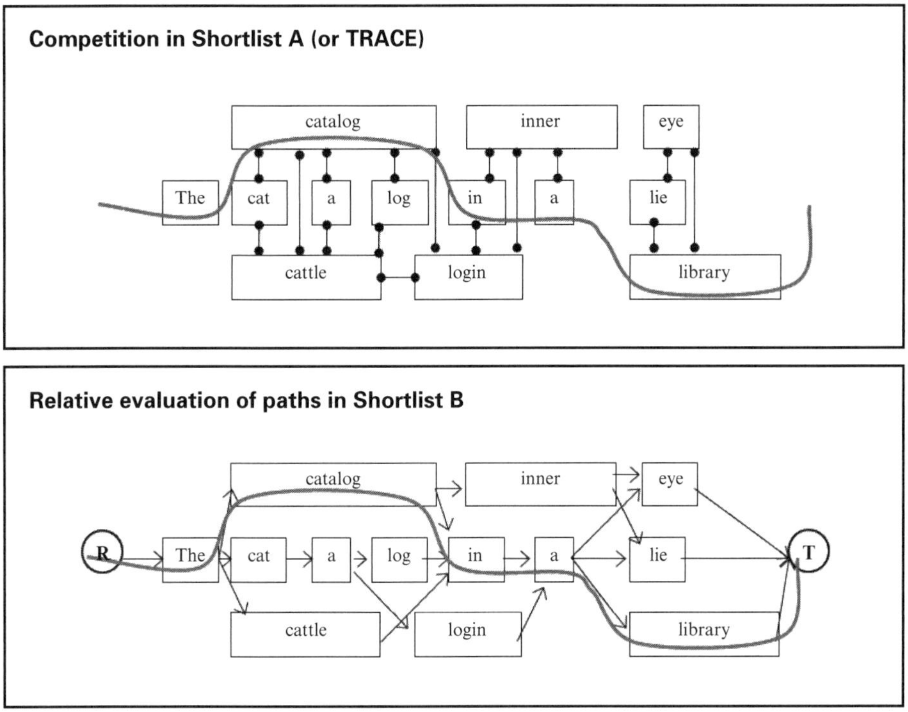

Figure 3.7
Shortlist A and Shortlist B process *The catalog in a library*. The upper panel shows the activated words in the Shortlist A simulation; inhibitory links (dark lines with dots at each end) represent the competition between word forms with a claim to overlapping portions of the input. The lower panel shows the most highly probable words computed by Shortlist B given the same input, and some of the possible paths through the set of supported words. The shaded line running through each figure shows the (identical) final accepted sequence of words in each case. The figure is borrowed from Norris and McQueen (2008), whose simulations used British English (in which *inner* is homophonous with *in a*).

can in fact be the case. The models are designed to explain lexical-level processes, and capturing that level is itself a significant achievement (recall that Shortlist A was the only second-generation model that could draw on a realistically large vocabulary). But because the prelexical input is thus not the primary focus of the models, it has generally just been simulated in some workable way, which may be more or less implausible—such as, in many cases, a discrete string of phoneme representations. In this respect, Shortlist B's relative probabilities of phoneme responses across time, derived from responses in an actual experiment, represent a notable and significant move forward.

Another advantage of Shortlist B is that effects of frequency are incorporated into the model in a natural way; frequency modulates the prior probabilities of lexical hypotheses. Despite the strong evidence for a processing role for frequency (see chapter 2), it was actually not easy to incorporate this concept into connectionist models. The Bayesian framework offers a way out of that problem, too. Thus the modeling of spoken-word recognition is making progress.

Of course, as we saw, there is a great deal of information in lexical representations, but not all of it plays a role in activating phonological representations. What does play a role depends on the makeup of the language-specific vocabulary. Segmental information is relevant in all languages, and in many languages certain suprasegmental features encode lexically distinctive information as well. There is more to come, in chapters 6 and 7, about what sources of information listeners successfully exploit.

However, the activation and competition processes are not the end of the story of word recognition in continuous speech, either. Although they alone can in principle deliver a resolution for a multiply parsable incoming continuous speech stream, listeners also command a formidable armory of techniques to deal with the continuity of speech and to detect boundaries within it (i.e., to segment speech). This is the topic of chapters 4 and 5 (and chapters 6 and 7 elaborate on this segmentation story, too).

4 Words: How They Are Extracted from Speech

The continuity of speech signals makes it necessary for listeners to segment utterances into their component words in order to understand what speakers have said. The activation and interword competition processes deliver word sequences, but segmentation can also be speeded if listeners exploit acoustic cues to word boundaries. The acoustic structure of speech indeed presents information not only about what words the speech consists of but also about where the boundaries between the words are or where they are likely to be; this chapter describes how listeners make use of this information. It also describes the laboratory methods that have been specifically devised for investigating segmentation. Cues to word boundaries are mostly probabilistic in nature, so that listeners' use of such information in speech processing shows sensitivity to the distributional structure of speech input. The rhythm of speech is widely used by listeners across different languages to determine the likely location of word boundaries, as is phonetic sequencing: that is, the phonotactic legality or likelihood of particular sequences of phonemes. Such boundary cues obviously differ from language to language, so that speech segmentation in listening becomes a language-specific undertaking.

So far, we have shown that word recognition in continuous speech involves concurrent consideration of multiple candidates, all of them lexical forms that are fully or partially compatible with incoming information. We have seen that the resulting superfluity of candidates is resolved by competition. Evidence for this picture of spoken-word recognition comes from many languages, and there is nothing to suggest that the process itself is language specific. We assume that activation and competition form the universal architecture of human speech recognition.

But that cannot be the whole story. The principal stumbling block is a logical one: Activation and competition are processes that involve an existing lexicon, and they do not have an inbuilt learning component. If they are claimed to be the only processes operating in adult recognition, then it follows that child learning and adult recognition involve different processes—for instance, that children must learn words in isolation before they can recognize them in continuous speech. As we shall see in chapter 8, this is not the case.

The second problem is more practical. Even if the process of lexical activation is universal, the units it applies to are not. As was laid out in chapter 2, vocabularies differ a lot in how they map units of sound to units of meaning. The universal architecture will thus inevitably be modulated by differences across languages—for instance, in how much activation there is at a given point (because the degree and positioning of embedding differs across languages) or in the type of information called on to resolve competition between activated forms (because the relevance of different aspects of phonological form in word identification also varies across languages). Thus the prelexical stage of listening may best be described as a universal architecture, but it must be one that can be implemented in a suitably adapted way for each individual language.

This inevitable language-specificity is also not the whole story. The competition process itself is an efficient way of selecting the correct sequence of words in speech input, but listeners can still speed this selection up in several ways. (If there is a way to speed up speech processing, listeners are likely to use it!) For instance, there can be pronunciation differences between phonemically identical sequences with and without a word boundary in them (*night rate* vs. *nitrate*). Listeners could use such acoustic information to exercise control over the competition process. Further, there might be language-specific probabilities of certain phonemic sequences occurring at word onsets or offsets. To take English as an example: there are phonemes and phoneme sequences that are completely ruled out in certain word-edge positions, and there are sequences that do occur in certain word-edge positions, but extremely rarely. Among the exclusions are the sound [ŋ] or the sequence [pt]; both can occur at the end of syllables and hence words (*strong*, *harangue*; *apt*, *precept*), but there are no words beginning with [ŋ] or [pt]. Conversely, the sound *h* or the sequence *pr* can occur at the beginning of words (*hot*, *harangue*; *pry*, *precept*), but there are no words ending with either.[1] The rarities include [sf] as a word beginning (*sphere*, *sphinx*) and [lb] as a word ending (*alb*, *bulb*); there are only a few English words of each kind. Listeners could also draw on knowledge of these rules and probabilities to speed up the process of competition.

Consider, for example, an input sequence such as [ɪlbɛə], which indeed contains such a phoneme pair that hardly ever occurs word finally. The sequence as a whole corresponds to, for instance, *ill bear*, but it could also activate *bare*, *air*, and *heir*. Taking the sequence probabilities into account might already make *air* and *heir* seem less likely, because *-lb* is such an unlikely word offset. In other words, information of this sort can be used to adjust the activations of words in the competition process according to the listener's past listening experience. Evidence that this happens is presented in section 4.9.

The process of breaking up the continuous speech stream into words is called lexical segmentation, and considering cues to and probabilities of word boundaries in this manner is one way to approach such segmentation. Instead of just letting the competition process produce the correct parse, all on its own, the listener can give it a helping hand by taking into account the knowledge built up from past listening. There is abundant experimental evidence that listeners exploit every bit of knowledge they can draw on for recognizing spoken words. Activation and competition are accompanied by processes that directly promote segmentation.

These processes are largely language specific. There is an oft-remarked perceptual illusion that speakers of foreign languages seem to talk faster than speakers in one's own language (the "gabbling foreigner" illusion; see chapter 10); its likely source is listeners' inability to segment speech in an unfamiliar language into separate words. An ERP (event-related brain potential) study by Snijders et al. (2007) examined the segmentation process for Dutch speech heard both by native speakers of Dutch and by English adults with no knowledge of Dutch. ERPs are the electrophysiological responses in the cortex to the apprehension of stimulus events; they can be measured from electrodes on the scalp. In each trial of the experiment, subjects first heard several repetitions of an isolated word (such as *hofnar* 'court jester' or *serre* 'conservatory'); the electrophysiological brain responses were collected as they listened. Both groups of listeners showed a changing response with increasing familiarity of the word, and this response was not significantly different across groups. That is, both the native and the nonnative speakers recognized that the repetitions involved several differently spoken tokens of the same form, even though only the native speakers knew what the word meant. Then sentences were presented, some containing the familiarized word and some not. The sentences did not predict the occurrence of the familiarized word (e.g., *Oma heeft een bijzondere serre vol planten* 'Grandma has a special conservatory full of plants'). Again, both native and nonnative brains detected the familiar words; but here, the responses measured in the native listeners' brains were significantly faster than those of the nonnative listeners. The native listeners also detected that there were other repetitions within the sentences; if they had been familiarized with *serre* and then heard some sentences containing the word *serre* and some containing *hofnar*, their brains also responded faster to *hofnar* when it turned up for the second time. The nonnative listeners' brains showed no indication at all of noticing these repetitions of words that they heard first in continuous speech. Snijders et al. suggested that the impression of faster speech in a foreign language is indeed due to segmentation problems, which reflects the fact that speech segmentation procedures are adapted to the native language.

For more on listening to foreign languages see chapter 10, and for the beginnings of speech segmentation in infancy see chapter 8. Segmentation in the native language is the concern of most of the next three chapters. This has been a central topic of my own research, and I tell some of that personal history, too, especially in the present chapter.

The acoustic cues that distinguish strings such as *nitrate* versus *night rate* are discussed in chapter 6. In the present chapter we consider principally the way that listeners can tailor their speech recognition processes for maximum efficiency by exploiting general probabilities associated with lexical segmentation in the native language. To begin with, let us consider the case of English stress.

4.1 What English Stress Is Good For

As we saw in chapter 2, taking stress into account in lexical activation produces a substantial payoff for the Spanish or Dutch listener, in the form of a huge reduction in embedding. In English, by contrast, it produces very little payoff. Stress in English is not separate from segmental structure, as is the case in Spanish; in English, segmental structure alone leads to pretty much the same outcome from the competition process as segmental plus suprasegmental structure. Accordingly, English listeners do not seem to bother much with suprasegmental information in lexical activation and selection. For them, segmental differences (such as between full versus reduced vowels) are far more important than suprasegmental differences (such as whether the same syllable with the same vowel, such as *ad-*, is stressed, as in *admiral*, or not, as in *admiration*; the example is from Cooper et al.'s (2002) experiment discussed in chapter 1).

Compare the English words *audience*, *auditorium*, *audition*, and *addition*. In *audience*, the initial vowel receives primary stress, in *auditorium* it receives secondary stress, in *audition* it is unstressed but not reduced, and in *addition* it is unstressed and reduced. To test the relative importance, for English listeners, of stress distinctions versus distinctions between full and reduced vowels, Fear, Cutler, and Butterfield (1995) presented listeners with tokens of such words in which the initial vowels had been exchanged between words. The listeners had to rate how natural the pronunciations sounded. Cross-splicings between any of the first three words of this set were rated as insignificantly different from the original, unspliced tokens. That is, *audience* with the vowel from *audition* and *audition* with the vowel from *audience* were judged to be as acceptable as *audience* and *audition* with their original vowels. The only cross-splicings that received significantly lower ratings were those between a reduced vowel (e.g., in *addition*) and any of the first three. That is, the listeners found the full/reduced vowel distinction very important but distinctions of stress level unimportant.

Other results also indicate that stress distinctions per se are perceptually irrelevant for English listeners. Listeners who heard a sentence context and a stress pattern, and then judged a candidate word for acceptability, often accepted words that were semantically appropriate for the context but that did not have the specified stress pattern (Slowiaczek 1991). For instance, they could hear *The florist watered the fresh . . .* followed by a noise with the stress pattern of *carnation*; if then asked whether *daffodil* was the appropriate word, they often said yes, although the stress pattern of *daffodil* is quite different from that of *carnation*. Phoneme detection is not slowed by a mis-stressed preceding word, even though the mis-stressing made an alternative word that mismatched the context (Small, Simon, and Goldberg 1988); for example, RTs to [p] in *the desert plain is barren*. . . were no slower if *desert* was stressed on the second instead of the first syllable, even though the word that was thus created (the verb *deSERT* or the noun *dessert*) did not fit into the sentence.

Response time in this study was significantly slowed if the mis-stressing created a nonword, however (e.g., *comet* pronounced as *coMET* or *polite* as *POlite*). Note that these mis-stressings change the nature of the vowel, too. Similarly, although mis-stressing does not prevent word recognition in noise if vowels remain intact (e.g., *resCUE*, *phoBIa*; Slowiaczek 1990), it does interfere with word recognition in shadowing when vowel quality is altered (e.g., *people* as [pəpʌl], *decide* as [di:sɪd]; Bond and Small 1983). Together, these findings suggest that distinctions of vowel quality are far more important for English word identification than distinctions of stress.

What is most important for listeners seems to be the vowel-quality opposition between strong and weak (or full vowels versus reduced). Distinctions of stress in English usually imply distinctions of vowel quality as well. Considered as sequences of strong (S) versus weak (W) syllables, *comet* is SW, *polite* WS; *carnation* is SSW, *daffodil* SWS. It turns out that we can discover what English stress is good for by considering the distribution of sequences of S and W syllables in the vocabulary. The distributions are not random; regularities exist that can prove very helpful in parsing the speech stream. The patterning of strong and weak syllables, in short, enables stress in English to guide segmentation.

The distributional asymmetries were revealed in a rather early corpus study. Today, corpus research is common and we enjoy the fortune of being able to study quite large corpora of spoken language (e.g., the British National Corpus [Leech 1992] or the Corpus of Spoken Dutch [Oostdijk 2000]). Long before the days of corpora of this size, there was the London-Lund Corpus of English Conversation (Svartvik and Quirk 1980). By today's standards, it is small—thirty-some hours of recorded conversation made up of 187,699 words (excluding proper names and nonwords). It contrasts with current practice also in that the recorded materials of this collection were never made publicly available. There was a good reason for this: the recordings were largely made without the knowledge of the recorded speakers at the time. Again, this too is very unlike the regulations that apply to today's corpus collectors.

However, it was a flagship among corpora and it made possible a wide range of studies that previously had been inconceivable. Among them was the study of the prosodic characteristics of words in the English vocabulary and in British English natural speech. This study, by Cutler and Carter (1987), was mentioned in chapter

2; it began with dictionary analyses that revealed that about half of all words in the English vocabulary are polysyllables with initial stress (e.g., *corpus*, *syllable*; the exact numbers were 50.6 percent in the *Shorter Oxford Dictionary of British English* and 48.1 percent in the *Merriam-Webster Pocket Dictionary of American English*). If polysyllables beginning with secondary stress (such as *characteristic* and *conversation*) and monosyllabic words (i.e., stand-alone strong syllables such as *speech* and *wide*) are added to the total, then about two-thirds of the vocabulary (73.0 percent and 77.6 percent, respectively) may be considered words that begin with strong syllables. The remaining one-third comprises weak-initial polysyllables (such as *initial* and *beginning*). Although these counts include function words, removing those from the vocabulary does not significantly alter the calculation because there are only a few hundred of them.

The proportions just listed do not translate to the statistics for real speech, however. Frequency counts already suggest what will happen—the average frequency of monosyllabic words is much higher than the average frequency of polysyllabic words, regardless of their stress pattern (Zipf's Law again). Indeed, when Cutler and Carter analyzed the London-Lund Corpus, they found that about 60 percent of the lexical tokens (that is, excluding function words) were monosyllabic. This may seem all the more remarkable in the light of the corpus content—the majority of the corpus consists of conversations in an academic environment! If any speakers are more likely than average to draw on a recondite vocabulary containing low-frequency polysyllabic words, one might have thought it would be academics. So indeed, the true proportion of monosyllabic words across all English conversations may be even higher. Nonetheless, around 60 percent of the lexical content of the London-Lund Corpus consisted of monosyllables—think of *book*, *teach*, *lunch*. Polysyllables with initial primary or secondary stress (*student*, *education*) accounted for another 31 percent; polysyllables with weak initial syllables (*curriculum*, *exam*) made up less than 10 percent of the lexical portion of the corpus.

That is still not the full story, however, because lexical words did not actually amount to the larger part of the corpus. The polysyllables with weak initial syllables, 10 percent of lexical words, were only about 4 percent of the corpus overall. More than half of all tokens in the corpus (59 percent) were function words (and, unsurprisingly, always the same function words—this large section of the corpus contained only 281 separate words). The majority of these could potentially be realized as weak syllables. Cutler and Carter (1987) suggested that an English listener would do well to assume that any strong syllable is very likely to be a lexical word (or the initial syllable of one), and any weak syllable is most likely to be a function word. The success rate of this assumption for location of the onsets of lexical words in the London-Lund Corpus would be very high (90 percent) and the false alarm rate would be very low: 74 percent of all strong syllables in the corpus are indeed the initial syllables of lexical words; of the residual 26 percent, more than half are noninitial syllables in either a lexical or a function word (e.g., *abut*, *about*), and the rest begin function words (e.g., *into*, *while*). Cutler and Carter also analyzed a short text that a speaker recorded for the purpose; the success rate of the proposed segmentation strategy with this passage was even higher.

Thus, English stress is indeed useful to listeners; it does not tell them so much about word identity, as we saw, but it is very informative indeed about where the beginnings of words are most likely to be found in a continuous speech stream. It is a segmentation cue that English listeners would be well advised to use in listening. A large body of experimental evidence now attests that listeners do indeed use stress in segmenting English speech.

4.2 Using Stress as a Segmentation Cue in English

One way to tell that listeners use stress as a segmentation cue is to observe the errors that sometimes result. Table 4.1 contains some examples of segmentation errors. Thus the rather unlikely line "She's a must to avoid," which occurred in a pop song of some decades ago (see example f), is reported to have been interpreted by very many listeners independently as "She's a muscular boy." In this case, the final syllable of the line (*void*), a stressed syllable, was interpreted as a new word (*boy*), and the two syllables before it (*to a-*), both unstressed word-initial syllables containing reduced vowels, were assumed not to be initial but to belong to the trisyllabic word *muscular*.

Table 4.1
Slips of the ear show the effect of segmentation preferences in English; syllables with stressed full vowels are misheard as word initial (a, b, c, d, f, g); syllables with unstressed reduced vowels are misinterpreted as noninitial (c, e, f). If a noninitial syllable with a reduced vowel is mistakenly interpreted as word initial, the word it makes will most likely be a closed-class (function) word (g; see also chapter 3).

	What speakers said		What listeners thought speakers said
a.	*I pledge allegiance to the flag*	→	*I led the pigeons to the flag*
b.	*by loose analogy*	→	*by Luce & Allergy*
c.	*she'll officially*	→	*Sheila Fishley*
d.	*. . . was illegal*	→	*. . . was an eagle*
e.	*How big is it?*	→	*How bigoted?*
f.	*she's a must to avoid*	→	*she's a muscular boy*
g.	*descriptive prose*	→	*the script of prose*

Exactly this pattern is found quite generally in mishearings by English listeners (Cutler and Butterfield 1992). In natural slips of the ear (such as in table 4.1), erroneous word boundaries are significantly more likely before strong (stressed) syllables than before weak syllables (*analogy* → *and Allergy*), whereas boundaries before weak syllables are correspondingly likely to be overlooked (*big is it* → *bigoted*). The same pattern appears in collections of jokes, puns, and folk etymologies. Think of the generations of American children who (legend has it) recited not *I pledge allegiance to the flag* but *I led the pigeons to the flag*; insertion of a word boundary before the stressed second syllable of *allegiance* is exactly the sort of segmentation mistake that was found to occur most frequently.

Following this analysis of natural slips, Cutler and Butterfield generated mishearings in the laboratory by presenting listeners with very faint speech input. Again the same patterns emerged: insertion of boundaries, where the input had none, tended to occur before strong syllables, and deletion of boundaries that were in the input tended to occur before weak syllables. Thus *conduct ascents uphill* might be reported as *the doctor sends her bill* (inserting boundaries before the strong final syllables in each word), or *sons expect enlistment* might be reported as *sons expectant listen* (inserting a boundary before the strong syllable *-list*, but also deleting the boundary before the weak syllable *en-*). Both the natural slips of the ear and the artificially induced misperceptions thus suggested that English listeners segment speech according to the heuristic: strong syllables are probably word initial.

The laboratory mishearings also allowed the types of error that subjects made to be compared against predictions from the structure of the vocabulary. Perhaps the observed patterns simply reflected what the vocabulary made available—the listeners reported more words like *listen* than *enlist* just because the vocabulary contains more words of the former sort (which, as we saw, it does). If that is the source of the patterns in the errors, then asymmetries in the vocabulary should also turn up in the errors. One asymmetry in the vocabulary concerns vowel occurrence; all full vowels tend to occur more often in a stressed first syllable than in a stressed second syllable preceded by an unstressed initial syllable, but this ratio is much more skewed for the vowel in *sons* and *conduct* (more than 13:1) than for the vowel in *send* and *expect* (around 4:1). The vocabulary thus predicts relatively more insertion errors for words with the first vowel than with the second. In fact, the mishearing patterns for the two vowels were similar. Across all the vowels used in the faint-speech experiment, the relationship with the predictions from the vocabulary was actually in the wrong direction. So the segmentation errors were not just a measure of the options given by the vocabulary. They were a result of the strong syllable heuristic guiding listeners' segmentation of the incoming speech.

One of the laboratory techniques of psycholinguistics, the word-spotting paradigm (see panel 11 in chapter 3), is especially intended for the study of speech segmentation. In fact, its very first use was to establish the role of stress in lexical segmentation in English (Cutler and Norris 1988). Recall that in a word-spotting experiment listeners hear short nonsense strings in which real words may be embedded, and their task is to press a button whenever they spot a known word and then to report the detected word. In *omzel* or *clibthish* they would not be expected to find words, but in *bookving* and *vuffapple* they should find *book* and *apple*, respectively. The technique allows researchers to focus on the segmentation problem; for instance, to compare the effects of segmenting a word from one minimal context versus another.

Listeners were presented with strings like *mintayf* (with two strong syllables) or *mintef* (with a weak second syllable, where the vowel was [ə]). Both contain the real word *mint* followed by a single vowel-plus-consonant; the only difference is that in one case the following vowel is strong (*ayf*) and in the other case it is weak (*ef*). Cutler and Norris (1988) proposed that if listeners were assuming strong syllables to be word initial, they would divide the strong-strong (SS) sequence *mintayf* into two parts, but they would not divide the strong-weak (SW) sequence *mintef*. That is, this minimal difference in the input strings was predicted to have a substantial effect on the way listeners treated them.

Indeed, as shown in figure 4.1, words like *mint* were much harder to find in *mintayf* than in *mintef*. So, it mattered whether the following vowel was strong or weak; in *mintayf*, listeners apparently postulated a word boundary before *-tayf*, so that correct detection of *mint* required recombination of speech material across

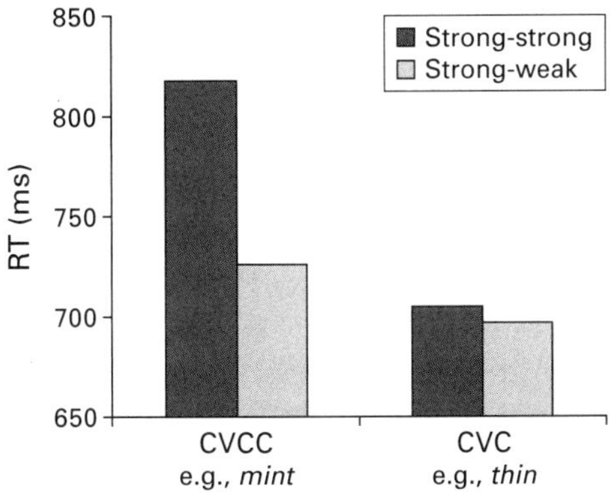

Figure 4.1
English listeners segment spoken nonwords at the onset of strong syllables but not weak syllables; so *mintef* and *thintef* are not segmented, but *mintayf* and *thintayf* are segmented (*-tayf*). When the target word is *thin*, this segmentation does not affect detection. But when the target word is *mint*, the segmentation interferes with detection (the detection RTs are slower). This is because the segmentation interrupts the word, and successful detection can only occur by reuniting *min+t*. (Word-spotting data of Cutler and Norris 1988.)

the segmentation point. The weak second syllable of *mintef*, in contrast, triggered no segmentation and hence had no adverse effect on detection of *mint*. Thus these word-spotting findings, just as the faint speech and the natural slips of the ear, pointed to a persistent assumption by listeners: strong syllables are so likely to be word initial that it is worthwhile segmenting speech input at the onset of every strong syllable. Experience with the distribution of strong and weak syllables in English speech fosters development of a heuristic that presumably pays off in efficiency of segmenting the speech heard every day.

4.3 Segmentation in a Language without Stress

Recall that stress is a phonological feature that is not universal across languages. Many languages have no stress distinctions; also, many languages have no vowel reduction and hence no distinction between syllables with full versus reduced vowels. Thus the facts about English that are relevant for segmentation are not going to be relevant for segmentation in all languages. There is a general point here: listeners will segment speech in whatever is for them the most efficient way, exploiting whatever their experience has taught them to be relevant information. This would only be the same experience if all languages were the same in all relevant respects. From this point of view it is not surprising that segmentation of continuous speech involves language-specific processing; instead, it would be surprising if it did not.

But there is also another point of view. Recall the most significant fact about language acquisition: the language that a child acquires is the language that the environment makes available. The child's specific genetic endowment does not induce one language rather than another. This suggests that the process of acquiring language, whether and however it involves innate specialization for linguistic structure or exploits general cognitive abilities, is much the same in all humans: it is universal, and it is not language specific. Segmentation of words from continuous speech is certainly part of acquiring language; babies can segment familiar word forms from continuous speech long before they can assign meaning to words, let alone produce words themselves (see chapter 8). From this point of view, then, one might expect that segmentation would be based on universal processes.

In early psycholinguistics, as described in chapter 1, this latter point of view was an important determinant of the research program. Against the background of that time, reports of crosslinguistic differences in speech segmentation came as something of a shock, as the following step-by-step historical account documents.

In most psycholinguistic research of the 1960s and 1970s, the language in which an experiment was carried out was not considered to be a variable that would influence the pattern of results as long as the phenomenon at issue was not itself language specific. The experiments on lexical ambiguity described in chapter 1, carried out in English and French, provide a case in point; lexically ambiguous words are found in both languages, and word length varies in both languages, so it was assumed that findings from one language would also be valid for the other.

Early experiments on the segmentation of continuous speech, too, were not always conducted in the same language. A major concern in the study of spoken-language processing during the 1970s was with "units of perception"—that is, abstract representations into which speech input would be recoded during listening and, in particular, the degree to which listeners could attain awareness of these representations. This debate was conducted between groups whose experiments were variously carried out in English (e.g., Savin and Bever 1970; Foss and Swinney 1973; Healy and Cutting 1976), in French (e.g., Segui, Frauenfelder, and Mehler 1981), or in Portuguese (e.g., Morais et al. 1979). Out of this debate emerged claims concerning the way in which continuous speech might be segmented into words.

An influential claim by Mehler et al. (1981) was based on evidence from the fragment detection task (see panel 5 in chapter 1). The claim was that listeners segmented spoken input syllable by syllable. Listeners (who were French) heard lists of words and responded whenever one of the words began with a designated target sequence, such as *ba-* or *bal-*. Responses were faster when the target corresponded to the initial syllable of the word. Thus *ba-* was detected more rapidly in *balance* (*ba-lance*) than in *balcon* (*bal-con*), whereas *bal-* was detected more rapidly in *balcon* than in *balance*—targets that corresponded exactly to a syllable were easier to detect than targets that were larger or smaller than a syllable. Figure 4.2a shows Mehler et al.'s results: a crossover pattern that came to be called the "syllable effect," and motivated the proposal that syllables are the units into which speech is segmented for lexical access. If the speech input was being divided up into syllables in any case, Mehler et al. argued, then matching the specified target against this necessary intermediate level of representation would lead to speedier responding than matching it against some arbitrary stretch of the input. Thus they interpreted their findings as evidence for syllabic segmentation.

An analogous experiment in English (with words like *balance* and *balcony*), however, failed to deliver the crossover pattern predicted by the syllabic segmentation hypothesis (see figure 4.2b). This experiment was conducted in 1982 by Dennis Norris and myself. We could have published the result by itself, as counterevidence to Mehler et al.'s claim. However, there was a reason why we had not expected to replicate their finding, and that reason lay in phonological differences between French and English. Consider the French word *balance* and the English word *balance*. Speakers of French agree that the French word is to be syllabified *ba-lance*. Speakers of English are far less sure about how to syllabify the English word—is the first syllable *ba-* or *bal-*? Phonologists, in fact, hold that a single intervocalic consonant preceded by a stressed vowel and followed by a reduced vowel—such as

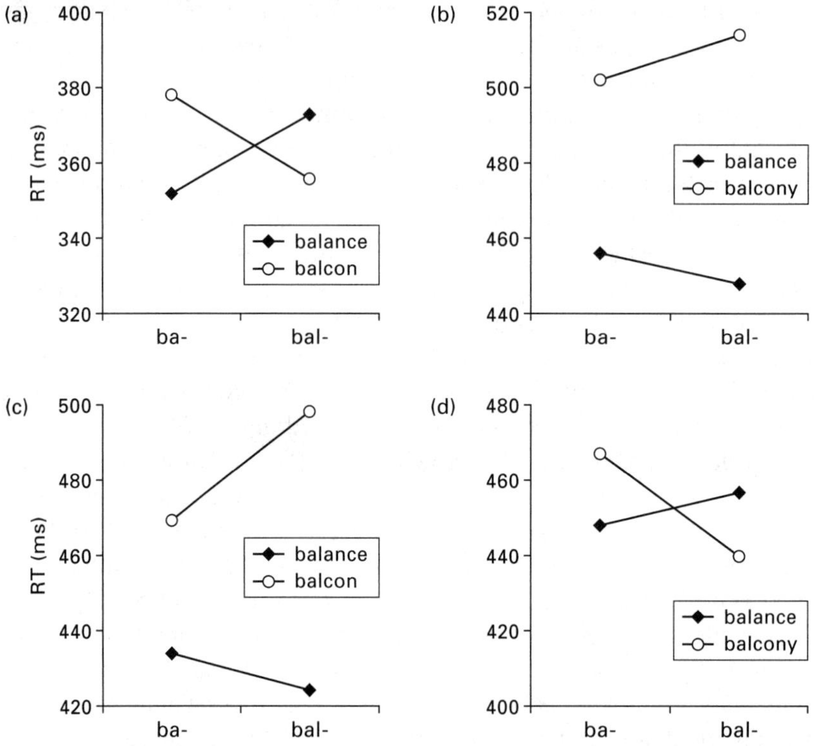

Figure 4.2
French listeners segment spoken words into syllables. (a) The target *ba-* is detected more rapidly in *balance* than in *balcon*, whereas the target *bal-* is detected more rapidly in *balcon* than in *balance*, in accord with the words' syllabification. English listeners do not show this pattern either with English words (b) or the French words (c), whereas French listeners do show it with English words too (d). (Fragment-detection data from Mehler et al. 1981 and Cutler et al. 1986.)

the [l] in English *balance*—is likely to be ambisyllabic; that is, to belong to both syllables at once (see, e.g., Kahn 1976). That would make the first syllable of *balance bal-* and the second syllable *-lance*, which means that dividing up an English word like *balance* into nonoverlapping syllables is impossible, and syllabic segmentation is, correspondingly, not an easy or obviously useful procedure to apply to speech input in English.

The criteria for ambisyllabicity (primary stress preceding syllable with reduced vowel) could not be met in French, in which English-like stress does not occur. Thus the intriguing possibility remained that both results (figures 4.2a and b) were simultaneously valid. In this case there were two possible explanations. The first was that syllabic segmentation was a universal procedure, that all listeners, whatever their native language, could command, but that listeners would only apply it to input in which it was useful. Thus they would certainly apply it if they were given French input, but they would be unlikely to apply it if they heard English input. The second explanation, more shocking to the prevailing assumptions of a universal language processing system, was that listeners from different linguistic backgrounds actually developed different sets of segmentation procedures. It seemed more interesting to test these explanations than to publish a simple counterexample to syllabic segmentation.

To test the first account, Mehler et al.'s (1981) French materials were played to English-speaking listeners who knew little French. If the listeners could use syllabic segmentation, they should do so with input that encouraged it. As figure 4.2c shows, they did not—their results with the French materials strongly resembled the results with English materials presented to listeners from the same population (as in figure 4.2b).

So, English listeners appeared not to have syllabic segmentation at their disposal even when it would help them with the experimental task at hand. What would French listeners do with English input? Presentation of our English materials to French subjects gave the dramatic result depicted in figure 4.2d: the characteristic crossover "syllabic" interaction appeared, even though the native listeners' performance with the same materials had suggested that syllabic segmentation was not a useful strategy for English. Thus French listeners were apparently inclined to apply syllabic segmentation to whatever spoken input they received, whereas English listeners did not apply it, whatever the input. Listeners from different language backgrounds, in other words, command different processing routines. Against the background of psycholinguistic universalism, the combined results depicted in figure 4.2 were startling (Cutler et al. 1983).

Clearly, it was no longer possible to assume that every part of adult processing should be shared by all language users; some parts of every listener's processing system might be language specific. But the argument for a universal basis retains its force—all children begin from the same point, so in some sense the system must be universal. The next challenge, therefore, was to seek the underlying universal commonality that is susceptible to this sort of language-specific implementation.

4.4 Stress and the Syllable: Basic Concepts of Rhythm

The phonetic literature offers a classic answer to the question of what links stress in English and the syllable in French. The answer is found in the distinction between stress-timed and syllable-timed languages, first proposed by Pike (1945) and particularly espoused by Abercrombie (e.g., 1967). These are categories said to hold for the underlying rhythmic structure of language, and English is cited as a typical language exhibiting stress-timing, whereas French is said to be syllable-timed. The distinction was intended to embrace all languages, preferably with each language unambiguously assigned to one or the other category. The proposal was based strictly on regularity of timing units (stress feet, syllables) and, in its strongest form, proposed isochrony: in a syllable-timed language, syllables are all (give or take some effect of the phonemes that make them up) equal in duration, but in a stress-timed language, stress feet all have the same duration.

Measurements of speech revealed that isochrony was far too strong a claim (see, e.g., Roach 1982; Laver 1994). The simple timing distinction did not do justice to real speech. Nonetheless, the timing claim clearly captured a real difference between languages. Consider, for instance, that typical poetic forms differ across languages. It is not possible to understand English poetic forms without the concepts of the foot and the stress beat, or ictus. A foot consists of a strong syllable bearing stress and, in poetry, a given number of weaker syllables (the number depending on the particular metrical form). For example, iambic pentameter is a five-beat line, each foot having two syllables with stress falling on the second. A well-formed limerick consists of five lines, with three stress beats in the first, second, and fifth lines, and two in the third and fourth (see example (4.1), which is not well formed at all but horribly violates one of the above rules!). In French poetry, by contrast, the number of syllables in a line defines the form (De Cornulier 1982).

(4.1) A limerick's rhythm is best
with the strongest of syllables stressed.
If you let the stress fall
on a weak syllable
All your readers will rightly protest.

To capture the idea that rhythmic structure varies across languages, broader definitions of rhythm include factors such as the variety and nature of syllable types in a language and the patterning of accents (e.g., Dasher and Bolinger 1982; Dauer 1987). It has also been suggested that languages could possess, to differing extents, features of both stress- and syllable-timing (Roach 1982; Dauer 1987); instead of stress- and syllable-timing forming two mutually exclusive categories, in other words, they might rather represent points on a continuum along which all languages could be placed. The criterion for determining a language's rhythmic structure was never really hard and fast, and given that isochrony cannot deliver a categorization, the issue remains a difficult one (see also section 4.7). The typical forms of poetry, however, undeniably provide strong indications of a language's preferred rhythmic structure.

The importance of this rhythmic contrast between English and French, in the light of processing language-specificity, was that it offered the underlying universal commonality. The use of stress in segmentation by English speakers, and the use of syllabic patterning in segmentation by French speakers, could arise from the same source: the use of rhythmic structure. A range of testable predictions arise. Obviously, one would predict that other languages that rhythmically resemble English should encourage stress-based segmentation, and other languages that rhythmically resemble French should encourage syllabic segmentation. Analyses of Dutch (Schreuder and Baayen 1994; Vroomen and De Gelder 1995) suggested that stress-based segmentation would also work well for that language, and indeed both the English word-spotting finding (Cutler and Norris 1988) and the faint-speech finding (Cutler and Butterfield 1992) were replicated in Dutch, in each case with results parallel to those that had motivated the claim of stress-based segmentation in English (Vroomen, Van Zon, and De Gelder 1996). Thus in Dutch as in English, listeners apparently exploit the high statistical probability that words begin with strong syllables, in that they act on the assumption that strong syllables in the speech signal are probably word initial.

Syllabic structure similar to French is found in other Romance languages such as Spanish and Catalan. Studies in those two languages (Sebastián-Gallés et al. 1992; Bradley, Sanchez-Casas, and Garcia-Albea 1993) indeed led to results echoing those that Mehler et al. (1981) had observed for French.

The fact that English (and Dutch) stress rhythm is crucially expressed in the strong/weak opposition (Fear et al. 1995) does not rule out a separate role for acoustic salience resulting from accent; of course, a form that is accented will be easier to detect. This has been shown in word-spotting experiments, with equivalent patterns appearing in French and in Dutch (Banel and Bacri 1997; Quené and Koster 1998). For segmentation, as shown by Cutler and Norris (1988), it is the difference between unaccented syllables with a reduced versus a full syllable that is crucial for English (and for Dutch). Full and reduced syllables can be equally lacking in stress, but a full vowel qualifies as strong and hence triggers segmentation, whereas a reduced vowel is weak and does not. This pattern has no direct reflection in French.

Although stress-based and syllabic segmentation had initially been supported by evidence from different experimental paradigms, converging evidence was provided for each; syllabic segmentation effects, for example, also appeared in French speakers' word stem completions (Peretz, Lussier, and Béland 1996) and phoneme detection (Pallier et al. 1993). Word-spotting also revealed syllabic effects in French (Dumay, Frauenfelder, and Content 2002), and priming studies showed sensitivity to syllable structure in Italian (Tabossi et al. 2000). There was also evidence from an experimental task in which different speech inputs are simultaneously presented to each listeners' two ears, generating auditory illusions in which listeners report hearing words that are actually amalgams of the two inputs. This task elicited syllabic effects in French (Kolinsky, Morais, and Cluytens 1995), in that the combinations tended to take a whole syllable from one input and a whole syllable from the other. It elicited stress-based effects in English, in that "migration" across ears of a single vowel occurred from weak but not from strong syllables (Mattys and Samuel 1997).

The concept of rhythm allows these disparate sets of results to be unified: listeners draw on assistance from the rhythmic structure of their language in dealing with the difficult task of segmenting continuous speech. Rhythm is not a concrete property that lends itself to simple measurement (e.g., in terms of timing intervals). It concerns the level of structure that is most involved in expressing regularity in utterances. In French and other Romance languages, that is syllables. In English and Dutch, it is stress. Because the basis of rhythm differs across languages, so does the way listeners segment speech, although there is a universal underlying commonality (in that rhythmic regularity helps all listeners).

4.5 The Metrical Segmentation Strategy: A Rhythmic Segmentation Hypothesis

The Metrical Segmentation Strategy (MSS) was proposed as a general form of the stress-based segmentation proposal made for English. The name MSS was intended to refer to what later became the rhythmic hypothesis (I can say this, because I did it; Cutler 1990), and it was conceived as a very general claim: whatever type of structure best describes the metrical forms a language prefers to use—for example, in poetry—that structure will also be useful for listeners in segmenting continuous speech. Metrical forms in English are stress based, as we saw above, and stress-based segmentation is useful for English listeners.

The name was not an optimal choice because the MSS was often taken as a synonym of stress-based segmentation, and hence thought to apply to English only. The term *rhythm* seems to be less closely associated than *metrical* with the notion of stress, so that the name *rhythmic segmentation hypothesis* now seems more likely to get the general point across. The rhythmic segmentation hypothesis is essentially the same: whatever rhythm best characterizes the phonological regularities of a language, that rhythm will be useful to listeners in segmenting speech. The most probable metrical structures of words are, as we saw, known to listeners. English words tend to be stressed on the first syllable (Cutler and Carter 1987). In the English vocabulary (disregarding frequency), the most common word type is an initially stressed bisyllable such as *lettuce* or *baggage* (Carlson et al. 1985). English listeners presented with ambiguous bisyllabic strings (*lettuce* or *let us*? *intense* or *in tents*?) choose a one-word solution more often for the trochaic, or initially stressed, strings (Cutler and Butterfield 1990b). French listeners, given similar strings (*bagage* ou *bas gage*?) produced exactly the opposite pattern: an iambic (finally stressed) pattern led to more one-word choices than a trochaic (Banel and Bacri 1994). This is consistent with the tendency for final accent in French stand-alone words (Fletcher

1991). But the important feature of the MSS/rhythmic hypothesis is that it is about segmentation alone. Listeners use rhythm to point them toward boundaries between words, not to predict the shape of words.

Given the continuous modulation of lexical activation and competition (see chapter 3), the most useful boundaries are onsets, as they bring new word candidates into consideration. Cutler and Norris (1988) found not only that spotting *mint* was different in *mintayf* and *mintef* but also that spotting *thin* was not different in *thintayf* and *thintef;* it was equally easy in each case. Segmentation should occur in *thintayf* but not in *thintef*, just as in *mintayf* but not in *mintef*. But interference with the responses only occurred when the segmentation captured the final segment of the embedded word (the *t* of *mint*, taken by *tayf*). When the embedded word is not divided by the segmentation (*tayf* contains no part of *thin*), detection is unaffected. Still, segmenting off *tayf* from *thin-tayf* makes the final boundary of *thin* very obvious. So if final boundaries were useful, the segmentation of *thintayf* should have made *thin* more accessible. But it did not; final boundaries appear to be irrelevant.

This point was also made on the basis of results from French experiments in which listeners were asked to reverse two syllables (e.g., given *jardin* they would be expected to say *din-jar*; Treiman and Danis 1988; Schiller, Meyer, and Levelt 1997). These experiments (Content, Kearns, and Frauenfelder 2001) showed, perhaps surprisingly, that French listeners did not always preserve the syllabic structure of the words. What they did preserve were the onsets of syllables—if a syllable was altered, it was the end of it that tended to suffer. Further, the "syllable effect" in fragment detection was more likely to be found when syllable-final consonants cohered with the preceding vowel, as, for instance, liquids such as [l] in *balcon* do (Content, Meunier, et al. 2001; Goslin and Frauenfelder 2008). These findings are difficult to reconcile with an account of syllabic segmentation in which whole syllables formed the access representation for word recognition; Content, Kearns, et al. (2001) proposed instead what they called a Syllabic Onset Segmentation Hypothesis (SOSH), whereby the onsets of syllables serve as alignment points for initiating new lexical hypotheses. This is, of course, exactly the proposal of the MSS/rhythmic segmentation hypothesis for the case of French: the initial boundaries of words are sought in segmentation, and listeners use rhythm to detect them; in French the rhythmic unit is the syllable, so the initial boundaries of syllables will be the point for segmentation.

Although it has once been claimed (Dumay et al. 2002) that the SOSH is a more general hypothesis than the MSS, the opposite logical relationship holds—the MSS/rhythmic segmentation hypothesis is the more general proposal, with the SOSH a special case of it for French (see Cutler et al. 2001 for a fuller account). For English, the SOSH would predict segmentation at weak and strong syllable onsets alike, given that weak syllables have onsets just as strong syllables do. But this does not happen, because weak and strong English syllables differ in their role in rhythmic structure. Instead, the SOSH captures for the French rhythmic unit, the syllable, the fact that the onset matters for segmentation, which is exactly what has been shown for the English rhythmic unit, the stress foot. Putting the two together, the rhythmic segmentation hypothesis gives the full explanation.

4.6 Testing the Rhythmic Segmentation Hypothesis

The most searching test of the rhythmic hypothesis, however, required another kind of rhythmic structure, as well as the demonstration that, in languages with that structure, there is the same kind of relationship to segmentation as observed for stress in English and the syllable in French. This, at least, was the motivation that drove the same groups who had established the French and English findings to extend their studies of segmentation to Japanese.

The rhythmic structure of Japanese is based on a subsyllabic unit, the mora. The mora is a unit of syllabic weight—light syllables (without coda, without long vowels) consist of one mora, and heavy syllables (with a coda or a long vowel) are bimoraic; this in turn means that a mora can be a vowel, or a vowel plus a syllabic onset, or a syllabic coda. The structure of Japanese syllables is very simple; there are no complex onsets, for instance, and only a very restricted range of codas is possible. The moraic structure of the names of Japanese beers exemplifies the various mora types: *Ki-ri-n*, *A-sa-hi*, *Sa-p-po-ro*. The rules governing Japanese poetic forms make it quite clear that the mora is the relevant rhythmic unit: A haiku, for example, consists of three lines of respectively five, seven, and five morae. Thus it is unimportant that in this classical haiku by Kakei (school of Basho, seventeenth century), the first five-mora line has three syllables and the last five-mora line has five syllables; only the number of morae counts.

(4.2)	*Shin shin to*	'In silence they fall
	ume chiri kakaro	into the garden bonfire
	niwabi kana	petals of the plum.'

The fragment-detection logic from the French studies was applied to Japanese in the form of a comparison of detection of targets like *ta-* and *tan-* in words like *tanishi* 'snail' and *tanshi* 'terminal' (Otake et al. 1993). Both of the fragments are nominally to be found in both of the words, but the mapping of the fragments to the moraic structure of the words is different. In *ta-n-shi*, *ta-* corresponds to the first mora and *tan-* to the first two morae. In *ta-ni-shi*, *ta-* again corresponds to the first mora, but *tan-* does not map neatly to morae at all, because it consists of the first mora plus half of the second. The hypothesis that segmentation makes reference to moraic

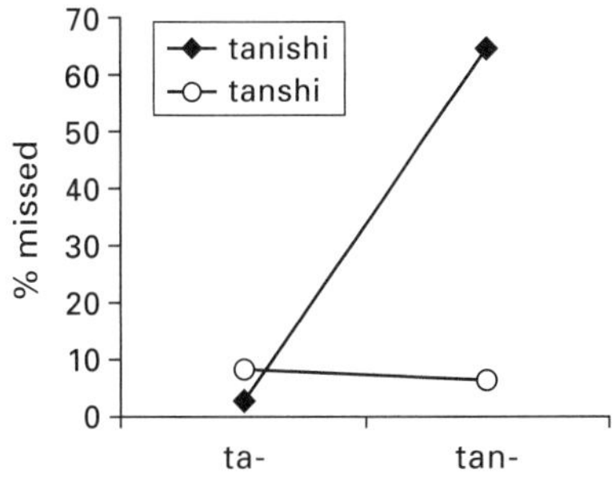

Figure 4.3
Japanese speakers segment spoken words mora by mora. They detect word-initial targets that are exactly one mora (*ta-* in *tanishi* or *tanshi*) or two (*tan-* in *tanshi*) but fail to detect targets not aligned with mora boundaries (*tan-* in *tanishi*). (Fragment-detection data from Otake et al. 1993.)

structure would predict that detection of the last target—*tan-* in *ta-ni-shi*—should prove extremely hard compared with any of the other three. This is, as figure 4.3 shows, exactly what the experiment revealed.

A similar effect could be demonstrated with phoneme detection. A single phoneme can be moraic—for instance, a vowel (as in the first mora of *A-sa-hi*) or a coda consonant (as in the last mora of *Ki-ri-n*). Phonemes that are moraic ([o] in *taoru* 'towel', [n] in *kondo* 'next time') are detected faster and more accurately than the same phonemes when they are nonmoraic ([o] in *etoku* 'mastery', [n] in *kanojo* 'girlfriend', Cutler and Otake 1994).

The comparison with Japanese also further strengthened the argument that segmentation effects reside in listeners' characteristic modes of processing (rather than being induced by the structure of the input). Just as French listeners had applied syllabic segmentation to English input that English listeners did not segment in such a way (Cutler et al. 1983, 1986), so did they segment Japanese words syllabically even though Japanese listeners did not (Otake et al. 1993). And Japanese listeners not only detected [n] faster in Japanese *kondo* than in *kanojo*, but also in English *candy* than in *canopy*, although, again, English listeners did not show this difference (Cutler and Otake 1994).

4.7 The Rhythmic Class Hypothesis

The idea of rhythmic segmentation prompted the rhythmic class hypothesis, because researchers naturally wanted to classify the possible types of rhythm that languages and listeners could exploit in this way. Surely there was unlikely to be an infinite set of possible rhythmic structures and associated segmentation strategies?

Impressionistic linguistic classification is unsatisfyingly subjective. Objective measurement of timing units, however, does not yield clear classifications, as described earlier. Two attempts have been made to develop a phonetic basis for grouping languages into rhythmic classes. One method assigns languages to a point in a space defined by the standard deviation of intervocalic intervals and the proportion of speech time taken up by vowels (Ramus, Nespor, and Mehler 1999; Ramus and Mehler 1999; Ramus 2002). The other approach uses a measure called the Pairwise Variability Index (PVI) to capture variability in the duration of successive vowels and in the duration of successive intervals between vowels in speech (Grabe, Post, and Watson 1999; Low, Grabe, and Nolan 2000; Grabe and Low 2002; Grabe 2002; see also Deterding 2001); again, different languages can be compared by plotting average values in a space defined by the two variability measures. Obviously, the two approaches are similar: each captures crosslinguistic differences in allowable syllable structures and in the degree to which syllables are affected differentially by, for example, stress. Assuming every syllable to have a vowel and every vowel to be in a different syllable, then intervocalic intervals and the duration of successive vowels will vary less when regularity is expressed in syllables than when regularity is expressed in units larger than the syllable. That is the principal insight. However, the absolute values delivered by the measures are not important; their main contribution is that, as figure 4.4 shows, they allow languages to be compared. The question about the set of rhythmic structures resolves to a question about the number of clusters in the space mapped by these comparative measures.

Each of the approaches passed the basic test of showing separation between languages that were traditionally viewed as stress- versus syllable-timed (e.g., British English vs. French), though the figure shows that the two measures do not yield exactly the same relationships when applied to the same samples from several languages. Extension of the measures to other languages also produced mixed results (Stockmal, Markus, and Bond 2005 for Latvian; Keane 2006 for Tamil; Loukina et al. 2011 for Mandarin, Greek, and Russian). The measures can, however, show differences between dialects of the same languages (Low et al. 2000; Deterding 2001; Grabe 2002) and between colloquial versus formal varieties of the same language (Keane 2006), so they offer an additional method for describing varietal variation. They may also be useful as a tool for measuring second-language learners' approximation to the native norm (Stockmal et al. 2005). However, the measures differ in which pairs of languages they distinguish best (Loukina et al. 2011); they vary across speech rates, with variation due to rate impinging on differences between languages more than on differences between dialects (Barry and Russo 2003; Deterding 2001); and they even vary across speakers of the same variety (Keane 2006). This variation suggests that the measures are not yet abstract enough to crystallize out whatever underlies the impressions that have caused linguists to propose

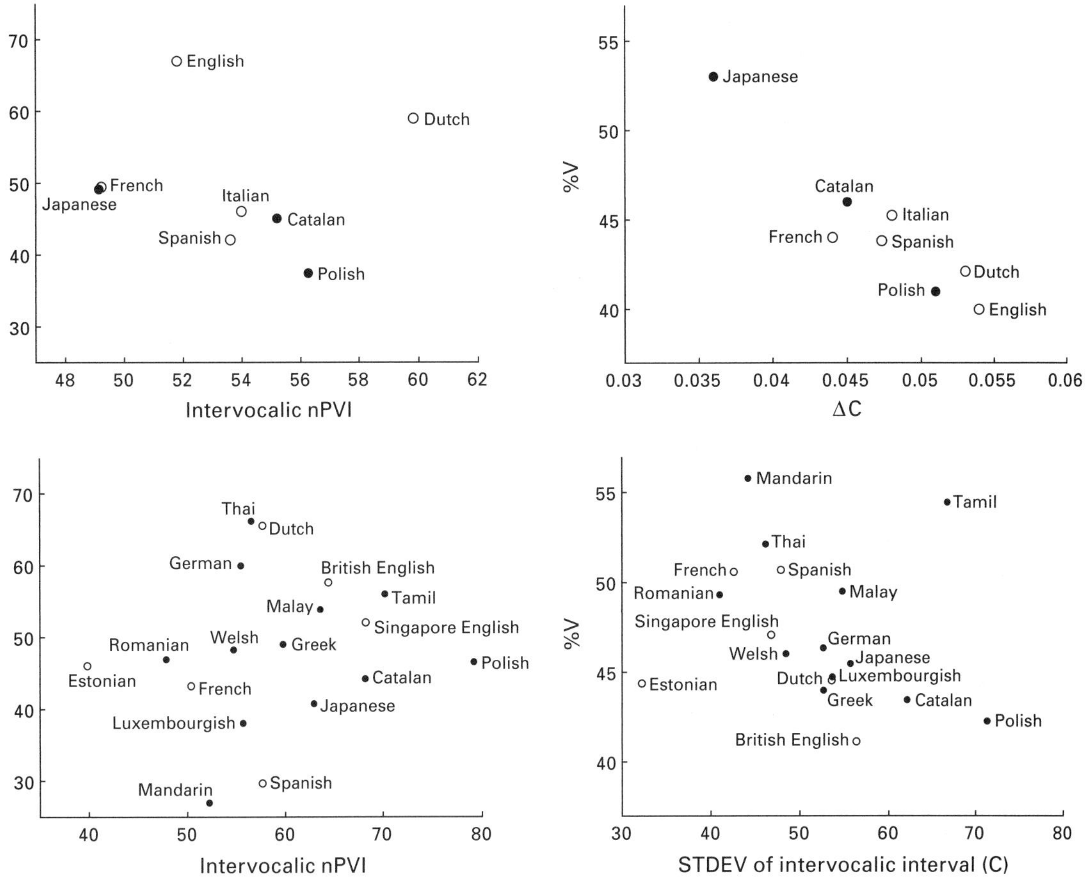

Figure 4.4
Measures of language rhythm compared: the two left panels show the normalized PVI measure (nPVI) of Grabe and colleagues; the two right panels show the vowel-based measure of Ramus and colleagues. In the upper row, eight languages (Polish, Spanish, Catalan, Italian, French, Japanese, Dutch, and British English), plotted in PVI space and in %V/ΔC space by Ramus (2002), and in the lower row, eighteen languages (all the above except for Italian, plus Mandarin, Thai, Malay, Tamil, Singapore English, German, Luxembourgish, Estonian, Romanian, Greek, and Welsh), plotted in the same way by Grabe and Low (2002). Language groupings allow comparison between the two measures.

rhythmic categories. It is possible that very large and carefully representative standardized samples from each language could produce greater stability in language placement. The problem is that both metrics require extensive measurement, which makes them even then quite labor intensive. Such analyses of large samples are thus unlikely in the near future.

4.8 Perceptual Tests of Rhythmic Similarity

In parallel to the development of their phonetic measure, Ramus and Mehler (1999) examined in perceptual studies whether the patterning of consonants and vowels might also be the basis for how listeners judged language rhythm. They resynthesized speech in English and in Japanese from several speakers, replacing (a) all vowels by [a] and each consonant by a generic consonant of the same broad class—stop, fricative, liquid, nasal, or glide, or (b) all vowels by [a] and all consonants by [s].[2] The timing of each original segment was preserved in the segment replacing it. In both versions, listeners were significantly better than chance at assigning different samples to the correct language category. They could do so even when intonation was removed. They could not perform the task successfully, though, in a third version (c) in which all vowels and all consonants were replaced by the same vowel. Ramus and Mehler proposed that judgments of language similarity by listeners are indeed based on the same dimensions of vowel-consonant variation that the rhythmic measures tap into.

Another way is to test rhythmic similarity implicitly, using the tasks that established the role of rhythm in segmentation. For both the smallest segmentation unit (the mora), and the next smallest (the syllable), similar response patterns have been shown across language pairs that are quite unrelated but have comparable rhythm. In the case of the mora, this was Japanese (as just described in section 4.6) and the Dravidian language Telugu, which is similar to Japanese in syllable structure and rhythmic patterning (and, interestingly, also in the role of the mora in poetic structures). When the Japanese materials of Otake et al. (1993) were presented to native speakers of Telugu in Hyderabad, India, detection of *tan-* in *tanishi* proved much harder than detection of any of the other target types (Murty, Otake, and Cutler 2007). This was just what the Japanese listeners in the original study had shown—that is, the Telugu listeners' results looked like figure 4.3—and a parallel result pattern appeared when Japanese listeners were presented with word lists in Telugu, too. The Telugu listeners did not show exactly the same pattern with the materials in their own language; but because there are as yet no computerized lexical databases of Telugu, the Telugu materials could not be controlled with respect to number of competitors and other factors that might affect native listeners' responses. Nor, for the same reason, could a set of nonsense materials for Telugu be easily constructed. Given such difficulties, presenting speech in an unfamiliar language is possibly the cleanest test of the rhythmic segmentation hypothesis. With these materials, the Japanese and Telugu listeners responded very similarly. Note that English and French listeners had not shown the same pattern of results with these materials (Otake et al. 1993), and Japanese listeners had also not shown this pattern with materials in English, French, or Spanish (Otake, Hatano, and Yoneyama 1996).

For the syllable, French again served as one member of the pair; the other was Korean. Previous work by Stockmal, Moates, and Bond (2000; Bond and Stockmal 2002) and Yoon and Derwing (1995, 2001) had indicated a syllabic rhythmic preference in Korean. Again, the poetic forms in the language are syllable based, too (see, for instance, the discussion of the classical *sijo* form by McCann 1976). Lexical databases for Korean also made it possible to construct competitor-controlled experimental stimuli. Koreans listening to Korean words proved to respond more accurately when the target was exactly a syllable (*ca-* in *camay* 'sisters', *cam-* in *campok* 'stakeout') than when it was more (*cam-* in *camay*) or less (*ca-* in *campok*)—exactly the pattern that French listeners showed with native and foreign speech (these listeners' accuracy patterns thus looked like the RTs in figures 4.2a and 4.2d; Kim, Davis, and Cutler 2008). The Korean listeners also showed the same response pattern with foreign speech, to wit, the original French materials of Mehler et al. (1981). The syllabic effect did not show up in RTs, but the RTs were very long by the standards of such experiments, and all the moraic effects, in Japanese and in Telugu, were mainly observed in accuracy rates, too. The rhythmic segmentation hypothesis was thus supported once again; across languages, irrespective of their etymological or typological relationships, similar rhythmic structure encourages similar segmentation procedures. As chapter 8 will describe, a language's typical rhythm is more or less the first aspect of linguistic structure available to an infant. Listeners' use of rhythm is primary and does not depend on knowing other phonological structures first.

4.9 Further Phonological Cues to Segmentation

Rhythm is, of course, not the only useful source of extralexical information (i.e., beyond the string of words actually being uttered) about where word boundaries occur in a speech stream. It is also not the only language-specific source of information. One other aspect of phonological structure that is clearly language specific is, as noted at the outset of this chapter, the sequencing of phonemes. Sequences that are perfectly okay within a syllable in one language may be completely prohibited syllable internally in another. Computerized detection of word boundaries can profit from use of this information (Harrington, Watson, and Cooper 1989). For instance, both German and English have the segments [p] and [f]. In German [pf] may occur at the beginning or end of a syllable—*Pferd* 'horse', *Kopf* 'head'. In English, [pf] as a sequence of segments only arises across a syllable boundary (*campfire*) or by insertion of an additional (epenthetic) segment in an [mf] coda (*triumph*, *lymph*, and *nymph*). The sequence [pf] is not a possible English syllable onset. Thus, a listener (human or machine) who does not yet know the English word *lope* would nonetheless do well to interpret the sequence [lo:pfɔr] as *lope+for*, simply because the parses *low+pfor* and *lowpf+oar* would each produce an illegal sequence, whereas *lope+for* is unexceptionable. In German, the sequence would not force such a decision. Similarly, English, Dutch, and German all have voiced stops—for example, [d] and [b]; but although these can be either syllable initial or syllable final in English (*bid*, *dub*), in Dutch and German they can only be syllable initial. A listener hearing a voiced stop in German or Dutch knows that it cannot be word final, whereas English allows no such decision.

Obligatory syllable structure constraints like this are called phonotactic constraints, and listeners can use them in locating word boundaries (McQueen 1998): Dutch listeners more easily spot *rok* 'skirt' in *fiemrok* (the sequence [mr] cannot be syllable initial or final) than in *fiedrok* ([dr] must be syllable initial because a syllable cannot end with the voiced stop [d]). Similar effects appear in Italian (e.g., for *lago* 'lake' in *riblago* versus *rinlago*, where [b] cannot be word final but [n] can, and [bl] can be word initial but [nl] cannot; Tagliapietra et al. 2009). These final voicing effects do not hold for many other languages, including English (indeed, *feed* and *rib* are actual English words). McQueen's *fiemrok* effect likewise does not hold for Czech and other languages that allow syllables to begin *mr-*. In other words, phonotactic segmentation effects are language specific. When the same rule holds across languages, of course listeners of each language should be equally able to make use of it. In English, German, French, and Italian, words can begin [kl] but not [nl], and English, German, French, and Italian listeners all spot [l]-initial words more easily after [n]-final than after [k]-final syllables (e.g., *lecture* after *moinlecture* versus *moiklecture*; Weber and Cutler 2006; Dumay et al. 2002; Tagliapietra et al. 2009).

Obligatory phonotactic constraints may be considered just one extreme of a continuum of sequence occurrence likelihood—sequences such as [mr] or [pf] have zero probability of occurrence within a syllable in English. As will be further discussed in chapter 6, listeners are sensitive both to obligatory and to optional sequence effects. It is reasonable to ask whether they are sensitive not just to rules barring particular sequences but even to where a sequence is placed along a continuum of likelihood. This continuum is called transitional probability (TP), and it is computed by counting for any pair of elements (phonemes within syllables, in this case, but it could also be syllables within words, or words within sentences) how often the pair occurs in sequence as a function of how often the components occur in total. Cairns et al. (1997) computed all the word-boundary transitional probabilities in the London-Lund Corpus and trained a simple connectionist network to predict the next phonetic segment at each stage of the input. Sensitivity to TP is displayed as higher error for sequences that occur rarely than for sequences that occur more commonly; the model did indeed develop such sensitivity, which allowed Cairns et al. to use it to predict where boundaries occurred in the input. Do human listeners similarly use TP regularities to predict where boundaries will fall?

Historical evidence may even be relevant here. Consider, for instance, that onsetless syllables are less frequent in English than syllables with a singleton consonant onset, and consider how *an*, the older form of the English indefinite article, has historically sometimes ceded its final consonant to an onsetless noun (so that *an ewt* became *a newt* and *an eke-name* became *a nickname*). A less probable word structure (onsetless) thereby became a more probable one (single consonant onset). In fact, listeners very rapidly pick up on phonotactic probabilities in the input they receive. English speakers who were asked to recite sets of nonsense syllables with varying built-in sequencing probabilities made speech errors that were skewed, in that they reflected the probabilities in whatever syllable set they had actually heard (Dell et al. 2000). Similarly, syllables that conform to some phonotactic probabilities built into a particular set of materials can be repeated faster than syllables that deviate from the built-in probabilities (Onishi, Chambers, and Fisher 2002).

Evidence that listeners take such probabilistic information into account in word boundary detection was garnered by Van der Lugt (2001) in a word-spotting experiment in Dutch. Many Dutch words begin *ga-*; few Dutch words begin *geu-*. Van der Lugt discovered that words with common onsets were easier to spot than words with rare onsets—so it is easier to find *galg* 'gallows' in *piengalg* than *geur* 'aroma' in *piengeur*. Note that this is a way in which segmentation can be recognized as an operation separate from word identification. In lexical decision, words that share their initial portion with many other words are recognized less rapidly than otherwise similar words with a rare initial portion, because more words produce more competition. So *mass* is recognized more slowly than *sad* because English contains many words beginning [mæ] and fewer beginning [sæ] (Vitevitch 2002). In Van der Lugt's experiment, one can think of the initial portion similarly activating many candidate words; and because word-spotting, like lexical decision, requires identification of the word, the greater competition presumably would slow this process. Thus the facilitation that arose is due entirely to the fact that the words needed to be segmented from a preceding context, and more words beginning in the same way clearly help this segmentation process. Segmentation is distinct from the word recognition process it serves. The effect of TPs has also been demonstrated in detection tasks, with both phoneme targets in English (McQueen and Pitt 1996) and syllable targets in Cantonese (Yip 2000). In both cases, as predicted by Vitevitch's and Van der Lugt's accounts, the effect was facilitatory. Facilitatory effects of probabilistic phoneme sequences in prelexical processing also contrast with inhibitory effects of neighborhood density in lexical competition (Vitevitch and Luce 1999).

Languages differ not only in what constraints there are but in how many. Korean has a very complex phonology, with certain phonemes changing their form obligatorily in specific contexts. Some of these changes only occur when a boundary is present or absent. The result is that certain sequences can be very informative about parsing of the input as a whole. So word boundaries in Korean are prohibited in the sequence [dʒi], legal but not highly likely in the sequence [di], and very likely in the sequence [nni]. These obligatory constraints and probabilistic patterns in Korean were examined together in a word-spotting experiment by Warner, Kim, et al. (2005). Korean listeners detected *i*-initial words such as *imin* 'migration' more easily in, say, [pjodimin], where a *-i* boundary is legal, than in [pjodʒimin], where a boundary is prohibited, and the most rapid responses of all came in the very likely boundary context [pjonnimin]. The listeners exploited both the prohibitory constraints and the statistical likelihoods.

Listeners also exploit other aspects of language-specific phonology for segmentation. Thus Finnish, as described in chapter 1, has a vowel harmony rule whereby certain vowels may not co-occur in a word. Two successive syllables containing such incompatible vowels should therefore be separated by a word boundary, and listeners are able to exploit this fact in speech recognition (Suomi, McQueen, and Cutler 1997). In word-spotting, a word such as *palo* 'fire' proved easier to detect in *kypalo* than in *kupalo*. The Finnish vowel [y] cannot occur in the same word as [a] or [o], but the vowel [u] can. Finnish listeners can, obviously, exploit their knowledge of the regularities of vowel harmony in speech segmentation. The great phonologist Trubetzkoy had written in 1939 that word-level vowel harmony rules such as this should be very useful to listeners in telling where word boundaries occurred in a string of syllables; Suomi et al.'s experiment proved his intuition correct. In Turkish, which has a similar vowel harmony rule, disharmony likewise leads to faster detection of bisyllabic targets embedded in nonsense strings (Kabak, Maniwa, and Kazanina 2010). Clearly, however, exploitation of vowel harmony is a strategy specific to languages that have this phonological feature.

In short, listeners use the probabilities of their language to good effect in segmentation. The need to segment speech is universal, because speech in all languages is continuous; but the cues that listeners can draw on differ from language to language, which makes the resulting behaviors language specific.

4.10 Which Segmentation Cue?

So, listeners can use a range of cues in segmenting speech. The rhythmic structure of their language, as well as the phonological constraints and probabilities of the native vocabulary, provide direct segmentation cues, but the multiple concurrent activation of words allows the lexicon to contribute segmentation information indirectly as well (see chapter 3). Significant segmentation information can be conveyed even by the fine detail of how segments and syllables are pronounced (more about this in chapter 6) or by the transitional probabilities within a particular listening situation (see section 4.11). Although the segmentation of speech signals is, indisputably, a nontrivial task, listeners are clearly not without the resources to deal with it.

Given that most of these cues will be simultaneously available, it is reasonable to ask whether some of them are more useful than others; whether listeners have a detectable preference for using some of them rather than others; and whether if more than one cue is concurrently used, each will contribute a separate segmentation benefit in an additive fashion. Analogous questions have exercised researchers studying infant vocabulary learning, where the heart of that topic is invoked; infants, having as yet no lexicon, have to start somehow, so what do they start with? (Some answers are in section 8.7 in chapter 8.)

Obviously, there must be a gradient of relative usefulness of segmentation cues. Consider that the clearest case of a word edge is adjacency to silence. When someone starts to speak, the beginning of the utterance is simultaneously the left edge of the first word in the utterance. This, with the greater informativeness of word beginnings in general, was the basis of the early left-to-right word segmentation proposals described earlier. Unless there is some *force majeure* that has stopped a speaker in midflow, silence following an utterance is likewise a pretty effective cue to the right edge of a word ending the utterance. Contrast a cue as obvious as this with the onset and offset frequencies described in the preceding section. You can't know that a word onset occurs in lots of words unless you know lots of words. So it is only logical to expect such phonological probabilities to be less easily available as segmentation cues than silence abutting a word edge.

A systematic attempt to map the relative strength of segmentation cues was undertaken by Mattys and colleagues (Mattys 2004; Mattys, White, and Melhorn 2005). Most of their experiments involved cross-modal priming given a fragmentary cue with a preceding nonsense context (this was sort of a combination of cross-modal fragment priming with word-spotting). Lexical decision responses for visually presented CUSTOMER, for instance, might be measured after the auditory prime *guspemcusto-*, which ends with the first two syllables of the target word, versus after a prime ending with distorted speech. With this method they compared which types of segmentation cue resulted in more versus less facilitation and whether the strength of the facilitatory effect was modulated by difficulty of the listening conditions. All their experiments were in English.

It is known that stress placement in English can have an effect on lexical access in acoustically less predictable speech—so, for instance, words with initial stress are easier to recognize, and their component phonemes easier to detect, if the input is spontaneous speech (McAllister 1991; Mehta and Cutler 1988; there is more on this in chapters 6 and 7). But this advantage for initial stress does not appear in read speech (i.e., speech carefully produced in the way it is in most psycholinguistic experiments). Similarly, Mattys and colleagues found no greater facilitation for initially stressed word fragments (*custo*- from *customer*) than for initially unstressed fragments (*cathe*- from *cathedral*) when the prime fragments were clearly spoken. But when the fragments were masked with noise, the initially stressed words were more effectively primed. Likewise, coarticulatory cues (created by having parts of the prime string spoken together or separated) were stronger than stress pattern cues in the clear speech, but again stress was the more effective cue in noise.

The conclusions drawn from these experiments were that the listeners preferred to rely on lexical and contextual information where they could; that they would then call on coarticulation cues and phonotactic constraints if they had to; and when things got really difficult they would fall back on stress. That is, the cues that were tested ranked in a three-tier hierarchy: the lexical level was the most useful, the segmental level the next most, and the prosodic level the third most useful. Moreover, listeners did not additively profit from multiple cues; having two was not better than one, because use would only be made of the highest ranked cue for the listening situation in question.

These attempts at a relative effectiveness ranking for segmentation cues are useful for spoken-word recognition research, but the last word may not have been spoken. In the noise-masked conditions in these studies, the signal-to-noise ratio (SNR) was –5 decibels, which is quite severe masking; the stressed syllables would be more robust against such noise. The automatic multiple activation documented in chapter 3 will occur whatever input is heard. If stressed syllables are the only clearly heard portions, then *custo*- will provide *cus*- as a basis for activating a set of lexical candidates, and the resulting set—*custard*, *customer*, *cusp*, and so on—will include the coming lexical decision target. But *cathe*- from *cathedral* will provide *the*-, which leads to activation of a set such as *theater*, *theme*, and *theory*. Segmentation may not have produced the facilitation difference, in other words; simple syllable-level intelligibility differences would lead to the same result. Further, the tasks Mattys and colleagues used in these studies (cross-modal priming and word detection) always involved an explicitly presented lexical target, so that the primary measure was word recognition, with segmentation success a secondary inference from it. It has been argued in this chapter and the preceding one that word-spotting, in which the listener has no prespecified target in mind and simply listens for any familiar portion in the speech input, is better able to provide a window on the operation of segmentation per se. Another "pure" segmentation task is artificial language learning (ALL), the topic of section 4.11. Mattys and colleagues have moved their research into more detailed exploration of the noise-masking effects (Mattys, Brooks, and Cooke 2009), but their cross-cue comparison cries out for replication with tasks that are purely focused on segmentation.

4.11 Learning to Segment an Artificial Language

ALL techniques were introduced in chapter 2 (see panel 9). These techniques provide a way of investigating the learnability of segmentation cues—quite a clean way, in that potentially confounding factors arising from knowledge of the native language can be excluded. By manipulating, for instance, the transition probabilities associated with word boundaries in a totally artificial language, or other constraints peculiar to this invented language, one can discover whether listeners can pick up on these sources of information just by being exposed to samples of the language.

Hayes and Clark (1970) were the first to realize the potential of this technique for studying segmentation. They concatenated sequences of "phonemes" (computer-generated square waves that were either dynamic or relatively unvarying; Hayes and Clark thought of the first as analogous in a way to consonants, and the second as analogous to vowels!). The phonemes made up "words" that were fixed sequences of six to eight of these sounds, alternating "consonants" and "vowels." The fixed sequences were concatenated in various orders in continuous streams. Subjects in their experiments listened to the resulting "speech" streams for about 45 minutes.

One has to hope that these heroic pioneers were paid well for doing this—participation in an artificial language experiment is not the most exciting of the laboratory tasks described in this book. Later experiments have shown that 45 minutes is much longer than listeners actually seem to need to pick up on the regularities in speechlike signals; 21 minutes suffices (Saffran, Newport, and Aslin 1996), so does 18 minutes (Onnis et al. 2004), and perhaps it was Be-Kind-to-Subjects Week when Vroomen, Tuomainen, and De Gelder (1998) ran their ALL experiment with only 10 minutes of exposure, because that worked too and it has been the most commonly used exposure period since then (e.g., Peña et al. 2002; Onnis et al. 2005). In one experiment, even two minutes proved enough (Peña et al. 2002).

In Hayes and Clark's study, after the initial exposure, the listeners heard sets of alternatives in which they were asked to distinguish the "words" they had actually heard from novel arrangements of the same "phoneme" set into "nonwords" with the same length and the same patterning of dynamic and steady-state elements. They could do this, as long as the total set of phonemes was not so small that everything sounded very alike anyway (this was the case if the "language" was made up of only four "phonemes"). So humans are good at extracting regularities from an auditory stream just by listening to it. Note that we now know that you must actually listen to it; you can successfully learn while doing another unrelated task (Saffran, Newport, et al. 1996), but if that other task is so hard that it requires all your attention, the standard of the resulting learning drops dramatically (Toro et al. 2005).

4.11.1 An ALL Renaissance

As described in chapter 3, artificial languages had already been proven useful as a test bed for studying syntactic processing. It nevertheless took a quarter of a century for Hayes and Clark's lead to be followed[3] in applying them to speech segmentation, although there had been some studies using prior presentation of nonwords (e.g., *stugadi*) and subsequent detection of these targets in continuous nonsense sequences (e.g., Cowan 1991). The ALL revival was launched by Saffran, Newport, et al. (1996) with an experiment that has formed the model for many later studies. Three hundred tokens of each of six three-syllable CVCVCV words, where V stands for any one of three vowels and C for any one of four consonants, were strung together in an unbroken sequence, and subjects in their study listened to this sequence with the task of figuring out what the words were. They were not told in advance how many words there were or how long these were. The 21-minute exposure was broken into three seven-minute chunks; but . . . *babupudutabapidabututibupidabupatubibabu pubupadababupu* . . . , and so on, in a monotone, seems to require listeners to muster a certain fortitude, even just for seven minutes.

At the end of the exposure the subjects were given two-alternative choices such as *babupu* versus *budabi*, or *tibupi* versus *pidabu*. They were asked to choose the real words (in this case, *babupu* and *pidabu*) from the alternatives. These alternatives could be either sequences that had never occurred in the input (e.g., *budabi*), or sequences that had occurred but across boundaries (e.g., *tibupi* in *tutibu pidabu* above). The subjects performed better on the first type of choice than on the second, but even on the second their performance was significantly above chance. Later experiments (Saffran et al. 1999) showed that listeners could equally well learn "words" that were made up of sequences of three nonspeech tones. Thus, sensitivity to the distributional structure of auditory experience is such that even relatively small amounts of input (certainly far less than the amount supporting young humans' distributional computations) enable listeners to calculate statistical regularities. Subjects in ALL experiments sometimes report that after a certain amount of exposure the words just seem to pop out of the speech stream. That is, the task may be boring, but it seems to be fairly easy. Sensitivity to the transition probabilities of the immediate input is seen in the repetition studies (e.g., of Onishi et al. 2002) described in section 4.9; it is thus also evident with simple listening tasks where no reproduction of the input is required.

4.11.2 ALL as a Test Bed for Segmentation Cues

Artificial language learning is not a one-off demonstration of sensitivity to statistics, however; it may be used to explore what else listeners can use in segmentation of speech. The error responses in Saffran, Newport, et al.'s (1996) study indicated that listeners were more sensitive to the final parts of words than the initial parts. And the addition of prosodic cues in a second experiment—three of the six words had their final syllable lengthened, or three had their initial syllable lengthened—showed that final lengthening further improved listeners' discrimination performance but initial lengthening failed to affect it. Constituent-final lengthening is certainly widespread across languages (Vaissière 1983) and may be universal; it may even result from general, nonlinguistic mechanisms, given that for at least a century we have known that regular sounds varying in duration tend to be heard as iambic sequences—that is, with the longer sound in final position (Woodrow 1909). Cross-linguistic tests of this ALL cue indeed showed that English, Dutch, and French listeners all significantly benefited from a final lengthening cue, whereas none of them made use of an initial lengthening cue (Tyler and Cutler 2009; see figure 4.5).

Final lengthening effects can thus be seen as knowledge that listeners bring with them to the ALL laboratory. Use of preexisting knowledge was similarly explored in the same task by Vroomen et al. (1998). Their artificial language was again a sequence of CVCVCV "words," but it included either a Finnish-like vowel harmony cue (all vowels in the word were front vowels, or all were back vowels) or a "stress" cue (this was actually a pitch contour that rose across the initial syllable of each

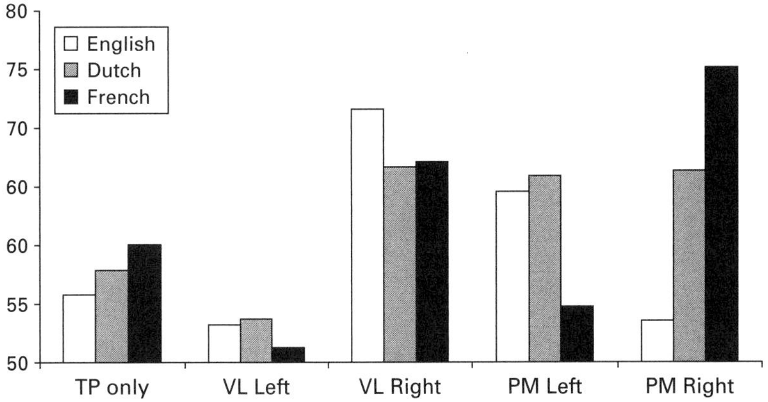

Figure 4.5
English, Dutch, and French speakers' percent correct identifications of "words" from an artificial language when the language contained no word-boundary cues other than the transition probabilities in the sequences (TP only) versus when cues were present—either a vowel lengthening (VL) cue or a pitch movement (PM) cue, consistently in word-initial position (Left word edge) or in word-final position (Right word edge). For all three groups, the VL cue is useful at right edges only. The PM cue is useful for English listeners only at the left edge, for French listeners only at the right edge, but for Dutch listeners in either position. (Data from Tyler and Cutler 2009.)

word, then gradually decreased to a baseline across the second and third syllables). Each of these cues effectively groups the three syllables of a word together (in contrast to the initial or final lengthening cues, which were realized on single syllables at word edges and hence were strictly cues to boundaries). Thus Vroomen et al.'s task should have been relatively easy, by ALL standards. Nonetheless, crosslanguage differences emerged when the materials were presented to Finnish, Dutch, and French listeners (in a short exposure period, as described earlier: five two-minute blocks). All the listeners again were able to perform the task; but although the Finnish were sensitive to both cues, the Dutch were only sensitive to the pitch-accent cue, not to vowel harmony. The French were sensitive to neither, in Vroomen et al.'s laboratory, but in a close replication of their study by Tyler (2006), French listeners did make significant use of the pitch-accent grouping cues. The same significant facilitation appeared even when Tyler obtained and reran Vroomen et al.'s original materials. There were some small differences between the conditions in which the studies were run, including that Vroomen et al. presented their materials by loudspeaker whereas Tyler made it easier for listeners to concentrate on the task by giving them headphones, so this is probably an object lesson in not making ALL tasks *too* challenging. The most important finding here is that only the Finnish speakers came to the laboratory equipped with knowledge that vowel harmony could be used to group syllables into words, and only the Finnish speakers used this type of cue in the ALL situation.

Tyler and Cutler's (2009) study tested for crosslinguistic differences in the use of a pitch-accent cue, too. Their cue, however, was not spread across the whole word; it was an edge cue, in the form of a F0 rise-fall across the vowel in either the initial or the final syllable of the artificial language (AL) words. In this case, French listeners significantly benefited from this cue on final syllables, but did not use it on initial syllables (see figure 4.5 again). English listeners, in contrast, used the cue on initial syllables but not on final syllables. This is fully in line with the generally final prominences in French but generally initial prominences in English (Fletcher 1991; Cutler and Carter 1987). Dutch listeners, who might have been expected to behave like their English linguistic cousins, actually proved to be more flexible—they could benefit from the pitch-accent cue in both edge positions. The reason for this is presumably that, as described in chapter 1 (and more fully to come in chapters 7 and 10), Dutch listeners are more sensitive to suprasegmental cues to lexical stress than English listeners are. Thus even though Dutch, like English, has a preference for trochaic structures (word-initial stress), when a clear pitch cue comes along in an artificial language, Dutch listeners can use it, whether it is in the usual position for prominence in Dutch or not.

Experiments in which identical AL materials are presented to listeners from different language backgrounds, such as those Vroomen et al. (1998) and Tyler and

Cutler (2009) conducted, hold much promise for the future. Meanwhile, noncontrastive ALL studies, examining the use of segmentation cues by various language populations, are accumulating rapidly. An ERP study by Sanders, Newport, and Neville (2002) actually failed to find any effect of learning from 14 minutes of exposure to Saffran, Newport, et al.'s (1996) original items. But when the (English-speaking) participants had to learn the six words of the AL and then listen to another 14 minutes of continuous AL speech, two small ERP effects appeared for the subjects who had shown the greatest learning. The effects were like effects observed in other studies, with real-word input: an N100 associated with word onsets, and an N400, both of which Sanders and Neville (2003a, 2003b) had observed, respectively with native-language and with nonnative words.

The N400 effect (but not the N100) appeared also in a Spanish study (Cunillera et al. 2006). Three conditions were compared: one like that of Saffran, Newport, et al. (i.e., the TP resulting from recurring words); one random condition where there was nothing to learn because words did not recur; and one where TP was accompanied by an added stress cue, as in Tyler and Cutler's study but here realized as higher pitch on the initial syllable of each AL word. The N400 component appeared whenever the input had TP cues (i.e., was made up of recurring elements rather than random syllables). A further effect of adding the stress cue to the TPs was also observed (a P200, i.e., positivity around 200 ms after onset, which can be interpreted as an auditory discrimination effect). This P200 also did not appear when the input was random syllables, so it was associated with parsing the AL into words via an explicit auditory cue. Interestingly, the same team (Toro-Soto, Rodríguez-Fornells, and Sebastián-Gallés 2007) also conducted an ALL study in which the higher-pitch cue was realized on the medial syllable of each trisyllabic AL word, hence presumably reflecting the native-language stress preference, which in Spanish is for stress on the penultimate syllable. Subjects failed to benefit from this cue at all. This result suggests that explicit segmentation cues in ALL are most helpful, perhaps only helpful, if they mark word edges.

So far, cross-cue comparison has not figured largely in the ALL segmentation literature. Though Tyler and Cutler (2009), for instance, compared two segmentation cues across listener groups, they did not compare the relative strength of the two cues within listeners. In the infant vocabulary acquisition literature, there have been comparisons of the relative strength of TP and stress cues (see chapter 8). For adults, however, only Fernandes, Ventura, and Kolinsky (2007) have addressed this issue. Coarticulatory cues and TP cues were compared in clear and difficult listening conditions. Syllables were recorded naturally (not synthesized as in most ALL studies) and were spoken together to provide coarticulatory cues, or not. Thus an AL word such as *lufaba* could have been recorded as a whole, or it could have been put together from separate recordings (e.g., of *lufa* and *ba*, or *lu* and *faba*). If TP and coarticulatory cues were in conflict, the latter proved to be the ones that more strongly determined participants' response patterns—at least, with the clear speech. In noise, the TPs determined responses. Even though the masking in this study was not extreme, the noise seems to have interfered with these unpredictable stimuli to an extent that the coarticulatory cues were no longer useful. Perhaps they were not even audible.

There is still much to be learned about how listeners select from the abundance of ways in which they can speed lexical recognition via segmentation, and many more systematic cross-cue studies would be helpful. Listeners presumably use the cues most effective for a particular situation; what has yet to be made is a complete inventory of which cues are most effective and when.

4.11.3 Dissociating Word-Level and Phrase-Level Segmentation in ALL

A series of ALL experiments by Peña et al. (2002) yielded a puzzling result pattern. The "words" in this study were *puliki*, *puraki*, *pufoki*, *talidu*, *taradu*, *tafodu*, *beliga*, *beraga*, and *befoga*; that is, they had the structure AXC, where the A and C syllables always predicted one another (*pu-ki*, *ta-du*, *be-ga*) and the X syllables were members of a closed set of three (*li*, *ra*, *fo*). The listeners successfully learned the set of words (after 10 minutes exposure). But they did not learn the underlying generalization. Presented with a new word such as *pubeki*, with a correct A_C combination but an unfamiliar X, listeners treated it in the same way as a sequence like *rakibe* (the end of one word and the beginning of another). The fact that *pubeki*, although new, conformed to the word rule, but *rakibe* did not, seemed to have no effect on the listeners' responses.

When an acoustic cue to the boundaries between the artificial words was available, in the form of a 25 ms pause before each word (N.B. actually below the duration at which a gap in the signal could just be noticed), listeners were able to group the words so effectively that they then behaved as if they had extracted the generalization. That is, in this condition *pubeki* was preferred to *rakibe*. Even just two minutes of exposure was enough to produce this generalization-based preference! But without the added acoustic boundary cue, even 30 minutes of exposure failed to produce a preference for the generalization—in fact, in that case listeners preferred *rakibe* (i.e., the string that, though a nonword, was part of their exposure experience). Peña et al. argued that consistent segmentation cues in speech signals allowed listeners to move from appreciation of statistical patterns to computation of a rule underlying the patterns. Note that this formulation would cover direct segmentation cues of any kind—that is, not just subliminal pauses but also language-specific word-edge and grouping cues—as long as they are physically instantiated beyond simple statistical co-occurrence.

The same result appeared in an ERP study by Mueller, Bahlmann, and Friederici (2008); although the authors in this case were more interested in the learning of syntax, and hence used rather longer strings, they too found that their subjects learned a dependency like the one Peña et al. (2002) had used. A pause—much larger than the below-threshold one in Peña et al.'s study—increased learning accuracy, as had indeed been found earlier for syntax learning with prosodically structured auditory AL input (Morgan et al. 1987). The main point of this ERP study, though, was that ERP signatures distinguished the condition with the segmentation cue from the condition without. In the test phase, there was one clear ERP effect that always distinguished correct versus incorrect examples of the AL, whether or not a cue had been available, but there was an additional effect that appeared only in the grammar-learning condition with the pause cue. In other words: we have seen that both in natural language recognition and in ALL, direct cues for segmentation can make an independent contribution to spoken-language parsing, over and above TP cues; a reflection of this contribution also appears in a neurophysiological measure.

However, the Peña et al. result also attracted criticism and a lot of follow-up studies exploring alternative accounts. First, it was suggested (Perruchet et al. 2004; Perruchet, Peereman, and Tyler 2006) that no real evidence showed that the AXC rule had been learned; listeners might have responded on the basis of just identifying the first syllable or the last syllable (i.e., learned an A-- rule or a --C rule); the result would have been the same. Perruchet and colleagues constructed a grammar with no A_C dependencies, but an A-- rule and a --C rule, and showed that listeners learned to identify the words when there were 25 ms gaps at word boundaries but not when the speech was truly continuous (i.e., they mimicked Peña et al.'s result in this respect). Next, Onnis et al. (2005) tested the importance of the fact that Peña et al.'s "words" all began with stop consonants (and their nonwords never). When they incorporated another phonological cue of the same type (A and C syllables always began with fricatives, X syllables never did), subjects also learned the words. Plosives were a better carrier of this phonological cue than fricatives, however; first, because replicating Peña et al.'s plosive-cue design produced significantly better learning than the fricative-cue design and, second, because subjects could learn the words when only a word-initial (A--) rule (and no A_C rule) applied, in the plosive-initial case, but they could not do this in the fricative-initial case. Reversing the roles of Peña et al.'s A syllables (*pu*, *ta*, *be*) and X syllables (*li*, *ra*, *fo*—see above) made words like *lipuki* and *fotadu*, and partwords like *taduli* and *kifota*; then, subjects showed a preference for the partwords (which began with stops) over the experimental words (which did not). This finding suggested an existing preference for stops as word onsets—a problem for all such studies.

In some ten experiments Newport and Aslin (2004) also consistently failed to find learning with the kind of CVCVCV strings that Peña et al. (2002) used, which incorporated A_C dependencies. But they succeeded in finding learning when the artificial languages involved other types of discontinuous dependencies (e.g., CVCVCV strings in which the consonants were always p-k-t- or the vowels were always -a-u-e). These kinds of dependencies actually occur in natural languages—consider the Finnish vowel harmony rule described in previous sections of this chapter. Languages do not, however, customarily construct words on the basis of the kinds of dependencies in which the first and third syllable of a word always co-occur but the middle syllable may vary; in lexical segmentation (either the real thing or an ALL analog), listeners should draw on the realistic probabilities available in natural languages, not on patterns that do not naturally occur. Bonatti et al. (2005) replicated Newport and Aslin's result, but with consonant frames, only not with vowel frames. Their presentation contained no immediate repetitions of a given frame, whereas Newport and Aslin's did; when Bonatti et al. added this to their design, they replicated Newport and Aslin's result with vowels, too. Bonatti et al. argued that vowels and consonants play different roles in language, and vowels in particular provide less reliable information concerning lexical identity. This is the argument used to explain the vowel-consonant processing differences described in chapter 1.

Note that discontinuous dependencies of the A_C type do occur in language, but not at the word level; they are more characteristic of syntax (e.g., verb agreement dependencies, or noun gender dependencies expressed in determiner and suffix), where they cannot be discovered by simple TP calculations. Adults can indeed learn A_C dependencies in CV-CVCV-CV strings (Gómez 2002); these strings were recorded as clear sequences of three words (i.e., with interword pauses), so it should have been clear to participants that this was a dependency above the word level.

This all shows that the ALL literature on segmentation is growing rapidly and that the debate about the basis for listeners' computation of the regularities in speech is not over yet. In a sense, the real action is not in the arena of adult listening but in infant vocabulary acquisition. Infants are not tutored about the regularities that will feature in the speech they are exposed to; they have to compute the regularities in the input for themselves. And most importantly, they solve the segmentation problem for themselves. Segmentation is thus a central topic in infant speech perception research. The importance of ALL techniques in the infant literature will be clear in chapter 8. Adults, the ALL research shows, certainly have the ability both to draw on known phonological regularities in segmenting novel input and to track and learn novel probabilities in such input. Listeners who have taken part in such an ALL experiment then find it easier to learn labels for novel objects if the labels correspond to the transition probabilities encoded in the ALL training (Mirman et al. 2008); that is, they can generalize from the learning that they have acquired. There are, as we saw, as yet very few crosslinguistic ALL comparisons; but the many other studies described earlier in this chapter, demonstrating exploitation of language-specific phonological regularities in segmentation, suggest that listeners use the ability to track probabilities in speech input to good effect in real life.

4.12 Conclusion

Segmentation is a listening operation made necessary by the continuity that is intrinsic to speech. The segmentation literature shows that both direct and indirect cues to boundaries can be found in speech, and because they are there and they are useful, listeners use them. In principle, the processes of multiple activation, and consideration in parallel of concurrent lexical hypotheses, could often deliver a correct parse of speech input, but additional sources of information are available and listeners do not ignore them. These sources of information, such as rhythmic structure, phonotactic constraints, and word-structure probabilities, are highly language specific. And there we are, back at the central theme of this book: language-specific structure ends up determining how listeners listen to speech. The most efficient way to segment speech is to exploit everything we know about the elements we want to segment it into—what these elements are, but also what they tend to sound like at the beginning and at the end, and what parts of them can and cannot be edges. Only our language-particular experience can tell us about such typical properties. My words are not necessarily like your words.

Segmentation is specific to speech and has no counterpart in reading print (though perhaps the study of how handwriting is read could profit from the work of speech researchers!). Segmentation has, as we saw, prompted the development of at least one new laboratory technique (word-spotting) and has been involved in a renaissance of ALL techniques as they became applied in the auditory word learning domain. There will be more on the topics covered here, especially in chapters 6, 7, and 8; but meanwhile, chapter 5 is devoted to a fundamental and near-universal constraint without which the segmentation that is based on activation and competition would be much harder for listeners to accomplish.

5 Words: How Impossible Ones Are Ruled Out

In this chapter, a powerful constraint on word structure, and hence on speech segmentation, is discussed in depth. The Possible Word Constraint captures the fact that across languages, a stretch of speech with no vowel in it is unlikely to be a stand-alone word. This constraint can be acquired early from the patterning of vowels and consonants in speech, and it has been shown to operate in the same way across a wide range of languages with differing phonological structures. Its discovery usefully illustrates the interplay between model and experiment in psycholinguistic research, and its operation as captured by spoken-word recognition models likewise provides a perfect illustration of how multiple activation and competition cooperate with segmentation cues. Across languages, the constraint proves to be almost universally useful. Its utility disappears only in the crucial case of a language that violates the generalization on which it is based—that is, in a language that allows vowelless stand-alone words of any word class.

Lexical activation and lexical segmentation, as reviewed in the preceding chapters, form a coherent account of the initial stages of word recognition. Universal and language-specific effects at this level likewise fit together seamlessly. We see that listeners make effective use of the probabilities that their language experience has led them to compute. As it happens, some of these probabilities are specific to their native language. But it is not necessarily the case that all are; many may well be universal. From the listener's point of view, though, there may be no difference between probabilities that are universal versus language specific—all might present themselves as the stuff of experience.

A model such as Shortlist (A or B) allows all these sources of information, and all the various probabilities, to modulate the activation and competition process in a straightforward way. They are all operative early in recognition, reducing activation and competition. This early level is where they can most efficiently be used, because of how much spurious activation speech can call up, whatever vocabulary is being recognized.

One of the strongest effects at this early stage is quite a simple one, and because it is ultimately based in the nature of the speech signal, it is potentially universal. It is the so-called Possible Word Constraint (henceforth, the PWC). Back in chapter 1 we considered speech sounds and how they come in two varieties: vowels and consonants. Both types of speech sound are processed as efficiently as the listener can manage, and either vowel or consonant information can immediately exercise effects on lexical activation. But because vowels and consonants differ in their acoustic properties, the way they are processed is in some ways different and their role in the structure of words is different. Here we see a consequence of these differences. The PWC is a way in which listeners exploit their knowledge of how vowels and consonants make up words, to rule out—quite automatically—a good proportion of the spuriously activated word candidates in speech. Such candidates are ruled out at the stage at which they are initially activated, purely on formal criteria and irrespective of what they mean or how they combine with other activated forms. The efficient and early operation of the PWC also acts as a framework that allows other probabilities to operate.

5.1 The Possible Word Constraint

The PWC was discovered in a word-spotting study where the appended context could be either a syllable or a single consonant (Norris et al. 1997). Thus *egg* was presented in the contexts *maffegg* versus *fegg*, *sugar* in *sugarthig* versus *sugarth*, *sea* in *seashub* versus *seash*, and *angry* in *nalangry* versus *langry*. The results, summarized in figure 5.1, were clear: single-consonant residues made word-spotting very hard indeed. The detection rate was significantly lower, and successful detection RTs were significantly longer for *egg* in *fegg* compared with *egg* in *maffegg*. For monosyllabic and bisyllabic target words, with preceding or following context, the result was always the same: single-consonant contexts made detection harder. The difficulty was not due to acoustic cues in the way the word forms were spoken in context, because cross-splicing between the contexts made no difference (so it was just as hard to spot *egg* in a *fegg* made of the *f* from originally uttered *fegg* and the *egg* from originally uttered *maffegg*, and just as comparatively easy to spot *egg* in a *maffegg* made of the *maff* from originally uttered *maffegg* and the *egg* from originally uttered *fegg*). Always, word-spotting was harder in single-consonant contexts.

The name PWC captures the effect's apparent role as a viability check on the potential components of a speech sequence. Only components that could possibly be words are worth considering. Suppose that one hears the input *We won't bring. . . .* The third syllable is fully compatible with the word *bring*, but also with *ring*. However, to accept *ring* would mean that part of the input, [b], would be left over. Can [b] be a word by itself? The structure of vocabularies across languages suggests that single consonants, or vowelless strings of consonants, are rarely possible words. A primitive constraint could exploit this generalization by ruling that any word candidate that left such a residue of the signal unaccounted for would thereby forfeit

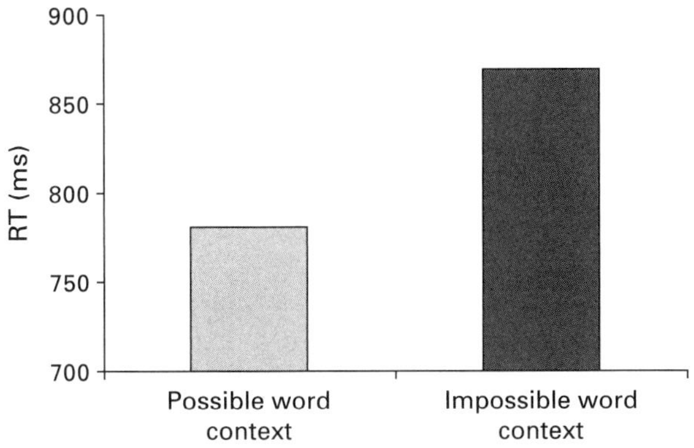

Figure 5.1
English listeners segment spoken nonwords, finding real words embedded in them, more rapidly if the leftover residue could itself be a possible word than if the residue is a single consonant and hence not possibly a word; thus *egg* is easier to find in *maffegg* than in *fegg*, *sugar* is easier in *sugarthig* than in *sugarth*, *sea* is easier in *seashub* than in *seash*, and *angry* is easier in *nalangry* than in *langry*. In each case, the easy version leaves a residue that might have been a word even though it is not—*maff*, *thig*, *shub*, *nal*—whereas the hard version leaves a residue that could not be a word—[f], [θ], [ʃ], [l]. (Word-spotting results from Norris et al. 1997.)

its own credibility. *Ring* would no longer be a credible competitor for *bring* because it would leave the residue *b*—that is, it would imply that *b* should be considered as a word candidate. Likewise *egg* in *fegg* would forfeit credibility due to postulating the impossible word candidate *f*. In this case (a word-spotting experiment where there was no other word on offer), listeners would indeed detect *egg*—but they would be rather slow in doing so. In *maffegg*, by contrast, *egg* would incur no penalty because the residue, *maff*, is not an impossible word. It is not an actual word—but it is a possible word, given that *map*, *muff*, and *gaffe* are all actual English words. Thus *egg* would be easier to spot in *maffegg*, and harder in *fegg*, because of the PWC violation in the latter case. The PWC simply recognizes that the smallest possible word candidate is a syllable. This is where the vowel-consonant difference comes in. A single consonant (or, indeed, any vowelless string of consonants) is simply not a possible word.

Note that residues—stretches of speech unaccounted for by the activated lexical representations—are not necessarily disastrous for the recognizer. They have to be admitted as a possibility in speech recognition. For someone who did not know the word *dove*, the utterance *That's a dove egg* would be unparsable if the recognizer did not allow for the possibility of learning a new word. Likewise, it is always possible that a mistake has been made, either in the speaker's production or the listener's perception, and recovery from such a mistake would again be impossible if residues were totally barred. Thus the PWC can be seen as a gatekeeper, exercising constraints on what might be a candidate for a new lexical entry, or what might be an erroneous sequence in need of reanalysis. These operations are necessary, and the PWC is thus necessary to constrain them.

It is important to realize that the PWC is not evidence of syllabic segmentation. In fact, if English listeners are given a task requiring explicit segmentation into syllables, no PWC effects appear. The fragment detection task (see panel 5 in chapter 1) can require listeners to detect a syllable target, for instance, and it makes no difference whether the target corresponds to a word (e.g., *bel*) or not (e.g., *beel*). It also makes no difference, in this case, what the rest of the string is: *bel* is detected equally easily in *belshig* and in *belsh* (Kearns, Norris, and Cutler 2002). But if the task is word-spotting, exactly the same syllable is detected (as the word *bell*) more rapidly in *belshig* than in *belsh*. In other words, the purpose of the PWC is to modulate segmentation of speech into word candidates. It distinguishes between syllables and consonants but only in the sense that consonants are not possible words. If the task does not require lexical processing (as detection of a fragment target does not), then the PWC is inactive. But as soon as lexical processing is going on, it springs into action. The PWC constrains word activation—in particular, with a view to getting rid of embeddings, such as *ring* in *bring* or *bell* in *belt*.

That alone makes it earn its keep, because computational analyses reveal that the payoff of the PWC in reduction of competition is substantial. To calculate what proportion of embedded words in English and Dutch would be excluded from competition by application of the PWC, Cutler, McQueen, et al. (2002) examined all embedded words in the CELEX English and Dutch dictionaries and ascertained what proportion of them left a vowelless residue of the matrix word between their edge and the nearest syllabic boundary. Such embeddings are the ones that the PWC would exclude. Thus *can* in *scan*, *cant*, or *scant* leaves a vowelless residue (or two) and would be excluded by the PWC, but *can* in *pecan*, *canny*, or *mechanic* could not be excluded and would enter into competition for recognition. The computations revealed that the PWC would exclude 73 percent of all embeddings in the English vocabulary and 61 percent of embeddings in Dutch.[1] Thus the PWC delivers substantial savings. This is true for final embeddings (*can* in *scan*, *ring* in *bring*), for initial embeddings (*can* in *cant*, *zoo* in *zoom*), and in particular for medially embedded words (*can* in *scant*, *ring* in *drink*), where the computations revealed the greatest savings of all. In frequency-weighted statistics compiled by summing frequencies of carrier words such as *zoom*, *cant*, and so on that begin with other monosyllabic CV (e.g., *zoo*) or CVC (e.g., *can*) words, the PWC again removed 64 percent of all spurious embeddings (Kearns et al. 2002). Applying the PWC is, clearly, well worth the listener's effort.

5.2 Implementation of the PWC in Shortlist

The discovery of the PWC was predicted by the Shortlist model (see Norris 2005). This came about as follows. Cutler and Norris's (1988) initial word-spotting experiment, described in chapter 4, compared detection of CVCC words followed by VC contexts in which the vowel was either strong (triggering segmentation of the second syllable) or weak (no segmentation). One target word was *jump* in the nonwords *jumpoove* and *jumpev*. This had been an easy target that had been detected by almost all listeners—albeit more slowly in *jumpoove* than in *jumpev*, as predicted. In 1988, when this study was published, the Shortlist model was not yet in existence. Once the first Shortlist paper had appeared (Norris 1994), Norris wanted to test the predictions of his model against materials from all the old experiments he could find. One such dataset came from the 1988 study. Here the model (armed with a version of stress-based segmentation; see Norris et al. 1995) showed that it could in general nicely simulate the 1988 response set—just as the listeners had done, the model settled less rapidly onto a final decision for target words followed by a strong vowel as compared to a weak vowel. But one item produced a deviant response: *jump*. The model never found *jump* in *jumpev*. Instead, it found *jumper*.[2]

This was not in any sense wrong. The model had been trained on British English and the input was in British English—the final *r* in a word like *jumper* is not pronounced by British speakers, so the word is spoken [dʒʌmpə] and thus it is indeed fully embedded in *jumpev* [dʒʌmpəv]. *Jumper* is longer than *jump* so it receives more activation (from five phonemes of input) than *jump* does (from four phonemes), which means that in the Shortlist competition it will triumph over *jump*. So far so good. The Shortlist model did exactly what it was supposed to do—it detected the embedded word that had received the most support from the input.

The question was why the performance of human listeners could not match the achievements of Shortlist. The experimenters had never noticed that *jumpev* inadvertently contained more than one embedded word, and none of the dozens of subjects tested in several experiments with this item had ever responded with *jumper* instead of with *jump*. Why? The PWC, and the experiments that demonstrated its robustness, were thus an answer to the challenge set by this mismatch between the performance of the model and the performance of human listeners. Without this mismatch, the PWC might have long remained undiscovered.

This anecdote incidentally illustrates how very useful computational modeling can prove for further theory development and how there is an interplay of theory and experimentation in scientific progress—in this case, the experiments motivated a model, the model challenged an aspect of the experimental results, the challenge led to further hypothesis formation and experimental testing, and, eventually, further theoretical advance was achieved.

The refinement of Shortlist A consisted of adding a procedure that reduced the activation of any candidate word in the competition when acceptance of that word would strand a vowelless residue of the input. The input *bring* might be fully compatible with recognition of *ring*, but accepting *ring* would leave the residue *b* unaccounted for, and *b* contains no vowel. Thus activation of *ring* was lowered. An analogous procedure incorporated the PWC into Shortlist B, in this case applied to the posterior probability of any path through the input in which a vowelless residue was unaccounted for. Here too, the input *bring* would be compatible with a path including *ring*, but that path would also contain *b*, and in consequence the probability of the path as a whole would be reduced.

Figure 5.2 shows Shortlist simulations using the materials of the PWC experiment (figure 5.1; Norris et al. 1997; there are more such simulations in that paper and in Norris and McQueen 2008). The two left panels show how Shortlist A operated in its original 1994 form for the words with preceding context (*egg*, *angle*) and with following context (*sea*, *sugar*) respectively; the two right panels show its operation with the same input in its 1997 version, with added PWC. Only the 1997 version successfully captures the figure 5.1 results.

Equipping Shortlist with the PWC led to a considerable simplification of the model. In order for Shortlist to account correctly for word recognition in continuous speech, it had to incorporate language-specific procedures for segmentation. For English, therefore, it had to account in some way for stress-based segmentation. In Shortlist A, such an account was accomplished by boosting the activation of candidate words with a strong initial syllable aligned with a strong syllable onset in the input, and penalizing candidate words without strong syllables beginning where a strong syllable began in the input (Norris et al. 1995). Thus in *true status* both words would receive a boost, as both begin with a strong syllable, but *rue* would not be boosted because its onset is not aligned with the onset of a strong syllable in the input, and *truce*, *ruse*, and *roost* would be penalized because they lay claim to the onset of a strong syllable (*sta-*) in the input, but they do not have a strong syllable with such an onset.

That modification of Shortlist A succeeded in simulating the competition results of McQueen et al. (1994) and Norris et al. (1995); but the modification is quite specific to English and would not work at all for the segmentation procedures used in other languages. The PWC implementation, in contrast, worked in a crosslinguistically adaptable way. Also, extra procedures to account for stress-based segmentation became unnecessary. The PWC was implemented as a simple (universal) constraint on initial lexical activation, with the following function: it reduced the activation of any candidate word form if accepting that word entailed that a vowelless residue of the input remained between the word's edge—either edge—and the nearest known (or hypothesized) boundary.

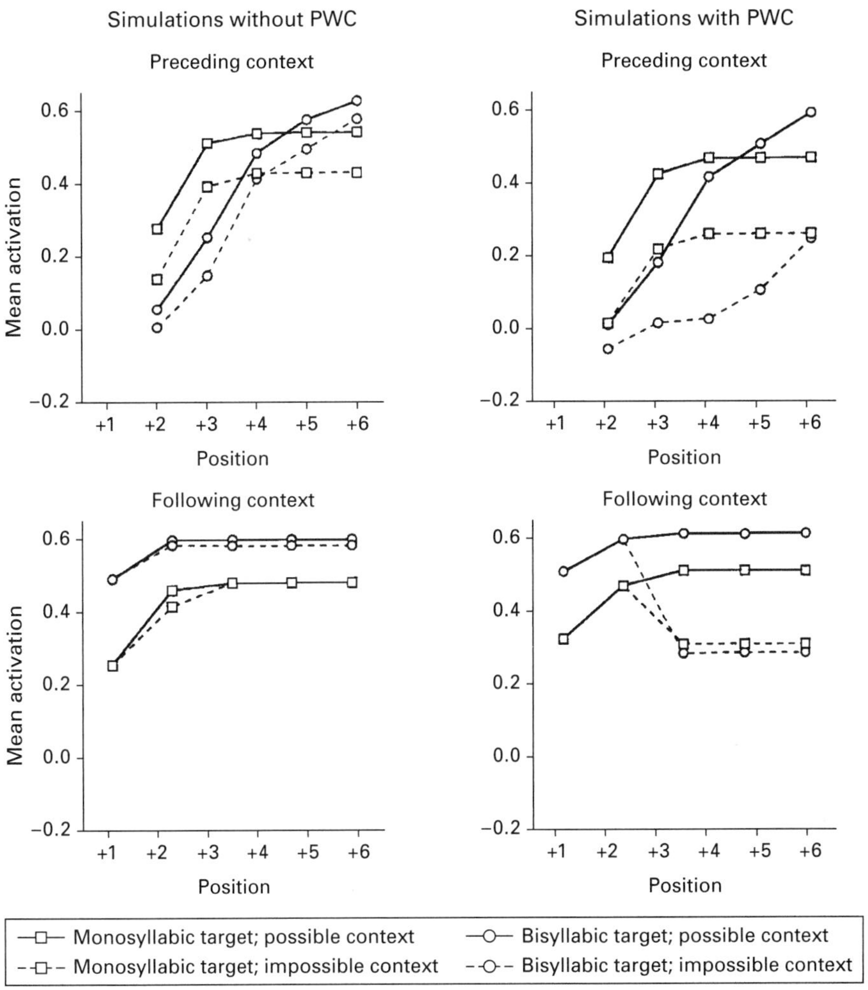

Figure 5.2
Shortlist simulations by Norris et al. (1997). Target words (squares: monosyllabic words, such as *egg*, *sea*; circles: bisyllables, such as *sugar*, *angle*) are embedded above in preceding context, below in following context; solid lines represent syllable context, dotted lines a single consonant. In panels on the left, Shortlist has no PWC mechanism, and the lines for the two contexts run parallel; that is, the model cannot capture the fact that word-spotting was far more difficult with single-consonant than with syllable contexts. On the right, Shortlist with a PWC mechanism successfully models the results in figure 5.1: it is much harder to spot *sea* in *seash* than in *seashub*, *angle* in *langle* than in *nalangle*, and so on.

Expressed in this way, it can be seen that there is a simple way to incorporate language-specific procedures, such as stress-based segmentation, into the PWC implementation. Boundary signals are language specific. For English, a boundary should be hypothesized to occur at the onset of every strong syllable. Not all strong syllables are always word initial, as was described in chapter 4, but English listeners behave as if strong syllables are very likely to be word initial, or in other words, they act on the hypothesis that this is so. Allowing such a hypothesis to control operation of the PWC captures this language-specific behavior. Similar hypotheses would cover all the other language-specific cues to segmentation. Phonotactic constraints are an obvious example; the sequence [pf], for instance, would receive an internal boundary in English because it never occurs within an English syllable. In a probabilistic model the strength of the relevant hypothesis could be varied, allowing this kind of phonotactic constraint to exert a stronger effect on the PWC's operation than, for instance, initial sequence frequency as tested in the experiments of Van der Lugt (2001).

Languages that do not contrast strong versus weak syllables, and where no relationship holds between stress and word boundaries—French and Japanese, among others—would not be usefully served by using strong syllables as boundary signals. Likewise, languages that allow syllables to contain, say, [pf], would be ill served by the English phonotactic sequence rules (thus, as we saw in chapter 4, [pf] is perfectly acceptable within a syllable in standard German—*Kopf*, *Pferd*). Listening in these languages would not involve the same constraints on the PWC as English demands. Instead, there would be other constraints, appropriate for each individual language. The formulation of the PWC itself would thus remain universal; it would always test for the presence of a vowel between an activated word's edge and the nearest such marker. What counts, in this test, as a marker of a likely boundary could be as language specific as necessary.

Consider McQueen's (1998) demonstration of the effects of phonotactic cues to speech segmentation in Dutch. The boundary cues of Dutch, of course, differ from those of English. In Dutch, [dr] is a necessarily boundaryless sequence (it can only be syllable initial), whereas in English this is not the case (words can end with [d] in English; there is a syllable boundary in the [dr] in *bedroom*). The relevant phonotactic rule applies to Dutch and other languages with syllable-final devoicing but not to English. Norris et al.'s (1997) simulation of McQueen's experiments used a Dutch lexicon and this Dutch-based rule. The simulation again mimicked the experimentally observed pattern of results: Because the sequence *dr* in *fidrok* must be syllable initial and cannot contain an internal boundary, the PWC placed a hypothesized-boundary marker before [dr], as a result of which a vowelless residue, [d], was stranded between this marker and the beginning of the embedded word *rok*. Detection of *rok* in *fidrok* was, in consequence, hard.

In the case of stress-based segmentation, procedures that were specifically stress based became unnecessary; the PWC alone, using strong syllables as boundary signals, enabled Shortlist to capture the pattern of results from all the relevant experiments. Cutler and Norris's (1988) finding that *mint* was hard to detect in *mintayf* fell out of the fact that a boundary marker was placed before *tayf*, so that between the end of *mint* (after [t]) and that marker (before [t]) there was just the [t] (i.e., no vowel). With the PWC implemented, Shortlist also no longer detected *jumper* in *jumpev*; *jumper* leaves the vowelless [v] between the word's edge and the clear marker constituted by the silence at the end of the string. *Jump*, in contrast, is easy to detect in *jumpev* because the contextual residue [əv] contains a vowel. That is to say, once it was equipped with the PWC, Shortlist behaved with Cutler and Norris's materials just as the listeners in the experiment had done. This clearly makes it a better model of human listening than any model without the PWC.

Shortlist with the PWC likewise correctly simulated the sensitivity of segmentation to the number of competitors beginning at the segmentation point (e.g., *table*, *tailor*, and *take* as competitors for the [t] of *mint* in *mintayf*; Norris et al. 1995; Vroomen and De Gelder 1995). Competition effects are, in any case, a feature of Shortlist; as soon as the PWC reduced the activation of the embedded word because of the vowelless residue, it could compete less effectively for its [t], and the number of other words competing with it determined how long it took for the listener to realize that the embedded word was, despite the strikes against it, the only real word available. More competitors delayed the realization; fewer competitors allowed it to happen earlier. Figure 5.3 shows simple examples of competition and the PWC in operation. McQueen et al.'s (1994) competition effects (*mess* in *domes*) are shown in the upper panel of the figure; the activation level of *mess* at its final phoneme is higher after [nə] than after [də]. The lower panel in the figure shows how activation of a longer word—*risible*—is also hit by a preceding vowelless residue. Presented in isolation, *risible* plateaus out before its end, because its uniqueness point occurs before the end of the word so no competitors remain. But when the word is preceded by a single consonant, the activation of *risible* never reaches that level even after segments of silence (i.e., the input's end). Further, a vowelless residue that activates a competing word (*prisible*, which activates *prison*) has a stronger effect than one that strongly activates no particular competitor (*trisible*). Norris et al. (1997) describe in detail simulations of experiments in English, using an English lexicon augmented with English-specific boundary cues, and also experiments in Dutch, using a Dutch lexicon augmented with Dutch-specific boundary cues. In both sets of simulations, Shortlist, with the PWC incorporated into its operation, accurately captured the patterns of human listening revealed in the experiments.

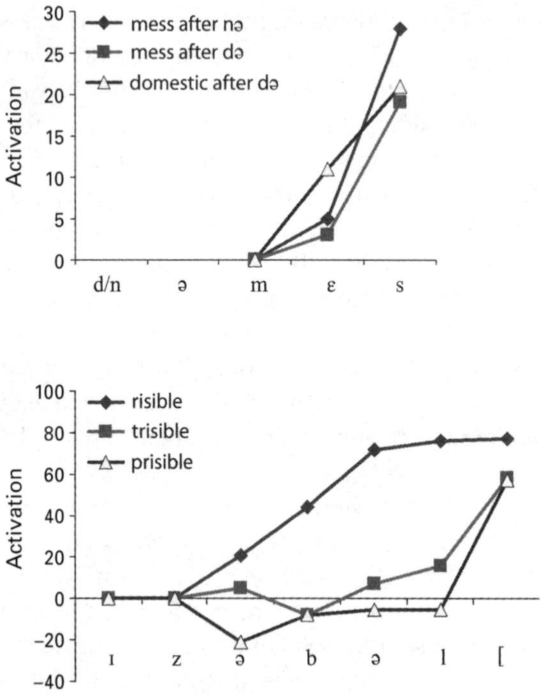

Figure 5.3
Shortlist simulations of activation of (a) *mess* and *domestic* given *domes* and *nemes*, and of (b) *risible* in isolation versus in the two PWC contexts *trisible* (activating no competitor) and *prisible* (activating *prison*). In (a), although all segments in the input are shown, *domestic* only appears in the competition at the third segment (too many other words begin [də]). In (b), the input is shown from the second segment on; again it is only at the third segment that *risible* as candidate starts its rise, even when presented in isolation.

5.3 Is the PWC Universal?

The PWC might appear to be a prime candidate for language-specificity, given that it is a constraint on what may enter into competition as a possible word, and languages differ in the possible forms that they allow words to take. In French, for instance, an open syllable with a short vowel can be a stand-alone word: *pas* 'step' [pa] and *lait* 'milk' [lɛ] have short vowels. But this is not possible in English. In English, there are no open (i.e., vowel final) syllables with short vowels such as [ʌ] in *puff* or [ɛ] in *let*. Thus, [lɛ] and [pʌ] are, in English, not possible words. English requires either a coda after the short vowel—as in *let* or *puff*—or a long vowel if the syllable is open—as in *low* or *pay*. As phonologists describe this, the minimal word in English is bimoraic, whereby the definition of the mora is the same as we encountered in chapter 4. An acceptable English word can be CV+C or CV+V, but it cannot be CV alone if V is short. French does not require bimoraicity of its minimal words—a monomoraic CV is a fine French word.

The patterns of language-specific phonological structure can result in other languages facing yet stricter constraints on what may count as a stand-alone word. The bimoraicity constraint (which in fact is quite common across languages of the world; McCarthy and Prince 1995) applies, for instance, to Sesotho, a Bantu language spoken in Lesotho and South Africa. But Sesotho has very simple syllable structure—no coda consonants and no diphthongs or long vowels. That means that the only way of satisfying the bimoraicity constraint is via more than one syllable, which makes the minimal stand-alone Sesotho word bisyllabic. In Sesotho, *rora* is a word, but *ro* cannot be a word. The stem *ja* 'eat' is itself monosyllabic, but the shortest words that are forms of this verb are the two imperative forms *ja-a* and *eja* 'eat!'.

Sesotho forms an ideal test case for the universality versus language-specificity of the PWC. The syllables *maff*, *shub*, *thig*, and so on are possible words of English, and so they did not violate the PWC in Norris et al.'s (1997) study, but they would not be possible words of Sesotho. Even open syllables, conforming to the constraints on Sesotho syllable structure, would not be possible stand-alone words of Sesotho. Sesotho word recognition could never involve any activated lexical candidates that were monosyllabic, because all the words in the lexicon have at least two syllables. Thus a language-specific PWC for Sesotho would inhibit words leaving anything less than a bisyllabic residue, because a bisyllabic string is the smallest possible word candidate in that language.

Cutler, Demuth, and McQueen (2002) carried out a word-spotting study in Sesotho. At the National University of Lesotho in Roma, Lesotho, undergraduates spotted words like *alafa* 'to prescribe' embedded in nonsense strings such as *halafa*, or *roalafa*, or *hapialafa*. The single consonant context *h* should make detection of the embedded word very hard, in Sesotho as in English. The bisyllabic context *hapi* should be relatively easy—*hapi* is not a word of Sesotho, but it might have been. The interesting case is the monosyllabic context *ro*. This contains a vowel, hence would not violate the PWC in the form implemented in Shortlist by Norris et al. (1997). If the PWC has a universal form whereby any residue with a vowel in it suffices to justify retention of a word candidate in the competition process, and only vowelless residues trigger rejection, then detection of *alafa* should be as easy in *roalafa* as in *hapialafa*. But if the PWC operation is sensitive to language-specific vocabulary structure, then the residue *ro* will count as an impossible Sesotho word and thereby trigger the PWC, with the result that detection of *alafa* will be as hard in *roalafa* as in *halafa*.

The results, shown in figure 5.4, were again crystal clear. In both error rates and response times, the *roalafa* case patterned like the *hapialafa* case. Sesotho listeners

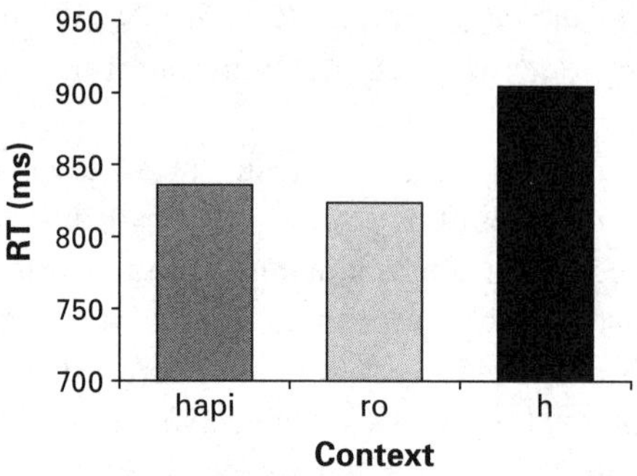

Figure 5.4
Sesotho listeners segment spoken nonwords, finding real words embedded in them, more rapidly if the leftover residue contains a vowel (e.g., *alafa* in *hapialafa* or *roalafa*) than if the residue is a single consonant (*alafa* in *halafa*). Crucially, it makes no difference whether the residue with a vowel could actually be a word in Sesotho (such as *hapi*) or not (such as *ro*). (Word-spotting data from Cutler, Demuth, et al. 2002.)

could detect embedded words in any context that contained a vowel. The *halafa* case was a different story—it was much harder to detect the embedded word when there was only a single consonant as context, just as in Norris et al.'s (1997) study in English. This result strongly suggested that the PWC might be universal—that is, it might operate to constrain lexical activation in exactly the same way whatever the characteristics of the vocabulary from which the activated words originated.

If the PWC is indeed universal, then syllables—any string containing a vowel—should always be good enough residues to let words stay in the competition process, regardless of whether they could be members of a specific vocabulary. This result should appear not only in Sesotho but also in, say, English, which, as we pointed out, does not allow monomoraic syllables such as [lɛ] and [pʌ] to be stand-alone words. Indeed, English listeners proved to detect, say, *canal* just as easily in [vɛ]*canal* as in *voocanal*—and in both cases far more easily than in *scanal*, where detection was really difficult (Norris et al. 2001). The results of this study thus looked just like the Sesotho results in figure 5.4. The fragments [vu] and [vɛ] both contain a vowel, but only the first could be—like *coo*, *do*, *sue*, and *shoe*—an English word. The bimoraicity constraint governing the stand-alone legality of English syllables, as well as the illegality of stand-alone single syllables in Sesotho, apparently does not count in the operation of the PWC—all that counts is whether a vowel is present.

It also did not matter in this study whether the vowel was full or reduced. *Sea* could be detected as easily in *seash*[əb] as in *seashub*—and in both cases far more easily than in *seash*, which made detection really difficult. Thus it also did not matter if the context consisted of a string such as [ʃəb] that could not be a stand-alone open-class word in English, where every stand-alone word has to have at least one full vowel. In all these cases, detection was difficult only when there was no vowel in the context. Viability of the context as a stand-alone word of the language-specific vocabulary was always irrelevant. The PWC appeared to have a universal implementation.

Thus, the sense in which the PWC justifies its name is somewhat abstract. The syllable is a viable residue because, across languages as a whole, the syllable is the smallest string that can be a word. The characteristics of the English vocabulary, or the Sesotho vocabulary, or any other vocabulary, are not at issue. Only the single generalization holds: a possible word should contain a vowel.

5.4 Exploring the PWC across Languages

Of course, this means that the results should hold in all languages—English, Sesotho, and the world's remaining thousands of languages. Thousands of experiments there have not yet been, but support for the PWC across languages has become quite widespread. The effect of the PWC has been observed in several experiments in Dutch, both word-spotting experiments (e.g., McQueen and Cutler 1998) and a cross-modal priming task (Vroomen and De Gelder 1997). In the latter study, priming of associates of words embedded in other words was measured (e.g., lexical decision responses to visual VUIL 'dirt' after spoken *advies* 'advice', which has embedded within it *vies* 'dirty'). Words embedded at the end of other words produced such priming when the preceding portion of the word was a whole syllable (*vies* in *advies*) but not when it was a single consonant (*wijn* 'wine' in *zwijn* 'swine'). This is exactly what the PWC would predict—the activation of *wijn* is reduced very quickly because it leaves an unviable residue, so it cannot activate associated words. Words embedded at the beginning of other words were also examined (although, because this experiment predated the publication of the PWC, there was no reason to compare syllables versus single consonants here). Again, words embedded in other words with only a single consonant residue (e.g., *paar* 'pair' in *paars* 'purple') produced no priming. This Dutch example is analogous to English cases such as *bell* in *belt*.

Interestingly, there was some priming when the word was embedded in a nonsense following context (*vel* 'skin' in *velk*, which is not a word). This is analogous to English cases such as *sea* in *seash*, and is again consistent with the English word-spotting results. In Norris et al.'s (1997) first experiment, with naturally spoken materials, bisyllabic words were not detected significantly more slowly with following consonantal as compared with syllabic context, such as *sugar* in *sugarth* versus *sugarthig*. (The PWC still affected these items: the error rate was significantly higher for the consonantal case, and in the second experiment, with cross-spliced materials, the PWC-induced disadvantage appeared both in response times and errors for all types of embedded word.) Also, in McQueen at al.'s (1994) competition study, described in chapter 3, *sack* was not responded to more slowly in *sackref* (the beginning of *sacrifice*) than in *sackrek* (which should activate no competitor; again, there was a competition effect only in the error rates for these items). From these reaction-time findings, it thus seems that a word's activation can quite often be detected before a following context has a chance to inhibit it.

In McQueen and Cutler's (1998) Dutch word-spotting experiment, nouns (e.g., *lepel* 'spoon') and verbs (e.g., *wonen* 'to live') were significantly harder to spot in consonantal contexts (*blepel, dwonen*) than in one-syllable (*kulepel*) or two-syllable (*dukewonen*) contexts. The effect of the PWC was the same for both nouns and verbs, as well as for both one- and two-syllable contexts. (This experiment was conducted as a control study at the time the Sesotho experiment was being prepared. The Sesotho experiment crucially involved a comparison between one- and two-syllable contexts, and we needed to know that there was no difference between these two types of contexts in other languages in which there would be no reason to predict a difference. Also, our searches of the Sesotho vocabulary had made it clear to us that we would have to use both Sesotho verbs and nouns as target words, so we also wanted to check whether there was likely to be a difference in susceptibility to PWC effects as a function of word class. In this case, a control experiment for a study in one language was carried out in another language. We could think of no reason why nouns and verbs should be recognized differently in Dutch versus Sesotho, and therefore there seemed to be no reason why the control should not be valid. In the event, both nouns and verbs also showed the same PWC effects in the Sesotho study, too.)

German is closely related to English and Dutch, and it is no surprise that just the same PWC effects are seen in German; *Rose* 'rose' is significantly easier to spot in *suckrose* than in *krose*, whereas lexical decisions to the two tokens with their preceding contexts removed do not differ (Hanulíková, Mitterer, and McQueen, 2011). Hanulíková, McQueen, and Mitterer (2010) also observed PWC effects in Slovak, the only Slavic language (as far as we know) in which such segmentation experiments have been conducted; again, the same effect appeared, with words such as *ruka* 'hand' proving easier to detect after a meaningless syllabic context (*dugruka*) than after a context consisting of a meaningless consonant only (*truka*).

Another language in which PWC effects were revealed was Japanese (McQueen, Otake, and Cutler 2001). In this study it was possible to observe a nice demonstration of the interaction of the PWC with language-specific segmentation cues. As the Japanese studies described in chapter 4 established, the boundaries that are relevant for segmentation in that language are mora boundaries. Thus we would expect that the domain of application of the PWC in Japanese would make reference to mora boundaries: rejection of an activated candidate word would occur if acceptance of the word would leave a vowelless residue between the edge of the word and the nearest mora boundary. McQueen et al. tested this prediction in the following way. Vowel-initial Japanese words such as *uni* were preceded by contexts consisting of a whole mora (e.g., *gya*) plus one other phoneme. That phoneme could be a vowel; the resulting *gyaouni* (moraic structure *gya-o-u-ni*) should make detection of *uni* easy. Or the phoneme could be a nonmoraic consonant; detecting *uni* should be extremely hard in *gyabuni* (*gya-bu-ni*, with the *u* of *uni* in the same mora with *b*). Both of these predictions were confirmed. The most interesting case is then the third possibility, in which the added context phoneme is a moraic consonant: *gyaNuni* (*gya-N-u-ni*). In this case there is no residual consonant between the word's edge and a mora boundary, because the word's edge is perfectly aligned with mora boundaries. This consonant context was therefore predicted to be as easy to deal with as the moraic vowel context—and this proved true. Mora boundaries are as relevant for segmentation of Japanese as stress-foot boundaries are for segmentation of English.

The only PWC studies in Chinese languages, it seems, are in Cantonese, in which Yip (2004a, 2004b) had to adapt the word-spotting task a little to address the issue. The problem is that the concept of the word is rather hard to define in Chinese languages, in which syllable-sized morphemes are put together to express concepts. Reasonably, Yip decided to use a syllable-spotting analog of the word-spotting task. As in word-spotting, there were no previously specified targets in his experiments; listeners had to respond when they detected any real (i.e., morphemic) Cantonese syllable in what they heard. Not every possible syllable is a morpheme in the Chinese languages; many syllables (i.e., combinations of legal onsets, rimes, and tones) are not used. Cantonese is actually a good language to test in from this perspective because its syllable structure is more complex than that of some other Chinese languages, such as Mandarin. Thus it has a larger range of potential syllables (including nonsense syllables). Existing syllables such as *kom1* (i.e., onset *k-*, rime *-om*, tone 1) or *peng1* (onset *p-*, rime *-eng*, again tone 1) were presented with preceding or following context that was either a nonexisting syllable such as *khow1* or *ta4*, a single consonant such as [ʃ] or [t], or a single vowel such as [a] or [i] (Yip 2004a). Listeners indeed detected *kom1* more rapidly in *khow1kom1* than with a preceding consonant only, and *peng1* more rapidly in *peng1ta4* than with a following consonant only. A preceding or following vowel alone was almost as easy as a preceding or following nonsense syllable. In other words, the PWC holds for speech recognition in Cantonese, too.

Likewise, detection of real words such as *bok3si6* 'doctor' was harder with preceding or following consonantal contexts than with syllabic or vowel contexts (Yip 2004b). An original manipulation in this latter experiment, again capitalizing on the structure of Cantonese, was a medial context. The example word *boksi* is quite typical of Chinese—two existing syllables together express the concept. When a nonsense context was inserted between the syllables, and listeners had the task of detecting the surrounding word, the results were the same as for preceding or following contexts: single inserted consonants (*bok-n-si*) were hardest, syllables (*bok-khim-si*) easiest, and vowels (*bok-a-si*) somewhere in between.

For French, *lire* 'read' was embedded in, for instance, *calire* or *flire*; it could be detected more rapidly in the former than in the latter, again just as the PWC would predict (Pallier 1997). Here, too, clever manipulations exploited language-specific factors. One concerned phonotactically determined syllable boundaries, which affect word-spotting difficulty in French as in other languages; in Dumay et al.'s (2002) word-spotting study, described in chapter 4, *lac* 'lake' was harder to spot in *zuglac* than in *zunlac* because the [g] combined to form a syllable onset with the [l], but the [n] did not. Pallier also found that detection of words like *usine* 'factory' was harder in *patkusine* (with an obligatory boundary between *t* and *k*) than in *palkusine* (where *palk* is a possible syllable in French—cf. *talc* 'talc', *quelque* 'which'). Though the phonologically determined syllable boundaries in *palkusine* would actually be *pal-ku-sine*, the syllable *palk* proved to be acceptable as a residue preceding *usine*.

As we saw in chapter 4, segmentation of French is based on syllabic rhythm. Thus one might have expected the phonologically determined syllabification to play a role in the operation of the PWC, just as strong syllables in English and mora boundaries in Japanese do. Pallier further pitted the PWC against the language-specific syllable boundaries by comparing detection of *lire* in *flire* versus *caflire*; the syllable boundary rules of French require this sequence to have a boundary before the *f*. If language-specific syllable boundaries control the operation of the PWC in French, then *caflire* would be just like *flire*, and *lire* would be equally difficult to detect in both these sequences. This result would mimic the result from Japanese in which, as we saw before, mora boundaries defined the domain over which the PWC was computed. However, it is not clear that exactly the same should hold for syllable boundaries. The syllable *caf* would be a legal French word (like *gaffe* 'gaffe', for instance). The syllable boundary in *ca-flire* is thus determined not by phonotactic constraints but by more abstract phonological considerations, which may not exercise strong controls on listeners' parsing of speech signals. If so, then one might expect that detection of *lire* would be significantly easier in *caflire* than in *flire*, just as detection of *lire* is significantly easier in *calire* than in *flire*. And that is indeed what was found.

Thus once again, the PWC seemed to be unaffected by language-specific syllable patterning. The French case is actually different from the Japanese case described before. In Japanese, extracting *uni* from *gyabuni* left the residue *gyab*, which was not only not a possible stand-alone word and not a possible syllable, it also could not be parsed into a sequence of morae. In contrast, the French residues were much less problematic. In every case in which embedded words could only be segmented from their contexts by violating French rules of syllabification, the contexts could have formed stand-alone French words. In the sequence *pal-ku-sine*, extracting *usine* leaves *palk*, which as we have seen resembles *talc*. In *ca-flire* extracting *lire* leaves *caf*, which resembles *gaffe*. The same holds for Dumay et al.'s (2002) sequence *zu-glac*: extracting *lac* leaves *zug*, and French contains words like *figue* 'fig', *fougue* 'fury', and *dogue* 'mastiff'. Consider also the Sesotho and English cases in section 5.3. In both Sesotho and English, syllables are viable residues even if they cannot be stand-alone lexical words—*ro* in Sesotho *roalafa*, [ʃəb] in English *seash*[əb], [vɛ] in English [vɛ]*canal*. Given this, it is unsurprising that residues that are indeed potential stand-alone lexical words also prove to be viable.

Figure 5.5 summarizes the results of the various PWC studies across languages. It can be seen that the PWC is a powerful and consistent effect. The consistency points toward a potential universal status for the PWC. Similar findings emerged in English, Dutch, German, French, Slovak, Japanese, Cantonese, and Sesotho. Some of these languages were chosen because their properties allowed the claim of universality to be put to a stringent test. It passed the test in all those languages.

5.5 Vowelless Syllables as a Challenge to the PWC

There is, however, still one stringent test that can be constructed. The universal account of what can and cannot be a word has three parts: (1) The units of lexical viability are the smallest elements with a claim to be stand-alone lexical words; (2) the basic unit of articulation, the syllable, is the smallest possible stand-alone word that languages can construct, so it forms the lowest threshold for lexical viability; and (3) syllables must minimally contain a vowel, so the threshold is operationalized in terms of presence of a vowel.

This simple and attractive account depends, however, on the validity of all its premises. The experiments so far have rigorously tested the first two of these. But what about the third? Do syllables indeed always contain vowels?

In fact, there are many cases in which they do not. Syllables consisting solely of consonants can be created in several ways (see Bell 1978 for an extensive list). For example, there are consonants that are more vowellike than others—the continuant consonants, especially the nasals and liquids, can act as syllable nuclei in many languages. English words such as *kitten* or *people* are phonetically transcribed [kɪtn̩, pipl̩] whereby the mark under the consonant in the unstressed syllables indicates a syllabic consonant. In languages such as Czech and Slovak, continuants can be the nuclei of stressed syllables, too—in each of these languages, the word for *wolf* is *vlk*, pronounced [vl̩k], and the word for *throat* is *krk*, pronounced [kr̩k] (the subscript marks again indicate syllabicity). This is perhaps not so problematic for the PWC if "vowel" in the formulation is understood to include such semivocalic continuants.

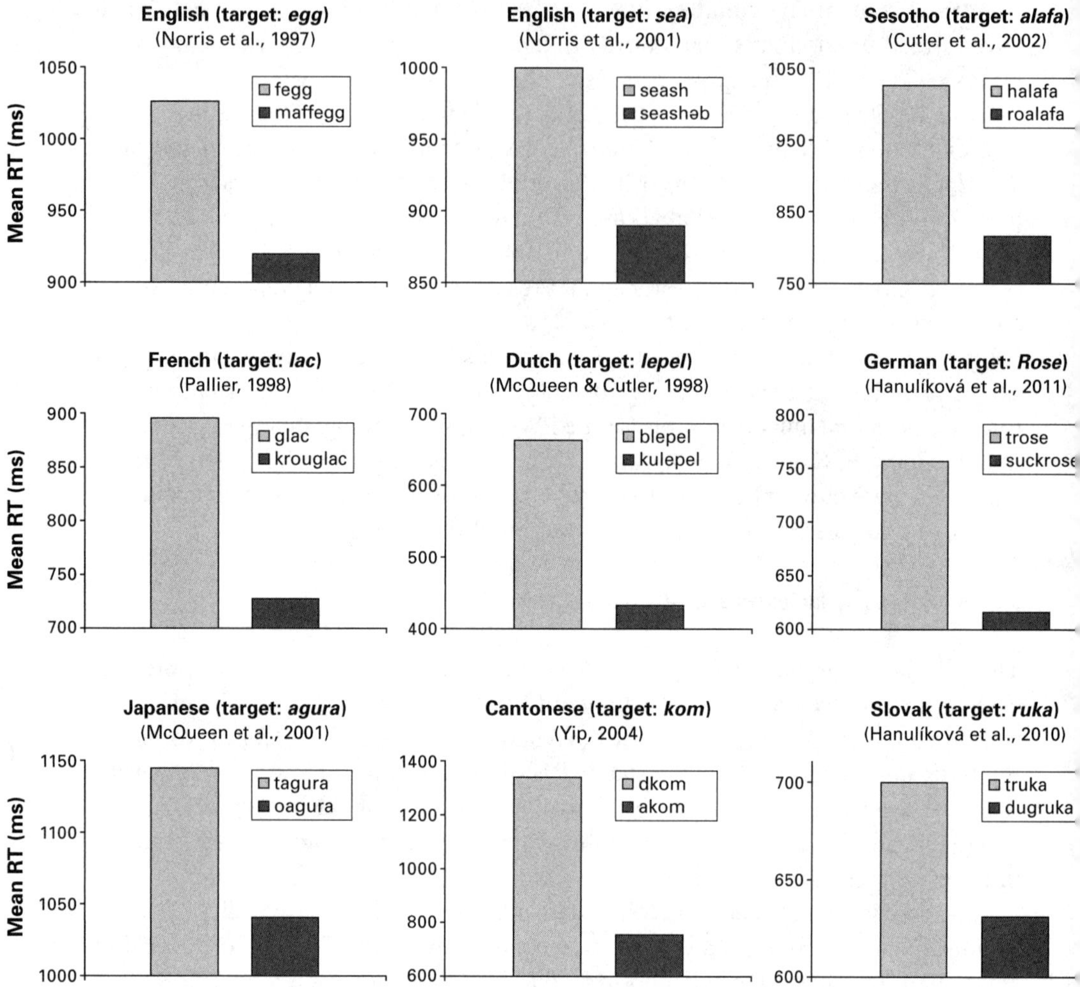

Figure 5.5

The PWC effect in comparable experiments in eight languages. In each case the task is word-spotting (or, in the Cantonese case, a close analogue), and in each case the same target word proves easier to spot when its adjacent context contains a vowel (dark bars) than when it does not (light bars), regardless of the length of the context or the position of the word with respect to the context. The effect is seen in RTs (as here) but also very often in detection accuracy. The effect size varies from around 10 percent of the grand mean (as in the Japanese, Sesotho, and English RT effects here, to as much as 40 or 50 percent (as in the Dutch and Cantonese effects shown here, and in Sesotho accuracy rates). Other types of tasks also produce statistically significant PWC effects. In cross-modal associate priming, embedded words prove to exercise priming only if they do not violate the PWC (e.g., *kort* 'short' was primed by embedded *lang* 'long' in *belang* 'importance' but not in *slang* 'snake'; Vroomen and de Gelder 1997); in infant speech perception tasks, twelve-month-olds detect repeated sequences that do not violate the PWC, but overlook repetitions if the PWC would be violated (e.g., *win* is detected as a repetition in *window* but not in *wind*; Johnson et al. 2003).

Syllables consisting solely of consonants can also be created when vowels that are supposed to be present are deleted. Chapter 6 describes many ways in which real speech is often not what it pretends in citation form to be; and one of these is that in real speech there are sometimes vowelless syllables. An English speaker can say *police* in one utterance, or, speaking more rapidly, *p'lice* on another occasion, for instance. This is far from the worst case of deletion—whole syllables can disappear in casual speech, and polysyllabic words can be represented by only one or two residual phonemes. Vowel deletion, and reduced speech in general, has been studied in experiments that are described in section 6.5 of the following chapter; the effects on word recognition are generally not beneficial.

However, there are also cases where a word's citation pronunciation contains a syllable with no vowel or continuant nucleus. These cases are much more problematic for our understanding of speech recognition and the role of the PWC in it. There are three ways in which this can happen. The first possibility is that vowels that are present in the underlying representation of a word in the speaker's vocabulary can be systematically absent in the word's pronunciation. Thus Portuguese speakers pronounce words such as *descalabro* 'disaster' with a vowelless initial syllable—[dʃkalabro]—and never pronounce them any other way. There is no residual vowel in this pronunciation, and fricatives such as [ʃ] are not as vocalic as liquids and nasals, and hence are less natural candidates for a syllable nucleus. Experiments on such vowelless syllables in Portuguese are described in section 5.5.1.

The second possibility is for the underlying phonology to contain a vowel that is suppressed in certain contexts by phonetic implementation rules. In Japanese, for instance, the high front vowels become devoiced when they appear between two voiceless consonants or between a voiceless consonant and silence (a word edge). Thus in *sukiyaki* the first *u* is devoiced because it is preceded by *s* and followed by *k*, both voiceless. This rule leaves the moraic rhythm unaffected—the vowel is still underlyingly there, but it is not actually pronounced. Pronouncing the vowel is not ruled out, as in hyperarticulated clear speech. This case, too, has been the subject of experiments (see section 5.5.2).

The third way in which vowelless syllables can appear, and the case that is potentially most problematic for a universal account of the PWC, is when the language's phonology allows them in underlying lexical representations. Sometimes this happens with closed-class words only—in Slovak, for example, prepositions can consist of single consonants. Only a few languages have been claimed to allow vowelless syllables even in open-class lexical words. They include some of the languages of the Northwest Pacific, such as Spokane and Bella Coola; some languages of the Caucasus, such as Georgian; and some Semitic languages, such as Tashelhit and Tarifit Berber. The claim is controversial, and some phoneticians argue that there is residual vocalization in nominally vowelless syllables (see, e.g., Coleman 1999 on

Tashelhit Berber). Examples of both variants of this crucial case have also been put to the test in word-spotting experiments, in Slovak and Berber respectively; they are described in sections 5.5.3 and 5.5.4.

5.5.1 Portuguese Utterances with Deleted Vowels

In Portuguese, a contrast of words like *agua* 'water' in single-consonant versus syllabic contexts produced the same PWC effect as in all other languages tested—*agua* was far easier to spot in *mofagua* than in *fagua* (Carvalho, McQueen, and Cutler 2002). The same happened for *belo* 'beauty' preceded by *mos* (a possible syllable with a vowel) versus *des* (a syllable that would always be pronounced without a vowel). Again *belo* was far easier to spot in *mosbelo* than in *desbelo*. This suggests that a syllable without a vowel is no more a viable word candidate in Portuguese than in any of the other languages examined in the studies described earlier.

The advantage of having the explicitly present vowel was attenuated in one case: where the context plus most of the word overlapped with an existing competitor word. This is an indirect competition effect, however. For instance, *calor* 'heat' with preceding context *des* overlaps with the first two syllables of *descalabro*. At first, [dʃkal] activates *descalabro*; this activation brings with it lexical support for the viability of the [dʃ] sequence. Once [kal] arrives, *calor* enters the competition, too, though at that point much less activated than *descalabro*. But the next phonemes to arrive, [ɔr], mismatch *descalabro* and knock it out of the competition, whereas they match *calor* fully; the result is that *calor* is spotted as fast in *descalor* as in *moscalor* with a pronounced vowel.

The curious possibility that a competition effect can apparently be facilitatory depends critically on the presence of the competitor being temporary. Consider McQueen et al.'s (1994) initial demonstration of such competition effects. In their study, sequences such as *domes* gave support both to the embedded word *mess* and to the longer competitor *domestic*; at the offset of *mess*, the longer competitor had actually received more supporting phonemes from the input. Only later incoming silence forced the competition to be resolved in favor of *mess*. In *nemess*, where no competitor was active, *mess* was detected more rapidly. Silence is not direct counterevidence for any lexical candidate, though it may signal the absence of expected matching evidence. But crucially, *mess* is fully embedded in *domestic*, whereas *calor* is not fully embedded in *descalabro* but only overlaps with one syllable of it. When the additional syllable of *calor* arrives, it provides new evidence mismatching *descalabro*, and this acts to remove the competition from *descalabro* entirely, so the activation of *calor* can rise. Thus the presence of the competitor is only temporary; but its presence acted to nullify effects of the preceding nonviable context. The parse of the input provided by lexical information remains available even if the word supporting it is no longer in the competition.

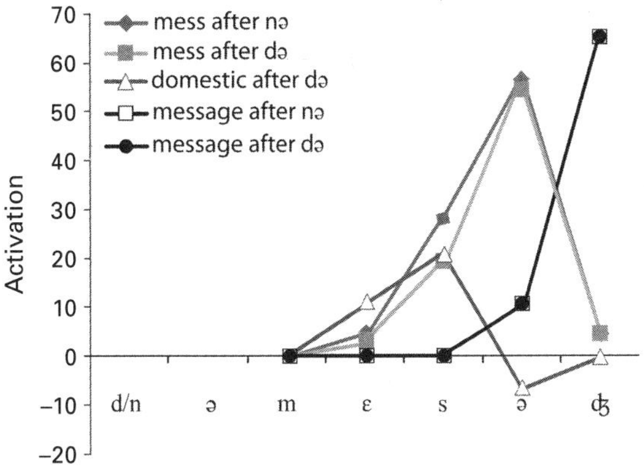

Figure 5.6
Shortlist simulation of activation of *mess* and *domestic* and *message* given *domessage* and *nemessage*. Up to the fifth input phoneme ([s]), the activation levels are as in the upper panel of figure 5.3; but adding the extra syllable *age* changes everything. The incoming vowel mismatches *domestic* and knocks it out of competition; this first enables *mess* to be as strongly activated as in the case with no competitor. But once the whole extra syllable is available, *message* is the clear winner. Moreover, the activation of *message* is identical in *nemessage* and *domessage*; *message* in these contexts stands for *calor* in *moscalor* and *descalor* in the Portuguese study described.

Without a Portuguese implementation of Shortlist, we cannot simulate the disappearance of this competition. But this account predicts that the same effect would result from later incoming mismatch information in any language. Had McQueen et al. added to their study of *mess* in *domess* versus *nemess* the similar case of *message* embedded in *domessage* and *nemessage*, they could have tested this in English. Simulations in English show that *message* would be recognized equally rapidly in each context. Figure 5.6 displays Shortlist simulations that can be compared with those in figure 5.3. Just as in the earlier figure, the activation level of *mess* at its offset is greater given the noncompeting input [nə]*mes*. But as soon as the signal continues and proves to contain the next phoneme of *message* instead of the next phoneme of *domestic*, a drastic effect on the activation of *domestic* results; it is knocked right out of the competition. The activation of *mess* rises steeply as a result (the incoming phoneme in this case being spoken for by activated function words that it matches); but *mess* too is knocked out when the last phoneme of *message*, which mismatches any candidate function words but matches the weakly activated *message*, arrives. Importantly, the activation of *message* is unaffected by the nature of the preceding context syllable that had so strongly affected the activation of *mess*. For longer words, recovery from temporary competition for an initial syllable is complete.

Thus the Portuguese case has proven very informative. Portuguese listeners have lexical representations of *descalabro* that are well matched by input without a vowel in the first syllable. But the existence of these lexical representations does not override the effect of the PWC in Portuguese. Vowelless syllables are no more generally acceptable in the early prelexical processing of a Portuguese listener than of a Dutch, English, or Sesotho listener. Recall that the effect of the PWC on activation is just as strong for long as for short words (Norris et al. 1997). In the Portuguese study, *belo* was hard to recognize after [dʃ] in the same way that *canal* was hard to recognize after [s] in English. Just as the possible structure of stand-alone words (e.g., in the Sesotho or English lexicon) does not affect the form of the PWC in a given language, so language-specific lexical content available to be activated leaves the relevance of the PWC in Portuguese intact.

5.5.2 Japanese Utterances with Devoiced Vowels

As recounted in section 5.4, the PWC is operative in Japanese. But vowel devoicing creates syllables without vowels when the vowels [i] or [u] fall between two voiceless consonants or between a voiceless consonant and silence. How does this devoicing influence word recognition? Suppose that listeners hear words like *gasu* 'gas' in following contexts such as *gasua* (where *gasu* should be easy to spot), *gasub* (where it should be extremely difficult to spot), and *gasuch*; will it matter that the latter is an environment for devoicing, given that it could be a realization of the underlying mora *chi* followed by silence? In fact, the operation of the PWC seemed to be unaffected by the existence of the devoicing rule in Japanese phonology; the *-ch* context proved just as hard as the *-b* context (Cutler, Otake, and McQueen 2009). Research to be described in section 6.4 of the next chapter corroborates this finding by showing that hearing consonants in sequence has the same processing consequences for Japanese listeners as for other listeners.

Longer preceding contexts, like those described in section 5.3, were also tested. Vowel-initial words such as *ase* 'sweat' were presented in contexts like *gyasase* or *gyazuase*, and words beginning with a voiceless consonant (e.g., *hamu* 'ham') occurred in contexts like *nyakuhamu* or *nyaguhamu*. The vowel-initial words (e.g., *ase*) formed a basic PWC test, and once again the context that made viable residues (*gya-zu*) produced easier detection than the context that left one consonant by itself (*gya-s*). The consonant-initial words like *hamu* again tested the devoicing case. Both *nyaku* and *nyagu* end with a CV mora, but the mora *ku-* before *ha-* triggers the devoicing rule, as both [k] and [h] are voiceless. Therefore, *nyakuhamu* should be pronounced [njakhamu]; that is, the context should become *nya-k*, like *gya-s*.

This time the devoicing context did not behave like a single-consonant context, however. Word detection was less accurate than after contexts like *nyagu*, but there was no effect in RTs. This was thus a similar result to the Portuguese one; apparently, the lexical-activation experience of Japanese listeners, like that of Portuguese listeners, included word candidates with devoiced syllables. A direct contrast of the presence versus absence of lexical support, as had been made in the Portuguese study, proved not to be so simple in Japanese, in which every mora is itself a word. However, some items in the experiment had fewer and others had more competitors activated by the end of context plus the initial mora of the embedded word (e.g., *kuha* in *nyakuhamu*). When there were few competitors, the embedded word was much harder to recognize in the devoiced context (e.g., *nyak-*) than in the voiced context (e.g., *nyagu*). But when many candidate words were available, the difference was attenuated and was no longer statistically significant, resembling the results from Portuguese and the English simulations in figure 5.5. Thus in Japanese, too, a viable interpretation of the input on the basis of lexical information appears to keep its force even when the word that motivated it has been knocked out of the competition. But the availability in the lexicon of words allowing vowelless syllables to be interpreted does not affect the PWC's role in prelexical parsing in Japanese; here too, it is a powerful tool for modulation of early lexical activation.

5.5.3 Slovak Utterances Containing Consonants That Might Be Function Words

In Slovak there are four prepositions of which the full form is a single consonant: *k* 'to', *z* 'from', *s* 'with', and *v* 'in'. This situation obviously takes the notion of "vowelless syllable" to its logical extreme; the obstruent [k] is as far from a vowel nucleus as one can get (on a continuum of sonority, vowels are held to be at the most sonorous end, and voiceless obstruents at the least sonorous end). As described in section 5.4, a PWC effect was demonstrated in Slovak by Hanulíková et al. (2010). A word proved to be harder to find if it was appended to a context consisting only of a consonant (such as [t]) than with a syllabic context; *ruka* 'hand' was harder to find in *truka* than in *dugruka*. But in the sequence *gruka*, the initial consonant could be the preposition *k* (it would be voiced to [g] if it occurred before [r], as here). This context was also tested in Hanulíková's experiments to determine whether single-consonant residues such as in *gruka* would function like a nonsyllabic consonant (because, after all, [g] is just an obstruent consonant) or like a viable word candidate (because *g*, *v*, and so forth could be prepositions). The subjects were instructed to detect words at the end of the nonsense strings they heard, so even if they treated *g* or *v* as a word, it would not be the word they responded with. The words were pronounced with initial stress as the citation form of a Slovak word requires, and the embedded word in combination with the preposition never constituted a grammatically acceptable sequence.

As figure 5.7 shows, the results for the [g] and the [t] cases differed: prepositional consonants such as *g* were indeed treated as something other than an ordinary isolated consonant. The words preceded by a single-consonant context that could

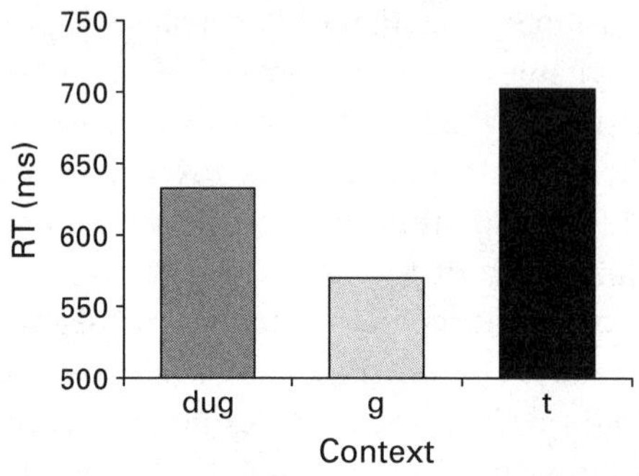

Figure 5.7
Detection of Slovak words such as *ruka* presented in syllable contexts such as *dugruka*, which the PWC predicts to be easy, and single consonant contexts such as *truka*, which it predicts to be hard; both of these predictions were supported. But the context *gruka*, with a single consonant that could be a preposition, was easiest of all. (Results from Hanulíková et al. 2010, experiment 2.)

have been a preposition were not harder to detect than in the syllable context—they were easier to detect, and certainly easier than with the nonprepositional [t]. A further experiment compared single-phoneme contexts that were vowels or consonants (Slovak has single-vowel prepositions, too). Word-spotting was easy with either vowel context (e.g., *e*, which is not a word, or *o*, which is) or with the consonant preposition (e.g., *g*), but again significantly harder with a nonword consonant as context (e.g., *t*).

This is an important result for our understanding of lexical activation and segmentation. It does not mean that the PWC plays no role in Slovak; if that were so, there would be no difference between the syllable context *dug* and the nonprepositional consonant *t*. There was a very significant difference, just as in all the other languages described so far. The Slovak results mean that a language can allow single consonants to be certain kinds of words without the users of the language suffering great processing disadvantage. The constraint can be applied in such a way that certain consonants can be exempted from it. The implications of this will be discussed further in section 5.7.

5.5.4 Berber Utterances with Vowelless Syllables That Might Be Content Words

This difficult case also had to be tackled. Experiments were run in both Tashelhit and Tarifit Berber, with testing conducted partly in Morocco and partly in the Netherlands, which has an extensive immigrant population from the Berber-speaking areas of northern Morocco (El Aissati, McQueen, and Cutler, 2012). Tashelhit and Tarifit allow sequences such as *kb bd* 'pour it for me', *txzntnt* 'and store them', or *tf'tk'ts'tt* 'you sprained it' (see, e.g., Dell and Elmedlaoui 1985, 1988). According to the phonological descriptions, any phoneme from anywhere along the sonority

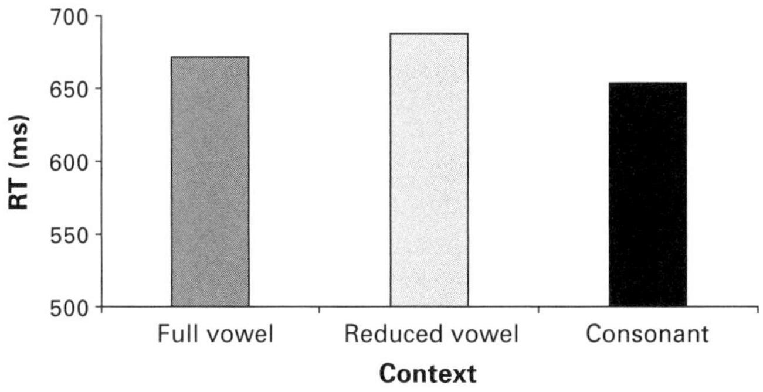

Figure 5.8
Detection of Tarifit Berber words such as *fad* presented in syllable contexts, with either a full or a reduced vowel, or in single-consonant contexts. The PWC predicts the first two contexts to be easier than the third, but the words were spotted with equivalent speed and accuracy in each of the three contexts. The PWC does not apply to listening in Berber, a language in which vowelless content words are allowed. (Results from El Aissati et al., 2012.)

continuum can function as the nucleus of a Berber syllable (so, even a voiceless consonant such as [t] or [k]). It is clear from the English glosses of these two examples that this is not a phenomenon restricted to a small segment of the (closed class) vocabulary, as in the Slovak case. Here a content word could have a pronunciation that happened to be vowelless.

Berber listeners in these experiments heard words such as *fad* 'thirst' or *batata* 'potato' preceded by contexts containing just a consonant (*ghfad*, *qbatata)*, a consonant with schwa (*əghfad*, *əqbatata*), or a consonant with a full vowel (*ughfad*, *aqbatata*). For the first time in all the series of PWC experiments, no trace of a PWC effect was detected. The type of context effectively made no difference to listeners' responses. The results of the Tarifit experiment (for which better dictionary resources allowed better balancing of the materials) are displayed in figure 5.8.

Combined with the Slovak result, this finding is exceptionally informative. It seems that application of the PWC to the segmentation of speech can be fully inhibited in a language where applying it could be counterproductive (in that some real lexical candidates would be ruled out). A constraint that would lower listening efficiency is (wisely) not applied.

5.6 The Origin of the PWC?

A constraint such as the PWC could, of course, be immensely useful in language acquisition, because it would allow infants to sort likely from unlikely candidates for membership of the vocabulary. Consider the following set of utterances that an infant might hear:

(5.1) Who's a pretty girl then? [huzəprɪtigɚlðɛn]
Did you quit eating that? [dɪdjukwɪtitɪŋðæt]
Just a little bitty more? [dʒʌstəlɪtlbɪtimɔr]
Look at the kitty! [lʊkətðəkɪti]

The longest single sequence that occurs in all four of these phonetic strings is [ɪti]. Should the infant hypothesize that this recurring string could be a word? In these sentences, it is not a word, and the PWC will protect the infant from the erroneous lexical hypothesis. In the first string, for instance, assigning lexical status to *itty* would leave the preceding *who's a pr* to be parsed as words. Phoneme sequence constraints, which were more fully described in chapter 4, rule out *pr* in syllable-final position, so that *who's a pr itty* could only be parsed with a syllable boundary before [p] or before [r]; both options would leave a vowelless residue between the beginning of *itty* and the nearest syllable boundary. Clearly, the operation of the PWC in this case would need infants to be sensitive to phonotactic constraints; as we will see in chapter 8, such constraints do play a role in the speech perception of nine-month-olds (Jusczyk, Luce, and Charles-Luce 1994).

A model of initial vocabulary acquisition (Brent and Cartwright 1996) was tested with computational simulations, in which it was given simulated speech input and could either consider any string of the input as a possible word or could consider only potential lexical candidates containing vowels (a PWC-like rule). The model performed more efficiently in the latter case.

Infants' sensitivity to the PWC was also tested directly (Johnson et al. 2003). Twelve-month-olds were familiarized with monosyllabic words like *rest*, *rise*, *may*, or *win* and then heard short texts in which the familiarized words occurred embedded in longer words, with either a vowelless residue (*pressed*, *prize*, *mate*, *wind*) or a residue containing a vowel (*caressed*, *arise*, *mating*, *window*). This task will be fully described in chapter 8; here it is enough to know that it demonstrates the beginnings of segmentation procedures in speech perception. In this kind of experiment, recognition of the familiarized words produces longer listening times for texts containing these words. These infants listened longer to the texts containing the bisyllabic carrier words, which suggested that they could detect the embedded familiarized words in those carriers (thus *rise*, *win* in *arise*, *window*). In contrast, they listened less to texts containing the monosyllabic carriers, which suggested that they had overlooked the familiarized forms in these contexts (i.e., *rise*, *win* in *prize*, *wind*). This substantial difference, shown in figure 5.9, suggests that even for twelve-month-olds, the PWC operates to rule out activation of embedded words such as *rise* in *prize*.

The wide generality of the PWC is consistent with a role in language acquisition. Infants are not programmed to acquire a particular language, but to acquire language, any language. The PWC helps them along the path to an initial vocabulary,

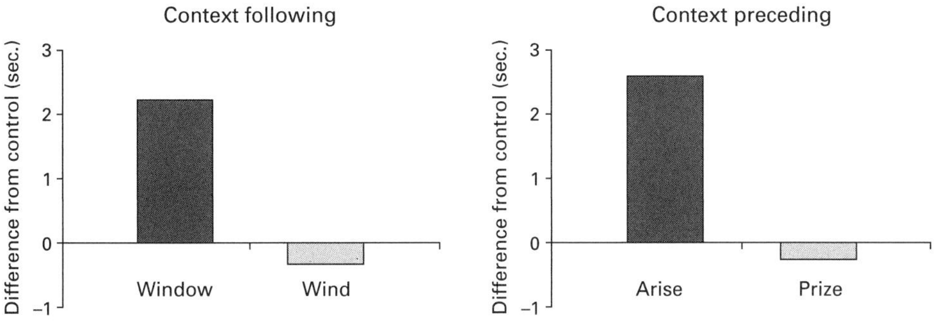

Figure 5.9
Twelve-month-old infants listen longer to texts containing a word that they have heard repeated beforehand. The figure shows the difference in listening time for a text containing a repetition compared with a control text containing nothing that was previously heard. Infants familiarized with the word *win* listen longer to a text containing occurrences of *window*, and infants who had heard *rise* before listen longer to a text containing *arise*, which suggests in each case that the embedded form has been detected. But there is no significant detection of *win* in *wind* or *rise* in *prize*, each of which would violate the PWC. (Data from Johnson et al. 2003.)

constrained in the most general way. In nearly all the vocabularies of the world, the generalization underlying the PWC holds true: there are no vowelless words. And as will become clear in chapter 8, the vowel-consonant difference is apparent in the earliest stages of infants' speech sound acquisition, in the form of earlier attainment of language-specific vowel than consonant representations. The putative source of this asymmetry is the greater salience of vowels (with their steady-state realization) than of consonants (crucially realized as transitional information); this could also lead to the earliest stored word forms being built on a vocalic core.

As we saw, however, using the PWC will not allow full acquisition of the vocabulary of Berber, and it will not help with four prepositions in Slovak. No infant experiments on this issue have yet been conducted in Berber or Slovak. There are two possible ways to interpret the infant finding from English in the light of the data we have. One is that infants try out rough constraints on what can and what cannot be a word based on the acoustic structure of speech, with their preference being motivated by the salience of the acoustic difference between vowel segments on the one hand and consonantal segments on the other. This account would predict that the PWC would be a universal preference, which children acquiring Berber would have to abandon. Given that Slovak speakers do apply the PWC, but just exempt prepositional consonants from it, the learning in their case would require merely adjustment of the scope of the constraint. The alternative account would be that infants try out lexical viability constraints based on the acoustic structure of the particular speech they hear, whereby speech with a high proportion of consonants and frequent vowelless strings would not induce the PWC. This could predict that Berber-acquiring infants might never show evidence of use of the PWC (and hence never need to learn to stop using it). The characteristics of infant-directed speech could perhaps make this latter account rather less plausible, however, so the question will be further discussed in chapter 8.

5.7 Conclusion

The discovery of the PWC has led to new insights into the operation of spoken-word recognition and the competition process it involves. In section 5.2 (and in Norris 2005) the process of discovery of the PWC was described as an interplay between modeling and experiment. This interplay has now continued for some years and has borne valuable fruit: without the prediction of the PWC, the experiments in Sesotho, Slovak, and Berber would never have been undertaken, and the insights that they have provided into the operation of word-recognition processes would likely still be undiscovered. The new insights enable us to appreciate how very efficient these processes are.

5.7.1 The PWC in the Speech Recognition Process

Speech input is interpreted in terms of the possible lexical mappings it offers in a moment-by-moment fashion, constantly updated as additional input renders some candidate words no longer likely, and introduces new candidates. The interpretation process refers not only to the ongoing representations of the input and to the stored representations of known words that the input has called up; it also refers to general criteria against which it tests the probability of each available candidate. The test criteria apply to the candidate word's role in the complete phonological parse of the input—specifically, to any residue entailed by acceptance of the word candidate.

The possibility of there being a residue cannot be totally excluded, because the processor can never be sure that the input is accurate or that the lexicon is complete. In any speech-perception operation, a misperception of the spoken message could have occurred, or the speech may have been distorted by environmental factors, or the speaker may have made a speech error or have pronounced a word differently to the way the listener knows, or the input could simply contain some word unknown to the listener and hence not present in the lexical store. All these eventualities must be allowed for; certainly, if a new word comes along, we want to be able to learn it. Nonetheless, strict criteria can be applied before the processor accepts that one of these cases holds. One criterion is that any residue with a vowel in it is a possible word, but any residue without a vowel in it is unacceptable. In nearly all languages, this criterion will hold for any new addition to the listener's vocabulary.

Figure 5.10 shows Shortlist simulations of how the PWC might help in such a case. Suppose you hear a particular accent for the first time. One of the words you hear is *fourf*, which your mental lexicon has never been required to deal with before. If the context does not present much competition (e.g., *it was my fourf cup of coffee*), it could be quite easy to determine that the intended word was what you know as *fourth*, even though the pronunciation mismatches the representation in your lexicon. But if there is competition (e.g., *we met a fourf time*, which is also compatible with *wee metaphor*), then the PWC is needed. With *fourth* not a candidate because it is mismatched on its final phoneme, the longer word *metaphor* will, without the PWC, become more activated than the shorter words in it. The PWC, however, rules out the parse *wee metaphor time*, with a stranded residue of [f], in favor of a parse involving *we*, *met*, *a*, and *time*, plus a potential novel word *fourf*. This is a viable residue—that is, a potential new word—because it has a vowel in it; so even though the lexicon so far does not contain *fourf*, the best the competition process can do is pass it on unidentified. This is the most desirable outcome in such a case. The listener can then add *fourf* as a new word or name to the lexicon, interpret it as a mispronunciation or accented pronunciation, or decide that it was actually a mishearing.

Thus the PWC helps listeners to identify new words and to rule out any interpretation of speech that is not going to be viable (because it contains an impossible candidate word). The way in which it does so should be similar across languages, given the near-universality of its guiding rule: that a possible word has to contain a vowel. It can be satisfied even by syllables that could not be stand-alone forms in the listener's language, as the Sesotho and English cases in section 5.3 showed, so it is not dependent on lexical experience. In the languages in which embedding statistics have been computed, it accounts for a dramatic reduction in the number of activated competitors. We do not have to worry about whether we are hearing *ring* every time we hear *drink*. The PWC does it for us.

In contrast to the generality across languages of the PWC's form and motivation, the manner in which a residue is demarcated during speech processing is quite language specific. This is because it is influenced by segmentation criteria such as phonotactic and rhythmic structures, which themselves are highly language specific. The PWC thus fits neatly into the activation and competition structure of word recognition; this process consists of a universal basis modulated by language-specific attunement. Experience with the language leads to modulation of how the PWC operates. If the PWC actually lowers efficiency, as would happen in a language where vowelless words are common, it can be never deployed. If it is inappropriate for a few specified consonants, those consonants can be exempted from its operation. If it is helpful, it can be integrated with the other segmentation criteria suggested by the language's phonology to optimize its functioning.

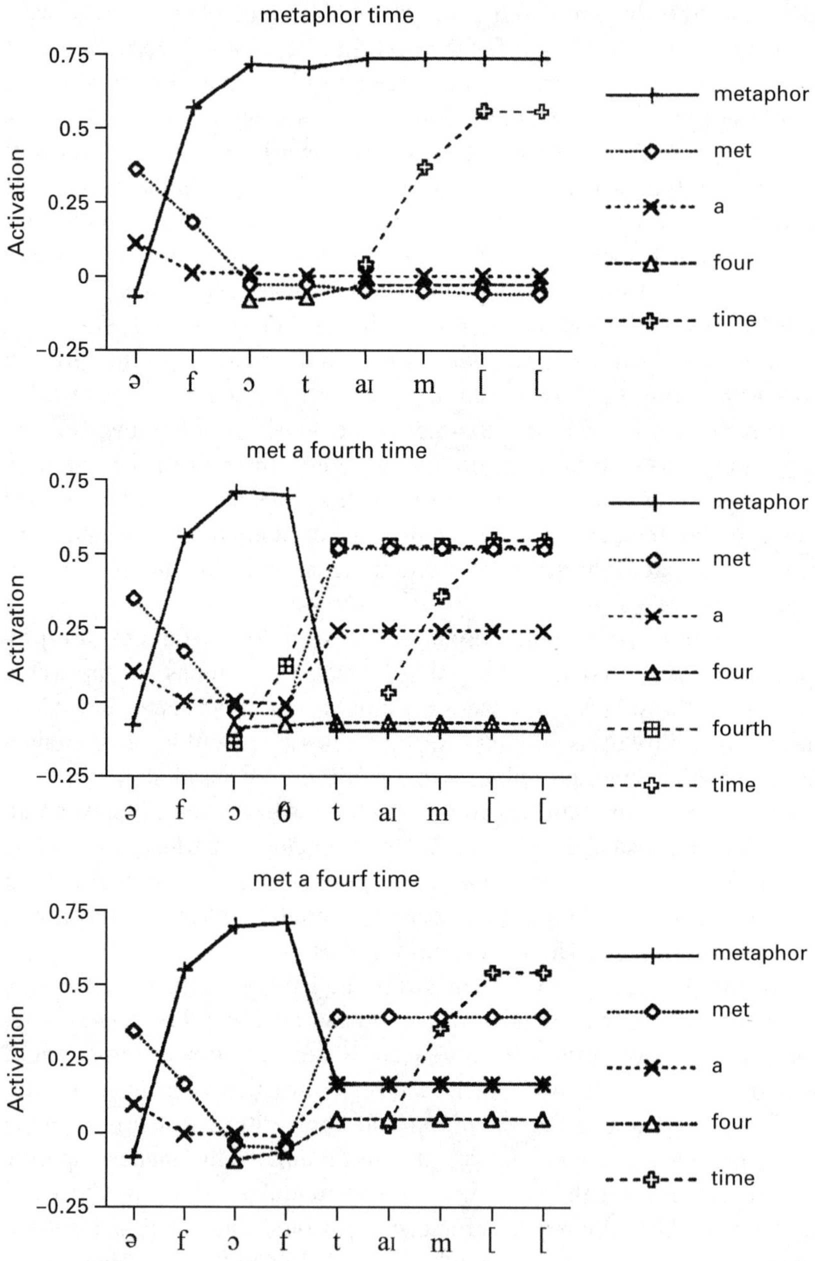
metaphor time
Activation
0.75
0.5
0.25
0
–0.25
ə f ɔ t aɪ m [[
metaphor
met
a
four
time
met a fourth time
Activation
0.75
0.5
0.25
0
–0.25
ə f ɔ θ t aɪ m [[
metaphor
met
a
four
fourth
time
met a fourf time
Activation
0.75
0.5
0.25
0
–0.25
ə f ɔ f t aɪ m [[
metaphor
met
a
four
time

Figure 5.10
Simulations of three similar inputs in Shortlist (including the PWC). In the top panel, the input *metaphor time* yields high activations for the two input words and little activation for competitors; although *met* and *a* are briefly activated, *four* never is because of the stiff competition from *metaphor*. The middle panel input is *met a fourth time*. As above, at the beginning of the utterance *met*, *a*, and *metaphor* compete, but *metaphor* is knocked out by the PWC when the final phoneme of *fourth* arrives. The disappearance of *metaphor* allows *met* and *a* to join *fourth* as final competition winners. In the lower panel, the input is again *met a fourth time* but spoken by someone from, say, East London who pronounces *fourth* as *fourf*. The model does not know this pronunciation. Because *fourf* mismatches the model's representation of *fourth*, and *metaphor* and *four* are competing, *fourth* is not activated. With no PWC, *metaphor* and *time* would be recognized, with [f] left over. But the PWC knocks *metaphor* out of the race because of this leftover [f]. The result is *met* and *time* as winners, with a potential new word *fourf* to be learned or interpreted by the listener. (Simulations by Norris et al. 1997.)

5.7.2 The PWC and the Open and the Closed Classes

The results from the PWC experiments shed light on what constrains lexical activation and competition. Slovak prepositions expressing location and direction, although they are members of a closed class, must be recognized as independent elements and presumably have independent lexical entries; recall the results of Haveman (1997; see chapter 3), which suggested that all closed-class words are lexically represented. The importance of the Slovak case is that four of these prepositions are single consonants. They can occur adjacent to other words; that is, in a position where the activation of those adjacent words would be reduced if a vowelless residue of the input was left over. But they do not cause the adjacent words' activation to be reduced. Note that this is not due to an eventual syntactic or semantic interpretation of the preposition+word combination. The combinations in the Slovak experiments were always ungrammatical (they made no sense, and inflections were wrong; e.g., *ruka* would always be inflected differently after *g* or any other preposition). In any case, the application of the PWC occurs well before activated words are accepted and interpreted; it constrains, as we saw, initial activation. Thus the modification of the PWC's operation in Slovak involves the speech segments in question, not the lexical entries they stand for. Experience with understanding their language has led the word-recognition system of Slovak listeners to adapt itself such that the PWC no longer applies across the board but exempts the small set of consonants that convey these prepositions.

One may then ask whether there might be other individual speech segments that systematically stand for lexical elements and can constrain the PWC's operation in the same way. As described in chapter 3, the model of morphological processing proposed by Baayen et al. (1997, 2003) holds that all elements in complex words (stems, full forms, and affixes) are lexically represented. This would mean that bound morphemes (such as affixes that code person, tense, or number) have independent representations even though they can never stand alone. Experiments in English have used [s] as a single-consonant context (because it can easily be placed before many word onsets to form strings such as *s-canal*), but [s] could also be a morpheme signaling person (*I walk*, *he walks*), tense (*walked*, *walks*), or number (*cat*, *cats*). Post hoc comparisons revealed no difference in the effects of phoneme contexts that could or could not be morphemes (e.g., *s-canal* versus *f-lapel*, in Norris et al. 2001); this suggests that these affixes may not play a fully independent role in speech processing.

An explicit test of this question was tried in Dutch, with for instance [t] and [s], which could both be morphological suffixes in Dutch, compared to [k] and [f], which could not (Mauth 2002). Words like *deur* 'door' or *geur* 'aroma' were followed by syllabic contexts (*deurtach*, *geurfum*), by consonant contexts (*deurk*, *geurf*), or by consonant contexts that could be suffixes (*deurt*, *geurs;* note that just as in the Slovak case these combinations were not at all meaningful). The findings were not fully conclusive; although the words were somewhat easier to recognize before "morphological" than "nonmorphological" consonants, syllables made recognition even easier. This pattern could reflect an independent role for inflectional morphemes that is nevertheless weaker than that of closed-class words such as prepositions. Further, [s] and [t] here are suffixes, as is the English [s]; we do not know what role might be played by prefixes with a comparable function. Prefixed tense or number markers are uncommon across languages (Hawkins and Gilligan 1988), but where they occur they might have as strong an effect as the Slovak prepositions. This has not yet been tested in any such language.

5.7.3 The PWC and the Segmentation Process

A prefix-suffix difference is plausible because the influence of the PWC is certainly strongest at the left edge of words. This is necessarily so because the PWC is a component of segmentation; as first noted in chapter 3, segmentation effects are always greater at word onset than at word offset (Cutler and Norris 1988; McQueen et al. 1994; Content, Kearns, et al. 2001). In the first report of PWC effects (Norris et al. 1997), effects on response time were always observed for words preceded by contexts (*fegg*, *maffegg*) but not always for words followed by contexts (*sugarth*, *sugarthig*). This makes sense in the framework of a process model in which speech input is interpreted in the temporal order in which it appears. In the rather artificial situation of the word-spotting task, with the segmentation operation reduced to a single appendage to a presented word, it is obvious that preceding contexts can exercise strong effects on a word's recognition, whereas following contexts may be less effective, especially if the word is highly probable (e.g., if it is a common word, or if it is long and becomes unique before its end).

Although the PWC's operation is closely entwined with the boundary effects that operate in segmentation, when phonotactic effects and PWC effects are directly compared, they prove to be independent, as a word-spotting study with words like *rok* 'skirt' in Dutch or *rack* in English showed (McQueen and Cutler, unpublished data). In both languages, there was a phonotactic effect (e.g., *rack* was easier to find in *bamrack*, with an obligatory boundary at the word's left edge, than in *bafrack*, with no such boundary) and a PWC effect (e.g., *rack* was easier to find in *bafrack* than in *frack*), but these were separate effects: *rack* was also significantly easier to find in *bamrack* than in *mrack*. Even though the phonotactic boundary is present in *mrack*, the PWC test is applied to the residue in this preceding-context case. Likewise, the PWC operates in tandem with allophonic cues to word boundaries (such as the aspiration that is present when English [t] occurs syllable initially but usually absent when [t] is syllable final; these effects are discussed in chapter 6). When tested together, the PWC and syllable-boundary effects were found to operate additively; segmentation was easier when both PWC and allophonic cues were present than when only one of the two was available (Newman, Sawusch, and Wunnenberg 2011).

5.7.4 The PWC: Two Further Avenues to Explore

Despite the efforts to explore the PWC in as many crucial phonological patterns as possible, there are still open issues that need experimental attention. For example, agglutinative languages such as Turkish have a very rich morphology that produces a large number of possible forms, few of which have high frequency. The nature of lexical representations for spoken-language processing in such languages is well worth exploring. If there are few stand-alone forms with high prior probability, it might seem as if only the much smaller units that make them up should be activated, but as Hankamer (1989) argues, simple sequential identification of such units would not necessarily yield the correct interpretation, because the form they take can depend on the context they appear in. Of course, some of the combinatorial units in such languages can surface as single consonants, so that again the PWC might serve as a tool for examining them.

The near-universality of the PWC also raises the issue of transfer in nonnative processing. Hanulíková et al.'s (2011) studies of the PWC in perception of Slovak and German included studies of German as a second language (L2) perceived by Slovak learners. These learners were able to adapt to German in some respects (for example, they could easily cope with the fact that the German stress placement was inappropriate for Slovak). However, there was a residual effect of their native constraints in their L2 processing; the consonantal context [k] (a possible Slovak preposition) led to faster RT for German words than the context [t] (not a word in Slovak). This was just like the Slovak native results but, of course, unlike the results from native speakers of German, who showed no [k]-[t] difference. The simultaneous effects of L2 and L1 constraints is reminiscent of Weber and Cutler's (2006) findings that Germans with good English could draw on both German and English phonotactic constraints (see chapter 4); the L1 transfer presumably reflects activation of L1 lexical representations even by L2 input, in accord with other demonstrations of this phenomenon (Spivey and Marian 1999; Weber and Cutler 2004; see chapters 9 and 10 for further discussion). It is an open question, though, whether transfer could occur in the other direction; could German learners of Slovak rapidly adapt their processing to include the possibility of single-consonant lexical entries? The PWC could prove to be a useful tool for examining L2 listening across languages that differ in the structure of lexical representations.

5.7.5 The PWC and the Vowel-Consonant Difference

As observed at the outset of this chapter, the PWC provides yet another demonstration that vowels and consonants behave differently in perceptual processing. It is not the only vowel-consonant difference that occurs across many languages; as described in chapter 1, listeners also know that vowels are more affected by context than consonants, and hence are more likely to be misidentified, so that consonants are more reliable than vowels as cues to lexical identity. Word-reconstruction studies showed parallel effects of this across differing languages. But vowel-consonant asymmetries linked to lexical access also raise questions about universality. In some languages, particularly Semitic languages such as Hebrew, the contribution of vowels and consonants to lexical structure differs far more than in Western European languages. Lexical representations in Hebrew are constructed around a triconsonantal root, with different vowels inserted into the root to form different derivational forms (*write*, *writes*, *wrote*, *writer*, *letter* all have the same root *ktb* in Hebrew, for example). Here the consonants are clearly primary in the lexical representations; thus the relative contribution of vowels and consonants in lexical recognition in such languages must be worth exploring. The PWC claim is that possible words necessarily contain vowels but not consonants. How exactly does the PWC constrain segmentation in a language where the vowels and consonants play different lexical roles?

The account of the PWC that has been sketched here involves abstract representations: the notions of vowel and consonant, and their role in syllables and words. Although the PWC operates early in lexical processing, it does not concern the initial acoustic input (PWC violations have no effect on listeners' classification of auditory input as "speech" versus "not speech," for instance: Berent, Balaban, and Vaknin-Nusbaum 2011.) Decisions based on the properties of nonlexical residues would be hard to implement without describing them in general, abstract terms; certainly an abstract statement is the only way to model the results succinctly. The account therefore assumes that abstract representations can play a role in the process of listening to speech. In this it joins all the other vowel-consonant proposals referred to in chapter 1, of course. The role of abstraction will be dealt with further in chapter 12.

The PWC has revealed an interplay of language-specific and universal constraints on the processes of activation and competition. From the listener's point of view, of course, this is no interplay at all; it is just maximal efficiency in the exploitation of all relevant information.

6 What Is Spoken Language Like? Part 2: The Fine Structure of Speech

The phonetic realization of sounds and words is variable; part of this variability is extralinguistic, including that due to differences between speakers and speaking situations, but part of it is linguistic. Thus sounds may be inserted, deleted, reduced, or effectively transformed into other sounds under the influence of adjacent phonetic context. Much of this linguistic variability is predictable, and much of it is, furthermore, language specific. Listeners need to compensate for the sources of variability in order to interpret speech signals. The research reviewed in this chapter shows that although many such contextual effects temporarily reduce the intelligibility of speech, listeners do indeed compensate effectively for them, and where appropriate this compensation is language specific. The availability of large corpora of natural speech has greatly expanded our knowledge of the fine detail of phonetic realization in speech and of how listeners deal with it.

With a limited repertoire of articulatory gestures, speakers contrast tens of thousands of separate lexical entries. The resulting task demands of listening to speech were documented in chapter 2. Speech processing involves automatic simultaneous activation of multiple candidate words that are fully or partly consistent with the input, as well as competition between these candidates, with the competition modulated by probabilistically weighted segmentation and selection procedures. As laid out in chapters 3–5, these seem to be the processes that best meet the task demands.

But the whole story of what speech is like does not finish there. For good reason, psycholinguists often act as if it does. In order to build testable models of the listening process, and to construct the experiments that distinguish between the models' predictions within a reasonable timeframe, they necessarily ignore much of the complexity involved. This kind of simplification and abstraction occurs in all fields in which the aim is to understand the general laws underlying highly complex processes. But all modelers of spoken-word recognition are painfully aware that speech is, in fact, far more variable than their models to date can capture.

Such variability is the topic of this chapter. It is a chapter that deals with an exciting subfield of language comprehension in which new discoveries are arriving at a great rate. How listeners cope with the variability in natural speech signals was viewed as a very hard issue to get an experimental handle on—and indeed it is; but new techniques, and the availability of large corpora of spontaneous speech, have permitted huge advances in our knowledge. The variability in speech has many sources and can range from largely predictable (e.g., effects of phonetic context and utterance structure) to quite unpredictable (e.g., some situation- and speaker-related factors), with many intermediate steps. There is now a formidable body of research on how listeners cope with all types of variability.

6.1 Predictable and Unpredictable Variation

Speech signals are subject to fairly unpredictable variation in every speaking and listening situation. This can be due to the nature of the communication channel (telephone systems attenuate the speech signal, for instance), the possible presence of background noise or other environmental sources of distortion such as echo, or interference to the listener's reception capabilities (e.g., from earplugs, a helmet, or an ear infection). All talker-related variation also falls in this category. Talkers differ in vocal tract size and shape; some are naturally endowed with articulators that produce clear speech, some naturally speak less clearly (Bond and Moore 1994). Further, anyone can suffer articulatory obstruction—from a cold in the nose, or from food in the mouth, or from injury—that can cause temporary or lasting effects on speech.

Such extralinguistic sources of variation naturally complicate the listener's task. They will do so across all languages, even though by accident the type of variation may differ across languages (e.g., there are, or were, languages never spoken over the telephone). Listening in noise has been intensively studied. We know that speakers adapt their speech in noisy conditions to make it easier for listeners, such as by adjusting amplitude ("Lombard speech"; Lane and Tranel 1971) and even formant structure (Van Summers et al. 1988). Listener adaptation to variation between talkers has also been well researched; there will be more on the effects of this variation, and how listeners cope with it, in chapter 11.

This chapter focuses on variability that is linguistic (and thus necessarily subject to language-specific realization). In every language, phonological rules govern the behavior of phonetic segments in sequence (see Goldsmith 1995). These rules permit segments to change character in certain contexts. Further, there are phonetic alterations that result from the effects that segments, or the articulatory movements that produce them, exercise on one another when they occur in sequence (see Hardcastle and Hewlett 1999).

Consider the spectrograms in figure 6.1. The utterance in all of them is the same: *The old postman knocked on the door*. Also the speaker is the same: a female speaker of English from the American Midwest. The speaker's natural utterance is

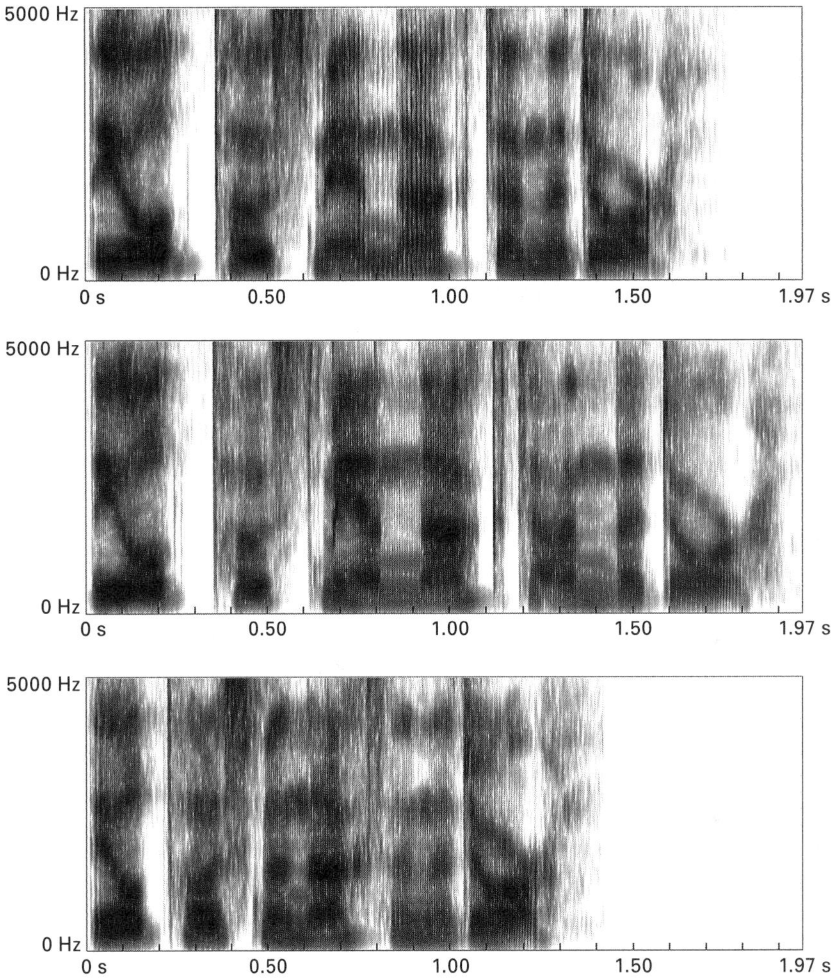

Figure 6.1
Spectrograms of the utterance *The old postman knocked on the door*, spoken by a female speaker of American English at a normal rate (a), carefully (b), and quickly and casually (c). The timeline is explicitly labeled every half second, but intermediate marks are placed at each 100 milliseconds along the signal. See the text for further explanation of the spectrographic representations.

in the top panel (a). The two other versions of the same utterance differ in speech style; in (b), the speaker was being careful, and in (c), she spoke casually. The three are obviously different in length, and there are many other clear differences. Look at the first gap in the spectrograms, for instance: it is the closure for the [p] on the stressed first syllable of *postman*. In (c) it is reduced to almost nothing (speech energy continues through the closure, in the upper regions of the spectrogram). No burst for the [d] of *old* is visible in (c), although one can be seen at 0.25 on the timeline of (b), and a residual burst at 0.275 in (a). (In both (a) and (c), the last sound of *old* in fact sounds more like a [b] than a [d], as a result of influence from the following [p].) At the end of *knocked* the three versions also differ; there are separate closures for the final [k] and [t] at 1.05 to 1.2 in (b), almost separate closures, with a bit of goodwill, at 1.0 to 1.1 in (a), but no closure at all in (c), where the relevant portion, about 0.75 to 0.85, shows continuous high-frequency energy (i.e., it has become a fricative).

More striking, though, are the points in which the three utterances do not differ. None of them show a closure (like the ones at the end of *knocked*) for the [t] in *postman*. In (b) a burst is visible at about 0.62, but in all utterances the high-frequency energy for the [s] continues to the [m]—the relevant portion of (a) is just after 0.6, and of (c) around 0.475. And in all of them the initial segment of the second *the*, after *on*, is not the fricative [ð] but a nasal continuation of the [n] before it, as can be seen by the continuing energy through the lowest bands of the spectrogram: at 1.2 to 1.3 in (a), at 1.35 to 1.45 in (b), and at 0.88 to 0.95 in (c). In other words, alterations in what might be the expected form of the utterance occur in all speech styles. Casual speech has more of them, but they occur in normal and even in careful speech, too. Despite the alternations, however, the utterance is perfectly intelligible in all three versions.

In earlier chapters, lexical activation in listening was shown to be a process of continuous adjustment, as incoming information favors or mismatches potential candidate words. As the example in figure 6.1 shows, the incoming information can vary due to the application of natural linguistic rules. The alteration of the final segment of *old* before *postman* is due to regressive assimilation, and the alteration of the first segment of *the* after *on* is due to progressive assimilation; section 6.2 deals with recent research on the effects of assimilation in word recognition. Deletion processes, such as the loss of the [t] in *postman*, are discussed in section 6.5. The other later sections of this chapter deal with different types of segment insertion (sections 6.3 and 6.4) and of variation in segment form (sections 6.6 and 6.7), and with perception of spontaneous speech exhibiting many such effects at once (section 6.8). Multiple processes thus affect the segmental realization of a given word, which results in substantial variability in the form of utterances. In the sections to come, we will see that listeners can usefully exploit the effects of many of these processes.

Listeners also know a lot about what happens to phonemes in sequence, and make use of this information, too. In chapter 3, we saw how some distant effects of one phoneme on another can be used to modulate word activation—coarticulatory information in the vowel signals the place of articulation of a following stop, for example, so that *job* and *jog* are distinct before the end of the vowel. Syllable-final stop voicing is also detectable from syllable-initial cues—for example, listeners can begin to distinguish *lack* from *lag* even during the [l], because the syllable, including the [l], tends to be longer with a voiced than with a voiceless coda (Hawkins and Nguyen 2003, 2004).

Listeners adjust their categorization decisions even to compensate for coarticulation between adjacent phonemes in speech. Two such effects with fricatives were documented by Mann and Repp (1980, 1981). In English, the lips are rounded for [ʃ] but spread for [s]; they are also rounded for vowels such as [u] and spread for vowels such as [i]. Yet there are no constraints that say that lip formation has to match in fricative-vowel sequences; *sue* and *she* are perfectly good English words, easily as good as (the matching) *shoe* and *see*. Lip position for a vowel can be anticipated during a preceding fricative. This can result, for example, in a rounded rather than spread lip position for [s] in *sue*, with a consequent partial alteration of the acoustic cues to fricative identity. Listeners will allow for this; so the same fricative with a little rounding will be judged as [s] if followed by [u], but as [ʃ] if followed by [i].

Likewise, the articulation of alveolar stops ([t,d]) versus velar stops ([g,k]) can be affected by the place of articulation of a preceding fricative. This underlies Mann and Repp's second listener compensation effect. Lip rounding, as for [ʃ], effectively lengthens the vocal tract; conversely, the vocal tract is shortened by lip spreading, as for [s]. Such effects can then persist into following sounds. As it happens, vocal tract length determines the distribution of energy in the release burst of the stop consonants, and this energy distribution is one of the strongest cues to whether a stop has alveolar or velar place of articulation. The result is thus that after [s] (e.g., in *boss cop*), a [k] comes to partially resemble a [t], whereas after [ʃ] (e.g., in *wash tub*), a [t] comes to partially resemble a [k]. Compensation occurs for these shifts, too, in that an ambiguous stop, that would get around 50 percent [t], 50 percent [k] decisions in a neutral context, tends to be judged more often as [t] after [ʃ], but as [k] after [s].

In Dutch, no such extensive labial difference holds between [s] and [ʃ]; the acoustic cues differentiating the two consonants principally result from tongue position. But a following rounded versus unrounded vowel still affects lip position, so that it shifts these acoustic cues, too. Listeners again take the shift into account in fricative categorizations, in that the roundedness of the following vowel influences their judgment of an ambiguous-frequency fricative (Smits 2001; Mitterer 2006). This is an example of how highly similar sounds can be articulated somewhat differently across languages, causing coarticulation patterns between pairs of similar sounds to be language specific. Even with similar articulations, the extent of coarticulation can vary across languages (Manuel 1999). Exactly the same input can be interpreted differently by listeners from different languages, as a function of their language-specific expectations about degree of coarticulation—for instance, about the different ways in which vowels influence each other across an intervening consonant in English, on the one hand, versus the Bantu language Shona, on the other (Beddor, Harnsberger, and Lindemann 2002).

So, listeners take adjacent information into account in interpreting sounds, and adjacent sounds influence each other in a language-specific way. This suggests that listeners learn the coarticulation patterns of their native language and incorporate them into prelexical processing. We saw that phonotactic sequence constraints are language specific and so must be learned, yet they clearly affect the probability weightings drawn on in prelexical segmentation. In the same way, coarticulation probabilities can be learned and built into prelexical probabilities. Indeed, both Smits (2001) and Mitterer (2006) argued for such an account of their findings, and Mitterer further showed that listener compensation in the prevocalic fricatives is affected by lip rounding (or spreading) visible on a video even when there are no accompanying acoustic consequences. The reason why listeners should adjust their prelexical processing to account for their experience of coarticulation patterns is, obviously, that the information can be effectively used in modulating lexical activation; listeners' ability to do this has already been documented in chapter 3, and there is more on the theoretical implications in chapter 12.

More global characteristics of the speech context, such as rate of speech, may also influence decision criteria for segments. Many distinctive cues to segment identity are durational, and any durational effect will take on different absolute values on different occasions, including as a function of rate of speech. Listeners adjust for this; their decisions about whether a syllable is [ba] or [wa] are affected by the duration of the vowel (Miller and Liberman 1979). The [b]-[w] distinction is cued by duration of the formant transition into a following vowel; [b] is an abrupt transition, [w] a more gradual one. Figure 6.2 gives a schematic depiction of this comparison: A syllable beginning with a constant ambiguous consonant is more likely to be categorized as [wa] if the vowel is short (because the transition sounds, in contrast, relatively long), but as [ba] with a long vowel (where the transition sounds, in contrast, rather short). Although the listeners in Miller and Liberman's study heard isolated CV syllables, they apparently inferred a rate of speech from the later-occurring vowel duration and adjusted their decisions about the consonant accordingly.

All of these compensatory adjustments, and more, allow listeners to reach the effectively phonemic decisions that underlie their decisions about words. As emphasized in earlier chapters, the phoneme categorizations are rarely explicit, and fea-

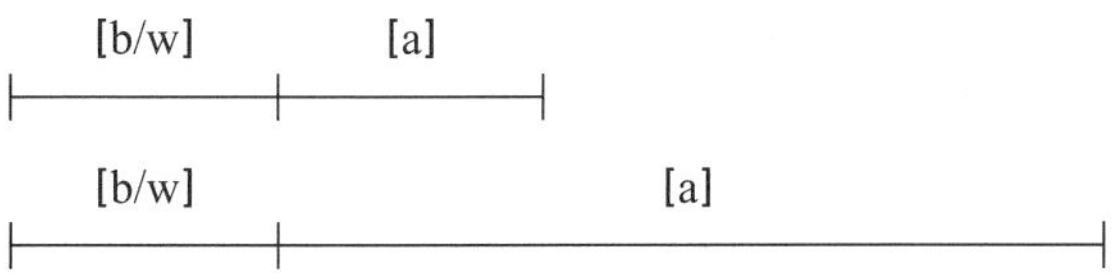

Figure 6.2
A schematic depiction of two CV syllables with the same consonantal portion (ambiguous between [b] and [w]) and a vowel that is either short or long. With a short vowel, the consonant comprises 50 percent of the syllable and so sounds very long. With a long vowel, the consonant makes up only 20 percent of the syllable and sounds short. The "long" or "short" impressions influence the listener's categorization of the consonant.

tural components of such segmental decisions even less so; all are means to a lexical end. Recall that single-feature versus multi-feature mismatches between two competing words reduce activation to an equivalent extent (Soto-Faraco et al. 2001), which suggests that what matters most to listeners is sorting out the lexical candidates. The usefulness of a feature depends entirely on its informativeness for distinguishing words. For example, the feature voicing in fricative phonemes is not very useful in distinguishing words in Dutch, because few minimal pairs contrast on this feature alone. As a result, Dutch listeners often simply overlook incorrect voicing in fricatives, whereas they do not overlook incorrect voicing in stops (Ernestus and Mak 2004). In German, speakers can allow a preceding voiceless sound (such as a word ending in [t]) to cause devoicing in a following sound (such as a word beginning with [v] or [z]); however, they do so less often for word-initial [v] than [z] (Kuzla, Cho, and Ernestus 2007). This is because devoicing the phoneme [v] could cause confusion with words beginning [f], but devoicing [z] could not cause confusion with word-initial [s] because no German words begin with [s]. Listeners are also more sensitive to the voicing realization of [v]-[f] than of [z]-[s] (Kuzla, Ernestus, and Mitterer 2010; and see further discussion in chapter 7). It is possible to construct situations in which listeners make use of the sensitivity they definitely possess to distinguish fine gradients of the goodness with which segments are realized (see section 6.6), but in general this sensitivity is exploited where, and only where, it helps to distinguish between candidate words.

The following sections thus describe research on the effects of segmental variability in word recognition. We recognize words, as described, by distinguishing them from other words, and this amounts to drawing phonemic distinctions. The variability of phonemic segments has not been easy to capture in models of word recognition, however, because the models cannot be formulated in terms of infinite variability. Usually, what is modeled is an idealized form presumably underlying the variable realizations; thus the question that has driven most work is the relation between underlying form and actually realized form. Not all of the recent work in this area has been carried out in English, but most of it has involved European languages. The inevitable result is little research attention to phenomena that do not occur in the languages spoken by the majority of psycholinguists. The roles in word activation of sandhi phenomena in tone languages, of word-initial consonant mutations, as occurs in Welsh, of vowel and consonant harmony phenomena, and of many other phonological accommodations are all awaiting the future attention of word-recognition researchers.

6.2 Segmental Assimilation Phenomena

In Japanese, the word for 'three' is *san*. Pronounced in isolation, the syllable *san* ends with a uvular nasal [saN]. In 'third', *san* becomes [sam]; that is, it ends with a bilabial nasal: *samban*. In 'March' (i.e., third month), *san* becomes [saŋ], and its final nasal is velar: *sangatsu*. And in 'thirty', *san* ends with a dental nasal [san]: *sanju*. Why the difference? Obviously, it depends on the following sound—Japanese requires place of articulation to be homogeneous in these sound sequences. So, if the second sound in a sequence is a labial like [b], then the final sound of *san* changes to a labial too; if the second is a velar like [g], then the final sound of *san* changes to a velar too, and so on. This homogeneity of place of articulation in consonant sequences in Japanese is obligatory. It is part of the phonology and is applied to loan forms as well as to native forms (thus *dansu paatii*, borrowed from English 'dance party', has a short form: *dan* from *dansu* plus *pa* from *paatii*, which together make not *danpa* but *dampa*). Like the effects in *old postman* and *on the* in figure 6.1, this is an assimilation.

Clearly, there is room for language-specificity in effects that are part of any language's phonology. And indeed, assimilation occurs across languages, but it varies greatly in the form it takes. Table 6.1 shows some examples of the range of possibilities. Assimilation effects vary in which segments they affect; they vary in which features are involved, they vary in direction, and they vary in whether they are obligatory.

The Japanese place assimilation case may seem quite familiar, because many languages show this effect. But consider the Hungarian assimilation of [lr] sequences to [rr], *balrol* 'from the left' becoming *barrol*; that type of assimilation is rarer across languages, so perhaps it is unfamiliar to most readers. Assimilation of place is likewise more common across languages than assimilation of voice or manner, but both of these also occur—voicing can be affected in English, too (many speakers produce less voicing of [z] at the end of *rose* in *rose petal* than in *Rose Bowl*). These cases are all influences in the same direction: later segments influencing earlier; this is called regressive assimilation. But earlier segments can also affect later ones, which is known as progressive assimilation. Examples of progressive effects in English

Table 6.1
Assimilation: Some examples. Assimilation phenomena are widespread; they include, for instance, the pronunciation of the English plural or verb suffixes that change form depending on the final segment of the stem that they are appended to. Assimilation affects adjacent segments, so that in a word like *cabin*, the assimilation of [n] to [m], matching to [b], can occur if and only if the second syllable is pronounced as a syllabic nasal rather than as a vowel+consonant.

Direction	Feature	Example Word	Canonical Segment Sequence	Output Segment Sequence
Regressive (an earlier segment changes its form to match a following one)	Place of articulation	*rainbow* (English)	[nb]	[mb]
	Voicing	*kaasboer* (Dutch)	[sb]	[zb]
Progressive (a later segment changes its form to match a preceding one)	Place of articulation	*cabin* (English)	[bn]	[bm]
	Voicing	*cabs* (English)	[bs]	[bz]

include the pronunciation of suffixes after stems ending with a voiced or a voiceless sound; the plural *s* in *backs* is pronounced [s] but in *bags* it is [z], and the past-tense inflection in *mopped* is pronounced [t] whereas in *mobbed* it is [d]. The end of the word influences the form of the following sound.

And even where assimilation effects appear similar in two languages, they can be obligatory in one but optional in the other. Consider the English word *sun*, which can be pronounced like *sum* in *sunbathing* or like *sung* in *sunglasses*. This is an effect of assimilation of place of articulation exactly analogous to the one we saw in Japanese. But the difference is that in English the effect is not obligatory; it is perfectly acceptable to pronounce *sun* as *sun* (i.e., without assimilation), in *sunglasses* or *sunbathing*. Such violation of the rule is not acceptable in Japanese.

When assimilation is optional, the likelihood of it being applied varies with lexical frequency; speakers tend to set a lower priority on clear phonemic realizations in words that they say often and listeners hear often (as discussed in chapter 2), and assimilation is one of the rules affected by this. In a large corpus of spoken Dutch, voice assimilation was significantly more likely in words of higher frequency (Ernestus et al. 2006). There are wide differences between individuals in the likelihood of assimilation and the degree to which it is applied (Ellis and Hardcastle 2002).

The variability in assimilation across languages means that exactly the same sequence of sounds can undergo assimilation in two languages but in quite different ways. For example, a sequence of [t] followed by [b] produces optional regressive assimilation in English, Dutch, and French, but not in the same way. In English, place of articulation is matched: [tb] becomes [pb], for instance in *ratbag*, which can then sound like *rapbag*. In Dutch or French, it is likely to be the voicing that is matched: [tb] can turn to [db], as in Dutch *houtblok* 'block of wood' or French *lutte brutale* 'brutal fight'. Listeners behave accordingly; speakers of English detect place-assimilated words more reliably than voice-assimilated words, whereas speakers of French show the inverse pattern (Darcy, Peperkamp, and Dupoux 2007).

6.2.1 Perception of Phonemes That Have Undergone Regressive Assimilation

The most well-studied form of assimilation is regressive assimilation of place, as in *green book* [grimbʊk] or *freight bearer* [frepbɛ:rə]. How listeners deal with this kind of alteration of underlying form has been examined in several studies with the phoneme detection task. So when English and Dutch listeners heard strings like *green book* (or the same in Dutch: *groen boekje*), detection of a target [n] in such strings occurred almost as often when the [n] was realized as [m] as when it was realized as [n] (Koster 1987). However, the detection time was slower for the assimilated form. The same result emerged from phoneme-detection studies in English looking at, for instance, detection of [t] in strings like *freight bearer* realized with or without assimilation (Gaskell and Marslen-Wilson 1998). Regressive assimilation of voice in French produces the same pattern for detection of [b] in *absurde*, where its pronunciation is [p] (Hallé, Chéreau, and Segui 2000).

Assimilated forms are responded to more slowly when they produce another, competing word (e.g., *sum* in *sun bright* with assimilation of the [n] to [m]) than when they do not (e.g., *chaim*, which is not an English word, in *chain broke*; Koster 1987). All these results suggest that listeners recover the underlying form of assimilated consonants very quickly, even though the surface phonetic form activates unwanted words with which it is compatible. The restoration of underlying form only happens in the case of a viable assimilation; "assimilated" forms are not restored if they lack the correct context to assimilate to. Gaskell and Marslen-Wilson found, for instance, that listeners did not respond to an underlying [t] in strings such as *freighp carrier*, where there is no following bilabial to account for the realization of the final [t] of *freight* as [p]. Thus it is not the case that listeners do not care about precise phonetic realization, so that any phoneme differing by one feature from the target will be able to activate the target to some extent; it is really the case that viable assimilations are restored and unviable "assimilations" are not. The latter are treated like random substitutions.

Given this ability of listeners to restore assimilated phonemes, it is reasonable to ask whether assimilations provide listeners with useful cues about what is coming up. In other words, does hearing a regressive assimilated form (such as [m] in *green book*) speed processing of the following phoneme that is the source of the assimilated feature? It might be said that the source phoneme has already been partly processed, in that one of its features has been signaled in the preceding sound.

Phoneme detection has been used to ask this question, too. And the answer has turned out to be no. Detection of [g] in *girl* is no faster if *sweet girl* is pronounced with [k] rather than [t] (Koster 1987); detection of [b] in *bearer* is no faster if *freight bearer* is pronounced with [p] rather than [t] (Gaskell and Marslen-Wilson 1998); detection of [b] in *buns* is no faster if *ten buns* is pronounced with [m] rather than [n] (Gow 2001). The same result appears for regressive voice as for place assimilation: detection of [b] in *boer* is no faster if *kaasboer* 'cheesemonger' is pronounced with [z] rather than [s] (Kuijpers, Donselaar, and Cutler 2002).

When assimilation is obligatory, violations delay phoneme detection; in Japanese, detection of [b] in *tombo* is faster than in *tongbo*, but this is perhaps less likely to be facilitation from the legal assimilation (i.e., the [m] predicting the upcoming [b]) than disruption of processing by an illegal sequence (i.e., after [ŋ] a [b] does not match the expectation of a velar, so reaction when it does occur is slow). Other nonviable cases involving optional assimilations also slow processing in English, where detection of [b] is slowed in the illegal sequence *freighk bearer* (Gaskell and Marslen-Wilson 1998) and the equally illegal *teng buns* (Gow 2001), and in Dutch, where detection of [k] is slowed in the illegal nonword *femk* (Weber 2001), and detection of [p] likewise in the illegal *kaazplank* (for *kaasplank* 'cheeseboard'; Kuijpers et al. 2002).

Thus regressive assimilation does not assist listeners' processing in any language, whether it is optional or obligatory. It is an effect for which listeners have to compensate. However, they do this with ease and they do it very early in processing. If listeners have to categorize utterances of *garden* versus *gardem*, they are extremely accurate when the words are presented in isolation or in a no-assimilation context such as *garden chair*, but they are much less accurate in an assimilation context such as *garden bench*. In the latter case, they mistakenly categorize [m] as [n] in many cases (Mitterer and Blomert 2003). In gating tasks with French voice-assimilation words, listeners accurately report [p] until the next segment appears and warrants a switch to [b] responses (Hallé et al. 2000). All these findings are not simply effects of lexical bias, because they can appear with nonwords (Hallé et al. 2000), and they can appear even when listeners are not paying attention to the categorization task, as was established with what is called a passive listening oddball paradigm (where electrophysiological responses in the brain are recorded as a repeating stimulus is presented, with an occasional different sound interspersed). With 15 percent unviable *tuimstoel* against a background of 85 percent *tuinstoel* 'garden chair', there was a robust reaction to the change—known as a mismatch negativity or MMN—but with 15 percent viable *tuimbank* against a background of 85 percent *tuinbank* 'garden bench', no significant response to the change appeared (Mitterer and Blomert

2003). Thus listeners noticed the change if there was no assimilation context for it, but it passed unnoticed if it was a justified assimilation. Mitterer and Blomert concluded that assimilation is compensated for early in perceptual processing.

6.2.2 Perception of Phonemes That Have Undergone Progressive Assimilation

Regressive assimilation warrants positive expectations. The listener hears the effect of the later phoneme before hearing that phoneme itself, and can expect the second to follow. The listener can use this effect to undo with great ease the effect on the assimilated phoneme; but there is no consequent speeding of processing of the second, or trigger, phoneme. That phoneme must be there (because it has exercised an advance effect); but although the existence of this positive expectation is clear from the fact that it can be violated (leading to an inhibitory effect on processing), it does not actively help the listener.

The case of progressive assimilation is rather different. What the listener first hears in such a case is the triggering phoneme itself; its effect continues into the following segment. Assimilation may not be complete; in the case of the progressive consonant assimilation in [nð] sequences illustrated in *on the* in figure 6.1, Manuel et al. (1992) report that slight articulatory differences remained (they measured English pairs such as *win those* versus *win nose*). However, from the listener's point of view, progressive effects principally act to rule out certain potential continuations. Thus after a high front vowel in German the velar fricative [x] cannot occur. The phoneme [x] can follow a back vowel (*hoch*, *lachen*) but is illegal after a front vowel; in *ich*, *echt*, or *Bücher*, the fricative is not velar but the palatal [ç]. In other words, progressive assimilation sets up the opposite kind of expectation from regressive assimilation. The expectations are negative—many continuations are possible, but a few are impossible. If a listener hears [lɪ] in German then many continuations may follow—*Linguist*, *Linnen*, *Littfasssäule*, including fricatives as in *lispeln*, *Lift*, and *Licht*. Just one fricative, [x], is ruled out. The listener has no idea with such sequences whether an assimilation environment is about to arise; only a very narrow negative expectation can be derived from the occurrence of a high front vowel. Anything can follow such a vowel—except [x].

What effect does violation of such a narrow negative expectation have? A phoneme detection experiment with German and Dutch listeners hearing Dutch nonwords such as *hicht* and *hacht* provided the answer (Weber 2001). In German, the fricative in *hicht* would have to be pronounced [ç]. But Dutch does not have the restriction that applies in German after high front vowels; in Dutch, the fricative in both *hicht* and *hacht* is pronounced [x]. For the Dutch listeners, detection of [x] in the two types of nonword was equally easy. For the German listeners, there was a difference. The [x] in *hicht* was detected significantly more rapidly—yes, more rapidly—than the [x] in *hacht*. Violation of the negative expectation—in other words, the appearance of the one sound that should not have been there—produced what in visual perception is called a "novel pop-out" effect: facilitation due to perceptual salience. The novelty of the sequence of a front vowel followed by [x] made it stand out. Violations of progressive assimilation did not facilitate responses if the sequences they created could occur somehow in German, such as across word boundaries (Weber 2002); only novelty induced pop-out. The novelty is relative to the listeners' experience, so of course it is language specific.

6.2.3 Obligatory versus Optional Assimilation in Word Recognition

Assimilation that is obligatory and assimilation that is optional induce different (i.e., language specific) expectations. Consider how speakers of Japanese and of Dutch would blend two names such as *Ranga* and *Serupa*, or *Mengkerk* and *Trabeek* (when asked to imagine names of townships formed by the fusion of two existing villages.) The Japanese should perceive the nasals (e.g., in *Ranga* or *Kumba*) as unmarked for place of articulation and might therefore produce assimilated forms in the blends. *Ranga* plus *Serupa* should then become *Ram-pa* and not *Rang-pa*, *Kumba* plus *Soroki* should become *Kung-ki* and not *Kum-ki*. Dutch, on the other hand, should perceive nasals as marked for place of articulation, which would lead them to produce unassimilated forms in the blends. *Mengkerk* and *Trabeek* should become *Meng-beek* and not *Mem-beek*; *Stambest* and *Sliekoop* should become *Stam-koop* and not *Stang-koop*. Both of these expected patterns indeed appear (Cutler and Otake 1998). The Japanese in this study even produced assimilated forms of the Dutch names as well (*Mem-beek*, *Stang-koop*), whereas the Dutch preferred unassimilated forms of the Japanese blends (*Rang-pa*, *Kum-ki*).

What does this combination of universal and language-specific processing effects mean for the recognition of words containing assimilated phonemes? In line with the phoneme detection results already described, cross-modal priming shows that legal regressive assimilation has no adverse effects on word recognition at all, and no facilitatory effects either. In *Sandra would only eat lean bacon*, *lean* facilitates the recognition of visually presented LEAN exactly as much whether it is pronounced *lean* or *leam* (Gaskell and Marslen-Wilson 1996; Gow 2001). Similarly, in the German sentence *Kannst du das Wort mal sagen* 'Can you just say the word', *Wort* facilitates recognition of visually presented WORT to the same extent whether it is pronounced with a final [t] or assimilated [p] (Coenen, Zwitserlood, and Bölte 2001). In French, there is equivalent priming of visual NOTE by *une note grave* 'a low tone', with the [t] assimilated in voice to the following sound, and by *une note salée* 'an expensive bill', with voiceless [t] (Snoeren, Segui, and Hallé 2008). Listeners are sensitive to assimilation patterns in their language; thus, voicing assimilation in French affects voiceless sounds such as [t] more strongly than the voiced counterparts such as [d], and Snoeren et al.'s listeners showed correspondingly greater facilitation with the [t]-final words such as *note* than with [d]-final words such as *guide* 'guide'. Notwithstanding this, assimilations that listeners have never heard but that preserve the homogeneity of place of articulation can be easy for them to process (Gow 2001); thus assimilation usually alters coronals rather than velars or bilabials, but if a bilabial is altered before a following coronal (e.g., *glum day* pronounced *glun day*), the result is easy to process, as evidenced by priming of GLUM after this *glun* (Gow 2001).

The assimilated words did not facilitate target recognition when they were presented in isolation without their sentence context (Coenen et al. 2001; Snoeren et al. 2008), and they did not facilitate target recognition when they were presented in an illegal context (i.e., with heterogeneous place of articulation such as *eat leam gammon*; Gaskell and Marslen-Wilson 1996). Progressive assimilations also did not facilitate recognition (Coenen et al. 2001); but in this case, the progressive assimilation applied across a word boundary (like the regressive assimilation), so that the assimilation affected a word-initial sound (e.g., *ich hab' Not* 'I'm in need' pronounced as *ich hab' Mot*). It is unclear whether priming in the case of an alteration of the final sound, but no priming in the case of alteration of an initial sound, should be ascribed to a difference between regressive and progressive assimilation or to a difference in relative importance of initial versus final sounds for word activation and recognition; further studies could sort this out.

Assimilation can result in a form that corresponds to, or resembles, a competing word, as we saw before. "Resembles" is the better term, it seems. In speakers' productions of phrases such as *She tried to get the right berries* (with the [t] of *right* assimilated to the following bilabial) versus *She tried to get the ripe berries*, the assimilated [t] is not exactly like a real [p]—it has spectral characteristics consistent with both labial and coronal place of articulation (Gow and Hussami 1999). Articulatory measures (e.g., of where the tongue hits the palate in [t] of *sweet girl*) likewise show that assimilation of the English place feature is rarely complete (Wright and Kerswill 1989). The French voice assimilation process, too, results in intermediate segmental realizations, especially with voiceless (more assimilable) segments, and particularly where a full assimilation would create another word (*rade sale* 'dirty harbor' could be heard as *rate sale* 'dirty spleen'; Snoeren, Hallé, and Segui 2006). In cross-modal priming studies of word recognition in cases of this latter type, *right* pronounced as *right* facilitated recognition of RIGHT (but not RIPE); *ripe* pronounced as *ripe* facilitated recognition of RIPE (but not RIGHT); and crucially, *right* pronounced with assimilation to a following bilabial facilitated only recognition of RIGHT (i.e., not RIPE; Gow 2002).

Note that these effects are specific to optional assimilations. They suggest that speakers' articulatory targets are unassimilated citation forms. When assimilation is optional, listeners not only undo the assimilation and reach the intended word but they can use fine phonetic detail in the signal to sort out competition between, say, *right* and *ripe* in favor of the intended word. When assimilation is obligatory, potential confusions such as *right* versus *ripe berries* cannot occur, and there will be no incomplete articulations, but listeners do not need to restore citation forms anyway.

6.2.4 Universal and Language Specific in the Processing of Assimilation

The perception of assimilated forms thus draws on early processing and experience-induced expectations. This makes it both in part universal and yet subject to language-specific expectations. Listeners use fine phonetic structure to resolve potential ambiguities arising from assimilation, and they draw on their language-specific knowledge to do so. Judgments about assimilation depend on lexical frequency (Ernestus et al. 2006), so they depend on reference to a particular language's vocabulary. But are the perceptual mechanisms involved in this processing also tailored by language-specific experience, or are they essentially universal?

The way to decide this issue is to present listeners with unfamiliar forms from a language they do not know. Perception of viable and unviable contexts for assimilation of liquid sounds ([l,r]) in Hungarian was compared across Hungarian and Dutch listeners, for example. Recall that this Hungarian assimilation converts [l] preceding [r] into [r]. Such liquid assimilation does not occur in Dutch, and the alveolar trill by which [r] is realized in Hungarian is also not very common as a realization of [r] in Dutch; so the Dutch listeners would not be familiar with the Hungarian forms at all. Mitterer, Csépe, Honbolygo, et al. (2006) mimicked the Hungarian assimilation in the Dutch words *knalrood* 'bright red' (which would provide a viable context for this assimilation) and *knalblauw* 'bright blue', which would not; both *knarrood* and *knarblauw* are nonwords in Dutch, although the former would be a legally assimilated phonetic sequence in Hungarian. In an MMN experiment with these stimuli, with the same design as used with Dutch place assimilation (see section 6.2.1), the Dutch listeners with no experience of this assimilation showed a significantly smaller MMN response when the deviant was viable (*knarrood* against a background of *knalrood*) than when it was unviable (*knarblauw* against a background of *knalblauw*). Also, both Dutch and Hungarian listeners showed a smaller MMN for the naturally occurring (viable) assimilation of Hungarian *balrol* 'from the left' than for the nonviable assimilation in *balnal* 'to the left'.

Similarly, the effect on phoneme detection of a viable Hungarian regressive voice assimilation was essentially the same for nonnative listeners with no Hungarian as for Hungarian listeners (Gow and Im 2004). Also, the effect of a Korean place assimilation was essentially the same for Korean listeners and listeners with no knowledge of Korean. In these experiments, the phoneme detection target was not the assimilated segment but the one after it (i.e., the assimilation source—the [b] in *ten buns*, to take an example from Gow's English work). The results are indeed similar to those of Gow (2001), which suggests that a simple detection task with the same materials is performed similarly by listeners across languages.

It is clear from all these results that first language (L1) phonology does not fully determine listeners' sensitivity to assimilation viability; basic auditory processes play a role. In categorical identification, a *balnal-barnal* continuum gives the same results as a *bal-bar* continuum (i.e., the following context has no effect on the [l]-[r] decisions), but a *balrol-barrol* continuum does not (Mitterer, Csépe, and Blomert 2006); here, both Hungarian and Dutch listeners make more *bal* judgments across the whole continuum (so the following [r] influences the [l]-[r] decisions). Thus all listeners judge the viable assimilation context to be more likely to contain the underlying [l], even though some of them had had no experience with such assimilation. Further, discrimination of stimuli on the unviable continuum was significantly better than the viable stimuli.

Mitterer Csépe, and Blomert's explanation was similar to Repp's (1983, 1988) account of compensation for coarticulation. When two similar consonants occur in succession, Repp proposed, the contrast between them is perceptually enhanced—the small differences between them are more salient to the listener than the large similarities. The existence of this auditory effect in listening to speech allows speakers in turn to exploit it by producing assimilations that lead to acoustically similar sequences. Sequences of two closely similar segments require less articulatory effort than sequences of two highly distinct segments (because the articulators have less far to travel between two close than between two more distant configurations), so assimilation benefits the speaker, too, which makes it even more likely. These effects are universal, even though which of the many potential assimilation phenomena occur in a language, and how they are realized, is highly language specific.

6.3 Liaison between Words

In French, some sounds are only pronounced in certain contexts. Thus, although *petit* 'little' is written with a final *t* in the masculine *il est petit*, it is pronounced [pəti] (whereas the feminine *elle est petite* sounds the *t*: [pətit]). If *petit* is followed by a word beginning with a vowel, however, the *t* resurfaces: *petit agneau* 'little lamb' [pətitanjo]. The *t* is called a liaison consonant because it emerges between two vowels, linking one to the other. Clearly, this effect does not occur in all languages (even with words that are just the same as in French; pronouncing English *secret* without any form of final [t] would be odd, and unacceptable, and pronouncing the written *s* of *debris* in *get the debris out* would be just as weird).

Liaison, in which a final sound is pronounced only when the following word begins with a vowel, raises interesting questions because of the way it interacts with segmentation of the speech stream. As we saw in chapter 4, French listeners draw on syllabic segmentation. But the circumstances that induce liaison make for an input in which syllable boundaries do not correspond to word boundaries. In the string *généreux Italien* 'generous Italian', for example, the fourth syllable will be *zi*—the liaison consonant at the end of the adjective surfaces to become the onset of the first syllable corresponding to the noun. In fact, the same resyllabification can happen with word-final consonants that are always pronounced—thus in *virtuose Italien* 'virtuous Italian' the fourth syllable will also be *zi*. The added problem with liaison is that, obviously, the final consonant of a word like *genereux* cannot be necessary for its recognition, given that in many contexts it is silent.

How words with such added syllable onsets are dealt with was examined in cross-modal priming, with visually presented ITALIEN preceded by spoken liaison strings such as *généreux Italien*, by other resyllabified strings such as *virtuose Italien*, or by undistorted strings such as *chapeau italien* 'Italian hat' (Gaskell, Spinelli, and Meunier 2002). There was no inhibition of recognition due to the resyllabification —ITALIEN was recognized equally rapidly in all cases. All three cases were normal pronunciations, of course. But the resyllabification has to have a legal source to be acceptable; thus AGNEAU 'lamb' was recognized faster after the prime *petit agneau* 'little lamb' (a liaison environment) than after *demi-t-agneau* (the nonsensical 'half t lamb', in which the *t* has no source; Spinelli, Cutler, and McQueen 2002). However, this difference was reduced when the two sequences of *t+agneau* were cross-spliced; the reason for this turned out to be that there were systematic durational differences between the liaison [t] (which was much shorter) and the spuriously inserted [t]. Thus, the speech signal may contain useful cues to inform listeners that a particular sound has its source in liaison.

Phoneme-detection response times are longer for liaison than for word-initial consonants (Matter 1986; Wauquier-Gravelines 1994; Dejean de la Bâtie and Bradley 1995), perhaps simply because the liaison consonants are acoustically less salient. Dutch resyllabified consonants are also detected more slowly—for example, in *de boot is . . .* ('the boat is', a resyllabification context), [t] is detected less rapidly than in *de boot die . . .* ('the boat that'; Vroomen and De Gelder 1999). This difference reversed when the source word onset was removed, which made the strings into nonwords: *oot is*, *oot die*. (The number of potential word candidates may also have played a role here, as well as the relative distinctiveness of consonants before a vowel versus a consonant.)

Resyllabification may, of course, differ across languages (so the acoustic differences between liaison and nonliaison consonants could be a French-specific effect). What is clear is that such acoustic differences could be very useful when liaison supports an alternative word. Thus in *trop artisan* 'too much a craftsman', liaison can produce a string that could also be *trop partisan* 'too much a partisan'. Such cases were again examined with cross-modal priming. Visual ARTISAN or PARTISAN was preceded by either spoken *trop artisan* or *trop partisan*, by the unambiguous strings *si artisan* 'so much a craftsman' or *si partisan* 'so much a partisan', or by a control prime *trop relatif* 'too relative'; once again, liaison did not delay word recognition (Spinelli, McQueen, and Cutler 2003). But the most interesting aspect of the results was that responses were fastest when the speaker had intended the word that was also the visual target—that is, ARTISAN was recognized faster when preceded by *trop artisan* than by *trop partisan*, whereas PARTISAN was recognized faster when preceded by *trop partisan* than by *trop artisan*. Measurements showed that the strings were not identical acoustically—the liaison consonants were again shorter than the nonliaison consonants. Lengthening the consonant in such an ambiguous string (e.g., in *un air* 'a tune' versus *un nerf* 'a nerve') actually shifts French listeners' judgments from the liaison interpretation (*air*) to the onset-consonant interpretation (*nerf*; Shoemaker 2010). It seems, therefore, that listeners receive and use fine phonetic cues that distinguish liaison consonants from nonliaison productions of the same sounds; liaison does not produce ambiguity at all (for native listeners; but see chapter 10 too!).

6.4 Segment Insertion in Words

Liaison may be thought of as a special case of segment insertion; the phonetic segment usually is not pronounced but is underlyingly always there and can be inserted when the context demands it. Insertion of segments without any corresponding underlying presence is known as epenthesis. Epenthetic segments are thus phonemes that are fully supported by the evidence in the speech signal but do not form part of the language user's underlying representation of the word. For instance, certain sequences of phonemes may require the articulatory system to make a transition through a state that is equivalent to production of another phoneme, as in *something*, in which getting from [m] to [θ] can produce a sound like [p]: *sumpthing*. If we speak aloud nonwords containing such transitions, such as *flomt* or *shengt*, there is a good probability that an epenthetic [p] will appear in the first and a [k] in the second. When nonwords such as these are read out from text by speakers and then presented to listeners for phoneme detection, strings like *flomt* elicit responses to a target [p], and strings like *shengt* elicit responses to [k] (Warner and Weber 2001). The epenthetic segments are sufficiently present to induce detection responses. Nevertheless, the epenthetic stops are acoustically less clear than intended versions of the same stops, and response times to the epenthetic stops are slower than to the intended stops. Thus again, acoustic cues in the signal can inform the listener about the status of a perceived segment.

Vowel epenthesis in consonant clusters leads to *film* being pronounced *fillum*, for example. Some languages, such as Japanese, have no consonant clusters, and in these languages vowels tend to get inserted into clusters in loan words from other languages (*glass* from English becomes *garasu* in Japanese, for example). Japanese listeners report VCCV nonsense strings like *ebzo* as trisyllabic (*ebuzo*) even when the middle vowel is not there at all (Dupoux, Kakehi, et al. 1999), and they exhibit little MMN response to an occurrence of *ebzo* after four occurrences of *ebuzo*, in comparison to French listeners' response (Dehaene-Lambertz, Dupoux, and Gout 2000). The phonological accommodation to this sequence constraint (as argued by Repp [1988] and as shown for assimilation by Mitterer and Blomert [2003], and Mitterer, Csépe, and Blomert 2006) seems to draw on quite early processes such as those involved in contrast perception. This does not mean that Japanese listeners really hear a vowel in such sequences, because in consonant sequences such as [ʃt] (Mann and Repp 1981; see section 6.1), both Japanese and English listeners adjust their responses to the second sound in the same way (Kingston et al., 2011). The adjustment reflects the contrast between the two adjacent sounds, and it would be blocked if a vowel were perceived between them.

In English, vowel epenthesis (as in *fillum*) is associated with nonstandard speech and thus its use is frowned upon. But in other languages vowel epenthesis is a speaker option with no such sociolinguistic connotations. In Dutch, for example, many speakers use forms with and without epenthesis equally often, allowing the likelihood of epenthesis to be affected by such factors as rhythmic structure; they are more likely to produce *tulp* 'tulip' with an epenthetic vowel (and hence with two syllables, a strong followed by a weak) in a rhythmic context consisting of a repeating strong-weak pattern (e.g., *Midden op de tafel stond een hele mooie tulp* 'In the middle of the table was a very lovely tulip') than in a repeating sequence of strong syllables (e.g., *Naast al dat onkruid zag ik nog maar één tulp* 'Near all those weeds I saw just one tulip'; Kuijpers and Donselaar 1998). For many speakers of Dutch, epenthesis simply offers an alternative way of saying words like *tulp*.

What do listeners make of epenthesis? First, it seems that words such as *tulp* produced with epenthetic vowels are nevertheless taken to be underlyingly monosyllabic. A reversal task is a way of looking at the syllabic structure of underlying representations (Treiman and Danis [1988] invented the task, and Schiller, Meyer, et al. [1997] showed how it could be used to look at syllable structure). Bisyllabic words can be reversed syllable by syllable (so the response to *workshop* should be *shopwork*) and monosyllabic words phoneme by phoneme (so the response to *pet* should be *tep*). When Dutch participants in this task are given words like *tulp*, with or without epenthesis, they treat them as monosyllabic: so, they say *plut* when asked to reverse either *tulp* or *tullep* (Donselaar, Kuijpers, and Cutler 1999). Nonsense words like *nulp* are treated as monosyllabic (giving *plun*), but if spoken with epenthesis (*nullep*) they are treated as bisyllabic (giving *lepnul*); this shows that listeners can hear the difference between the strings with and without epenthesis. In the real-word case, therefore, the epenthesized form must simply have contacted the same lexical representation as the monosyllabic version did. Apparently this is a unitary representation, and it is monosyllabic.

Not only did the epenthesized utterance contact the lexical representation, it contacted it more easily than the monosyllabic utterance did. Auditory lexical decisions were faster to *tulp* when it was spoken with epenthesis than without, and word-spotting responses were also faster to embedded forms with epenthesis (*tullepmuik*) than without (*tulpmuik*; again both results from Donselaar et al. 1999).

So epenthesis creates a form that is not identical with the lexically represented form; it is a bisyllabic form, although the lexical representation is apparently monosyllabic. Figure 6.3 shows spectrograms of the same Dutch speaker saying *wolf* 'wolf' without epenthesis and *kolf* 'flask' with epenthesis; the bisyllabic nature of the second word can be clearly seen. Yet despite this mismatch between surface form and lexically represented form, the version with epenthesis is easier to understand. Why should this be so?

Perhaps epenthesis produces a more easily perceived phoneme. In Dutch, as in English, there are two articulatory forms of the phoneme [l]. Before a vowel, [l] is said to be "clear" (articulated principally with the tongue tip), whereas in syllable-final position it is "dark" (articulated more with the back of the tongue). Indeed, measures of Dutch speakers' articulations of words like *film* (without epenthesis), *fillum* (*film* with epenthesis), and *Willem* 'William' (with two syllables and hence a real, nonepenthetic vowel between the [l] and [m]) show the [l] in *fillum* to be articulated just like the [l] in *Willem* and very differently from the [l] in *film* (Warner et al. 2001). So it is not surprising that phoneme detection on the materials from the epenthesis word-spotting experiment—*tullepmuik*, *tulpmuik*, and so on—produces faster detection of [l] in nonwords with epenthesis (e.g., *tullepmuik*) than in nonwords without epenthesis (*tulpmuik*; Donselaar et al. 1999). The inserted vowel makes the [l] clear, and it is apparently easier for listeners to hear a segment as [l] if it is clear than if it is dark. This then appears to be the reason why epenthesis makes words easier to process—the sounds are identified more rapidly and hence the word as a whole is processed more rapidly. As with all the other orderly forms of variation, the variant form does not make lexical access slower; the reason is that in this case access is in fact speeded, as a byproduct of articulatory clarity.

If you want to buy low-fat milk in a Dutch shop you ask for *halfvolle melk*; with epenthesis, you would say *hallufvolle melluk*. The results of this series of experiments suggest that the latter form will get you your milk more quickly.

6.5 Segment Deletion

Variability in a spoken word's form arises by way of insertion but also by deletion of sounds. Deletion often occurs with vowels, as when *family* loses its middle vowel

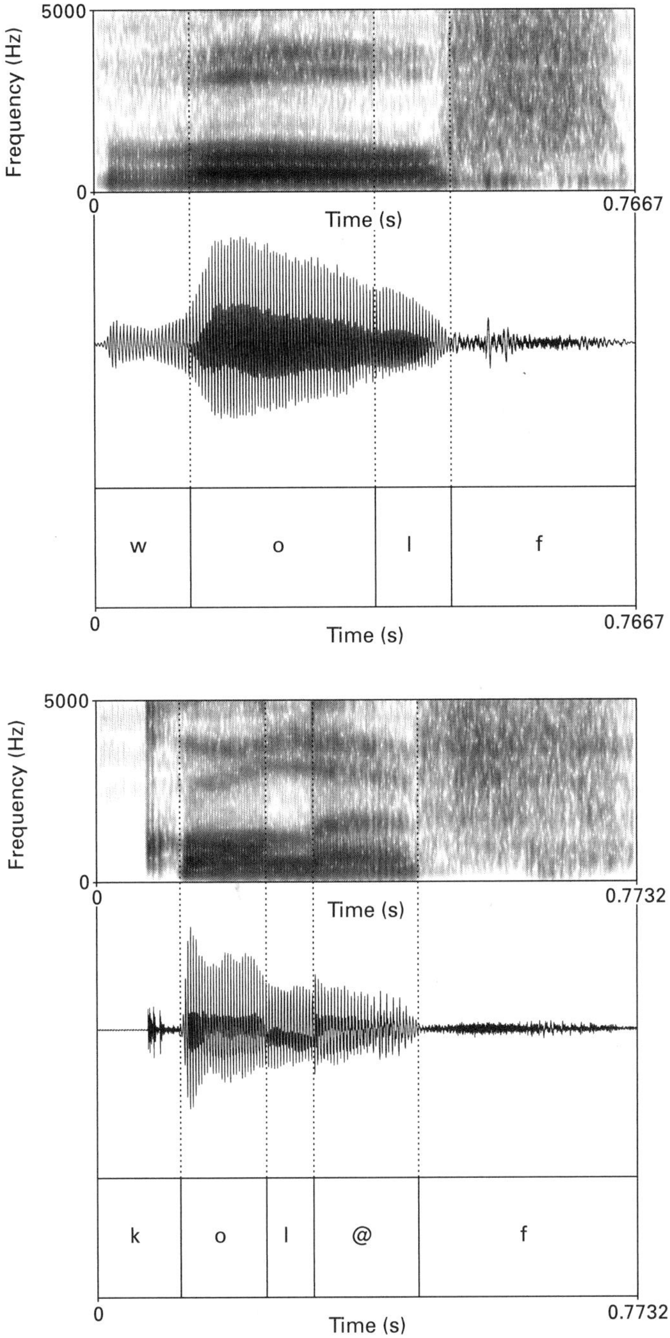

Figure 6.3
Spectrograms and waveforms of the words (a) *wolf* 'wolf' and (b) *kolf* 'flask', produced by the same female speaker. The upper panel (a) shows no vowel epenthesis for *wolf*; the word is just one syllable, as is especially clear in the smooth waveform. The lower panel (b) shows a vowel between the two final segments of *kolf*; the word is spoken as two syllables, and again, the increase in amplitude for the second syllable can be seen in the waveform, even though this syllable is, of course, much weaker than the stressed first syllable.

and is pronounced *fam'ly*, or *suppose* loses its first vowel and is pronounced *s'pose*. It is essentially obligatory in some cases: in French, *galerie* would always be pronounced *gal'rie*; and it is quite usual in many other cases, for example in *mostly* or *postman* where the [t] is deleted (see figure 6.1).

The epenthesis results imply that forms with vowel deletion will be harder to identify because sequences of consonants are intrinsically harder to process than the same consonants separated by a vowel. Indeed, identification and acceptability scores are lower for vowel-deleted versions of English words like *believe* (*b'lieve*) or *family* (*fam'ly*) than for versions with a (reduced) vowel present (LoCasto and Connine 2002). Lexical decision responses are slower for words with deleted segments in French (Racine and Grosjean [2000] compared cases like *s'maine* versus *semaine* 'week') and in Dutch (Kuijpers, Donselaar, and Cutler [1996] compared cases like *vet'raan* versus *veteraan* 'veteran'). There is a processing cost for children's perception of such forms, too, and it is unaffected by whether the children can yet read (Spinelli and Racine 2008), which shows that the effect is not one of spelling-sound (mis)match. Identification of consonants has long been known to be facilitated by availability of a following vowel context (Liberman et al. 1954; Van Son and Pols 1995), and this effect has been called on to explain such effects as faster phoneme detection responses to consonants in singleton onsets versus clusters in English (Treiman et al. 1982), slower detection of a word-initial consonant in French when a following vowel is elided (Matter 1986), and slower detection of Dutch consonants in syllable coda than in onset position (Vroomen and De Gelder 1999). These effects of vowel deletion and the effects of vowel insertion described in section 6.4 thus seem to be two sides of the same coin. It is harder to recognize forms such as *vet'raan* (Kuijpers et al. 1996) or *s'maine* (Racine and Grosjean 2000), as the underlying forms *veteraan* and *semaine* because some of their segments are realized in a phonetic context that is perceptually less than optimal.

Apparently counter to this argument, in one study the English prime *police* pronounced as *plice* facilitated lexical decisions to the same word heard again immediately afterward, more than the bisyllabic prime *police* did (Utman, Blumstein, and Burton 2000). But another very similar experiment did not find this result; in the conditions most comparable to those of Utman et al., LoCasto and Connine (2002) found vowel-present forms to be less facilitated by vowel-deleted forms than by vowel-present forms. In Utman et al.'s experiment, one third of the items were identical pairs, a further third were pairs such as *p'lice police*, and the remaining third were unrelated pairs such as *decide police*; thus the full form could be followed by a related or by an unrelated word, but a reduced form was always followed by a related word. Subjects could have adopted a strategy of assuming that a form like *p'lice* would be followed by *police*, leading to the observed facilitation (with no need to assume that *p'lice* was perceived as *police*). Two of LoCasto and Connine's priming studies differed only in whether the experimental design supported a strategy of this kind; when the strategy was possible, listeners' responses were significantly faster. It thus seems likely, in line with all other results from English, Dutch, and French, that *police* is actually easier to recognize with the vowel than without it, mainly because consonants are easier to perceive when separated by vowels than when abutted to one another.

Vowel deletion can also create competitors from the existing vocabulary. Using cross-modal identity priming, as ever the tool of choice for probing lexical activation, Spinelli and Gros-Balthazard (2007) examined the recognition of French words with and without their first-syllable vowels. When vowel deletion activated potential competitors (e.g., *pelouse* 'lawn', where *pl-* could be an onset, as in *plume* 'pen'), recognition was significantly harder, in comparison with the full form. When vowel deletion resulted in an illegal sequence so that no potential competitors could be activated (e.g., *renard* 'fox'; no French words begin *rn-*), the processing cost was negligible. Thus the effect of having to process two consonants in sequence can be invisible where lexical processing is fast.

Finally, it is also possible that deleted segments leave an acoustic trace just as the underlying forms of other noncanonical segments do. *Support* without its first vowel is not the same as *sport*, in other words. Measures of contact between tongue and palate showed that there was often longer contact in French sequences such as *d'rôle* from *Il n'a pas de rôle* 'He has no role' than in *drôle* from *Il n'est pas drôle* 'He isn't funny'; Fougeron and Steriade 1997). Listeners were good at using this difference to judge which sequence an excerpted [padrol] had been taken from. Similar results appear for pairs such as *sport* and *support* in English (Manuel et al. 1992). So liaison in French, accidental epenthesis in Dutch consonant sequences such as [mt], and assimilation in English sequences such as *right berries* and French sequences such as *rade sale* all turn out to be detectable from subtle acoustic correlates, and in just the same way there can be perceptible cues in consonant sequences like [sp] or [dr] to show when they have arisen as a result of deletion rather than being intended as consonant clusters.

In fact, segment deletion is the end of a continuum of phonemic realization, running from exaggeratedly clear articulation through all degrees of reduction to full deletion. Among other things, that implies that there is no real boundary between this section and the next.

6.6 Variant Segmental Realizations

Not only are segments inserted or deleted, but they vary almost infinitely in precisely how they are realized. An example, well studied in the past few years, is the realization of [t] in word- or syllable-final position. In English, a fully released [t] is possible, an unreleased [t] is also possible (and most usual), and a glottal stop is also possible. In Dutch, word-final [t] is released when words are spoken in isolation, but hardly ever released and frequently deleted in some contexts (Janse, Nooteboom, and Quené 2007; Mitterer and Ernestus 2006). Variation in realization of final segments should not be very problematic for listeners, because, as discussed in chapters 2 and 3, words may have few or no competitors left by the time their final segment arrives. It might seem that for this reason speakers would avoid variation early in words. But in fact variation can occur anywhere. Variation in the voice onset time (VOT) of initial stops (a subphonemic level of variation) and variation in the overall duration of vowels and consonants (hence, variation at the phonemic level) have also been extensively studied. Because of the slightly different issues arising, experiments on the word recognition effects of variant segmental realization in word-initial versus word-final position have also been slightly different; thus they are presented separately in the subsections that follow.

Listeners are certainly sensitive to the way in which phonemes are realized, as becomes very clear when they are asked to judge the goodness of phonemic tokens (Miller and Volaitis 1989; Volaitis and Miller 1992; Hodgson and Miller 1996; Allen and Miller 2001). Like members of any cognitive category, phonemic category members are more versus less prototypical, and listeners find it a tractable task to rate this prototypicality, or goodness, on a scale from 1 to 10. Their judgments take into account the immediate phonetic context and the temporal structure of the signal in which the phoneme in question occurs.

This fine-grained sensitivity is also obvious in the results from studies of how segmental variation affects word recognition, which are described in the following sections.

6.6.1 Word Recognition and Word-Final Subphonemic Variation

English words ending with [t] (e.g., *combat*, *flute*) produce equivalent associate priming in whichever form the final stop is realized (Deelman and Connine 2001; Sumner and Samuel 2005). The same is true for priming and word detection of Dutch words (Janse et al. 2007). However, the released [t] variant leads to significantly faster phoneme detection (Deelman and Connine 2001), which suggests that acoustic processing is easiest for this form. Words spoken with released [t] also produce significantly greater repetition priming effects than other variants (Sumner and Samuel 2005), which suggests that the released version corresponds best to the word's lexical representation. Recall also that, as described in chapter 2, the phoneme-detection advantage for released variants holds most strongly when the released variant is also phonologically preferred in the language (Cho and McQueen 2006); match to lexically stored representations thus seems more important than acoustic clarity alone.

Production and corpus studies show that [t]-reduction in Dutch is most probable after [s] and before any bilabial consonant (Mitterer and Ernestus 2006). (Actually the same is true in English; the [t] in both English *postman* and Dutch *postbode* might be regarded as especially vulnerable.) Before [n], on the other hand, [t]-reduction is quite unlikely. The availability in Dutch of locative prepositions beginning with [b] (*boven* 'above') and [n] (*naast* 'next to') allowed Mitterer and McQueen (2009a) to demonstrate listeners' knowledge of this patterning. Subjects in an eye-tracking study saw a display of printed words that might, for instance, include both *tas* 'bag' and *tast* 'touch', arranged above or next to various shapes. The distributional patterning makes [t]-reduction very likely in *tast boven* and less likely in *tast naast*; indeed, listeners were more likely to look at *tast* as they heard *tas boven* than as they heard *tas naast*. They have thus built their knowledge of the reduction patterns in the language into prelexical processing in such a way that lexical activation can be efficiently modulated.

Listeners also take their previous experience of the distribution of [t]-reduction into account when they are presented with artificially manipulated tokens of Dutch nonwords such as *blast* or *blant*[1] and asked to judge whether or not a [t] is present (Mitterer and Ernestus 2006). The nonwords ended in one of five ways, shown in figure 6.4, varying from a clearly produced [t] to no [t] at all. The stronger the acoustic evidence for [t], the more likely listeners were to judge that a [t] was present, of course. But independent of that, they were also far more likely to judge it present after [s] (in *blast*, for instance) than after [n] (in *blant*), which indicates that the effects of preceding context were known to them; and they were always more likely to judge it present before a bilabial (*blant prima*) than before an alveolar (*blant nauwelijks*), which indicates that the effects of following context were also familiar to them.

These listeners were also more likely to report a [t] in a supporting lexical context; a word-nonword continuum *orkest-orkes*, where the word end is *orkest* 'orchestra', produced more [t] responses than the continuum *moerast-moeras*, where the word end is *moeras* 'swamp'. Janse et al.'s (2007) word-final [t] study also included stimuli such as *mest* 'dung' in which full deletion of the [t] produces *mes* 'knife'; the availability of another word modulated activation in their study, in that full deletion of the [t] led to no more priming for MEST than in a control condition. Here, however, the lexical difference principally appeared with the manipulations midway along the clarity continuum, not with clearly present or absent [t]; the lexical information was of most use when acoustic information about the final sounds was indeterminate.

6.6.2 Word Recognition and Subphonemic Variation in Word Onsets

It takes less time to decide that *queen* is a word if *queen* is heard just after *king* than just after an unrelated word such as *bell*. But what if *king* had been mispronounced

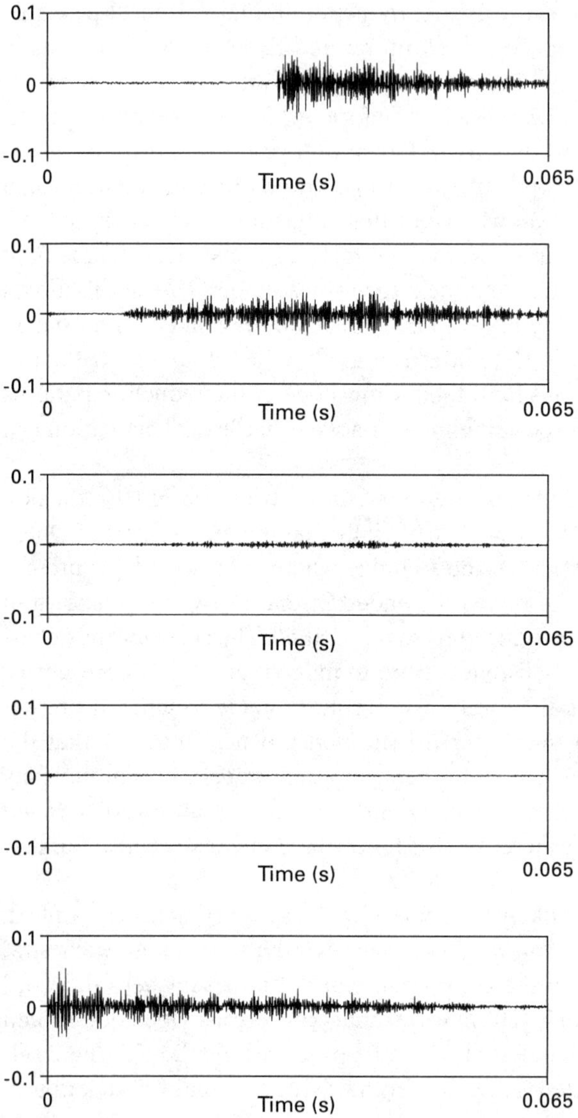

Figure 6.4
The five different versions of [t] that Mitterer and Ernestus (2006) appended to the two Dutch nonsense fragments *blan* and *blas*. The top version is the clearest: a canonical closure followed by a release. Below it is a clear release burst with virtually no closure preceding it. The third version is similar to the second, but the release burst is much weaker. The last two versions are severely reduced: just a closure in the fourth version; and, on the bottom, no actual [t] at all but just a lengthening of the consonant before it. Still, listeners report those versions as [t] if the surrounding phonetic context is one in which deletion of [t] happens frequently.

or realized in some nonstandard way? Shortening the VOT of the initial stop of *king* to only one-third of its normal duration (so that *king* really sounded more like *ging*) greatly reduced the benefit for responses to the following related word (Andruski, Blumstein, and Burton 1994; Utman, Blumstein, and Sullivan 2001). The benefit was restored if the second word occurred not immediately after the first but a few hundred milliseconds later; the first word had presumably by then been understood as *king*, more slowly than usual because of the abnormal VOT. Auditory-auditory identity priming (e.g., lexical decision to *king* after *king*) also showed reduced facilitation when initial VOT was reduced (Utman et al. 2000). Effects of how well phonemes are realized seem to be stronger in word-initial than in word-final position.

But what use to the listener is sensitivity to acoustic goodness? Surely, from the listener's point of view the goal is, as ever, to identify the words that are in the signal and to rule out the similar words that might be partially supported but were not actually intended. That is, the goal is always to achieve categorical distinctions. We might expect, therefore, that goodness distinctions that carry categorical implications weigh more heavily for the listener than distinctions without categorical import. Consistent with this, Andruski et al. observed no significant effect of shortening the initial VOT of *king* by one-third, although shortening it by two-thirds had reduced facilitation. The two-thirds reduction was more likely than the one-third reduction to make the [k] sound like a [g].

Gradient effects of within-category variation on lexical activation did appear in an eye-tracking study conducted (in English) by McMurray et al. (2002), already mentioned in chapter 3. Listeners were asked to click on given pictures in a display including, for instance, a bear and a pear, where the name in the instructions was spoken with a VOT somewhere between [b] and [p]. Recall that we already know from the study of Connine et al. (1994), also described in chapter 3, that a word containing an initial ambiguous sound (e.g., a synthesized word form that could equally well be *ghost* or *coast*) can equally activate both potential candidates. McMurray et al. went a step further by demonstrating the gradient nature of the parallel activation; the more the initial consonant resembled a [b], the stronger the activation of *bear*; the more it resembled a [p], the stronger the activation of *pear* (where activation was measured in terms of proportion, across subjects, of looks to the corresponding picture). The stimuli in this experiment were not very natural in that they varied solely in VOT; in this case, what the listener had to work with in the signal was precisely mirrored in the pattern of responses.

The very same *pear-bear* pair figured in another study (in Dutch, in which *beer* means *bear* and *peer* means *pear*) that showed listeners' preference for categorical responses (Van Alphen and McQueen 2006). Cues to the voicing distinction in Dutch and in English differ—English has a contrast of short VOT (voiced consonants) versus long VOT (voiceless), whereas the Dutch contrast is between negative VOT, or prevoicing, in the voiced stops [b] and [d], and positive VOT in their voiceless counterparts [p] and [t]. Actually, speakers sometimes fail to produce prevoicing in initial [b] and [d], so that listeners have to fall back on other cues to the difference from [p] or [t]; despite this, the presence versus absence of prevoicing is easily the most effective perceptual cue to voicing (Van Alphen and Smits 2004).

When listeners in a same-different judgment task were asked to distinguish between pairs of stimuli varying in word-initial prevoicing, from zero prevoicing through six periods of prevoicing to twelve periods of prevoicing, they could always do so—six versus twelve periods of prevoicing was judged to be different, just as six versus zero was. Thus the differences were always perceptible. However, not all differences affected word recognition, Van Alphen and McQueen found. In cross-modal identity priming, listeners heard, for instance, *blauw* 'blue' and then decided whether visually presented BLAUW was a word. The initial sounds of the primes varied in prevoicing. Sometimes this could cause confusion with another real word—for instance, *beer* could become *peer*, or the nonword *brins* could become *prins* 'prince'. In precisely these conditions, results with zero prevoicing differed from results with some prevoicing (six or twelve periods). There was no effect of how much (i.e., six and twelve periods gave the same results). With zero prevoicing, the prime always sounded more like it began with [p]. With zero prevoicing, then, the nonword *brins* facilitated the visual target BRINS less and PRINS more, and the real word *beer* facilitated PEER more (than the same primes with at least some prevoicing to make the input sound like [b]).

This finding shows that it was clearly important to the listeners to accomplish the categorical distinction between [b] and [p]; the mere presence of prevoicing sufficed to achieve this. How much prevoicing did not matter. Note that Van Alphen and Smits's (2004) measurements had established that the average amount of prevoicing in natural stops was equivalent to somewhere in between the six and twelve periods used in the word recognition study—that is, six periods here was a bit less than usual, and twelve periods a bit more. But perceptually, they functioned in the same way. Any prevoicing satisfied the listener that the stop was voiced. These listeners were not using the prevoicing in a gradient way but categorically.

Competitor effects also appeared in Andruski et al.'s (1994) study; the effect of the VOT manipulation was magnified if instead of *king* (of which the voiced counterpart *ging* is a nonword in English) the prime was a word such as—again!—*pear* (with its real-word counterpart *bear*). Thus *pear* with two-thirds less VOT primed *fruit* significantly less than *pear* with its normal VOT. Utman et al.'s (2000) study also contained a mix of items with word and nonword voiced counterparts (e.g., *keep*, which would become *geep*, versus *cause*, which would become *gauze*), but alas they did not analyze this feature of their results. McMurray et al. (2002) did not use items such as *blue* or *prince* or present trials with only a *pear* or only a *bear*; their study only had the condition with competitor (though their later studies indicated gradient activation in the absence of a competitor; McMurray, Tanenhaus, and Aslin 2009). Further analyses of the extent of gradient effects are clearly called for, and in particular we need to know more about the relation between strength of the acoustic evidence for a phoneme and the modulation of phonological-form activation and competition, as well as the relative impact of acoustic goodness in word-initial and word-final position.

6.6.3 Word Recognition and Phonemic Variation

VOT variation is durational, so it is clear that listeners can process fine temporal structure. The French liaison case provided further proof of this. There is another level at which segments can vary in the duration of their realization—they can be lengthened or shortened overall, owing to prosodic and positional factors. Listeners are sensitive to this kind of variation, too. In chapter 7, research by Davis, Marslen-Wilson, and Gaskell (2002) and by Salverda et al. (2003; see chapter 2) will be described. Their findings, from cross-modal priming and eye-tracking, showed that listeners compute the implications of a vowel's duration for the status of a syllable it is in: if the vowel is longer, the syllable is reckoned more likely to be a stand-alone word; if it is shorter, the syllable is reckoned more likely to be part of a longer word. Embedding (especially at word onset) poses problems for listeners, so if use of such cues could rule out embedded forms, it could be a great help.

These studies are dealt with in chapter 7 because it is prosodic structure that determines such variation in vowel duration. The prosodic shape of a word determines the syllable duration. Prosodic structure also results in lengthening of vowels in the final syllables of prosodic constituents, and as we will see in chapter 7, listeners exploit this information, too. Additionally, prosodic structure can affect the duration of consonants; they are strengthened at the beginning of a prosodic domain. Sensitivity to this type of variation can help listeners find the correct parse of potentially ambiguous strings of segments such as *truck stop* versus *trucks top*. Research by Cho, McQueen, and Cox (2007) and by Shatzman and McQueen (2006a), also described in chapter 7, indicates that listeners indeed possess this sensitivity.

Interestingly for the present argument, however, we will see that listeners did not make use of all the potential cues in the consonants Shatzman and McQueen examined. The Dutch sequences *eens pot* 'once jar' and *een spot* 'a spotlight' consist of the same sequence of phonemes but differ in how the phonemes are realized: among other differences, the [s] is longer and higher in amplitude in *een spot* than in *eens pot*, whereas the closure duration of the [p] is longer in *pot* than in *spot* (see figure 6.5). The duration of [s] was correlated with listeners' eye-tracking responses. But other differences did not correlate with the results in word perception at all. The

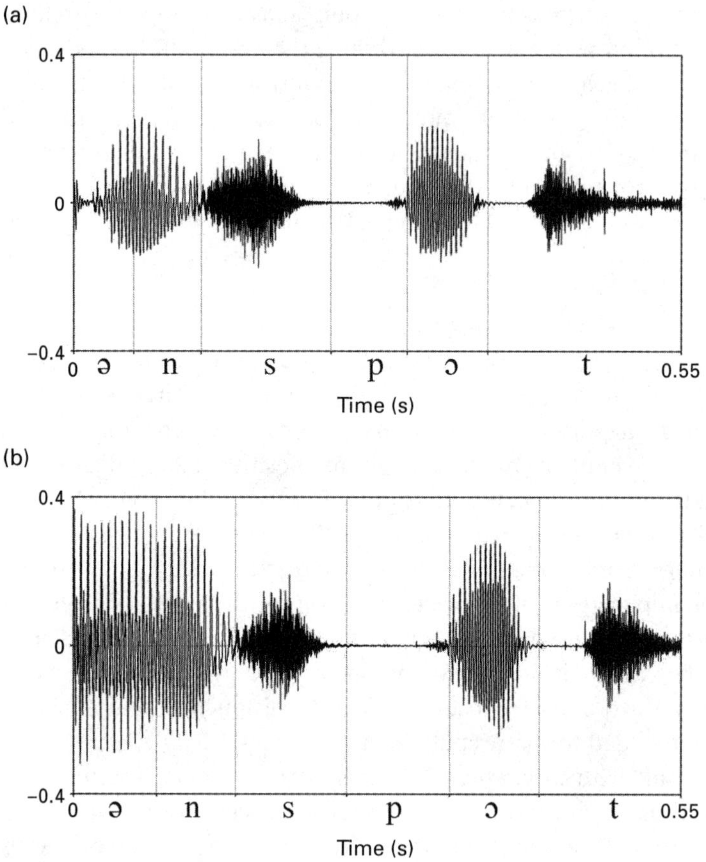

Figure 6.5
Waveforms of (a) *een spot* 'a spotlight' and (b) *eens pot* 'once jar', spoken by a female speaker of Dutch in the context *Zij heeft wel . . . gezegd* 'She did say . . . '. Every segment is different in these two utterances: the duration and amplitude of both the vowel and the consonant in the first syllable *een*, the duration of the [s] and [p] segments, and of the vowel and coda of the second syllable. But one difference was important to the listeners who took part in Shatzman and McQueen's (2006a) study; their eye-tracking performance was correlated with the duration of the [s]. If it was longer, they looked more at an object with a name beginning *sp-*; if it was shorter, they looked there less. In this figure, the word-initial [s] is 16.8 percent longer than the word-final [s] (in Shatzman and McQueen's experiment, the average difference in initial versus final [s] across all their utterance pairs was 18.7 percent). Although some other differences were as large, this one was the one that listeners used. The experiment is discussed in detail in section 7.3 of chapter 7.

cue that is most clearly affected by the prosodic structure—the overall duration of a word-initial versus word-final segment—was the cue that listeners used most. As will be elaborated in chapter 7, these durational cues inform listeners about a word's place in the prosodic structure. The eye-tracking results suggest that duration of a complete segment is not used for directly distinguishing between potential competitor words. Subphonemic cues such as VOT, in contrast, distinguish competitors differing only in the feature (voicing) of which VOT is the principal signal.

6.7 Phonemic Neutralization

Quite a few languages exhibit a particular, phonologically determined form of segment variation: distinctions that are contrastive in some positions are neutralized in other positions. Word-final devoicing is a very common neutralization phenomenon. In Dutch, German, and Polish, for instance, contrasts of voicing appear in syllable-initial but not in syllable-final position. In final position, obstruents are obligatorily voiceless.

This pattern strongly affects listener expectations, and it also affects the perception of second languages that do allow voicing contrasts in final position; some of this evidence is discussed in chapters 9 and 10. The interesting aspect of neutralization for the present discussion is that the voicing contrast is neutralized only on the surface; underlyingly, it is preserved, and it must feature in lexical representations, because it often reappears in morphologically related forms where the neutralized phoneme is no longer syllable final. Thus in Dutch, the singular forms of *lont* 'fuse' and *hond* 'dog' rhyme, but the plurals *lonten* and *honden* do not—the underlying voicing contrast has reappeared. This raises interesting issues concerning the relationship of surface and lexical forms in word recognition; that is to say, it brings neutralization into the domain of this chapter.

In the languages mentioned, there is evidence that, once again, speech signals offer fine acoustic cues to an apparently obscured distinction (for Dutch: Ernestus and Baayen 2003; for German: Port and O'Dell 1985; for Polish: Slowiaczek and Dinnsen 1985). But the phonetic evidence has been mixed, and the presence of such cues (called "incomplete neutralization") seems to be more likely when, as in the Dutch case, the orthography also cues the underlying difference. And thus it is perhaps not surprising that, again, listeners can tune in to these cues and use them in word recognition; in particular, the cues can be used to distinguish word pairs that would otherwise be homophonous. This is true for Polish pairs such as *kot* 'cat' versus *kod* 'code' (Slowiaczek and Szymanska 1989); interestingly, not only Polish but also American English listeners (with no knowledge of Polish) could profit in this study from the acoustic cues. In a two-alternative forced-choice task, these two groups of listeners produced respectively 61 percent and 59 percent correct responses (a nonsignificant difference); both groups were understandably biased to choose the voiceless alternative, but signal-detection analyses indicated that both groups were also making use of the acoustic information in the signal.

The same was true for Dutch pairs such as *wed* 'bet' versus *wet* 'law'; speakers did not necessarily produce cues to the underlying voicing distinction, and where they did produce cues they were not always the same, but listeners could nonetheless reliably use whichever cues were produced (Warner et al. 2004). Speakers also made, and listeners used, cues to similar orthographic distinctions that had no underlying correlate of a voicing contrast (e.g., *baden* 'bathe' and *baadden* 'bathed' differed in [d] duration). This latter finding suggests that the phenomenon of incomplete neutralization is not a reflection of a linguistic process but rather a speaker choice based, for communicative reasons, on the assumption that listeners will need lexical distinctions. Effects of lexical analogy are similarly found in the spelling of nonwords; for instance, a nonword with a long vowel is more likely to be treated as having an underlyingly voiced final segment than a nonword with a short vowel (Ernestus and Baayen 2003). This reflects the same asymmetry in real words of Dutch. When obstruent-final Dutch words are pronounced with a voiced final segment, listeners find the resulting (incorrect) forms more acceptable for *hond* (with a morphological relative pronounced with [d]) than for *lont* (no [d] relatives), and for *kwaad* (with a long vowel) than for *glad* (short vowel; Ernestus and Baayen 2006). Thus, reference to patterns in the lexicon affects interpretation of phonetic contrasts in the input.

6.8 Multiple Concurrent Variations

The research reviewed in sections 6.2 to 6.7 has comprehensively demonstrated listener sensitivity to fine phonetic structure. All this extensive body of work has adopted the usual scientific approach of focusing on one change at a time. By this method, separate effects of each particular type of phonetic variation—assimilation, deletion, featural goodness disparity, or whatever—may be ascertained. But of course, real speech rarely involves such localized deviations from canonical form (although see the discussion of individual speakers' pronunciation of phonemes in chapter 11). Far more usually, real speech involves many alterations, reductions, and deletions all at once.

The effects of background noise, reverberation of the speech signal, and attenuation (filtering) of parts of the signal have all been intensively studied; of course, they all make the listener's task even harder. But they are outside the scope of this chapter, because although they certainly mask fine phonetic structure, they do not systematically alter it. Speech rate is another factor that can influence listeners' ability to understand utterances, but fast speech alters fine phonetic structure via casual articulation, not by its speed alone. Rate effects are often studied by compressing speech input (e.g., Dupoux and Green 1997); that is, speed is examined alone, with articulation controlled. Such compression studies show that listeners are tolerant of considerable increases in the speed of speech; even speech compressed to 50 percent of its natural duration is fully comprehensible after a short amount of practice.

Of course, very fast rates force listeners to curtail some aspects of processing in order to keep up. Aydelott and Bates (2004) compared the effects of filtering and compression on the patterns of facilitation and inhibition for listeners' lexical decisions to the final word in predictive sentences such as *Cut the string with a pair of*. . . . Filtering, which reduced the acoustic quality of the signal, resulted in much less facilitation for the expected continuation. Compression, which forced listeners to process faster but left signal quality unimpaired, reduced the inhibitory effect of an unexpected continuation. Given the distinction between phonological and conceptual activation, this result suggests that impairment of signal quality affects the activation level of phonological representations, whereas fast speech forces listeners to curtail processing at all levels. Inhibitory effects result from violation of expectation; input arriving at a faster than comfortable rate does not allow time for expectations to be generated.

Until recently, the recognition of real spontaneous speech was hardly studied in the psycholinguistic laboratory. In one exception to this, Mehta and Cutler (1988) recorded an hour of spontaneous conversation between two young academics who had not previously met, selected several sentences from the speech of one of them, and then caused him to return to the laboratory a week later and record the same sentences again from a written transcript. Phoneme-detection studies with these two matched sets of sentences from the same speaker showed differences that reflected the characteristics of the two types of speech. Thus, only in the read sentences were later targets detected faster than early targets; this was because only the read speech exhibited smooth prosodic contours that supported listener prediction of rhythmic structure and sentence length. Only in the spontaneous productions, by contrast, were targets in stressed syllables and in accented words detected faster than unstressed, unaccented targets; this was because the acoustic differences associated with contrasts of stress and accent were far greater in the spontaneous than in the read speech.

This result suggests, of course, that the entire body of psycholinguistic findings based on carefully constructed, manipulated, synthesized, and read speech may not provide a full picture of listening in the most common case; the characteristics of normal speech have simply not been captured in the laboratory. When the different ways in which a word may be spoken vary in their frequency, the most frequently encountered variants are easier to recognize than less frequently heard forms

(Connine 2004); if laboratory speech differs from the normal case, then researchers are potentially missing whole dimensions affecting ease of recognition.

The availability of large corpora of real speech is changing this state of affairs. The Switchboard corpus of American English (Godfrey, Holliman, and McDaniel 1992), for example, consists of approximately 240 hours of speech; the Corpus of Spoken Dutch (Oostdijk 2000) comprises 800 hours, more than a quarter of it spontaneous face-to-face conversation. Recent studies have mined such corpora for experimental word-recognition stimuli and for a fuller picture of how reduction is applied. Thus speakers do not simply reduce the quality of their speech across the board; reduction is more likely in high-frequency than in low-frequency forms (Pluymaekers, Ernestus, and Baayen 2005). This is good news for listeners, whose frequency-based guesses are thus quite likely to be correct (although see Bell et al. 2009 for evidence from Switchboard that content and function words are affected asymmetrically).

It is clear that listeners maintain some stored knowledge of variants; having encountered a particular variant earlier makes it more easily recognizable on a later occurrence (Pitt 2009), just as the frequent variants are more easily recognized (Connine 2004). But also, listeners reconstruct what they are hearing; many different lines of evidence attest to this. First, phoneme-detection responses can occur when there is no acoustic evidence for the target phonemes in the signal at all (Kemps et al. 2004). Second, if listeners are asked to repeat back (or "shadow") reduced speech, their productions are lengthened to a relatively greater extent than if they are repeating canonical forms (Brouwer, Mitterer, and Huettig 2010), which suggests that they have reconstructed underlying forms from the reduced inputs. Third, consider the relative recognition accuracy for spontaneously produced words (Ernestus, Baayen, and Schreuder 2002). Words that were highly reduced, somewhat reduced, or hardly reduced at all were presented to listeners in or out of context. When words were in their original context, listeners were generally able to identify them, but out of context this was not necessarily the case: 10 to 15 percent of low-to-medium reductions, and nearly 50 percent of the highly reduced forms, were misidentified. This result does not suggest that the reduced forms were available in memory as such; it suggests that the recognition success in context largely relied on reconstruction.

In fact, what is often first activated by a reduced form, in or out of context, is a surface competitor compatible with the acoustic structure of the heard form. Eye-tracking studies using natural utterances culled from the Corpus of Spoken Dutch showed that a casual pronunciation of *wedstrijd* 'match' (missing the stop consonant after the first vowel) initially activated *wesp* 'wasp', and a casual pronunciation of *beneden* 'down' (with the initial stop assimilated to a nasal and the onset of the third syllable deleted) likewise first activated *meneer* 'mister' (Brouwer 2010). Although listeners do use context to reconstruct severely reduced words, their decisions about identity of reduced forms rely most heavily on whatever acoustic cues are available (Van de Ven 2011), and only really strongly supporting context makes a big difference in the likelihood of reduced forms being correctly identified at first go (Brouwer et al., 2013).

In other words, it seems that reduced speech at least has the potential to be dangerously misleading. Normal natural conversation can find listeners making extensive use of context and other resources to reconstruct and recognize what speakers are saying. Given this, it is not very surprising that listeners adjust the criteria they apply to activated words, requiring less exactitude of acoustic form when they know that speech input may be reduced than when they expect only canonical forms (Brouwer, Mitterer, and Huettig 2012). Such adjustment will increase the likelihood that the intended word is included in the activated lexical candidate set, and not excluded because of a minimal mismatch that, in an ideal listening situation, would be quite enough to rule a competitor out.

6.9 Conclusion

Most of the speech that listeners hear is spoken spontaneously. Read speech is heard in news broadcasts, rehearsed speech is heard in radio broadcasts and in the theater and movies, synthesized or concatenated speech may be encountered by some of us on the telephone or computer or from devices we own. But all of these types of speech together account for only a tiny proportion of our listening experience. Spontaneous speech is the norm.

Yet, for all the practical reasons that are easily imaginable, most psycholinguistic studies of word perception have presented listeners with something other than this normal case. The main reason for this has to do with achieving the controlled conditions that are needed if we want to be able to draw definitive conclusions from the outcome of experiments. Controlling the content of speech (syntactic form, semantic complexity, etc.) is impossible in a spontaneous situation—telling a speaker what to say makes the utterances no longer spontaneous. Some cleverly contrived experimental situations in which speakers describe diagrams or pictures have yielded small and reasonably well controlled corpora, but much more hope is offered by the huge natural corpora such as those used for the research described in section 6.8. These too have a disadvantage: talker identity is not controlled, so that such experiments typically present listeners with tokens from multiple talkers. As will be seen in chapter 11, this approach has its own problems. However, our knowledge of how listeners deal with the nature of real speech is now growing fast.

It would be nice if spontaneous variant forms always evinced greater acoustic clarity, as section 6.4 showed can happen with epenthesis, but alas they do not;

mostly, as we saw, they lead to reduction and ambiguity. They are effects for which listeners need to compensate. But compensate they do, and often remarkably well. Even the presence of reduction itself can be informative. Fowler and Housum (1987; see also Fowler 1988) had subjects listen to a radio broadcast in which a given word occurred more than once. The acoustic clarity was greatest for the first occurrence; later occurrences were somewhat reduced. When subjects were presented with a probe word and asked to decide whether it had indeed occurred in the story, their responses were faster for tokens that were later occurrences rather than initial occurrences. The reduction served as a signal to listeners that this was not a newly introduced word but something that already figured in the discourse.

Many spontaneous speech processes, we have seen, also provide listeners with cues to the underlying structure. This happens across languages; and across languages, listeners are adept at exploiting such cues. The variability of speech may be manifested in language-specific ways, but there seems to be no reason to assume that the ability to deal with variability is anything but universal. Because the existence of high variability in speech signals is itself universal, so is whatever listeners do to deal with it.

7 Prosody

Prosodic structure differs across languages in many ways, so that listener use of prosodic structure inevitably also differs across languages. This has implications, for instance, for whether prosodic cues to word identity play a role in lexical activation and competition; even in two languages with similar prosody, the use of the prosodic structure differs if the payoff for the listener differs. So, suprasegmental stress cues affect lexical activation in Dutch and pitch accent cues affect activation in Japanese, but the same kinds of cues to stress have very little effect in English. There are also prosodic universals that appear in how prosody expresses salience and juncture; these have perceptual implications, and indeed experiments reveal that such prosodic effects are highly informative for listeners, with similar results being found across languages. As yet, prosody is poorly integrated into models of speech processing, and cross-language comparisons of the perceptual exploitation of prosodic structure are remarkably few.

This is another chapter with a personal slant, because it was prosody that propelled me into crosslinguistic research. This book could thus be said to owe its existence to prosody. My dissertation research was not crosslinguistic, but it concerned prosody: the central issue was how stress and accent placement in sentences affected listeners' comprehension (for the contemporary reports, see Cutler 1976a, 1976b; Cutler and Foss 1977). The problem with results of this kind for a psycholinguist is that they will not necessarily hold universally, because stress and accent are not universal. Of all dimensions of linguistic structure, prosody varies particularly widely across languages (for discussion, see Himmelmann and Ladd 2008).

Therefore, it cannot be the end of the story to have demonstrated that accent placement in English affects phoneme-detection responses, because many languages do not have English-like accent patterns. To finish the story satisfactorily, we have to ask also: What role does this processing of accent fulfill in understanding spoken English, and what processing would fulfill that role in those other languages? Psycholinguists all really believe in a common universal basis for every listener's language processing, as discussed in chapter 1. Whenever processing effects have been observed that must be language specific, then, we need to seek the universal factors underlying the effects. Thus consideration of crosslinguistic differences, and of the interplay of universal and language-specific components of processing, is simply unavoidable if one works on prosody.

Nonetheless, this has not led to a central role for prosody in models of spoken language processing. It is interesting to consider why prosody is so difficult to fit into processing models. Even now, with prosody research currently the biggest growth area in phonetics, and the topic of a growing set of conference series (e.g., the Speech Prosody conferences from 2002 on), prosodic research is still not well integrated in psycholinguistic theorizing.

Prosody research has always been bedeviled by miscommunication, which may be part of the problem. There are varying definitions of the term, so that researchers may find themselves talking at cross purposes. Here is what prosody can mean:

1. For students of poetry, the term refers to the norms of verse metrics.
2. For phonologists, it denotes the abstract organization that determines the grouping and relative salience of phonological units.
3. For most phoneticians and psycholinguists, the best definition would be: the linguistic structure expressed in the suprasegmental properties of utterances. This is how the term is used in this book.
4. For speech researchers in applied phonetics and engineering, the term can denote the suprasegmental properties themselves—the pitch, tempo, loudness, and timing patterns of speech.

Obviously, all these definitions are similar, and some overlap to a considerable extent; all four of them would include accent, stress, and rhythm as aspects of prosody. Moreover, they all relate in some way to the original Greek meaning of *prosoidia* (a sung accompaniment), though that hardly helps researchers communicate if they are using different definitions.

A more fundamental problem for the integration of prosody in processing models may be the discrete representations used in most such models; these would be hard to adapt to allow a role for prosody, just as they would be hard to adapt to the role of fine structure discussed in chapter 6. Certainly, no modeler has succeeded in fully incorporating prosody into spoken-word recognition. Automatic speech-recognition models built by engineers to process real speech have also notoriously failed to make effective use of prosodic information (I am aware of two engineering projects specifically aimed at using lexical stress in word identification in English and Dutch, respectively; neither resulted in a working application: Sholicar and Fallside 1988; Van Kuijk and Boves 1999).

The most prosodically insightful researcher that linguistics ever knew, Dwight Bolinger, referred to intonation as "around the edge of language" (Bolinger 1964). Perhaps it is thus no surprise to readers that prosody gets a chapter to itself in this book instead of being seamlessly integrated into all the other chapters as one of the central aspects of linguistic structure. The chapter covers a larger-scale topic than most of the preceding chapters; there is surely a whole book to be written about prosody's role in understanding and speaking. So, the chapter will focus on the crucial issues for the present book's theme: the interplay of universal and language-specific in prosodic processing. Sections 7.1 and 7.2 consider lexical-level prosody; the later sections extend the discussion to the processing of words in their prosodic context—that is, in the prosodic phrases and intonation contours of utterances.

7.1 Prosody in the Lexical Activation and Competition Processes

Models of spoken-word recognition are incomplete if they do not accord prosody an explicit role, because we have already seen that listeners can use it; as they recognize words, they can (if appropriate for their language) extract linguistic structure from the suprasegmental properties of speech. In chapter 3 we briefly discussed types of suprasegmental information and the level of structure they encode. Lexical tone, as in Chinese languages, is suprasegmental variation that is realized entirely within a syllable. Having tone in a language is not in principle different from an expansion of the phoneme inventory—syllable nuclei would have the same degrees of freedom in a language with five vowels and four tones as in a language with twenty vowels. Tones may be affected by adjacent context, as segments are, but their identity does not depend on higher levels of structural organization.

Stress, by contrast, is bound to higher prosodic structure. Stressed syllables are the syllables that may serve as the locus for accentual prominence. At the same time, stressed and unstressed syllables will differ acoustically, which allows stress to operate to distinguish words from one another. Listeners make use of stress distinctions to the degree that it facilitates word recognition in their vocabulary; the relevant evidence was laid out in chapters 1 and 2. Stress is not the only type of prosodically determined suprasegmental variation that lends itself to this use; later in this section, we also consider evidence from pitch accent in Japanese. All of these types of prosody are absolutely not universal across languages, but as we have already seen, listeners' exploitation of such language-specific prosodic information still contributes to our understanding of spoken-language recognition in general.

7.1.1 Stress

For a detailed review of speech perception research on lexical stress, going far beyond what can be included here, see Cutler 2005a. Here we concentrate on how the research results differ across languages.

In lexical stress languages, stressed syllables are acoustically reliable. The study of Fear et al. (1995), described in chapter 4, included a comparison of the acoustic realization, in the speech of twelve English speakers, of four types of syllables: syllables with primary stress, with secondary stress, with no stress but a full vowel, and with a reduced vowel. There were highly significant differences. The differences were not so much between syllables with primary versus secondary stress—only in their duration did these two really differ; rather, the differences were between these two types of stressed syllable, on the one hand, and unstressed syllables, on the other. The stressed syllables were longer, they were louder, they had higher fundamental frequency (F0), and their vowels were less likely to be centralized. Similarly, in segmentally matched English syllables differing in stress, such as *mu-* from English *MUsic/muSEum*, the syllables with primary stress (*MU-* from *music*) proved significantly longer and louder, had more energy higher in the frequency spectrum ("spectral tilt"), and had a higher minimum, maximum, and average F0 than the unstressed syllables (*mu-* from *museum*; Cutler, Wales, et al. 2007). So even where vowel quality is the same, stressed syllables in English are acoustically more salient than unstressed syllables.

In figure 7.1, American English pronunciations of the verb *perVERT* (top three panels) and the noun *PERvert* (bottom three panels) can be compared. The vertical lines show where this word begins and ends. Each of the three displays shows differences between the stressed syllables (the second syllable of the upper word and the first syllable of the lower word) and their unstressed counterparts. The broadband spectrograms show especially clearly how the stressed syllables are longer. The waveforms further show how they have more energy (i.e., are louder) than the same syllables are when unstressed. The narrow-band spectrograms show how the higher regions of the frequency spectrum have more energy (i.e., are darker in the picture) in the stressed versus the unstressed syllables, and also how the harmonic bands (formants) are spaced further apart in the stressed syllables. Given that the formants are harmonics of the fundamental frequency, wider spacing means that the fundamental is higher. So all the durational, F0, and amplitude effects of stress are visible in this figure.

These acoustic differences make stressed syllables more perceptible. In English, stressed syllables are more readily identified than unstressed syllables when excised from a context (Lieberman 1963), and speech distortions are more likely to be detected in stressed than in unstressed syllables (Cole, Jakimik, and Cooper 1978; Browman 1978; Cole and Jakimik 1980; Bond and Garnes 1980). Gated words are recognized earlier if initially stressed (Wingfield et al. 1997), and in gated presentation of spontaneously spoken—but not of read—sentences, stressed syllables are recognized earlier than unstressed syllables (McAllister 1991). Also in spontaneous speech, word-initial target phonemes are detected more rapidly on lexically stressed than unstressed syllables (Mehta and Cutler 1988). Note that acoustic differences between stressed and unstressed syllables are relatively large in spontaneous speech,

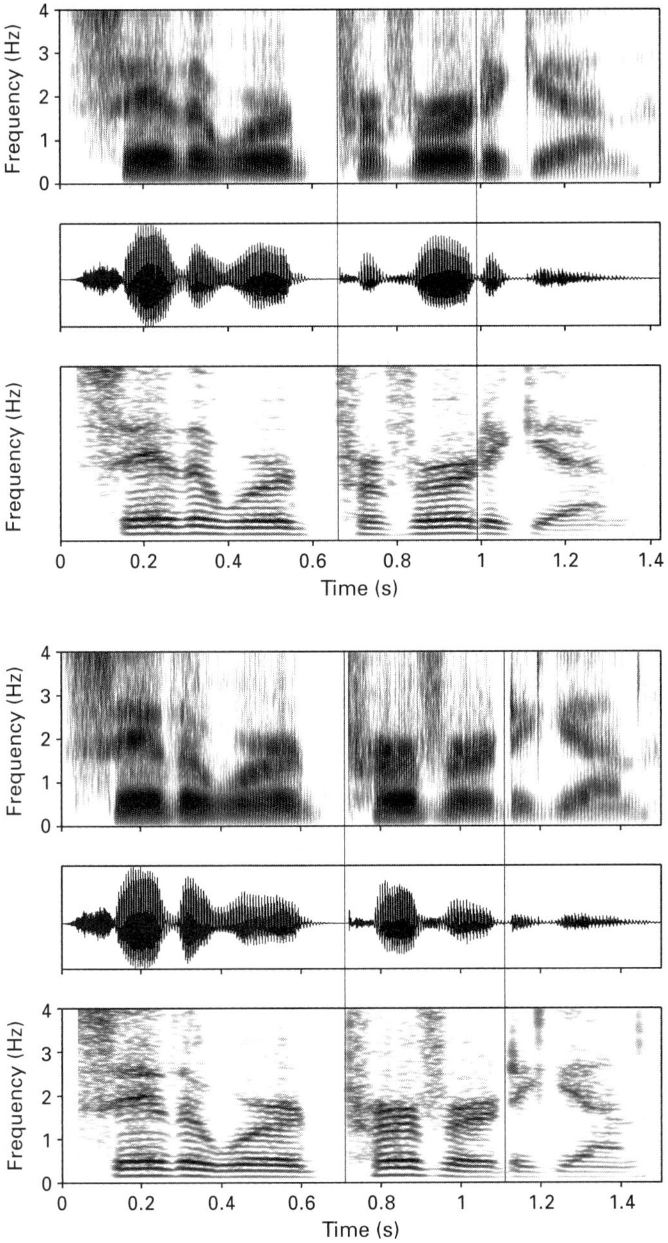

Figure 7.1

Spectrograms of the verb *perVERT* (top three panels) and the noun *PERvert* (lower three panels), spoken in the carrier sentence *Say the word . . . again* by a male speaker of American English. For each word, the panels show, respectively, a broad-band spectrogram on top, a waveform in the middle, and a narrow-band spectrogram below. The figure is modeled, in homage to the late Ilse Lehiste's outstanding example in suprasegmentals research, on a figure originally created by Lehiste and Peterson (1959).

and these phoneme-detection differences do not always arise with read speech; there, detection is in general faster in words with initial stress, irrespective of where in a word the target phoneme occurred (Mattys and Samuel 2000). In that case the advantage is for initially stressed words as a class, rather than for stressed syllables as an acoustically distinct set.

We saw that stress patterning in English provides important information to listeners segmenting speech (see chapter 4). By far the majority of lexical words in the vocabulary, and in typical speech samples, have strong initial syllables, and listeners exploit this statistical regularity by treating strong syllables as likely to be word initial. The suprasegmental cues to a particular syllable's stress level do not convey as much useful information to the listener in English as these cues do in some other free-stress languages, and we saw that listeners use suprasegmental cues to stress in word activation to a lesser extent in English than in, say, Spanish or Dutch.

This adds up to a picture in which for English listeners it is important to know whether a syllable is strong or weak, but regardless of saliency considerations, it is not usually important to compute its stress level. Knowing the stress pattern of an English word in advance does not help recognize it (this has been tried in various experimental setups, including lexical decision: Cutler and Clifton 1984; and primed lexical decision and shadowing: Slowiaczek, Soltano, and Bernstein 2006). Strong/weak decisions do not depend on stress pattern but can be made on the basis of segmental information—strong syllables contain full vowels, and weak syllables contain reduced vowels. Hence, English listeners assign greater weight to segmental than to suprasegmental distinctions between words. There is abundant empirical evidence supporting this assertion.

English listeners attend to the distinction between full and reduced vowels more than to stress distinctions among full syllables, as was shown by the cross-splicing study of Fear et al. (1995). In the perception part of this study, listeners heard tokens of words such as *audience*, *auditorium*, *audition*, and *addition*, where the initial vowels had been exchanged between words; they then rated cross-splicings among any of the first three of these as not significantly different from the original, unspliced tokens. Lower ratings were received only by cross-splicings involving an exchange between a reduced initial vowel (e.g., in *addition*) and the initial vowel of any of the other three words in the same set. Especially the vowels in stressed syllables seem to be important to listeners. Comparison of the disruptive effects on word recognition of types of segmental distortion reveals that distortion of vowels in stressed syllables is most disruptive (Bond 1981). The number of features involved in disruption of a stressed vowel is irrelevant; any replacement of such a vowel is harmful (Small and Squibb 1989). Likewise, phantom word recognitions, which can happen when different dichotically presented inputs are heard at once, are inhibited by mispronunciations in stressed syllables (Mattys and Samuel 1997).

If the vowels stay unaltered, though, very little detrimental effect ensues when English words are incorrectly stressed. Listeners are unaffected by stress correctness in judging acceptability of such words in context (Slowiaczek 1991), and word recognition is achieved despite mis-stressing, both in shadowing and in word identification in noise (Bond and Small 1983; Slowiaczek 1990). An asymmetry sometimes appears in the effects of mis-stressing: Taft (1984) found that responses in a monitoring task were slower only with mis-stressed forms of initially stressed words (*cacTUS*); for initially unstressed words when mis-stressed (*SUSpense*), RTs were actually somewhat faster than with correct stress. In a semantic decision task, mis-stressing without vowel alteration had less adverse effect on recognition than mis-stressing that changed vowels (Cutler and Clifton 1984); once again, if vowels were intact and stress was erroneously brought forward (*canteen* as *CANteen*), there was no significant detrimental effect at all. Even recognition of high-frequency words such as *forget* and *person* was disrupted by stress shifting later (*perSON*) but not by a forward shift (*FORget*), even when vowels changed in the latter case (Field 2005). All of this reinforces the argument already made in chapter 3—that the contribution of the initial portion of the word is crucial for recognition—and suggests that a strengthened syllable is more useful in this process than a weakened one. Experience with strengthened forms may be relevant (e.g., in stress shifting: *CANteen service worker*), or it may be that strengthening makes the consonants clearer, as lexical access is fairly tolerant of vowel mispronunciation anyway (Van Ooijen 1996, described in chapter 1). But for the stress story, it remains true that word recognition by English listeners is not particularly sensitive to mis-stressing.

Crosslinguistic comparisons show, however, that mis-stressing is more harmful in other stress languages. Thus Dutch experiments on the perception of mis-stressed words (using gating: Van Heuven 1985; Van Leyden and Van Heuven 1996; or a semantic judgment task: Koster and Cutler 1997; Cutler and Koster 2000) have shown that mis-stressing interferes with word recognition in that language, and at least in Koster and Cutler's (1997) study the effects of mis-stressing were of similar magnitude to the effects of segmental mispronunciation. The mis-stressing effects are again asymmetric; but interestingly, the asymmetry is in the opposite direction from that observed in English. Mis-stressing of initially unstressed Dutch words (*PIloot* instead of *piLOOT*) is more harmful than mis-stressing of initially stressed words (*viRUS* instead of *VIrus*) both in gating (Van Heuven 1985; Van Leyden and Van Heuven 1996) and semantic decision (Koster and Cutler 1997). In German, the same result appeared when ERPs were recorded as listeners made decisions about correctly stressed versus mis-stressed words (Friedrich 2002): *KAnal* instead of *kaNAL* 'canal' produced a deviant ERP response, whereas *kaNU* instead of *KAnu* 'canoe' did not.

It certainly seems that listeners in these languages do attend to the stress of the initial syllable, and again, the probable reason for the difference from English is the activated competitor population. Where stress information plays a significant role in the modulation of activation, the competitor populations for stressed and unstressed initial syllables are likely to differ. Because an overwhelming majority of Dutch and German words have initial stress, more inappropriate competitor words will be activated by an initial stressed syllable and fewer by later stress. Thus the adverse effect from mis-stressings that produce initial stress will be greater. Although this should also hold for the English vocabulary, because most English words also have initial stress, the effect is not the same because the English listeners are apparently using only segments to modulate lexical activation, and not stress as such. Where stress has no role in the activation and competition process, the competitor population given a correctly stressed and a mis-stressed input with the same vowel is likely to be much the same. Mis-stressing that has no effect on segmental structure will then exercise little effect on recognition. The advantage for brought-forward stress in some English experiments was probably due to clearer articulation arising from the stress placement.

Just as the effect of mis-stressing is greater in Dutch and German than in English, so do crosslinguistic differences arise when listeners are presented with truncated words and asked to select (usually in a two-way forced choice) the source word. In Dutch, listeners can correctly choose between two words with segmentally identical but differently stressed initial syllables (e.g., *ORgel* 'organ', *orKEST* 'orchestra', or *CAvia* 'guinea pig' *kaviAAR* 'caviar') from only the first syllable, and between members of a minimal pair (e.g., *VOORnaam-voorNAAM* 'first name') from either syllable alone (Cutler and Donselaar 2001; van Heuven 1988; Jongenburger 1996). Such decisions are sensitive enough to make allowance for the suprasegmental context (e.g., speech rate; Reinisch, Jesse, and McQueen 2011). The high proportion of correct responses in Dutch (for example, 85 percent for first and 80 percent for second syllables in Cutler and Donselaar's study) was not equaled in English, however (Mattys 2000); there, two-syllable and one-syllable word-initial fragments averaged, respectively, 62 percent and 54 percent correct responses (although both these values are actually above chance). Similarly, English listeners correctly assigned only 59 percent of initial syllables of source words such as *MUsic* versus *muSEum* (Cooper et al. 2002). These were the very tokens for which significant acoustic cues to the stress distinction had been measured (by Cutler, Wales, et al. 2007). The English listeners had an overwhelming bias to choose the initial-stress member of the pair, so that especially for the secondary stress cases (*muSEum*) their performance was poor—in fact, it was significantly below chance. Dutch listeners in Cooper et al.'s English study actually outperformed the native listeners, scoring 72 percent correct overall, including above-chance scores for the *muSEum* cases. The responses of Cooper et al.'s Dutch listeners per token correlated appropriately with the measured differences in F0, amplitude, and duration, which suggests that they were able to make use of all these dimensions of information. The English listeners, on the other hand, made use of F0 (which showed the largest differences) but not of the other dimensions (Cutler, Wales, et al. 2007). The task of deciding where a single syllable like *mu-* comes from forces listeners to attend to acoustic cues to stress. In this case, English listeners can latch on to a salient cue and use it. Their natural processing, however, does not seem to exploit this information even though it is available.

The English-Dutch asymmetries in the use of suprasegmental information in lexical activation (see chapter 1) therefore carry through even to non-time-limited judgments about the source of single syllables. Studies with minimal pairs also show the same crosslinguistic asymmetries in activation, of course; pairs like *VOORnaam* and *voorNAAM* 'first name' do not prime each other in Dutch because they are perceived as clearly different (Cutler and Donselaar 2001), but pairs like *FORbear* and *forBEAR* do prime each other in English because the differences between them, though present, are overlooked (Cutler 1986).

The use of stress information in activation is paralleled by effects of stress on competition. Dutch listeners in an eyetracking study look to the correct member of a pair such as *OCtopus-okTOber* before the point at which segmental information differentiates the words (Reinisch, Jesse and McQueen, 2010). Recall that detection of English *mess* was faster in *nemes* than in *domes*, presumably because of competition from *domestic* in the latter case (McQueen et al. 1994). Similarly, Dutch *zee* 'sea' was detected more rapidly in *luZEE* (activating no competitor) than in *muZEE* (activating *museum*; Cutler and Donselaar 2001), But when *zee* was embedded in *MUzee*—that is, the first two syllables of Dutch *museum* again, but with the stress shifted from the second to the first syllable—the stress shift removed the activation of *museum* and the competition it caused for the detection of *zee*: in this condition, the detection of *zee* was not significantly slower than in the *luZEE* condition, which suggests that *museum* had not been activated. Again, stress information directly affects lexical activation in Dutch.

We might expect to see the same result if this experiment were replicated in Spanish, given the Spanish fragment priming results described in chapter 1. As for English—well, as we also saw in chapter 1, the experiment could not be done in English. There are too few three- or four-syllable words in English in which the first two syllables are strong, and when we add the constraint that the second syllable has to be an unrelated monosyllabic word—we give up. Constructing such materials will never work. Consider English *museum*, one of the few English polysyllabic words with strong first and second syllables. In the Dutch study of Cutler and Donselaar, *museum* could be included in the materials because *zee*, the second syllable, is a real Dutch word by itself. But in English *museum*, the second syllable [zi:] is not a real word. There are enough embedded words to stock an experiment like that of McQueen et al. (1994) many times over—*mess* in *domestic*, *neck* in *connection*, *fish* in *sufficiency*, and so on; but in none of these can the stress be shifted without the quality of the vowels also changing.

The bottom line for stress effects in lexical processing was already described in chapters 1 and 2. In any language, information will be used to the extent that it significantly helps in the reduction of competition. What is a significant reduction may vary across listeners or across listening conditions, but the lexicostatistical data discussed in chapter 2 suggest that a rough threshold of less than one activated competitor per real word is sufficient. Competition can be brought down to this level in Spanish and Dutch only by exploiting stress in activation, which is why doing so is more useful in Spanish and in Dutch word recognition than in English. In English, stress is unnecessary for this purpose.

Stress information would also be useful to German listeners, as Cutler and Pasveer (2006) showed. We do not have data from German that would be directly comparable to the word-spotting results of Cutler and Donselaar in Dutch, nor to the fragment-priming results from Spanish, Dutch, and English. From a fragment priming study in German we know that a one-syllable fragment (e.g., *me-* from *MEdium* 'medium' versus *mediZIN* 'medicine') can produce significant facilitation if it matches the visually presented target word but not if it mismatches; that is, not if it was taken from a word with the contrasting stress pattern (Friedrich 2002). With fragments varying in length, facilitation did not significantly increase with increasing fragment size (Friedrich, Kotz, and Gunter 2001). In ERPs, too, prime-target pairs that matched versus mismatched in F0 correlates of stress were responded to differently (Friedrich et al. 2004). Direct tests for inhibition and competition in German are still needed; however, the lexical statistics suggest that the German pattern in such tests would be very like the Dutch pattern.

Moreover, the lexical statistics suggest that the role of stress in lexical activation in any lexical-stress language in the world will simply follow from the structure of the vocabulary: if paying attention to suprasegmental stress cues not only enables listeners to distinguish between competitors beginning with the same segments but also facilitates exclusion of embeddings, then listeners will use such cues in the earliest stages of lexical processing. In principle, English listeners ought to be able to modulate activation by attending to the stress level of individual syllables, because the differences are clearly audible, as Cutler, Wales, et al.'s (2007) measurements showed. Indeed, Cooper et al.'s (2002) priming study showed some facilitation for matching primes, as can be seen in figure 1.3 in chapter 1; the suprasegmental cues do not go entirely unremarked in certain experimental settings, at least. Further, stress was relevant in determining the competitor population for predicting recognition of words in gating in English (Wingfield et al. [1997]; N.B., the effect of stress was not directly tested with pairs such as *admiral* and *admiration* here). But modulation of activation requires that mismatching words be rejected, and crucially, English listeners appear to do little of this[1]. Cooper et al.'s listeners showed no inhibition when the stress of the prime mismatched the target. And this is simply because it does not pay off for English listeners to attend to stress for this purpose. It does pay off for Spanish and Dutch listeners; thus in Spanish and Dutch, stress cues do modulate activation.

7.1.2 Pitch Accent

Stress is not the only type of lexical prosody that listeners use in activation. Pitch accent in Japanese shows similar effects. This pitch accent system is another way prosodic distinction between words makes contrasts in minimal pairs; in Standard Tokyo Japanese (henceforth Tokyo Japanese), for example, *ame* pronounced with a high-low accent pattern means 'rain', and *ame* with low-high accent is 'candy'.

A brief summary[2] of the Tokyo Japanese system is that words can be unaccented or accented; in unaccented words, the first mora is labeled low (L) and all subsequent morae are labeled high (H), whereas in accented words, one specific mora of the word is marked for accent and is labeled H. If this marked mora is the first in the word, all subsequent morae will be labeled L—a two-mora word would thus have the pattern HL, a three-mora word HLL, and so on. If the marked mora is the second or a later mora in the word, the first mora will be L, all other morae between the first and the marked mora will be H, and morae after the marked mora will be L. So, the distinguishing characteristic of a pitch accent is a fall from high pitch to low pitch on anything following it. Unaccented words (LH, LHH, LHHH, etc.) are referred to as Type 0; Type 1 words (HL, HLL, HLLL, etc.) have the accent on the first mora, Type 2 (LH^, LHL, LHLL, etc.) on the second, and so on. (The caret ^ is used to distinguish accented from otherwise identical unaccented strings. So LHHH is Type 0, or unaccented, but LHHH^ is Type 4, or accented.) The accenting rules apply to native words, including proper names, and also to loan words; to give a few familiar illustrations, *Nissan* is a Type 0 word (*ni-s-sa-n*, LHHH), *Toyota* is a Type 1 word (*to-yo-ta*, HLL); *Mitsubishi* is Type 2 (*mi-tsu-bi-shi*, LHLL), *Kokakoora* 'Coca Cola' is Type 3 (*ko-ka-ko-o-ra*, LHHLL), and *Makudonarudo* 'McDonald's' is Type 4 (*ma-ku-do-na-ru-do*, LHHHLL).

Although there are yet further complexities in the pitch accent system of Tokyo Japanese, the above description should make one interesting property of the system clear: there are only two possible ways to label the first two morae of a word, HL- or LH-. So, important pitch-accent distinctions are expressed in the initial portions of Tokyo Japanese words. Besides the minimal pairs such as *ame*, there are many sets of words that overlap segmentally but not suprasegmentally in the first two syllables—thus *nagasa* 'length' has an HLL accent pattern, and *nagashi* 'sink (noun)' is LHH. This means that, although both begin *naga-*, the accent pattern of the first two syllables is HL in one case and LH in the other. This obviously makes the pitch accent system of great interest to researchers in spoken-word recognition: do Japanese listeners make use of these word-initial patterns?

They do indeed. Cross-modal fragment priming, with which the role of stress in Spanish and Dutch lexical activation was established, was also applied to the Japanese pitch accent case (Sekiguchi and Nakajima 1999). When listeners heard whole or truncated words such as *jidou* HLL 'children' or *jidou* LHH 'automatic', then just as in the stress studies, there was facilitation of the recognition of visually presented words if they had matching accent but not if they had mismatching accent. (With the truncated words, there was also some evidence of competition-induced inhibition, but the difference between mismatching and control primes was not statistically significant. This may be because Sekiguchi and Nakajima's items were minimal pairs, rather than fragments that began otherwise quite different words such as *nagasa-nagashi*, or *principe-principio* in Spanish and *octopus-oktober* in Dutch.)

In minimal pairs, of stress or of accent, one member of the pair can be more frequent or familiar than the other. In English, *INsight* is more common than *inCITE*; in Japanese, *sonchyou* LHHH means 'respect', which is quite frequent, compared to *sonchyou* HLLL 'village headman', which is infrequent. In cross-modal priming the relative frequency interacted with the effect of accent pattern; when the target was the more familiar form, a mismatching prime was as facilitatory as a matching prime, but when the target was the less familiar form, a mismatching prime was as ineffective as the control (Sekiguchi 2006). This result suggests that activation is modulated by frequency and by accentual information at the same time (which can be naturally accounted for in a probabilistic activation framework).

Beginnings such as *naga-* HL from *nagasa* versus *naga-* LH from *nagashi* can certainly be rapidly distinguished. Listeners in a gating study heard initial fragments of words such as *nagasa* or *nagashi* and guessed what word they were hearing (Cutler and Otake 1999). The fragments systematically increased in the amount of phonetic information on offer. Simply for reasons of convenience, gating studies often use a constant fragment size, but instead, these fragments ran to the midpoint of each measured phoneme. The first fragment of *nagasa* or *nagashi* thus terminated at the midpoint of the *n*, the second contained all of the *n* and terminated at the midpoint of the following *a*, and so on. Thus it was guaranteed that each new fragment would add information concerning one additional phoneme. The listeners' guesses in response to each fragment were examined, and each guessed word was scored as matching or mismatching the input in initial accent pattern (HL versus LH). The first fragment produced a roughly fifty-fifty split; that is, there was no

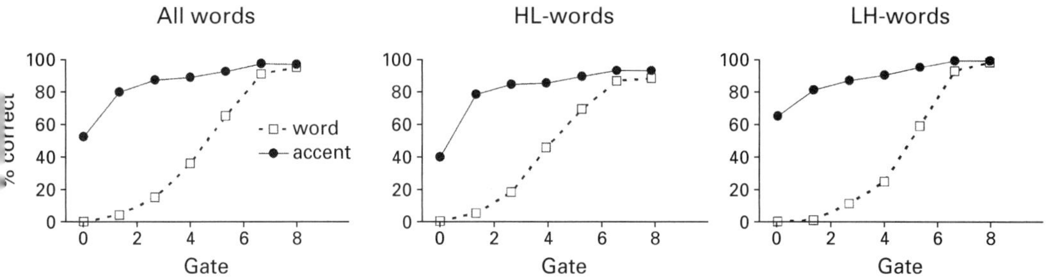

Figure 7.2
Proportion of Japanese listeners' correct word guesses (squares) given gated fragments of real words, and proportion of guesses matching the target word in pitch accent pattern (circles), overall (on the left) and separately for words beginning HL- (middle) and LH- (right). Words themselves were not guessed correctly until six or more phonemes had been heard, but from gate 2 on, over 80 percent of the guessed words had the same pitch accent pattern as the target word. Listeners' guesses were also influenced by lexical statistics of Japanese: there are more LH- words than HL-. With no pitch accent information (gate 1), listeners guess 40 percent HL- and 60 percent LH- (almost exactly the proportion for three-mora words in the vocabulary). When pitch accent information comes in (from gate 2), accent is correctly guessed. The word itself is guessed more slowly for LH- (i.e., there are more LH- competitor words).

accent information in the initial consonant of these words. Indeed, listeners' guesses at this point nicely reflected the structure of the vocabulary, in which LH- words are more common: see figure 7.2. But from the second fragment on, the guessed words overwhelmingly (in more than 80 percent of the cases) had the same initial accent structure (HL- or LH-) as the input word. Thus very little information is needed for Japanese accent to distinguish between words; even when all that the listener had heard of the word was the first consonant and half the following vowel (e.g., *na-* from *nagasa* HLL or *nagashi* LHH), cues to accent pattern were available and could be effectively exploited.

These Tokyo Japanese listeners revealed use of pitch-accent information in two further tasks. In forced-choice identification, listeners could quite accurately judge whether an isolated syllable had been extracted from a Type 1 versus a Type 0 or Type 2 word (e.g., they could tell whether *ka* had been extracted from *kako* HL versus *kaki* LH, *baka* HL versus *gaka* LH, *kame* HL versus *kami* LH^, or *naka* HL versus *haka* LH^). Overall, the listeners' correct response rate was 74 percent. Again, this finding shows that acoustic cues to pitch-accent distinctions are available within a single syllable. Interestingly, however, the correct response rate was higher for initial syllables (80 percent, the same rate as in the gating study) than for final syllables (68 percent); just where the information is most needed to distinguish an intended word from competitors, it is most available to listeners.

In repetition priming, Cutler and Otake (1999) also tested for homophony. If accent completely disambiguates minimal pitch-accent pairs (e.g., *ame*), then lexical decision responses to one member of the pair should be unaffected by having heard the other member previously. If accent does not disambiguate, however, both words may be activated regardless of which word is heard, and then, priming will occur on the second occurrence. No minimal-pair priming occurred: response time to decide that *ame* HL is a real word was faster if *ame* HL had been heard earlier in the experiment, but not if *ame* LH had been heard. Thus pitch-accent information rules out activation of words that are otherwise segmentally identical. (Note that this is the same result as Cutler and Donselaar [2001] observed for minimal stress pairs such as *VOORnaam* and *voorNAAM* in Dutch.)

Misaccenting experiments have also been conducted. Misaccented words in Tokyo Japanese, presented in isolation, were harder to recognize than the same words with correct accent (Minematsu and Hirose 1995). Also, Type 1 four-mora words (HLLL), presented incrementally in successively larger fragments, could be recognized on the basis of less information than Type 0 (LHHH) or Type 2 (LHLL) words. As the four-mora vocabulary of Tokyo Japanese contains less than 10 percent Type 1 words, this result suggests that listeners were effectively using accent to narrow down the set of potential candidate words.

In short, the suprasegmental structure of Tokyo Japanese words is as useful as the segmental structure in narrowing down a set of potential word candidates. The accumulated results provide strong evidence that Tokyo Japanese listeners make early and effective use of pitch-accent information in recognizing spoken words. Note that speakers from other dialect areas of Japan inevitably also have extensive exposure to Tokyo Japanese, given that it is the standard variety (e.g., for broadcast media); and indeed, speakers of other varieties can also make good use of pitch-accent information in identifying words spoken in the Tokyo variety (Otake and Cutler 1999; there were, in fact, some interesting differences between the native and nonnative dialect users, to be discussed further in chapter 11).

In some Scandinavian languages, word-level tonic accent is distinctive in a similar way to Japanese accent. Such accent differences can distinguish between unrelated words or between morphological variants of a single stem. Just as in Japanese, only a portion of a syllable was needed for listeners to be able to correctly identify the original carrier from gated forms of the same Norwegian verb (Efremova, Fintoft, and Ormestad 1963). The Norwegian accent distinctions between verb forms are signaled, like the Tokyo Japanese pitch-accent distinctions, via fundamental frequency variation. Where such distinctions provide cues that listeners can profitably use in discriminating words, it appears easy for listeners to benefit from this.

7.2 Irrelevant Lexical Prosody

As described in chapter 3, many languages exhibit word-level prosodic structure that is effectively irrelevant for lexical identification. For instance, languages may have stress that obligatorily falls at a particular position in the word. In comparison to stress in free-stress languages, however, the acoustic realization of stress in such languages is weak (see Dogil 1999 for Polish; Rigault 1970 for Czech and French; Fonagy 1966 for Hungarian). In fact, Dogil (1999) found no consistency at all in the acoustic reflections of stress in Polish. Dogil proposed that word stress in Polish is an abstract feature defining the position with which intonational movements in the utterance context may be associated.

Languages with noncontrastive stress do not form a unitary class, however (see, e.g., Peperkamp and Dupoux 2002). In some languages (e.g., Finnish and French), prominence is unaffected by grammatical factors; listeners should be able to learn early in life that stress plays no useful contrastive role and can be ignored. In other languages (e.g., Hungarian and Polish), prominence rules affect lexical (content) words and grammatical (function) words differently. This pattern should be harder to learn, with the result that some sensitivity to stress contrasts may develop. Peperkamp and Dupoux suggested that overall listener sensitivity to stress cues in adulthood depends on the function of stress in the native language; even though stress is not used in lexical identification, listeners may be more sensitive to stress distinctions (for instance, in a foreign language) if their native language is a member of the latter rather than the former class.

Indeed, speakers of French have great difficulty detecting stress contrasts, such as deciding whether a nonsense token *bopeLO* matches an earlier token of *bopeLO* or *boPElo*, whereas the same contrasts are easy for speakers of Spanish, which distinguishes words via stress (Dupoux et al. 1997; Dupoux, Peperkamp, and Sebastián-Gallés 2001). The performance of Finnish and Hungarian speakers resembled that of French speakers, whereas speakers of Polish fell between the French and the Spanish levels (Peperkamp, Vendelin, and Dupoux 2010). These results were right in line with the predictions concerning relative cross-language sensitivity.

It is tempting to assume that fixed stress located at a word edge might be useful in lexical segmentation. However, there are reasons for caution with this assumption. In Finnish, for instance, stress is initial, but in the absence of intonational prominence effects, Finnish stressed syllables are in fact not distinct in F0 from unstressed syllables (Suomi, Toivanen, and Ylitalo 2003). The principal acoustic correlate of word stress in Finnish is segmental lengthening within a word's first two morae, even if the second mora is also the second syllable (Suomi and Ylitalo 2004). This finding suggests that Finnish stress would not be easy for listeners to use in segmentation. Indirect evidence consistent with this can be deduced from Suomi et al.'s (1997) study of vowel harmony described in chapter 4. Their word-spotting target words were recognized no less rapidly in lexical decision if excised from a preceding context (e.g., *palo* from *kupalo*) than from a following context (e.g., *palo* from *paloku*). Although the former type could be considered not to have been uttered with canonical stress, this had no deleterious effects on word recognition. Clearly marked word-initial accentuation, however, exercised a stronger effect on segmentation than vowel harmony in the study of Vroomen et al. (1998); but as the Suomi et al. (2003, 2004) analyses show, Finnish stress is only marked in such a way when it carries intonational prominence. Interestingly, in Slovak, which Peperkamp and Dupoux would group with Polish rather than with Finnish, fixed stress does seem to play a role in segmentation. Hanulíková et al.'s (2010) Slovak listeners had difficulty recognizing words if a preceding syllabic context had been accorded word-initial stress. There is obviously room for more exploration of the relative contribution of word-edge fixed stress to segmentation in different fixed-stress languages.

The same message as always concludes the discussion of lexical prosody, however: listeners will use whatever makes a difference for them. The function of lexical prosody in the native phonology can nevertheless affect the overall sensitivity to prosodic realizations, even in other languages. (This issue will be raised again in chapter 10.)

7.3 Prosodic Contexts and Their Role in Spoken-Word Processing

The focus of this book is listening to spoken language, and so most of the research discussed concerns prelexical and lexical processing; at these levels the processing story is modality specific. Higher levels of processing have been largely assumed (rightly or wrongly) to be less modality specific, and in any case, most comprehension research above the lexical level has been visually based. Prosody has no visual analog, however (except perhaps the pale reflection of some prosodic effects in punctuation). To study prosodic processing, we have to use spoken language. There is certainly evidence that the processing of spoken words is affected by the surrounding prosodic structure, above the lexical level. That evidence has a place in the story told in this book.

The principal evidence falls into two categories. A word's place in the utterance intonation contour affects how it is processed, in that listeners use prosodic cues to salience and modulate their word processing accordingly. A word's place in prosodic phrasing also affects how it is processed, because listeners use fine phonetic cues to prosodic structure to determine grouping and juncture in utterances. As it happens, these two categories correspond to the two functions that Bolinger (1978) identifies as the only two prosodic universals. Prosody is used across languages to form accents and to form closures (1978, 471); that is, it is used to signal semantic salience and to mark boundaries or juncture in utterances. Exactly how a language achieves these prosodic effects can vary, but according to Bolinger all languages will do them both, somehow. Such an interplay of universal function with language-specific realization fits with everything else we have seen of word processing so far.

7.3.1 Processing Prosodic Salience: Words and Intonation Contours

Suppose we construct sentences that begin the same way but differ in which words are accented, and hence most salient, as in example (7.1).

(7.1) a. The couple had quarreled over a BOOK they had read.
b. The couple had quarreled over a book they hadn't even READ.
c. The couple had quarreled over a book they had read.

The first six words in each case are the same, but the seventh word, *book*, is accented in version (a) but not in version (b). In (7.1b), accent falls later. Suppose that we now excise the word *book* from each of (7.1a) and (7.1b) and replace it in each case with an identical token of the same word from a third recording, say of (7.1c), spoken without any contrastive accent.

Measurements will show the words excised from the (c) version to be shorter than the words from (a) but longer than the words taken from (b), and there will probably be differences in amplitude and pitch contour, too. But most importantly, the rest of the utterances will also differ in timing pattern, pitch contour, and amplitude distribution. The result of the cross-splicing exercise will then be two sentences in which *book* occurs in acoustically identical form, at the same point, but in which the prosodic contour surrounding that word differs.

This was the technique that I used in the research mentioned at the outset of this chapter. It is illustrated in figure 7.3. The experiments (Cutler 1976a) demonstrated that listeners monitored the prosodic contour of sentences and directed attention to where accent would fall. Response times should, of course, be faster if the target-bearing word is really accented. Thus if the unmodified versions of (a) and (b) are presented to listeners, the phoneme-detection RTs will be faster in (a). But that could just be for acoustic reasons—an accented target-bearing word is clearer and hence easier to hear (Hawkins and Warren 1994), so accented words produce faster responses in phoneme detection (Shields, McHugh, and Martin 1974; Cutler and Foss 1977). In the cross-spliced versions, however, there are no acoustic differences at all in the target-bearing word. Nevertheless, there is a difference in phoneme-detection responses.

In the (7.1) sentences, the [b] of *book* is detected significantly faster in the cross-spliced version of (7.1a) (in which the first six words have a prosodic contour suggesting that accent will fall on *book*) than in the cross-spliced version of (7.1b) (in

Target: /b/
(a) The couple had quarreled over a book they had read
(b) The couple had quarreled over a book they hadn't even READ
(c) The couple had quarreled over a book they had read

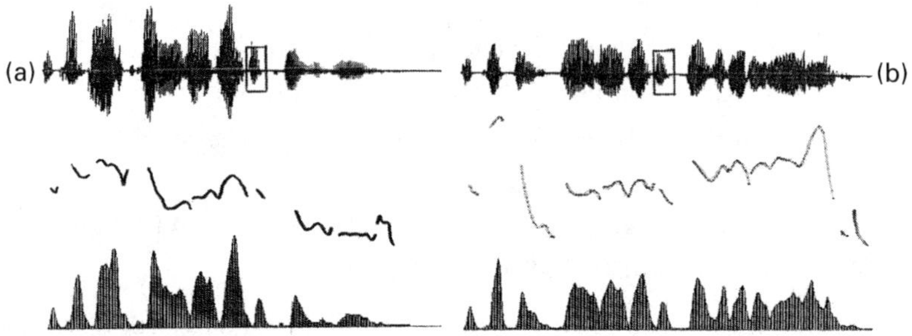

Figure 7.3
The process by which the experimental materials of Cutler (1976a) were constructed. Listeners detected target phonemes such as [b]—in this example, they would respond to the first phoneme of *book*. In utterances (a) and (b), the underlined word *book* is identical (it is actually two copies of the same spoken token, extracted from a third utterance (c) and inserted into (a) and (b) in replacement of the same word as originally spoken there). The intonational context surrounding *book* in the two utterances differs because (a) was originally spoken with contrastive accent on *book* and (b) with contrastive accent elsewhere; utterance (c) was spoken without any contrastive accent. In the waveforms (top figures), the box marks the target word. The same six words precede *book* in each case, but the timing of those words can be seen from the waveforms to be very different in (a), where accent fell on the target word, versus (b), where accent fell later. The pitch contours (middle figures) and amplitude contours (bottom figures) also show significant differences between the first six words in (a) versus (b). In the experiment, listeners' detection was affected by this difference in realization.

which the first six words have a prosodic contour suggesting that no accent will fall on *book*). Up to the point at which the target occurred, the only difference in these two utterances was in the prosodic structure; it must have been the prosody, therefore, that was responsible for the difference in the subjects' detection times. The cues in the prosody enabled them to direct their attention to the point at which accent would fall. Because accent signals semantic salience, the listeners were effectively directing attention to the semantically most central part of the utterance.

In this case, it should be possible to produce the same effect by manipulating semantic salience in some other way (keeping the prosody constant). The relative semantic centrality of words in a sentence can be changed by altering the context around the sentence. Thus in the sentence *The woman on the corner was wearing the blue hat*, the color of the hat is central if the sentence follows a question *Which hat was the woman wearing?*, but the woman's location is central if the sentence follows a question *Which woman was wearing the hat?*. In a naturally spoken exchange, this switch in centrality would be accompanied by a switch in sentence accent placement. But for the purposes of an experiment, one can present exactly the same token of the answer sentence, preceded by either one of the two different questions. Then the semantic salience effectively alters, but the prosody stays the same.

When this experiment was conducted (Cutler and Fodor 1979), the listeners' phoneme-detection responses changed with the alteration in semantic structure. If their phoneme target in this example sentence was [b]—so that they would respond when they heard *blue*—they were faster after the question asking about the hat than after the question asking about the woman. But it was the other way around if their phoneme target was [k], so that they would respond when they heard *corner*; in that case they responded faster after the question about the woman than after the question about the hat. In other words, the question seemed to direct listeners' attention to the part of the sentence that would answer it—that is, to the semantically central portion of the sentence. This finding suggested that the accent effect could therefore be restated as a focus effect—listeners direct their attention as rapidly as possible to the most important part of a speaker's message, using whatever means they can (surrounding context or prosodic structure) to get them there.

If this explanation is correct, then the two effects should not be independent. Either focus or prosody will get you to the semantically most important part of a sentence, but as the goal is the same in each case, there is no real need to use both sources of information together. If both are available, either one will do. Statistically speaking, this translates to a prediction that if Cutler's (1976a) cross-splicing study and Cutler and Fodor's (1979) question study were combined into a single big experiment, the accent effect and the focus effect should interact.

It took a few years to get around to testing this prediction, but Akker and Cutler (2003) found out that it was quite correct. The experiment used sentences like *The tourists from Denmark photographed the crocodile hunter*, preceded by one of two focusing questions (*Which tourists . . . ?* and *Which hunter . . . ?*) and spoken in one of two accent versions, with primary accent on *Denmark* or on *crocodile*, respectively. The phoneme target could be (in this case) either [d] or [k]; the target-bearing words were always cross-spliced from a third version of the sentence, so that as in Cutler's (1976a) experiment only the surrounding prosody provided an indication of where accent should fall. That meant eight versions of each sentence (two questions times two accent locations times two targets).

How did this turn out? First, each of the effects that had been found earlier reappeared. Focused targets ([d] after *Which tourists . . . ?*, [k] after *Which hunter . . . ?*) were detected significantly faster than unfocused ([d] after *Which hunter . . . ?*, [k] after *Which tourists . . . ?*). Identical targets cross-spliced into in a location predicted by the preceding prosody to be accented ([d] when accent had originally fallen on *Denmark*, [k] when accent had originally fallen on *crocodile*) were detected significantly faster than the same targets spliced into prosody predicting that accent would fall elsewhere. But these two main effects also interacted—when the target was focused, the effect of accent was significantly reduced. This was exactly as predicted from the hypothesis that the two effects were not orthogonal but two sides of the same processing coin.

The same experiment was also conducted in Dutch. The relation between semantic focus and accent placement is broadly the same in Dutch and English (Gussenhoven 1983; Gussenhoven and Broeders 1997), so, unsurprisingly, the results of the experiment were the same as in English. That is, targets focused by the question were overall responded to faster than targets that were not in focus, and targets predicted to be accented were responded to faster than targets predicted to be unaccented, but the two effects also interacted such that the accent effect was not significant for focused targets. In chapter 10, readers can find out what happened when Akker and Cutler (2003) gave Dutch listeners the English questions and answers to listen to.

Eye-tracking studies confirm that cues to contrastive accent are rapidly exploited by listeners for selection of an appropriate referent, such as one of several items in a display. Suppose that a display contained a large red circle, a small red circle, a large blue square, and a small yellow triangle; in this instance, correct selection was possible once listeners had got as far as hearing the word *small* in the utterance *the SMALL red circle*; the contrastive accent allowed the listener to decide on the one member of the subset of small items that contrasted with some other display item just in being small (Sedivy et al. 1995). Similar results appeared for repeated versus newly mentioned items in a four-element display (Watson, Tanenhaus, and Gunlogson 2008). Ito and Speer (2008) made their listeners' task much harder by giving them dozens of items to choose from, but again they were able to show that the participants used accent patterns to identify specified items in the display. If instructed to take a green drum and subsequently to take a blue drum, subjects looked most quickly to the blue drum when *blue* bore contrastive accent; if instructed to take a blue ball and then a blue drum, their looks were faster when *drum* bore contrastive accent.

In that study, contrastive accent on a preceding phrase (e.g., *And now . . .*) had little effect on how quickly listeners looked to the target. This null result may be specific either to English or to the complex selection task Ito and Speer used, however, because a strong effect of the accent in such phrases did appear in Dutch, in a more classic eye-tracking setup (a simple four-element display, including objects with phonetically similar names such as *zegel* 'stamp' and *zetel* 'seat'; Braun and

Chen 2010). Similar stimuli also revealed a discourse contrast effect in English; listeners saw, for instance, four objects, among them a *candle* and a *candy*, and heard paired instructions such as *Put the candy below the triangle*, followed by *Now put the candle above the square*. In the second instruction, accent fell either on the noun *candle* or on the prepositional phrase *above the square*. Clearly, accent on *candle* is more appropriate in this example. When contrastive accent instead fell on *above the square*, listeners were more likely to look early to the competitor object (the candy); apparently, they assumed that the absence of accent on *cand-* meant that the previously named item was being named again (Dahan, Tanenhaus, and Chambers 2002). Exactly how the accents in such utterances are realized also affects where listeners look (Chen, Den Os, and De Ruiter 2007). Given the weight of all this evidence, there can be no doubt that the role of accents, signaling salience and hence newness in discourse, is useful to listeners.

The realization of contrastive accent differs across languages (Hay, Sato, et al. 2006), but the effects always assist listeners. In English and Dutch, accent on new information and deaccenting of given information makes utterances as a whole easier to process (Bock and Mazzella 1983; Nooteboom and Kruyt 1987; Terken and Nooteboom 1987). Although the interpretation of deaccented material as given information can result in rapid access to that given context (Fowler and Housum 1987), focused words are better retained in memory and recalled (Birch and Garnsey 1995), perhaps because they are processed more deeply so that more aspects of lexical semantics become available (Blutner and Sommer 1988).

Contrastive accent can even call up contextual alternatives. In a cross-modal priming study (actually in Dutch), sentences such as *Dirk photographed a flamingo* were spoken either with contrastive accent on the final word or with a noncontrastive contour. Visual lexical decision responses to target words that were associates of the final spoken word (e.g., PINK, given *flamingo*) were unaffected by the intonation pattern of the sentence; but responses to contextual alternatives (e.g., PELICAN) were much faster with the contrastive intonation than with the noncontrastive (Braun and Tagliapietra 2010). The presence of contrastive accent on *flamingo* apparently caused the listener to consider what *flamingo* could be contrasting with. As described in chapter 3, Norris, Cutler, et al.'s (2006) cross-modal priming studies showed that listeners' responses to the presence of contrastive accent were even more global—contrast resulted in greater availability of lexical semantics in the whole sentence, not just on the focused word itself. This was explained as contrast causing the listener to relate the sentence meaning to a wider context, a process requiring extension of semantic analysis. Nonetheless, as Akker and Cutler's (2003) study indicated, the location of accent is sought out by listeners so that focused material will be rapidly processed. All these results confirm the important role of focused material in comprehension.

7.3.2 Processing Cues to Juncture: Fine Prosodic Detail

The realization of words in speech is affected by prosodic phrasing as well as by intonation, and this returns us to the fine phonetic detail that was the topic of the preceding chapter. Listeners' attention to such structure was abundantly documented there, and indeed, boundary cues have already been at issue. Consider for example Spinelli et al.'s (2003) demonstration that the duration of a consonant in a French utterance reveals to listeners whether it is a segment inserted by the liaison rule or a segment that belongs to a nonvarying part of a word. This can indicate whether the segment is word final (the final segment of *dernier* in *dernier oignon*) or word initial (the initial segment of *rognon* in *dernier rognon*). Although French liaison is in some ways a special case, variation of segment duration as a function of boundary placement is quite general across languages (Keating et al. 2003), and evidence that listeners capitalize on this variation is steadily accumulating.

Segments vary with position in the syllable. For instance, in Italian *silvestre* the [l] is longer and the [i] shorter than in *silencio*, because the first syllable of *silvestre* is *sil* and the first syllable of *silencio* is *si*. Listeners respond faster in an associative priming task if a priming fragment matches a word related to the target than if it does not (RUMORE 'noise' is responded to faster after *sil* from *silencio*, where the prime fragment actually crosses a syllable boundary, than after *sil* from *silvestre*; Tabossi et al. 2000). Segments also vary with position in the word. Gow and Gordon (1995) found no activation of LIPS given *tulips*, which, they argued, reflected the absence of word-initial strengthening in the [l]. Listeners can correctly choose between segmentally identical strings that vary in segment duration, both in English (*grade A* versus *gray day*; Lehiste 1960) and in Dutch (*die pin* 'that pin' versus *diep in* 'deep in'; Quené 1992).

To make these choices, listeners rely on duration. Subjects in an eye-tracking experiment were asked to click on pictures of objects they heard mentioned in a spoken Dutch sentence (Shatzman and McQueen 2006a). The sentence might be, for instance, *Ze heeft wel eens pot gezegd* 'She once said jar'—and then they would click on a picture of a jar. In all the sentences they heard, however, a word-boundary portion (e.g., *-s pot*) had actually been taken from another recording by the same speaker. This was either another recording of the identical sentence or a recording of another sentence—for this example, *Ze heeft wel een spot gezegd* 'She did say a spotlight'. This latter utterance is segmentally identical to the first, and because there was no picture of a spotlight, clicking on the jar was always the subjects' only effective option. But they were faster doing so when they heard the identity-spliced sentence; the cross-spliced sentence not only slowed down their looks to the jar, it also induced many looks to a competitor picture of a spider (*spin* in Dutch).

Figure 6.5 in the preceding chapter showed a waveform of this pair of sentences with clearly visible durational differences. Measurement of all the segment durations in the actual experimental materials revealed many differences, but importantly, only one of them correlated with the subjects' pattern of responses in the experiment. In *een spot*, the [s] was significantly longer than in *eens pot*. The bigger the difference in duration, the bigger the advantage of the identity-spliced over the cross-spliced items in proportion of looks to the target. In a following eye-tracking study, then, the duration of the [s] was directly manipulated. Listeners were much faster at looking to the jar, and much less likely to look at the spider, given the same utterance of *Ze heeft wel eens pot gezegd* with a shortened [s] than with a lengthened [s]. Thus the effect of segment duration on listeners' placement of word boundaries in a continuous utterance was clearly demonstrated.

A noteworthy finding in Shatzman and McQueen's (2006a) study is that listeners do not use all the cues they might. Ten different durational and other measurements were made in their study, and five of these revealed significant differences between the *eens p-* versus *een sp-* sequences; but only one of the five, duration of [s], was related to the listeners' behavior. Clearly, these listeners had learned to concentrate on one aspect of the signal, presumably because this aspect is more reliably related to the presence of a word boundary. Listeners' use of local prosodic cues to boundaries is thus also modulated by experience. This is not surprising, because although prosodic boundary cues may feature in the speech signal in all languages, the form that such cues take is language specific.

A nice demonstration of this concerns the VOT of word-initial [t]. In prosodically stronger positions—when the word is accented versus not accented, for example, or when the word is at the beginning versus in the middle of a prosodic domain—this VOT in Dutch is significantly shortened (Cho and McQueen 2005). By comparison, the VOT of [t] in English becomes longer in exactly these cases (Lisker and Abramson 1967; Pierrehumbert and Talkin 1992). Cho and McQueen argued that in both cases the strengthening resulted in enhanced contrast with the closest segmental competitor (for [t], that would be the voiced counterpart [d]). In English, both voiced and voiceless stops have a positive VOT; voiceless stops are produced with glottal opening and with accompanying aspiration as well, whereas voiced stops are not aspirated. Longer VOT, they argued, enhances the glottal opening gesture, which in turn enhances the contrast with [d]. In Dutch, however, voiceless stops are not aspirated, and voiced stops have a negative VOT (i.e., they are prevoiced). The contrast between [t] and [d] concerns whether the VOT is positive or negative, and a positive VOT can be emphasized by enhancing the closing gesture of the glottis. This enhances the contrast with [d] and results in shorter VOT. So the effect is universal—stronger prosodic positions produce enhancement of contrast with segmental competitors—but the realization of the effect depends on the characteristics of the language-specific phonetic inventory. In German, the effect is different again; German stops show the greatest prosodic strengthening effects in the duration of their closure (Kuzla and Ernestus 2011).

Thus prosodic strengthening influences how articulatory features cue phonetic contrasts, but the cues also differ across languages. It is useful to listeners if prosodic strengthening mainly affects acoustic features that are not carrying another distinctive load; the various effects could potentially then be computed independently. Strengthening affects word-initial segments, and in the German case, for instance, where the closure is affected, word-initial closure will signal voicing distinctions (such as between [t] and [d]), so it may be perceived independently of phoneme identity. But we have just seen in chapter 6 that there are many other effects exercising influence on the fine phonetic detail of the speech signal. Do such effects interact, like speech rate does with duration as a cue to stress (Reinisch et al. 2011)? What if, for instance, prosodic strengthening exercises an effect on cues to voicing at exactly the point where a voice assimilation process could be triggered by mismatching features of subsequent consonants, as described in chapter 6?

This could indeed happen in German. As in other languages (see Cho 2004; Cho and Keating 2001), assimilation in German is more common across a prosodically weaker (e.g., word) than a stronger (e.g., phrase) boundary. Prosodic strength expresses itself in the duration of a postboundary word-initial consonant; thus assimilation is most likely where there is only a short duration for it to be expressed on. Consider the German utterance *auf Wiedersehen* 'good-bye'. German allows progressive devoicing assimilation and this is an appropriate environment for it; the initial sound of *Wiedersehen*, [v], would become devoiced and hence longer and more [f]-like after the [f] of *auf*. German fricatives, like German stops, show independent effects of prosodic strengthening and contrast (Kuzla et al. 2007), but this independence is clearly not maintained when such assimilation comes into play. Still, the listener is not disadvantaged; the boundary in *auf Wiedersehen* being prosodically weak, the initial sound is as short as it can get, so that even when lengthened the [v] does not really sound long enough to be a true [f]. The contrast should still be clear to the listener.

Perceptual experiments (Kuzla et al. 2010) showed that listeners indeed took both prosodic boundary strength and immediate phonetic context into account when they had to judge whether a sound was, say, [v] or [f]. Interestingly, both the production and perception effects were sensitive to the implications for word recognition. Although German words can begin with [v] or [f] or [z], they never begin [s]. Therefore, devoicing assimilation of [v] could create a lexical competitor (the beginning of *Wiedersehen* could activate *Fieber* 'fever' or *Fiedel* 'fiddle', and more), but devoicing assimilation of [z] would never activate a competing word. The acoustic effects of assimilation turned out to be much stronger where no competitor was possible—reasonably so, given that acoustic alterations could have no disastrous consequences for understanding there. Further, listeners confined their compensation for the prosody-assimilation interaction to the [f]-[v] case; that is, to the case where it was important to tease the separate effects apart because otherwise an unwanted word might be activated. Thus just as for the use of prosodic dimensions (such as stress) in lexical access, listeners make use of prosodically generated fine detail in listening when, and only when, there is a word-recognition advantage to be gained.

The consequences of listeners' use of prosodically conditioned boundary cues for the activation of and competition between word candidates were also explored in English and French. The English study (Cho et al. 2007) compared sentences such as *John bought bus tickets for his family* versus *When you get on the bus, tickets must be shown*. These two sentences share the sequence *bus tickets*; but in the second sentence, a prosodic domain boundary falls between these two words. In this latter case, where the initial [t] of *tickets* begins a prosodic domain, we would expect this segment to be strengthened (i.e., have a longer VOT; this is English). Note also that there are potential competitors that begin with the sequence that straddles the word boundary: *bus+t* (*bust*, *busty*). Cho et al. created spliced versions of their sentences, in which the initial CV of the second word (e.g., *ti-* of *tickets*) came either from another utterance with the same prosodic structure or from an utterance with the other of the two prosodic structures tested. These sentences became the spoken input in a cross-modal priming study, in which the visual lexical decision target was one of the two critical words (BUS or TICKETS).

Recognition of TICKETS turned out to be unaffected by the prosodic structure, but recognition of BUS was faster if the first syllable of the word following it (*ti-* in the sentence *John bought bus tickets . . .*) had been spliced in from the sentence in which it was domain initial and hence stronger. In *John bought bus tickets . . .*, there is no prosodic domain boundary in the original utterance, so the word *bus* is presumably subject to active competition from *bust* and words like that. An extra cue to the presence of a boundary, in the form of a strengthened initial segment of the following word, helps listeners to sort *bus* out from its competition (and in turn to recognize visual BUS more rapidly).

In French, lexical access in sentences containing word sequences such as *père silencieux* 'silent father' or *père repugnant* 'repugnant father' was examined with word and phoneme detection tasks (Christophe et al. 2004). The first of these sequences contains the potential cross-word embedding *persil* 'parsley'. The detection-time measures showed slower responses when this competitor was available. But here, too, no such competitor-induced inhibition was observed if a phonological phrase boundary fell between the two words in such a sequence. Both the English and the French studies show how the processing of prosodic structure can immediately pay off in word recognition.

Prosodic cues can also distinguish between alternative interpretations of strings such as *hamster*; that is, longer words with shorter words embedded within them. But in both gating and in forced-choice identification (in English), listeners given, say, *dock* did not suggest polysyllabic completions, whereas the same fragments from, for example, *doctor* did elicit polysyllabic completions (Davis et al. 2002). In a cross-modal priming study by the same authors, sentences such as *On Saturdays the dock teemed with people* and *On Saturdays the doctor was always busy* were used as primes, and the monosyllabic versus bisyllabic words DOCK and DOCTOR were the visual targets. Priming at the end of the initial syllable of the prime word in the sentence was significantly greater when word and target matched—that is, *dock* produced greater priming for DOCK and *doc-* from *doctor* produced greater priming for DOCTOR. The listeners were clearly able to tell whether the syllable *doc* was a stand-alone word or the first syllable of a longer word.

Essentially the same results appeared in the first experiment in the Dutch study by Salverda et al. (2003), which has already been mentioned. Subjects instructed to click with their mouse on the picture of a hamster were less likely to look at a competing picture of a ham if the first syllable of *hamster* had been taken from another utterance of *hamster*, but they were more likely to look at the ham if the first syllable of *hamster* had been taken from an utterance of *Zij dacht dat die ham stukgesneden was* 'She thought that that ham had been cut up' (N.B. *ham* and *hamster* are cognates in English and Dutch).

Davis et al. (2002) rejected a prosodic explanation of their results on the grounds that there was no prosodic boundary in their sentences (e.g., after *dock* in *On Saturdays the dock teemed . . .*). But prosody is not just a matter of syntactic boundaries, and a second eye-tracking experiment by Salverda et al. (2003) showed that prosody did indeed underlie listeners' decision making in these studies of embedded words. Suppose listeners are instructed to click on the hamster picture with a sentence in which the first syllable of *hamster* actually comes from a utterance of *Zij dacht dat die ham steriel was* 'She thought that that ham was sterile'. The word *steriel* is stressed on the second syllable. That means that the sequence *ham ster-* in that sentence is stressed-unstressed, just as the two syllables in the bisyllabic word *hamster*. In contrast, *stukgesneden*, from the earlier cross-splicing sentence, is stressed on the first syllable, so that *ham* there is a stressed syllable preceding another stressed syllable. In this case, listeners were less likely to look at the ham if the first syllable of *hamster* had come from the stressed-unstressed context *ham steriel*. The difference could be traced to duration; the syllable *ham* was longer if it was itself a word, and it was longer still if it was produced before another stressed syllable than before an unstressed syllable. Listeners' looks were directly responsive to the duration; fewer looks to the monosyllabic competitors were even induced by syllables that had originally been produced as monosyllabic words, but were (uncharacteristically) short, than by syllables that had originally been produced in a bisyllable, but were (uncharacteristically) long. Thus lexical activation and competition are affected by this type of prosodic computation.

To take the story a step further, a further eye-tracking study in English involved instructions such as *Now click on the cap* and *Put the cap next to the square* (Salverda et al. 2007). We know that *cap* will be longer than the same syllable in *captain*, and it will be further lengthened when it is the final word in the sentence. The crucial factor in this experiment was the presence of competitor pictures—for *cap*, the display also included a captain and a cat. With the target word's name in final position in the instruction sentence, subjects looked significantly more often at the monosyllabic competitor picture (e.g., the cat) and significantly less often at the polysyllabic competitor picture (e.g., the captain) than when the target's name was sentence medial. The population of potential lexical competitors is immediately determined by, among other things, the fine durational structure of the utterance.

The processing of prosodic cues to word length and to the placement of interword boundaries has thus brought us back to listeners' abilities to exploit fine detail of utterances. If listeners can profit from such fine expression of prosodic structure, it is clear that coarser detail should be accessible to them, too. Indeed, it has long been known that clause and phrase boundary effects in the expression of prosody are available to listeners. Major syntactic boundaries can be determined from "delexicalized" versions of utterances—that is, from versions in which the words are not intelligible, as in spectrally scrambled speech (De Rooij 1975), hummed speech (Collier and 't Hart 1975) or filtered speech (De Pijper and Sanderman 1994). Note that the mapping from syntax to prosody is not direct; so using prosodic cues to choose, for instance, between two alternative interpretations of the same sequence of words (such as *James phoned his friend from Edinburgh*) can only succeed if the prosodic constituent structure of the two interpretations differs (Nespor and Vogel 1983; Shattuck-Hufnagel and Turk 1996). To the extent that clear cues to boundaries are present in phrase-final lengthening, or in the intonation contour, listeners will conclude that a boundary is present, and use this information in reconstructing syntactic and discourse structure. Studies on this issue, conducted over several decades in a range of languages (mostly European languages, but also Japanese and Korean) are reviewed in Cutler, Dahan, and Donselaar 1997 and Wagner and Watson 2010.

7.4 Universal Processing of Prosodic Structure?

So, how universal is the processing of intonation and prosodic structure? For the role of intonation and accent placement in signaling semantic salience (Bolinger's first universal), all of the evidence described in section 7.3.1 came from English and Dutch. Given that the relation of accent to focus is essentially the same in these two languages (as we saw), how universal can we assume the perceptual results to be? The accent-focus relation is itself far from universal. In Italian and Catalan, the focus contrasts that are expressed as accent contrasts in English and Dutch may become word-order variation instead (Vallduví 1992; Ladd 2008), and accents provide less discourse structure information for listeners in Italian than in Dutch (Swerts, Krahmer, and Avesani 2002). In Korean and Japanese, which do not use intonationally determined pitch accents, other prosodic effects, such as local pitch range expansion, are argued to be functionally analogous to the accent contrasts of English or Dutch (Venditti, Jun, and Beckman 1996). Ladd (2008) presents an extended discussion of crosslinguistic differences in the expression of focus.

Without more relevant evidence, we have thus not reached the end of the salience story. It may be the case that, wherever consistent accent contrasts exist, listeners will be skilled at processing them rapidly and extracting whatever information they provide, focal or otherwise. Note that the powerful mechanism of categorical perception is at play in interpreting accent peaks in English; listeners do not judge accents in terms of degrees of emphasis but in terms of whether emphasis (focus, contrast) is present or absent (Ladd and Morton 1997). It may be that listeners can rapidly exploit the acoustic realization of contrasts in salience however such contrasts are expressed, by accent or otherwise. But until we have the evidence, we cannot tell for sure.

The role of prosody in signaling juncture (which Bolinger also held to be universal) has been studied in many languages, but very little of this research has been comparative. Similarities of prosodically realized juncture effects across languages have been documented in the linguistic literature (Vaissière 1983; Keating et al. 2003), but differences have not been subjected to detailed study. Beckman and Pierrehumbert (1986) compared Japanese and English in terms of a prosodic hierarchy in which intonational phrases are composed of smaller prosodic phrases, which in turn are composed of prosodic words, which in turn are composed of syllables. Even supposing such a hierarchy to be universal, the levels that it manifests may differ across languages, and how it is realized in phonetic effects can certainly be language specific (see, e.g., Cho and McQueen 2005). Clearly, then, there is room for a lot of work on the corresponding language-specificity of prosodic processing.

Consider the following two simple prosodic judgment situations, revealing crosslinguistic similarity and crosslinguistic difference, respectively. In both cases, listeners were presented with utterance fragments and asked to make an essentially prosodic judgment about how they would continue. First, listeners heard extracts from a corpus of natural Swedish speech and judged whether the fragments they heard had been followed by a major prosodic break, a minor prosodic break, or no break (Carlson, Hirschberg, and Swerts 2005). Native Swedish listeners and American listeners with no knowledge of Swedish performed equivalently accurately—and not only could they reliably distinguish between the three prosodic categories, they could do so almost as accurately given single-word fragments as multiword fragments. Native Chinese listeners without knowledge of Swedish also produced reliable judgments, but only if given the multiword stimuli. Acoustic analyses showed that there were correlates of boundary strength in F0 and in segmental glottalization, and the judgments were correlated with these measures. Carlson et al. proposed that marking juncture is a universal prosodic function, and this encourages universality in how listeners exploit the available acoustic cues—regardless of whether they can make sense of what they are hearing.

A rather different conclusion emerged from a study by Grosjean and Hirt (1996), however. Here sets of recorded sentences of increasing length (e.g., the sentences in (7.2) and (7.3)) were presented incrementally in a gating paradigm. Listeners (native to the relevant language) made continuous judgments as to which sentence was being presented; that is, in effect they judged how long the sentence was going to go on.

(7.2) a. Earlier my sister took a dip
b. Earlier my sister took a dip in the pool
c. Earlier my sister took a dip in the pool at the club

(7.3) a. Avant-hier, le garçon a volé un porte-monnaie
b. Avant-hier, le garçon a volé un porte-monnaie dans la cour
c. Avant-hier, le garçon a volé un porte-monnaie dans la cour de l'école
'The day before yesterday the boy stole a wallet in the yard at school'

English listeners could clearly tell in the course of the word *dip* whether the sentence terminated on that word or not, and they were also quite efficient at distinguishing longer from shorter continuations. French listeners, however, could only distinguish termination from continuation; they were quite unable to discriminate between the two continuation options. Acoustic measures revealed systematic differences in the English sentences as a function of length of continuation, but there were no corresponding differences in the French sentences. The cross-language differences in structural realization thus led to crosslinguistic differences in exploitation of the structural effects. There are likely to be many more similar cases waiting to be discovered.

Next consider how listeners may use prosody in making overall judgments about language (identity, for instance, or similarity to the native norm). In the discussion of the rhythmic class hypothesis in chapter 4 (see section 4.7), we saw that rhythmic classifications are ultimately based in strong subjective impressions, even though it has proved very difficult to back up these judgments with consistent and reliable acoustically based metrics. Still, these impressions have more basis in fact than the equally strong impressions that foreigners talk fast (see chapter 10, section 10.1.1); it was clear from the evidence in chapter 4 that languages really do differ in rhythm and in other aspects of prosodic structure. It also seems that listeners can with some success identify, discriminate between, or judge the similarity of languages that they do not know. In a long tradition of experiments, listeners have been asked to identify languages from speech samples lacking all segmental (and hence lexical) information—for example, low-pass filtered or spectrally inverted speech. In general, performance at the identification task is above chance, although listeners are better at making the binary distinction "my language" versus "not my language" than at actually identifying foreign languages (Cohen and Starkweather 1961; Bond and Fokes 1991), even if they are only choosing from a set of three languages on which they have received previous training (Ohala and Gilbert 1981).

In other studies the judgment task has been identification not of the language but of the rhythmic category; in such cases, listeners with phonetic training outperform untrained listeners. Whether or not the segmental information in the speech stimuli is preserved, listeners' categorization responses show a reasonable measure of agreement (consistent with the strength of the subjective impressions regarding rhythm), but the overall level of performance is not impressively high (Miller 1984; Benguerel 1999). For individual languages, however, the judgments in these experiments tend to echo the results of the rhythmic-class measurements and experiments described in chapter 4; some languages (such as English or Japanese) are easy to classify and listeners tend to agree, whereas others (such as Polish) are harder and evoke disagreement.

A rather more tractable task is deciding whether two speech extracts are in the same language or not. Stockmal, Moates, and Bond (2000) succeeded in constructing an experiment with eight different bilingual speakers who provided them with same-voice samples from language pairs such as Akan and Swahili, or Hebrew and German. English-speaking listeners who knew none of the test languages could generally succeed at this task. The features they used to do this apparently included rhythmic structure, given that language pairs with similar rhythm were harder to distinguish than different-rhythm pairs. The team also found that listeners can learn to distinguish a particular (but still unknown) target language from rhythmically similar and different alternatives (Bond, Stockmal, and Muljani 1998; Bond and Stockmal 2002).

Despite its long tradition, this line of research has not yielded evidence that listeners form specifically prosodic representations of languages. Salient phonetic details also contribute to listeners' judgments, and spurious similarity can be reported on the basis of geographical attributions (Stockmal, Muljani, and Bond 1996). However, although listeners' grouping of language samples was indeed affected by phonetic

Figure 7.4
In English, a phrase such as *Capitol Disposal Service* is prosodically disambiguated. Accent falls differently when the first word is the object of the disposal (cf. *waste disposal service*, where accent would usually fall on *waste*) versus when it signifies the name of the disposal company (cf. *Wayne's disposal service*, where accent would usually fall on *disposal*). This joke works in a visual form precisely because, as pointed out at the outset of this chapter, the prosodic structure that could disambiguate it is not represented in the written form of English.

factors (such as the presence of glottal articulations in a sample), these factors were not very important in the rankings that listeners gave on a scale of similarity to English, their L1 (Bradlow et al. 2010). Listeners form undeniably real impressions of how languages sound, but we do not know whether in doing so they draw on universal knowledge of prosodic structure.

7.5 Conclusion: Future Developments in Perceptual Studies of Prosody?

Most psycholinguistic research has been carried out with written materials, and prosody is usually not represented in writing (see figure 7.4). This may be one reason why there are still many untrodden paths in the study of prosodic processing. But further, it seems clear from the review in this chapter that, although prosodic research itself is currently blossoming, and although such research forces one to acknowledge language-specific effects, implications of this language-specificity have not been drawn for comparative studies of prosody in perception. A detailed picture of the universal versus language-specific components of prosodic processing is thus not available.

In all areas of prosody, there is a lot of work on structural similarities across languages, and a growing amount of work on structural differences across languages, but in most areas there is virtually no work on consequent differences in prosodic perception across languages. Only the comparative processing of lexical prosody has attracted substantial research attention in recent years. In the first part of this chapter, we saw that the processing of lexical prosodic structure can be explained in the same terms as the processing of other lexically distinctive information. There may well be a similar conclusion to be drawn for the processing of prosodic salience and of junctural information, but despite claims for a universal central role of prosodic juncture computation in listening (Frazier, Carlson, and Clifton 2006), the evidence on which relevant conclusions can be based has yet to be gathered. At the sentence level, there have been many studies showing perceptual consequences of specific prosodic structures in one or another language, and there is a significant literature on intonational universals (see, e.g., Ladd 1981, 2008; as well as Bolinger 1978); but there have been only a handful of comparative studies examining the perception of identical sentence-level patterns by speakers of prosodically differing languages (e.g., Gussenhoven and Chen 2000; Makárova 2001). Crosslinguistic perceptual comparisons may be the next major growth area in prosodic research.

8 Where Does Language-Specificity Begin?

Native listening begins as soon as it can. Even before birth, the infant brain is presented with, and learns, relevant information about the language of the environment. Although infants speak their first words only by about age one, they amass information about their native language from birth on and throughout the first year. This knowledge starts with more global structure such as rhythm but proceeds rapidly to finer detail; by the end of the first year, infants have learned the relevant phonemic contrasts of their language, the typical structure of words, and much distributional and sequence probability information. In this learning process they are aided by the speech input they hear, which is structured to facilitate acquisition of linguistic knowledge. In the second half of the first year they develop the ability to segment word forms from speech, and thus they are ready by the end of the year to build a vocabulary and launch spoken communication. This chapter outlines the story of learning to listen during the first year, including an account of the laboratory methods developed for testing infant listeners. The story charts the origins of native listening, in the infant brain's adaptation of listening procedures to deal in the most efficient manner possible with the language input it receives.

Speech perception necessarily precedes speech production. It is tempting to think that babies' use of language begins with their first spoken words, but as this chapter will show, it begins much, much earlier. It is only from about age one that little native speakers deliberately communicate with spoken words. At least half a year earlier, though, their speech production shows language-specificity. During the second half of their first year, infants' babbling gradually takes on more and more of the typical phonological form of the input language—in phonetic repertoire (de Boysson-Bardies and Vihman 1991; Blake and de Boysson-Bardies 1992), in intonational patterns (Hallé, de Boysson-Bardies, and Vihman 1991; Whalen, Levitt, and Wang 1991), and in rhythmic structure (Levitt and Wang 1991; Levitt and Utman 1992). By eight months of age—still well before recognizable words are consistently produced—an infant's babbling has acquired sufficiently language-specific attributes that listeners can recognize their native language in it; French listeners, for instance, can pick out the babbles of infants acquiring French from the babbles of Arabic and Chinese infants (de Boysson-Bardies, Sagart, and Durand 1984).

If there is language-specificity in early speech production, then language-specific structure has been learned from the input. Native listening begins much earlier than any production. It begins even before birth. We know this from studies that have measured babies' preferences for one kind of auditory input over another soon after birth; these studies are described in more detail in section 8.2. The auditory system develops to a point at which loud sounds from outside can be perceived by six months postgestation (Birnholz and Benacerraf 1983); by the time of birth, frequency information that enables discrimination between voices (Kisilevsky et al. 2003) can be perceived, as can musical sounds (Lecanuet et al. 2000). Mothers realize, of course, that auditory input is perceived by the baby in the womb; the fetus responds to external sounds and clearly expresses preferences, such as reducing activity in response to music or kicking when the vacuum cleaner starts up. Thus it is clear that language input, too, could be audible in the womb and available for the baby to learn from. Analysis of the hearing abilities of unborn infants suggests that discriminative learning about auditorily structured stimuli would be feasible from the third trimester of pregnancy (Querleu et al. 1988). For individuals with normal hearing, in other words, the acquisition of the environmental language can begin before birth. A lot depends, of course, on how much can be usefully heard in the womb, and as it happens, a significant part of our knowledge of this has come not from experiments on human fetuses but from studies of sheep.

8.1 What Fetal Sheep Might Extract from the Input

Because of such factors as the amount of tissue between the fetus in the womb and the world outside, there is a reasonably good match between the auditory environments of the human infant in its mother's womb and the lamb in the womb of a ewe. The researchers in the fetal-sheep projects used a tiny hydrophone (i.e., a microphone for recording in liquids); when this was placed near the fetal lamb's ear, they could record the auditory stimuli reaching the ear in utero. Their recordings showed that, perhaps contrary to what one might expect, the mother's heartbeat was not the dominant element; adults who listened to the recordings clearly heard external sounds, certainly those above 65 decibels, although all sounds were attenuated compared to recordings made on the animal's skin (Armitage, Baldwin, and Vince 1980; Gerhardt, Abrams, and Oliver 1990). Music was clearly perceptible, and even timbre was well preserved (Abrams et al. 2000). When the research progressed to the making of auditory brain-stem recordings of the fetal lambs, it was further established that the fetus's brain was clearly giving a response to the sounds from outside (Abrams and Gerhardt 1996; Pierson et al. 1997).

Lists of words and nonwords were also played to the sheep, and recordings were made of what could be heard in the sheep's uterus. These recordings (and reference recordings from outside the sheep) were then presented to human listeners to see how much of the phonemic information in the speech material was intelligible to the adult human ear. Of course, the recordings made outside proved more intelligible. But the in utero recordings were also surprisingly well identified; the phonemes in a small response set (e.g., *wig rig gig pig big* or *dig*?) were reported fully correctly in about 45 percent of the adult listeners' responses (Griffiths et al. 1994). The listeners' errors indicated that voicing was better preserved than place or manner information; it seemed that the internally recorded signals had effectively been low-pass filtered by the mother's body and the intrauterine fluids. Nonetheless, the quality of the signal is certainly sufficient to provide a developing fetus with speech experience—subject, of course, to the limitations on its utility imposed by the developmental state of the fetal auditory system.

8.2 What the Human Fetus Extracts from the Input

The human fetus gradually becomes able to make use of the auditory information available in the womb. The sort of work done with sheep will not be exactly replicated with human babies; but recordings have been made in human wombs during the birth process, along with the normal fetal monitoring process, and the results of these investigations show that, like the sheep, the human infant has a good and rich auditory environment. The mother's voice, it was found, is even better preserved than other voices heard from outside (Richards et al. 1992). The response of a human fetus to stimuli from the world outside can be assessed by measuring the fetus's heart rate, which can be done with a sensor from outside the mother's body; the mother's voice makes the fetus's heart beat faster than another woman's voice (Kisilevsky et al. 2003).

Infants that are born a month or two prematurely can discriminate vowel sounds shortly after birth as reliably as full-term babies (Cheour-Luhtanen et al. 1996), which suggests that they already have efficient auditory processing. DeCasper et al. (1994) asked mothers to read a short rhyme aloud every day to their unborn baby, from the thirty-third to the thirty-seventh week of pregnancy. At the end of this four-week period the babies—still unborn, of course—were tested with recordings of the same rhyme as well as another, unfamiliar rhyme, spoken by someone else and played from a loudspeaker positioned over the mother's abdomen. Measurements were made of the fetus's heartbeat during this presentation. When the familiar rhyme was played, the heartbeat was lowered, but the unfamiliar rhyme had no such effect. It is obvious that the human fetus not only perceives the auditory environment in some detail but learns and retains information from it.

Most studies of what the human fetus extracts from auditory input have approached the question via perception experiments with newborn infants—usually two to four days old, sometimes even younger. At that age the ability to separate streams of input occurring in different frequency bands is in place; auditory stream segregation, as this is called (Bregman 1990), is an essential prerequisite for the perception of meaningful streams of sound such as speech, given that these are usually presented against a background of other auditory signals of different kinds. Mismatch negativity (MMN) responses in the brains of newborn infants presented with a recurring 50-millisecond tone showed that streams were segregated. In adult brains, an MMN results when one of the tones in such a repeating stimulus is presented with a different amplitude. If the repeating sequence is interleaved with other tones of similar frequency, the repetition is no longer obvious and there is no MMN. But if the sequence is interleaved with the same number of other tones but these have quite different frequency, auditory stream segregation allows sequence and tones to be kept apart, and an MMN is again observed. Exactly this also happens in the newborn brain (Winkler et al. 2003). Thus although the mother's voice will have been heard against different noise backgrounds, the mechanisms were in place to enable it to have been perceived as the same voice each time.

And it is indeed recognized at birth. Two-day-old infants change their patterns of sucking at a pacifier such that they get to hear recordings of their mother's voice rather than recordings of other female voices (DeCasper and Fifer 1980). That is, they clearly prefer the mother's voice, which means they must recognize the difference between it and other voices. They do not show such preference for the father's voice, even though they can be shown to tell the difference between two male voices (DeCasper and Prescott 1984; Ward and Cooper 1999). Spence and DeCasper (1987) compared the strength of the maternal preference for two versions of the mother's voice: unfiltered, versus low-pass filtered at 1 kilohertz. Unfamiliar voices were preferred in the unfiltered form, but newborns showed no preference for either version in the case of the mother's voice, presumably because they were more familiar with that voice, including in the low-pass filtered form in which they must chiefly have heard it in the womb.

Newborns also prefer the mother's language. They suck longer to hear recordings in that language than in another, for instance (Moon, Cooper, and Fifer 1993); exposed to a set of recordings of women talking in Spanish or English, two-day-olds with English-speaking mothers sucked longer to hear the recordings of English, whereas two-day-olds with Spanish-speaking mothers sucked longer to hear the recordings of Spanish. Unsurprisingly, newborns also have a preference for natural speech over reversed speech (Peña et al. 2003), and this preference is expressed in the left hemisphere of the infant's brain, which suggests that speech specialization is developing before birth.

Prebirth training has been combined with newborn testing. For instance, newborn infants were presented with a story that they had heard many times prenatally because it had been read to them daily, throughout the last six weeks that they had spent in the womb. The newborns preferred listening to the story they had been trained on rather than a previously unheard story (DeCasper and Spence 1986). Importantly, it did not matter whether the stories were both read by the infant's mother or were both read by a stranger; in either case, there was a preference for the familiar over the unfamiliar story. The stories were quite long (500–600 words each), and more than half of the words in each story were not unique to that story but also occurred in the other stories. Control infants who had received no prebirth training showed no preference among the pairs of stories. It appears that the prebirth training allowed the infants to store quite a lot of detailed speech information, which enabled them to recognize the story when they heard it again after they were born.

Some of what infants have learned while in the womb even supports the kind of discriminations relevant for speech. At two days they can discriminate between real syllables (such as *pat* or *tap*) and pseudosyllables (without a vowel nucleus, e.g., *pst* or *tsp*; Moon and Fifer 1990), and importantly, they prefer to listen to the former (Moon, Bever, and Fifer 1992). They can also discriminate between CV syllables differing in initial phoneme (*pa*, *ta*; Bertoncini et al. 1987; Bertoncini et al. 1988) and can discriminate two-syllable sequences that have been extracted from a single word from those containing a word boundary (e.g., *mati* from *mathematicien* or from *panorama typique*; Christophe et al. 1994; also Christophe, Mehler, and Sebastián-Gallés 2001 for Spanish stimuli with stress pattern held constant). However, although they can further discriminate speech inputs that differ in number of syllables (Bijeljac-Babic, Bertoncini, and Mehler 1993), they do not appear to differentiate between syllables that are heavy versus light (Bijeljac-Babic et al. 1993; Bertoncini et al. 1995) or between syllables with full versus reduced vowels (Van Ooijen et al. 1997). Such discriminations are reserved for life after birth. The studies of prebirth and neonate responses have, however, made it clear that an astonishing amount of learning is possible in the womb.

8.3 Discrimination, Preference, and Recognition

The rest of the baby's first year of life is spent homing in on the structure of the native language. Studies of very early listening have enormously expanded our knowledge of this process in recent years, and the research field itself is growing rapidly. In the 1980s there were, worldwide, only a handful of infant speech perception labs. Now there are probably hundreds. It goes without saying that experimental testing of infants younger than one year old presents considerable challenges to the investigator; the growth in the field has been made possible by the development of standardized procedures for such testing.

Three principal questions have been asked in research on infant speech perception. The first concerns what infants can discriminate in speech input—are two different speech signals (sounds, words, or whatever) indeed registered as different by the infant? The second question goes a step beyond this and tests whether the infants exhibit preferences in listening—if two signals can indeed be discriminated, is one of them more attractive to the infant listeners than the other? In part dependent on these is then the third question, which asks whether recognition has occurred—is the appearance of a discrimination or preference between two inputs based on the infant having registered that one of the two has been received before?

The theoretical underpinning of the recognition question is simple. Consider two inputs that differ only in whether or not they have been presented earlier. If the two elicit different behavioral responses, then this difference is ascribed to the earlier experience (and the trace it has left in memory). The usual way of ensuring that test inputs differ only in whether they are familiar is to ensure that there are also two groups of participants, with one group receiving exposure to half the test stimuli and the other group receiving exposure to the other half. The behavioral response in question will usually involve either discrimination or preference.

The discrimination question also has a simple rationale: if a difference is reflected in some behavioral measure, then the difference is not only perceived by the sense organs (audition, in this case) but also registered by a cognitive system that exercises control over the behavior. Preference, however, raises more difficult theoretical issues. Preference tasks are particularly useful with infants four months or older. In such tasks, a gradable response—such as how long an infant maintains a headturn—distinguishes which of two speech inputs an infant is more inclined to listen to. But on exactly what grounds does an infant prefer one input to another? Is the preferred signal more pleasant than the dispreferred one? Can an input that is familiar be expected to be more attractive than an input that is unfamiliar, or is the reverse the case—an input that is novel will be more attractive than one that is well known (and by implication, boring)?

In fact, all three of these potential sources of preference—pleasantness, familiarity, and novelty—appear to play a role in infants' perception, both visual (Roder, Bushnell, and Sasseville 2000) and auditory (Burnham and Dodd 1998). In language acquisition, however, they come into play at different stages and depend in part on the stimuli and task. Simple stimuli such as sine waves can elicit a familiarity preference from younger infants and a novelty preference from infants just a few weeks older (Colombo and Bundy 1983). Whether the infant prefers the familiar or the novel may depend on the amount of exposure (Houston-Price and Nakai 2004). The cognitive task being addressed can also play a role. For instance, when infants are first acquiring the ability to recognize words, in the second half of the first year of life, a preference for familiar signals dominates in experiments in which real words and sentences are presented, as will be described later (see section 8.7 on). At this time of life, that is, it seems that infants are actively trying to build up a stock of familiar speech patterns. They are in search of the reassuringly recurrent.

Here are some of the most commonly used testing procedures in infant speech perception research (especially the research discussed in this chapter). More extensive discussions of procedures can be found in the edited volume by Friederici and Thierry (2008), as well as in Jusczyk 1997 and Fernald et al. 2008.

8.3.1 The High-Amplitude Sucking and Visual Fixation Procedures

These are simple measures of discrimination. High-amplitude sucking is the method used in most of the experiments with neonates described previously. The method was introduced to infant studies by Eimas et al. (1971), whose test subjects were one or four months old. The strength with which infants suck on a pacifier decreases as they become habituated to the situation. If presence or intensity of an auditory signal is contingent on the sucking response, then it too will decrease as the infants become more used to the input. A change in the input will lead to an increase in sucking rate, however—if it is detected. Thus an increase in sucking rate after a change has been introduced is a sign that the change has been detected (see figure 8.1).

The visual fixation procedure is similar, in that habituation and release from habituation again form a response to auditory input; however, the dependent measure is fixation on a visual stimulus such as a checkerboard (e.g., Best, McRoberts, and Sithole 1988).

8.3.2 The Headturn Preference Procedure

This is a simple measure of preference. In the most common form of this method, too, presentation of the speech input is (in part) contingent on the infant's behavior. The infant is seated on a caregiver's lap facing forward in a booth; there is usually some static visual stimulus in front of them. On either side are loudspeakers. Speech is presented from one or other loudspeaker and at the same time a light flashes on that side, attracting the infant's attention; this presentation continues as long as the infant maintains the headturn to that side, but stops if the infant turns back to the front. Experiments usually compare two types of input; longer listening times are held to be a measure of how much the infant wants to listen to a given input (i.e., of preference). The method was first used (in a slightly different form) by Fernald (1985) to show that four-month-olds preferred to listen to speech spoken in the style usually used for addressing infants, rather than to speech between adults. As described here, its first use was Hirsh-Pasek et al.'s (1987) demonstration of a preference in seven- to ten-month-olds for speech that was interrupted at sensible points, such as at clause boundaries, rather than in the middle of a clause.

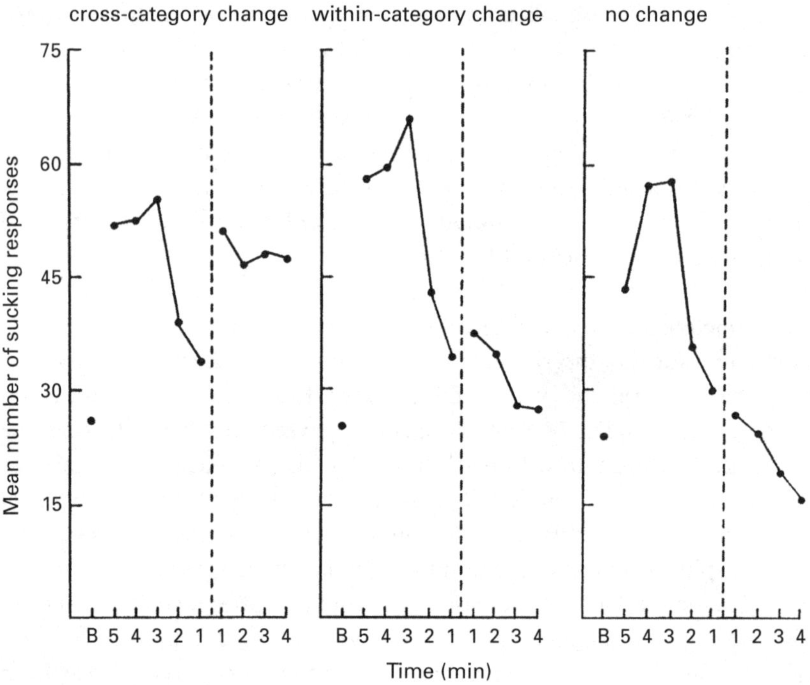

Figure 8.1
Four-month-old infants alter their sucking rate, showing that they have noticed a categorical change in an auditory stimulus. Their sucking rate at baseline (B) increases when a stimulus is heard; at the point indicated by the dotted line, the same input has repeated and sucking rate has diminished. In the right panel, the same input continues unchanged, and sucking rate further diminishes. In the left panel, the input changes in VOT across a category boundary (e.g., from *ba* to *pa*) and sucking rate revives. In the middle panel, the input changes by exactly the same amount of VOT, but the values of VOT are consistent with the same phonemic interpretation (e.g., two different tokens of *pa*). Sucking rate does not alter significantly. (Data from Eimas et al. 1971; reproduced with permission.)

8.3.3 Looking Tasks

In conditioned headturn experiments, infants learn that a reinforcer (e.g., a moving puppet) will appear whenever a particular auditory signal is heard. Their headturn to look at the location where the reinforcer will appear thus indicates that they have indeed perceived the signal. Perception might involve discriminating a change, such as in the phonetic structure of an input (Kuhl 1979); or it could involve accepting an input as a member of a particular category, such as the name of a nonsense object (e.g., Stager and Werker 1997).

Looking at pictures in response to instructions (e.g., *Where's the ball?*; Swingley 2003) is a useful method once infants have representations of word meaning. Especially informative is the speed with which infants move their eyes in a given direction

(Swingley, Pinto, and Fernald 1999; Swingley and Aslin 2002; see Fernald et al. 2008 for more).

8.3.4 The Infant's Brain

Event-related potentials (ERPs) are the brain's electrophysiological responses to input received from the world outside. The measurement of auditory evoked potentials in the infant brain has been a test method in use since the 1970s (e.g., Molfese, Freeman, and Palermo 1975). All brain responses are highly variable, and perhaps especially those in infant brains, which change quite rapidly during the first year of life: dendritic growth and pruning, and cortical folding, are going on throughout that period (Mrzljak et al. 1990). Also, when babies are born, the skull is not fully closed up; the fontanels, or holes in the skull, gradually close during the first year or so of life, and the degree to which the skull is closed affects the nature of the EEG signal (Flemming et al. 2005). These complications entail that interpretable ERP patterns are only found after averaging over a lot of trials per subject and a lot of subjects per study. This makes ERP research harder to do than behavioral research, particularly with young infants who are not good at sitting still for long experiments. It is common to see reports in infant ERP studies that fewer than half the tested infants completed the study (e.g., Kuhl et al. 2006 report 64 completions and 118 failures to complete). Nonetheless, ERP measures, and other measures such as optical tomography (Peña et al. 2003) and near-infrared spectroscopy (Bortfeld, Wruck, and Boas 2007; Gervain et al. 2011), have provided substantial information about the cortical responses associated with the observed speech perception behavior.

8.4 The First Stages in Language-Specific Listening

Newborn infants prefer the environmental language over others (see section 8.2), and that means that even before birth they have amassed information about language. The low-pass filtering affecting auditory input in utero (see section 8.1) means that perhaps the single best-preserved aspect of speech is its prosodic structure—in particular, the rhythm and intonation.

Infants' sensitivity to rhythmic structure has long interested researchers. Neonates' brain responses, even when asleep, are stronger to speech and song than to prosodically degraded speech (Sambeth et al. 2008). Two- to three-month-olds have quite advanced rhythmic sensitivity; they can, for instance, discriminate different rhythmic groupings in sequences of short tones (Demany, McKenzie, and Vurpillot [1977], using the visual fixation procedure). This sensitivity may be evidence of months of rhythmic perception practice already. The familiar rhyme recognition in the womb (DeCasper et al. 1994) is probably carried by rhythmic structure, as is the neonate's preference for the environmental language. Neonates have been shown to prefer the maternal language over another language (Moon et al. 1993), even when the utterances are produced by the same bilingual speaker (Mehler et al. 1988), and to be unable to discriminate between two foreign languages (Mehler et al. 1988). These findings were, however, modulated by later studies taking rhythmic class (see chapter 4) into account; newborn infants could indeed discriminate between foreign languages when these were from different rhythmic classes (English, Japanese); they failed to discriminate only when foreign languages were from the same class (English, Dutch; Nazzi, Bertoncini, and Mehler 1998).

During the months after birth, sensitivity to the rhythm of the maternal language is gradually refined. Early on, even the maternal language is represented in quite general rhythmic terms: so two-month-olds acquiring English still fail to discriminate English from Dutch (Christophe and Morton 1998). But five-month-olds acquiring English can make this discrimination, and make it as well as the discrimination of unfamiliar languages from different rhythmic classes (Japanese, Italian; Nazzi, Jusczyk, and Johnson 2000). The five-month-olds cannot, however, discriminate two unfamiliar languages from the same rhythmic class, either the native one (Dutch, German) or a nonnative class (Italian, Spanish). There is a wealth of evidence from this stage of life consistent with gradual refinement of sensitivity to temporally marked structure in speech. Thus infants presented with audio input with pauses inserted in it prefer the pauses to be placed at the boundaries of prosodic units such as clauses in speech or musical phrases, rather than breaking up these units (Hirsh-Pasek et al. 1987; Krumhansl and Jusczyk 1990). Larger units such as clauses induce earlier and more robust effects than smaller units such as noun phrases (Jusczyk et al. 1992; Nazzi, Kemler Nelson, et al. 2000; Soderstrom et al. 2003). These sensitivities to auditory structure are extremely important in that they could provide the basis for exploiting the prosody of speech input to learn about language-specific syntactic structure (a hypothesis known as "prosodic bootstrapping"; see Gleitman and Wanner 1982 and papers in Morgan and Demuth 1996 for more discussion, and Christophe et al. 1997 for a specific proposal).

8.5 Refining Language-Specific Listening: The Phoneme Repertoire

If there is one famous achievement of the field of infant speech perception, it is the establishment of the developmental progression from universal to language-specific phoneme categorization in the first year of life. Chapter 1 made it clear: psycholinguistics is founded on the fact that children are born without language and acquire whatever language they are exposed to. Phoneme contrasts are a part of this process because, as laid out in chapter 2, languages differ greatly in the makeup of the phoneme inventory (if not so greatly in its size). When they begin acquiring language, infants do not know what contrasts will be relevant for distinguishing words of their language; when acquisition is complete, they do.

8.5.1 Universal Listeners: The Early Months

The need to learn what is relevant for the native language could mean that infants gradually learn to distinguish phoneme contrasts, starting from a point where they do not distinguish them at all. But that is not what happens. Infants start by distinguishing phoneme contrasts too well, in that they can successfully make distinctions that their language does not use phonemically. The course of phonetic acquisition is learning to restrict this excellent discriminative power to only the contrasts relevant in the native language.

Eimas et al.'s (1971) classic study showed that one- and four-month-old infants discriminated voicing contrasts in much the same way that adult listeners do. If a syllable on a synthetic [pa]-[ba] continuum, with a VOT of 20 milliseconds, changed to a syllable with a VOT of 40 milliseconds, the infants' sucking rate dishabituated, which indicated that they had registered the change (see the left panel of figure 8.1). English-speaking adults would categorize such stimuli as *ba* and *pa*, respectively (i.e., as containing different phonemes). If the syllable with a 20-millisecond VOT changed to one with a 0-millisecond VOT (or a syllable with a 60-millisecond VOT changed to a one with a 40-millisecond VOT), there was no significant dishabituation (middle panel of figure 8.1). Adults would categorize stimuli with 0- and 20-millisecond VOTs as both being *ba*, and stimuli with 40- and 60-millisecond VOTs as both being *pa*; that is, in both cases the syllables would be held to contain the same phonemes. The infants apparently did the same.

This performance does not reflect the relevance of the [p]-[b] contrast in English (the language Eimas et al.'s [1971] infant subjects were acquiring). Infants can also discriminate contrasts with which they can have had no previous experience—that is, contrasts that are not used in their environment. The literature on speech perception by English-learning infants up to six months of age shows discrimination for consonant contrasts from Thai (Aslin et al. 1981), Czech (Trehub 1976), and Hindi (Werker and Tees 1984a), none of them corresponding to English contrasts. American six-month-olds also discriminate certain German vowel contrasts (Polka and Werker 1994). Infants acquiring Japanese can discriminate the English [r]-[l] distinction (Tsushima et al. 1994; Kuhl et al. 2006), and infants learning Kikuyu can discriminate English contrasts not found in Kikuyu (Streeter 1976).

Further, the ability of all these infants to behave as "universal listeners" (Werker 1995), discriminating any speech contrast they are presented with, does not imply specifically phonetic inborn sensitivities, even though, as we saw, this ability is present at birth (Bertoncini et al. 1987; Bertoncini et al. 1988). Phonemic discrimination has also been demonstrated in a variety of nonhuman animals (e.g., Kuhl and Miller 1978; Kluender, Diehl, and Killeen 1987). The phonemic contrasts that human languages select for their phoneme repertoires tend to come from a range of naturally distinguishable acoustic contrasts. This, of course, is exactly what one would want. When Lisker and Abramson (1964) measured where along a VOT continuum different languages draw a boundary between stop-consonant categories, they found the variation to be "so far from random that we may speak of three general phonetic types" (p. 422). These types corresponded simply to how many voicing contrasts were distinguished; languages with just a voiced-voiceless distinction (e.g., English, Cantonese, Hungarian) tend to draw the relevant boundary at much the same point, languages with three types of voicing (such as Thai or Armenian) tend to have their two boundaries at similar points, and so on. Of course, some sounds are more common than others (Maddieson 1984), and some realizations of a particular sound are more common, too; interestingly, newborns prefer to listen to more common realizations (e.g., the trilled [r] of Spanish) than to less common (American [r]; Hernandez, Aldridge, and Bower 2000).

8.5.2 Language-Specific Listeners: What Happens Next

The early ability to categorize is remarkable, but just as remarkably, those early universal sensitivities are soon no longer in evidence. By the end of the infant's first year, discrimination is in general reserved for contrasts that form part of the native repertoire.

That is, of course, effectively the adult pattern. The Thai, Czech, and Hindi contrasts, discriminated so successfully by English-learning infants early in life, are not at all easy for English adults, and Japanese adults notoriously have difficulty with [r] versus [l]. Adult listeners are very bad at perceiving foreign-language contrasts that do not occur in the native language. At some point, therefore, the infants have to turn into adults; and phonetically speaking, this is to a large extent achieved during the rest of the first year of life. Classic work by Werker and her colleagues has demonstrated that stop-consonant contrasts that (English-learning) infants could indeed discriminate at six months are not discriminated at ten to twelve months (Werker et al. 1981; Werker and Lalonde 1988; see figure 8.2). The same infants who discriminated a nonnative contrast successfully at six months have lost the ability to make this discrimination four months later (Werker and Tees 1984a). Japanese-learning infants likewise cannot discriminate [r] from [l] by the end of their first year (Tsushima et al. 1994; Kuhl et al. 2006).

For consonants, then, initial language-specific knowledge appears to develop between six and twelve months. Vowels can be learned earlier. Kuhl et al. (1992) tested American and Swedish infants on a vowel perception task in which adults show a strong "perceptual magnet effect" for prototypical vowels of the native language: for example, nonprototypical tokens of [i] are perceived as more similar to the prototype [i] than to each other, even though the actual physical difference between pairs of stimuli is equated (Kuhl 1991). The Swedish infants showed a stronger magnet effect for Swedish [y] than for English [i], whereas for the American infants

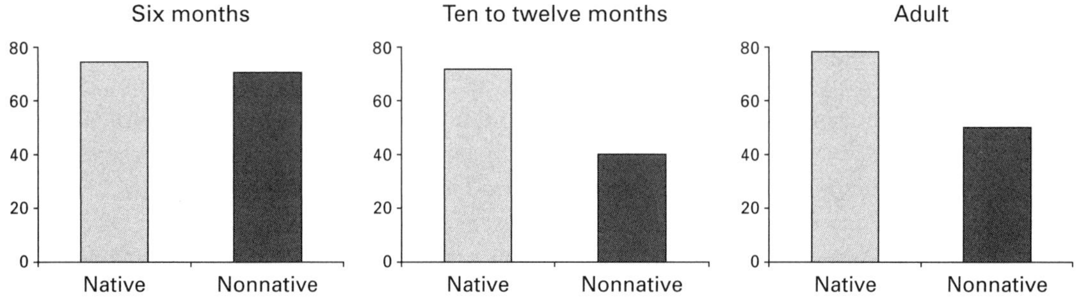

Figure 8.2
At six months of age, infants discriminate nonnative stop-consonant contrasts as well as they discriminate the contrasts from the language they are acquiring (left panel). By ten to twelve months, their discrimination is better for the native than for the nonnative contrasts (middle panel), just as is the case with adult listeners (right panel). (Data from Werker and Lalonde 1988.)

the magnet effect was stronger for the English than the Swedish vowels. The language-specific vowel prototypes thus appeared to be in place by six months of age.

As the phonetic repertoire becomes established, sensitivity also develops for prosodic patterns and for the language-specific rules of phoneme sequencing. At nine months, infants discriminate stress contrasts only if their language has them (Spanish and English yes, French no: Skoruppa et al. 2009, 2011), and listen longer to legal (*raks*, *snef*) than to illegal sequences (*ksar*, *fesn*; Friederici and Wessels 1993) and to highly probable (*vate*) versus improbable sequences (*thage*; Jusczyk et al. 1994). These preferences are phonetically based, given that low-pass filtered versions of the stimuli do not elicit preferences. Nine-month-olds likewise prefer rare words that are legal in their own language over prosodically matched foreign words that violate native phonotactics (Jusczyk, Friederici, et al. 1993). And Dutch infants, from nine months on, show no sensitivity to voicing contrasts in word-final position (*ket*, *ked*), although they easily discriminate the same contrasts in word-initial position (*tos* versus *dos*; Zamuner 2006). This is in keeping with Dutch phonology, which allows voicing contrasts only in prevocalic position.

8.5.3 How Universal Listeners Become Language Specific

Explaining the course of phonetic acquisition has been the most central question for infant speech perception researchers.[1] The earlier success with vowel than with consonant contrasts, for example, has several possible explanations. First, vowels are longer and may therefore have been more distinct in the womb; they also carry most of the prosodic information to which infants have begun to be sensitive before birth, and this could have focused infants' attention on them. Second, though not independently of this, memory processes seem more critical in vowel than in consonant perception (Cowan and Morse 1986), given that (adults') mental representations of vowels gradually become more diffuse over time. Comparison of infant and adult memory revealed longer-lasting echoic traces in infants (Cowan, Suomi, and Morse 1982). Assuming that the speed of speech processing is not at a maximum very early in life, and that longer stimuli are more easily stored than shorter, then it seems likely that infants will succeed in creating stored representations of vowels before they succeed in storing more transient speech sounds, such as stop consonants. Third, consider that (as noted in chapter 1 and since) vowels are affected more than consonants by surrounding phonetic context in speech. More variable realizations make contrasts easier to learn (Thiessen 2007; Singh 2008).

The change from good to poor discrimination for nonnative contrasts can be described in three possible ways, Aslin and Pisoni (1980) observed: (a) as initial absence of discriminatory skill, which must then be induced; (b) as partial ability initially, with discrimination being enhanced, maintained, or lost in line with experience; and (c) as good initial skills that are either lost or maintained depending on experience with a particular contrast. The first option is obviously ruled out by the evidence of very early discrimination skills. The discussion has thus centered on whether (b) or (c) is a better account, with the current consensus favoring a bit of both. Infant consonant discrimination is best for contrasts that are perceptually distinct, but it is less good for less distinct contrasts such as weak fricatives (Eilers, Wilson, and Moore 1977; Polka, Colantonio, and Sundara 2001). Also, more-salient contrasts of the native language are discriminated earlier than less-salient contrasts (Narayan, Werker, and Beddor 2010). Aslin and Pisoni's choice was a version of (c) in which initial skills are entirely auditory in nature and as good as they can be, given the degree of distinctness of the input and the processing abilities of the infant brain. However, there is evidence for enhancement of initial skills, as proposed for (b). Consider that the less-salient contrasts are indeed well discriminated by adult listeners for whom they are phonemically relevant; this is improvement that must have come about by experience. One difficult contrast is the English [r]-[l]; Kuhl et al. (2006) observed equivalent performance in English- and Japanese-learning infants at six to eight months, but at ten to twelve months the performance of Japanese infants had dropped off whereas that of English infants had significantly improved.

The way in which experience attunes performance has been examined in studies of statistical learning. If the input presents a clearly bimodal distribution along some continuum of contrast, six- and eight-month-olds learn a distinction between the continuum endpoints, but they do not learn this from a unimodal distribution (Maye, Werker, and Gerken 2002). The contrast manipulated here is a natural one in English (unaspirated voiceless versus voiced alveolar stops; e.g., [t] in *stay*, [d] in *day*), and infants can discriminate it (Pegg and Werker 1997). The lack of learning in the unimodal case thus suggests that distributional information in the input not only can sharpen discrimination of a contrast but can also diminish it. Enhancement can also occur for contrasts that infants have never before needed to distinguish (Hindi stops), and bimodally distributed training of a featural contrast on one of two places of articulation (velar or dental) generalizes to the same contrast at the other place of articulation (Maye, Weiss, and Aslin 2008). Sensitivity to distributional information is a powerful learning mechanism.

What is now quite clear is that discriminatory abilities are not irretrievably lost as a result of this experience. Adults can perfectly well discriminate unfamiliar foreign contrasts when these are not in danger of being captured by native-language phonemic categories (Best et al. 1988, described in chapter 9). Although the same infant brains show discrimination of phonetic contrasts at six to seven months but no longer show it at eleven months (Cheour et al. 1998; Rivera-Gaxiola, Silva-Peyrera, and Kuhl 2005), other responses in the eleven-month-olds' brains suggest that the acoustic differences involved are nevertheless registered (Rivera-Gaxiola, Silva-Peyrera, et al. 2005). The dramatic changes in the second half of the infant's first year, especially the reduction in the range of phonetic contrasts that are discriminated, attest to the infant's efficient use of speech in the environment. Phonetic skills continue to show reductions across childhood (Burnham 1986). But ability has not been lost; rather, the ability to focus on what is relevant for linguistic communication has increased.

8.6 How the Input Helps

There is a style of speech sometimes called "motherese" or, less colorfully, infant-directed speech. In comparison with speech between adults, speech directed to infants has a slower articulation rate, longer pauses and shorter continuous sequences, more frequent stresses, higher pitch, and a wider intonational range (Fernald and Kuhl 1987; Fernald and Simon 1984; Fernald et al. 1989; Garnica 1977; Stern et al. 1983). The two styles are quite different; we all recognize motherese when we hear it.

Note, however, that some of these effects may not be universal. Although rising contours predominate in infant-directed speech in the stress languages English (Sullivan and Horowitz 1983; Kitamura et al. 2002), German (Fernald and Simon 1984), and Dutch (Van de Weijer 1999), falling contours are more associated with the same style in the tone languages Mandarin (Grieser and Kuhl 1988; Papousek and Hwang 1991) and Thai (Tuaycharoen 1978; Kitamura et al. 2002). In fact, a recognizable style of infant-directed speech is itself not universal; in some cultures, infants hear much normal adult speech but not necessarily any speech in a special infant-directed mode (Heath 1983; Schieffelin 1985; Schieffelin and Ochs 1983).

Universal or not, there is abundant evidence that infants who are exposed to the infant-directed speech style prefer it over speech between adults, from an early age and across languages (Cooper and Aslin 1990; Fernald 1985; Werker and McLeod 1989; Pegg, Werker, and McLeod 1992; Werker, Pegg, and McLeod 1994). The pitch characteristics of speech to infants were first held to be responsible for this preference (Sullivan and Horowitz 1983; Fernald and Kuhl 1987). But later studies showed that, in fact, it is the affect expressed in this style that really makes it attractive (Kitamura and Burnham 1998, 2003; Singh, Morgan, and Best 2002). Exaggerated prosody, typical of infant-directed speech, is also found in highly emotion-laden adult speech (Trainor, Austin, and Desjardins 2000), which suggests that the special style used for talking to infants may primarily be emphasizing the communicative function and the emotion it involves; in so doing, it perhaps convinces the infant that interpersonal communication is an enjoyable activity. Infants' preference for affective infant-directed speech is stronger at four to five months of age than at eight to nine months (Werker and McLeod 1989), and indeed, around nine months, when word acquisition is beginning, the predominance of affect expression in the speech that infants receive gives way to an increase in directive utterances (Kitamura and Burnham 2003).

8.6.1 Van de Weijer's Corpus

One study covered the entire input heard by an infant in the crucial six- to nine-months period: the doctoral dissertation of Van de Weijer (1999). The infant, a little girl, was accompanied at all times by a digital tape recorder (handily stowed in a bicycle basket!—perhaps not so surprising, given that this research was carried out in the Netherlands. The basket was handy because it could be easily hooked to the side of the infant's crib or on nearby furniture). The microphone dangled from the basket and hung by her ear, so that whatever she heard was recorded. The recorder was switched on as soon as she woke up, and it was off only while she slept. In this way everything she heard could be captured.

Some 800 hours of recordings were made in the three-month period. This is a treasure house of material. Much of the treasure is still untouched—transcription and analysis of 800 hours of recordings is far beyond what a single human being can accomplish in the (relatively) short period of doctoral research. Van de Weijer analyzed about one fifth of the data—the first week, the middle week, and the last week, which amounted to approximately 150 recorded hours. Altogether, some 85,000 utterances were transcribed and analyzed.

From this study, we know that the greater part of what infants hear is not necessarily directed to them personally. This baby heard, on average, just over two and a half hours of speech per day. That was the sum of all utterances, excluding any silence or pause. Figure 8.3 shows the breakdown of the sum: around 20 percent was

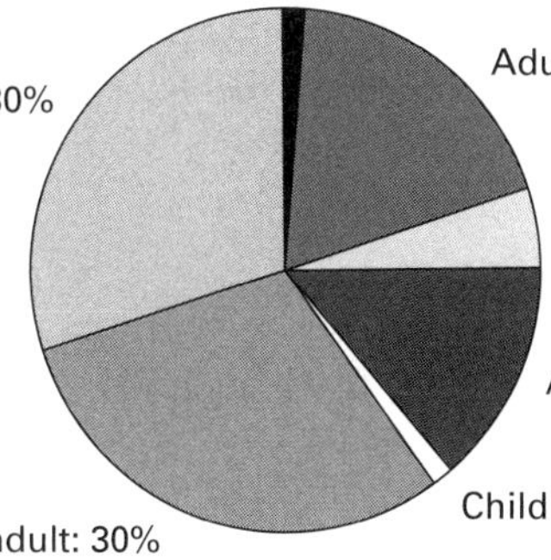

Figure 8.3
The daily average speech input received by a normally developing infant between the age of six and nine months, as a function of speaker and addressee. The average total input for a day is 2.56 hours; 14 percent of that (the speech addressed directly to the infant by an adult speaker) thus amounts to 21.5 minutes. (Data from Van de Weijer 1999.)

speech between adults in the environment, and around 60 percent was speech between adults and the infant's older sibling. Just 14 percent of the input was speech uttered by an adult directly to the infant—that is, on average 21.5 minutes of speech per day.

The characteristics of this latter speech were certainly different from the same adults' speech among themselves or to the older child. The mean length of the infant-directed utterances was shorter—just over two and a half words, compared with just over three words to the older child, and four and a half words in adult speech (note that long utterances never predominate in speech, even among adults!). The infant-directed utterances contained fewer different words—less than half as many different words as the same adult speakers used to the older child. And the type-token ratio in the speech to the infant was lower; that is, each word that was used was more likely to be reused. Further, in comparison to the other types of speech, the infant-directed speech contained more unique word-boundary sequences—that is, sound sequences that occurred across word boundaries but never within words. And finally, the words spoken to the infant contained significantly fewer other words embedded within them than the words in the two other types of speech.

But although the utterances to the infant were shorter, it was not the case that she mostly heard isolated words. Far from it. Less than 9 percent of the words (of all types) that she heard occurred in isolation; so, more than 91 percent occurred in longer sequences. Even in the speech to the infant herself, 86.7 percent of words occurred as part of longer utterances, and only 13.3 percent were single-word utterances. That is: what the infant heard was, in general, continuous speech.

At the time of writing, the infant in question has become a teenager doing well in high school. From this evidence, at least, it seems that language acquisition is well supported by the type of speech input that this infant received between the ages of six and nine months.

8.6.2 The Phonemic Cues in Infant-Directed Speech

Infant-directed speech appears in some respects to be tailored to the language learner's needs. In English, Swedish, and Russian, the vowels [a], [u], and [i] (which fall at the edges of the vowel space of any language) are located further from one another in the vowel space of infant-directed speech samples than in the adult-speech vowel space (Kuhl et al. 1997). The same was true of the same three vowels in the content words in the Dutch corpus just described (Van de Weijer 2001a). Thus the vowel space presented to infants is expanded, which makes the vowel categories more distinct and hence putatively more easily learned. Computer models certainly learn these three vowels more readily from infant-directed than from adult-directed speech samples in English (De Boer and Kuhl 2003), and they construct appropriately different sets of vowel categories given infant-directed input in English versus Japanese (Vallabha et al. 2007). The vowel space expansion does not simply follow from the suprasegmental characteristics of infant-directed speech, or from the features that express affect, because speech to pets, though it resembles speech to infants both in suprasegmentals and in rated affect, shows no such vowel-space expansion (Burnham, Kitamura, and Vollmer-Conna 2002). This is, of course, consistent with an assumption on the part of speakers that the addressees to which they direct such speech are not very likely to learn language from it.

Consonants, too, are especially distinct in infant-directed speech—for instance, the spectrum for English [s] has more higher-frequency energy whereas that for [ʃ] has more lower-frequency energy, and this distinction is enhanced in infant-directed compared with adult speech (Cristià 2010). Infant-directed speech also groups phonemes more clearly into words, in that the range of word and syllable onsets and offsets is smaller than in adult speech (Van de Weijer 1999), and many sound sequences occur only within words, whereas others occur only across word boundaries (Hockema 2006). When adults are teaching their infants phonemic contrasts, they emphasize the aspects most relevant to the phonology of their language; Werker et al. (2007) had English and Japanese mothers teach their infants pairs of names such as *Gidda* and *Geeda*, and found that the English mothers emphasized the spectral differences between the (vowels in the) names, whereas the Japanese mothers emphasized the durational differences (short vowel with geminate consonant versus long vowel with single consonant). Infants' attendance to such factors in the speech they hear is reflected in their own productions: their babbling changes in accord with speech input they have just received (Goldstein and Schwade 2008).

But it would be too simplistic to say that phonemes are always more clearly articulated in infant-directed speech than in adult speech. They are not. For instance, the same vowels [a], [i], and [u] in the function words in Van de Weijer's corpus were less distinct in the infant-directed than in the adult speech (Van de Weijer 2001a). Some consonants in infant-directed speech collected by Sundberg and Lacerda (1999) were also less differentiated in VOT, and hence potentially more confusable, than in a parallel adult speech sample. The infants to whom this speech was addressed were three months old; at that age infants are not learning the consonant repertoire of their language, so there is no point in making consonants extra clear for them, Sundberg and Lacerda argued. Stress distinctions are known to be important at that age, and these were particularly clear in Sundberg and Lacerda's corpus.

Phoneme sequence distortion such as elision and assimilation occurs less often in infant-directed than in adult speech (Bernstein Ratner 1984a, 1984b), but speech to somewhat older children is replete with such processes and other reductions (Bard and Anderson 1983, 1994; Shockey and Bond 1980). Words excised from infant-directed speech are also less intelligible for adult listeners than words excised from adult speech (Bard and Anderson 1983). Interestingly, when large corpora of speech to infants and to adults were presented to an automatic speech recognition system by Kirchhoff and Schimmel (2005), the vowel categories proved to overlap more in the infant-directed speech than in the adult speech. The effect of this was that the system could generalize better from infant-directed speech to adult speech than vice versa, because the learning was more restricted and hence less generalizable in the adult speech case. Given that the corpora came from the laboratory that had produced the first report of highly separated vowel categories (Kuhl et al. 1997), some explanation seems in order. Kirchhoff and Schimmel pointed to the size of the corpus and the fact that the speech contained many repetitions. If speech for infants is making linguistic structure clear, and this includes emphasizing the discourse function, then we might expect that second-occurrence words could be significantly reduced (as described in chapter 7). Then there would be a tradeoff—discourse structure could be made especially clear, at the expense of loss of demarcation between vowel categories across the sample as a whole.

8.6.3 Speech Segmentation: The Role of Infant-Directed Speech

Parents are overjoyed when their child finally produces a spoken word. But this happens only around the end of the first year. Before that, the child has put in a full year of preliminary work. The speech input has encouraged this work by making speech attractive. A central task has been mastering the phoneme repertoire, so that the child knows which acoustic distinctions will (or will not) signify lexical distinctions. Speech input has, to a certain extent, facilitated this learning, too. But does infant-directed speech specifically help the beginning of vocabulary acquisition?

If infant-directed speech contained many words in isolation, or many words always in initial position in an utterance, or always in final position, then the infant would have less need to segment these words from adjacent speech context. Recurring patterns could also highlight word forms. Thus *what a gorgeous baby*, *what a sweet baby*, and *what a noisy baby* frame *gorgeous*, *sweet*, and *noisy*, respectively. (By contrast, *what a pretty baby*, *what a happy baby*, and *what a noisy baby* would presumably suggest a frame *what a __ y-baby* with inserted word forms *pret*, *hap*, and *noise*. It's not as easy as it might seem.) Specific proposals supporting such a function of infant-directed speech were made by Brent (1996; Brent and Cartwright 1996), and supporting evidence appeared in analyses of speech to slightly older children (nine to fifteen months). This included a positive relation between a word appearing in isolation in the mother's speech and the child producing the same word (Brent and Siskind 2001). As early as four and a half months, infants show a preference for hearing their own name, possibly the word they most often hear by itself (Mandel, Jusczyk, and Pisoni 1995).

Van de Weijer's (1999) data suggest that words in speech directed to a younger infant do not in general occur in isolation. Most of the single-word infant-directed utterances in his corpus were indeed occurrences of the infant's name, and otherwise fillers (e.g., *hmmm*) or social utterances (*hi!*). Consistent with Brent and Siskind's findings, though, a comparison of the speech directed to the infant versus to the older sibling in Van de Weijer's corpus revealed some significant differences; many more of the isolated words spoken to the older child were declaratives (*nice!*), imperatives (*look!*), and interrogatives (*ready?*; Van de Weijer 2001b). Isolated words increase, then, when word learning is established. In speech to twelve-month-olds, again, most words occurred in fluent speech, not in isolation (Aslin et al. 1996). Even when parents in this study were explicitly asked to teach their infants words, they still produced the target words in isolation only about 20 percent of the time. They did not choose more detectable word boundaries over less detectable (e.g., in teaching the word *wrist* they did not favor contexts such as *his wrist* or *my wrist*, which are easier to segment, over *your wrist* or *her wrist*, which are harder). Other attempts to have adults teach words to prelinguistic infants (E. Johnson p.c.) also produced mostly continuous speech. So, the strongest form of support that early speech input might have provided for initial vocabulary acquisition—lots of isolated words—does not seem to hold. Perhaps it would conflict with the other useful functions of speech input for infants (facilitating spoken interaction, in particular).

However, other aspects of early speech input may more than make up for this. The prosodic structure appears to help; nonsense strings, in which only intersyllable transitional probability cued a potential parse, were successfully segmented by seven- and eight-month-olds if presented with typical infant-directed prosody but not if presented with typical adult contours (Thiessen, Hill, and Saffran 2005). Recall also that words in Van de Weijer's infant-directed Dutch speech tended to reoccur, and that word-boundary phoneme sequences were more distinct from word-internal sequences in infant-directed than in adult speech. Both of these patterns could provide at least some further support for segmentation. Distinct boundary sequences have also been found in a French corpus of speech to infants (Peperkamp et al. 2006) and in child-directed English (Hockema 2006), and more strongly marked syntactic boundaries were found in infant-directed than in adult English by Bernstein Ratner (1986).

Finally, variability should also not be underestimated. Pronunciation variability results from more frequent reoccurrence of the same words anyway; it also results from more exaggerated intonation, and mothers speaking to infants tend to alternate recurring tokens of the same word between accented and deaccented forms (Bortfeld and Morgan 1999). Further, just as more variable tokens in infant-directed speech facilitated the learning of vowel categories by a machine (Kirchhoff and Schimmel 2005; see section 8.6.1 in this chapter), so word recognition at the very earliest stages (seven and a half months) is facilitated if training tokens are more variable (Singh 2008).

8.7 Beginning on a Vocabulary

Studies of the input thus show that construction of an initial vocabulary will be helped if infants can extract recurring word forms from the continuous-speech contexts in which they hear them. And indeed—infant speech perception research has established that the ability to segment running speech is firmly in place in the second half of the first year of life.

This new line of research became possible when Jusczyk and Aslin (1995) adapted the Headturn Preference Procedure (HPP; see section 8.3.2) as a two-phase task. Infants were first familiarized with words and then tested on whether they could recognize the same words embedded in spoken texts. In the initial study, seven-and-a-half-month-olds first heard multiple tokens of a couple of short words (for instance, *bike* and *cup*, spoken in the animated manner typical of speech to infants), then listened to four short texts—several sentences in a row, each containing an occurrence of a particular word. In two of the texts, the repeating words were the ones they had been familiarized with; table 8.1 shows an example text with *bike*. The other two texts were constructed around other words (which had served as first-phase familiarization for other infants in the study). In the second phase, the infants listened longer to the texts containing the words they had heard in the first phase. This can only mean that they could tell the difference between the two sets of texts, and they preferred to listen to the texts with familiar words—so they must have been able to detect the words, which they had previously heard in isolation, even though now they appeared in a longer stretch of continuous speech.

Table 8.1
Test text from Juszcyk and Aslin 1995. Seven-and-a-half-month-old infants listened longer to this text if they had previously heard the word *bike* in isolation than if they had heard another word.

His bike had big black wheels. The girl rode her big bike. Her bike could go very fast. The bell on the bike was really loud. The boy had a new red bike. Your bike always stays in the garage.

Six-month-olds did not succeed in segmenting the texts, however. But with seven-and-a-half-month-olds the experiment also worked the other way around: after a first phase in which the texts were presented, listening times were longer for the key words in the familiarization texts than for other words. Subsequent experiments showed successful segmentation of bisyllabic words such as *doctor* and *hamlet* also (Jusczyk, Houston, and Newsome 1999; see figure 8.4). The familiarization-and-test experiments have since been replicated many times and in numerous languages, although for bisyllables at least, the age at which successful segmentation has been demonstrated has been later than the seven and a half months in the studies by Juszcyk and colleagues (e.g., nine months for Dutch: Kuijpers et al. 1998; twelve months for French: Nazzi et al. 2006).

Thus toward the end of the first year of life, infants can extract newly encountered word forms from natural speech. It is important to emphasize that what appears to be going on here is simple registration of a recurring acoustic-phonetic pattern. The matching of meaning to word forms must be the primary goal of vocabulary acquisition, and infant memory abilities appear sufficient to support word-form storage by

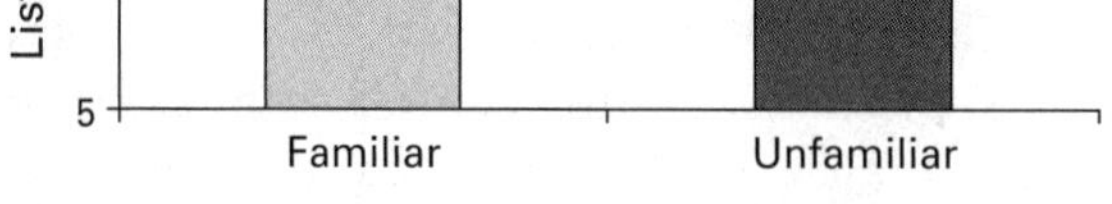

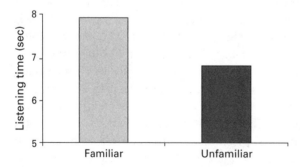

Figure 8.4
If infants are familiarized with previously unknown words such as *hamlet*, by hearing them repeated several times, they then recognize them when they are heard in a text; this is shown by the fact that they listen longer to the texts with the words they had been familiarized with than to texts with other words (that other infants had been familiarized with). The method was invented by Jusczyk and Aslin 1995; these data are from Jusczyk, Houston, et al. (1999).

this age (e.g., at six months there appear to be stored traces for *Mummy* and *Daddy*: Tincoff and Jusczyk 1999; Bortfeld et al. 2005). From nine months of age, infants can successfully be taught high-frequency concrete nouns such as *book* and *apple* (Schafer 2005). Nonetheless, no link to meaning is likely for an infant presented with words like *hamlet*, and still less for the nonsense forms presented in some of these studies (Johnson 2005a; Mattys and Jusczyk 2001). Yet the infants manage to recognize the acoustic-phonetic reoccurrence.

A further piece of evidence underscores this point: segmentation was observed when the Dutch materials of Kuijpers et al. (1998) were presented to nine-month-olds acquiring American English (Houston et al. 2000). Words such as *kusten* 'coasts' or *pendel* 'pendulum' were familiarized in the first phase, and in the second phase the infants heard short Dutch texts, structured like the text in table 8.1, with six occurrences of the familiarized or control words. Recall that English and Dutch have highly similar prosody, and bisyllabic words with strong-weak structure are typical for both languages. It is no surprise that Dutch infants showed results (figure 8.5, left panel) just like those found for English by Jusczyk, Houston, et al. (1999; figure 8.4). But the American infants were just as successful in recognizing *kusten*, *pendel*, and so on in spoken Dutch as the Dutch-acquiring infants had been (figure 8.5, right panel). Eight-month-old American infants can find real words in Italian that are spoken in an infant-directed manner, too (Pelucchi, Hay, and Saffran 2009).

Very young infants, as we saw, do not distinguish English from Dutch. Well before the word-learning stage, however, infants succeed in distinguishing their native language from rhythmically similar other languages (Jusczyk, Friederici, et al. 1993;

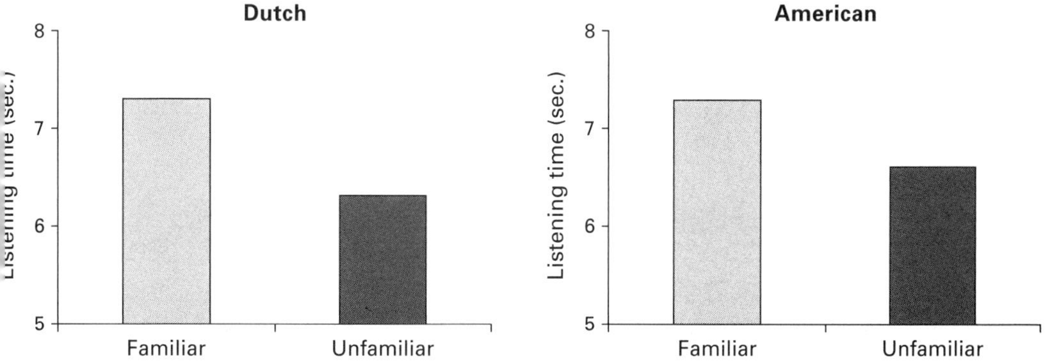

Figure 8.5
American infants never previously exposed to Dutch successfully segment Dutch words from Dutch texts (right panel). Their performance is statistically indistinguishable from the findings with the same materials and Dutch-acquiring infants (left panel. Data from Houston et al. 2000.)

Nazzi, Jusczyk, et al. 2000). Therefore we might expect that, given a choice between listening to English or Dutch, Dutch infants would prefer Dutch, and English infants would prefer English. But if they do not have the choice, and are just given the foreign language to listen to, they deal with this input in the same way as they deal with input in their maternal language—they successfully store newly heard word forms and discover them when they reoccur in running speech the like of which they would never have heard before. The last part of the first year of life is marked by a search for recurring forms that are candidates for a match to meaning—that is, material for the newly developing vocabulary.

8.7.1 Segmentation Responses in the Infant's Brain

An adaptation of the two-stage Juszyk and Aslin (1995) procedure made it suitable for the collection of ERPs (Kooijman, Hagoort, and Cutler 2005). Dutch-acquiring ten-month-olds heard in a first phase ten animated productions of a bisyllabic word such as *sauna* or *python* (these Dutch words have the same meanings as their English counterparts; that is, they are not words known to the average ten-month-old). In a second phase they then heard eight sentences. Four of these contained the familiarized word, and the other four contained another word (which, again, had served as first-phase familiarization for other infants in the study). Infants familiarized with either *sauna* or *python* might thus then hear the text in table 8.2. This interleaving was the main change that made it possible to collect interpretable ERPs. Kooijman et al. looked in each second-stage trial at the infant's responses to the familiarized word and to the other repeated word; as the example shows, the words were matched with respect to position in the sentences and immediately preceding sounds.

Averaged across infants and trials, the brain response to the familiarized versus control words clearly differed. Figure 8.6 shows the response at a frontal electrode to the familiarized word (solid line) and the matched unfamiliar control word

Table 8.2
Test text from Kooijman et al. 2005. Ten-month-olds' brain response to whichever repeating word they had previously heard in isolation (*sauna*, *python*) differed from the responses to the word not heard before.

Naast een sauna hebben ze daar ook een zwembad. In een warme sauna kun je goed ontspannen. Daar zie ik een boze python liggen. De python ziet er nogal gevaarlijk uit. De sauna is behoorlijk ver weg. Dat is een lange python met scherpe tanden. Met een python moet je altijd voorzichtig zijn. Na het sporten is een lekkere sauna heerlijk. (In English: 'As well as a sauna they have a swimming pool there. In a warm sauna you can relax well. I can see a nasty python lying there. The python looks rather dangerous. The sauna is quite far away. That is a long python with sharp teeth. With a python you always have to be careful. After playing sport a nice sauna is wonderful.')

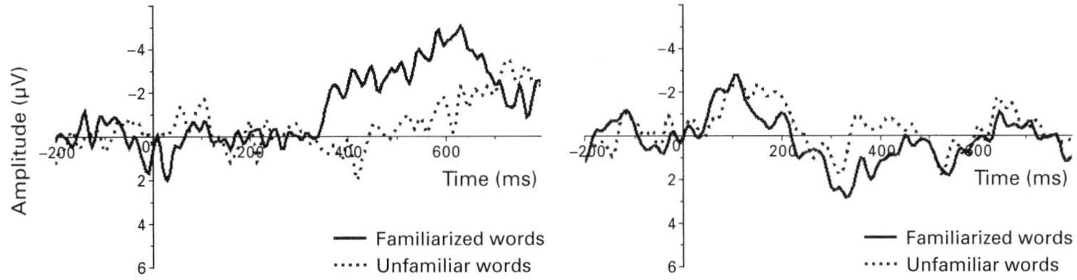

Figure 8.6
Words just heard in isolation are recognized by infant brains when they recur embedded in a text of the kind in table 8.2. The left panel shows ten-month-olds' ERP responses to familiarized (solid lines) versus unfamiliar words (dotted lines), from 0 to 800 milliseconds after word onset. The right panel shows seven-month-olds' ERP responses to the same materials. (Data from Kooijman 2007.)

(dotted line). The vertical axis shows signal amplitude (with negativity plotted upward, as is customary in ERP reports), and it crosses the horizontal axis (time) at word onset. In the left panel, there is clearly greater negative amplitude in the response to the familiarized word than to the control word. A difference in the same direction was observed in the familiarization phase of each trial (where ERPs were also collected): first occurrences of a word produced a positive-going response, but there was a steady reduction in positivity across the ten occurrences during familiarization. This is the same sort of response as observed for familiar as opposed to novel words at eleven months (Thierry, Vihman, and Roberts 2003). In adult ERP studies, repeated presentation of a word elicits increasingly more positive-going ERPs (Rugg 1985), but in the eleven-month-olds' brains more familiar items produce less positivity. Note that the infants' brains discern very rapidly that a word is familiar. Thierry et al. found the eleven-month-old familiarity response within 250 milliseconds; here the difference between the two signals is significant from 350 milliseconds after word onset. So less than half a second suffices for a ten-month-old to recognize a familiar word form's occurrence in a continuous speech context.

Kooijman (2007) presented the same materials to seven-month-old Dutch-learners, too. Kuijpers et al. (1998) had found no evidence of segmentation by Dutch seven-and-a-half-month-olds. But a segmentation response—that is, a clear difference between the ERPs to familiarized versus control words—did appear in the seven-month-old brain. The pattern, shown in the right panel of figure 8.6, differed from that in the ten-month-olds. First, it had a different location, and second, it differed in polarity (and also a bit in timing). Such differences are not easy to interpret because of the rapid cerebral development in the first year of life. But principally, what is most striking is the similarity between the seven- and ten-month-olds' results. In the HPP studies, there was a segmentation effect at nine months of age but none at seven months. In ERPs, there was a significant effect at ten and also at seven months.

Of course, the materials in the ERP study might have been somehow more easily segmentable than those used in Kuijpers et al.'s (1998) HPP. But an HPP study with the ERP materials elicited no significant preference for familiarized words with seven-month-old listeners. So the response in their brain was not transformed into a preference strong enough to keep their head turned longer toward one stimulus rather than the other. Again, this asymmetry between the brain response and the behavioral response is not easy to interpret. It could be that infants at seven months distinguish familiar from new words but display no preferences. This seems rather unlikely, given that they display other preferences (see section 8.8). Alternatively, it could be that they cannot yet translate their brain response into a clear perception of distinction that can then influence behavior. This is the account offered by McLaughlin, Osterhout, and Kim (2004) for a similar asymmetry in adult L2 learners (whose brain distinguished better between real words and nonwords after a few months of instruction than their lexical decision responses did). On this interpretation, brain responses may need to become relatively established before they can support voluntary behavioral responses. The effect in the seven-month-old brain is a precursor of the behavioral effect observed some weeks later in development.

In French, a similar asymmetry appeared with French twelve-month-olds tested with HPP and with Kooijman et al.'s (2005) ERP paradigm. Using HPP, Nazzi et al. (2006) had found that segmentation was driven by the final (accented) syllable of words such as *putois* 'skunk'; familiarization with just the final syllable led to a preference for sentences containing these words, but familiarization with the whole word did not. With ERP the familiarity response in the brain—a negativity just like that observed by Kooijman—was indeed elicited by the words in test sentences after familiarization with the same whole words (Goyet, De Schonen, and Nazzi 2010). The French infants were a little older than the Dutch infants tested by Kooijman, but again the brain response appeared to be ahead of the behavioral effect.

8.7.2 Determinants of Segmentation

Words that are extracted from speech contexts in experiments of this kind can be retained for at least two weeks; the familiarity preference is still in place then (Juszcyk and Hohne 1997). But not all words can be extracted with equal ease. Words at the edge of an utterance, where they are bounded on one side by silence and only on the other one by speech, are easier to extract than words that are utterance medial (Seidl and Johnson 2006, 2008). For English learners, it is the stress pattern that mainly determines segmentation success. At seven and a half months, infants successfully detect bisyllables with stress on the first syllable (*doctor*, *hamlet*) but not words with second-syllable stress (*guitar*, *device*; Juszcyk, Houston, et al. 1999). If the latter are consistently followed by the same unstressed syllable, in fact (e.g., in every sentence *guitar* is followed by *is*), then the strong-weak bisyllabic sequence (here, *tar is*) is treated like a word and segmented out. The evidence of this is that these pseudowords are looked at longer in the test phase of the experiment. However, if variable contexts follow words like *guitar*, then just the strong syllable (e.g., *tar*) is extracted. Similarly, trisyllabic words with initial stress (e.g., *cantaloupe*) can be extracted from texts, but in trisyllables with final stress (e.g., *cavalier*), just the final syllable is extracted (e.g., *-lier*; Houston, Santelmann, and Jusczyk 2004).

Dutch infants, like English infants, segment speech principally at strong syllables (Kooijman, Hagoort, and Cutler 2009). When Dutch ten-month-olds were familiarized with words stressed on the second syllable (e.g., *getij* 'tide'), their brain response in the test phase looked just like the one found with initially stressed words (*python*, *sauna*), but only if this brain response was measured from the onset of the stressed syllable in the input rather than from the onset of the whole word. Also, the infants who heard words like *getij* produced a (reduced) familiarity response to words with the same stressed syllable in initial position (e.g., to *tijger* 'tiger').

Only at ten and a half months of age, Juszcyk, Houston, et al. (1999) found, could English learners successfully extract weak-strong words like *guitar* as wholes; ten-and-a-half-month-olds are also sensitive to whether the unstressed syllable of such an English word is mispronounced (Johnson 2005b), so they have really formed a representation of the whole word. As will be described later (see section 8.10), at nine months of age, infants know the most likely structures for words of the language and show sensitivity to phonotactic sequence probability. Phonotactics can also affect the likelihood of a word being segmented from continuous speech (Mattys and Juszcyk 2001). Another ability seen at ten and a half months, but not yet in place six weeks earlier, is sensitivity to allophonic cues (e.g., the difference in how [t] is pronounced in *nitrate* versus *night rate*; Jusczyk, Hohne, and Bauman 1999). By twelve months, infants can differentiate highly similar phrases such as *toga lore* versus *toe galore* (Johnson 2008). These findings thus suggest that, up to nine months of age, segmentation is most strongly dependent on the prosodic knowledge that infants have acquired about the language and its words. Successful use of more subtle cues to word boundaries takes longer.

Prosodic structure and most word boundary cues are language specific. There are also, however, mechanisms of segmentation that could be universal. For instance, infant perception conforms to the Possible Word Constraint (PWC; Johnson et al. 2003; see chapter 5). Because adult experiments revealed considerable crosslinguistic similarity in PWC effects, it is very likely that Johnson et al.'s finding with infant English learners would replicate for infants learning many other languages. As yet there is no evidence on whether it would also replicate with learners of languages that allow vowelless words, though. It is interesting to note that in infant-directed Berber speech, words or syllables without vowels may be produced in a reduplicative form with more vowels than the citation form has (e.g., *susu* for *sksu* 'couscous';

Bynon 1977). Perhaps the PWC will turn out to be indeed a universal mechanism (that Berber acquirers must learn to discard). The next sections discuss further suggestions of universal segmentation mechanisms.

8.8 Statistics—A Universal Segmentation Cue?

Infant listeners can track distributional structure in the input (see section 8.5.3); this ability could offer a universal route into language-specific vocabularies (see, e.g., Brent 1996). Consider the set of utterances encountered in chapter 5: *Who's a pretty girl then? Did you quit eating? Just a little bitty more? Look at the kitty!* The sequence [ɪti] occurs in all four of these inputs. Would infants gain anything by forming an initial assumption that this recurring string is a word? And if so, do they actually have the ability to track the distribution of such sequences? The attempt to answer this question has prompted one of the most exciting recent lines of work in infant perception. To cut to the answer—it seems that infants can indeed extract from certain speech inputs some purely statistical information concerning potential word forms.

Saffran, Aslin, and Newport (1996) gave eight-month-olds a few minutes of exposure to continuous strings such as *golabubidakupotadobidakugolabu*, made up of repetitions of three-syllable nonsense words such as *bidaku*, *golabu*, and so on. That is to say, the infants participated in an artificial language learning study (ALL: see panel 9 in chapter 2). Obviously, it will be beyond them to make a two-alternative forced choice between words and nonwords, as adult subjects do. Instead, their preference was tested. After the initial exposure, the infants heard repetitions of three-syllable strings that were either one of the "words" that had made up this stream (e.g., *bidaku*, *golabu*) or a sequence that had indeed occurred but was not a constituent element (e.g., *bubida*, *dakugo*). They listened significantly longer to the latter type of item, which showed that they were able to distinguish between the "words" and the spurious sequences (referred to as "partwords"). Note that in this type of experiment, in which the infants have had a relatively long—by infant standards—and quite boring initial exposure, the novelty preference seen in Saffran, Aslin, et al.'s results is the standard pattern (at eight months, at least; not necessarily at other ages: Thiessen et al. 2005; Johnson and Seidl 2009).

The only cues to structure in the exposure phase were the transitional probabilities across the syllables (high within "words," low across word boundaries); there was no intonational variation and no pauses or other word-boundary markers. Discrimination was successful even with materials in which the frequency of the partwords was matched to that of the real words (Aslin, Saffran, and Newport 1998). Eight-month-olds also extracted recurrent tone sequences, analogous to the trisyllabic "words" in Saffran, Aslin, et al.'s (1996) study, using transitional probabilities alone (Saffran et al. 1999). For older infants (seventeen months), tracking the transition probabilities paid off in ability to learn the "words" as object labels in a subsequent task (Graf Estes et al. 2007), which suggested that the transfer from segmentation to word acquisition is a reality.

The infant ALL research, with its important implications for a potential universal explanation of the beginnings of speech segmentation, has provoked debate, just as the analogous research with adult listeners did (see chapter 4). Johnson and Jusczyk (2001) brought transitional and stress cues into conflict, by stressing the final syllable of "words" (e.g., *golaBU*). This meant that, at test, stress would fall on the initial syllable of a partword (e.g., *BUbida*). Under these circumstances, the infants listened longer to the "words" at test, which suggests that they had used the stress cue for segmentation, in defiance of the transitional information. At eleven months, infants still used such a stress cue in preference to the statistical cue (Johnson and Seidl 2009), even though, as we just saw, they are no longer solely reliant on prosodic structure at that age.

In a replication of the stress versus statistics study, stress again overrode statistics for nine-month-olds: but with a younger age group (six and a half to seven months), the transitional cues overrode the stress cues (Thiessen and Saffran 2003). Thus perhaps transitional cues are a universal tool that all infants can start with but will stop using as soon as they discover what the distributional regularities of the input language are. Using those regularities would be the most effective way to extract the words really in the input. Exposure to a list of thirty nonsense words with a consistent stress pattern, either trochaic (*DApu*, *BIdo*, etc.) or iambic (*daPU*, *biDO*, etc.) certainly induced infants to use stress cues of the relevant sort in segmenting artificial-language input (Saffran and Thiessen 2005). Even six-and-a-half-month-olds did this. Just this short exposure, Saffran and Thiessen suggested, was enough to convince the infants that it would be worth relying on a stress cue in segmenting. The putative universal cue, transitional patterns, was abandoned when something potentially more reliable, or more salient and hence easier to compute, was on offer.

In fact, stress regularity enhances the value of transitional cues in real speech (Curtin, Mintz, and Christiansen 2005), so it is only in artificial-language experiments that infants have to choose. Curtin et al. found that both seven- and nine-month-old English learners segmented artificial input as if stressed syllables were always word initial. Nonetheless, a universal cue that could serve as a starting point for everyone is an attractive idea. Could real speech input—particularly infant-directed speech, which actually seems to be quite effective in encouraging segmentation—offer infants sufficient transitional information to start the vocabulary building process in this way?

One reason for some skepticism toward this proposal is the rather unnatural uniformity of the "word" sets in most of the relevant experiments. In Saffran and colleagues' early studies, for instance, all the utterances were made up of words of three syllables; other studies have used sets of two- or four-syllable "words." But real language is not at all like that. Real language has a range of word lengths, skewed according to Zipf's Law (as in this hundred-word paragraph: 73 words of one, fourteen of two, eight of three, four of four, and one of five syllables).

There have been several attempts to move transitional probability studies closer to real language. Pelucchi et al.'s (2009) study with English-learning eight-month-olds hearing Italian speech included a test of the use of transitional probability. After hearing Italian sentences, the infants were tested with bisyllabic words that had actually occurred in the sentences, and other bisyllables that had not occurred as whole words but were made up of syllables that had occurred in the sentences. They preferred the words that they had heard as wholes (i.e., with these real-speech materials, there was a familiarity preference again). They also preferred words, again all bisyllabic, that were made up of syllables that never occurred elsewhere (and so had high transitional probability) over lower-probability words made up of syllables that occurred elsewhere in the materials as well. Clearly, the infants were sensitive to the transitional patterns in this real-language input. However, as in the studies in the preceding section, the words had a uniform structure. This was not the case in a study by Johnson and Tyler (2009); their six- and eight-month-old listeners heard artificial languages in which the words were all bisyllabic, or all trisyllabic, or a mix of two and three syllables. With the uniform-length languages, infants succeeded—even at six months, which is younger than had previously been demonstrated with such materials. But neither group succeeded in segmenting the mixed-length language. This is not good news for the argument that the statistical learning results should scale up to the task of learning real language.

8.9 Open and Closed Lexical Classes—A Universal Segmentation Cue?

One of the most salient differences in speech is that between content words and functors—words of the open versus closed lexical classes. As described in chapter 2, English function words are usually monosyllabic and usually weak, in keeping (by Zipf's Law) with their high frequency of occurrence. Content words, in contrast, are never fully weak—at least not in citation form. This difference is highly perceptible and, as described in chapters 3 and 4, known and used by adult listeners. Studies of artificial language learning showed that the frequency asymmetry between functors and content elements is a prerequisite condition for learnability of grammatical structure (Valian and Coulson 1988). Although not all languages have the same types of functional elements, the frequency asymmetry between functional and content elements, with its consequent differences in acoustic realization, is putatively universal. Both the frequency difference between the two word classes and its acoustic reflection also appear in infant-directed speech. In Van de Weijer's (1999) corpus, 53.7 percent of the infant-directed words were functors, and the token frequency of the functors was much higher than that of the content words; further, as described earlier (see section 8.6.2), the vowels in infant-directed closed-class words were less distinct than adult-directed equivalents, whereas those in infant-directed open-class words were more distinct (Van de Weijer 2001a). As noted in chapter 2, speech to Mandarin and Turkish infants from eleven months of age contains highly significant frequency and acoustic differences between the two classes (Shi et al. 1998). Thus the distinction may well be picked up quite early by infant listeners.

Indeed, newborns can discriminate between sets of functors and sets of content words, both extracted from infant-directed speech (Shi, Werker, and Morgan 1999). By six months, infants prefer to listen to the content-word rather than the functor lists (Shi and Werker 2001); this is perhaps because the content words are acoustically clearer and more interesting, given that the same preference appears when Chinese infants are presented with these English lists (Shi and Werker 2003). But this does not mean that infants are ignoring the weaker words. In contrast: ten-and-a-half-month-olds prefer to listen to passages in which the function words are in their normal form over the same passages in which the functors have been replaced with stressed syllables or unstressed syllables with short full vowels such as *gek* and *aff* (Shady 1996). The materials for Shady's experiment were synthesized; the same materials presented in infant-directed speech were discriminated by infants at eleven though not at ten months (Shafer et al. 1998). Interestingly, Shady found that her infant subjects did not notice if content words were substituted; only the function words mattered. These were, one could argue, serving as a frame in which content words could be showcased.

This is the conclusion that can be drawn from two sets of studies by Shi and colleagues, too. First, English-learning thirteen-month-olds presented with novel nonwords prefer them to be accompanied by real function words of their language rather than segmentally similar monosyllables—they listened longer to sequences of nonwords (e.g., *tink*, *breek*) paired with the real functors *the*, *his*, *her*, and *its* (*the tink!*, *his tink!*, and so on) than to the same nonwords paired with the pseudofunctors *kuh*, *ris*, *ler*, and *ots* (*ots tink!*, *ler tink!*; Shi, Werker, and Cutler 2006). Eight-month-olds had no preferences among these stimuli; eleven-month-olds had a weaker preference than the thirteen-month-olds (which, however, became stronger over the course of the experiment). A second set of experiments (Shi, Cutler, et al. 2006) then examined whether segmentation was facilitated by knowledge of the functor inventory. In the familiarization phase of a two-part HPP procedure, infants heard the above nonwords preceded by real functors or pseudofunctors, and in the test phase, they heard the nonwords alone. If they had segmented the nonwords from the preceding weak syllable, the nonwords should be familiar, and hence preferred in the test phase. If they had not segmented them, they should sound like novel forms, and no preference should appear. Eleven-month-olds did indeed prefer the nonwords that had been preceded by real functors, such as *tink* if preceded by *the* or *her* rather than *kuh* or *ler*. Eight-month-olds, however, showed a different preference: they recognized any nonword that they had heard preceded by a functor (real or not) with a reduced vowel, such as *tink* preceded by *the* or *kuh* (both with [ə]) rather than by *her* or *ler* (both with [ɚ]).

The pattern that emerges is thus that the clear acoustic separation between the frequent functor elements and the less frequent lexical elements is apparent to infants very early on. Well before the actual phonetic form of any individual functor is known, the prosodic weakness of functors enables them to be used as a background against which potential candidate lexical words can stand out. Segmentation of speech for initial vocabulary acquisition is thereby facilitated. Although it is, in principle, the frequency difference between functors and lexical items that underlies this, in practice these English-learning infants are profiting from the fact that highly frequent elements are acoustically reduced, whereas less frequent elements are not.

This facilitatory effect could potentially be universally applied. It should be noted that sensitivity to the precise form of functor elements has been observed at earlier ages in German (seven to nine months: Höhle and Weissenborn 2003) and French (six to eight months: Shi, Marquis, and Gauthier 2006). In both of these languages, the prosodic difference between function and lexical items is less salient than in English. In English, the stress-based segmentation preference and the open- versus closed-class separation go hand in hand, each facilitating the other in that the weakness of functors enhances the salience of stressed syllables, while an assumption that stress is word initial allows a weak initial syllable of a sequence to be interpreted as a functor. There will be cross-language differences in how word-class asymmetries are exploited in launching an initial vocabulary; but the fact that the open and closed classes differ is likely to be valuable to all.

8.10 The First Perceived Words

Infants successfully extract recurring word forms from speech, but this does not immediately provide them with a huge working vocabulary; the link to meaning takes a while longer. But segmentation success does yield useful knowledge in its own right. Consider that, as we saw in earlier chapters, language-specific knowledge about the vocabulary is exploited in adult lexical recognition. English listeners know that words tend to begin with strong syllables, and they use this information in segmenting continuous speech. It turns out that this fact about English is so salient that it is one of the earliest pieces of knowledge English speakers acquire about their vocabulary.

Table 8.3
Some of the 96 pairs of strong-weak and weak-strong English words used in the study of Juszcyk et al. (1993); six-month-olds showed no preference between the two word sets, but nine-month-olds preferred the set more typical of English.

Strong-weak pattern, typical for English:	pliant crossing manger ponder mantle cautious
Weak-strong pattern, atypical for English:	comply across remain upon demand macaw

Nine-month-olds, not yet in possession of a working vocabulary, have this knowledge (Jusczyk, Cutler, and Redanz 1993). In an HPP study, infants heard lists of bisyllabic English words with either the typical strong-weak stress pattern or an atypical weak-strong pattern (see table 8.3). Nine-month-olds significantly preferred (i.e., listened longer to) the typical words. This was not just because these words were acoustically more attractive: six-month-olds did not prefer either list. Nor was it because the older infants recognized some of the (generally low-frequency) words: they also preferred hearing the strong-weak pattern when the speech was filtered such that the prosodic structure was clear but no words could be identified. The nine-month-olds just liked to listen to speech with the prosodic shape typical of the vocabulary they were ready to acquire. They knew already what the typical shape of English words was.

Converging evidence comes from studies of infants' rhythmic segmentation itself. Recall that six-and-a-half-month-olds could be induced to show either an iambic or a trochaic preference with artificial language materials, given the appropriate training (Saffran and Thiessen 2005). Similarly, six-month-olds preferred in a test condition whatever prosodic pattern had been presented in a familiarization condition, although nine-month-olds preferred trochaic patterns irrespective of whether that was consistent with the familiarization (Morgan 1996). The seven-month-olds in Curtin et al.'s (2005) study, who had segmented an artificial language on an initial-stress basis, also preferred to listen in a test phase to the artificial "words" spoken (in a real sentence context) with initial stress. This indicated, Curtin et al. argued, that the infants had encoded the stress pattern as part of their stored memory of the new word forms. In other words, it seems that quite early on, infants acquiring English consider that word forms ought to be typical of English.

8.10.1 The Form of the First Words

Word forms are recognized long before production starts. The first words that infants actually produce are words they have frequently heard in their environment (Hart 1991); and consistent with this, eleven-month-olds prefer to listen to lists of frequent words rather than lists of words they are less likely to have heard (Hallé and de Boysson-Bardies 1994). Infant brains respond differently to frequent versus rare words, within a quarter of a second of a word's presentation (Thierry et al. 2003), a preference that is in place by eleven months but not yet present at nine months (Vihman et al. 2004).

With the earliest stored word forms, infants' representations appear to be reasonably exact. Jusczyk and Aslin's (1995) seven-and-a-half-month-olds did not listen longer to the texts containing *cup* or *bike* if they had been familiarized not with these words but with the nonwords *tup* or *gike*. Eight-month-olds can tell the exact form of nonwords they have just been familiarized with from mispronounced versions (Stager and Werker 1997), and eleven-month-olds listen longer to real words that they actually know, like *nose* and *puss*, than to nonwords that differ just in the initial phoneme, like *mose* and *tuss* (Swingley 2005a). Vihman et al.'s (2004) eleven-month-olds did the same with frequent versus mispronounced bisyllables (*doggy*, *noggy*). All of these results suggest that infants store even their early word forms not in vague or approximate form, but quite accurately.

However, some experiments have shown a paradoxical drop in this capacity for exact lexical representation. For fourteen-month-olds, initially mispronounced versions of newly learned forms (e.g., *din* for *bin*) can be acceptable variants (Stager and Werker 1997; Pater, Stager, and Werker 2004). This only happened, however, when the new forms were being learned as names for novel objects. If these forms were presented without such a referent, but just with a neutral visual display, mispronunciations were indeed noticed. Mispronunciations of already known words (e.g., *ball* as *doll*, or *baby* as *vaby*) are also noticed at fourteen months (Fennell and Werker 2003; Swingley and Aslin 2002), with vowel mispronunciations spotted as readily as consonant mispronunciations (Mani and Plunkett 2007). The drop in accuracy with new names is only temporary; by seventeen to twenty months of age, infants perform just as accurately in word learning tasks as in other recognition tasks (Werker et al. 2002; Swingley 2003; Swingley and Aslin 2000). ERP studies confirm the developmental course: no ERP reflection of the difference between correct words (*bear*) and single-feature mispronunciations (*gair*) appeared in the brain of fourteen-month-olds tested by Mills et al. (2004), but a clear difference could be observed at twenty months. By that latter age, preferential looking studies also show that children detect any type of phonological feature mismatch in the way a word is pronounced (White and Morgan 2008), and for vowel mispronunciations this featural sensitivity appears even earlier (Mani, Coleman, and Plunkett 2008).

Werker and colleagues explain the temporary dip in ability to detect mispronunciations as reflecting how hard it is for new word learners to construct a lexical representation combining form and meaning. Before age one, word-form recognition is easily performed, but only the most frequent and familiar forms are lexically represented together with their meaning. By fourteen months, infants are capable of constructing lexical representations for newly encountered meanings, but they are still novices at the task; the storage of accurate phonetic form suffers at the expense of storage of meaning. Once they have managed to master the trick of storing both together, however, there is no stopping them; it is in the second half of the second year of life that language acquisition sees the phenomenon known as the vocabulary spurt, when a rapid increase occurs in the number of words known. This spurt is visible in both comprehension and production (Reznick and Goldfield 1992), consistent with its dependence on a processing component drawn on by both, such as the lexicon.

8.10.2 What Is Relevant for the First Words

It could hardly be otherwise: the distributional structure of speech input affects early word learning. Using the Van de Weijer (1999) corpus of Dutch input and a corpus of English speech to six infants over a 10-week period collected by Korman (1984), Swingley (2005b) computed the co-occurrence frequencies of syllables in these corpora and examined whether simple statistical analysis would enable words to be extracted. The answer was yes: most of the syllable groups with high co-occurrence frequency were indeed words. Moreover, this frequency computation yielded, for each language, a bias toward a trochaic word stress pattern. As we saw in section 8.7, both English and Dutch infants develop such a bias in the first year of life.

As the lexicon grows, new words become easier to learn if they are distinct from the ones already known (Swingley and Aslin 2007). Also, lexical representations tend to be more accurate the more tokens one has heard of a word (Swingley 2007) and the more talkers one has heard saying it (Rost and McMurray 2009). A word is also better learned if the phonemes it consists of have been encountered in a variety of phonetic contexts (Thiessen 2007). In this latter study, fifteen-month-olds were tested in the paradigm of Stager and Werker (1997) and displayed the same lack of phonetic accuracy when the original testing conditions were replicated with a pair of monosyllables (*daw*, *taw*) but a recovery of phonetic sensitivity when the phonetic contrasts had been trained in more varied contexts than in the original design (*daw*, *dawbow*, *tawgoo*).

Distributional structure differs, of course, across languages; learning about the first words is thus appropriately language specific. Infants at this stage pick up very quickly on phonotactic probabilities built into speech input (Chambers, Onishi, and Fisher 2003), just as adults do (as described in chapter 4). Languages differ, for instance, in what is and is not relevant for distinguishing words. In English, words vary in duration because of the effects of obstruent voicing (vowels before voiceless obstruents are shorter), of emphatic stress (emphasized syllables are longer), or of position in a phrase (final syllables are longer). However, duration itself is not a means to distinguish two otherwise identical English words. In languages with phonological quantity, this is different: two words can differ solely by having, for example, a short versus a long (but spectrally equivalent) vowel. A Japanese example is *su* 'vinegar' versus *suu* 'inhale'; a Dutch example is *tak* 'branch' versus *taak* 'task'. Japanese infants acquire sensitivity to this distinction gradually in the second half of the first year (Sato, Sogabe, and Mazuka 2010). At age one, both Dutch- and English-acquiring infants are as sensitive to duration variation as to variation in vowel quality (e.g., *taak* versus *tak* or *teek*; Dietrich 2006). In word-learning tasks at seventeen to eighteen months, however, these language groups differ. Vowel quality is treated by both as a potential distinction between words, but only Dutch infants treat durational variation in this way; English infants do not (Dietrich, Swingley, and Werker 2007). The Dutch infants have learned by then that duration is a factor to be attended to for word identity, whereas the English infants have learned that as far as word identity goes, duration can be ignored.

The mispronunciation detection studies described in section 8.10.1 also show cross-language differences; in English and Dutch, both with predominant initial stress, eleven-month-olds notice changes in word-initial phonemes but may overlook changes toward the end of a word (Swingley 2005a; Vihman et al. 2004), whereas in French, with phrase-final accent whereby later parts of words are more salient than earlier parts, eleven-month-olds overlook word-initial changes but detect changes at the onset of a final syllable (Hallé and de Boysson-Bardies 1996).

In short: infants are attuned to the structure of the speech they hear around them, and the learning they display has its basis in that structure.

8.11 More Than One Language in the Input?

An obvious question arises at this point: what if the environment presents the infant learner with more than one system of phonetic and lexical structure?

The answer is: no problem, infant learners are quite capable of dealing with mixed linguistic input. Newborns of bilingual mothers, exposed to two languages in the womb, show equal preference for the two languages at birth, but they also show that they can distinguish between them (Byers-Heinlein, Burns, and Werker 2010). By four months of age, infants have formed separate representations of the linguistic systems they are exposed to (Bosch and Sebastián-Gallés 1997, 2001). This is all the more remarkable given that the two languages in this latter study were Catalan and Spanish, which do not differ in rhythm. Monolingual and bilingual four-month-olds were first familiarized with speech in the mother's language (either Spanish or Catalan), then tested with speech in the other language; bilingual and monolingual infants alike detected the language change. Rhythmic similarity is not enough to make two languages confusable, given sufficient exposure to either one.

With a measure of how rapidly infants looked at a picture of a face (see section 8.3.3), Bosch and Sebastián-Gallés found that infants from monolingual homes, Catalan or Spanish, oriented faster to native-language speech than to speech in another language (either a rhythmically different one like English or a similar one like Spanish or Catalan). Infants from bilingual homes, however, oriented faster to speech in English or Italian than in either of their environmental languages (in which they showed no preference). Bilingual infants, as a result of their separation of two systems, seem to have developed sensitivity to the existence of differing linguistic systems in general.

As phonological acquisition continues through the first year, bilinguals continue to show phonological competence in both languages. Phonotactic constraints tend to be better learned in a language that is dominant in the input; at ten months, both Catalan monolinguals and Catalan-dominant bilinguals know which coda clusters are legal in Catalan, but Spanish-dominant bilinguals show less knowledge (Sebastián-Gallés and Bosch 2002). Bilinguals' phonemic acquisition can also be affected by how difficult individual contrasts are. Vowel contrasts present in Catalan but not Spanish were discriminated by monolingual Catalan learners at four, eight, and twelve months, but their bilingual agemates only had good discrimination at four months and again at twelve months; in between, at eight months, they appeared not to be able to tell the vowels apart (Bosch and Sebastián-Gallés 2003; Sebastián-Gallés and Bosch 2009). This temporary dip in vowel acquisition may be specific to this language pair (note, for instance, that there are many Spanish-Catalan cognate words), or it may be a downside of the variability with which vowels occur. Consonants seem to show no such dip. English and French six- to eight- and ten- to twelve-month-old bilinguals and their monolingual agemates show equivalent performance in distinguishing versions of [d] which differ in frequency in the two languages (Sundara, Polka, and Molnar 2008). The same equivalence characterizes monolingual English and bilingual French-English infants' acquisition of bilabial voicing distinctions ([p], [b]; Burns et al. 2007).

Thus, being exposed to two languages makes more work for the infant. But it does not seem to cause serious confusion, and the most recent evidence suggests that bilingual acquisition is an eminently tractable task.

8.12 Individual Differences in the Development of Speech Perception

The skills being exercised in the first year of life, although they do not yet support active communication, are directly laying the foundations for language use later on. Recent studies have revealed links between performance on speech perception tasks in the first year of life and later language development. Some of the variance in speech and language development is accounted for by individual differences in neuroanatomy, just like variance in other domains, such as right- and left-handedness, colorblindness, quality of singing voice, sporting skill, and musicianship. Molfese and Molfese (1985, 1997) compared discrimination of certain phonetic contrasts in auditory evoked potentials at birth with verbal scores on standardized tests at age three. The left hemisphere responses of children who later had higher scores showed phonetic discrimination that was absent in the responses of children whose later verbal scores were lower.

This is not the full story, however, because the input that children receive also has an impact on their speech perception development. As described before, infant-directed speech tends to have phonetic and distributional properties that are favorable to the development of phonetic contrast perception and word-boundary detection. At least for the former skill, a direct relationship between the input and speech perception skills has been discovered; the more expanded the mother's vowel space when addressing her infant (and hence the clearer her speech), the better her infant tended to perform in a phonetic discrimination task (Liu, Kuhl, and Tsao 2003). This relationship was established both for six- to eight-month-old infants and ten- to twelve-month-olds; that is, both at the beginning and at the end of the period in which the language-specific phonemic repertoire is being perceptually acquired.

Whatever the sources of individual differences—and they are likely to be many—these differences correlate significantly with language development later on. A standard measure for this is the MacArthur-Bates Communicative Development Inventory (CDI; Fenson et al. 1994, 2000), which is a checklist of a child's vocabulary filled in by parents. The CDI has been normed across ages, and versions now exist for several languages. Vocabulary size as reflected by CDI scores, at thirteen, sixteen, and twenty-four months, is positively correlated with both the rapidity (i.e., number of trials to reach a discrimination criterion) and the accuracy of vowel discrimination at six months (Tsao, Liu, and Kuhl 2004). In fact, the phonetic performance in this study accounted for over 40 percent of the variance in later vocabulary (with socio-economic status controlled). Responses to nonnative phonetic contrasts are likewise related to later CDI scores (Rivera-Gaxiola, Klarman, et al. 2005); in an MMN experiment, eleven-month-olds fell into two groups, one showing an ERP response around 200 milliseconds (P200), the other showing a response around 400 milliseconds (N400). Across five CDI production measurements collected between eighteen and thirty months, the P200 group systematically scored higher than the N400 group. These relationships continue throughout development: Stronger ERP reflections of semantic anomaly detection in the second year of life are likewise predictive of better performance on picture-description tasks in the third year (Friedrich and Friederici 2006).

Sensitivity to temporal structure in auditory input is also related to later language ability. The better that children performed on a gap-detection task at six and twelve months, the longer were their average utterances a year to eighteen months later, and the larger their CDI-rated vocabulary (Trehub and Henderson 1996). The lower the interstimulus interval at which seven-and-a-half-month-olds could discriminate between two auditory stimuli differing in fundamental frequency, the better their receptive and expressive language scores a year to two years later—in particular, in the second half of the second year, when, as we saw, vocabularies expand rapidly (Benasich and Tallal 2002).

Most significantly for the arguments constructed in this book, it appears that these skills are not independent. The beginnings of vocabulary development are directly related to later vocabulary size and use. Newman et al. (2006) examined the later vocabularies of over 400 children who had participated, somewhere in the age range of seven and a half to twelve months, in six studies of segmentation from the Jusczyk laboratory (most of the studies have been described in this chapter). Vocabulary was again measured with the CDI, filled in by the parents when the children were two years old. From the responses, the 15 percent of children with the largest vocabulary (on average 646 words) and the 15 percent with the smallest vocabulary (on average 73 words) were selected. The question that Newman et al. asked was whether these children had shown the same result as the majority of subjects in the experiment in which they had participated as infants or not. There was a highly significant difference between the two groups: of the infants who later had a larger vocabulary, 71 percent patterned with the overall group result, but of the infants who later had a smaller vocabulary, only 38 percent showed the majority result. The result in question was, of course, successful detection of familiarized words in the HPP test phase. Thus the ability to segment word forms from continuous speech in the first year of life is directly related to the ability to communicate effectively at age two.

It was particularly striking that this difference even appeared in individual studies reexamined by Newman et al. (2006). Thus 82 percent of the high-vocabulary children tested by Mattys and Jusczyk (2001) showed the sensitivity to phonotactic word-boundary cues that they reported for the group as a whole, but only 43 percent of the low-vocabulary children showed this effect. In the experiment that demonstrated the relevance of the PWC for infant word-form segmentation (Johnson et al. 2003), 88 percent of the high-vocabulary group but only 46 percent of the low-vocabulary group had originally shown the PWC effect (i.e., detected *win* better in *window* than in *wind*, and so on).

Newman et al. also examined infants' ability to discriminate between input in different languages (as demonstrated, e.g., by Nazzi, Jusczyk, et al. 2000) but found that performance in this rhythmically sensitive decision task was unrelated to later vocabulary size. Segmentation of words is what drives word learning. The same relationship was visible when examined via the ERP segmentation response (Junge, Hagoort, et al. 2010; Junge, Cutler, and Hagoort 2010; Junge et al., 2012). A stronger ERP response in a segmentation task at ten months was positively

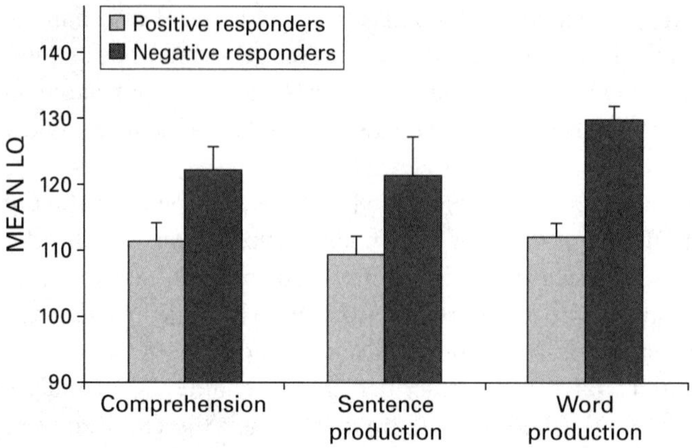

Figure 8.7
At three years of age, infants who had participated in the ERP segmentation study shown in figure 8.6 were tested on their vocabulary and their language comprehension and production skills. On all measures, higher scores were achieved by the small group who at seven months of age had shown a negative-going segmentation response (like that shown by ten-month-olds; black bars) than by the larger group who had shown a brain response in the opposite (i.e., positive) direction (shaded bars). (Data from Junge, Cutler, et al. 2010.)

correlated with higher scores, only two months later, on a CDI component; and the shape of an ERP response at the same age was related to success in a word recognition task at sixteen months. Moreover, among the seven-month-olds for whom segmentation had been evidenced by a significant familiarity effect, but in the opposite direction to that at ten months (see figure 8.6 in section 8.7), there had been some infants who had already shown the ERP response typical of ten-month-olds. When their language quotient (LQ) was tested at age three, the latter group, with the "maturer" brain response at seven months, proved to score higher on all measures than the group whose seven-month-old brain response had not been so developed (see figure 8.7). Segmentation of words from speech is an essential prerequisite for the launching of language use.

8.13 Conclusion: Languages Train Their Native Listeners

Individual language learners thus clearly differ in how rapidly and efficiently their brains can respond to the structure in the speech input they receive. But equally clearly it is the input, and not the genetic endowment, that determines what is learned. There are differences across languages that affect the course of this learning, too. Speech sounds differ in how distinct they are and hence in how quickly they are successfully discriminated (sections 8.5.3 and 8.11), so languages with relatively many nondistinct phonemes should make life a little harder for their acquirers. More than one language in the input can also slow down phonetic acquisition briefly (section 8.11): infants seem wisely to take extra care to get the separate systems right.

Likewise, the structure of the vocabulary and the number, salience, and reliability of word-boundary signals will affect the course of initial vocabulary acquisition. Several such effects have been noted in this chapter. Phonetic sensitivity is greater for more salient syllables, and because languages differ in which syllables are more salient, so are there cross-language differences in where mispronunciations in the earliest words are detected (section 8.10.2). In some languages, function words are nearly as distinct as content words, whereas in others there is an obvious prosodic difference between them; this too affects how rapidly function words are acquired and how easily the function-content word difference can be exploited in lexical segmentation (section 8.9). Even when the same type of information exercises the same effect in two similar languages, there can be subtle differences in the course of learning how to use it. Consider the initial segmentation of English and Dutch (section 8.7).

Dutch infants learn to extract bisyllabic words (such as *pendel*) a month or so later than infants in America learn to extract *hamlet* and the like. This developmental asymmetry was ascribed to the same English-Dutch difference that also underlies English- and Dutch-speaking adults' asymmetric use of suprasegmental stress cues in spoken-word recognition (see chapters 1 and 2). English has more vowel reduction than Dutch. In both languages, words tend to begin with strong syllables, and adult listeners tend to segment speech at strong syllable onsets (see chapters 2 and 4). But the more extensive use of vowel reduction in English makes the vowel-based difference between strong and weak syllables more salient, and hence likely to be more useful for segmentation by both adult and infant listeners in English than it is in Dutch.

In both languages and in similar measure, the input to infant listeners encourages early acquisition of this segmentation procedure. In the English infant input corpus of Brent and Siskind (2001), just over 3 percent of lexical words were weak initial (words such as *giraffe* and *suggest*, which do not conform to the strong-initial segmentation procedure). Recall that in Cutler and Carter's (1987) statistics for English speech between adults, such words made up around 10 percent of the lexical word counts; the speech to infants is thus significantly more skewed toward the strong-initial procedure. In Van de Weijer's (1999) Dutch corpus, the counts were strikingly similar: 11.7 percent of lexical words in the adult speech component of the corpus disfavored strong-initial segmentation, but in the infant-directed speech it was less than 3 percent of such words.

Despite these parallels, the segmentation strategy appears easier to acquire when the strong-weak difference is more salient in the speech input. The task that Dutch learners face is more complex than the English learners' task: for word recognition in Dutch, suprasegmental as well as segmental stress information needs to be exploited. Learners have to work out which type of information to use when.

Direct evidence that the stress differences are more salient for infants in English than in Dutch would be hard to come by. There are very few studies assessing early sensitivity to stress, and those that exist concern suprasegmental differences in segmentally identical syllables—the differences that are eventually ignored in favor of vowel quality by English listeners but used by Dutch listeners (and presumably Germans; see chapter 2). English two-month-olds equally well distinguish bisyllables contrasting segmentally in the first syllable (*bada* vs. *gada*), or in the second (*daba* vs. *daga*), or contrasting in stress (*BAda* vs. *baDA*; Jusczyk and Thompson 1978, using sucking measures). At eight months and at twelve months, English learners can still discriminate purely suprasegmental contrasts of an unfamiliar language (Spanish; Skoruppa et al. 2011). On the other hand, German five-month-olds detect a change from *baBA* to *BAba* but not vice versa, whereas four-month-olds detect neither (Weber et al. 2004, using ERP measurement in an MMN paradigm). The change-detection patterns shown by infants learning German (predominantly initial stress) versus French (predominantly final accent placement) in this MMN task are the mirror image of each other; that is, the French infants detect a change from *BAba* to *baBA* but not vice versa (Friederici, Friedrich, and Christophe 2007). This asymmetry suggests that language phonology influences stress sensitivity early on, but we do not yet know the developmental progression that turns infants' suprasegmental discrimination abilities into adults' language-specific choices (i.e., mostly ignoring suprasegmental information for processing English words, but attending to it for German and Dutch words).

Quite informative, however, is a finding in the study of Vihman et al. (2004) described in section 8.10.1. English-learning eleven-month-olds in that study noticed when a consonant in a familiar word was mispronounced (e.g., *doggy* became *noggy*), but they did not notice mis-stressing (*baby* as *baBY*)—that is, there was no significant difference in their response to correctly stressed versus mis-stressed familiar bisyllables. The words in this study were presented in isolation, which means that in fact the eleven-month-olds were behaving just as adult English listeners (who ignore stress pattern information in word recognition and use it only in segmentation). Such adult listeners can certainly attend to suprasegmental differences between syllables if they have to, of course (Cooper et al. 2002). Just as adults' inability to distinguish foreign phoneme contrasts does not imply that the ability to distinguish these contrasts acoustically has been lost (Best et al. 1988), neither have adult English speakers lost the acoustic sensitivity to suprasegmental contrasts that they showed both early in the first year of life (Jusczyk and Thompson 1978) and later (Skoruppa et al. 2011). What adults have learned, though, is that this sensitivity does not help much with word recognition.

Thiessen and Saffran (2004) showed that there is a change in English learners' use of suprasegmental stress cues in segmentation between nine and twelve months, with the twelve-month-olds' use of such cues more closely resembling the adult response pattern. Vihman et al.'s (2004) finding, which concerned known words, suggests that eleven-month-olds' response pattern in word recognition is likewise becoming adultlike. As soon as vocabulary acquisition begins in earnest, then, language users learn which cues to use for word recognition (and which to ignore). If the suggestion is correct that Dutch requires the acquisition of more complex abilities during initial vocabulary acquisition, Vihman et al.'s study should produce a different result if replicated with Dutch learners of the same age. There is a lot more yet to be discovered about how the foundations of native listening are laid in the first year of listening life.

9 Second-Language Listening: Sounds to Words

The efficiency of native listening rests in the exquisite adaptation of speech processing to the structure of the mother tongue. Listening in a second language draws on the same architecture as listening in the first language, but the adaptation to the first language means that this efficient adult listening system is maladapted to differently structured input from another language. In this chapter, the extensive body of research on second-language phoneme identification is first summarized; the most important factor in perception of second-language phonemes is the mapping between the phonemic repertoire of the two languages involved. Then the effects of phonemic misperception in word recognition are analyzed. Lexicostatistical analyses of a target-language vocabulary suggest that second language listening is likely to suffer from extensive unnecessary lexical activation and hence added competition; this has indeed been abundantly demonstrated in laboratory studies. Again, the mapping between the two vocabularies also adds difficulty, and the first-language vocabulary can be activated by second-language speech, too, which makes listening in a second language noticeably harder than listening in the first.

No user of a second language needs to be told that it is harder to listen to and understand speech in the second language than in the first. There may be infinite gradations of language mastery, but as a rule of thumb, using any language first encountered after puberty presents difficulties unknown in the language(s) used since early childhood. Some of these problems arise in listening to spoken language, which brings them onto the terrain of this book.

Languages learned in childhood are conventionally referred to as first language, or L1, and languages learned after puberty as second language, or L2. Research on the L1/L2 mismatch is driven both by important theoretical issues (is language acquisition biologically constrained and subject to a critical period?), and by equally important practical problems (in today's global economy, how can acquisition of a functional L2 be improved?). The practical side has dominated listening research, and many training studies have been undertaken. The growing focus on neurobiology has brought L2 listening into the biological arena, too.

9.1 First-Language Listening and Second-Language Listening

There is no single reason for the L2 listener's difficulties. Successful listening requires at least that listeners can:

- distinguish minimal interword contrasts (i.e., phonemic contrasts),
- activate words from memory,
- segment continuous speech into its component words,
- and construct sentences from the resulting words.

The preceding chapters have documented these steps for the L1. No a priori reason would lead us to expect the architecture of L2 listening to be different. So if L2 listeners can successfully perform these four tasks, they will have achieved comprehension skills for their new language. The problem for such listeners is that, for each one of these four operations, the path to success is beset by separate, possibly insurmountable, difficulties:

- Distinguishing phoneme contrasts in an L2 is a well-known source of error that hardly needs to be described; for an indication of how embedded the phenomenon is in English-language popular culture, the reader can Google the phrase *flied lice*. Problems arise when the phoneme contrasts required by the L2 differ to a greater or lesser degree from the contrasts that distinguish the words of the L1. The trainability of the most difficult perceptual distinctions is very much an open question; some researchers would hold that certain problems are indeed intractable.
- Activation of L2 words can draw on mechanisms already used in the L1, but the listener's L2 vocabulary is likely to be very much smaller than that in the L1, and even the L2 words that are known will have been heard less often. This is, obviously, a problem that will persist until a very great deal of experience with the L2 has been accumulated.
- Segmentation of continuous speech into its component words will be complicated when the sequence constraints and boundary-related probabilities that work well for the L1 are not exactly the same as those encouraged by the L2. Given that listeners are, as we saw, highly sensitive to fine-grained probabilistic differences, and given that these will inevitably differ across vocabularies, the tractability of this problem is also moot.
- Finally, comprehension of spoken sentences is similarly complicated when the L1 and L2 differ in what casual speech processes are allowed, how prosody is used, and how syntactic and semantic relations are encoded. As if this were not enough, constraints of the cultural discourse context can then add further layers of perplexing difference.

Hence there is potential for added difficulty in every step. There has been so much research on aspects of this topic in the past two decades that it too would fill a book in its own right. Here it fills two chapters; this first chapter covers research on the perception of L2 phoneme contrasts and the initial activation of L2 vocabulary.

9.2 Distinguishing Non-L1 Phonetic Contrasts

As outlined in chapter 8, listeners use the phonemic categories of the L1 from early in life. By puberty, L1 categories are extremely well practiced, and it is not surprising that any speech input will tend to get assigned to these existing categories. The challenge for an L2 learner is not only to set up a new, alternative partitioning of phonetic space into phonemic categories but also to ensure that input in the L2 contacts these new categories rather than those of the L1.

Substantial theoretical progress has been achieved by viewing the problem in terms of the categorization in this section's title: L1 versus not-L1. The central issue is then how the L1 phonemic categorization experience affects interpretation of input in another language, irrespective of whether that other language is a learning target. That is, the categories of the L1 determine how listeners interpret speech input. The implications of this for L2 listening have been acknowledged since the first writings about phonemes (Polivanov 1931[1]).

Laboratory demonstrations of L1-specific categorization also have a history spanning more than 50 years. In chapter 2, the study of Lotz et al. (1960) was described, in which three types of English prevocalic stop consonants were presented to English, Spanish, Hungarian, and Thai listeners. Each listener group responded in accord with their L1 categories. Thai listeners reported three distinct categories (voiced [b] in *bill*, voiceless [p] in *pill*, unaspirated [p] in *-pill* from *spill*). English listeners grouped the unaspirated *-pill* with *bill* rather than *pill*, because syllable-initial [p] in English should be aspirated, whereas Spanish and Hungarian listeners grouped it with *pill*, because in both languages [p] is always unaspirated.

Adult speech perception is thus highly constrained by L1 phonemic categories. But this does not mean that the adult perceptual system has lost the sensitivity required to distinguish non-L1 contrasts. Adult English speakers who cannot distinguish unfamiliar contrasts of an Amerindian language (uvular versus velar ejective stops) or of Hindi (retroflex versus dental alveolar voiceless stops) when the contrasts are presented syllable initially, do discriminate the same stops if they are presented without vowel context so that they do not sound like speech (Werker and Tees 1984b). Mismatch negativity responses in a passive listening task are also observed for contrasts for which category decisions cannot be reliably made (Rivera-Gaxiola et al. 2000). Adult perceptual sensitivity is sufficient to discriminate the contrasts, but the highly practiced categorization processes of the L1 that are engaged by speech exclude acoustic distinctions that are not relevant to the L1.

9.2.1 The Perceptual Assimilation Model

If sensitivity is unimpaired, how exactly do L1 categories constrain listeners' interpretation of non-L1 input? According to the Perceptual Assimilation Model (PAM; Best 1994, 1995; Best, McRoberts, and Sithole 1988) there are six principal ways to treat a non-L1 contrast.[2]

1. *Single-category assimilation*: The contrasting sounds are both assimilated to the same category in the L1. This is usually assumed to be the case with, for instance, English [r] and [l] for Japanese listeners, which leads to the *flied lice* confusion type (but see later sections of this chapter for recent modulations of this assumption). A single-category assimilation of this sort is the most difficult non-L1 contrast to perceive.
2. *Two-category assimilation*: The contrasting sounds may be assimilated to the L1, but to different categories. This is the case with French unaspirated stops for English speakers. These two-category contrasts are easy to perceive, because the sounds are assimilated to categories that also contrast in the L1 (e.g., English listeners will categorize French [b] and [p] as such, even though aspiration would form part of the corresponding English distinction).
3. *Category-goodness difference*: Both sounds are assimilated to the same L1 category, but one is a far better match to it than the other. This is the case with Hindi stops for English speakers; dental stops match well to English, whereas the retroflex stops are a poor match. These contrasts should be difficult but perceptible; they should appear as differences in the relative "goodness of fit" to the L1 category. Note that this case highlights the difficulty of assigning L1 to non-L1 relationships unequivocally to one of these classes. Even with a single-category situation, there may be a slight difference in category goodness for the two non-L1 sounds. Can listeners increase their sensitivity to this dimension of goodness, and by doing so move a non-L1 contrast from single-category to category-goodness status?
4. *Uncategorized versus categorized case*: One contrasting sound is assimilated to a L1 category, but the other falls outside all L1 categories. This might arise with a contrast in place of articulation where both L1 and L2 use one place of articulation, but the other is used only by L2 and is also so different from L1 articulations that not even a poor L1-category match is feasible. Such an uncategorized versus categorized comparison resembles the category goodness case, but correct categorization should be easier, perhaps even as easy as for a two-category comparison.
5. *Both uncategorizable*: Both sounds may be uncategorizable though within the phonetic space of the L1 (e.g., a contrast from a phoneme-rich inventory, for listeners with a restricted L1 inventory). Such cases can in principle be hard or easy, depending on the acoustic-phonetic distinction involved and the precise L1 categories available; an example could be the English dental fricatives in *thin* and *than* for

listeners from an Australian language such as Arrente, without fricatives but with dental place of articulation for nonfricative contrasts.

6. *Nonassimilable*: Finally, it might be the case that both sounds may be uncategorizable and outside all L1 categories. Because the world's languages have selected their phonetic stock from a relatively limited range, such cases are rare, but an example is found in the click contrasts used in many African languages. For speakers of nonclick languages, these are unlike any native sound.

The nonassimilable case (6) provides a useful window onto adult perceptual capabilities in the absence of relevant auditory experience, and Best et al. (1988) exploited this by presenting Zulu click contrasts to English-speaking listeners. Discrimination performance was excellent—as good, in fact, as that of adult Zulu speakers. Infants, needless to say, could also perform the same discrimination. Thus the perceptual narrowing for phonetic contrasts in adult listening does not imply that the necessary phonetic capabilities have been lost. The lack of relevant auditory experience has not, for instance, caused sensorineural atrophy anywhere along the auditory processing path. The capabilities remain intact; but once the phonological organization of speech sound percepts into L1 categories is in place, these categories take priority for reasons of efficiency. Speech recognition requires that phonemic categories be identified rapidly, and therefore it is expedient for categorization according to the L1 system to override the detailed phonetic analysis that, in principle, remains possible.

The model's predictions regarding the different kinds of category mappings have been well supported in experimental tests (e.g., Polka 1991, 1992). Even the relative difficulty of the uncategorized-categorized and both uncategorizable cases patterned as predicted (Aoyama 2003). A particularly convincing demonstration involved American listeners and three further contrasts from the Zulu language. These were (a) a pair of lateral fricatives that the Americans were predicted to map to two separate English categories; (b) a voiceless aspirated versus an ejective velar stop, which were predicted to differ in category goodness, being interpreted as a fairly good versus a quite poor realization of English [k]; and (c) a plosive versus implosive bilabial stop, which were predicted to assimilate to the single English category [b]. The model thus clearly predicts that these listeners should find the (a) case easiest to discriminate, the (b) case somewhat harder but still possible, and the (c) case hardest of all. This was indeed what was found (Best, McRoberts, and Goodell 2001).

9.2.2 The Speech Learning Model

The practical problems of acquiring the phonetic system of an L2 and using it in both production and perception have been studied over many years by Flege, whose Speech Learning Model (SLM; Flege 1995, 1999, 2003) offers an account of phonetic learning in both L1 and L2. In Flege's view, there are no language-external factors (such as biological age) that insuperably constrain phonetic perception or production. The learning process is effectively continuous. An existing L1 affects acquisition of an L2, but acquisition of an L2 also affects the L1 system. Language users do their best to keep separate systems apart and distinct; for example, Dutch native speakers with good English proficiency shift the boundary of their categories [t] and [d] as a function of whether they believe they are hearing Dutch or English (Flege and Eefting 1987), and Spanish learners of English adopt different perceptual strategies as a function of the relation between their native variety and the particular variety of English they are learning (Escudero and Boersma 2004). How successful these attempts are depends on many factors (see, e.g., Flege, Munro, and Fox 1994), with age of initial exposure to the L2 and mapping of given L2 contrasts to the L1 system exercising the largest effects.

Flege's model is focused on learning, and its particular forte is accounting for why some types of contrast are more difficult than others to learn (and to apply, in production and in perception, respectively). There are alternative learning accounts, such as the claim that a match between the L1 and L2 in the relevant features involved in a contrast is required for successful learning; this has accounted for asymmetries in Chinese versus Japanese learning of English [l]-[r] (Brown 1998), and for the course of Japanese learning of Russian sounds (Larson-Hall 2004). Nonetheless, the SLM has a good track record in predicting degree of learning difficulty for speech sounds of an L2. The following two sections deal with such cases of learning where the outcome may not be immediately intuitive.

9.2.3 Familiar Phonetic Contrasts in Unfamiliar Positions

In some phonological systems, certain contrasts may occur only in restricted positions. Thus both English and Dutch contrast voiced versus voiceless obstruents (e.g., [d] versus [t], [s] versus [z]). In English, such contrasts may occur either syllable initially or syllable finally, but in Dutch, voicing can contrast only syllable initially. All syllable-final obstruents in Dutch are voiceless. So, how do Dutch listeners cope with English contrasts such as *pad* versus *pat* or *peace* versus *peas*? Many other languages share this restriction with Dutch. In general, how do listeners process phonetic contrasts that are in principle familiar to them but appear in an unfamiliar position?

The answer is: quite well, in fact. Dutch listeners, for instance, can discriminate voiced from voiceless English syllable-final obstruents by applying to syllable-final decisions the same procedures that they use for syllable-initial decisions (Broersma 2005). Interestingly, though, this is not what L1 listeners do. For English listeners, the strongest cue to syllable-final voicing is the duration of the preceding vowel. The vowels in *pad* and *peas* are significantly longer than the vowels in *pat* and *peace*, and even though there are undeniably other cues as well, the vowel difference is so strong that English listeners can usually rely on it alone. Dutch listeners have experience with processing vowel duration, but for them it distinguishes between vowels and hence words (e.g., *taak* versus *tak*; see chapter 8). In these fricative-categorization experiments, English listeners relied more on vowel duration than Dutch listeners. If duration was held constant, the English listeners' responses became less categorical, whereas Dutch listeners made more effective use of the residual nondurational cues than English listeners did (Broersma 2008, 2010). Also, the Dutch listeners were able to be more flexible than the L1 listeners in use of the vowel-duration information; in the initial practice trials of the constant-duration experiment, the Dutch listeners' responses were indeed significantly influenced by vowel duration, but unlike the L1 listeners they were able to set aside use of this cue once it became clear that it was, in this case, uninformative.

The same kind of discrimination has been tested with other language pairs. Fricative voicing contrasts occur syllable finally in French as well as in English and do not occur in this position in either Swedish or Finnish. If both final fricative duration—not varied in Broersma's (2005) study—and vowel duration are separately manipulated in synthesized pairs of English CVC words such as *peas-peace*, English listeners integrate the two durational cues. French listeners, who also have syllable-final voicing contrasts, rely mainly on the fricative duration (as per the French native cues), and Swedish and Finnish listeners, who do not have syllable-final voicing contrasts in their L1, both use vowel-duration cues only (Flege and Hillenbrand 1986). Thus in this study again, all listeners had some degree of success, albeit not in the nativelike manner. Integration of more than one cue to a contrast, the authors proposed, seems hard for adults to acquire. The cue here might be said to be unitary, in that only duration was manipulated, across two positions; still, these listeners' failure to achieve the L1 integration is consistent with research on how auditory categories are learned, to be described in chapter 11—even given explicit feedback, learners find it very hard indeed to simultaneously use more than one cue to a contrast (Goudbeek, Cutler, and Smits 2008).

Chinese listeners also offer an interesting case study for English syllable-final voicing contrasts. Cantonese, for instance, allows obstruent codas, but only voiceless ones, whereas Mandarin allows no obstruent codas at all. Cantonese listeners proved to judge English syllable-final [t]-[d] contrasts much more successfully than Mandarin listeners (Flege and Wang 1989). Thus, just some experience of one end of the continuum in that position helped listeners process a continuum of contrast. Editing the stimuli to remove cues in the release burst significantly worsened these Cantonese listeners' discrimination performance, although English listeners' discriminations were unaffected by the editing (Flege 1989). Cues in the release burst are not, as we saw, the primary cue for syllable-final English voicing distinctions, only for the syllable-initial case. Chinese has syllable-initial voicing contrasts, so these listeners had knowledge of how release bursts signal voicing distinctions in one position. They could apply this knowledge to discrimination of the same contrast in another position, just as Broersma's Dutch subjects drew on such knowledge when durational cues for final English contrasts were unreliable.

Another study of the perception of English syllable-final [t]-[d] contrasts (Crowther and Mann 1992) involved Japanese and Mandarin listeners. Neither of these languages has coda obstruents (although, as we have seen, Japanese has geminate intervocalic obstruents, as in *Rokko* or *Sapporo*). The two languages differ in their use of vowel duration; Japanese distinguishes short versus long (doubled) vowels as well as the short versus long (geminate) consonants, whereas Mandarin has no durational contrasts for either vowels or consonants. Japanese listeners outperformed Mandarin listeners in categorization of the English syllable-final stops, again putatively because of their greater L1-induced sensitivity to durational distinctions involving consonants (even though never in coda position). Some degree of familiarity with a contrast or with some component of it can be turned to good use in distinguishing nonnative use of comparable distinctions in previously unfamiliar positions.

9.2.4 Effect of Category Goodness Differences

Flege's SLM makes a prediction about the kind of L1-L2 mapping that, in Best's PAM, involves goodness of fit to a single L1 category. The better the fit to the native category, the more effectively the native category will capture the input, so that, somewhat paradoxically, the two L2 categories should differ in how easily they can be learned, with the L2 category that fits less well to a native category being easier to learn, and the one that fits better being harder!

As noted, single-category assimilation and category-goodness mismatch are close neighbors; even where perceptual performance points toward assimilation, there may still exist slight differences in goodness of match to a single L1 category. Such a difference in goodness seems to hold, after all, for the English [r]-[l] distinction for Japanese listeners. Japanese has a single category spanning the English [r]-[l] contrast, and Japanese (and other Asian) speakers' difficulties with this English contrast are legendary (the *flied lice* search surely bore this out). It is the most well-studied contrast in L2 speech perception since Goto 1971 (and see Yamada 1995).

However, English [r]-[l] is definitely asymmetrical with respect to the single native Japanese category. Japanese [ɾ] is an alveolar tap, which to many nonnative listeners sounds more like a deficient realization of [d] than of either [r] or [l]—for instance, Dutch listeners who were supposed to be detecting [d] often responded to [ɾ] (Otake et al. 1996). In most dialects of British and American English, [l] is a lateral approximant and [r] a postalveolar approximant. Because only [l] shares place of articulation (alveolar) with [ɽ], it is [l] that, to Japanese ears, more closely approaches [ɽ]—certainly in prevocalic position, which is where Japanese listeners have trouble with the English distinction.[3] When Japanese listeners are asked to rate the goodness of tokens of prevocalic English [l] and [r] as instances of Japanese [ɽ], the [l] tokens receive the higher ratings (Takagi 1995; Iverson et al. 2003). English [l] is also, more often than [r], falsely identified as [ɽ] (Iverson et al. 2003).

This clear difference in goodness motivates the prediction that the less good category [r] should be mastered before [l] by Japanese learners of English—their production of the harder category should earlier approach the native target, and their discrimination should improve more for contrasts involving the harder category than for contrasts involving the easier category. That turned out to be indeed the case (Aoyama et al. 2004). Note that Kuhl's perceptual magnet model (e.g., Kuhl and Iverson 1995), which was encountered in chapter 8, predicts the same asymmetry: the smaller the perceptual distance between the L2 and L1 categories, the more effective assimilation to the L1 category will be and the less the difference will be noticed. The discrimination results of Iverson et al. (2003) were interpreted as support for Kuhl's model of discrimination, whereas the learning results of Aoyama et al. were held to support Flege's model of learning. Best's PAM model is not in any sense contradicted by these results, either, although the [r]-[l] case highlights how hard it is to assign contrasts to the classes distinguished by PAM; many continua of variation are involved in non-L1 perception. This effect of category goodness seems in any case to be firmly grounded in empirical evidence. Perceptual closeness between similar but not identical L1 and L2 categories, which might be held to make life easier for L2 listeners, in fact makes it harder.

As this last case highlights, the main models of L2 phoneme perception all make many similar and common-sense predictions. It is impossible to do justice here to the huge literature on L2 speech perception (which is, incidentally, further outdone by an even vaster literature on L2 speech production). The collections of papers in Strange 1995, Birdsong 1999, and Bohn and Munro 2007 are recommended for further details. Most empirical work in L2 speech processing has focused on phonetic category assignment, for the very good reason that the nature of the L1-L2 interaction is founded on the relationship between separate linguistic systems; at the speech processing level, the systems in question are the language-specific repertoires of phonemic contrasts. This line of work fits seamlessly with the central argument of this book—namely, that the way we process speech is determined by our native repertoire of sounds and vocabulary of words.

In the L2 acquisition literature, models such as SLM and PAM (for the L2 extension of PAM, see Best and Tyler 2007) are sometimes called "phonetic" models, in contrast to "phonological" models that focus on the phonological feature sets relevant to each language (e.g., Archibald 1998; the learning accounts referred to in section 9.2.2). This is an artificial distinction; successful mastery of either L1 or L2 speech communication requires both phonetic accuracy and phonological competence. Modeling the interaction of phoneme repertoires has certainly proven a fascinating and fruitful endeavor, as the research reviewed in this section demonstrates. More recently, such L2 speech perception studies have also been undertaken from within a phonological framework (e.g., Escudero and Boersma 2004; Hayes-Harb 2005).

The L2 phonetic literature is highly developed because phonetic systems have been well understood for many decades. Research on spoken-word recognition, in contrast, has chiefly developed since the advent of electronic dictionary resources and computational modeling techniques in the 1980s (see chapter 2). It is thus also only recently that researchers have addressed the issue of where L2 speech perception goes after phonemic processing—that is, they have begun to study the activation of L2 words. The application of this new knowledge to the L2 case is now, however, bearing interesting fruit, and it forms the topic of the rest of this chapter.

9.3 The Activation of L2 Vocabulary

Once L2 speech input has been phonetically interpreted, with greater or lesser certainty, word candidates will be activated and will compete for recognition, just as in L1 listening. The L2 listener's vocabulary will almost inevitably be smaller than that of the average L1 listener. Some words will be heard that have not previously been encountered—the "out-of-vocabulary" problem, as it is called. In this case the L2 listener has to try to create a new lexical entry (something that of course also happens, if not so often, in the L1; see the discussion in the first section of chapter 5).

But what is the effect of the small vocabulary size on recognition of a known L2 word? Does having a smaller vocabulary benefit the recognition of known words, simply because the remainder of the vocabulary offers less interfering competition? Consider an L2 listener who knows the English word *balance* but only one other word beginning with the same stressed first syllable, namely *balcony*. Compare this listener with an extremely literate native English speaker who also knows *ballad*, *ballast*, *ballot*, *balalaika*, *ballerina*, *balustrade*, *ballyhoo*, and *balneology*. Which listener experiences more competition for the spoken input *balance*?

If the phonetic problems described in the first sections of this chapter did not exist, the L2 listener might indeed have a slight advantage in the form of less competition. But the phonetic problems themselves have implications for vocabulary activation, and the effects are so dramatic that the amount of competition besetting L2 listeners almost always outstrips that which L1 listeners experience.

Inability to distinguish phoneme categories in the L2 can have an impact in at least three ways on lexical processing. First, it can result in pseudohomophones—

that is, the inability to distinguish minimal pairs such as English *write* versus *light* or *grow* versus *glow*. Second, it can cause spurious word activation, whereby non-words such as *loof* in *aloof* or *ret* in *retina* may actually be identified as real words (i.e., heard as *roof* as in *a roof*, *let* as in *let in a*). And third, phonemic confusion can induce temporary ambiguity, with a larger set of competitor words remaining active for a longer time for the L2 listener in comparison with the L1 listener (consider, for example, that *register* might become distinct from *legislate* only at the sixth rather than at the first phoneme).

9.3.1 Pseudohomophones in Lexical Activation and Competition

How can we determine whether two words are effectively perceived as homophones? One way is to use the lexical decision task to assess whether the two words each activate the other's lexical representation. The repetition priming phenomenon, which has figured in several earlier chapters, is the key here. Repetition priming causes a faster "yes" response when a word is heard for the second time. For example, the fifth item in *caramel feeper sooch aunt caramel* should be responded to faster than the fifth item in *cavalry feeper sooch aunt caramel*. If, by analogy, we find that responses to *light* are faster in *write feeper sooch cousin light* than in *pause feeper sooch cousin light*, we may assume that *write* in the former string has activated the lexical representation of *light*, causing repetition priming when *light* occurs a little later.

This technique was used to show that pseudohomophony bedevils the processing of even quite high-level bilinguals. In Barcelona, all children use both Spanish and Catalan from the beginning of their schooling on. Some children are also exposed to both languages before they begin school, but some come from monolingual family backgrounds and so do not become bilingual until they start school. For some of these, the process of becoming bilingual means encountering a larger phonetic repertoire than that of the L1: Catalan has more phonemes than Spanish does, and some Catalan contrasts involve distinctions between two sounds that would each be possible tokens of the same category in Spanish—in other words, they are single-category cases, the hardest contrasts for an L2 listener to distinguish. Pallier, Colomé, and Sebastián-Gallés (2001) found that for adult bilinguals who had started with Spanish only during their preschool years, some Catalan pairs were effectively homophonous, in that repetition priming occurred when the two were presented as part of the same lexical decision experiment. So pairs such as *pera-Pera* ('pear' versus 'Peter') contrast the vowels [e] and [ɛ], where Spanish only has [e]; the bilinguals who began with only Spanish would respond faster to *pera* if *Pera* had occurred earlier in the list.

Japanese and Dutch listeners presented with English words showed the same effect (Cutler and Otake 2004). None of these L2 listeners had any problem doing lexical decision in English; they could all accurately pick out the real words in sequences such as *duck shoff ocean vinch canthy peanut*. The priming experiment involved two types of word pairs. There were pairs like *grass-glass* and *write-light*, which differed only in containing [r] versus [l]; these should be very hard for the Japanese. And there were pairs like *cattle-kettle* and *gas-guess*, which differed in [æ] versus [ɛ]; these should be difficult for speakers of Dutch, which only has [ɛ]. Indeed, the Dutch listeners showed repetition priming for the [æ]-[ɛ] pairs, and the Japanese listeners showed repetition priming for the [r]-[l] pairs. Thus a Dutch listener's response to *kettle* was faster if they had heard *cattle* earlier in the experiment (compared to a control word such as *window*), and a Japanese listener's response was faster to *light* if they had heard *write* earlier in the experiment (compared to a control word such as *pause*). Exactly the pairs that a listener found hard to distinguish led to repetition priming. Repetition priming suggests that these pairs are functionally homophonous, just like real homophones such as *meet* and *meat*.

Whenever a real homophone is encountered, listeners have to have recourse to context to select its interpretation. There is no way to tell whether a speaker has said *meet* or *meat* except, for instance, by working out that the word is functioning as a verb or a noun. In other words, homophones cause the listener a little bit of extra work. This may not be terribly arduous work—in fact, it surely is not; otherwise, languages would not display such an enthusiastic acceptance of homophones.[4] Nevertheless, work it is, and clearly the addition of pseudohomophones to the L2 listener's lexical processing means that L2 listening involves more homophone-disambiguating work than L1 listening does.

9.3.2 Spuriously Activated Words in Lexical Activation and Competition

The inability to distinguish between two phonemes can cause a nonword to sound like a word. If [r] and [l] in syllable-initial position are indistinguishable, then *ret* will sound like *let* and *loof* like *roof*; if the vowels [æ] and [ɛ] sound like the same vowel, then *daff* will sound like *deaf* and *lem* like *lamb*. We can call nonwords of this kind "near words"—they differ from actual words only in that a single sound in the real word is replaced by an acoustically near sound in the nonword.

Such near words are quite hard to reject in lexical decision, even for native listeners. Pressure to respond as quickly as possible can lead to small differences between phonemes going undetected (so *daff* might receive the response appropriate for *deaf*). This happened about 25 percent of the time in experiments with English listeners in our laboratory (Broersma and Cutler 2008, 2011). The study also included Dutch listeners with high proficiency in English, as shown in their performance with real words (*share*, *wish*) and clear nonwords (*plog*, *strisp*); the native English listeners responded "yes" to 95 percent of the real words and 11.5 percent of the nonwords, and the Dutch listeners' corresponding proportions were not significantly different, at 89 percent and 10 percent. The most striking result, however, was the

Dutch listeners' responses to the near words—these were accepted as words over 60 percent of the time, significantly more often than in the English listeners' responses. This finding suggests that the L2 listeners had experienced considerable spurious activation of words by these nonwords in the input. They systematically heard "words" where there were none to be heard. Further recall Broersma's (2005) demonstration that Dutch listeners proficiently discriminated the (familiar) English voicing contrast in (the unfamiliar) syllable-final position. Even though they could do that, near words differing from real words in the same contrast (*groof*, *flide* based on *groove*, *flight*) were erroneously accepted as words in lexical decision (Broersma and Cutler 2008).

Spanish-dominant Catalan-Spanish bilinguals similarly accept near words in Catalan lexical decision (Sebastián-Gallés, Echeverría, and Bosch 2005). In the Catalan word *galleda* 'rooster', for example, the second vowel is pronounced [ɛ]; substituting [e] for the intended vowel makes it a nonword. The bilingual listeners were actually told to watch out for near words of this type, but they still failed to avoid making false positive responses to nonwords like *galleda* with [e].

Are near words a problem for L2 listeners in real life? One might think that they are not, in fact. As a rule, speakers do not torture nonnative listeners by willfully uttering nonwords at them. But willful utterance of nonwords is not the issue; inadvertent utterance of nonwords is the problem, and it happens all the time. The near word *daff* occurs in the real word *daffodil*, *lem* occurs in *lemon*, *ling* in *linguist*, and *rad* in *radical*—whenever one of these real words is uttered, an embedded near word (*deaf*, *lamb*, *ring*, *lad*) has been inadvertently produced. As demonstrated in chapter 3, real embedded words can be activated and can cause competition in listening. The lexical decision results suggest, therefore, that L2 listeners experience competition that native listeners are spared—competition from embedded near words.

Cross-modal priming results confirm that such competition does indeed occur. Near-word fragments extracted from real words or from word sequences (e.g., *daff* from *daffodil*, or *groof* from *big roof*) cause repetition priming for the words they resemble (*deaf*, *groove*; Broersma and Cutler 2008, 2011). In cross-modal priming, as we have seen, a visually presented target word such as DEAF should be accepted faster if it is preceded by a spoken form of the same word (in comparison to a control word). Indeed, DEAF was recognized faster if preceded by *def-* extracted from *definite* than if preceded by a control prime (e.g., *souf-* from *souffle*), The responses of native listeners (English undergraduates) after a matching prime were 6 percent faster, and the responses of L2 listeners (Dutch undergraduates) were 13 percent faster. This matching-prime effect was statistically equivalent for the two groups. The groups differed, however, when a near-word fragment was used as the prime (e.g., DEAF was preceded by *daff* from *daffodil*). For the native listeners, this led to responses that were slower (by 3.5 percent) than in the control condition. For the L2 listeners, in contrast, the effect was basically the same for the near word *daff* as for the matching prime *def*—responses after *daff* were 12 percent faster than after a control prime.

This finding suggests a worrying conclusion for the L2 listener. A native listener spots a mismatch between an input and any real word and uses the mismatch to reduce competition. The native results here were referred to in chapter 1; as laid out there and in chapter 3, the inhibition of DEAF when *daff* has been heard is evidence of this effective use of mismatch. Soto-Faraco et al.'s (2001) Spanish listeners could use vowel mismatch to inhibit SARDINA after hearing *sarda-*, and the English listeners do the same in inhibiting DEAF after hearing the beginning of *daffodil.* But the same information has led to an increase in competition for the L2 listener. Recognition of DEAF was assisted by hearing *daff* just as much as by hearing *def*, so that every time these listeners hear *daffodil*, words beginning *def-* (*deaf*, *definite*) are also activated. Embedded near words occur quite frequently, as will be discussed in section 9.4; these results indicate that they really do cause spurious lexical activation and hence added competition for L2 listeners.

9.3.3 Prolonged Ambiguity in Lexical Activation and Competition

This is not the end of the explosion of added competition for the L2 listener. It is also possible for competition to persist for longer in L2 than in L1 processing. Consider again the competition that can be expected given a word beginning *bal-*—lexical candidates such as *balance*, *balcony*, *ballast* could all become temporarily active and compete until incoming further information favors one over the others. Likewise the input *bel-* could initiate competition between *bellow*, *belly*, or *belfry*. But if an L2 listener cannot distinguish [æ] from [ɛ], then all of *balance*, *balcony*, *ballast*, *bellow*, *belly*, and *belfry* are potential candidates, and the amount of competition is effectively double that experienced by the L1 listeners who can profit from use of the [æ]-[ɛ] distinction.

Prolongation of L2 competition has been demonstrated in eye-tracking (see panel 6 in chapter 2). Lexical decision tasks (repetition priming, cross-modal priming) provide evidence of the results of lexical recognition, but they do not offer a window into spoken-word recognition as it unfolds. Eye-tracking does provide such a window, revealing processing at a stage before it is certain what word is being heard, so that alternative word candidates are still competing for recognition. The task is simple; listeners instructed to *click on the candle* will almost always do just that without noticeable hesitation. If the display then contains a *candy* as well as a *candle*, their eye fixations during the first syllable of the incoming target word will reveal that *candy* and *candle* are both, momentarily, acceptable word candidates. Fixation proportions to pictures in this task correspond quite closely to simulated activation levels of lexical candidates in computational models of spoken-word recognition (Allopenna et al. 1998).

Weber and Cutler (2004) compared the eye-tracking responses of Dutch and British English listeners shown a four-picture display. Among the four pictures were pairs of items with names that began with syllables such as *bal-* and *bel-*. For instance, there might be a ballot box and a belly button, or a palace and a pelican, or a racket and some records, or a panda and a pencil. Instructions (in English) asked the subjects to click on one of the displayed items. Figure 9.1 shows what happened. If the target item was the panda, the proportions of looks to the picture of the pencil showed that the competitor (i.e., the word *pencil*) was activated for longer for the Dutch L2 listeners than for the English L1 listeners. This longer activation can be clearly seen in the proportion of looks graphed in the left panel. Correspondingly, the looks to the correct target (here, the panda) rise more rapidly for the L1 listeners than for the Dutch listeners (right panel). The L1 ability to distinguish the vowels in the first syllables of the pictures' names enabled the

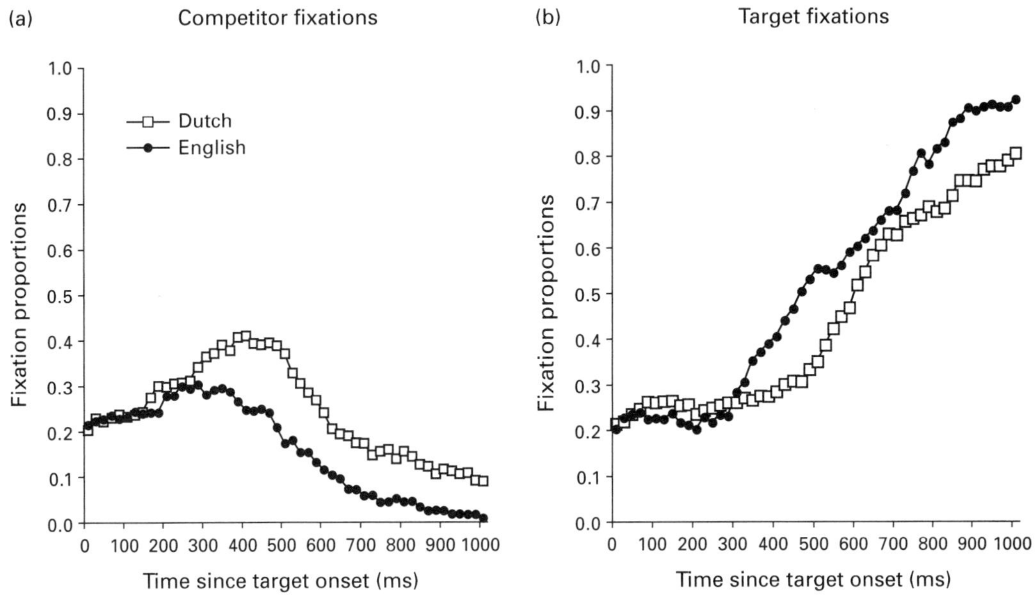

Figure 9.1
Eye-tracking data for Dutch and British English listeners given spoken instructions such as *Click on the panda* and a visual display containing inter alia a panda and a pencil; fixation proportions across time for (a) the competitor picture (here, the pencil) and (b) the target picture (here, the panda) in the first second from onset of the target word. Dutch listeners look more at the competitor picture, and less at the target picture, in this time period. In contrast, the native listeners' looks to the competitor drop away rapidly and their gaze goes increasingly to the correct target, starting from the earliest possible moment (200 milliseconds after target onset, which is roughly the time needed to launch an eye movement). (Based on results from Weber and Cutler 2004.)

British listeners to reduce the competition earlier. The L2 listeners, in contrast, experienced a prolongation of ambiguity as to whether they were really hearing *panda* or *pencil.*

Neighborhood computations within the vocabulary allow some words to be classified as harder than others, because there are more words like them; on this metric, *kin* is harder than *king*, in that if first or last sounds are substituted, both can produce other real words, but only *kin* produces other words via a vowel change (*can*, *keen*, *coon*, *cane*, etc.; Luce et al. 1990). It turns out that L2 listeners are also far more susceptible than native listeners to the effects of this difference, too, even when they are definitely familiar with the words (Bradlow and Pisoni 1999). Here, too, uncertainty about what sounds they are actually hearing is likely to be a responsible factor.

Finally, recall that competition involves phonological representations, but their activation does not flow on automatically to conceptual representations in the L1 (see chapter 3). Prolongation of ambiguity can also be seen in the finding that such a flow-on can happen in L2 listening (Rüschemeyer, Nojack, and Limbach 2008). In cross-modal priming and in an ERP study, Russian listeners to German as an L2 showed evidence of associative priming (e.g., to LACHS 'salmon' when they heard *Tisch* 'table'), which presumably reflected activation of a conceptual representation (in this case, of the rhyme neighbor *Fisch* 'fish'). This only happened for L2 listeners; L1 listeners showed no such activation, which was consistent with the English results of Norris, Cutler, et al. (2006). This finding, too, suggests that uncertainty about the initial interpretation of spoken input persists longer in L2 than in L1 listening; multiple phonological representations may pass activation to conceptual representations, where in efficient L1 listening such unnecessary conceptual activation is avoided.

9.4 The Lexical Statistics of Competition Increase in L2 Listening

How extensive are the word-recognition problems caused by L2 listeners' phonemic confusions? This section describes some lexical statistics computed[5] to answer this question (Cutler 2005b). The severity of the problem for any individual listener, of course, depends on the number of phonemic confusions the listener makes. It also depends heavily on the size of the listener's vocabulary. Exact computations are therefore impossible; we can at least, however, find out how much potential addition to the competition process a given phonemic confusion can cause in the worst case. We can assume that any problematic word an individual L2 listener knows (e.g., *write* for a Japanese listener or *cattle* for a Dutch listener) will have as many homophones or embedded words on average as the population of words with the same problematic phoneme.

It does make a difference whether the confusion we choose is vocalic or consonantal. The contribution of vowels and consonants to vocabulary structure is not symmetric; for English words from two to fifteen phonemes in length, for instance, there are about 2.2 times as many lexical neighbors resulting from a consonant replacement (*cat* becoming *mat*, *pat*, *rat*, *sat*, *cap*, *can*, *cash*, etc.) as from a vowel replacement (*cat* becoming *kit*, *cot*, *cut*, *coot*, etc.; this asymmetry is quite similar across languages; Cutler et al. 2000.) We therefore made the calculations for one of each—choosing once again the English [æ]-[ɛ] confusion made by Dutch and German listeners, and the [r]-[l] confusion that is such a problem for Japanese and Chinese listeners. These replacement statistics already suggest that the latter confusion will cause (even) more problems than the former.

Using the CELEX English lexicon, with its more than 70,000 word types and its frequency statistics from a 17.9-million-word corpus, we could calculate the statistics both for the pseudohomophony resulting from phonemic confusions and for the spurious embedding and added ambiguity the same confusions cause. We assessed the extent of each separately.

1. To tally pseudohomophones, we ascertained for each word containing one confusable phoneme whether replacing it with its confusable alternative produces another real word—for example, for every word containing [æ] we tested whether replacing [æ] by [ɛ] produced a word. Then, *and* becomes [ɛnd], which is a word (*end*), so a pseudohomophone would be created; but *ant* becomes [ɛnt], which is not a word.
2. Even when the answer on pseudohomophony is no (i.e., the *ant* case), we then still checked whether the resulting string ([ɛnt]) occurs embedded in other words (e.g., in *rent* or *mental* or *entertain*). This gives a measure of the possibility for spurious lexical activation, as of *ant* in *entertain* (for the *and* case, an example is *and* in *endless*).
3. Finally, we assessed the added temporary ambiguity by calculating how many words begin in the same way—if the third phoneme of *stack* is heard as [ɛ], how many words beginning [stɛ] (*step*, *steady*) will be added to the competitor set activated by *stack*?

9.4.1 Lexical Statistics of Pseudohomophony

Pseudohomophony turns out, contrary to many L2 users' intuitions, not to be an extensive problem. Confusion between [æ] and [ɛ], for example, adds fewer than 150 homophones to the English vocabulary. *Bland* and *blend*, *cattle* and *kettle*, and *flash* and *flesh* become homophones for Dutch listeners or for others who cannot distinguish between these vowels, whereas of course they are not homophones for English native listeners. The exact number depends on the direction in which one substitutes. Replacing [æ] by [ɛ] adds 137 homophones to the lexicon. Substitution in the opposite direction does not give exactly the same number because some words contain instances of each phoneme. For instance, *access* in the above count becomes *excess*. But if we replace [ɛ] by [æ], we would have to replace both tokens of [ɛ] in *excess*, and the result would be a nonword. Replacement of [ɛ] by [æ] in fact adds 135 pseudohomophones.

The situation for confusion of [r] and [l] is a little worse—around 300 homophones are added. *Glass* and *grass*, *write* and *light*, and *parrot* and *palate* are homophones for Japanese or any other listener who cannot distinguish [r] from [l], where English native listeners have no trouble keeping these pairs apart. Again the count is asymmetric (*rightly* becomes *lightly* if [r] goes to [l], but *lightly* becomes a nonword if [l] goes to [r]; *celebration* becomes *cerebration* if [l] goes to [r], but *cerebration* becomes a nonword if [r] goes to [l]). Replacing [l] by [r] adds 287 cases; replacing [r] by [l] 311 cases. It should be noted that the [r]-[l] counts do not include any words with [r] in syllable-final position. Although American speakers would pronounce, say, *peer* with a final [r], Japanese listeners would be unlikely to confuse *peer* with *peel* because, as we have already noted, they are generally capable of making this phonetic distinction syllable finally (Sheldon and Strange 1982). It was not necessary to exclude such cases from the present count, however, given that we used the CELEX British English transcriptions, in which no syllable-final [r] is pronounced.

Given that listening in any language involves a certain amount of homophony, and actually there are hundreds more real homophones in English, the additional load caused by any one such phonemic confusion would seem to be relatively minor. Computing the exact size of the additional load is probably not possible because we would need a precise definition of what counts as homophony to determine the "real" count. We can tally the number of words in CELEX for which there is another word with the same pronunciation but different spelling—like *meet* and *meat* or *bury* and *berry*. There are 660 such words in CELEX. But many homophone pairs have the same spelling—the *bank* of the river and the *bank* that administers money, for instance. Those are clearly different meanings, but what about the *mouth* of the river and the *mouth* of the human—is that a clearly different meaning, or is the former usage a metaphorical derivation from the latter? The *mouse* under the floorboard and the *mouse* attached to your computer? *Room* as part of a house (*bedroom*, *dining room*) and *room* as space (as in *There's room in my car*)? Furthermore, as already noted, languages regularly create new homophones by assigning new meanings to existing words. Wherever one tries to draw the line between what is and what is not a homophone, it is clear that dealing with possibly different meanings of a single auditory sequence is something listeners have to do a great deal of. Each phonetic confusion made by an L2 listener then just adds a little more complication to an already complicated task.

9.4.2 Lexical Statistics of Spurious Embedding

The spurious activation of pseudoembedded words is far more serious. *Chess* in *chastise*, *deaf* in *daffodil*, *testicle* in *fantastical*, *ant* in *rent*, *rag* in *regular*, *flag* in *phlegmatic*—there are scores of such cases for the [æ]-[ɛ] confusion. We examined these in detail. One question we asked was whether the confusion caused equivalent difficulty in either direction—that is, were there more problems of the *deaf* in *daffodil* kind ([æ] perceived as [ɛ]) or of the *rag* in *regular* kind ([ɛ] perceived as [æ])? Another reasonable assumption was that there would be a role for the PWC (see chapter 5). Just as this widespread constraint efficiently helps L1 listeners get rid of real embeddings, so it should help L2 listeners get rid of spurious embeddings. On this assumption, embeddings that strand vowelless residues (*ant* in *rent*, *pen* in *span*) would be less problematic than embeddings that leave whole syllables if they are removed from the carrier word (*ant* in *entertain*, *pen* in *panda*).

The [æ]-[ɛ] embeddings are indeed not equally common in either direction. The spurious embeddings that arise if [æ] is perceived as [ɛ] (*egg* in *fag* or *agriculture*, *stem* in *stamp* or *stampede*) comprise 7,090 cases, whereas perception of [ɛ] as [æ] (*ant* in *rent* or *entertain*, *lass* in *bless* or *lesson*) yields nearly twice as many, namely 13,658 cases. Of course, embeddings occur more often, for obvious reasons, in longer words, and longer words are encountered less frequently than shorter words. So, do embeddings perhaps cause little listening problem in reality? We can test this by taking into account the frequency of occurrence statistics and weighting each word that contains an embedding according to its relative likelihood of occurrence. A word that occurs on average once per million words would be weighted 1, but a word that occurs 90 times as often would be weighted 90. The CELEX frequency statistics come from a written corpus, so they do not provide a direct estimate of the problem confronting the listener, but asymmetries in such a written corpus should also show up in a spoken corpus. And the above asymmetry indeed reappears in the frequency-adjusted count: in every million words, this count suggests, 25,631 spurious embeddings will result when [æ] is misperceived as [ɛ], but 92,284 will result from [ɛ] misperceived as [æ].

These numbers are considerably reduced, as expected, by application of the PWC. Embeddings that leave no vowelless residue reduce to 3,636 cases for misperceptions of [æ] as [ɛ] (*egg* in *agriculture* but not in *fag*) and 8,054 cases for misperceptions of [ɛ] as [æ] (*ant* in *entertain* but not in *rent*). Frequency-adjusted estimates then suggest 14,193 spurious embeddings per million words for misperceptions of [æ] as [ɛ], and 64,198 per million words for misperceptions of [ɛ] as [æ].

Having computed all this for [æ] and [ɛ], we then conducted the same exercise for the consonantal confusion [r]-[l]. Once again we distinguished embeddings that strand vowelless residues (*crow* in *clone*, *let* in *pretzel*) from embeddings that leave whole syllables of the carrier word (*crow* in *clothing*, *let* in *retina*).

The embedding problems in each direction are again asymmetric. Perception of [l] as [r] yields 15,381 spurious embeddings (*crow* in *clothing* or *clone*), whereas perception of [r] as [l] leads to 1.65 times as many cases, namely 25,470 (*let* in *pretzel* or *retina*). Frequency-adjusted estimates suggest 59,079 spurious embeddings in every million words due to misperceiving [l] as [r], and 108,873 per million due to misperceiving [r] as [l].

Application of the PWC again reduces these numbers, especially the very large [r]-as-[l] numbers. If vowelless residues are ruled out, embeddings caused by misperceiving [l] as [r] reduce by about 25 percent to 11,458 cases (*crow* in *clothing* but not in *clone*), whereas the reduction is nearly 40 percent, to 15,428 cases, for misperception of [l] as [r] (*let* in *retina* but not in *pretzel*). Frequency-adjusted estimates then suggest 49,508 spurious embeddings per million words due to misperceiving [l] as [r], and 69,923 per million words for misperception of [r] as [l].

These numbers are still dramatic. Although the near-universal nature of the PWC implies that L2 listeners should mostly be able to avoid the embeddings that leave a vowelless residue of the input (*crow* in *clone*, *egg* in *fag*), an enormous number of spuriously activated words remain. Phoneme confusions can thus cause a substantial increase in lexical competition in L2 listening via spurious activation of embedded words.

9.4.3 Lexical Statistics of Prolonged Ambiguity

The third type of problem that phonetic confusability causes for the L2 listener's spoken-word processing is simply delay in reduction of competition. Weber and Cutler's (2004) Dutch subjects were unsure whether they were being told to click on the panda or the pencil picture until they heard the second syllable, whereas the British subjects were sure it was the panda as soon as they heard the vowel in the first syllable.

To compute the lexical statistics underlying this problem we tallied the extra competitors remaining active at the point of a substituted phoneme. For instance, for every English word with an [æ] in it, if that [æ] is replaced by an [ɛ], how many words in the lexicon are there that are the same up to that point? Thus *abandon* would be truncated to [əbæ], which would be retranscribed as [əbɛ]; the search would then deliver words beginning [əbɛ], such as *abet* and *abed*. Likewise, *stack* would become [stɛ] and the count would include *step* or *steady*.

The temporary ambiguity at issue in this computation concerns initial activation only, so the PWC has no role, because it constrains competition but not initial activation. Across the 7,926 CELEX English words containing [æ], replacement by [ɛ] adds an average of 138.03 competitors per word. Replacement of [ɛ] by [æ] adds on average 135.77 competitors. The consonantal tallies are, as predicted, even higher; so, replacement of [l] by [r] adds on average 264.85 competitors, whereas replacement of [r] by [l] adds on average 305.04. All these, of course, are added competition; the legitimate competitors (e.g., for *abandon*: *aback*, *abash*) should also play their

Table 9.1
Mean number of added competitor words for four potential phoneme confusions, as a function of position of the phoneme in the carrier word (from first to fifth phoneme; examples for [r] replacing [l]: words beginning with [r] competing with *lock*, with [fr] competing with *flop*, with [bɛr] competing with *belly*, with [dɪsr] competing with *dislike*, and with [sɪmər] competing with *similar*).

	Position: First	Second	Third	Fourth	Fifth
[æ]-[ɛ]	583	174.99	27.39	3.09	1.39
[ɛ]-[æ]	903	177.99	32.75	2.13	1.01
[l]-[r]	2,412	349.12	9.85	2.61	0.76
[r]-[l]	1,623	208.51	18.15	2.35	0.80

role, just as they do for the L1 listener. The L1 listener has no trouble from the added competition—that is the difference.

These averages across all words are again quite alarmingly high. Of course, the earlier in the word the confusable phoneme occurs, the more competitors remain; table 9.1 shows that the largest contribution to the means is made by misperceptions in a first or second phoneme. From the sixth phoneme on, misperception on average adds less than one viable competitor; for instance, if the seventh phoneme in *democratic* is thought to be [ɛ] instead of [æ], no competitor is added because there is no word beginning *democre-*. But the rapid drop-off in competitor addition in table 9.1 does not allow us to discount the severity of the temporary ambiguity problem. Misperceptions in third or fourth position in the word clearly still add competition; and the preponderance of short words in real speech means that most misperceptions that occur will be in these early word positions anyway, because these early word positions are usually all the positions there are.

9.4.4 Lexical Statistics Extrapolated

Any phonemic confusion will probably induce similar problems—so the more phonemic confusions a L2 listener makes, the more spurious activation will be induced and the more this listener's word recognition will be affected by unwanted competition that L1 listeners can avoid. Vowel confusions are slightly less troublesome than consonant confusions. But these statistics show that any single phonemic confusion brings substantial potential for lexical confusion in its wake. Even the restricted vocabulary of an L2 learner will be subject to plentiful confusion. Beginning learners probably make more phonemic confusions; but as increased proficiency reduces phonemic confusion, a growing vocabulary provides more potential competition. There is no wonder that, as the experimental evidence has attested, pseudohomophony, spurious activation, and temporary ambiguity cause real trouble for the L2 listener at the word-activation level.

9.5 The L1 Vocabulary in L2 Word Activation

As if phonetic discrimination difficulties did not sufficiently burden the L2 listener with added competition, further sources of competition abound. Consider the following situation. A Dutch speaker of English sees the display in figure 9.2, which contains a swing, a desk, a lid, and a flower, and is instructed to look for a desk. The listener first briefly looks at the lid and only then at the desk. Why would this happen? Consider an English listener who knows Dutch doing the same experiment. This time the instruction asks about a lid, in Dutch: *Zie je een deksel?* 'Can you see a lid?'. But the English native speaker first looks at the desk.

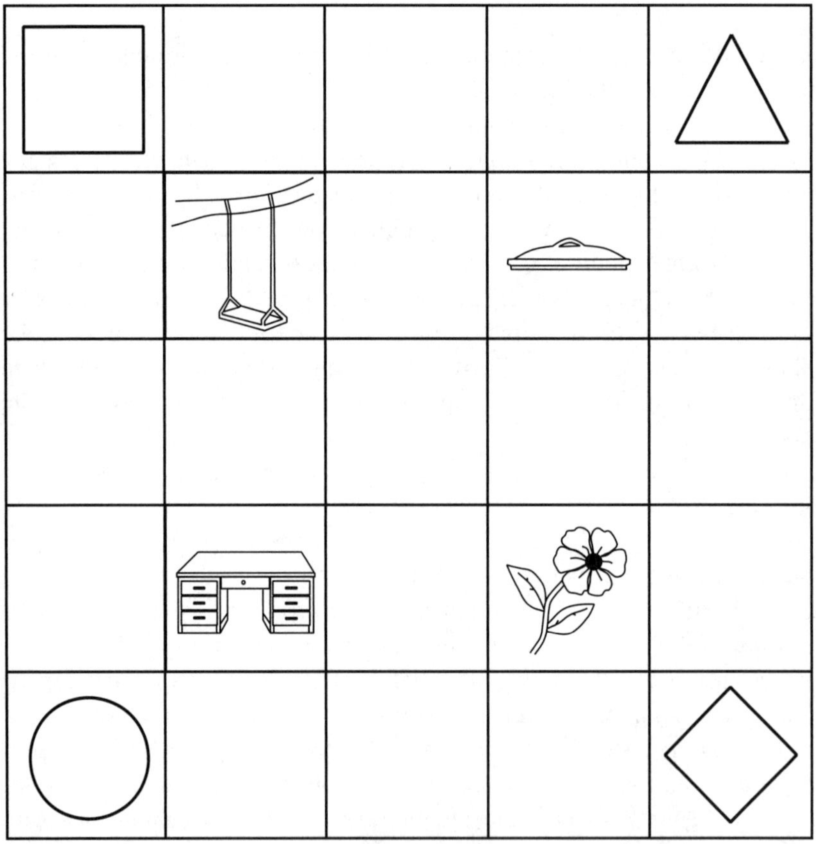

Figure 9.2
Display used by Weber and Cutler (2004) for an eye-tracking experiment testing the availability of the L1 vocabulary in L2 listening.

Clearly, what is happening is that the L1 vocabulary is proposing words for recognition although the input is in the L2. The Dutch speaker knows perfectly well that only English is coming in, but still the input *Look for a de-* activates, among other words, the L1 candidate *deksel*, which indeed matches one of the items in the display. This item then competes for attention with the target picture. The English listener experiences the same problem when *Zie je een de-* activates, among other words, the L1 candidate *desk*.

The example comes from the study by Weber and Cutler (2004), although they did not do the experiment with English listeners to Dutch. In their control experiments, English listeners (with no knowledge of Dutch) did not look at a lid when instructed to click on a desk—so there was no intrinsic similarity causing confusion between the pictures themselves. Dutch listeners also did not look at the desk when asked about a *deksel*. That means that the L1 vocabulary was interfering with L2 recognition but not vice versa.

In contrast, in similar experiments with Russian-English bilinguals (Spivey and Marian 1999; Marian and Spivey 1999) interference between vocabularies occurred in both directions. In these experiments, subjects were instructed to move objects on a table, with instructions presented in Russian and in English in separate sessions. The objects sometimes included pairs like Weber and Cutler's *desk-deksel*; that is, an object with a name in English that was phonologically similar to the name of another object in Russian (e.g., a marker pen and a stamp, which is *marka* in Russian). One study produced more interference from L1 to L2, whereas the other study produced more interference from L2 to L1. Clearly, both forms of competition were, in principle, possible for this listener group. Spanish-English bilingual listeners presented with Spanish words such as *playa* 'beach' and displays containing an English distractor such as a pair of pliers, also experienced English (L2) competition for processing of the L1; *pliers* and *playa* were both activated (Ju and Luce 2004).

Why did these subjects show L2 effects in L1 listening, though Weber and Cutler's Dutch listeners showed no trace of L2 activation when listening to their L1? Possibly, it was because of daily listening experience, which for Spivey and Marian's and Ju and Luce's listeners was strongly L2 dominant—they were all resident students in an English-speaking country, spending most of their day listening to lectures and other speech in their L2. Weber and Cutler's subjects, in contrast, were living in the Netherlands and were presumably L1 dominant. The effect of the alternative vocabulary perhaps depends not only on whether it is an L1 or L2 but also on relative strength or accessibility of each vocabulary for the listener in question. However, even an L1 that is not dominant at the time of testing can interfere with processing of a dominant L2 (Nguyen-Hoan and Taft 2010), so possibly multiple factors play a role here.

Beyond general considerations of L1/L2 accessibility, there are also variations in accessibility across sub-sections of the vocabulary. One type of input that tends to activate an alternative vocabulary, for example, is input that crosses the vocabulary boundary. Cognates are words that have the same etymology in two languages, such as English *father* and Dutch *vader* or Spanish *padre*. Motivated by evidence from word production and word reading suggesting that cognates have a special status in bilingual lexicons, Blumenfeld and Marian (2007) tested for such a special status in spoken-word recognition also, with an eye-tracking study in which listeners who knew both German and English heard instructions in English. Some nontarget items had names in German that resembled the target names—for instance, a *shirt* 'Hemd', given instructions to look at a hen. As found before (Spivey and Marian 1999; Weber and Cutler 2004), interference from these competitors was stronger when the interfering language was stronger—so, subjects with German as L1 and English as L2 had more German interference than English speakers with German as L2. However, when the target word was cognate with its German translation, such as a *guitar*, which is *Gitarre* in German, the interference also appeared for the latter group. In that case, a competitor would get looked at; for example, given the *guitar* as target, English speakers with German as L2 were more likely to glance at the picture of prison bars (*Gitter* in German). Blumenfeld and Marian also manipulated how much competitor and target overlapped in onset, and again, this factor had more influence with cognate targets. Cognates thus seem to activate an L2 lexicon even for L1 speakers using the L1 in the L1 culture, and to activate a "wrong" lexicon more strongly than noncognate words do.

Listeners are usually able to identify the language a word is spoken in, as studies of code-switched words and *faux amis* have shown (these latter "false friends" are words that sound alike in different languages and may seem to be meaning-related cognates but actually are not, such as the form [ʃu] representing *shoe* in English and *chou* 'cabbage' in French). We have very fine-grained prototypes for our native phonetic categories; English listeners detect (French-)accented pronunciation equally well from whole phrases, from single syllables, from phonetic segments, or even from just the release burst of a stop consonant (Flege 1984). Ju and Luce (2004) exploited this sensitivity in their eye-tracking study described earlier; the Spanish-English bilinguals instructed to look at the *playa* 'beach' were far more likely to look at the English distractor (the picture of a pair of pliers) when the VOT of the [p] in *playa* had been lengthened to resemble a typical English rather than a typical Spanish [p].

Listeners use speech context to evaluate acoustic-phonetic forms in multiple ways, and for listeners who know more than one language, language identity plays such an evaluative role. Figure 9.3 shows French-English bilingual listeners' categorizations of ambiguous syllables varying along a continuum from English *day* to French

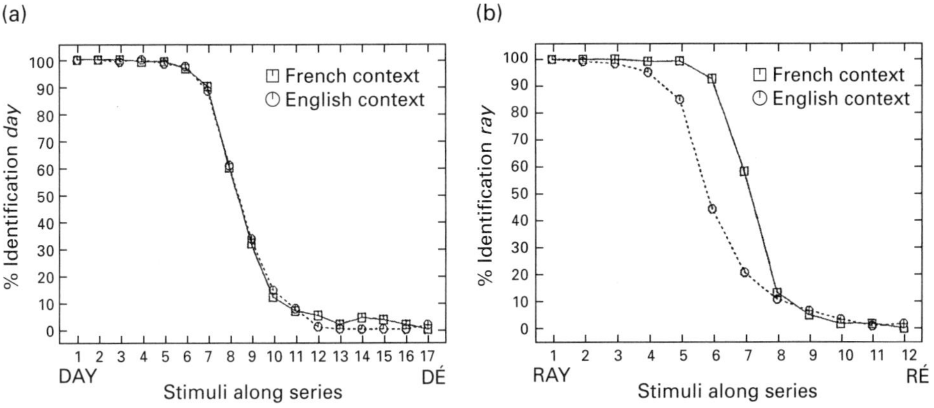

Figure 9.3
French-English bilingual listeners' identification of CV syllables as English or French words. For syllables beginning [d], pronounced similarly in the two languages (left panel), it makes no difference whether the surrounding speech context is in French or English. However, for syllables beginning [r], which are realized differently in French and English (right panel), the context makes listeners' judgments choosier: French context reduces choices of the French word, English context reduces English word choices. (Data from Bürki-Cohen et al. 1989.)

dé or from English *ray* to French *ré*; the task was to identify the syllables as (more like) the English or the French word (Bürki-Cohen, Grosjean, and Miller 1989). Word-initial [d] is pronounced similarly in English and French, but word-initial [r] is pronounced differently. Out of context, a smooth categorical function appeared for each continuum. With a lead-in sentence in either English (*We have to categorize* . . .) or French (*Il faut qu'on categorize* . . .), the same smooth function appeared for [d] irrespective of language (left panel of the figure). But the *ray-ré* continuum (right panel) shifted as a function of context language. Listeners became more particular about what they would accept—so the English context actually reduced the number of identifications of *ray-ré* as English *ray*. The language context had a contrastive effect, which highlighted the mismatch of the variably pronounced phoneme when its realization was ambiguous.

Not only the phonetic form, but also the relative probabilities of each vocabulary may be rapidly exploited. In another experiment by Grosjean (1988), French-English bilinguals heard gated sentences such as *Il faudrait qu'on slash les prix* 'The prices will have to be slashed', where *slash* is a code-switch, or, as Grosjean prefers to call it, a "guest" word from English. The gated guest words were recognized earlier as such if they began with sequences more common in English than in French (e.g., *sl-* as in the example) than if they began with sequences (such as *fi-*) for which the French vocabulary provides more activation.

Even cross-language pairs transcribed identically in IPA, such as the *shoe*/*chou* example cited before, show language-specific differences of realization. Dutch and English have some such pairs, such as *lief* 'beloved' versus *leaf*, both transcribed [li:f]. Dutch undergraduates' lexical decisions for English visual targets such as LEAF in cross-modal priming were facilitated by both the English and Dutch spoken primes: *leaf* or *lief* (Schulpen et al. 2003). The facilitation was somewhat less for the Dutch than for the English prime, however, which suggested that the slight differences in acoustic-phonetic realization had been translated directly into differences in strength of activation for the English words.

In chapter 6, we saw how listeners continuously evaluate the acoustic-phonetic realization of speech input to establish lexical identity, and in chapters 3 and 4 we saw how the probabilities of vocabulary structure are also efficiently exploited. It is clear that speech is processed in fine detail in just the same way in L2 listening, and probabilistic information may be accessed just as efficiently in L2 listening, too. Part of the use to which listeners put this information is in distinguishing, as far as they can, the L1 from the L2 vocabulary.

9.6 The Relation between the Phonetic and the Lexical Level in L2

In the L1, accurate discrimination of phonetic form is presumed to allow rapid activation of lexical candidates, and we have seen that detection of a mismatch allows the unwanted candidates to be discarded at the earliest opportunity (Soto-Faraco et al. 2001). In the L2, accurate discrimination of phonetic form cannot be guaranteed. This leads, at the word-activation level, to the many problems documented in preceding sections of this chapter.

The relation between phonetic processing and the lexicon in L2 is not controlled simply by discrimination accuracy, however. If contrasts are indistinguishable, there might seem to be obvious consequences at the lexical level: whether a Japanese listener to English hears *write* or *light*, both will be activated. However, things turn out not to be quite as simple as that. Even though pseudohomophony appears in lexical decision (Pallier et al. 2001; Cutler and Otake 2004), the two members of a pair such as *write* and *light* may not be equally activated, especially where L2 phonemic contrasts differ in goodness of fit to an L1 category. This was revealed by an asymmetry first seen in the eye-tracking study of Weber and Cutler (2004).

As described earlier, Dutch listeners were likely to look first at a picture of a pencil when they were supposed to look at a panda, or at a picture of a pelican when instructed to look at a palace. However, the reverse did not apply—instructions to look at the pelican in Weber and Cutler's study did not induce looks to the palace, and instructions to look at the pencil did not induce looks to the panda. Looks to a pelican instead of a palace might seem like a preference for animate targets, were it not for the looks to a pencil which should have gone to a panda! Figure 9.4 com-

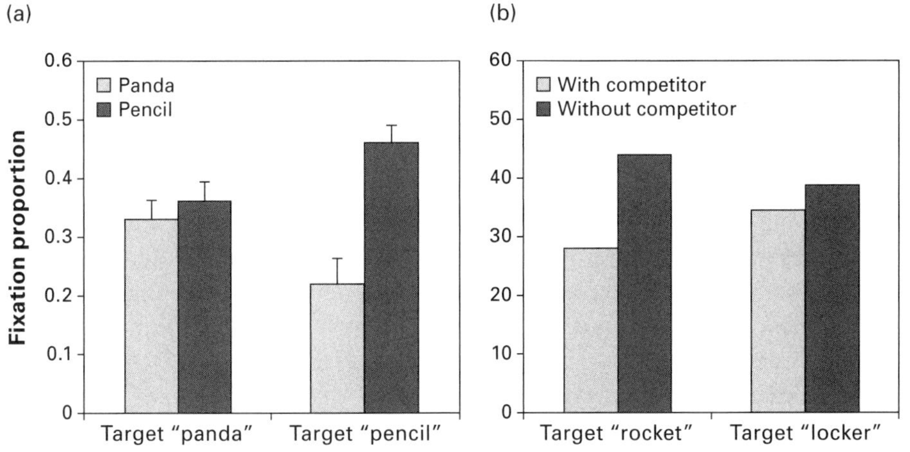

Figure 9.4
Fixation proportions in eye-tracking experiments with Dutch (left panel) and Japanese (right panel) listeners to English. The target names contained confusable phonemes ([æ]-[ɛ] for the Dutch, [r]-[l] for the Japanese). The effect of a competitor is not equivalent for the two contrasted phonemes, and this can be shown in two ways. The left figure shows how often Dutch listeners looked at each type of picture given each type of target; whatever the spoken target was, they looked more often at the picture with a name containing [ɛ]. Thus [æ] was subject to more competition from [ɛ] than vice versa. Competitors were always present in the Dutch experiment, but in the Japanese experiment, competitors were present or absent. The right figure shows how often Japanese listeners looked at the correct target, as a function of whether a competitor was present. There is a big competition effect for [r] (presence of a competitor significantly reduces looks to the target) but not for [l] (presence of a competitor does not significantly influence looks to the target). In each case, the names on the left (with [æ] and [r]) are more affected than those on the right (with the dominant phonemes [ɛ] and [l]).

pares the relative competitor effect; [ɛ] words competed strongly with [æ] words but not vice versa. In these listeners' lexicon, therefore, English words containing [æ] or [ɛ] must be distinct, with *pelican* or *pencil* containing a vowel different from that in *palace* or *panda*. The listeners could not successfully make this distinction in their acoustic-phonetic processing—whether they heard *pelican* or *palace*, the first syllable was interpreted as *pel-*, and whether they heard *pencil* or *panda*, they interpreted the first syllable as *pen-*. But *pel-* and *pen-* were then mapped to *pelican* and *pencil*, not to *palace* or *panda*. Despite the extensive literature on L2 speech perception, such asymmetry of phonetic and lexical processing had not previously been observed; it was only with eye-tracking that the mapping of phonetic information to lexical entries could be examined with sufficient sensitivity.

Maintenance of a distinction at the lexical level is perhaps not so surprising, especially because most foreign language teaching relies heavily on reading and writing. Proficient L2 users who are taught their L2 in the classroom will certainly be aware that minimal pairs such as *cattle* and *kettle*, or *light* and *write*, are supposed to be different. Confusions in writing are not reported to be common in the same way as confusions in speaking and listening—that is, writing about *kettle ranches* or *essay lighting* does not seem to be a frequent L2 error. In the initial stages of L2 phoneme learning, older learners, who can draw on more varied learning resources, do better than younger learners, even though the younger learners have an advantage in the long term (Jia et al. 2006). By maintaining such a lexical distinction, L2 users of course show evidence of proficiency. What is remarkable is that, first, this distinction coexists with failure to make the same distinction in phonetic processing and that, second, the mapping is asymmetric—whatever the Dutch listeners heard, [æ] or [ɛ], it was preferentially mapped to words with [ɛ] in the lexicon. One of the two English categories, [ɛ], was clearly dominant.

Why should Dutch listeners, however, consistently treat both English [æ] and [ɛ] as [ɛ]? Two explanations for this result in Weber and Cutler's (2004) study seemed possible. One was that [ɛ] is perceived as a closer match than [æ] to the nearest L1 category. Indeed, Dutch has only one vowel where English has [ɛ] and [æ]; the Dutch vowel is written in IPA as [ɛ] although it is, in fact, typically lower than English [ɛ]. The other explanation invokes influence from orthographic knowledge. Words written with *e* (such as *pet*, *pen*) are pronounced similarly, with a short front central vowel, in Dutch and English, but words written with *a* are pronounced differently—*a* represents a back vowel in the first syllable of *paleis* 'palace' and *panda* 'panda' in Dutch. According to this explanation, both [æ] and [ɛ] would be perceived as a front central vowel, and given that only *e* can orthographically represent a front central vowel, only words written with *e* would be matched.

The two alternative explanations for category dominance can be teased apart by considering also the Japanese case. Japanese famously has only the one phoneme [ɽ] where English distinguishes [r] versus [l], and phonetically, as we saw earlier, Japanese [ɽ] is closer to English [l]; [l] is more often than [r] perceived as [ɽ] and receives higher goodness ratings as a match to [ɽ] (Takagi 1995; Iverson et al. 2003). In alphabetic transliterations of words of Japanese, however, [ɽ] is represented by *r* (as in *tempura*, *karaoke*, *Narita*). Thus an explanation involving acoustic-phonetic similarity to the nearest L1 category would in this case predict dominance for [l], whereas an orthographic account would predict dominance for [r]. Cutler, Weber, and Otake (2006) undertook another eye-tracking study to answer this question. At the same time, their study allowed a test of whether the phonetic-to-lexical asymmetry was specific to vowel categories, and whether it would only be seen with highly proficient L2 users such as the Dutch speakers of English. The new study involved the English [r]-[l] distinction and Japanese listeners who were instructed to click on pictures in a display containing, for example, a rocket and a locker. If an asymmetry were to appear with these listeners, it could not be specific to Dutch speakers of English, and if it appeared with this consonantal distinction it could not be specific to vowels.

The results, shown in figure 9.4b, were very clear. The Japanese listeners also showed asymmetric lexical confusions. Instructed to look at the rocket they significantly often looked at the locker, but instructions to look at the locker did not induce them to look at the rocket. Thus asymmetry is general—maintenance of a distinction at the lexical level can quite often coexist with inability to make the distinction in speech input. And a phonetic explanation in terms of similarity to the nearest L1 category seems the best explanation of why one of the two L2 categories should dominate the other in perceptual processing.

The lexical statistics of the [r]-[l] and [æ]-[ɛ] contrasts, presented earlier in section 9.4.2, make it clear that the dominance pattern cannot be explained by relative confusability of the two L2 categories within the English vocabulary. The categories that dominate are the vowel [ɛ] and the consonant [l]. The lexical statistics show that, in the vowel case, more problems arise from misperception of the dominant [ɛ] as [æ] than vice versa, whereas in the consonant case more problems arise from misperception of the nondominant [r] as [l] than vice versa. In other words, the two cases pattern in opposite directions, suggesting no simple lexical explanation of dominance (even though differences in lexical familiarity can also cause asymmetry in L2 listening performance with non-L1 contrasts; Flege, Takagi, and Mann 1996).

A phonetic explanation of the dominance pattern is that L2 input is primarily interpreted in terms of L1 categories. Each L2 category is coded in terms of its match to an L1 category. In the case of two L2 categories covered by a single L1 category, the coding will represent one L2 category as a better match than the other to the L1 category. That is, Dutch speakers of English will represent English [ɛ] as a fairly good match to Dutch [ɛ], and English [æ] as a less good match to it; Japanese speakers of English will represent English [l] as a better match than English [r] to Japanese [ɽ]. Whatever category occurs in the input, the L1 category will be activated and an estimate will be made of the degree to which the input matches this category. In fact, this perceptual estimate will tend to be unreliable, because perceptual magnet effects (Kuhl and Iverson 1995) will make the degree of match seem closer than it actually is. Thus, input containing the dominant category will be rated as a better match to the L1 category than it actually is, and will thus be even more likely to be routed to lexical representations containing the dominant category. Input containing the nondominant category will likewise be rated as a less poor match to the L1 category than it actually is, and will therefore also attain a higher probability of being routed to lexical representations containing the dominant (better matching) category. The net result is that whichever of the two categories occurs in the input, there will be a greater likelihood of its being perceived as the dominant category and hence activating, in the first instance, lexical entries containing the dominant category.

The asymmetry in mapping phonetic information to the lexicon further delays L2 listening with unnecessary competitor activation; the eye-tracking studies revealed slower looks to the targets containing the nondominant category than to the targets containing the dominant category. In Weber and Cutler's (2004) experiment, correct looks to targets such as *panda* or *palace* seemed to require about 200 milliseconds longer than correct looks to targets such as *pencil* or *pelican*—effectively, *panda* could not be recognized until the arrival of the disambiguating phoneme (i.e., the [d]). Likewise, in Cutler et al.'s (2006) study, correct looks to targets such as *rocket* took about 150 milliseconds longer than correct looks to targets such as *locker*.

Not only is the speed of lexical access in these cases asymmetric, but also the strength of competition is asymmetric. In particular, it will be hard to get rid of competition from a spuriously embedded word that contains the dominant member of an asymmetrically mapped phonetic contrast. Consider again the case of the Dutch listener hearing *daffodil* and first activating the spurious embedding *deaf*. If the lexical representation of *daffodil* is coded as having a different vowel than the lexical representation of *deaf*, then the two will not actually compete for the vowel that is heard in the input; this will be heard as the vowel that belongs to *deaf*, and *deaf* will be, and remain, a more viable lexical candidate than *daffodil*. The same goes for *pen* in *panda*, and, in the [r]-[l] case, *leg* in *regulate* or *blue* in *brunette*. In each case the spurious embedding, containing the dominant category, will receive greater support than the (corresponding part of) the carrier word.

Shortlist simulations summarized in figure 9.5 reinforce this point. The activation of the word *deaf* was compared across four separate simulations: one with the input *deaf*, one with the input *definite*, one with *daffodil*, and one with the nonword *deffodil*. In each case Shortlist drew on its normal British English lexicon of 26,000 words. When the input was *deaf* (plus some segments of silence), the candidate *deaf* was quickly activated and its level of activation stayed high. When the input was *definite*, *deaf* was initially activated, but it was knocked right out of the competition when the accrued evidence of the input made it clear that *definite* was the better candidate. These two simulations represent listening either by L1 listeners, or by the Dutch L2 listeners, with their preference for hearing the dominant vowel category.

When the input was *daffodil*, *deaf* was not activated at all. This simulation would represent L1 listening only, because, as we saw, the Dutch listeners would indeed activate *deaf* in this case, given that for them the first syllable of *daffodil* would be interpreted as *deff*. The fourth input, *deffodil*, therefore represents what happens when the Dutch listeners hear *daffodil*. There is no need to change Shortlist's lexicon, because these listeners' lexical representations are indeed accurate—it is only their phonetic processing that miscategorizes the vowel. With *deffodil* as input, *deaf* is activated and, crucially, it remains activated; *daffodil* does not succeed in

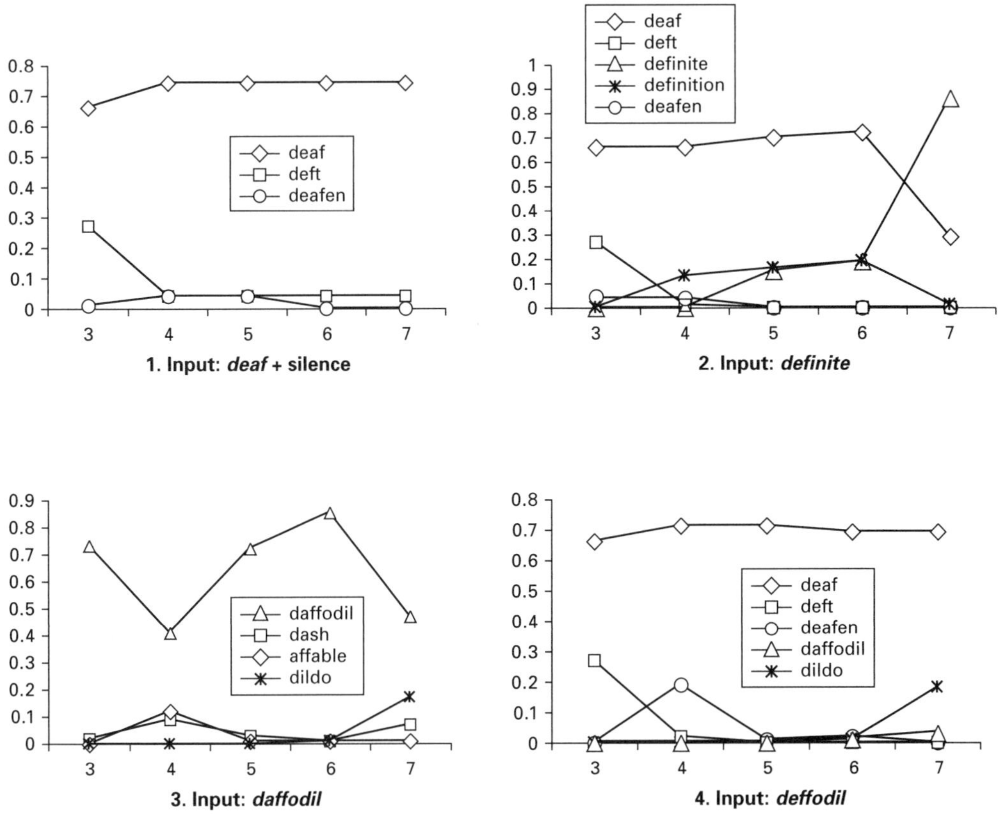

Figure 9.5
Shortlist simulations given four separate inputs, showing activation in each case from the third input segment (always [f]) to the seventh. With the input *deaf* (followed by silence), only *deaf* is highly activated; its activation rises a little with the first segment of silence (because all competitors, including the closest competitor *deft*, are mismatched) and stays high. With the input *definite*, *deaf* rises less rapidly at the fourth phoneme, because the total competitor set is larger (e.g., *deficit*, *deference*). However, *deaf* remains available until, at the seventh phoneme, [t], the evidence for *definite* becomes definite; competition from *definite* then removes *deaf* from the candidate set. Either of these two simulations could represent processing by native or by nonnative listeners. With the input *daffodil*, only *daffodil* itself is highly activated, although there are competitors for parts of it such as *affable* and *dildo*. There is however no activation at all for *deaf*. This simulation only corresponds to native processing. With *deffodil*—the input *daffodil* with its first vowel miscategorized, assumed to correspond to *daffodil* as processed by Dutch listeners—*deaf* is activated, and crucially, *daffodil* itself offers no effective competition, because its lexical representation does not match the vowel perceived in the input. Here *deaf* remains active through the seventh and final phoneme. In fact, the activation pattern for *deaf* given *deffodil* most resembles the pattern for *deaf* given *deaf*.

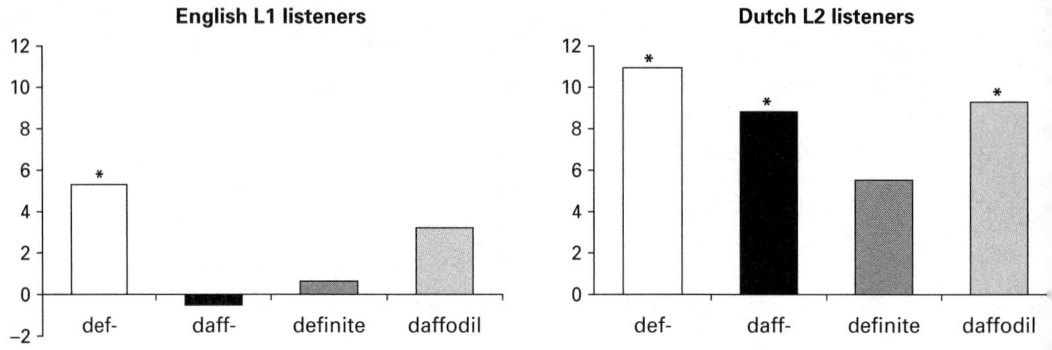

Figure 9.6
Priming effects (%) for English L1 listeners (left panel) and Dutch L2 listeners to English (right panel) in four cross-modal priming conditions. The priming effects were calculated by determining the difference between the mean RT for the primed condition versus RT for a condition with an unrelated control prime word, and are expressed as percentages of the control prime RT to allow better comparison across the two listener groups. In all cases, an example target word for visual lexical decision is DEAF; the corresponding four primes for this target are *def-* (the first syllable extracted from an utterance of *definite*), *daff-* (from *daffodil*), *definite*, and *daffodil*. An asterisk indicates that the priming effect is significant. Only *def-* primes DEAF for L1 listeners, but *def-*, *daff-*, and *daffodil* all prime DEAF significantly for the Dutch L2 listeners. (Data from Broersma and Cutler 2011.)

knocking it out of the competitor set (in the way that *definite* managed) because *daffodil*, with its correct lexical representation, is partly mismatched by the input *deffodil* and therefore only musters a weak amount of activation, insufficient to compete with that of the fully matched candidate *deaf*.

The pattern of activation in these simulations exactly matches the response patterns of the listeners in Broersma and Cutler's (2011) cross-modal priming study described in section 9.3.2, and summarized here in figure 9.6. When L1 listeners heard *def-* (from *definite*), *daff-* (from *daffodil*), untruncated *definite*, or untruncated *daffodil*, their lexical decision responses to a visually presented DEAF were significantly facilitated only in the first case; *def-* matched DEAF, but *daff-* did not, and *definite*, though it would have activated DEAF early on, soon knocked it out of competition. When Dutch L2 listeners heard the same four primes, their responses to DEAF were significantly facilitated by *def-*, by *daff-*, and by *daffodil*. Only in the case of *definite* was the facilitation not significant, which suggests that for these listeners, too, the longer word knocked its shorter embedding out of competition. Competition that is "real" (such as *deaf* in *definite*) is dealt with in a similar way by L1 and L2 listeners. The crucial finding is that competition from the carrier word to the embedded form did not happen with *daffodil*; there, the spurious embedding was activated and remained activated. The accurate lexical representation of *daffodil* failed to provide the competition required to knock out the shorter word that had been brought into play by the inaccurate phonetic processing. Thus spurious competition (such as *deaf* in *daffodil*) is not only confined to L2 listeners; it is also particularly persistent and hence particularly troublesome competition.

9.7 Conclusion

Nonnative listening is hard because native listening is easy. By now, the relation between phoneme repertoires, and the effects of L1-L2 repertoire mismatch on the perception of L2 phonemic contrast, are well understood, as is the course of learning to distinguish contrasts in L2. However, from the listener's point of view, listening is never consciously about perceiving phonemic contrasts. It is about understanding messages. The central point in this chapter has been the serious implications for L2 word recognition of problems occasioned by phonemic (mis)perception.

We have seen that the relationship between levels of processing in L2 is not as simple as one might have expected; ability to perceive an L2 contrast does not necessarily mean that this ability will be correctly deployed to discriminate words, and inability to perceive a contrast does not necessarily rule out accurate encoding of the contrast in lexical entries. The theoretical implications of this mapping asymmetry will be revisited in chapter 12. Here, the practical implications for the L2 listener have been reviewed, and they are not good news: inaccurate phonetic processing causes additional, sometime spurious competition, and this competition can be harder to get rid of than the competition that results if all phonetic processing is accurate. This chapter having brought us from the phoneme to the word level in L2 listening, chapter 10 goes on from there to consider lexical processing in speech context.

10 Second-Language Listening: Words in Their Speech Contexts

The specialization of listening for the native language also causes difficulties for the second-language (L2) listener at levels above the phoneme and word. Segmenting continuous speech draws on procedures specialized for the native language, its rhythm, and its phoneme sequence probabilities and constraints; these may be counterproductively applied to speech input in the L2. Idioms and casual speech processes of the L2 can also cause trouble, as can prosodic structure, syntax, and sentence semantics. These difficulties, and those arising from phonetic and lexical processing, accumulate, so that effective comprehension can be substantially impaired. Extralinguistic factors add further difficulty: Voice recognition is easiest in the native language, for instance, and understanding speech in a noisy environment is notorious for causing difficulty for L2 listeners. However, there are also some rays of hope; thus, native listening specialization can sometimes offer a compensatory benefit in a second language, and with experience, it is possible to improve L2 listening in many dimensions.

Acquisition of a second language is sometimes necessary for survival, often the basis for a career, frequently motivated by love, and always, always useful. The practical value of L2 instruction has produced a huge literature. Much of it, naturally, concerns the beginning stages of L2 acquisition. But the goal of the L2 learner is to function in the new language. In some cases (migrant workers are usually cited here), a low level of L2 mastery may suffice. In other cases (students, executives in multinational companies), very high levels of mastery can be needed to achieve career goals. Listening skills then involve understanding lectures, participating fully in meetings and conferences, and conversing with native speakers in both formal and informal settings. Sounds and words must be processed in their speech contexts.

The architecture of the system that supports the initial stages of listening to speech should be generally the same for L1 and L2. But as already documented, L2 phonetic processing and lexical activation rarely match performance levels achieved in the L1. Subsequent stages also presumably rely on the same architecture as in L1, and sometimes perhaps even on the same representations. Consider, for instance, that Dutch speakers of L2 English show repetition priming for translation equivalents in each language in auditory lexical decision; hearing *air* in English facilitates responses to *lucht* 'air' in Dutch, and also vice versa, without it making any difference whether the English and Dutch words were phonologically similar (Woutersen, De Bot, and Weltens 1995). This symmetry suggests that common conceptual representations may be activated even when the preceding phonological competition involves quite different representations. No matter how much processing is shared between the L1 and L2, however, L2 listening is less efficient. This is true even at very high levels of proficiency (the listeners in the lexical studies described in chapter 9 were far from beginners). The processing of words in speech contexts, as we shall see, certainly shows L2 disadvantage.

10.1 Segmenting Continuous L2 Speech

The difficulty of listening to continuous L2 speech cannot be simply predicted from success in L2 phoneme discrimination and word recognition; listeners who perform well in these tasks can still often have great trouble listening to natural continuous speech (e.g., a lecture in the L2). This is because segmentation of speech involves its own specific procedures, over and above the processes of lexical activation and competition (see chapters 4 and 5). Segmentation draws on listeners' knowledge of the probabilistic patterns of word-boundary occurrence, and this knowledge is highly language specific. Moreover, as artificial language learning studies demonstrated (see chapter 4), listeners apply their L1 segmentation procedures to input in languages other than the L1.

In the following sections, evidence is reviewed from studies of segmentation of speech in a real, not an artificial, foreign language. If segmentation processes appropriate for the L2 do not match the phonology of the L1, listening to the L2 becomes even harder. In the ERP study of Snijders et al. (2007) described early in chapter 4, brain responses to repetition of words in isolation were comparable in native and nonnative listeners, but when the same repeated words were embedded in a simple natural sentence of seven or eight words in length, responses were slowed for the nonnative listeners but speeded for native listeners. In other words, the L1 listeners could exploit the appropriate segmentation procedures for this input, but the nonnative listeners could not. At a more advanced level, segmentation may still be a problem, in that segmentation hypotheses may be hard to abandon; L1 listeners prove more willing than L2 listeners to revise their guesses about gated presentations of ambiguous sequences (e.g., the first two syllables in *eaten up*, *eat an apple*, *eat enough*; Field 2008). Sticking too long with a wrong segmentation hypothesis can certainly put a brake on listening efficiency.

10.1.1 The "Gabbling Foreigner Illusion": Perceived Speech Rate in L1 versus L2 as a Segmentation Issue

There is a common impression that foreign languages are spoken faster than one's native language; Snijders et al.'s (2007) study addressed this and fingered segmentation as its source. Obviously, the general impression cannot be true. But putting the perceptual basis of such judgments to empirical test has proven quite difficult.

British English listeners tested by Lorch and Meara (1989) could extract quite a bit of relevant phonetic information from 20-second samples of continuous speech in unfamiliar languages. However, the listeners showed a strong recency effect (i.e., a tendency to be more accurate about the final portions of what they heard), which indicated that committing the unfamiliar material to memory was not easy. A similar recency effect appeared when Dutch and American English speakers heard Arabic sentences and then decided whether a subsequent probe word had occurred in the sentence (Swingley 1995). American English listeners with no knowledge of French who were asked to detect the words *taux*, *seau*, *taupinière*, or *societaire* in spoken French stories could detect the four-syllable words quite accurately, but the one-syllable words were detected only slowly and with many false alarms (Goldstein 1983). Thus, there are clearly limitations on what listeners can do with non-L1 input (e.g., commit it to memory); however, it does not seem that the input goes by in an impenetrable blur. When comprehension is impaired for any reason, rate of speech may get the blame. Schwab and Grosjean (2004) played short stories in French at slow, normal, and fast rates of speech to L1 listeners and L2 (German L1) listeners, and collected comprehension scores and estimates of speech rate. The L2 listeners were less accurate in estimating rate than the L1 listeners (in particular, they overestimated faster rates), and at slow and normal rates, they tended to overestimate the rate of the stories that they had comprehended less well.

This result strongly suggests that the "gabbling foreigner" effect has its source in the L2 listeners, not in the speakers. But how should it be tested? Comparing the rate of speech across different languages is itself not a simple task, because it depends on knowing how speech rate should best be measured (see Roach 1998 for a list of the problems here). Tauroza and Allison (1990) addressed the measurement question in an analysis of British English conversation and radio talks and interviews, from 126 speakers in all. They established that there were more words per unit time in conversational speech than in radio speech (which was read or at least rehearsed). But this did not mean that people were speaking faster in conversation, because the words used in conversation tended to be a little shorter than those used on the radio. Tauroza and Allison therefore rejected rate of word production as a measure. In syllables per unit time, their conversational and radio samples did not significantly differ (the grand average was 4.25 syllables per second).

But even syllables per second may not be the right measure, if one wants to compare across languages. All languages have syllables; but some languages allow a wide range of syllable structures (thus the words *awe* and *screeched* are both monosyllabic in English), whereas others allow only a very limited range (e.g., only [C]V[V] in Hawaiian). Trying for a direct test of the reality of listeners' impressions of foreign speech rates, Osser and Peng (1964) measured phonemes per unit time. They found no rate difference between Japanese and American English on this measure. Their conclusion was that subjective impressions of speech rate are formed within the framework of a listener's native language phonology, and that this can mislead—for instance, Japanese listeners may hear English consonant clusters as strings of syllables, whereas English listeners may interpret the high frequency of vowels in Japanese in terms of the speech rate that so many vowels would imply for English.

In a rating study in which German and Japanese listeners heard short excerpts of German and Japanese spontaneous speech, Pfitzinger and Tamashima (2006) provided laboratory evidence for the subjectively well-attested illusion. The samples came from ten different speakers in each language, and they varied in number of phonemes and syllables, but they were all 625 milliseconds long (this having been shown to be long enough for listeners to make reliable judgments but not so long that local speech rate fluctuations are probable; Pfitzinger 1999). The listeners, none of whom knew the non-L1 language at all, arranged these short excerpts from both languages along a continuum of perceived rate, under no time pressure, and with the opportunity to compare stimuli and revise their ratings as often as they wished. Even with such an unpressured situation and such restricted speech samples, the "gabbling foreigner illusion" appeared: the German excerpts were rated 7.5 percent faster by the Japanese than by the German listeners, whereas the Japanese excerpts were rated 9 percent faster by the German than by the Japanese listeners. Both results were significantly different from chance, but the two listener groups did not differ significantly in how much they overrated each other's language, which suggests that the illusion affects all listeners to much the same extent. However, the German listeners were more likely to overrate the fastest Japanese stimuli—that is, the ones containing more phonemes/syllables—whereas the Japanese listeners also overrated the slower German stimuli. This is consistent with Osser and Peng's suggestion that consonant clusters may have played a role in inducing the illusion for Japanese listeners (German, like English, allows many consonant clusters that never occur in Japanese).

10.1.2 L1 Rhythm and L2 Segmentation

Exploitation of the rhythmic structure of language to inform segmentation decisions begins early in life (see chapter 8), which leads to procedures that are highly overlearned. Moreover, the rhythmically based procedures for facilitating speech segmentation differ a lot across languages (see chapter 4).

Although L2 learners' segmentation difficulty is the practical problem to which this research can eventually be applied, again the theoretical advances have in the first instance been made with studies of the perception of speech in an unknown foreign language. From such studies we know that segmentation procedures are not induced by the input structure but are part of the listener's processing system. French is clearly best segmented syllabically—that is what native French listeners do; but neither English listeners (Cutler et al. 1986) nor Japanese listeners (Otake et al. 1996) apply syllabic segmentation to French. Japanese lends itself to a moraic segmentation strategy, but neither English nor French listeners call on such a procedure when they hear Japanese (Otake et al. 1993).

In contrast, listeners apply segmentation procedures that they have learned for their L1—that is, procedures that facilitate listening in their L1—even to input in another language that in no way encourages those procedures. Thus, English listeners do not use syllabic segmentation because such a procedure is not efficient for English; stress-based segmentation is the efficient strategy for English. Japanese listeners also do not use syllabic segmentation, because syllabic segmentation is likewise inefficient for Japanese; moraic segmentation is the preferred strategy in that case. Notwithstanding what all these native listeners do, French listeners apply syllabic segmentation to English input and also to Japanese input (Cutler et al. 1986; Otake et al. 1993). Even though the L1 syllabic procedure is unsuited to the foreign language, it seems that it is automatically applied.

Similarly, moraic segmentation is not the most appropriate procedure for segmenting French, Spanish, or English; native speakers of these languages do not use such a procedure. Japanese listeners, however, apply moraic segmentation to input in French or Spanish (Otake et al. 1996) and to English words (Cutler and Otake 1994). Note that this latter study was a fully crossed design—parallel experiments in Japanese and in English, both with English and Japanese listeners. It showed effects of the L1 in both listener groups' responses to the non-L1. As described in chapter 1, English listeners doing phoneme detection detect consonants more easily than vowels. The input does not have to be in the native language for this difference to show up; Cutler and Otake's English listeners produced the same asymmetry when detecting phonemes in Japanese words or in English words. The targets were the consonant [n] and the vowel [o]; whatever the language, and whether the target was a mora by itself or part of one, the English listeners always detected [n] more easily than [o]. Japanese listeners did not show the same pattern, however. For them, the vital factor was whether the phoneme target was itself a mora. No matter whether it was a vowel or consonant, the target was detected more accurately and more rapidly if it was a mora by itself. And no matter whether it occurred in Japanese or in English, [n] was detected more accurately and more rapidly if it could be considered moraic—thus [n] was detected more easily by Japanese listeners (but only by Japanese listeners) in English *candy* than in *canopy*.

These results from non-L1 listening suggest that L2 listening should be easier in an L2 with the same rhythmic structure as the L1 than in an L2 that has a rhythmic structure different to that of the L1. Also, "nativelike" segmentation of a given language by L2 listeners should only be possible for listeners whose L1 encourages the same segmentation procedure. Listeners with other languages will apply their different procedures, inefficiently. The evidence in favor of the rhythmic class hypothesis (see section 4.7 of chapter 4) indeed gave some support for this suggestion, and further supporting evidence from bilingual listening is described later in section 10.8.

10.1.3 L1 Phonotactics in L2 Segmentation

Can listening to an L2 in which one has achieved a certain proficiency also be plagued by inappropriate use of L1 segmentation procedures (just as it is plagued by inappropriate L1 phonetic categorizations, as described in chapter 9)? Or can L2 listeners quickly acquire the appropriate probabilities and apply them to segmentation of the L2 input?

Highly proficient L2 listeners include, for instance, the students in a school for simultaneous interpreters. Such listeners, with German L1 and English L2, undertook English word-spotting in an experiment by Weber and Cutler (2006) partly described already in chapter 4. These German listeners, and American English-speaking controls, all spotted words more rapidly when the word boundaries were signaled by a phonetic sequence that would be illegal within a syllable; [nl], for instance, is such a sequence for both languages. It was thus easy to spot *lecture* in *moinlecture*. It was much harder to find *lecture* in, say, *moyklecture*, as [kl] occurs inside syllables in both languages (e.g., English *cluster*, German *Klasse* 'class'). The whole experiment was in English, and in addition to the word boundaries that are clear in both languages (e.g., with [nl]) and those clear in neither language (e.g., with [kl]), there were two further crucial boundary types, of which examples with *lecture* are *moycelecture* and *moyshlecture*. In the first item, *lecture* is preceded by [s], which can form an onset with [l] in English words (*sleep*, *slow*, *slump*, *slot*, and so on) but is illegal in word onsets in German. In the second item, *lecture* is preceded by [ʃ], and here the possibilities are reversed: no native English words begin *shl-*, but many German words do: *Schlange* 'snake', *schlimm* 'bad', *schleppen* 'haul', and *Schloss* 'castle', for example.

These cases contrasted a phonotactic cue for segmenting English but not German ([ʃl]) with a cue for segmenting German but not English ([sl]). Effective use of phonotactic probabilities in the testing language, English, would require listeners to use the former but not the latter. They should detect *lecture* more rapidly after *moysh-* than in the control no-boundary condition (*moyk-*), but they should show no difference between the *moyce-* and *moyk-* cases. English listeners did exactly this. The left panel of figure 10.1 shows the percentage facilitation in RT for the English cue (*moysh-*) and the German cue (*moyce-*) over the control (*moyk-*) for these participants; there is significant facilitation in the former case, but nothing much at

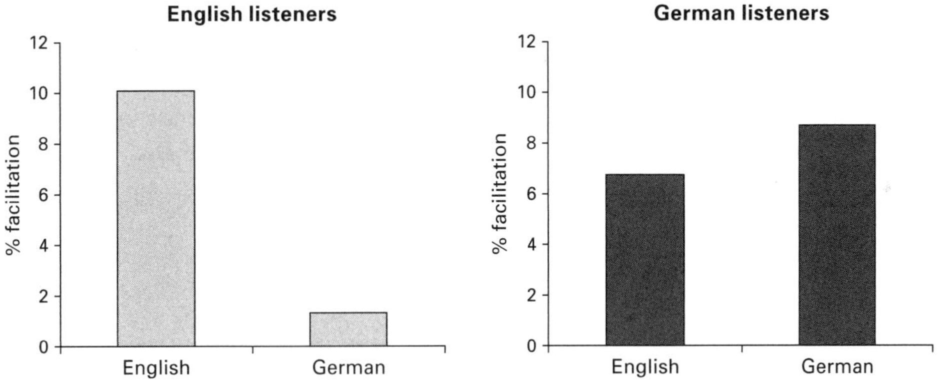

Figure 10.1
How much benefit do segmentation cues give? English listeners (left panel) detect English words more than 10 percent faster given an English-specific segmentation cue (e.g., *lecture* after *moysh*, which could not combine with the [l] onset) than in a control condition. They get no significant benefit from a German-specific cue. German listeners (right panel) with good English also benefit (although to a lesser degree—about 7.5 percent) from the English-specific cue. But they benefit more from a German-specific cue, even though it is actually counterproductive in English (in *moycelecture*, [s] and [l] could indeed combine to a new onset).

all in the latter. The right panel of the figure, however, shows that the German students of English interpreting responded differently. They detected the embedded words after contexts of both the *moysh-* and *moyce-* type more rapidly and accurately than after control contexts such as *moyk-*. The fact that they could find *lecture* more easily in *moyshlecture* than in *moyklecture* means that they did not simply treat the L2 like their L1, nor were they unaffected by the L2 segmentation probabilities. Both [kl] and [ʃl] can be word initial in German, so German listeners should treat them equivalently. These highly proficient listeners to English did not do this, so they had clearly acquired appropriate phonotactic knowledge for the L2. But they also found *lecture* more easily in *moycelecture* than in *moyklecture*, which means that they were not behaving like native English listeners, either. The probabilities of the L1, German, were so strongly in place that they played a role, even though they were not at all valid for the input, which the listeners knew to be in their L2. Thus even highly proficient L2 listeners apparently cannot avoid letting L1 phonotactics influence their segmentation of speech.

German listeners could ignore the possibility of a German boundary in *moyshlecture* but could not suppress the impossibility of a German boundary in *moycelecture*, and the reason why is presumably due to the nature of the constraint. The constraints that these German listeners observed were all positive cues to the presence of a boundary ([sl] in the L1 and [ʃl] in the L2 should always contain a boundary). Both the L1 constraint that they could appropriately suppress, and the L2 probability that they were impervious to, were however negative cues; that is, they were indications that a boundary is unnecessary ([ʃl] in the L1 and [sl] in the L2 may be word initial). Converging evidence for this explanation comes from a study of how Spanish listeners to English parse potentially ambiguous sequences (Altenberg 2005). For instance, [gre:væt] in English could be *grave at* or *gray vat*; positive boundary cues such as a glottal stop before the initial vowel of *at* proved much more useful for parsing such sequences than negative cues such as the absence of a glottal stop before the vowel in *vat*. An intervention study by Al-jasser (2008), involving pretest, intervention, and posttest, showed that explicitly instructing L2 listeners about English phonotactics, again using positive constraints such as the necessity of a boundary in sequences like [dl] and [gm], significantly reduced both their RTs and their errors in English word-spotting.

Note that as we saw in chapter 5, the implementations of Shortlist (Norris et al. 1997; Norris and McQueen 2008) with an explicit role for phonotactic segmentation information would predict just such a stronger effect of positive boundary information: Only clear boundary cues play a role in the model, so that strings with ambiguous boundaries (e.g., *moycelecture*) must be resolved via competition between alternative word candidates. The empirical evidence is not yet plentiful, but it indicates that L2 listeners can learn to exploit phonotactics effectively, in the same way as in their L1, with the strongest and clearest constraints being the ones most immediately accessible.

10.2 Casual Speech Processes in L2

Second-language teaching has begun to pay attention to the way words in real speech differ from words in their canonical pronunciation, and the implications of this for L2 learners (e.g., Brown and Kondo-Brown 2006). But so far there is very little research on how L2 listeners deal with the phenomena that filled chapter 6.

Consider liaison in French, in which sounds that are absent in words spoken in isolation appear in the same words when they are followed by a vowel in continuous speech (e.g., *petit* 'little', which ends with the vowel [i], whereas in *petit ami* 'little friend' a [t] separates the two medial vowels). English listeners instructed to detect word-initial phonemes in French, their L2, responded to liaison phonemes, although L1 listeners did not make such errors (Dejean de la Bâtie and Bradley 1995). This result suggests that words beginning with those sounds had been activated for the L2 listeners. The word-initial vowel in liaison sequences (e.g., the [a] of *ami*) was detected equally rapidly by L1 and L2 listeners, but the L2 listeners were significantly slower at detecting a word-initial consonant in a pseudoliaison sequence (e.g., the [t] of *talent* in *grand talent* 'great talent'; Matter 1986). Nonnative users of French (in Matter's study they were Dutch) thus seem aware of the potential for segmentation mistakes with the liaison phenomenon in their L2. They also know that there is a difference in how word-initial versus liaison consonants are realized; the liaison consonants are shorter, as was described in chapter 6, and the same consonants are judged more likely to be liaison realizations if they are artificially shortened, but more likely to be word-initial if they are lengthened, by L1 and (English) L2 listeners alike (Shoemaker 2010).

Liaison is an obligatory connected-speech process that is explicitly drawn to the attention of L2 learners of French, but other processes described in chapter 6 are rarely mentioned in a language class. All the assimilation, reduction, deletion, and insertion processes described there appear, in some form or other, in every language. For the L2 learner, the effect of such processes on listening will be determined by whether their occurrence is familiar from the L1, in much the same way as L1 phoneme repertoires affect perception of L2 phonemes.

An example of a process that is likely to be familiar to many L2 learners is /t/-deletion. This process patterns very similarly in Dutch (utterances of *postbode* 'postman' mostly contain no detectable /t/) and in German (the same holds for utterances of *Postbeamter* 'postal worker'). When German learners of Dutch were asked to judge varying realizations of [t] in such Dutch words, their responses were just like those of Dutch listeners tested by Mitterer and Ernestus (2006; see section 6.6.1 of chapter 6): they were sensitive not only to the strength of the acoustic evidence for the presence of [t] but also to effects of preceding acoustic context ([t]-deletion is more likely after [s] than after [n]) and to lexical and syntactic support for underlying [t]. Only in one case did their judgments deviate from those of the L1 listeners: they were relatively more likely to report [t] in verbal inflections. This is exactly where patterns of [t]-deletion differ across German and Dutch: deletion of [t] as a morphological ending is disfavored in German but acceptable in Dutch (as in English: cf. *postbox, passed by*). Tuinman (2011), who conducted this L2 study, concluded that the German listeners were sensitive to this difference between their L2 and their L1, and overgeneralized perceived deletion in the L2 precisely where the L1 would prohibit it.

But there are also processes that are less likely to be familiar. For instance, the [r]-intrusion process, by which British English phrases such as *law and order* can come to sound like *Laura Norder*, is unknown in many languages. Dutch is one such language. Dutch users of English who were asked by Tuinman, Mitterer, and Cutler (2011 [a]) to judge whether a British English phrase contained *ice* or *rice* based their choice most strongly on the way words are spelled; they chose *rice* more often in *saw ice* than in *more ice* (see figure 10.2). Neither *saw* nor *more* is pronounced with final [r] in isolation in British English, but the spelling of *more* gives a source for an [r] to surface in continuous speech. These Dutch listeners paid relatively little

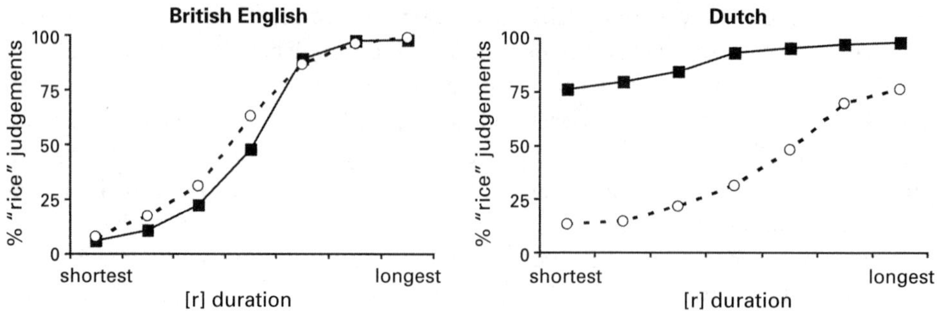

Figure 10.2
Casual speech processes unfamiliar from the L1 are not efficiently dealt with by L2 listeners. In British English, the sound [r] may intrude at a word boundary such as *saw ice*, making the phrase sound like saw *rice*. Native listeners do not get confused by this; the intrusive [r] is shorter than an intended [r], and native listeners' *ice-rice* categorization responses given a continuum varying in [r] duration are driven by the duration alone (left panel). This is not the case for Dutch listeners to English (right panel). Their responses are above all affected by the spelling of the words; in the context *saw [r]ice* (dark squares) they make significantly more *rice* judgments than in the context *more [r]ice* (open circles), because their knowledge of the spelling of *more* provides an alternative source for the sound [r]. The native listeners do not show this effect (at most points along the continuum their responses show slightly more *rice* judgments after *more*). (Data from Tuinman et al., 2011a.)

attention to the duration of the [r] sound, which was manipulated to vary from very short to very long. In contrast, British English listeners hearing the same items were completely unaffected by spelling; they based their judgments on the duration alone. Just as with the sounds that appear as a result of French liaison, the intrusive [r] sound is actually weaker than a "real" [r], and just as French listeners use the duration to tell a liaison from a word-initial sound, so do British English listeners use duration to distinguish intrusive and intended [r]. The Dutch listeners to English, unlike Shoemaker's (2010) English listeners to French, failed to match this L1 sensitivity to duration. The [r]-intrusion process was neither familiar to them from their L1 nor was it obligatory in the L2, so that the need for particular attention to it in L2 instruction did not arise.

When L2 listeners' sensitivity to word-boundary processes falls short of what L1 listeners can muster, consequences ensue for listening efficiency. For instance, the competitor population can be affected, as Tuinman, Mitterer, and Cutler (2012) showed. British English listeners in a cross-modal priming experiment who heard a sentence containing a potential intrusive [r], as in *Canada aids*, showed no facilitation of visual lexical decision for RAIDS. But Dutch listeners to English, their L2, given the same sentences where an intrusive [r] could occur, did show facilitation for target words such as RAIDS. The unfamiliar word-boundary processes thus exacerbated the number of competitor words that the L2 listeners had to deal with while understanding sentences.

Together these results suggest that the mapping between L1 and L2 is as important in the interpretation of casual speech processes in speech perception as in categorization within a phoneme repertoire. Casual speech processes that are already familiar from the L1 may be easy to adapt to in L2; subtle differences can even be detected in their precise patterns of occurrence across L1 and L2 and can be accommodated to in L2 listening. Unfamiliar casual speech processes, however, are difficult to adapt to in L2, and the listening consequences of this can be severe.

10.3 Idiom Processing in L2

Idioms are a known source of comprehension problems for many L2 listeners. They are difficult learning targets because they are unpredictable both semantically (why is it disastrous to *kick the bucket*?) and syntactically (why is one *under the weather*, rather than in it? how can one *shoot the breeze*? why do, by and large, prepositions never conjoin with adjectives, except in *by and large*?). This unpredictability makes it necessary to understand idioms as units—effectively, they function as large words. This is true for idioms in speech or in written text. But there turn out to be added problems associated with listening to idioms.

Many studies of idiom comprehension in L1 have used cross-modal associative priming, and the results have suggested a quite complex picture. There seems to be activation of the meaning of the idiom as a whole (FORGIVE is primed by *George wanted to bury the hatchet*; Titone and Connine 1994), but there also seems to be activation of its literal components (CRAVATTA 'tie' is primed by *Suo fratello fosse nato con la camicia* 'His brother was born with the shirt', that is, was born fortunate; Cacciari and Tabossi 1988). Some studies have shown no activation of literal meaning for the final parts of an idiom (Swinney 1981) or for the parts of highly predictable nondecomposable idioms such as *burn the midnight oil* (Titone and Connine 1994). This suggests that even though literal components may be (briefly?) activated along with the idiomatic meaning, the idiomatic meaning soon dominates. It seems that L1 listeners process idioms as efficiently as the input allows.

Again, L2 listening seems to be different. Polish listeners to English (final-year university students who were highly fluent in their L2) showed no consistent priming for idiom-related meanings at all but consistent priming for the meanings of the literal components (Cieslicka 2006). This study was modeled on that of Titone and Connine (1994) and used a subset of the same materials, and the idiomatic meanings were known to this L2 population. Nonetheless, *George wanted to bury the hatchet* here primed AXE but did not prime FORGIVE, which suggested that the idiomatic reading of the phrase was not as rapidly available to these L2 listeners as to the L1 listeners in the earlier study.

This may be simply because the L2 listeners did not recognize the idioms as such as they heard them. In most cases, idiomatic phrases differ prosodically from syntactically equivalent nonidiomatic phrases. This has been shown in studies comparing the productions of idiomatic versus literal versions of strings such as *bury the hatchet* or *skating on thin ice*; the two versions usually differ in pitch contour, timing, and pause distribution. L1 listeners can readily distinguish the two readings on the basis of these prosodic cues (Van Lancker and Canter 1981). Vanlancker-Sidtis (2003) asked both highly proficient and less proficient L2 listeners to do the same, for example, to categorize isolated strings (such as *He didn't know he was skating on thin ice*) as an intended idiom or a literal utterance. In a second task, they had to choose the idiom from a paired presentation of the idiomatic and the literal utterance of the same string. The materials were also presented to two L1 groups: speakers of American English (because the idioms were in some cases specific to American English) and non-American native speakers of English.

The Americans had no problem with either task, scoring above 80 percent correct even on the isolated strings; the non-American English speakers scored almost as well. The L2 listeners scored above chance only on the easier paired task, and then it was only the more proficient listeners who did so, with 64 percent correct. Even this group, however, scored below 60 percent for the (harder) isolated-string task. The less proficient listeners' scores were not different from chance (50 percent) on either task. Clearly, the prosodic signal that an idiomatic interpretation was required had passed these listeners by. As if interpreting idioms were not complex enough, L2 listeners are thus additionally handicapped by apparent deficits in the interpretation of the L2 prosody, with the result that they miss out on information that might have helped.

10.4 Prosody Perception in L2

Indeed, L2 prosodic processing is not the equal of L1 prosodic processing. This is true of word-level prosodic structure, and of higher-level prosodic structure as well. As with connected-speech processing, there has been recent attention to prosody in L2 acquisition (e.g., Trouvain and Gut 2007). But recall that it was noted in chapter 7 that the processing of prosody has hardly been studied crosslinguistically. Until that gap in the literature has been remedied, prosodic processing in L2 can also not be fully understood.

10.4.1 Word-Level Prosody and Suprasegmentals

At the word level, there is again evidence from perception studies with unknown languages As described in chapter 7, speakers of nonstress languages have great difficulty encoding, and retaining in memory, meaningless stress distinctions in nonsense materials that cause no problem at all to speakers of stress languages (Dupoux et al. 2001; Peperkamp and Dupoux 2002). The Dupoux-Peperkamp project is focused on infant learning of L1 phonology, but their model also makes predictions about adult listening. In their proposal, stress contrasts are like segmental contrasts; any contrast that distinguishes words in the L1 can be encoded and distinguished elsewhere, too. Distinguishing between words, of course, defines a lexical stress language. But fixed stress languages also differ in how easy it is (for an infant) to discover that stress placement is actually fixed and hence noncontrastive; some such languages (e.g., Polish) require full knowledge of content word boundaries, whereas others (e.g., Hungarian) require only knowledge of the distinction between content and function words (Peperkamp and Dupoux 2002). Knowledge of a content-function word distinction is acquired early, before the vocabulary contains very much in the way of entries at all (see chapter 8). Hungarian infants can therefore decide that their language does not have contrastive stress (and thus stop paying attention to stress) earlier than Polish infants can. This in turn means that although both languages have fixed stress, Hungarian listeners are more likely than Polish listeners to be "stress-deaf" in the way that Dupoux et al. (1997) first found for French listeners. Peperkamp and Dupoux (2002) tested Hungarian and Polish listeners in the stress-deafness tasks and found that this was indeed so.

In accord with what Peperkamp and Dupoux's analyses would predict, French listeners to L2 English could not perform significantly better than chance at distinguishing stress in English word pairs such as *mystery-mistake*, regardless of their level of English proficiency (Tremblay 2008). Further, extensive studies by Archibald (1992, 1993, 1997, 1998) have also produced results in accord with the Peperkamp and Dupoux analysis. These studies examined the acquisition of English stress by speakers of various languages: lexical stress languages (e.g., Spanish), fixed stress languages (e.g., Polish and Hungarian), and nonstress languages (e.g., Chinese and Japanese). Speakers of languages without stress succeed, where they succeed at all in learning correct English stress, on a case by case basis; their errors are unpredictable and inconsistent. Speakers of languages with fixed stress are at great risk of applying their L1 principles to English words, which indicates that they are effectively deaf to the English stress; however, they are consistent in their errors, which makes it clear that they recognize the need for computation of metrical structure in their L2. Speakers of other stress languages are most likely to assign stress correctly in English, even in cognates with different primary stress placement in the two languages (e.g., English *FORmal*, Spanish *forMAL*). They may assign too much weight to the parameters determining stress in the L2 (e.g., typical stress position, correlation with word class; Guion, Harada, and Clark 2004), but they are clearly not stress-deaf. They may even do better at stress detection than L1 natives (see section 10.7).

Just as stress distinctions are hard for nonstress language users, so are tone distinctions for listeners from nontone languages (Shen 1989). English listeners draw on their native knowledge of English pitch patterning in interpreting Chinese tones (Broselow, Hurtig, and Ringen 1987) Similarly, perception of Japanese pitch-accent distinctions by English and French listeners falls far below native levels and is influenced by the L1 system (Nishinuma 1994; Nishinuma, Arai, and Ayusawa 1996). But speakers of tone and pitch-accent languages likewise show L1 influence in judging English stress; for example, they attend more to pitch change than English listeners do (Archibald 1997; Grabe et al. 2003; Watanabe 1988). For pitch judgment tasks in general, speakers of tone languages show influence of their L1 (Bent, Bradlow, and Wright 2006; Burnham et al. 1996), whereas speakers of nontone languages often show influence of their musical experience (Burnham et al. 1996; Wong and Perrachione 2007; Wong et al. 2007).

10.4.2 Prosodic Cues to L2 Syntactic Boundaries

The distinction between an idiomatic reading and a literal reading of the same string could be termed a syntactic distinction, given that idiomatic strings are like large words. The fact that L2 listeners have difficulty with prosodic cues to this distinction might then suggest that L2 listeners generally have difficulty with prosodic cues to syntactic structure. However, the available evidence indicates that syntactically determined prosodic structure is quite well perceived in an L2. This is not so surprising if marking juncture is indeed a prosodic universal. Recall that early on, infants prefer pauses to occur at syntactic boundaries rather than within constituents, and this preference appears across languages. The ability of listeners to use boundary cues in unfamiliar input should then perhaps be expected, either on the basis that listeners can look for universal structural cues, or because they will usually be able just to respond to familiar reflections of the native language.

Consistent evidence is again available from studies of listening to quite unfamiliar speech. Wakefield, Doughtie, and Yom (1974) presented English listeners with half an hour of speech in Korean and then tested their ability to choose between two versions of a sentence—one with a pause inserted at a constituent boundary or a word boundary, and the other with a pause inserted such that it interrupted a constituent or a word. Their listeners, none of whom had had any prior exposure to Korean, chose the noninterrupting pause significantly more often than chance. In a similar experiment by Pilon (1981), some listeners had no pre-exposure at all, whereas others were exposed to sentences and some to random word lists in Korean, where these in turn were made up of vocabulary that was either the same as or different from the test sentences. Pilon then tested all listeners on utterances in which pauses either occurred at the boundary of syllables, words, and syntactic constituents or interrupted them. The results were clear: there were no effects of pre-exposure at all. Listeners who had heard no Korean performed just as well as listeners who had heard any Korean words in any sequence. All subjects judged pauses at constituent boundaries to be more natural than pauses elsewhere. A similar conclusion can be drawn from a study in which British English listeners heard spoken Czech and detected beeps coincident with the speech (Henderson 1980). When a beep coincided with an intonational fall in the speech, response times were slower, which suggested that structural processing was under way at that moment. All of these results suggest that prosodic cues to syntactic units are readily available, even to listeners who have no prior knowledge of the language and no exposure to it.

Few studies have directly addressed this issue in L2. English listeners and Hebrew learners of English were found to make similar use of prosody to disambiguate phrasing ambiguities such as *They talked about the problem with the builder* (Berkovits 1980). Harley, Howard, and Hart (1995) made life a little harder for their listeners; they cross-spliced pairs of (unambiguous) sentences such as *The new teacher's watch has stopped* and *The new teachers watch baseball games*, interchanging the final two-word sequences so that the prosodic cues conflicted with the syntactic information. Listeners had to show recognition of the sentence subject (e.g., *watch* or *teachers*). L1 listeners in their study ignored the misleading prosody, but Cantonese-native L2 listeners did not; their responses tended to follow the prosodic cues. These results are again consistent with the suggestion that the prosodic cues are more available because they are common across languages, not specific to the L2.

10.4.3 Prosodic Cues to L2 Semantic Interpretation

The use of accents to highlight semantically central parts of the message was also proposed to be universal. If there is parallel crosslinguistic use of prosodic cues to syntactic boundaries, is there also parallel crosslinguistic processing of prosodic cues to semantic focus?

There appears to be no counterevidence to this suggestion. But there is evidence that even when the L1 and the L2 require exactly parallel prosodic processing, this processing is less efficient in the L2 than in the L1. Exploitation of accentual cues to focus is efficient in L1 (see chapter 7): cues to upcoming accented words direct listeners' attention quickly to the location of sentence focus. Phoneme detection is faster on words in accented than in unaccented position (Cutler 1976a), and on words in focus than not in focus (Cutler and Fodor 1979). This search for accent subserves a search for focus, because the two factors interact when both are manipulated in one experiment: if targets are not focused, detection is faster in accented than in unaccented position, but if targets are focused, there is no extra effect of accent (Akker and Cutler 2003; see figure 10.3). Once listeners have the focus, they no longer need accent to tell them where it is.

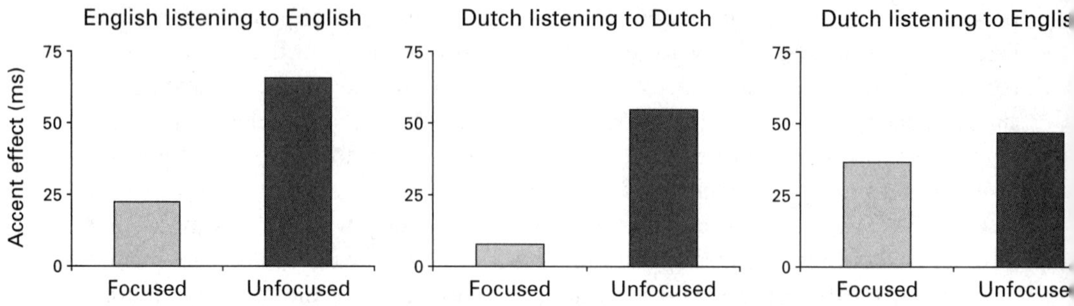

Figure 10.3
An interaction in the responses of native listeners is absent from the responses of L2 listeners. The accent effect (faster RTs to target words in accented versus in unaccented position) varies as a function of focus when English or Dutch listeners are processing their native language; there is a large accent effect when the target is not focused, but this effect is greatly attenuated under focus (left and middle panels). For L2 listeners, however (Dutch listening to English, right panel), there is no significant attenuation; the accent effect is significant regardless of focus. (Data from Akker and Cutler 2003.)

Akker and Cutler found this pattern with English listeners hearing L1 English sentences and with Dutch listeners hearing L1 Dutch sentences. Focus placement in English and Dutch is close to identical (Gussenhoven 1983). However, the L1-like interaction did not materialize when Dutch listeners (proficient in English) heard the English materials, as figure 10.3 shows. Instead, there was a strong effect of focus, as well as a strong effect of accent position, but the two effects were independent of one another. It was as if the Dutch listeners had adopted a fail-safe, belt-and-braces approach whereby two sources of the same information were better than one. Nowhere in Akker and Cutler's data was there any indication that their L2 listeners varied in proficiency or that the listeners' prosodic processing was itself slowed, say, by imperfect phonetic processing. The lack of an interaction is more likely to arise from the way these listeners integrated prosodic and semantic information. If the L2 listeners were processing the focus structure relatively slowly, it might be worth their while to continue processing prosodic cues to focus for longer than L1 listeners needed to.

In a rare exploitation of cross-language prosodic difference, Braun and Tagliapietra (2011) repeated with L2 listeners their demonstration that contrastive accent calls up options for the contrast. In their earlier study (see chapter 7), Dutch listeners' responses to contextual alternatives (e.g., PELICAN, given *Dirk photographed a flamingo*) had been speeded when the final word in the sentence bore contrastive accent, in comparison to responses after the same sentence with a noncontrastive intonation contour. Prosodic accounts of German claim that the contour that served as noncontrastive in their Dutch study actually signals contrast in German. They reasoned, therefore, that German speakers of L2 Dutch might treat it as contrastive in Dutch, too, and when they repeated their study with such L2 listeners, that is what they found. The Germans showed priming from both contours, so they had not adjusted their prosodic processing to deal with this difference between their L1 and the L2.

These results for focus and for contrastive intonation add to the finding of deficient processing of prosodic cues to idiomaticity in L2 (Vanlancker-Sidtis 2003). Also relevant is a finding by Pennington and Ellis (2000): prosodic cues to semantic structure are difficult for L2 listeners to retain in memory. L2 listeners first heard twenty-four sentences, then in a recognition phase they heard twice as many sentences and had to say which ones they had heard before. Sometimes a sentence was presented with changed prosody, implying a change in semantic structure, but about four times out of five the L2 listeners did not notice this. When the listeners were explicitly told to attend to prosody, their performance improved somewhat for focus placement changes (*Is HE driving?* vs. *Is he DRIVing?*) but not for other changes involving prosodic structure, such as question versus statement or noun-compound structure (*light housekeeper* vs. *lighthouse keeper*). All together, the evidence suggests that L2 listeners have quite some difficulty with prosodic cues to sentence semantics.

10.5 Higher-Level Processing: Syntax and Semantics in L2

The prosody evidence raises questions about its relation to syntactic and semantic processing in L2; however, most research on this has involved written materials. Moreover, although syntactic and semantic competence in L2 have been more intensively studied than any other aspect of L2 achievement, either from instructed L2 acquisition (e.g., Ellis 1994) or uninstructed (e.g., Perdue 1993), the focus has usually been on the learner's output success. Perceptual issues have rarely been central. We can only infer, mostly from indirect sources, how L2 listening comprehension might differ from L1 in these domains.

Review of a large body of research on L2 syntactic processing, mostly visual but including some in the auditory modality, led Clahsen and Felser (2006) to conclude that adult L2 learners compute shallower and less-detailed syntactic representations than those of L1 users. This seems to suggest actual processing differences between the L1 and L2. But note that there is a continuum of this sort in L1 also; some L1 users in some situations compute richer and more detailed syntactic representations, or maintain syntactic alternatives longer in memory, than others (MacDonald, Just, and Carpenter 1992). As Brown (2008) has described, under stressful conditions even L1 listeners can ignore parts of a linguistic input (e.g., modal expressions) or can refrain from full syntactic analysis of incoming sentences and instead attend chiefly to the nouns they contain; Brown suggests that the threshold at which such selective listening would be invoked is likely to be reached earlier for L2 listeners. Perhaps the accumulated evidence thus suggests processing similarity in L1 and L2 but a lower level of L2 than L1 progress along the shared continuum of processing depth. Even at high levels of proficiency in L2, syntactic processing can fall below the L1 level in subtle ways (e.g., Sorace 1993). There can be interference effects, of course. Acoustic cues to gross syntactic structure, such as number of branching phrases, may feature in some languages but not in others (Grosjean and Hirt 1996), which can lead to unrealized expectations in L2. Mismatch between L1 and L2 in availability of features such as noun gender, case marking, determiners, or inflectional marking can likewise cause interference. But the principal difference between L1 and L2 higher-level processing may be less one of kind than of degree.

The overall picture seems consistent with the following account: at higher levels of the comprehension process, difficulties for L2 listeners have accumulated, to a level at which processing is seriously impaired. In chapter 9 we saw that L2 deficiencies in phonetic processing have a potentially massive impact on the word activation and competition process. In this chapter we have seen that L2 processing of word-level prosody can be as deficient as L2 phonetic processing; contrasts may be effectively indistinguishable. Further, lexical segmentation in L2 lags behind that in L1 whenever rhythmic and other strategies from the L1 interfere. None of these deficiencies is an absolute bar to comprehension. Each, however, increases ambiguity or slows down the rate of processing.

In consequence, there is a disastrous cumulative effect as the different problems proliferate across the course of processing an utterance. It is as if the system silts up and all processing is slowed. Add to that the simple but equally disastrous effects due solely to lack of practice; facilitatory benefits of high frequency of occurrence (of words or of structures) will be less available to those whose degree of exposure is as yet insufficient to underpin strong biases. Equally beneficial effects of automaticity in much-used processes will not appear if the degree of use is as yet insufficient. Consistent with this is the conclusion by Mueller (2005) that ERP reflections of controlled syntactic processing tend to be similar in L2 and L1 but reflections of automatized processing show less similarity. Consider then that the L2 user's degree of control over processing extends to the depth to which processing is undertaken (just as for all language users; MacDonald et al. 1992). In order to cope with speech input in real time, as processing at each level of the system slows, the only real option for an L2 user may be to curtail processing at a relatively shallow level. This could lead, for instance, to restriction of detail in syntactic representations or failure to reactivate the referent of a pronoun or trace (Love, Maas, and Swinney [2003] showed that L2 listeners do this less than L1 listeners). In most cases, reference to context will suffice to resolve residual ambiguity. L2 listeners are quite likely to need to refer to context to resolve ambiguity at the lexical level anyway (see chapter 9), so that there may even be little extra cost in invoking the context to clear up syntactic ambiguity too.

10.6 Why Is It So Hard to Understand a Second Language in Noise?

L2 listening becomes disproportionately difficult under noisy conditions. We are all familiar with the experience. Sitting in a noisy bar with a group talking in the L1 may be difficult, but it is certainly doable; in fact, it is usually fun. Sitting in the same noisy environment with a group talking in one's L2 is a different matter entirely—hard, frustrating, finally exhausting.

Even though no L2 user needs to be convinced that this phenomenon is real, science keeps demonstrating it in the laboratory anyway (Black and Hast 1962; Gat and Keith 1978; Nábělek and Donahue 1984; Mayo, Florentine, and Buus 1997; Bradlow and Alexander 2007; a detailed comparison of thirty-five such studies can be found in the review by Garcia Lecumberri, Cooke, and Cutler [2010]). But just why is L2 listening in noise so hard?

Noise masking is described as either energetic or informational. The former refers to purely auditory perception; the intensity of the noise makes the nature of the signal imperceptible. The second refers to the various ways in which the noise mask may compete with the underlying signal. Some of these are highly relevant for a comparison between L1 and L2. Thus, the more speakers (up to about eight) that contribute to a competing speech mask, the more it interferes (Simpson and Cooke 2005); competing speech maskers cause greater interference if they are in the L1 rather than a foreign language (Garcia Lecumberri and Cooke 2006; Van Engen and Bradlow 2007); and reversing L1 speech makes it less interfering as a masker whereas reversing foreign speech makes it more interfering (Rhebergen, Versfeld, and Dreschler 2005). The latter increase is due to an energetic masking effect that should hold for the L1 speech, too, which suggests that the informational effect is actually much stronger because it not only overrides this energetic effect but is actually significant in the opposite direction. Hoen et al. (2007) propose that the greater part of the strong informational masking effect comes from lexical competition—competing speech activates competing words.

10.6.1 Mainly a Phonetic Effect or Mainly a Higher-Level Effect?

It is possible that the breakdown of phoneme perception described in chapter 9 has a major role to play in the susceptibility of L2 speech perception to noise interference. Perhaps L2 listeners require higher-quality acoustic input to achieve phoneme discriminations, so that the front end of their system simply fails to deliver when the quality of the acoustic input is poor. Then, the whole listening in noise problem could be seen as propagating through from the phonetic processing level. Certainly, it has repeatedly been suggested that improving L2 listeners' use of acoustic cues to phonemes would improve their whole speech perception both in general (Jamieson and Morosan 1986) and in noise (Hazan and Simpson 2000).

Most studies of L2 speech perception in noise have, reasonably, presented listeners with real words in real sentences. This does not really test the phonetic explanation, because noise could be affecting the word recognition and syntactic processing levels, not only phoneme perception. There are indications that higher-level processing might actually be quite important in the interference effect. First, the biggest effects of noise in L2 listening occur with sentences that are highly predictable (Mayo et al. 1997). This finding suggests that L2 listeners exploit predictability less efficiently than native listeners. Second, L2 listeners' recognition performance for sentences in noise correlates significantly with a measure of linguistic predictability of the materials (letter-by-letter guessing, by other participants, of visually presented versions of the same sentences; Van Wijngaarden, Steeneken, and Houtgast 2002). Less effective use of context, especially reduced exploitation of semantic predictability, could be a major factor in L2 listening difficulty in noise.

Cutler, Weber, et al. (2004) tested the phonetic explanation. They constructed 645 syllables consisting of a vowel plus consonant (e.g., *uf*, *ig*) or a consonant plus vowel (e.g., *foo*, *ga*). These were all such possible syllables using all the phonemes of American English (except the reduced vowel, schwa). Each syllable was presented once for vowel identification and once for consonant identification, in each of three levels of noise: very mild (16-decibel signal to noise ratio [SNR]), moderate (8 decibel), and fairly severe (0 decibel). There were sixteen native American listeners and sixteen L2 listeners (Dutch, with, as usual, good English). The 645 syllables times three SNRs times two presentations times thirty-two listeners made for 123,840 responses—very large indeed, as L2 listening studies go.

Noise affected the phoneme identification of the L2 listeners; their performance dropped from 68 percent under mild noise to 62 percent under moderate and 50 percent correct under severe noise. However, it also affected the performance of the L1 listeners: they dropped from 81 percent to 76 percent to 63 percent. The L2 listeners, in fact, performed at about 80 percent of native performance at every noise level; that is, the effect of noise on the L2 listeners' identifications was not disproportionate.

In other words, noise seems to affect the phoneme identification performance of native and nonnative listeners rather equivalently. Thus, the especial difficulty of listening to the L2 in noise is not really because phonetic processing is more disrupted for L2 than for L1 listeners, but mainly because we cannot recover from these effects as well in our L2. In the native language, we make effective use of contextual redundancy, of our knowledge of likely transitional probabilities, and of our large vocabulary and greater syntactic flexibility; all this extra knowledge helps us to recover from the effects of noise on phoneme identification. L2 listening does not have the resources to support such recovery.

Another contribution to this debate was made by Garcia Lecumberri and Cooke (2006), who also presented L1 and L2 (this time they were Spanish) listeners with an English phoneme identification task with no possibility for lexical recourse. The phonemes were consonants, and they were presented in a constant context (both preceded and followed by [a]), with the noise beginning a constant period in advance. The main aim of their paper was to compare different types of competing noise. They found that multitalker babble (the type of noise used by Cutler, Weber, et al. and many others) had the most severe effects on both L2 and L1 listening. Competing speech from one other talker was easier to deal with, especially if it was incomprehensible; so the L1 listeners, who knew no Spanish, had less problem with competing Spanish than with competing English, whereas the L2 listeners were affected by both Spanish and English. This resembles the effect, well known to L2 listeners, that it is easier to tune out speech in an unfamiliar tongue. The Spanish listeners in this study failed to tune out English either because they were students of English and thus listened to it regularly, or as a side effect of the fact that the task was discrimination in English.

However, Garcia Lecumberri and Cooke also found that noise affected consonant identification far more for their L2 than for their L1 listeners. Figure 10.4 shows the results of these two studies, for the most comparable conditions tested. In Cutler, Weber, et al.'s results, in the left panel (a), the lines for the English and Dutch listeners run parallel; that is, the effects of noise on L1 and L2 listening are equal. This

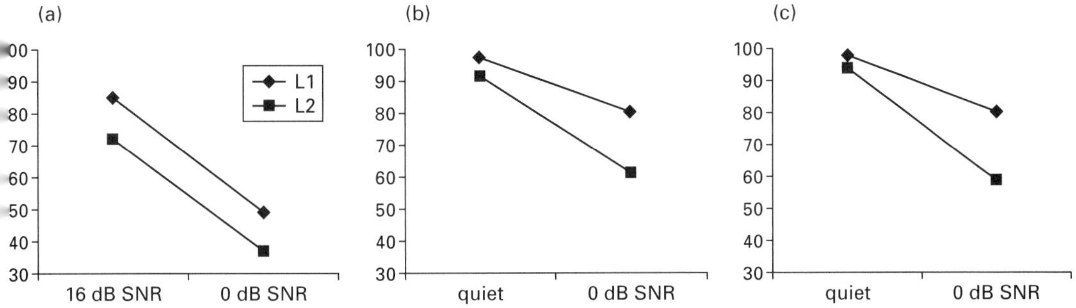

Figure 10.4
Listening to American English phonemes in noise is affected to about the same extent for L1 (British English) and L2 (Dutch) listeners if there is absolutely no contextual support (left panel). A constant phonetic context and predictable timing allows L1 listeners to avoid being as much affected by noise as either Spanish (middle panel) or Dutch (right panel) L2 listeners. (Data from Cutler, Weber, et al. 2004; Garcia Lecumberri and Cooke 2006; Cutler, Garcia Lecumberri, et al. 2008.)

was the result in their study overall, and it appeared in the subset of their study most resembling Garcia Lecumberri and Cooke's study, too. In the latter's results for the babble condition versus quiet shown in the middle panel (b), there is a much greater difference between the English and Spanish listeners in noise than in quiet—in other words, there are greater effects of noise on L2 than on L1 listening.

There were differences between the studies, two of which seemed particularly relevant here. First, it could be that Cutler, Weber, et al.'s (2004) L1 listeners were underperforming because of the high unpredictability of the VC and CV stimuli—there was no constant phonetic context, and the syllables differed in duration and were center-embedded in the noise, so that even the moment of onset could not be predicted. If L1 listeners profit from any predictability in the listening situation to a greater extent than L2 listeners do, then even the small increase in predictability offered by Garcia Lecumberri and Cooke's (2006) VCV tokens could have helped the L1 listeners preserve their performance in noise. Second, however, it could also be that Cutler, Weber, et al.'s L2 listeners were overperforming in comparison with the average L2 listener, simply because Dutch listeners to English are generally more skilled than Spanish listeners are.

To decide between these accounts, Cutler, Garcia Lecumberri, and Cooke (2008) presented the materials from the 2006 study to Dutch listeners. If the discrepancy in the two results was due to the relative English proficiency of the Dutch versus Spanish listeners, then the result in panel (a) of figure 10.4 would be repeated: Dutch listeners would maintain a performance decrement roughly constant to L1 across the two conditions. If the discrepancy was due to task differences, then the result in panel (b) of figure 10.4 would reappear: Dutch listeners would differ more from the L1 control group in babble than in quiet. Panel (c) in the figure shows what happened: the latter prediction came out. Thus the difference between the two original results happened because the tasks were different. Comparing (a) and (c) in the figure makes it clear that the Cutler, Weber, et al. task was harder for L1 and L2 listeners alike. Overall, it thus appears that noise masking itself can have equivalent effects on L1 and L2 speech, but L1 listeners are definitely better at recovering from disruption.

In a further experiment in this series (Cutler, Cooke, et al. 2007), English, Dutch, and Spanish listeners heard a larger set of American English consonants, again in a constant vowel context, under two types of masking: a competing talker or signal-correlated noise. Both the Dutch and Spanish listeners were more affected than the L1 listeners by signal-correlated noise, which suggests again that the L1 listeners had been able to exploit low-level predictability in the stimuli. But although the Spanish listeners found the competing talker as disruptive as the noise, the Dutch listeners' performance with the competing talker only decreased to the same extent as the L1 listeners' did, which implies that, at least in the face of this more ecologically valid disturbance of listening, the Dutch listeners' superior experience with English helped them maintain their performance levels.

10.6.2 The Multiple Levels of L1 Advantage

Thus, answering the question of why listening is harder in noise in an L2 than in the L1 is not a simple matter. It depends on the relation between the L1 and L2, the type of noise, and the type of speech input. The effect of noise on identification of Mandarin tones, for instance, runs quite parallel for L1 and L2 listeners (Lee, Tao, and Bond 2010). Of course, if L2 listeners' phonetic processing breaks down to such an extent that less than 50 percent of the input is correctly categorized, and L1 performance remains above 50 percent correct even if disrupted, there is no doubt that L1 listeners will be in a better position to reconstruct the input; phonetic processing does play a role and can be shown to predict L2 word recognition in noise fairly directly (Meador, Flege, and MacKay 2000). Word activation in L2 is generally slower, too: gating studies show that L2 listeners need more of an input before they come up with the correct word (Nooteboom and Truin 1980), as do even bilinguals in their nondominant language (Sebastián-Gallés and Soto-Faraco 1999). So if phonetic processing is slowed by noise, the word-recognition level could be hit by a substantial knock-on effect.

However, not all of the L2 disadvantage in noise should be ascribed to phonetic misidentifications plus the effects they then trigger at higher levels; at all levels, L1 listeners recover from disruption better than L2 listeners do. Direct tests of the degree to which L1 and L2 listeners use different types of information to interpret speech in noise show that L1 listeners tend to make more use of higher-level—lexical—information than L2 listeners anyway, and they increase their reliance on it still further when listening is difficult (Mattys et al. 2010).

Take away the means of recovery—support from contextual redundancy, for instance—and L1 listeners lose their advantage. Thus Mack (1988) presented L1 and L2 listeners with semantically anomalous sentences such as *A jaunty fork raised a vacant cow*, either spoken naturally or in a poorly synthesized version; it was the L1 listeners who showed the proportionally greater increase in errors from the naturally spoken to the synthesized condition. Mayo et al.'s (1997) finding that L1 listeners significantly outperformed L2 listeners on the Speech Perception in Noise test (Kalikow, Stevens, and Elliott 1977) only held for highly predictable sentences (e.g., *Stir your coffee with a spoon*; there was no significant L1 advantage with low-predictability sentences such as *We spoke about the knob*). Phoneme identification in noise by all listeners benefits from cue enhancement (selective amplification of the acoustic cues critical for particular phonetic distinctions; Hazan and Simpson 1998), but neither L1 nor L2 listeners receive significantly greater advantage (Hazan and Simpson 2000). That is, in the absence of any contextual support, simple acoustic effects, either positive or negative, can be equivalent for L1 and L2 listeners. Any contextual support there is, however, is better used by the L1 listener.

Indeed, when noise-masked speech is deliberately spoken clearly so that, for instance, it can be easily segmented into words, this benefits L1 more than L2 listeners (Bradlow and Bent 2002). The materials in this study were quite plausible sentences such as *The bus left early*, so the L1 listeners could in fact benefit at many levels. Clear speech, Bradlow and Bent argued, is actually designed for maximal benefit to L1 listening. In line with this, English speakers who are trying to be clear emphasize exactly the boundaries that English listeners overlook—namely, those before weak syllables (Cutler and Butterfield 1990a); when speakers thought that a listener (actually, a stooge) had misheard *He called in to view it* as *The cold interviewer*, their repetitions of the first utterance proportionally strengthened boundary cues before *to* more than those before *view*. English listeners assume that words begin at strong syllables (see chapter 4); the clear speech alterations thus compensated for this segmentation bias. Little wonder that clear speech has less benefit for L2 listeners, if they have not mastered these native biases in the first place. Bradlow and Alexander (2007) combined predictability cues with clear speech cues in noise and found that L2 listeners' performance was improved if they had both cues at once (rather than no cue or just one); for L1 listeners, in contrast, the two types of information had separate, additive effects.

At the lexical level itself, we saw in chapter 9 that word-recognition success is not a simple consequence of the success with which the individual phonemes of known words can be identified; phonetic contrasts that are correctly distinguished in phoneme-level tasks may still be misidentified in "near words," even where there is no interference from noise (Broersma 2002; Broersma and Cutler 2008, 2011; Hayes-Harb 2007). As an L2 listener's vocabulary in the new language expands, it provides more accurate statistical support for transition probabilities and sequence restrictions in the L2 (Hayes-Harb and Masuda 2008). But the size of an L2 vocabulary will generally remain smaller than that of the L1 vocabulary, and thus it will simply offer less recovery support in difficult listening conditions. Note that L2 listeners seem to be more sensitive to the number of phonologically similar competitors in the vocabulary than L1 listeners; Marian, Blumenfeld, and Boukrina (2008) found that L2 but not L1 listeners named pictures more rapidly when the (German) word targets had a common onset (such as *Dach* 'roof') than a rare onset (*Platte* 'record'; many German words begin [da] but few begin [pla]). In the same study, competitor population size influenced the effects of L1 interference in L2 eye-tracking. Recall that Bradlow and Pisoni (1999) likewise found that L2 listeners to English showed greater effects of the number of phonologically similar competitors in the language than L1 listeners did (see chapter 9). All this suggests that L2 listeners are highly susceptible (to an even greater extent than L1 listeners) to the precise makeup of their vocabulary.

It is not only lexical and higher-level cues that L1 listeners benefit from; the results of Cutler, Garcia Lecumberri, et al. (2008) suggest that even the slightest low-level cues available in speech materials can be used. A constant vowel context helps, and so does a constant period of preceding noise. We have already seen (in chapter 1) that constant vocalic contexts simplify consonant detection (Costa et al. 1998; Swinney and Prather 1980). A constant amount of preceding noise could help by making the speech onset temporally predictable. Compared to noise that is temporally contiguous with the speech, such leading noise improves intelligibility of CV syllables (Ainsworth and Cervera 2001); and predictability also elicits more accurate performance in pitch discrimination (Bausenhart, Rolke, and Ulrich 2007) and gap detection (Rolke and Hofmann [2007], using visual materials). Sensitivity to the information in such low-level structure allows L1 listeners to recover from effects of noise, just as use of high-level plausibility can help them. In both cases, the lesser experience of L2 listeners translates to lesser ability to make use of the recovery information on offer.

Recognizing speech in noise can require the listener to attend to different aspects of the speech signal, including different subsets of the many cues to phoneme identity (Parikh and Loizou 2005; Jiang, Chen, and Alwan 2006). This too can interact with L1-L2 effects, given that the makeup of the phoneme repertoire affects how a particular phoneme is identified across languages (Wagner et al. 2006). The outcome need not be a disadvantage for L2 listeners. In Cutler, Cooke, et al.'s (2007) speech-in-noise in experiment with both Dutch and Spanish listeners to English, the two groups' performance on most consonants ran parallel: each L2 group was more seriously affected by noise than the L1 group. However, a different pattern appeared with the fricative/affricate subset of the materials; there, Dutch listeners were less seriously affected by noise than either L1 listeners or the Spanish group. This result was interpretable in the light of Wagner et al.'s (2006) finding that transitional information is useful for fricative identification in English and Spanish (which both have not only [f] but also [θ]) but not in Dutch (which has no [θ]). Gating experiments in the same languages by Wagner (2008) showed that cross-language differences in sensitivity to transitional information do not generalize to other phoneme classes (e.g., stops). So, if the presence of a noise masker seriously disrupts the use of transition information, then the paradox of the better performance of the Dutch group with these consonants would be explained: in their case, their native experience with fricative identification, not relying on the cues that were fragile under noise, served them better than the other two groups' native-language experience that induced attention to the cues that had been particularly disrupted.

Many sources of information are thus less available to L2 listeners than to L1 listeners. Even high-functioning bilinguals have less accrued experience with a language than monolinguals do, and are correspondingly more affected by noise in listening (Mayo et al. 1997; Rogers et al. 2006). Listeners' knowledge of relative lexical frequencies of occurrence, of transitional probability, and of contextual plausibility for an L2 all fall below that of their L1 knowledge. Even when speech has been especially carefully enunciated, the adjustments will be less useful to the L2 listener. In L2, ultimately, everything ends up taking longer. This leads L2 listeners to skimp on sentence-level processing, we suggested—not because they cannot do it in principle, but because in practice they have no time for it. The absence of an elaborated syntactic framework then potentially further reduces the likelihood of recovery from listening disruption. In section 10.7 we consider yet another type of listening performance that is harder in L2. All of these separate problems contribute to the disadvantage for L2 listeners in noisy listening situations. The explanation for this disadvantage, it seems, is not primarily to be found in the initial impact of the noise on processing but in the ability to recover from the disruption it causes, by recourse to multiple sources of information.

10.7 Voice Recognition in L2 versus L1

Identification of speakers seems to vary as a function of what they are speaking. American English listeners tested by Thompson (1987) identified speakers producing native English most accurately, speakers producing accented English less accurately, and speakers producing native Spanish less accurately still. This pattern suggests that recognition accuracy varies with familiarity of their output to the listener. But in another study, speaker recognition accuracy did not differ for accented versus nonaccented voices speaking the same language (Goldstein et al. 1981), which seems to suggest that familiarity of the language may be what matters. So Goggin et al. (1991) carefully controlled speaker identity by collecting productions of texts in English and in German from six German-English bilinguals. They then presented one text followed by all six speakers' productions of another text. The subjects' task was to identify the speaker of the first text among the six speakers of the second text. Native English speakers were significantly better at picking the speaker when all the passages were presented in English rather than in German. Then the same materials were presented to native German speakers, and they were significantly better at picking the speaker when all the passages were presented in German rather than in English. Given that the set of speakers was exactly the same, this study showed that it was the L1 that was associated with high accuracy in speaker identification.

Voice identification was again better in the L1 in a study with English and German words again spoken by fluent bilinguals; English listeners were trained to identify the ten speakers with English words only or with German words only or they were not trained; then they had to decide for pairs of words whether the speaker was the same or different (Winters, Levi, and Pisoni 2008). Irrespective of training, these English listeners always showed better speaker identification when both the spoken words were in English than when they were in German. Training (with either language) improved performance to an equal extent. The training effect in a study of Chinese and English voices (Perrachione and Wong 2007) was also significant but was independent of the L1 effect; despite improvement across training sessions, English speakers stayed better at identifying English talkers than Mandarin talkers, and Mandarin speakers stayed better at identifying Mandarin talkers than English talkers.

The basis for the L1 advantage was examined by Schiller and Köster (1996; Köster and Schiller 1997) who tested (a) German speakers, (b) English, Spanish, or Chinese speakers who knew German, and (c) speakers of the same three languages who knew no German, all on recognition accuracy for six male voices speaking German. The groups who knew no German performed worse than all the groups who knew German. Within the four groups who did know German, no statistical difference in performance was observed between German L1 listeners and English listeners with German L2; however, the Spanish and Chinese L2 groups performed significantly less well than the native Germans and the English L2 speakers. English is phonologically closer to German than either Spanish or Chinese is, so this suggests that the L1 advantage is in part phonological. Rhythm (stress based in both English and German) is not enough by itself, because reiterant speech, which mimics natural utterances with repetitions of a single syllable and thus preserves rhythm but obliterates syllable weight and segmental structure, removed the language familiarity effect (Schiller, Köster, and Duckworth 1997). Phonetic segments differ in how useful they are for voice discrimination (Andics, McQueen, and Van Turennout 2007), so crucial segmental similarities between an L2 and the listener's L1 may facilitate voice recognition; other similarities in phonological structure may also play a role.

Talker recognition was not at issue in chapter 8, but it is relevant to note here that even seven-month-olds can better distinguish speakers in the language they are acquiring than in an unfamiliar language. The evidence comes from a study by Johnson et al. (2011) in which the infants listened to three voices speaking either in the native language or in a foreign language. When they showed signs of getting bored, the input changed to a different voice speaking either the same language as before or a different language. The infants always noticed a change of language but only noticed a change of talker when the language being spoken was the native one. These seven-month-olds obviously could not understand what was being said. This, too, suggests that familiarity with the phonological structure of the input is a crucial factor.

Voice discrimination (especially on the basis of small speech samples) is a hard task. Recall the finding of Lorch and Meara (1989), reported in section 10.1.1, that some phonetic information can be extracted from brief samples of unfamiliar speech, but committing the extracted information to memory (as required for identification) is not easy. Even a relatively natural but difficult speech perception task, shadowing in the native language, can be so attention consuming that a midstream change of talkers passes unnoticed (Vitevitch 2003a). A lot more research seems to be needed here, with special attention to the phonological relation between the listener's L1 and the L2 in which voice recognition is undertaken. But it is interesting that the ability to discriminate between speaker's voices may depend at least in part on phonological processing. Recent neural studies of voice recognition (Andics et al. 2010; Perrachione, Pierrehumbert, and Wong 2009) show that acoustic processing of voices is separate from identification of voices, with the latter involving left hemisphere neural circuitry used for language processing. Voice identification seems to draw on L1 experience even from infancy, before speech conveys meaning, and this L1 advantage persists.

10.8 A First Ray of Hope: When L2 Listeners Can Have an Advantage!

When listeners apply their L1 capacities and procedures in L2 listening, it may not necessarily be to their disadvantage. It is easy to think that L1 listening cannot be bettered—why should L1 listeners miss any trick to listen with maximum efficiency? In fact, however, we have seen in the earlier chapters that L1 listening is not always maximally efficient. Some procedures that could be used are not used where the payoff that they return is apparently not worth the cost of their implementation. Consider an example from chapters 1 and 7: English listeners' use of stress cues in word recognition. English listeners can recognize words on segmental information alone; they do not really need to use suprasegmental stress cues. So although such cues exist and could help them distinguish, for instance, *ele-* in *elephant* versus *elevation*, they make less use of such information than Spanish and Dutch listeners make of equivalent information in their native languages. There are good reasons for the English listeners' choice, as we have seen—the relative payoff in reduction of embedding is very small, compared to the payoff in Spanish or Dutch.

English listeners do not find it easy to decide whether a single syllable taken from an English word is stressed or not. This is not surprising—as Fear et al. (1995) showed, English listeners easily distinguish between full and reduced syllables but not between full syllables with primary, secondary, or no stress. Dutch listeners, in contrast, distinguish individual syllables such as *voor* or *naam* from *VOORnaam* versus *voorNAAM* with ease (Cutler and Donselaar 2001). When Cooper et al. (2002) asked English and Dutch listeners to categorize syllables such as *mus-* from English *music* versus *museum*, they found, then, just the result that these findings in toto would predict—the L2 (Dutch) listeners performed better than the L1

(English). Recall that Tremblay's (2008) French listeners did not succeed on this task. The Dutch listeners, however, brought from their L1 an ability to process prosodic stress cues. Applied to the L2, this ability would surely return less payoff than they were accustomed to in the L1; nevertheless, apply it in English they did, with the result that they extracted from the English speech signal just a little more information than the L1 listeners did.

Analysis of the acoustic cues in Cooper et al.'s materials (Cutler, Wales, et al. 2007) made it possible to compare what cues each listener group used in the categorization task. The Dutch listeners made sensible use of F0, duration, and intensity—differences in each of these were associated with a higher proportion of correct responses. The native listeners also made use of the F0 cues, which showed by far the most significant differences between the primary (e.g., in *music*) and secondary stress syllables (e.g., in *museum*). Oddly, at first sight, a few correlations for the native listeners' results seemed to go in the wrong direction (this never happened for the Dutch listeners). For example, the longer a secondary-stressed syllable, the more likely it was to be correctly classified as secondary stressed—although syllables were systematically shorter with secondary than with primary stress. This correlation makes sense if one considers that in longer syllables, F0 cues are more perceptible. The only way to perform such a classification task ("Where does this token of *mus-* come from?") is by listening to the acoustics; the picture that emerges is that the native listeners really did their level best and managed to latch on at least to the usefulness of the F0 cues, even though they do not normally use any of these cues in recognizing words. The Dutch listeners, in contrast, simply called on their L1 experience and used all the cues in the way they normally do.

Dutch listeners also displayed greater sensitivity in interpreting Fear et al.'s (1995) cross-spliced words (*audition* with the vowel of *audience*, *auditoria*, or *addition*, for example) than the original native listeners had shown. The native group had effectively tolerated any cross-splicing except where vowel quality was altered. Dutch listeners presented with the same materials by Cutler (2009) were particularly more sensitive to what an unstressed full vowel should sound like; replacement of such a vowel (as in the first syllable of *audition*) by a more stressed vowel (e.g., from *audience* or *auditoria*) was rated significantly worse by these listeners than by the native listeners. The acceptability ratings of the Dutch listeners proved to be more strongly related to suprasegmental than to segmental properties of the stimuli, in contrast to the English listeners' original responses (see figure 10.5). Whereas for the English listeners vowels were either full or reduced, the Dutch listeners apparently had—from their L1—a more graded representation—in particular, a more precise concept of an unstressed syllable with a full vowel.

A similar pattern of greater L2 sensitivity appeared in Broersma's (2005, 2008, 2010) studies of phonetic categorization described in chapter 9, in which Dutch

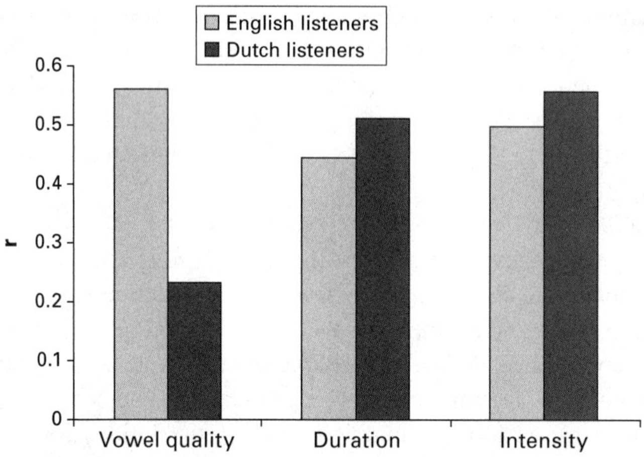

Figure 10.5
Correlation coefficients for the relationship of rated acceptability of cross-spliced English words (e.g., *audience* with the vowel of *audition*) with acoustic measures, for English L1 and Dutch L2 listeners. For the L1 listeners, the segmental measure vowel quality is more strongly related to the judgments than the suprasegmental measures of duration and intensity. For the L2 listeners, vowel quality plays a weaker role than suprasegmental cues. (Data for English from Fear et al. 1995 and for Dutch from Cutler 2009.)

listeners judged voicing contrasts in syllable-final position, a position in which all native obstruents in Dutch are voiceless. Broersma's Dutch listeners performed well with these familiar contrasts in an unfamiliar position, by using the same cues that they would use for syllable-initial distinctions. The English L1 listeners, who tended to rely almost exclusively on vowel-duration cues, had nothing to fall back on when such cues were unavailable; but the Dutch listeners efficiently processed the remaining cues, thereby achieving a sharper categorical division of the continuum than the L1 listeners' responses showed. Here the Dutch listeners were not taking the shortcut that is characteristic of L1 listening, and this allowed them to use acoustic information overlooked by L1 listeners.

Wherever cues present in productions of a contrast are not phonologically significant enough in the language to warrant exploitation by L1 listeners, they are open to superior exploitation by L2 listeners whose L1 phonology does make it worth attending to those cues. Gottfried and Beddor (1988) found that French listeners made no use of variations in vowel duration as a cue to vowel identity. In speaking, their vowel productions showed systematic variation in vowel duration as well as spectral information, but in perceptual identification they used the spectral information alone. English listeners presented with the same French stimuli, however, were able to make use of both temporal and spectral variation. In English, Gottfried and Beddor pointed out, temporal and spectral information trade off to distinguish vowels (and indeed, the English listeners reported that they were assimilating the French stimuli to English categories). In French, however, duration can be an unreliable cue to vowel identity, so French speakers have learned to ignore it. But the durational information is still there for listeners to exploit if, for L1 reasons, their processing systems have included it. Goudbeek et al.'s (2008) Spanish listeners were similarly reluctant to exploit duration as a cue for distinguishing between Dutch vowels, but American English listeners made full use of duration as a cue with the same unfamiliar vowels.

No doubt there are many more such cases. Kubozono (2002) discovered one of a different kind. In Japanese, a single vowel may constitute a mora. The distinction between short and long vowels is thus a distinction between one mora or two, so that it is crucial for rhythm perception and all that depends on it—segmentation, for example (see chapter 4). However, this distinction is sometimes partly neutralized, especially in word-final position. In the word *kookoo* 'high school', for example, the ratio of length of the first *koo-* to a monomoraic initial syllable (e.g., *ko-* in *koke* 'moss') is greater than that of the second *koo-* to a monomoraic final syllable (e.g., *ko-* in *yoko* 'side'). Despite this, enough cues remain for Japanese listeners to be extremely accurate in distinguishing minimal word pairs contrasting only in final vowel length (such as *sado* 'Sado Island' versus *sadoo* 'tea ceremony'). They can do this whether the words are heard in sentence context or in isolation, and in audio only or audio-visually. In the latter case, the listeners only use cues in the audio signal, though, not cues in the visible gestures. With only visual information (videos of the speakers saying the words), their performance on the final vowel contrast fell to chance (50 percent). However, L2 listeners (with varying language backgrounds, resident in Japan, and speaking Japanese for on average two years) achieved 75 percent correct discrimination of this same contrast on the visual signal alone! Thus, Japanese speakers do provide a visual correlate of the long-short final vowel contrast (lip configuration, Kubozono suggested). L2 listeners learn to use it. The L1 listeners, in whom the moraic rhythm of their language may have developed exquisite temporal sensitivity, rely exclusively on the auditory timing.

Finally, L1 expectations also do not necessarily lead to slower processing. Consider Weber's (2001) study described in chapter 6, in which German listeners detected the velar fricative [x] in Dutch-pronounced nonwords like *hicht* and *hacht*. The Dutch pronunciation violates German assimilation rules; in German, [x] cannot follow the vowel [ɪ], and real German words like *Licht* 'light' contain a different consonant sound. The German listeners were actually significantly faster in detecting [x] in environments like *hicht* that would be impossible contexts in their L1. Dutch L1 listeners showed no difference in response speed to the two nonword types.

Reviewing these results, we see L2 listeners doing their very best with what they have. Sometimes, by accident, what they have (in the form of their L1-tailored processing system) is actually better suited to some aspect of some input than the L1 listeners' probabilistically weighted processing. Such advantages may well be few; mostly, what L2 listeners have (a smaller vocabulary, far less relevant experience from which to develop probabilistically based strategies, and L1 biases that are nearly all inappropriate for the L2) cannot help at all but simply makes listening in the L2 far harder than in the L1.

10.9 A Second Ray of Hope: The Case of Bilinguals

Bilinguals, as Grosjean (1989) has forcefully argued, are not two monolinguals in one person. Grosjean's point was underlined by a surprising result found by Cutler et al. (1989, 1992) in a study of segmentation by early bilinguals. For the metrically based segmentation procedures, it appeared that these bilinguals could command no more than one of the differing procedures that were characteristic of their languages.

This group of bilinguals, all final-year pupils at bilingual high schools in London and Paris, had acquired both English and French from a very early age. Most of them had been raised bilingually by one French- and one English-speaking parent. They were, to all intents and purposes, native speakers of both languages. As we saw in chapter 4, French listeners typically segment speech at syllable boundaries, whereas English listeners typically use a stress-based segmentation strategy. The bilinguals took part in fragment detection and word-spotting experiments (using the materials of Cutler et al. [1986] and Cutler and Norris [1988], respectively). For any one experiment, the results of the group as a whole gave an unclear pattern, unlike any of the original findings with nonbilingual groups. However, this turned out to be because the bilinguals were not a homogeneous group. Cutler et al. (1989, 1992) partitioned the group and examined the comparative performance of subgroups in each experiment. The first partitioning they chose, by country of residence, was perhaps the most obvious: approximately half of the group were resident in the United Kingdom, half in France. This also failed to produce results that resembled those found with monolinguals. Similar failure attended a partitioning of the group by language of either parent.

Another partitioning was based on the bilinguals' answer when they were asked to express a preference for one of their languages. Although all averred that they spoke each language equally happily, they were willing to fantasize in answer the question, "Suppose you had a dread disease, and the only way to save your life was a brain operation that would result in the loss of one of your languages; which one would you keep?" They were told to ignore pragmatic criteria; in fact, all the subjects found answering this question both enjoyable and easy. Their answer was deemed their preferred language. The notion of a preferred language was obviously not strange to them, because the participants started guessing their classmates' answers, with great success!

When the bilinguals were divided into groups by preferred language, their results fell into a pattern that, as figure 10.6 shows, clearly resembled the previous findings. Those who had chosen English performed like English monolinguals with both the English and the French materials; in English word-spotting, they showed stress-based segmentation, and in French syllable detection they did not show syllabic segmentation. Those who had chosen French, in contrast, showed no stress-based segmentation in the word-spotting experiment, but they did show syllabic segmentation in syllable detection in French.

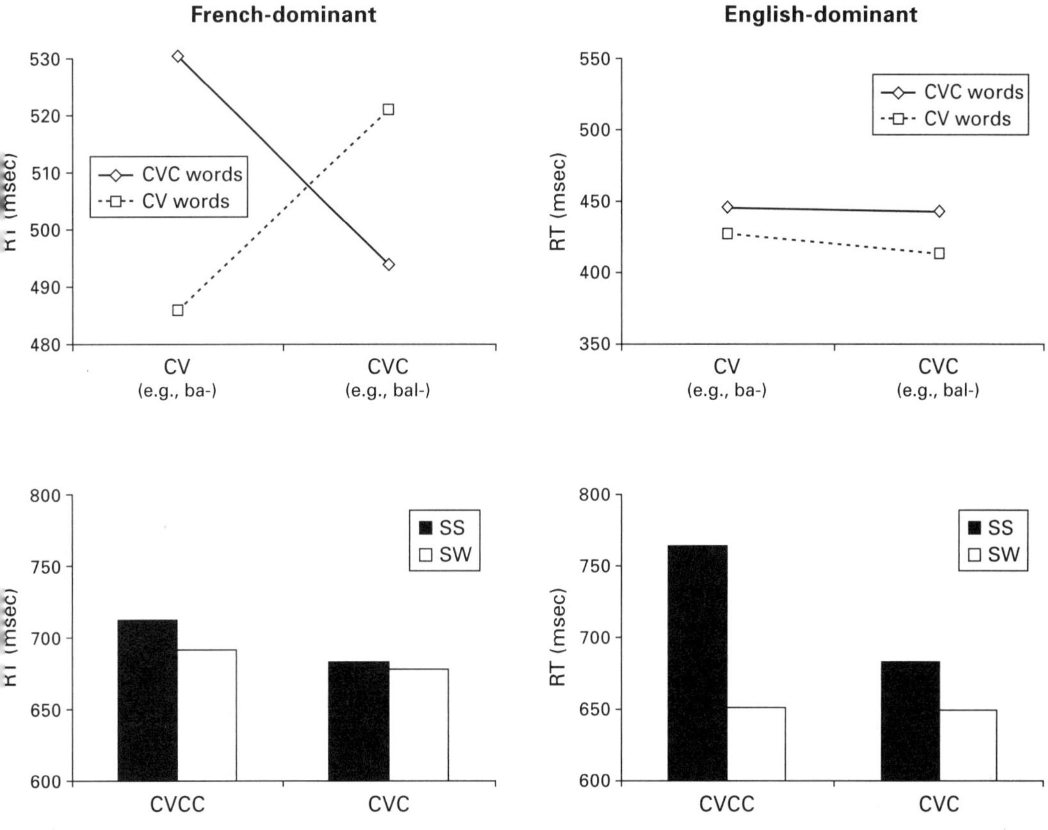

Figure 10.6
Fragment detection in French (upper panels) and word-spotting in English (lower panels) by balanced French-English bilinguals revealed to be French dominant (left panels) or English dominant (right panels). Compare the upper panels with figure 4.2a in chapter 4; the response pattern seen there appears here only for the French-dominant bilinguals. Compare the lower panels with figure 4.1; the pattern seen there is here displayed only by the English-dominant bilinguals. (Data from Cutler et al. 1992.)

This finding suggested that the bilingual listeners, despite their exceptional mastery of both English and French, could call on only one rhythmic segmentation procedure—either the procedure typical of French or that typical of English, but not both. If nothing else, this underlines the rather anomalous status of these segmentation heuristics in listening: clearly, they are not strictly necessary for effective listening. Models of spoken-word recognition can succeed in simulating recognition of continuous utterances by the use of multiple activation of lexical forms and competition between simultaneously active candidates, with no explicit procedures of segmentation. And bilinguals with only one rhythmic segmentation procedure at their disposal can still faultlessly comprehend two rhythmically different languages.

The use of only a single rhythmic procedure could indicate that the procedures have their roots in the initial launching of segmentation, when infants first exploit language rhythm to assist in segmenting speech into words. Perhaps such rhythmic assistance is needed only once? A test of this explanation would require experiments with infants exposed in bilingual environments to rhythmically differing languages, and to date no such studies have been conducted. It is also not clear yet whether the bar on the use of multiple procedures in adulthood is absolute. Some procedures may lend themselves more than others to late acquisition; for example, Bradley et al. (1993) and Sanders, Neville, and Woldorff (2002) have suggested that stress-based segmentation may be available to at least some L2 learners of English. (Both studies tested L2 listeners to English with Spanish, i.e., a stress language, as L1; see section 10.3.1 for constraints that may apply in making English segmentation procedures accessible to listeners with nonstress L1s).

A further important finding, however, emerged from a third experiment with the bilingual listeners. Not only did Cutler et al. (1992) test syllable detection in French (in which French monolinguals show evidence of syllabic segmentation), and word-spotting in English (in which English monolinguals show stress-based segmentation), they also tested syllable detection in English. Cutler et al. (1986) originally found that English listeners showed a null effect in syllable detection. The responses of Cutler et al.'s (1992) bilingual listeners, including the French-preferring bilinguals (see figure 10.7), patterned like those of the English listeners in the earlier study—no evidence of syllabic segmentation appeared.

Thus, although the bilinguals with a preference for French did command a syllabic segmentation procedure, and did make use of it when listening to French, they did not apply it inappropriately to their other language, English. This pattern contrasts with the inappropriate application of syllabic segmentation to English by the French listeners in the 1986 study, who did not have fluent mastery of English. Bradley et al. (1993) similarly showed that Spanish-English bilinguals did not use syllabic segmentation with English, and Kearns (1994) replicated Cutler at al.'s (1992)

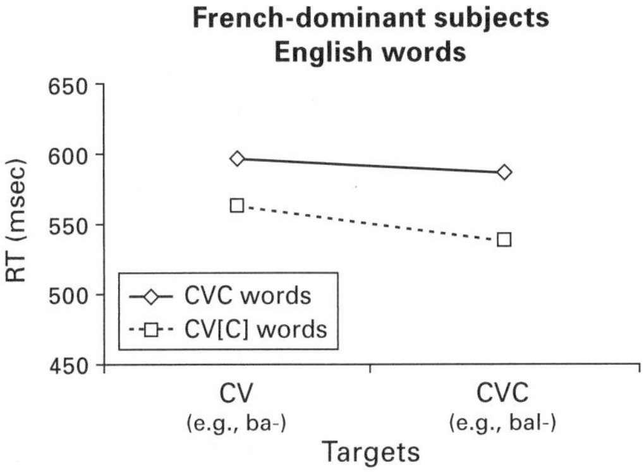

Figure 10.7
Fragment-detection performance of French-dominant bilinguals with English words, in the same study as in figure 10.6. Compared with figure 4.2 again, the French-dominant bilinguals can be seen to resemble the original English listeners, not the original French listeners.

French-English bilingual result with sentence stimuli rather than the word lists used by Cutler at al. (1986). All of these results thus suggest that with sufficient experience with more than one language, inappropriate application of language-specific segmentation procedures can be avoided.

The degree of similarity between a bilingual's languages is also relevant. Any procedure a listener has available ought to be equally applicable to any language for which it is useful. Thus, if a bilingual commands two languages with the same metrical structure, an available segmentation procedure should be usable with both. Indeed, studies by Van Zon (1997) with Dutch-English bilinguals, all of whom were clearly dominant in Dutch, showed that they used stress-based segmentation procedures when listening both to Dutch and to English. On the other hand, French-dominant French-Dutch bilinguals, also tested in Van Zon's study, did not use stress-based segmentation with Dutch. They behaved like the French-dominant French-English bilinguals of Cutler et al. (1992), whose results are shown in figure 10.6. In each case, French-dominant bilinguals did not have the stress-based procedure available. Both the English-dominant and the Dutch-dominant bilinguals did.

10.10 The Language Use Continuum

The bilinguals described in section 10.8 are bilinguals by anybody's definition. Yet their processing of their two languages was in at least one respect asymmetric. Such asymmetries are, in fact, typical of the use of more than one language. Technical vocabularies provide many instances of asymmetry, from speakers with apparent L1 mastery of two languages who know a technical vocabulary in only one (for instance, the French-Dutch bilingual from Belgium who trains as a chef in Paris), to speakers with apparently little knowledge of an L2 whose command of a given technical vocabulary in that L2 is perfect (e.g., the Russian-native air traffic controller in Kursk whose spoken English outside the control tower is no better than rudimentary). Most people's experience includes at some time use of more than one language; the lifelong monolingual is rare (see Grosjean 1997). If L2 is any language acquired after childhood, there is also a vast range of L2 proficiency, from emigrants who have made a professional living writing or performing in an L2, through top performers in international politics, business, or academia whose principal working language is not their L1, way on down to holiday phrasebook users and accomplished beggars with a small line of patter in an L2. The term "L2" captures the populations discussed in this chapter. But really any use of more than one language is bilingualism, and it is impossible to draw a hard and fast line between bilinguals on the one side and L2 users on the other. Asymmetry in usage is not the criterion, because there will always be asymmetry of some kind. Simply, the degree to which we master more than one language varies along a continuum of infinite gradations.

In fact, there will be many such continua, because linguistic experience varies at every level. Vocabulary size is often pointed to: bilinguals tend to know fewer words in each of their languages than a monolingual knows in the same language (although if both vocabularies are counted, the bilingual's total tally is higher). This does not mean that the bilingual knows more or fewer concepts, though, because some words tend to be known in one language only (often words used in the home context; Bialystok et al. 2010). Individual differences of vocabulary affect lexical activation and competition. But there is likely to be similar variation in experience of distinguishing phonetic contrasts; in the metalinguistic knowledge (e.g., of spelling) that affects lexical coding independently of input discrimination; in knowledge of idioms and syntactic forms and register variations—the list seems endless, and the various competencies will certainly not develop strictly in parallel. The result is that on this array of separate continua, each individual language user will display an individual profile of abilities.

10.11 Conclusion: Universal and Language Specific in L1 and L2

What of that important theoretical issue raised at the beginning of chapter 9? Is language acquisition biologically constrained and subject to a critical period, making for an absolute difference between those languages that can be termed L1 versus those that are L2? Neuroimaging evidence presented by Kim et al. (1997) suggested separate areas of brain activation for L1 and L2. In a task involving silently describing events from the recent past, areas within the left inferior frontal gyrus (Broca's area) were activated. Kim et al. asked their subjects to perform this task in two languages. When both the languages had been spoken from infancy, the areas activated were the same, irrespective of language. But when one language was the L1 and the other an L2 acquired in adulthood, the areas were different.

Broca's area is crucially involved in language production, but its role is coordination of the selection and unification processes involved, rather than lower-level processing (Hagoort 2005; Sharp et al. 2005; Thompson-Schill 2005; Thompson-Schill et al. 1997). This type of coordination does not seem likely to be language specific, although differences in amount of accrued practice could lead to differences in the automaticity of processing. Another aspect of Kim et al.'s study is relevant here, however. As well as looking at areas in the inferior frontal gyrus, they also looked at the superior temporal gyrus (Wernicke's area), which is associated with language reception. In Wernicke's area, there was no difference in area of activation as a function of L1 versus L2. Snijders et al. (2007) also found no significant differences in what brain areas were activated in their native and foreign listeners' brains (though great differences in how much activation there was). Listening to language activates the same areas of the brain in L1 and L2, more strongly in general for L1.

This is consistent with Mueller's (2005, 159–160) conclusions from her review of ERP studies of L2 processing: "the results . . . in the lexical-semantic domain point to similarities between L1 and L2 speakers rather than to differences," and "differences between L1 and L2 processing are more quantitative than qualitative in nature." In other processing domains, too, L1 and L2 processing seems to pattern similarly except for the effects of practice. Both in segmentation (Sanders and Neville 2003a, 2003b) and in syntactic processes (Hahne and Friederici 2001; Weber-Fox and Neville 1996), early negativities reflecting automatized responses are significantly reduced in an L2. L1 and L2 lexical processing in priming tasks, we saw, is likewise similar (Woutersen et al. 1995). Noise affects the apprehension of speech signals equivalently in L1 and L2, even though recovery from the effects of noise is far easier for the (more experienced) L1 listener. The pattern seems to be most consistent with the application of universal processing procedures in listening to speech, regardless of what language the speech is in. There is large variation, however, in the automaticity with which the procedures are applied, as a function of familiarity with the language, and in the extent of the resources that listeners can draw on. The precise way in which the procedures are applied can also vary as a function of the probabilities of the language with which one has had most experience.

The language use continuum is one of infinite gradations. The listener takes up a position on a continuum of listening proficiency, and perhaps it is even a different position for different kinds of listening situations. Speech input varies along continua, too. There is a general continuum of familiarity that runs from a completely unknown language, through minimally known L2, to various levels of L2 proficiency, to nonpreferred L1, and to an only or preferred L1. At the furthest end of this continuum, with an unfamiliar non-L1 that may be not recognized as speech at all (Best et al. 1988), nonlinguistic processes kick in. Otherwise, listeners do the best linguistic processing they can, with amount of experience being the strongest factor in determining how good that is. Again, the processing level they can achieve may vary separately with input type. Consider, for instance, that even highly proficient L2 users show reduced ability to adapt to speech in different language varieties and dialects (a topic at issue in the following chapter).

The hopeful conclusion of some of the research presented in this chapter is that it must be possible to move along the continua. Cutler et al.'s (1992) study with bilinguals suggests, in particular, that it is possible to learn to avoid applying L1-influenced processing inappropriately. The French-preferring listeners in that study apparently commanded only one segmentation procedure but did not apply this procedure where its use was inefficient. Clearly, procedures developed to exploit the rhythm of a particular language will be inefficient when applied to a language with different rhythm; this finding suggests that enough experience with a differing language can induce avoidance of such inefficiency. The procedure is available for use, but its application is inhibited with input in the language in which it does not pay off with improvement in listening efficiency. Language experience is the key; the principal open question is how much experience is "enough."

11 The Plasticity of Adult Speech Perception

Native listeners excel in adapting rapidly to newly encountered talkers, to dialectal variation, to unfamiliar accents, to new words, and to language change. All such factors can cause initial minor processing difficulty that is, however, rapidly overcome. Listener adaptability rests on the inherent plasticity of categorical decisions in speech perception; the boundaries of L1 phonemic categories are not immutably fixed but can be adjusted as the listening situation requires. Category decisions are adjusted to take account of sequence constraints, phonetic context, rate of speech, and higher-level probabilities; they are also adjusted to deal with individual pronunciation idiosyncrasies. Perceptual learning of this latter kind is speaker specific and long lasting, and, most importantly, it generalizes beyond the learning situation to facilitate continued communication. In all this, however, early-acquired languages command an advantage over later-acquired languages; it is principally in the native language that the flexibility and robustness of speech perception is expressed.

Categorical perception, defined as the detection of minimal differences that distinguish words, has played a central role in the story so far. Forming new L2 categories presents a difficult learning challenge (see chapter 9). When the discrimination of categorical contrasts in L1 is compared with the results from L2, and the influence of L1 on L2 performance is considered, it is tempting to think that the categories of the L1 may be essentially fixed. But that cannot be a correct depiction of the real L1-L2 asymmetry. Recent findings suggest that the categories of the L1 should actually be viewed as quite mutable, which may make them less fixed than more newly learned categories.

There is good reason why categories ought not to be immutably fixed—speech contains variable realizations of the categories that listeners have to identify. For example, variation in cross-category distinctions can arise due to dialectal variety (see section 11.2), to foreign accent (see section 11.3), or to the differences between individual talkers' vocal tracts (see section 11.4). The evidence shows that listeners are able to recalibrate the perceptual criteria for sounds to adjust to the wide range of possible forms a speech sound can take. A crucial factor here is that the listener's experience with the range of possibilities is inevitably greater in the L1 than in a later-acquired L2. This variable experience alone may induce greater flexibility of L1 categories.

Besides the variability argument, however, there is another issue that will be considered first—and that is language change. It amounts to a particularly potent argument for why phonemic categories cannot be regarded as fixed.

11.1 Language Change

If the phonemic categories of a language were fixed, then the language would presumably not change. But languages do change, all the time. It is easy to set up an experience of this; listen to any radio broadcast, or the soundtrack of a newsreel or movie, from several decades past. It sounds charmingly (or repulsively) old-fashioned. The language has changed since it was recorded.

There are several components to pronunciation change across a language community. Older speakers die and are replaced by younger speakers with different speech patterns, for one thing. But this is not enough to account for the relative rapidity of change. Nor are the changes that afflict individual speakers' voices as they age (e.g., Russell, Penny, and Pemberton 1995). Change occurs not only in average values across the community but in the pronunciations that individual members of the community strive for.

To demonstrate this, one would ideally want to be in possession of high-quality recordings of a speaker saying essentially the same thing every year for 50 years or so, with, of course, no awareness that the characteristics of his or her pronunciation were under scrutiny. It is to the phonetician Jonathan Harrington that we owe the insight that such a collection of recordings could be naturally located (Harrington, Palethorpe, and Watson 2000a, 2000b, 2005; Harrington 2006). With the permission of Buckingham Palace, he analyzed the pronunciation of the Queen of England as recorded in her Christmas messages, preserved in the highest of fidelity by the British Broadcasting Corporation (BBC). There were words that turned up each year without fail in these messages—*happy* and *Christmas*, for example, and *people, year, family, my husband and I* . . . ; in other words, this was just the corpus needed to answer questions about changes in an individual's speech.

Harrington and his colleagues analyzed around 3,000 vowels from these broadcasts, concentrating on the broadcasts from the 1950s and 1980s (a thirty-year time span is quite enough to test for changes in pronunciation, and the Queen's voice in the 1980s was arguably not yet showing severe effects of aging). They compared the recordings with an average of measurements of the same vowels from recordings of five female BBC presenters in the 1980s. The results were dramatically clear: all of the Queen's vowels had shifted over that thirty-year period, and they had shifted toward the positions where the average 1980s measurements fell. Note that the shift did not bring the Queen all the way to the 1980s average—her speech was still distinct from that of the other speakers. But her 1980s pronunciations were much closer to the 1980s average than her 1950s vowels were.

Consider the vowel [u] as in *you* or *do*; it varies naturally as a function of phonetic context, being rather more back in *fool* than in *few*, but it has been on average moving from a more back to a more front position in British English. Along that dimension, the measured pronunciations of [u] showed that furthest back were the Queen's utterances in the 1950s and the furthest front were the average of the 1980s speakers; the Queen's 1980s utterances fell in between. Three more vowels are shown in figure 11.1; they showed exactly the same change. Dimension by dimension, the same could be said of all the measured vowels—the Queen's pronunciation effectively tracked the changes that were occurring in British English (maintaining always a conservative distance, but not letting this distance grow as British English in general changed). The same was true of the diphthongs they measured (as in *my* or *how*)—these too resembled the 1980s population average to a greater extent in the Queen's recordings from the 1980s than in those from the 1950s.

The speech of this individual talker thus changed as the speech of the community changed. The Dutch linguist Marc van Oostendorp was inspired by Harrington's work to undertake a similar analysis of twenty-seven successive Christmas messages by Queen Beatrix of the Netherlands, concentrating on the pronunciation of [r], which is known to be undergoing change in Dutch. This Queen too proved to be changing along with her community (Van Oostendorp 2008). Similar individual changes have been reported for vowels of thirteen Montreal French speakers across the period 1971–1984 (Yaeger-Dror 1994), and for vowels of thirty-seven British English speakers over the period 1949–1966 (Bauer 1985). Susceptibility to a change

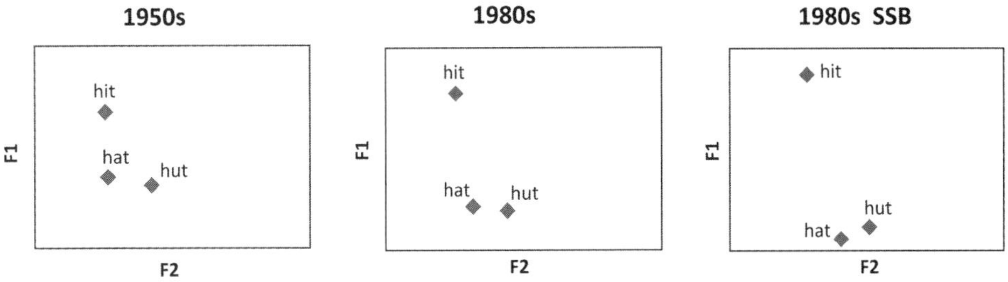

Figure 11.1
Three of the Queen's vowels (the vowels in *hat*, *hit*, *hut*). The left figure shows her average vowels in the 1950s, the middle figure her average in the 1980s, and the right figure the comparison 1980s average for other female speakers of standard southern British English (data from Harrington et al. 2000b). The vertical axis represents first-formant frequency and the horizontal axis second-formant frequency, on the Bark scale (frequency in terms of the critical bands of human hearing). Within each rectangle, the vertical dimension can be thought of as representing mouth opening (upper = less, lower = more), and the horizontal dimension as representing where in the mouth the vocal tract is constricted (left = nearer the lips, right = further back). On these dimensions, the Queen's 1980s vowels are nearer than her 1950s vowels to the British female 1980s average.

can certainly differ across individuals (Sankoff and Blondeau 2007, for [r] in Montreal French), and such individual differences could reflect differences in the distributions of speech input received (Scobbie 2005). The central point, however, is that if individual change tracks community change, then the change must be perceptually driven (whatever precipitated it in the first place). Listeners hear how the speakers around them realize phonemes of the language. They adjust their criteria for phoneme realization accordingly. As realizations within a community change, listeners' perceptual criteria change along with them, eventually altering the criteria for phoneme production targets. Each listener may thus also be affected as a speaker—even the most conservative listeners and speakers can eventually change.

11.2 Language Varieties and Perception of Speech in Another Dialect

Languages shape listeners' perceptual processing but so do the varying forms of a language.[1] In two dialects of a single language, it could be that listeners distinguish among the same sets of word candidates, or perform the same parsing operations, but attend to different sources of information to do so. Consider again the rhythmic structures that listeners use to segment continuous speech into words. English is the stress-timed language par excellence, and English listeners exploit this aspect of the phonology in segmentation. They show no sign of the syllable-based segmentation that French listeners use (see chapter 4). Yet, according to Deterding (2001) and Low (Low, Grabe, and Nolan 2000; Grabe and Low 2002), Singapore English displays syllabic rhythm. Might it be that listeners with Singapore English as L1 would profit from the use of syllabic segmentation when listening to speech in their native variety? Although this particular issue has apparently not been experimentally tested, there is abundant evidence of cross-dialectal differences in what information listeners exploit and for what purpose.

11.2.1 Cross-dialectal Differences in Perceptual Cues for Phonemes

One example comes from vowel perception in French. Standard French vowels hardly show any durational differences, and accordingly, listeners who speak that variety of French show little sign of exploiting temporal information in distinguishing between vowels (in contrast to English listeners, who know that some of their vowels differ a lot in average duration as well as in spectral quality; Gottfried and Beddor 1988). But other varieties of French make more use of durational cues; Swiss French, for instance, systematically uses duration to distinguish word pairs such as *voie* 'road' and *voix* 'voice' that are homophones in standard French, and pairs such as *côte* 'hillside' and *cotte* 'petticoat' that are distinguished only by spectral cues in standard French. Miller and Grosjean (1997) presented listeners from each of these dialect areas with standard French words on a spectral continuum from *côte* to *cotte*, with three different vowel durations. The listeners from the standard French dialect area made no use of duration in categorizing the tokens; their identification functions were the same irrespective of vowel length. But the Swiss French listeners (and a control group of American English listeners, too) were affected by the—irrelevant—duration manipulation; their identification functions were different when the tokens had long, versus medium, versus short vowels. Information that is ignored in one dialect area is attended to in another dialect area of the same language.

The English listeners in Miller and Grosjean's study were Americans, so this result joins Gottfried and Beddor's demonstration that American English listeners attend to vowel duration in distinguishing certain contrasts. Recall that English is not a so-called quantity language; that is, it does not distinguish word pairs just on the length of a particular vowel (or consonant) alone. But there is a lot of systematic variation in phoneme duration. In particular, [æ] in *bat* in American English is about one and a half times as long as [ɛ] in *bet*. Indeed, American listeners take duration into account in distinguishing this contrast (Hillenbrand, Clark, and Houde 2000).

This is not necessarily the same in other varieties of English. Although vowels in Australian English, for example, can also show durational cues to contrasts (Harrington and Cassidy 1994), the durational difference between [æ] and [ɛ] is far less in Australian than in American English. This asymmetry affected performance in a study by Cutler, Smits, and Cooper (2005) of cross-dialectal vowel perception. Australian English listeners heard the vowel discrimination subset from Cutler, Weber, et al.'s (2004) study of American English phoneme perception in noise, described in chapter 10. The acoustically similar [æ]-[ɛ] distinction was one of the hardest (most easily confused) for both groups, but the Australian listeners made many more errors than the American listeners had. It seems probable that under noise masking this contrast was particularly hard to distinguish by spectral cues. The American group, with knowledge of the additional difference in duration, could then base their decisions largely on that. The Australian listeners, not expecting such a distinction, failed to profit from it. Another difference between these two varieties is that Australian English vowels are generally tenser than the same vowels in American English. Again, the Australian listeners were more likely than the Americans to identify the American-spoken tense vowels as lax (e.g., to identify the vowel in *caught* as the vowel in *cot*).

Not only at the segmental level are there cross-dialectal differences in the relevance of types of information, but also at the level of segmentation. Speakers of American English can use the form of an intervocalic consonant as a perceptual cue to the presence or absence of a phrase boundary between two words, reflecting the fact that application of certain phonological effects is inhibited if there is a phrase boundary between the words. This is true, for instance, of intervocalic flapping (which turns the [t] in *writer* into a flap) and of palatalization (which turns *did you* into *didju*); each is, in principle, allowed across words (as in *visit India, did you*) but is inhibited if the two words belong to separate phrases. Thus there is unlikely to be a flapped form in *Each time we visit, India surprises us* or a palatalization in *I did, you know*. American listeners know this, and use it in choosing how to interpret strings such as *Each time we visit India is in the middle of the dry season* or *Mary remembered you like lightning*. These are syntactically ambiguous, and the presence of flapping or palatalization can signal that *visit India* or *remembered you* belong to the same phrase.

British English listeners can hear each of these American differences, but they fail to use the presence or absence of flapped or palatalized segments effectively in choosing between alternative readings of such strings. Long-time British-native residents of the United States, though, produce a sort of intermediate performance, which suggests that experience helps, but it is not really easy to learn to use a new source of information for the L1 (Scott and Cutler 1984). Interestingly, the degree to which Scott and Cutler's U.S.-resident British exploited the two types of phonological alternation in listening differed; they used flapping more successfully than palatalization. This can be explained in terms of the listeners' native variety. British English does not have flapping (so the U.S. form was distinctive for British listeners) but does have palatalization (e.g., in *Tuesday* or *duty*, which include a prevocalic glide in British English and hence provide an environment for palatalization to occur). The palatalization alternation was more difficult to exploit perceptually in the way American listeners do, not only because it occurs in more environments in British English, but also because it is effectively preempted for a different communicative function: in British English its use is nonstandard, so that hearing someone say [tʃuz]*day* instead of [tjuz]*day* tells the listener about the social background of the speaker. Thus even with long-term exposure to another variety, the ability to attend to certain cues can apparently still be affected by the requirements of the native variety.

Thus casual speech processes such as flapping and palatalization can differ across varieties of a language, just as they can differ across languages. The [r]-insertion in environments such as *idea of* provides a British-American example in the opposite direction, because it occurs in English in Britain but not in most parts of America. U.S. listeners in Philadelphia, who participated in both the *ice-rice* categorization study and the cross-modal priming study of Tuinman, Mitterer, and Cutler (2011a, b, see chapter 10), produced an interesting asymmetry in that their categorization responses differed from those of British listeners, but their word-recognition responses did not. In categorization of tokens varying along a continuum of duration, they were significantly less sensitive to the duration variation than the British listeners were, and their responses were affected by the availability of an alternative source for [r], in that they gave more *rice* responses after *saw* than after *more* (the

British listeners were unaffected by this factor). That suggests that their relative unfamiliarity with the [r]-insertion process had not equipped them with the appropriate sensitivity to the relevant durational cue. In cross-modal priming, though, they showed no evidence of sustained competition from unintended words—so RAIDS was not facilitated after they heard *Canada aids* with intrusive [r] (Dutch listeners to English did show this facilitation, but British listeners did not). That in turn suggests that their less-efficient processing of the phonetic evidence for [r] did not cause less-efficient word recognition. Perhaps the slight difficulty posed by another variety of the L1 is easy to recover from (just like noise masking is relatively easy to recover from in the L1).

11.2.2 Mismatching Contrasts across Varieties, and the Effects on Word Recognition

In English, the strongest cross-dialectal differences are in vowels. There are consonantal differences, too: most British speakers do not sound out postvocalic [r] (e.g., in *dark hair*) but most Americans do; most Scots distinguish the onsets of *wear* and *where* whereas most other English speakers do not; Indian English allows retroflex consonants; in some London-area dialects, minimal pairs such as *thought* and *fought* become homophones; and so on. Also there are prosodic differences—terminal rises of different kinds in Newcastle, Belfast, Australian, or Californian English, variation in the prosodic realization of stress in Indian or Welsh English compared with most other forms, and so on. But vowels figure most strongly (see Wells 1982 and Foulkes and Docherty 1999 for overviews of English dialectal variation). Often, the dialect differences show up as lexical distinctions that are made in one variety but collapsed in another. *Look* and *luck* are homophonous in Yorkshire English, and *look* and *Luke* are in Scottish English, but speakers of most other varieties expect a three-way distinction among *look*, *luck*, and *Luke*. In many American dialects *marry* and *merry* do not contrast, whereas other English listeners expect a distinction. In British English, *paw*, *poor*, and *pour*, or *fought* and *fort* are indistinguishable; Americans and Scots expect them, in differing ways, to contrast.

Differences between dialects cause confusions in both directions. If you speak a dialect that confuses *poor* and *paw*, will both be activated when you hear either? Presumably so, given that whichever intended version of a homophone is heard, both versions are activated (Grainger, Van Kang, and Segui 2001; the strength of activation varies with relative frequency of the two forms). Oddly enough, though, the activation effects in word recognition of such vowel mismatches have (to my knowledge) not been assessed across varieties but only in the context of language change within a variety. For example, a change is going on in New Zealand English, whereby the vowel in *square* is merging with the vowel in *near*, so that pairs such as *cheer* and *chair* come to sound the same (more like what *cheer* used to sound like than what *chair* used to sound like). When speakers of this variety hear speech from other English speakers who do contrast these vowels, what happens? Do they correctly assign the speaker's pronunciations to the separate categories, so that *cheer* only activates *cheer* and *chair* only activates *chair*; or are both words activated whatever they hear; or is the activation asymmetric, with *cheer* activating both words but *chair* only activating *chair*? In an auditory associative priming study, Warren, Rae, and Hay (2003) discovered that the last pattern held true. Their listeners recognized both *shout* and *sit* more rapidly after hearing *cheer* than after a control prime, whereas after they heard *chair*, only *sit* was facilitated, not *shout*. Within this language community, such a pattern should minimize misunderstanding.

In some cases, language change seems to happen more rapidly in perception than in speech production. Even though speakers actually maintain a distinction in their production of two sounds, the difference between their two types of utterance has become so small that listeners in their community no longer make use of it. These cases have been most notably described by Bill Labov, who calls them "near mergers." Labov, Karen, and Miller (1991) showed that a distinction that was disappearing in Philadelphia—the contrast of *furry* with *ferry*—was sufficiently preserved in locals' speech tokens for non-Philadelphians to score almost 100 percent correct on identifications of minimal pairs; but other Philadelphians—that is, speakers who made exactly that distinction in their own speech—were quite unable to categorize the minimal pairs correctly. Labov et al. argued that the categorical distinction has effectively been lost for this community; as far as the listeners' phonemic representations are concerned, the categories have merged. The distinctions that appear in speech are treated as epiphenomenal, similar to effects of adjacent context on phonetic realization (e.g., how [k] sounds after [s] versus after [ʃ]; see chapter 6). Speakers of other dialects, who have maintained the separate categorical representations, can accurately pick up on the small acoustic correlates of the contrast. Language change, in other words, can increase or reduce differences between dialect groups, and this can have consequences for cross-dialectal communication.

11.2.3 Intelligibility and Dialect Mismatch

The evidence so far suggests that adult listeners with a mature command of the L1 should, with sufficient experience, adapt fairly easily to another dialect of their language. Evans and Iverson (2004, 2005) found that listeners altered their goodness ratings for British English vowels as a function of the perceived dialect (Northern versus Southern British) of the carrier phrase in which the vowel occurred. This did not happen so much for Northern listeners who were living in the North, but it did happen for Northerners who were living in the South. Northerners who had lived longer in the South tended to modify their own accent, though this had only limited effect on their perceptual sensitivity to dialectal differences in vowels.

This indeed suggests that listeners can adapt to a regional accent quite rapidly. At the psychoacoustic level, discrimination is correspondingly good. The main finding of Cutler et al.'s (2005) study of cross-dialectal vowel perception was in fact that dialect mismatch affected overall performance hardly at all. Recall that L2 (Dutch) listeners consistently performed below the level of L1 listeners (Cutler, Weber, et al. 2004). In the follow-up comparison of speakers of a non-American variety of English with the same task, Cutler et al. (2005) kept the variation in consonant context low (just [b] and [v]) but increased variability by mixing CV and VC tokens in a single block. Thus [i] could be heard in [iv], [vi], [ib], or [bi], and it could be heard at any of three signal-to-noise ratios (SNRs) and needed to be distinguished from the fourteen other vowels in the experimental set. This effectively maximized the chances for vowel errors. The Australian listeners' performance was compared with that of both the American and Dutch listeners for the same subset of the materials, and they proved quite as good at the task as the American listeners, at all SNRs (see figure 11.2). Although small effects of the dialect difference could be discerned in the results (see section 11.2.1), performance was in general unaffected by dialect; the overall American and Australian percent correct was identical at the lowest noise level (16-decibel SNR), the Australians were a tiny bit (3 percent) better at 8-decibel SNR, and the Americans were 2 percent better at 0-decibel SNR. No cross-dialect differences were statistically significant; phoneme perception within dialects of the same L1 is robust.

Of course, how easily listeners cope with a particular dialect depends on the amount of experience they have with it. A completely new dialect can be startlingly

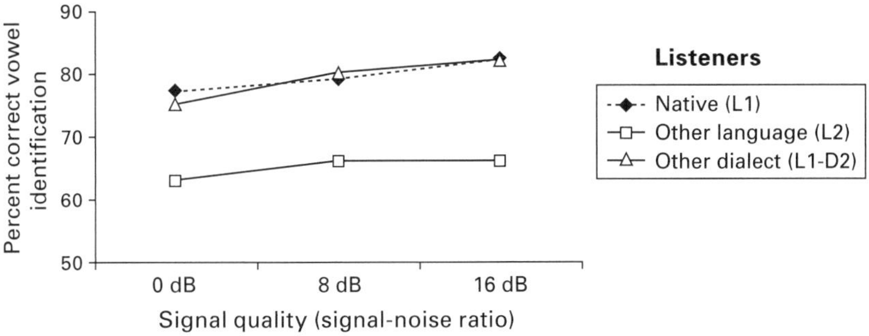

Figure 11.2
Identification of American English vowels in heavy (0 decibel), mild (8 decibel), or minimal noise (16 decibel), for native listeners versus listeners with another language (Dutch) or another dialect (Australian English). Dialect mismatch does not have the disastrous effect that language mismatch has on listening under difficult conditions!

incomprehensible. The further the dialect is from the native variety, the harder understanding can be. But experience does help. Listeners are better at judging which general dialect areas speakers come from (e.g., the American South) than specific areas within them (for instance, the Southwest—e.g., Texas—vs. the Southeast—e.g., Florida), and the errors that they make reflect their experience, in that for instance confusions between dialects were reduced for listeners who themselves had led a more mobile life (Clopper and Pisoni 2004, 2006).

In noise, local dialects proved more intelligible than nonlocal, according to an early report (Mason 1946). But Clopper and Bradlow (2006) found no effects of mismatch in speaker and listener dialect for the perception of noise-masked high-predictability sentences (e.g., *I ate a piece of chocolate fudge*). However, they did find that the most common dialect they tested (General American) produced the best listener scores, which suggests possibly again a simple effect of familiarity (this dialect is especially predominant in the American broadcast media). The more familiarity, the better the listener can recover from the effects of noise.

Dialects can differ on all dimensions, as noted before, and this includes the suprasegmental as well as the segmental dimensions. Lexical tone is expressed by F0 in South Vietnam, for instance, but by both F0 and voice quality in North Vietnam. Perceptual confusion measures for normalized CV syllables with different tones reveal that Southern Vietnamese listeners are more likely to confuse pairs that vary mainly in voice quality, whereas Northern Vietnamese listeners are more likely to confuse pairs that do not vary in voice quality and are similar in F0 contour (Kirby 2010). The local variety has thus induced attention to different critical information in the signal. In Japan, similarly, there is variation across varieties in the pitch-accent distinctions that Tokyo listeners make good use of in word recognition (see chapter 7). On Kyushu Island in the south of Japan, and in the Ibaraki area north of Tokyo, the local varieties make no accent distinctions. However, listeners from these areas hear a lot of pitch-accent distinctions because they hear a lot of speech in Tokyo Japanese (the dominant variety). The word guesses of Kyushu and Ibaraki listeners given the gated word-initial fragments of Tokyo Japanese words used in Cutler and Otake's (1999) pitch-accent study showed early use of the accent information, like the guesses by the original listeners from the Tokyo area. However, signal-detection analyses revealed that the accentless speakers' sensitivity to pitch information in the speech signal was significantly lower than that of the Tokyo listeners, and their bias (tendency to respond with the pattern most likely in the vocabulary) was significantly greater (Otake and Cutler 1999). Reduced experience with pitch-accent distinctions thus made their processing of pitch accent less efficient and perhaps less confident; but still, when accent distinctions featured in the speech they heard, they were able to use them in recognizing words.

In general, then, listeners can adapt to dialects; the ability to do this is a side effect of the flexibility that helps us understand any current conversation, including conversations involving many speakers.[2] More relevant evidence is summarized later in this chapter in sections 11.4 and 11.6. A small cost of this flexibility is that we are not very good at dialect categorizations. But why should listeners be good at this? If we can understand what is said, why do we need to know about the origin of the person who said it? Such information can sometimes be helpful, but the help it provides has little to do with recognizing words. Thus it remains the domain of Professor Higgins-like specialists.

11.3 Perception of Foreign-Accented Speech

We also adapt to foreign accents in our L1. We perceive the difference from a standard very rapidly; recall that listeners can detect the presence of foreign accent even in subphonemic fragments of speech (see chapter 9). The way we do this is just by using our customary sensitivity to the fine phonetic structure of speech. For instance, native listeners are not very sensitive to single-feature mispronunciations that tend to occur quite often in casual speech, such as noncanonical voicing, but they are far more sensitive to mispronunciations of the same magnitude that occur only rarely (Ernestus and Mak 2004). Exactly the same is true in foreign accent perception—incorrect voicing, which also happens in native production, is quite likely to be overlooked in a foreigner's speech, whereas the incorrect realizations that stand out are the ones that native speakers are less likely to perpetrate (Magen 1998).

Any deviation from expected form renders speech harder to recognize under difficult listening conditions; foreign accent is no exception. Foreign-accented speech is generally less well recognized in noise (Munro 1998; Bent and Bradlow 2003). Particularly if mispronunciation causes confusion with other words—that is, particularly for words from dense lexical neighborhoods—foreign accent causes word misperception (Imai, Walley, and Flege 2005). However, there are some interesting features in this overall pattern. Individual differences between talkers are considerable. Even without noise, recognition can be slowed for the speech of some foreign talkers but not for that of others (Munro and Derwing 1995). Likewise, some talkers with a foreign accent are no harder to understand in noise than L1 talkers (Munro 1998). The easier-to-understand speakers are generally those with higher L2 proficiency, of course. They may be naturally clearer speakers (see the next section). But there is also another factor. Among Bent and Bradlow's (2003) listeners were some who were L2 users themselves, from the same language background (Chinese or Korean) as the speakers whose utterances were presented in noise. For these L2 listeners, English from any high-proficiency talker with their own L1 was as intelligible in light noise as English from a native talker. This perhaps reflects prior exposure to such an accent, especially given that the benefit was only observed for speech from the better talkers. Higher proficiency presumably includes greater consistency in realization of phonemic targets, whereas speakers with lower proficiency produce more variable output.

Experience tells us that we indeed often understand perfectly well what foreigners are saying despite recognizing that they are not native speakers; and even if we initially experience difficulty with a particular speaker's pronunciation, we usually can adjust rapidly. This adaptation can be very rapid. As little as one minute (two to four sentences) of exposure to an L2 speaker is enough to almost entirely remove RT differences to foreign-accented versus L1 productions in a probe recognition task with unpredictable sentences (Clarke and Garrett 2004). Likewise, exposure to just a few words of English manipulated to sound like a French accent suffices to shift category boundaries between phonemes (Clarke and Luce 2005). Adaptation is likely to be speaker specific (see also section 11.7). Training with accented words produces generalization to new words spoken by the same speaker but not to words spoken by another speaker (Jongman, Wade, and Sereno 2003). However, adaptation also generalizes if training is general; training on the productions of several different talkers from the same L1 background allowed listeners to recognize the speech of a novel talker with the same accent more accurately (Bradlow and Bent 2008).

11.4 Perceptual Effects of Speaker Variation

Speakers differ in how intelligibly they talk; all of us can speak especially clearly when we try (Bradlow and Bent 2002), but some people just naturally speak more clearly than others (mainly because of face and mouth structure; Bond and Moore 1994). Correspondingly, some talkers elicit better performance than others from listeners in word-recognition tasks (Munro 1998; Nygaard 2005). Listeners are also sensitive to differences in how talkers realize phonemes; for instance, realization of VOT boundaries for stops may vary independently of speech rate (Allen, Miller, and DeSteno 2003), and listeners pick up on the talker-specific choice and generalize it when they identify new tokens (Allen and Miller 2004), even to other phonemes within the same broad class (Theodore and Miller 2010). Similar variation across talkers exists in the degree of separation between fricative categories, again affecting listeners' phonemic identifications (Newman, Clouse, and Burnham 2001). Talkers differ in the duration they assign to segments (Crystal and House 1988) and in how they realize vowels (Peterson and Barney 1952; Hillenbrand et al. 1995), and this too can affect phoneme identification (Uchanski and Braida 1998). In fact, the realization of any speech sound is subject to substantial individual variation. In general, though, we are quick to learn the idiosyncrasies of a particular talker; for instance, transcription accuracy improves with increasing familiarity with a talker's speech (Nygaard and Pisoni 1998). Listeners who were trained to identify previously unfamiliar voices found it easier, once they had learned the voices, to identify words spoken in noise by these voices than by others (Nygaard, Sommers, and Pisoni 1994).

Even if speakers are equally intelligible, though, the fact that such training takes time to occur shows that adjusting to different speakers costs effort. There is abundant experimental confirmation of this (see Luce and McLennan 2005 for a review). If words are spoken by a single talker rather than by multiple talkers, listeners repeat the words more rapidly and more accurately, and they also identify words more accurately when they are noise-masked or degraded (Mullennix, Pisoni, and Martin 1989). There are similar effects of talker variability in recall tasks—early items in a serial recall list are recalled better if the list was spoken by one rather than several talkers, and "preloaded" items (to be held in memory during a subsequent task, then recalled) are recalled better if the intervening task involved listening to only one talker (Martin et al. 1989). These authors explained their results in terms of greater processing cost incurred by understanding speech from separate talkers.

If lists like this are presented at very slow rates, listeners should have enough time to attend fully to the voice information, which means that more information about each item actually gets encoded. This was tested by Goldinger, Pisoni, and Logan (1991; also Nygaard, Sommers, and Pisoni [1995], with a different task), and the results were reversed; items were recalled better from lists spoken by multiple speakers rather than only one. The talker detail that is encoded seems to be indeed tied to the individual talker, in that the recognition memory advantage for same rather than different voice on second presentation is unaffected by how many different voices are drawn upon or by whether speaker sex matches across presentations (Palmeri, Goldinger, and Pisoni 1993). Talker-specific information must also have been stored if the training results of Nygaard and colleagues, described above, are to be explained. It is not just a matter of auditory detail remaining constant, because although fragments of previously heard words can be completed more successfully if presented in the same voice as before, it does not help at all to keep other acoustic factors (e.g., amplitude) constant in such a task (Schacter and Church 1992; Church and Schacter 1994). Despite this, listeners can actually tell if amplitude and rate of speech change (Bradlow, Nygaard, and Pisoni 1999); it thus appears that listeners record a lot of detail, but response speed and accuracy in the word memory tasks is only affected by factors relevant to phoneme identity.

Talker variation can therefore slow down processing, especially in tasks involving recall from episodic memory. However, switching between speakers does not always make it harder to recognize speech. In contrast to memory recall, there are no deleterious effects of talker variation in simple lexical decision (Luce and Lyons 1998). Nygaard, Burt, and Queen (2000) found that beneficial effects of talker match in recognition memory were observed not so much with items that were typical but rather with items that were atypical of the item population in some way (in their experiments this meant spoken very fast or very slow or very loudly or very softly). Level of processing is relevant; the deeper that items can be processed, the smaller the effect of talker variation (Goldinger 1996). Talker variation affects processing that is slow or difficult (such as lexical decision when the nonwords are very word-like), but it does not affect easy processing (such as lexical decision when the nonwords are really easy to tell from words; McLennan and Luce 2005). McLennan and Luce also refer to further findings of theirs showing that low frequency (and thus harder) words benefited to a greater extent from talker match than high frequency (thus, easier) words.

It is probably rare for most of us to encounter a situation in which talker identity changes from word to word, as was the case in many of these experiments. Much of our everyday listening may fall rather into the categories that seem to be less affected by talker variation. Thus it is probable that switches between speakers rarely cause us to make an error or fail to understand. Nevertheless, under certain circumstances such switches can certainly cause us extra processing load, and the reason for this is that in listening, we store information about individual talkers. Some theoretical implications of this will be discussed further in chapter 12. But there are also practical implications. Those who have visited Barcelona will recall that in the underground trains there, an audio system announces each upcoming station. The station name, spoken in one voice, is preceded by the Catalan frame *Pròxima estació* 'Next station', in another voice. At least for visitors to the city, unfamiliar with the stations in the underground system, possibly unfamiliar with the language, and struggling to perform this recognition memory task on an announcement heard in a very noisy environment, it is arguable that the Barcelona city fathers have constructed exactly the situation that will maximize deleterious effects of voice change.

11.5 The Learning of Auditory Categories

There is a productive line of research on the learning of new categories for visual perception. When adult learners are given feedback on categorization decisions, learning of new categories is rapid. Without such feedback, learning is possible, but significantly slower.

But clearly the learning of L1 phonetic categories—as described in chapter 8—cannot rely on supervision and the provision of feedback. Infants extract the categories from the input they receive without feedback of any kind, either direct (that is, tutorial) or indirect (for instance, by comparing to an existing lexicon). Unsupervised learning of auditory categories is thus perfectly possible in infancy. In adulthood, as it turns out, it is very difficult. Using training and test methods based on the experiments in visual perception, Goudbeek, Smits, and Swingley (2009) trained adult listeners on new auditory categories, with or without supervision. The categories could be speech sounds (vowel contrasts from an unknown language) or nonspeech signals (whereby the dimensions of variation, however, were the same durational and fundamental frequency continua as distinguished the vowels). The dimensions varied either unitarily (so that a contrast just in duration or just in frequency distinguished two novel categories) or in tandem (so that one dimension's information value depended on the contribution of the other dimension). This sort of interdependence is typical of categories in speech, which means, again, that it must be learnable in infancy.

Unidimensional categories, based either on duration or on frequency, could be learned both with and without supervision. But for multidimensional categories, the story is not so straightforward. Both types of category (speech and nonspeech) could be learned in a supervision paradigm (where subjects received feedback on their performance in every trial). This had also been observed with visual complex categories. But without the feedback supervision, learning in the auditory case was unsuccessful. (In the visual experiments it had just been slower). So, complex multidimensional categories could not be learned if all that was provided was what infants get: exposure to auditory input. Of course, the undergraduate subjects in Goudbeek et al.'s studies must have learned just such complex categories entirely from exposure to input, at an earlier time in their lives. But either that earlier learning now preempted their ability to learn new categories without being explicitly instructed about their performance or the existing categories provided perceptual interference that precluded formation of new categories, unless feedback gave explicit assistance in the task of forming them. Either way, it is clear that learning entirely new categories in the auditory domain is a nontrivial task. This is useful background knowledge against which to consider the evidence on the next question to be considered: the adaptability of existing phoneme categories.

11.6 The Flexibility of L1 Categories

"Flexibility" is the term used by Repp and Liberman (1987) in summarizing the wealth of empirical demonstrations that the boundaries between phonemic categories can be shifted. Categorical perception is the basis of lexical processing, as we have seen; whatever can distinguish one word from another must be apprehended as efficiently as possible. Categorical assignments are not the whole of the prelexical processing story, though; activation is gradient, and there can be correspondingly gradient subcategorical effects on activation (see chapter 6). Further, many articulatory and contextual effects can alter the realization of phonemic categories. One way for listeners to deal with this is to alter the boundaries between categories accordingly—to expect a distinction to be realized differently in one context than in another, for example. This certainly happens.

11.6.1 Category Adjustment Caused by Phonetic Context

Compensation for coarticulation shifts categorization responses, in a way that was already described (see chapter 6). Listeners' [t]-[k] boundaries shift toward [k] after [s], but toward [t] after [ʃ], exactly correcting for the perceptual carryover effect of articulation that makes stops more [t]-like after [s] (spread lips) but more [k]-like after [ʃ] (rounded lips; Mann and Repp 1981). A preceding liquid similarly affects stop-consonant categorization (Mann 1980), and boundary judgments between [s] and [ʃ] are affected by the nature of a following vowel—a rounded vowel such as [u] in *sue-shoe* expands the [s] category in comparison to an unrounded vowel such as [a] in *sa-shah*, because the rounding can be ascribed to the vowel and not only to the fricative (Mann and Repp 1980). The most widely referenced demonstration of the dependence of consonantal identifications on subsequent vowels is that exactly the same noise burst is judged as a [p] if prefaced to [i] or [u], but the sound is judged to be [k] if prefaced to [a] (the "pikapu" effect of Liberman, Delattre, and Cooper [1952]). There are many more such accommodations that have been empirically demonstrated (see Repp and Liberman's [1987] review). Articulatory gestures constantly modify one another, and listeners convert their experience of this into expectations about how phonemic information will be acoustically realized in speech.

11.6.2 Category Adjustment Caused by Phonotactic Regularity

Sequence constraints within a language can also affect listeners' category boundaries. There are English words beginning with *tr-* (e.g., *train*, *tree*, *troop*) and *sl-* (e.g., *sleigh*, *sleep*, *sluice*), but there are no English words beginning with *tl-* or *sr-*. Massaro and Cohen (1983) found that ambiguous stimuli on a continuum of glides from [r] to [l] were more often judged [r] in the context [t_i], but [l] in the context [s_i]. In other words, English listeners reported sequences of phonemes that are allowable in words of their language (e.g., *tree*, *sleep*) but avoided sequences that—though pronounceable—do not occur (e.g., *tlee*, *sree*).

With a different paradigm, a similar effect was demonstrated in French. Stimuli that began with sequences such as *tla-* (phonotactically illegal in French, just as in English) were presented in gated fragments. Early fragments were correctly identified as [t]. But as evidence for the [l] appeared, listeners shifted their responses to [kl] rather than [tl] (Hallé et al. 1998). Likewise, French listeners found it hard to categorize the stops on a [tl]-[kl] or [dl]-[gl] continuum but had no difficulty with exactly the same stops on a [tr]-[kr] or [dr]-[gr] continuum. English listeners showed the same asymmetric performance as the French. But the Hebrew language allows all these clusters, and Hebrew listeners had no difficulty with any of the continua (Hallé and Best 2007). Category boundaries can only be firmly placed if the language allows the result.

11.6.3 Category Adjustment Caused by Inferred Rate of Speech

In chapter 6, the classic experiment of Miller and Liberman (1979) was described. Listeners' decisions about the identity of a syllable-initial phoneme could be determined by whether a following vowel was long or short, because durational information determining the phoneme's identity sounded respectively short or long by comparison (see figure 6.2 in chapter 6). Although the stimuli were isolated syllables, the listeners apparently inferred an overall rate of speech from them and used this to adjust their phonemic category decisions.

This inferred rate of speech can also alter listeners' perceptions of the internal structure of the phonemic category. We saw that members of a phonemic category vary in perceived "goodness"—some tokens are just better, or closer to the listener's prototype for the category, than others. This distribution of goodness ratings is effectively the internal structure of the category, and it changes with inferred rate (Miller and Volaitis 1989). Understandably, the peak of the goodness ratings curve falls at a higher VOT value for longer syllables and at a lower VOT value for shorter syllables. But the ratings curve is also flatter for longer syllables, such that a wider range of VOT values receives equally high ratings. This nicely matches the actual effects of rate of speech—in slow speech, VOT in stop consonants does vary more than it does in fast speech. Not only are category boundaries determined by listeners' experience, but goodness of within-category positions is, too, and it can be finely adjusted even on a scale allowing infinite gradations, such as rate of speech.

11.6.4 Category Adjustment at All Levels of Processing

There are many kinds of effects on category boundary perception. Some are quite low level. There are contrast effects (Diehl, Elman, and McCusker 1978), whereby an ambiguous stimulus paired with a clear endpoint tends to be identified more often as the opposing endpoint category than it otherwise would be; and there are range effects (Sawusch and Nusbaum 1979), whereby contracting or expanding or skewing the range of stimuli presented from a given continuum causes the boundary to shift along the continuum in such a way that the response categories are equalized (so presentation of more stimuli from one end of a continuum leads to expansion of the category at the other end, to deliver more responses from that underrepresented category).

Perhaps the lowest-level effect is selective adaptation (Eimas and Corbit 1973; Ades 1976). This occurs when heartless experimenters subject hapless listeners to many repeated presentations (5,400 in Eimas and Corbit's study!) of a single stimulus that corresponds to one endpoint of a continuum; the effect on subsequent categorization of a continuum of stimuli is expansion of the category corresponding to the other endpoint. For instance, hearing *ba* many times encourages one to hear an ambiguous sound as *pa* rather than *ba*. Anything but another *ba*!

This effect is definitely a low-level auditory one because an acoustic form exercises the same effect regardless of how it would be categorized. Thus in *spa* the [p] has no aspiration and a shorter VOT than in *pa*, with the result that it actually sounds more like [b]; and adaptation with *ba* or with *spa* have the same effect on a [p]-[b] decision (i.e., expansion of the [p] category; Sawusch and Jusczyk 1981). In Diehl et al.'s (1978) response contrast paradigm, though, *spa* has the effect of a [p], not of a [b], which shows that selective adaptation is not due to a contrast effect. Audiovisual effects on categorization also leave the selective adaptation effect intact: in the McGurk effect (McGurk and McDonald 1976), a spoken *ba* paired with visual cues to an articulated *ga* seems like a *da*, but even when paired with the visual *ga* cues, a spoken *ba* causes the adaptation that spoken *ba* should (Roberts and Summerfield 1981). The way input is phonetically interpreted thus has no role in selective adaptation; the effect purely involves fatiguing of the auditory processors invoked by particular stimuli.

Other effects, by comparison, are quite high level. Thus an ambiguous sound between [d] and [t] is more likely to be reported as [t] if prefaced to [i:k] (because *teak* is a word and *deek* is not), but as [d] if prefaced to [i:p] (because *deep* is a word but *teep* is not; Ganong 1980). This is an effect of lexical identity on phonetic categorization, with theoretical implications that have prompted a productive line of research in word recognition (to be discussed further in chapter 12). The lexical effect can be mediated by lexical stress; the same [d]-[t] shift is brought about by *-Igress* (giving *tigress*) versus *-iGRESS* (giving *digress*; Connine, Clifton, and Cutler 1987). Of course, a difference in lexical tone between two words gives the same lexical effect on a continuum from one Mandarin tone to the other, and then only for native, not for nonnative, listeners (Fox and Unkefer 1985).

There are also effects of sentential context; thus an ambiguous sound between [p] and [b] is more likely to be reported as [p] in *She likes to jog along the -ath*, but as [b] in *She ran hot water for the -ath* (Miller, Green, and Schermer 1984), and judgments on a [t]-[ð] continuum can be shifted toward [t] before a verb (e.g., *to go*) but toward [ð] before a noun (e.g., *the gold*; Isenberg, Walker, and Ryder 1980; Van Alphen and McQueen 2001). All these higher-level effects do not alter the way the acoustic input is initially perceived, but they do alter the way its import is evaluated (more on this in chapter 12). Thus the phonetic categories of the L1 are not fixed; they can be adjusted whenever language processing can benefit as a result.

11.7 Perceptual Learning

Perhaps the most important reason to adjust our categorical decisions about speech is to apply what is called "normalization" of the input. The physiology of individual speakers' articulatory organs can vary widely, leading to differences in the precise range of sounds uttered. But listeners need to know how contrasts between phonemes are realized, and if a newly encountered speaker makes a particular contrast in a way never previously heard, listeners have to adjust for this or they will not be able to decide which words have been spoken. Exactly how this happens is still the subject of considerable theoretical debate (summarized in the following chapter). But that it happens, and happens very rapidly indeed, is beyond question; many decades of experiments have made this outcome very clear.

A mid-1950s experiment by Ladefoged and Broadbent has now become a classic. They constructed vowel continua—from *bit* to *bet*, for example—which listeners then heard preceded by the sentence *Please say what this word is*. The formant structure of the preceding context was manipulated to simulate speakers with essentially the same dialectal setting but different vocal tracts. In their original experiments with synthesized stimuli (Broadbent, Ladefoged, and Lawrence 1956; Ladefoged and Broadbent 1957), and in later replications with natural speech (Dechovitz 1977; Ladefoged 1989; Mitterer 2006), listeners' decisions about which word they had heard differed for each token as a function of the context. For instance, the same [bVt] token was identified as *bit* after a context with a lower second formant (F2) but as *bet* after a context in which F2 was higher. Ladefoged and Broadbent interpreted their finding as an auditory analog of identifying colors in different illuminations (where identifications can likewise alter if the context—the type of illumination—alters). As with the visual effects, the size of their vowel-interpretation effect decreases with increasing distance between context and target (so a 10-second interval between sentence and [bVt] token produces about 50 percent less adjustment; Broadbent et al. 1956).

The important feature of the Ladefoged and Broadbent finding is its robustness. Although there was some indication that the listeners' own dialect influenced their particular judgments, all listeners were influenced by a change in the context to some extent. Indeed, this simple effect is very compelling, and, like the effects described in section 11.6, it requires remarkably little surrounding context to exercise its influence.

Rapid adaptation of this kind is part of everyday speech perception. Not only do we interpret phonetic segments differently in different contexts, but we can very rapidly learn to deal with an unusual realization of a particular phoneme irrespective of context. For instance, our experience tells us that we adapt quickly to talkers with, for instance, a speech impediment or a nonlocal accent; at least, we adapt if we are adult listeners and the language being spoken is our mother tongue. Most of us are familiar with the experience of noticing that a speaker's accent is peculiar in some way, and initially having to make an effort to work out what is being said; but we are also familiar with the consequent rapid adaptation. The strangeness in the speaker's productions is very soon unproblematic. We have adapted to it.

11.7.1 Lexically Induced Perceptual Learning

Rapid adaptation to a deviant pronunciation can be induced with lexically induced perceptual learning, a two-phase experimental paradigm developed by Norris, McQueen, and Cutler (2003). Subjects first performed lexical decision on 200 words and nonwords. Among the words there were twenty ending with [s] (e.g., words like *glass*, *morose*, and *tremendous*) and twenty ending with [f] (e.g., words like *beef*, *carafe*, and *handkerchief*—although actually, the experiment was in Dutch). After prior testing with [s]-[f] categorization, a sound between [s] and [f] had been found that elicited approximately 50 percent decisions for each category. This truly ambiguous sound, which we can refer to as [f/s], then replaced all the final [s] sounds for one group of subjects in the lexical decision experiment. For those subjects, the [f]-final words were heard in their normal pronunciation. Another group of subjects heard the ambiguous [f/s] sound replacing all final [f] sounds and heard the [s]-final words pronounced normally.

After the lexical decision phase, the subjects had a second task. They heard a series of syllables and had to judge whether each was more like *ef* or *es* (phoneme categorization). The results in this phase showed a dramatic adaptation effect. When listeners had heard the ambiguous sound replacing [s] in words, their [s]-[f] boundary moved so that the [s] category became more inclusive; when they had heard the ambiguous sound replacing [f], their boundary moved to make the [f] category more inclusive. Figure 11.3 shows this effect. The figure shows the proportion of [f] judgments for five stimuli between [f] and [s] (none of them actually good renditions of either the [f] or the [s] endpoint). The middle stimulus is the [f/s] that had replaced either [f] or [s] in lexical decision. The listeners who had heard this sound replacing [f] call it [f] over 80 percent of the time in the phoneme categorization task. The listeners who had heard the same sound as [s], however, give it only about 30 percent [f] decisions (and hence 70 percent [s]). But their responses differ not only to that particular sound but also to the other sounds along the continuum. Each group has expanded the whole category to which the [f/s] supposedly belonged, to include such a deviant realization. Thus, hearing a deviant production of [f] or [s] twenty times is quite enough to produce a significant shift in the phoneme-category boundary. Listeners adapt their perception to a speaker's odd production.

This category adaptation facilitates word recognition. Evidence from several control groups in the study underlined this. No shift in the boundary appeared at all if the ambiguous sound was heard in nonwords (e.g., *gleef*, *canoss*, or *internoaf*).

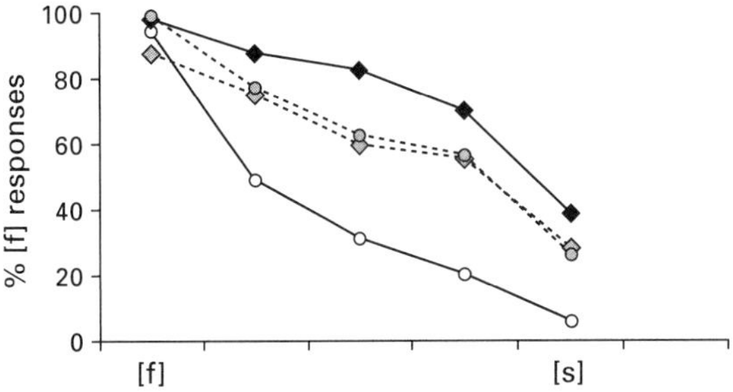

Figure 11.3
Phonetic categorization of a continuum between [f] and [s], following exposure to an ambiguous [s/f] sound in a preceding lexical decision experiment. Listeners who had heard the ambiguous sound replacing [f] in words (solid lines and black diamonds) show an expanded [f] category. Those who had heard [f/s] replacing [s] in words (solid lines and white circles) show an expanded [s] category. However, listeners who had heard [f/s] in nonwords, contrasting with either [f]- or [s]-words (the remaining two conditions, with dotted lines) experience no [f]-[s] category boundary shift. (Data from Norris et al. 2003.)

The lexicon had to provide information about what the ambiguous sound was supposed to be. Hearing words containing [s] and the ambiguous sound in nonwords could set up a contrast, which would lead listeners to deduce that the funny sound must, by elimination, be [f]; but this did not happen. Figure 11.3 shows the results of this control condition, too. There is no shift at all for the nonword exposure condition accompanied by real words with either [f] or [s]. So, contrast alone did not induce learning about category boundaries. Nor was the effect of category adaptation by lots of exposure, described earlier, responsible for the results—just hearing words with [s], and no [f] anywhere in the lexical decision list, also produced no boundary shift. The category expansion was confined to the groups who had heard the ambiguous sound in real words.

Further studies showed the perceptual learning to be developed early and to be very robust. The earliness was shown in studies with children: the effect was fully in place at six years of age. Figure 11.4 shows perceptual learning in six-year-olds, twelve-year-olds, and adults tested by McQueen, Tyler, and Cutler (2013); there is essentially no difference across the three age groups in the strength of the effect. Lexical decision being a bit taxing for children, the first-phase task in this study involved picture verification, and animals with [f] or [s] in their names—for instance, the subjects clicked on a picture of a giraffe, dolphin, or flamingo. The second task similarly involved a choice between characters named *Simpy* or *Fimpy*.

Robustness was evidenced by the appearance of the same learning in other sorts of tasks. The tasks used in the study with children showed that there was nothing special about the lexical decision training originally used, and indeed many different

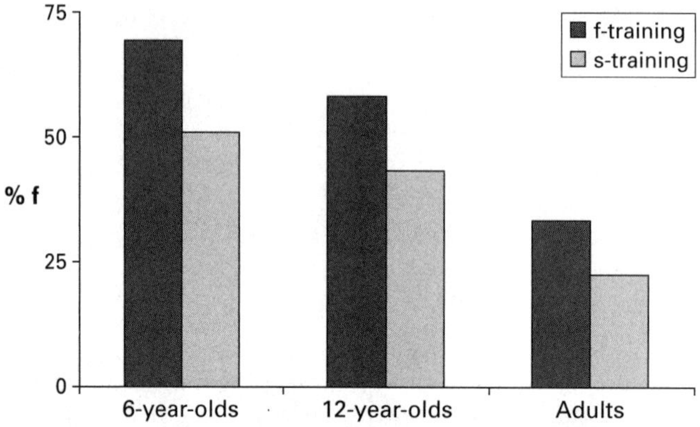

Figure 11.4
Perceptual learning at three ages: 6 years, 12 years, and adult. Choices of *Fimpy* averaged over seven steps on a [f]-[s] (*Fimpy-Simpy*) continuum, as a function of prior training with the most ambiguous sound on this continuum replacing [f] in words like *giraffe* (dark bars) or [s] in words like *platypus* (light bars). Although the older one gets, the less one tends to choose *Fimpy*, training with the sound replacing [f] always induces more *Fimpy* choices and to an equivalent degree across ages. (Data from McQueen et al., 2013)

types of training proved effective—learning was still robust if the words did not have to be processed as words at all, but listeners merely tallied how many words they heard (McQueen, Norris, and Cutler 2006a), or performed same-different judgments (Clarke-Davidson, Luce, and Sawusch 2008). When the training words occurred in a story (Eisner and McQueen 2006), the shift was just as robust as when they appeared as lexical decision stimuli. The phonemes in that story occurred in different positions in the words, so a constant position was also unnecessary; and even if position in the word is kept constant during training, the perceptual learning can transfer at test to occurrences of the same phoneme in a different position (Jesse and McQueen 2011). Also, when the second-phase task was discrimination rather than categorization, there was a shift in the discrimination peak (Clarke-Davidson et al. 2008). As categorization and discrimination results go hand in hand (see figure 1.1 in chapter 1), this result, too, shows that listeners' category boundaries had been altered.

The most important constraint on the appearance of adaptation in the first perceptual learning studies is that it only occurred when the phoneme was heard in real words. Listeners needed to know what the phoneme was supposed to be, if they were to learn how to deal with the deviant pronunciation. But lexical identity is actually not the only type of information that can be used for such learning. Visual speech cues, such as the difference in the gestures for articulation of [aba] versus [ada], will also do the trick (Bertelson, Vroomen, and De Gelder 2003). A comparison between training with lexical information versus such visual speech cues shows that the patterns of learning they produce are closely equivalent (Van Linden and Vroomen 2007). Thus, all that listeners need to achieve adaptation to an unusual phoneme is something, anything, telling them what it is supposed to be.

If need be, this can work in nonwords, even. Recall how phonotactic constraints affect phoneme category assignments in gating (Hallé et al. 1998) and categorization (Massaro and Cohen 1983). In English, [sr] is an impossible syllable onset, and so is [fn], but [sn] and [fr] are fine, as in *sneak* or *freak*. So if one and the same ambiguous [f/s] occurs before [n], it should be interpreted as [s], but if it occurs before [r], it should be interpreted as [f]. This interpretation should then carry over to a later categorization task, just as the lexical effect did. Nonwords such as *snuter* and *frulic* in the lexical decision phase of a perceptual learning study did indeed produce learning (Cutler, McQueen, et al. 2008). English listeners interpreted [f/s]*nuter* as *snuter* and not *fnuter*, and [f/s]*rulic* as *frulic*, not *srulic*. In phonetic categorization, their categorization function then showed a corresponding shift. Thus the learning effect of Norris et al. (2003) is not dependent on lexical information. As long as the altered sound occurs in a speech context, and one way or another this context makes it clear what phoneme the strange sound is supposed to be, listeners rapidly and efficiently adapt the relevant phonemic category specification to suit.

11.7.2 Specificity of Perceptual Learning

There are a lot of obvious questions to ask about this rapid adaptation. It is supposed to be useful and efficient; it should help us understand words more rapidly and thus speed up communication. But consider the following scenario. We are talking in English to a group of Americans, and a speaker of Scottish English joins the conversation. Clearly, the adaptation effect will allow us rapidly to overcome the initial strangeness of the Scottish accent and any initial difficulty in understanding this new speaker. But will this mean that understanding the rest of the group, all of them Americans, becomes harder?

Such an outcome would not really be efficient for communication. Therefore, the adaptation should be speaker specific—we should be able to adjust our phonetic categories for interpretation of the new speaker's speech without any consequent effect on interpretation of the speech of others. This means that in an experiment like that of Norris et al. (2003), there should be no adaptation if the lexical decision stimuli in the first phase and the phonetic categorization stimuli in the second phase are spoken by different speakers. Indeed, second-phase testing with an [f]-[s] continuum based on speech from someone other than the person who spoke the first-phase training stimuli fails to produce adaptation (Eisner and McQueen 2005). However, if the fricatives were actually the same fricatives in both the training and the test, the adaptation occurred even if the listeners thought that the speaker was different. Eisner and McQueen demonstrated this by testing with a continuum in which the training speaker's fricatives were appended to another speaker's [ɛ] vowel, and also by training with the test speaker's fricatives inserted into another speaker's words in the lexical decision phase. (Making this kind of hybrid syllable is possible with voiceless fricatives, given that no issues of continuity between the voicing in the vowel and the following consonant arise.) In both cases listeners showed learning across the continuum, consistent with a shift in the category boundary. These results suggest that the adaptation is very specific; it does not generalize to other talkers or to other segmental realizations.

However, there is less speaker-specificity with stop consonants (Kraljic and Samuel 2006, 2007). Ambiguous stops (e.g., a sound between [d] and [t]) induced learning in medial position in words (e.g., in *academic* or *cafeteria* but, again, not in nonwords), but here the learning effect generalized to a different (and different sex) speaker at test. Even more remarkably, the boundary shift for stops, though somewhat smaller than the shifts observed for fricatives, also generalized to another stop consonant continuum ([b]-[p], given training with [d]-[t]). In a direct comparison across fricatives and stops, Kraljic and Samuel (2007) confirmed that the learning was indeed speaker specific for fricatives (in this case [s]-[ʃ]) but generalized across speakers for stops ([d]-[t] again).

This difference reminds us that phoneme classes are not all equally effective at cueing talker identity. Fricatives are quite good at this (Newman et al. 2001), but stops are less informative than fricatives (Andics et al. 2007). Although VOT in stops does vary systematically across speakers (Allen and Miller 2004; Allen et al. 2003), it is an intrinsically temporal cue and thus highly sensitive to any factors affecting speech timing, such as rate of speech (indeed, factoring out speech rate change significantly attenuates speaker-related variation; Allen et al. 2003). Kraljic and Samuel argued that listeners will learn as much useful information as they can, and the fricative variation allowed them to learn to restrict the boundary shift to a particular speaker's productions, whereas the stop variation provided less information, although enough to support learning at the featural level (thus supporting the generalization to other sounds with the same features).

11.7.3 Durability of Perceptual Learning

We would also presumably want this speaker-specific adaptation to last reasonably well. Next time we meet the same speaker, it would be useful to be able to build on the experience from the previous encounter. Talker-specificity effects in word-recognition tasks (see section 11.4) are both rapid in onset and known to last. Correspondingly, the lexically induced perceptual learning lasts for at least 25 minutes (Kraljic and Samuel 2005)—unless listeners are exposed to normal pronunciation of the sound in question by the same speaker. In that case, the adaptation disappears as rapidly as it first arose. The longest test of the adaptation's persistence so far is 12 hours (Eisner and McQueen 2006), and it proved not to matter whether the listeners slept most of that time away or spent it on normal daily activity including conversations with many other talkers—that is, an initial evening test followed 12 hours later by a morning test produced a persisting robust adaptation effect, and so did an initial morning test followed by a second test in the evening of the same day.

The only thing that can effectively and quickly reduce the adaptation is hearing the same speaker produce nondeviant renditions of the same phoneme. A clear production by another speaker has no effect, but a clear production by the speaker responsible for the apparently deviant production abolishes the phoneme boundary shift right away (Kraljic and Samuel 2005). For visually induced boundary shifts, unlearning has been studied too. Just as Norris et al. (2003) had established with control conditions that their perceptual learning effect was not due to selective adaptation, Bertelson et al. showed that the learning based on visual speech cues patterned quite differently from selective adaptation, both in its nature (Bertelson et al. 2003) as well as in the way it built up (Vroomen et al. 2007) and in the way it dissipated (Vroomen et al. 2004). Thus the perceptual learning is not an adaptation effect at a low processing level; it is learning for the purposes of facilitating communication.

11.7.4 Generalization of Perceptual Learning

Finally, if perceptual learning is really intended to produce better communication, then the crucial test is that it must generalize to the rest of the lexicon. There will be no improvement in understanding a new speaker if the learning only applies to words that have already been heard. Those words may not come around again; meanwhile the unusual phoneme will be spoken in many other words in the course of a conversation. Ideally, hearing a speaker produce an unusual [f] in *beef* and *carafe* should help us process the same speaker's later utterances of *handkerchief*, *office*, *forty*, and so on.

This generalization cannot be tested by means of a phonetic categorization task in the second phase of a perceptual learning study—generalization across words must be tested with a word-level task. But it must be a task that gives a different result depending on how the ambiguous phoneme is categorized. So the best example to use is a minimal pair, which can only be distinguished by the categorical decision—*knife* versus *nice*, for instance. Subjects who have heard [f/s] as [s] in the first phase should later interpret [naif/s] as *nice*, whereas those who have heard [f/s] as [f] should interpret [naif/s] as *knife*. McQueen, Cutler, and Norris (2006) used cross-modal identity priming to test for this. Would [naif/s] yield more facilitation of lexical decisions to visually presented NICE or KNIFE? (N.B. Again, the materials of this study were actually in Dutch. The target words were minimal pairs like *doof* 'deaf' versus *doos* 'box').

As predicted, first-phase training to interpret [f/s] as [s] led listeners to interpret [naif/s] as *nice*, so that they showed significantly greater facilitation for NICE. First-phase training to interpret [f/s] as [f] produced the opposite: greater facilitation for KNIFE. *Knife* and *nice* had not been heard in the first phase, of course; nor had any of the other minimal pairs used in the cross-modal experiment. Thus the adaptation had generalized to other words in the lexicon. The argument for a facilitatory effect on word recognition was thus supported.

Generalization has also been observed for vowels of an artificial dialect involving systematic vowel lowering (Maye, Aslin, and Tanenhaus 2008; Bardhan, Aslin, and Tanenhaus 2006). The training was with a synthesized story (Maye, Aslin, et al.) or with naturally spoken accented words combined with visual referents (Bardhan et al.), and in each case listeners perceived new words at test in accord with the dialect training. Perceptual learning for individual talkers' production of Mandarin tones also generalizes to new words with the same tones (Mitterer, Chen, and Zhou 2011). It should be noted that these three findings not only reinforce the evidence for generalization but also demonstrate that the perceptual learning effects are not restricted to consonants. Nevertheless, it is not yet known whether the relative learning course for vowel and consonant adjustments is the same. Listeners exhibit greater tolerance for variable realization of vowels and greater reliance on consonants for lexical identity (see chapters 1 and 2), which may affect this type of perceptual learning.

Finally, the priming that words with the ambiguous sound exercise after training is quite as strong as the priming exercised by naturally spoken tokens of the same words (Sjerps and McQueen 2010; and in their study, learning again generalized to untrained words). There is no lesser status to an adjusted category; it is the category we use for normal word recognition.

11.8 Learning New Words

If we only know four words beginning [skwɪ]—say *squint*, *squirrel*, *squid*, and *squib*—then coarticulatory cues in the vowel are likely to distinguish these four for us quite effectively before we actually hear the postvocalic consonant that is the nominal uniqueness point. The [n] and the [r] and the [d] and the [b] will all cause fairly different realizations of the vowel. But if we then learn one other word beginning in the same way, the recognition of the whole set of words may be affected. We might learn *squiffy*, meaning drunk, or *squill*, a type of lily, or *squit*, meaning an insignificant person, or *squinch*, an architectural support. *Squiffy* has a labial (more precisely, a labiodental) after the vowel, so it will make *squib* slower to recognize than the other three original words. *Squill* ends with a lateral, which may take time to tell apart from the rhotic of *squirrel*. *Squit* differs from *squid* only in voicing of the last consonant, and *squinch* differs from *squint* only in having an alveolar affricate instead of an alveolar stop at its end. Depending on which new word we learn, some of the original words will stay recognizable at the vowel, and the recognition of others will become delayed.

What are the effects of new vocabulary on the recognition of words we already know? Gaskell and Dumay (2003) taught listeners new lexical items such as *cathedruke* or *shrapnidge* by presenting them repeatedly in a phoneme detection task. There were two sets of new words, presented in training to two separate subject groups. The listeners then performed a lexical decision test that included the real words on which the new items had been based (e.g., *cathedral*, *shrapnel*), and here both groups received all the base words. Their lexical decisions (e.g., to *cathedral*) were a little faster when they had learned the new competitor (*cathedruke*) than when they had not. This facilitation probably means that the new words had activated their real-word bases. But in a lexical decision test several days later, irrespective of whether the new words had been heard again in the interim, responses to the real words (*cathedral*, etc.) were slowed (compared to the other group's responses). This inhibition suggests that the memory trace of the new item was acting as a competitor. For this consolidation to take place and the new item to act as a competitor, it was, however, essential that the learner had had a night's sleep in between (Dumay and Gaskell 2007). A consolidation effect for intervening sleep was also found for perceptual learning about identification of words spoken by a not-very-good speech synthesizer (Fenn, Nusbaum, and Margoliash 2003).

Once in place, a lexical representation should in principle be available both for use in production and for participation in perception—for instance, by competing with similar-sounding words supported by speech input. But the studies by Gaskell and his colleagues suggest that such active participation does not follow automatically from the presence of a stored representation of the word. Other evidence from vocabulary acquisition likewise indicates that full instantiation of a lexical representation is a gradual process. For instance, consider that, as mentioned earlier, Americans who had been learning French for six months produced significantly different ERP responses to real words and nonwords but could not categorize them above chance in lexical decision (McLaughlin et al. 2004). If L2 learners' brains correctly distinguish real words from nonwords at an earlier stage than their explicit lexical decision responses do, again it seems that lexical representations may be initiated, but not yet fully available to be deployed in language use.

In search of evidence for such a dissociation in adult vocabulary acquisition, Leach and Samuel (2007) first taught undergraduates a set of totally new words via repeated exposure in a phoneme detection task. Then they tested recognition of the forms—for instance, by presenting them against a background of noise. Over a period of five days (during which the training continued), the amount of noise that listeners could tolerate while still achieving correct recognition of the new forms significantly increased. This improvement suggested that representations of the new forms were in place. A version of the two-stage perceptual learning task (Norris et al. 2003) was then added, to check whether the new forms could support learning in the way that known words do. Here the first stage induced learning with a recognition paradigm; listeners heard a set of words and had to indicate for subsequently presented words whether they had been in the set or not. Some of the newly learned forms in this first stage contained a phoneme with a deviant pronunciation. Then in the second stage, phonetic categorization assessed whether the boundary for the phoneme category had shifted. There was indeed a significant, albeit small, perceptual learning effect; the newly acquired forms had thus been able to supply the requisite lexical support.

In a second version of the multiday learning study, Leach and Samuel taught picture associations for the new forms rather than using phoneme detection. With this training, the newly learned forms supported significantly more perceptual learning, especially in the later days of the training period. The degree to which noise toleration improved across the training period, however, was just the same as with the phoneme detection training. So establishing an initial lexical representation is achieved as well through phoneme detection as through picture association, but picture association, with its link to some referent for the new form, is more effective in making a new lexical representation available for use—lexical "engagement," as Leach and Samuel termed it. Once this establishment has occurred, the new words get involved in lexical competition, and indeed, their presence can still be observed for months afterward (thus subjects who learned *cathedruke* were quite lastingly affected for later recognition episodes of *cathedral*; Tamminen and Gaskell 2008).

11.9 Extent and Limits of Flexibility and Plasticity

Learning about the sounds of the native language in the first year of life produces deep and long-lasting effects. Additional learning about speech continues throughout life. Plasticity in the adult speech processing system is currently a "hot" research topic, in part because it raises important issues with obvious practical implications—speaker recognition, language change, and adaptation to hearing impairment, among others. Exploration of plasticity in adult speech perception has also led to new insights into the architecture of speech recognition (see chapter 12).

Adults must be able to learn about speech variation; they need such learning to recognize talkers and to benefit (in increased ease of processing) from familiarity with voices. The same learning also underlies language change and allows listeners to cope with such change and to adapt to dialect variation. Further, it allows us to deal with unusual speech input—speech that is distorted by poor amplification, for instance, or the synthetic or otherwise manipulated speech that listeners encounter, ever more often, in interactions with automated systems. Some listeners have to adapt more than others. Cochlear implant recipients, for instance, need to learn how to interpret the transformed input they receive (see Clark 2002; Fu and Galvin 2007). And many aging listeners have to deal with reduction in their hearing capacity and learn about how it changes the available cues to speech sounds (see Sommers 2005).

The perceptual learning about ambiguous sounds that has been demonstrated in the laboratory depends on listeners being able to use some cue (such as lexical identity) to tell them what the strange sounds are supposed to be. Learning about other unusual speech input is subject to exactly the same rule. For instance, listeners can make a fair showing at understanding sine-wave speech (consisting just of a sinusoid, patterned to follow the central resonant frequency of a vocal tract producing an utterance), as long as they know it is supposed to consist of real words (Remez et al. 1981). This is rather remarkable given that such signals seriously attenuate the information content, compared to normal speech. Another really difficult input is noise-vocoded speech, which removes spectral cues while leaving the temporal characteristics of speech intact (Shannon et al. 1995). This too can become interpretable, but only if the training materials are sentences, made up of real words (not necessarily plausible or even meaningful: sentences like *The effect supposed to the consumer* are roughly as effective as sentences like *The police returned to the museum*; Davis et al. 2005). Importantly, though, training with nonwords fails to produce learning. Presenting clear speech first and the distorted input second makes for more effective training than vice versa (Hervais-Adelman et al. 2008). So, as in the studies with ambiguous phonemes, learning about how to interpret attenuated or noise-distorted speech is guided by higher-level (especially lexical) information.

Meaningful stimuli that are not speech can serve to guide the learning, too: so normal-hearing listeners, presented with the kind of transformed signal that a cochlear implant delivers, could extract useful clues about what it would do to speech from hearing what it did to the sounds made by animals, cars, and musical instruments (Loebach and Pisoni 2008). Note, however, that in one way weird-speech perception results and phoneme-learning results differ. Learning about synthetic speech consolidates after sleep (Fenn et al. 2003), but learning about an ambiguous sound is unaffected by sleep (Eisner and McQueen 2006). This could mean that the phoneme and the synthetic speech studies tap different levels of learning, but it could also simply be the case that the amount of learning involved determines whether there is scope for additional overnight consolidation.

The robustness of perceptual learning raises the question of whether other low-level categorical decisions in linguistic processing can be similarly adapted. Indeed,

Figure 11.5
Interpretation of ambiguous letters is learned in the same way as interpretation of ambiguous speech sounds (see section 11.7); if the middle letter in this set is first seen in words like *WEIGH*, a later categorization task with an H-to-N continuum shows that the subject's H category has grown bigger, but if the same ambiguous letter is first seen in words like *REIGN*, the categorization responses show that the N category has expanded (continuum used by Norris, Butterfield, et al. 2006).

an analog of the phoneme adaptation using an ambiguous letter instead—see figure 11.5—also produced adaptation of letter perception if it was presented in real words but not if presented in nonwords (Norris, Butterfield, et al. 2006). Nonlinguistic categories can be adapted in just the same way: exposure to an ambiguous color applied to a banana versus a carrot causes the boundaries between the colors yellow and orange to shift correspondingly in a subsequent color categorization task (Mitterer and De Ruiter 2008). Letter categories or color categories can expand to embrace a deviant exemplar, just as phoneme categories can.

The plasticity in adult speech perception can thus be seen as a powerful adaptive tool that makes language processing even more efficient. The mechanisms drawn on for the retuning of phoneme categories are general learning techniques that form part of the extensive range of human cognitive abilities (see Gilbert, Sigman, and Crist 2001 for a discussion of perceptual learning as a general cortical attribute). Native-language control in speech processing is itself in the service of maximal efficiency, and the ability to learn useful adaptations for specific cases (e.g., individual talkers, changing pronunciations, unusual listening conditions) is no different. Whether this adult perceptual flexibility and plasticity extends even across multiple languages is the next question that arises.

11.9.1 The Effects of Bilingualism on Cognition

First consider bilingualism, the active use of more than one language. This proves to have far-reaching implications for cognitive processing beyond the realm of language. There is a remarkably simple tool in the repertoire of cognitive psychology, known as the Simon task; in this paradigm, the subject has two response buttons and has to press, say, the left button if a blue patch appears on the computer screen and the right button if a yellow patch appears. Response time is slower when locations of visual stimulus and response are not congruent (e.g., a yellow patch appears on the left side of the screen; Simon and Wolf 1963). The "Simon task cost" is the extra time needed in the incongruent compared with a congruent or neutral condition; it is held to represent the time needed to inhibit an inappropriate response (e.g., pressing the left button).

This cost is significantly attenuated, however, in bilinguals who have maintained use of more than one language throughout life (Bialystok et al. 2004). The bilinguals were tested in communities where languages were routinely used together, in India, Hong Kong, and Canada. Further, the size of the cost in the Simon task tends in general to increase with age; but in the lifelong bilinguals, the age-related increase began later, and was less marked, in comparison with matched monolingual controls.

Switching between languages in everyday speaking, the authors suggested, develops facility in doing what the Simon task measures: inhibiting unwanted responses. Quite general added benefits of cognitive control result from the language switching, even in such simple applications as this task. The crucial cognitive control component appears to be response selection (Bialystok, Craik, and Ryan 2006); this was shown with a task where subjects had to press a response key on the opposite side of a stimulus presented in peripheral vision. If the stimulus appeared out on the left, the subject had to press a key on the right, and so on. These responses were slower than responses where the stimulus and the response position matched. Again, lifelong bilinguals experienced less cost due to the mismatch than monolinguals, and this was particularly so in older age ranges.

The implications of this work were further supported by the group's analysis of the onset of symptoms of dementia in a large group of aging individuals (Bialystok, Craik, and Freedman 2007); in lifelong bilinguals, the onset of serious symptoms was delayed by about four years, again in comparison with matched monolingual controls. Children acquiring more than one language even show cognitive benefits before they start schooling. Three-year-old bilinguals outperform monolingual age-mates on theory of mind tasks involving working out that another person has a false belief (Kovács 2009); between six and eight months, infants acquiring just one language reduce use of visual cues to linguistic information in speech, but infants acquiring two languages maintain this ability (Weikum et al. 2007); and seven-month-olds acquiring two languages outperform those acquiring one language at replacing one learned experimental response by a newly learned one (Kovács and Mehler 2009). Thus, language processing both draws on and feeds into cognitive processing in general.

11.9.2 Early Exposure

For learning language later than early childhood, early exposure to some language is critical. Adult learners of sign languages do better if they have had early exposure to spoken language than if they have had no early language experience, and adult learners of spoken language do better if they have had early exposure to language (any other language, spoken or signed) than if they have had none (Mayberry, Lock, and Kazmi 2002). But does early exposure to a particular language leave indelible traces?

Some studies suggest not. Brain imaging studies of Korean adoptees in France showed no evidence of differential processing for the language to which they had been exposed in childhood compared to another foreign language (Pallier et al. 2003). The same adoptees' performance on several perceptual tasks using Korean phonemes, words, or sentences did not differ from the performance of a matched group of (nonadopted) French speakers (Pallier et al. 2003; Ventureyra, Pallier, and Yoo 2004).

But other studies, not involving cross-culture adoptees, have revealed significant benefits of early experience with a language, especially one learned later. Early experience of hearing Spanish spoken in the home allows undergraduates in Spanish classes to perform as well as native speakers on several measures of phonological perception and production, significantly outperforming their classmates who had had no such experience (Au et al. 2002). There is a further benefit from having actually spoken a little Spanish early on (Au et al. 2008), and the same pattern holds for early exposure to Korean in the home (Oh et al. 2003). In the Korean group, Au and colleagues' production measures showed native-equivalent performance if there had been early speaking experience, but not if the early experience had been only perceptual, whereas their perception measures showed benefits of both types of early experience. Any early language experience helps in some way.

11.9.3 Training L2 Speech Perception

One benefit that bilingualism might be thought to bring, but does not, is sensitivity to unfamiliar phonetic contrasts; bilinguals are just as bad at discriminating phoneme contrasts that are not in the repertoire of either of their languages as monolinguals are at discriminating contrasts not in their one language (Werker 1986). Irrespective of how many languages one acquired early, late acquisition of a new language is generally associated with disadvantages in both perception and production. The person who can discover the way to overcome these disadvantages will be ensured of lasting fame and fortune. It has not happened yet.

There have been some successes; three weeks of intensive training can improve the performance of Japanese learners of English in distinguishing between [r] and [l] (Logan, Lively, and Pisoni 1991), and the improvement persists for months at least (Lively et al. 1994). The training also has beneficial effects on the same learners' production of words containing [r] and [l] (Bradlow et al. 1997). Crucial for the success of such a training program is that the training exemplars are variable—they are produced by multiple speakers, and the phonetic environment is varied, too. Training with synthetic stimuli produces a small learning effect, but it does not generalize to natural speech tokens (Strange and Dittmann 1984), and training with a single speaker's productions does not generalize to other speakers, either (Lively, Logan, and Pisoni 1993). The variable training methods are also successful with suprasegmental contrasts, such as Chinese tones for learners with a nontonal L1 (Wang et al. 1999), and Japanese consonant-length contrasts (geminate vs. singleton consonants) for American listeners (Hirata 2004).

Training techniques that highlight particular relevant aspects of the acoustic-phonetic input, and hence should encourage L2 listeners to attend to those features, have also been explored with some success (e.g., Hazan and Simpson 1998, 2000; Jamieson and Morosan 1986; McCandliss et al. 2002). But no technique yet in existence can succeed in bringing the perception of a difficult L2 contrast up to native levels for learners who started late on the L2. The one factor that works, of course, is starting early (Flege 1999; Flege, MacKay, and Meador 1999).

Perceptual learning techniques can be used to improve adaptability to L2 speech. It is much harder to adjust to an unfamiliar dialect in the L2 than in the L1, but knowing what the words are supposed to be is a big help. Mitterer and McQueen (2009b) exposed Dutch listeners, all proficient in English as an L2, to extracts from movies spoken in heavily accented English (Scottish or Australian). The movies were presented without subtitles, or with L1 (Dutch) subtitles, or with L2 (English) subtitles; listeners were then tested on previously unheard speech excerpts. The best perceivers of the new speech samples were the subjects in the L2-subtitle condition; knowing as you hear something like [pɪt] in the soundtrack that it is the word *put* (in the Scottish movie) or *pet* (in the Australian movie) really helps you to acquire knowledge that is generalizable to new input. Just knowing what it means is no help; the subjects who saw Dutch subtitles actually performed worse than those who saw no subtitles at all. Thus the learning only worked if it engaged the relevant L2 phoneme categories. The implications of this study for self-help in L2 perception are obvious.

11.10 Conclusion: Is L1 versus L2 the Key Distinction?

Adaptability and generalization are key elements of human cognition. In this chapter we have seen that speech processing benefits from both of these. Our language abilities are, however, integrated with general cognitive abilities, and the adaptability of our adult brains allows for reciprocal influences of many kinds. The way in which the native language allows sharper focus of attention on voice discrimination was described in chapter 10, consistent with the evidence, described in section 11.7.2 of this chapter, that speaker identity is cued in phonemes and that phoneme category retuning will be phoneme specific and speaker specific to the extent that this is possible. There are many such flow-ons. Consider that users of sign language, whose language processing requires them to develop special facility with visual imagery, perform mental rotation more rapidly than nonsigners (Emmorey 2002). Having multiple native languages also has significant effects on cognition in general (and cognitive control and attention in particular), as described in section 11.9.1. However, the evidence reviewed in chapters 9 and 10 shows convincingly that adult cognitive flexibility does not stretch to processing second language as efficiently as a first.

Studies of language processing in the brain have multiplied in recent years. They have revealed brain changes consequent on acquisition of a second language (Mechelli et al. 2004), as well as differences in the processing of L1 versus L2 in the brain (Mazoyer et al. 1993; Kim et al. 1997; Chee, Soon, and Lee 2003), and considerable individual differences in brain structure that are correlated with differences in L2 speech perception and production abilities (Callan et al. 2004; Golestani, Paus, and Zatorre 2002; Golestani and Zatorre 2004; Golestani and Pallier 2007; Golestani et al. 2007). Note that this would be expected, given the range of individual differences in phonetic acquisition skills (see chapter 8).

Even early bilinguals differ in how well they can discriminate sounds of the nondominant language, and these differences are reflected in the size of mismatch negativities for speech sounds even when auditory capabilities are otherwise matched across good and poor discriminators (Diaz et al. 2008; the subject population was the Spanish-Catalan bilinguals in Barcelona again). Auditory abilities certainly do predict speech perception abilities (see chapter 8), but speech-specific abilities overlaid on general auditory capacity clearly play a role, too.

Consistent with the proposal that L1 and L2 categories differ in relative plasticity, brain reflections of such a difference have also been measured (in the same bilingual population; Sebastián-Gallés et al. 2006). Catalan-Spanish bilinguals made lexical decisions on correct Catalan words (*gall*[ɛ]*da* 'bucket'), nonwords differing from words just in a vowel that Spanish listeners confuse (*gall*[e]*da*), or nonwords with a nonconfusable vowel. Spanish-dominant bilinguals performed poorly with the confusable nonwords (replicating the results of Pallier et al. 2001; see chapter 9). ERP measurements showed that, although erroneous responses to these nonwords by Catalan-dominant bilinguals resulted in an error detection response in the brain, error responses by the Spanish-dominant group did not. Thus the behavioral difference between the two bilingual groups was paralleled by a difference in this ERP pattern. But on another ERP component (the N400 measure elicited by the stimuli) the two groups showed matching response patterns. Sebastián-Gallés et al. explained the N400 effect as evidence of lexical activation, and thus indicative of toleration of variant pronunciations. In a bilingual community, variant pronunciations will certainly have formed part of all listeners' experience. Their conclusion was that the plasticity differences evident in perception experiments correspond to differences between L1 and L2 plasticity in the brain; that is, the Catalan-dominant listeners had more adaptable representations of the Catalan words than the Spanish-dominant listeners did. L1 representations are not only stronger and more sharply defined, but also more adaptable.

All the evidence reviewed in this chapter has supported such an account. Although listening in the L2 tends, in far too many respects, to be fragile and inflexible, native listening in the L1 is characterized by great robustness and apparently unlimited flexibility.

12 Conclusion: The Architecture of a Native Listening System

The efficiency of native listening rests on an architecture designed for optimal utilization of speech information, as soon as this becomes available. Language-specificity in speech processing flows from this architecture: Listeners use whatever information is most useful in their language-specific case. All listening involves abstract representations, at all levels of phonological structure from phonemic units to prosodic patterns. But it also involves considerable storage of encountered perceptual episodes. Again, both types of information, abstract and episodic, are employed because both are useful. The flow of information in speech processing is, in principle, unidirectional; information cascades continuously through levels of processing, allowing higher-level probabilities to influence how much lower-level information may be needed for a decision. All these architectural features are, once again, universal in nature, but their operation is modulated where needed by language-specific detail. And finally: a lot of work still remains to be done!

Listening to speech feels like about the easiest thing we do, but the separate operations it consists of—such as segmenting a continuous stream of input into its discrete components, or selecting words from among a vocabulary extending into the hundreds of thousands—are, as we have seen, highly complex. The argument of this book has been that the efficiency with which these complex operations are carried out derives from the fact that they are, at all points, exquisitely adapted to the characteristics of the mother tongue.

This process of adaptation begins in the earliest stages of listening, in infancy. The more listeners come to know about the typical patterns in a language, the more they can refine their listening to take account of the language-specific probabilities. Information that is critical for distinguishing between phonemes and words is exploited at the earliest possible opportunity. Information in the signal that does not significantly facilitate phoneme and word decisions, however, may be ignored.

Because phoneme repertoires and vocabularies differ across languages, the information critical for listeners in one language may be irrelevant for listeners in another. In this way, the processes that make up listening to speech come to be different across languages too.

Nevertheless, it remains true that listeners start from the same point. Babies are open to whatever language input the environment may throw at them. This is the fundament on which psycholinguistics rests: language processing is universally made possible by the cognitive abilities of the human brain. Thus understanding the process of listening involves us in the interplay of universal and language specific. As the case studies in chapter 1 made clear, we can only acquire the full picture by comparing language processing across languages. Universal aspects of language structure tell us both about universal effects of structure on processing and about how such effects can be shaped by variation across languages. Language-specific aspects of linguistic structure can tell us more about how the processing system can adapt to deal with structural variation, in the most efficient way.

In this final chapter, some principles governing the architecture of the native listening system are presented, based on the evidence summarized in preceding chapters. The main questions concern the nature of representations in speech processing, the type of information represented, and the flow of information within the system.

12.1 Abstract Representations in Speech Processing

There are abstract representations involved in listeners' processing of speech, both at the prelexical and at the lexical levels. This does not mean that abstract representations are the only ones, and all incidental detail is lost; that is certainly not the case. But evidence for retention of veridical detail in speech perception has prompted recent suggestions at the other extreme: that abstract representations in spoken-word recognition can be dispensed with, and just incidental detail is enough (see section 12.2.1). That is not the case, either; several types of evidence compel the conclusion that abstraction plays a central role in listening.

Such a central role for abstract representations in speech processing is appropriate given the capacity of human cognition for abstraction and generalization. Humans are theorizing machines; we make and test hypotheses, and we extract rules from the collections of instances that form our experience. This capacity can be seen in the learning of language in many ways, and certainly in our processing of speech; it is one of the main reasons why listening is so efficient. It is fair to say that abstraction is one of the premier achievements of the human mind, and explaining how it happens is now an important goal of cognitive (neuro)science. One might wonder why anybody would want to deny it.

12.1.1 Abstract Prelexical Representations

The perceptual learning discussed in chapter 11 provides strong evidence for abstract representations at the phonemic level. Through hearing phonemes in words, the listener learns about how the phonemes are pronounced, and shows evidence of this learning in phonetic categorization responses on a continuum of simple nonlexical tokens. Most importantly, the learning generalizes, as we saw, from the few words actually heard in the training phase to other words not previously heard from the talker in question.

Our experience leads us to expect such generalization: when we adapt to a new talker, we understand whatever we hear even though we have no stored memories of particular words from that particular person. So, hearing someone pronounce [f] in an odd way in *beef*, *carafe*, and *handkerchief* really should help us to understand the same person's later pronunciations of, say, *dwarf* or *hoof* and to distinguish between potential minimal pairs (e.g., realize that an utterance of *knife* is not *nice*).

Generalization is thus crucial to the claim that the rapid adaptation observed in the perceptual learning experiments serves to facilitate communication. There will be no improvement in understanding the speaker if only the few words heard in the training phase of a learning experiment are affected. Waiting for exactly those words to reoccur may be ultimately rewarded, but given the structure of vocabularies (hundreds of thousands of words made from only a few dozen phonemes), it is likely that while the listener is waiting, the same phoneme has occurred in many other words uttered by the same speaker. Communication is only facilitated if these words are recognized more rapidly because the deviant phoneme is identified more rapidly; that is, if the learning has generalized.

The evidence of generalization was described in chapter 11. Subjects who heard an ambiguous [f/s] replacing [s], in the first phase of a perceptual learning experiment, later interpreted previously unheard minimal-pair words ending with this ambiguous sound as the *s*-final alternative (e.g., they heard [naif/s] as *nice*). Those who heard the [f/s] replacing [f] interpreted the ambiguous form as the *f*-final interpretation (e.g., they heard [naif/s] as *knife*). As a result, in a cross-modal identity priming task, [naif/s] yielded more facilitation of lexical decisions to visually presented NICE or KNIFE, respectively (McQueen, Cutler, et al. 2006; Sjerps and McQueen 2010).

Thus, twenty words in a short training session induced a phonemic category boundary to shift, and the shift generalized more or less immediately to words not heard in training—perception of any word in the lexicon involving the same phoneme was appropriately adjusted. The generalization to words in which the trained sound occurs in new phonetic contexts implies that the learning concerns phonemic categories, independently of the forms in which they have just been encountered. The learning is not just incrementation of extra episodes of experience; it is happening at an abstract level. Listeners must have at their disposal phonemic representations—abstract forms standing for the sound that is common to *carafe*, *handkerchief*, and *knife*, and indeed to *fate*, *fresh*, *office*, and *muffle* as well.

Such a level of abstraction is absent from models of word recognition in which input is compared against stored veridical traces of speech perception episodes. A model of that type thus lacks the flexibility to profit from experience accrued in the training phase of perceptual learning experiments (see section 12.2.2). Human listeners, however, definitely do profit from the training and use it to improve their future speech perception performance.

12.1.2 Abstract Representation of Phoneme Sequence Probabilities

In the first demonstration of perceptual learning about phoneme category boundaries (Norris et al. 2003), learning was induced by lexical information (e.g., [f/s] at the end of *gira-* or *platypu-*) but not by nonwords that provided no clue either way (*liff/liss*? *gleef/gleece*?). But when phonotactic structure provides unambiguous information about what a phoneme should be (i.e., it must be [f] if it precedes [r], but it must be [s] if it precedes [n]), listeners exploit this in the same way that they exploit lexical information, even if the information has in this case been imparted not by real words but by nonwords. So, [f/s] at the beginning of *-nuter* or *-rulic* also induced appropriate category boundary shifts (Cutler, McQueen, et al. 2008). Thus not only does phonotactic structure directly influence phonetic categorization (Massaro and Cohen 1983), it can also be interpreted in such a way that perceptual learning occurs. Phonotactic sequence constraints figure in listeners' store of knowledge about their language.

Knowledge of phonotactics is used in segmentation of continuous speech, where at a prelexical level it constrains the activation of potential word candidates (e.g., McQueen 1998). All phonotactic knowledge, about possible and impossible sequences and about likely versus unlikely transition probabilities, is acquired through experience with the patterns in the language-specific vocabulary; nonetheless, in these uses the knowledge is abstractly coded and independent of lexical processing. Lexical and transitional probability information have separable effects on phoneme categorization (Pitt and McQueen 1998; also see section 12.4.3). Repetition of spoken forms and same-different judgments both show different effects of transitional probability manipulations in words versus in nonwords (Vitevitch 2003b; Vitevitch and Luce 1998), which again indicates that the transitional probability information is represented in its own right. Listeners pick up very rapidly on transitional probabilities and patterns built into speech input, and generalize from them (Dell et al. 2000; Onishi et al. 2002; Wilson 2006); experience with the language has alerted listeners to the usefulness of such information in the first place, but the usefulness is great enough to warrant explicit representation of the regularities in prelexical processing.

12.1.3 Abstract Representation of Prosodic Patterning

In chapters 4 and 7, we saw how listeners' knowledge of prosodic patterns controlled their responses in experiments. One such pattern concerned the location of primary stress in words—in English and Dutch, words are most likely to be stressed on the first syllable, and listeners act on this probability in segmenting speech streams. Another concerned the duration of isolated syllables versus syllables within longer words—thus, the relative activation of *dock* and *doctor* varied, given a longer or shorter version of their common syllable in a priming study (Davis et al. 2002), as did the relative looks to pictures of a cap or a captain in an eye-tracking study (Salverda et al. 2003, 2007). But is such prosodic knowledge independently represented, or is it just the case that, for instance, a long *cap* better matches stored traces of the monosyllabic word than stored traces of the first syllable of *captain*?

This can be sorted out by teaching listeners new words and carefully controlling the exact acoustic nature of the episodes they hear. In an eye-tracking study, Shatzman and McQueen (2006b) first had subjects learn the names for some nonsense objects, including pairs with names such as *nim* and *nimsel*. Natural recordings of the set of paired words produced much longer average durations for the monosyllabic names than for the first syllable of the bisyllabic names. The recordings presented to the subjects were manipulated, however, so that the segmentally identical syllables in a training pair were the same length. For *nim* and *nim(sel)*, this was 275 milliseconds (whereas the natural stand-alone *nim* had been 329 milliseconds long and the natural *nim-* of *nimsel* 221 milliseconds). After the training, all stored traces of each type of *nim* in the subjects' experience had the same duration. There then followed a test phase, in which the subjects had to click on one of the objects. The crucial syllable in the instruction they heard either had the same duration as in training, or it was of longer (329 milliseconds) or shorter (221 milliseconds) duration.

Episodic models, in which lexical memory consists of traces of listening experience, would predict that the version corresponding to the training exemplars should most efficiently activate the target's name. Models that also allow abstract prosodic knowledge, however, would predict effects for the longer and shorter versions; the longer version should be more likely to encourage looks to the object with the monosyllabic name, and the shorter version more likely to encourage looks to the object with the bisyllabic name. Exactly this latter difference appeared. A *nimsel* was looked at faster if its first syllable was spoken shorter than if it was long, whereas a *nim* was looked at faster if it was spoken longer than if it was short. The matching competitor effects showed the same pattern: *nimsel* with a long first syllable encouraged more looks to the competitor *nim* than *nimsel* with a short first syllable did, and a short utterance of *nim* encouraged more looks to the competitor *nimsel* than a long *nim* did. Also, the *nimsel* was looked at more if named with a short first syllable than with the trained 275-millisecond syllable; the training exemplar, though exactly matching all instances in the listeners' total experience of *nimsel*, was not the best at calling up the target's name for recognition.

With the same technique, Sulpizio and McQueen (2011) addressed the lexical stress case. Most three-syllable words in Italian have penultimate stress (e.g., *geLAto* 'icecream'), but a minority (less than one-fifth) of such words have initial stress (e.g., *FEgato*, 'liver'). Sulpizio and McQueen found, first, that Italian listeners used acoustic cues to stress in the recognition of the minority set but not in the recognition of the majority case with penultimate stress. Thus they appeared to assume a default stress pattern, but to be attentive to acoustic indications that such an assumption was inappropriate. Sulpizio and McQueen then taught their listeners novel trisyllabic names for nonsense objects, with among the names some minimal stress pairs such as *TOlaco* and *toLAco*. All of the training examples were again manipulated, in this case by reducing some of the acoustic cues to stress: the amplitude and duration of the first two vowels of each word in a pair were always matched.

In the test phase, listeners heard either the same exemplars as in training, or other versions of the nonsense words that had been provided with a full range of stress cues (i.e., including amplitude and duration). For the nonsense words with the majority pattern (*toLAco*, etc.), it made no difference which exemplars the listeners heard; both were recognized equally rapidly. For the initially stressed items (*TOlaco*), however, recognition was significantly faster with the full-cue exemplars than with the reduced-cue exemplars that had already been heard.

In Shatzman and McQueen's (2006b) study, a *nimsel* with a 221-millisecond *nim* was a better *nimsel* than every *nimsel* their subjects had ever encountered (all of which had a longer *nim*). In Sulpizio and McQueen's (2011) study, *TOlaco* with a full range of stress cues was a better *TOlaco* than any of the instances (all with a reduced range of cues) that the listeners had previously heard. Listeners are clearly able to call on abstract knowledge of prosodic patterning, including the tendency for polysyllabic names to have shorter first syllables and the likely location of primary stress in words of their language's vocabulary. Moreover, they apply this knowledge to the recognition of words for which no matching prosodic variation has accrued in their experience. It is not only their word-specific experience that determines how the words are recognized. They exploit their knowledge about prosody, abstracted from experience with many different words, as well.

12.1.4 Underlying Representations in the Lexicon

There is evidence that words are lexically represented in canonical form (see chapter 6). Although listeners may more frequently encounter noncanonical pronunciations (*pos'man* with deleted [t], *fillum* with vowel epenthesis) than pronunciations of the canonical form (*postman*, *film*), the core form stored in the lexicon is the canonical one. Such evidence embraces, for instance, listeners' categorization of productions such as *fillum* as monosyllabic (the canonical form) rather than bisyllabic (which is what they have in truth become; Donselaar et al. 1999). It also includes faster lexical decisions and stronger priming effects for canonical than for variant word pronunciations (Sumner and Samuel 2005; Ranbom and Connine 2007).

The canonicality issue also provides a handle on the question of representational abstraction. In a study of priming effects on word repetition and lexical decision, McLennan, Luce, and Charles-Luce (2003) used prime and target utterances of the same word that were both casually spoken, both carefully spoken, or one of each. If the lexicon contains veridical traces of perceptual experience, then a mismatch in form between prime and target should inhibit responses; if the lexicon contains canonical form representations, then careful articulations should produce greater facilitatory priming effects. The results supported both these conclusions! Crucially, the results differed with task difficulty (and by implication, with the depth of processing required by the task). Only easy processing (lexical decision with nonwords that were not at all wordlike, and hence easy to tell from words) produced the veridical-trace pattern. Easy tasks apparently allowed responses to be made at a shallower level of processing, which could be achieved on the basis of traces of the earlier perception. All types of processing that were in any way harder (for instance, the repetition task requiring a spoken response, or lexical decision where the nonwords were distractingly wordlike) led to a greater likelihood of canonical forms being engaged. Note that the much longer-term priming investigated by Sumner and Samuel (2005) also engaged canonical forms.

Also relevant is another investigation of variant pronunciations described in chapter 6—namely, Deelman and Connine's (2001) study with words ending in [d] or [t]. Associative priming showed no differential effects of the form of [t] or [d] in such a word's pronunciation, which suggested that the lexicon held only a single conceptual form of the word, regardless of the input form. In phoneme detection, reduced variants of [t] and [d] elicited slower responses, which in turn suggested that these variants were less effective at accessing phonological representations. Evidence that conceptual and phonological representations are separated in the lexicon was reviewed in chapter 3, and its implications are considered in the following section.

12.1.5 Separate Lexical Representations of Word Form and Word Meaning

Phonological representations are activated by speech input and participate in the competition process. Conceptual representations are not immediately activated. This was the conclusion warranted by the discussion in chapter 3. Assuming a formal separation between conceptual and phonological representations brings comprehension models in line with models in speech production, where researchers have needed such a distinction to explain, inter alia, patterns of frequency effects in picture naming. If form and meaning were conjointly represented, then a hare and a swan, very similar in frequency, should be equally easy to name, and it should not matter that the name *hare* has a homophone *hair* with a much higher frequency. But it does matter; naming time is determined by the highest-frequency homophone (Dell 1990; Jescheniak and Levelt 1994). Production researchers have therefore assumed that the phonological form has a separate representation, contacted by each meaning. In spoken-word recognition, in contrast, separation between the conceptual and phonological components of lexical entries may seem unnecessary; a homophonous form like *hare/hair* could activate two lexical entries, with fortuitously identical phonological form but different semantic content. Some models of lexical access in comprehension have indeed explicitly proposed that access to form entails access to meaning (e.g., Gaskell and Marslen-Wilson 1997).

However, comparing across the two alternative versions of cross-modal priming revealed that the priming patterns for a word's form and its meaning were not correlated (Norris, Cutler, et al. 2006). Hearing *lease* either in isolation or in a sentence facilitated recognition of the same word form, LEASE, whereas recognition of the conceptually related word RENT was facilitated when *lease* had been heard in isolation but not necessarily when *lease* had been heard in a sentence. Hearing *police* (especially in a sentence) led to inhibition of LEASE, which showed that the lexical representation of *lease* had been activated but had lost out in the competition; but there was never any trace of an effect on RENT of having heard *police*, either in isolation or in a sentence. It was certainly not the case that the pattern of phonological-form activation predicted the pattern of conceptual-form activation.

The implication of this dissociation is the separability of phonological and conceptual information in the stored representations of words. Effects arising in the form- (or identity-)priming version of cross-modal priming (*lease*-LEASE) reflect phonological activation consequent on any occurrence of the word form, intended or not. Such effects have no necessary implications for conceptual activation (e.g., the inhibited activation of embedded words appears to concern their phonological form alone). Effects in associate priming (*lease*-RENT) do not constitute a general touchstone for lexical access. They are dependent on activation of lexical semantics, which may or may not result from activation of phonological form, as a consequence of the phonological form's success in competition. A simple unitary model of lexical entries, in which phonological and conceptual representations are inextricably united, is therefore untenable; the lexicon contains separate representations of form and of meaning.

12.1.6 Phonological Representations and Where They Come From

The primary contact between speech input and the lexicon occurs via the phonological representations. Hearing speech causes phonological representations to become active and enter the competition process. Each separate known form has a distinct stored representation; whenever we learn a new word, we have to construct a phonological representation and store it, if we want to recognize the word when we hear it again.

It is easy to assume that the phonological representations found in the lexicon will have been entirely determined by the prelexical representations computed during the processing of speech. If we hear two forms as distinct, and thus derive distinct prelexical representations for them, then lexical forms constructed for them will also be different; but if we hear them as indistinguishable, they will be assigned identical phonological representations prelexically, and hence the representations in the lexicon should also be identical.

However, this simple state of affairs cannot hold. Evidence from L2 learning makes it clear that lexical phonological representations are abstract and can be codetermined by other sources of knowledge than our prelexical phonetic perceptions, and that this can lead to an asymmetry: distinctions that are maintained in the lexicon do not line up with distinctions that can be apprehended in the input.

Note that the L2 situation offers a useful window onto the relationship between prelexical and lexical processing. In the L1, at least the very earliest stages of word learning in infancy must be fully dependent on the input. But in an L2, even the initial acquaintance with phonological form can be influenced by sources of information beyond the nature of the input. L2 learners already have an L1, for example; this means they have a set of phonemic categories. As we saw, this may help or hinder the formation of the correct set of categories for interpreting speech in the L2. They also have a good deal of knowledge about how words are structured phonologically, and again, this can be helpful or unhelpful to the extent that the L1 and L2 do or do not match. Further, adult learners bring expectations to the task of language learning—about how concepts map to nouns and verbs, about how language should be used in different communicative situations, and so on. Finally, the L2 learner can receive explicit instruction, either formally from a teacher or less formally from, say, workmates, and can draw on orthographic representations of new forms as well as spoken input. L2 learners exploit every type of help they can get with the language learning task, and one result is that they set up phonological representations in the lexicon that include information they have not extracted from the input.

The evidence was described in part in chapter 9 (see section 9.6). Dutch listeners cannot tell the difference between spoken *pan* and *pen*, and Japanese listeners cannot tell the difference between spoken *rock* and *lock*; but their lexical representations for words beginning *pan-* and *pen-* (or *lock-* and *rock-*) are distinct (Weber and Cutler, 2004; Cutler et al. 2006). L2 listeners can maintain a phonological distinction at the lexical level that they show no sign at all of being able to discriminate in speech input. Where has this distinction come from? Not from prelexical processing; it must have come from one (or more) of the other sources of information listed above.

One of the listed possibilities was knowing how words of the L2 are written. Following up Weber and Cutler's study, Escudero, Hayes-Harb, and Mitterer (2008) taught Dutch speakers of English the supposed English names for some nonsense figures, including pairs like *tanzer* and *tendik* that differed in the first vowel, like *panda* and *pencil*. When the nonsense names were taught using only the spoken forms, the two were confused equally often with each other in a subsequent test with eye-tracking; the instruction *look at the tan-* produced about the same proportion of looks to the tanzer as to the tendik, and so did the instruction *look at the ten-*. These listeners could not tell the vowels apart and so treated the two initial syllables as versions of the same syllable. When the nonsense names were taught using the spelled as well as the spoken form, however, the eye-tracking results were quite different: the instruction *look at the tan-* produced looks to the tendik as well as the tanzer, but the instruction *look at the ten-* led the listeners to look overwhelmingly at the tendik only. This mimics the result that Weber and Cutler had observed. The additional orthographic information enabled these listeners to realize that the vowels were different, and hence to store different representations of the novel words' first syllables, in the same way as they did for known English words such as *panda* and *pencil*. But just as with real English input, the availability of this lexical distinction did not imply that the listeners could make a corresponding distinction in phonetic processing.

Thus L2 listeners use abstract knowledge about phonological distinctions—derived from orthography, for instance—to shape the stored phonological forms. Once they know there is supposed to be a distinction between two phonemes, they store the distinction, even if they cannot reliably hear it at all. Although this is very easy to see in the L2 case, where the phonemic confusions involved are predictable from the L1-L2 mapping, there is no reason to rule it out in L1. Only in infancy, in the very earliest stages of word learning, are we restricted to spoken traces of word forms; as soon as we can interact with others, we are open to explicit instruction and hence to other sources of information about words. Once we learn to read, the possibilities expand further. Many words that educated adults know have been learned from reading and may indeed never have been heard (sometimes even with the result that the stored phonological form is quite incorrect; see Zwicky 1979 and Frith 1980 for some implications of this). Further, as Hanson, Shankweiler, and Fischer (1983) showed, deaf adults who have never experienced spoken input can succeed in constructing phonological representations of English words based on their knowledge of orthography. The lexical representations that language users draw on are richly supplied with phonological information, only some of which has been drawn from prelexical processing of speech input.

12.2 Specific Representations in Speech Processing

Listeners retain extensive records of the specifics of their speech processing experience. This can include a great deal of fine phonetic detail, as described in chapter 6. Although variant pronunciations contact a core lexical representation of their canonical form, the relative frequency of each variant also plays a role in processing, which indicates that information about patterns of variation is also stored (Connine, Ranbom, and Patterson 2008). The record further includes speaker-specific information, as described in chapter 11. Switching speakers in a laboratory listening situation increases, in general, the difficulty of recognition, whereas predictability of the speaker makes processing easier. In a recognition task involving a small set of speakers, even having a photo available can mitigate the effect of speaker switch on recognition accuracy, which suggests that listeners can deliberately make use of talker knowledge in word processing (Hay, Warren, and Drager 2006). The evidence already presented in this book, especially in those two chapters, makes it quite clear that listeners exploit such specific detail in processing utterances. In the first models of speech perception, it seemed most important to capture listeners' ability to perceive wildly differing tokens of sounds, words, and utterances as instances of the same set of categories—that is, to account for abstraction across variable inputs. But now it would be eccentric to claim that all of the variability is discarded. Listeners make use of the variations too.

In linguistics, recent years have seen an upsurge in interest in processing models in which stored traces of specific language experience replace abstract representations. The impetus for this came initially from the sociolinguistic literature on language change and dialect variation (some of which also appeared in chapter 11). Careful analyses revealed surprisingly specific patterns of variation, such as vowel-quality differences as a function of the ethnicity of a person referred to (Hay, Jannedy, and Mendoza-Denton 1999) or of the frequency and lexical neighborhood of a word being uttered (Jurafsky, Bell, and Girard 2002; Wright 2003). Sound changes in progress do not necessarily affect all susceptible words at once, and lexical storage of new words can differ across talkers, leading to effectively word-specific pronunciations (Pierrehumbert 2002; Yaeger-Dror 1994). Pierrehumbert cites examples such as *realize* versus *realign*; speakers differ in whether or not they differentiate the *real-* portions of these words, and are more likely to make such a distinction if they consider *realign* to be a productive combination of *re-* and *align*. Yaeger-Dror describes a vowel change in Montreal French that affected words like *mer* 'sea' and *paire* 'pair' but did not affect *mère* 'mother' and *père* 'father', which once were homophones of *mer* and *paire*.

Listeners take such factors into account in making decisions about word identity (see, e.g., Johnson 1990; Hay et al. 2006). Frequency of individual words in a minimal pair also modulated perception of phonemes affected by a near-merger in progress (Hay et al. 2006). The linguistic interest resulting from these discoveries drew gratefully on developments in psychological modeling aimed at accounting for talker-specific word recognition effects (see section 11.4 of the preceding chapter). It may indeed be among linguists that this work has had its greatest theoretical impact; in the decade or so that episodic models of spoken-word recognition have been around, publications reporting specificity effects in speech perception have rarely failed to note their consistency with the claims of the episodic models.

12.2.1 Modeling Specific Traces

The class of models in which stored representations are constructed exclusively from specific traces of experience is known variously as exemplar or episodic modeling. The underlying theory is simple. Individual instances of separable aspects of experience (objects, words, or whatever) leave veridical traces in memory. New instances of experience are compared against the stored traces, and categorical decisions are made on the basis of a similarity metric (e.g., this is a dog because it resembles the traces labeled "dog" more than any other traces). The more traces are laid down, the more they form clusters from which a prototype can be derived for each category label.

This type of modeling has its roots in memory research (Hintzman 1986; Nosofsky 1988, 1991). It was first applied to word recognition by Goldinger (1996, 1998), whose model of lexical access was a version of the memory model MINERVA-2 (Hintzman 1986). The approach was rapidly applied also to speech sound perception by Johnson (1997), Lacerda (1995), and Pierrehumbert (2001).

In MINERVA-2, each episode of previous experience lays down a trace in long-term memory (LTM); in Goldinger's adaptation of the model to spoken-word recognition, these traces are episodes of heard words. The traces are passive, but similar traces effectively group by resonating together. Whenever a new input is presented to the model, not only is a trace of it stored, but its form (acoustic properties, in the spoken-word case) activates all traces in LTM in proportion to their match to it. This is the way that word recognition occurs in the model: An aggregate echo of all activated traces is formed, and the content of this echo indicates the most likely lexical match.

A model of this type effectively captures frequency effects, because there will be more traces of frequent words (or frequent variants of a word), which makes the aggregate echo more intense as well as more strongly similar to the most frequent input. It also captures recency effects and talker-specificity effects, especially if recent traces are allowed to be weighted more highly than older ones. It accounts for many subtle effects, such as the greater impact of talker match on lower-frequency than on higher-frequency words (because the echo activated by a higher-frequency input will be diluted by many participating traces).

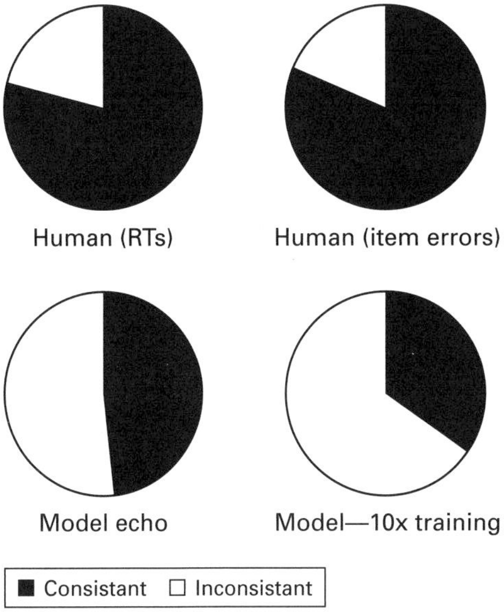

Figure 12.1
Proportion of responses consistent versus inconsistent with training, for humans and for an episodic model. In the upper two panels for the human results, dark segments give the proportion of subjects responding faster, and the proportion of items more accurately responded to, on consistent than on inconsistent trials at test. Consistent responses have an advantage on both measures. The lower panels show the episodic model's response at test with a word consistent or inconsistent with training. With the same amount of training as the human subjects, the model is unaffected and responds at chance (lower left); with ten times as much training, its performance becomes even worse.

12.2.2 The Necessity of Both Abstract and Specific Information

Strictly episodic models for word recognition, such as Goldinger's (1998) model, cannot, however, explain the generalization of perceptual learning (see chapter 11, section 11.7). In such a model, acoustic traces corresponding to the training experience in a learning experiment can be stored, but these traces have absolutely no implications for all the other passive traces stored in memory. Specifically, traces of training (with *carafe*, *handkerchief*, etc.) cannot affect the match between *nai*[f/s] and previous traces of *knife* and *nice*, which is the relevant issue in the second part of McQueen, Cutler, et al.'s (2006) generalization study.

Figure 12.1 shows the outcome of simulations with an implementation of MINERVA-2 (Hintzman 1986), like the one Goldinger had constructed. These simulations by Cutler et al. (2010) directly tested how an episodic model would respond to the generalization stimuli. The figure uses a summary form that allows comparison of the human data of McQueen, Cutler, et al. (2006) and the output of the model:

in both cases, what is represented is the proportion of responses consistent with training. As the responses on each trial involve a binary classification (e.g., *knife* vs. *nice*; or [f] versus [s] as the final phoneme), chance would be fifty-fifty.

The human data are summarized in the top two panels. Whether the results are presented as a view of the subject RTs (speed of response on consistent vs. inconsistent trials, top left) or the item errors (likelihood of correct "yes" responses on consistent vs. inconsistent trials, top right), the pattern is the same: consistent trials do much better. The listeners are overwhelmingly likely to interpret *nai*[f/s] in a way consistent with whatever training they received, and, when they do so, to respond faster.

The bottom two panels show, for the model, the percentage of times that the echo content was more similar to the training-consistent than the training-inconsistent interpretation of the test word. It is clear that the model performs very differently from the humans. With the same amount of training as the humans (lower left), the interpretations delivered do not differ significantly from chance, although there is a small indication that the inconsistent interpretation is chosen more often. Then the simulation was rerun, giving the model ten times as much training as the humans had received (ten exposures to the whole training set), to see if the model was being affected by the training at all. This rerun showed that the model certainly was learning; the model now (lower right) showed a significant preference for the training-inconsistent interpretation—that is, it produced exactly the opposite pattern of results from the human data in the upper panels.

The reason for the reverse effect was nothing to do with the ambiguous sounds themselves, in fact; it was because the training set contained, besides the ambiguous sound, also a contrasting unambiguous sound ([f] in the [s]-training case, or [s] in the [f]-training case). Words matched by this unambiguous phoneme were strengthened by the training. This made their representations stronger and more likely to be chosen at test. The ambiguous [f/s], however, simply had an equal effect on all the portions of words it weakly matched—*f*-words and *s*-words alike—and so it had no influence at all on what choices were made at test. (A further rerun with the unambiguous training only, omitting the ambiguous items, confirmed that exposure to the unambiguous sound had this strengthening effect; the presence or absence of an ambiguous phoneme played no role.)

This is not just a problem for this particular version of this particular model. Crucially, the model learned nothing about the [f/s] from the pattern of where this sound appeared in training. For the human listeners, the ambiguous sounds were phonemes, and they learned without apparent effort, from just a few exemplars, how to interpret them. For the model, the ambiguous sounds were nothing but uninformative noise. This is because the model has no abstract representations. Thus, to capture the human listening data from perceptual learning, abstract representations are necessary. However, as described earlier, abstract representations are not sufficient, given that a model with only abstract representations fails to capture the evidence for storage of information about episodes of speech experience.

12.2.3 What Determines Retention of Speaker-Specific Information

As described in chapter 11, the perceptual learning about phonemes helps us adjust to pronunciation variability across talkers, and in line with that, the learning is in good part speaker specific and segment specific. For fricatives, which carry quite a lot of information about speaker identity, learning is specific to a particular speaker's utterances of the segment in question (Eisner and McQueen 2005; Kraljic and Samuel 2007). For stop consonants, which are less informative about speaker identity, learning occurs at a level, possibly a featural level, which is less speaker specific and hence permits some generalization (Kraljic and Samuel 2007).

Listeners are also sensitive to when speaker-specific information should usefully be stored. When an ambiguous fricative between [s] and [ʃ] occurred in a single phonetic context only (e.g., always preceding [tr], as in *district*, *orchestra*, *destroy*, etc.) and so was putatively a dialectal feature of that one context, no adjustment of the [s] category occurred, although the boundary was indeed adjusted if the occurrence of the sound was context independent—occurring, for instance, in words like *dinosaur*, *obscene*, and *hallucinate* (Kraljic, Brennan, and Samuel 2008). The listeners apparently inhibited any implications for the speaker's production of that category as a whole if there was an apparent contextual restriction. Similarly, listeners did not learn when they watched a video and the ambiguous tokens only occurred when the speaker had a pen in her mouth; and they did not learn when they had previously heard the same speaker utter unambiguous versions of [s] (Kraljic, Samuel, and Brennan 2008). Thus, if listeners can attribute a deviant pronunciation to a potentially transient phenomenon, they again inhibit category adjustment.

These results are important because they constrain the uptake of speaker-dependent information. Listeners only store this when it is informative about a particular speaker's idiosyncrasy and hence potentially generalizable to future output from the same speaker. That is, they only store it when it is useful in that it will help them with future listening. Storing speaker-specific information is not an automatic, indiscriminate registration of each and every episode. Speaker information is stored for use; if it is no use, it is ignored.

12.3 Continuity, Gradedness, and the Participation of Representations

The processes that derive lexical candidates from speech input are, as laid out in chapters 6 and 7, exquisitely sensitive to the fine details of speakers' pronunciation. This is the most important reason why lexical activation from speech is a continuous process rather than a series of irrevocable commitments to intermediate classificatory decisions.

The 1970s debate on "units of perception" (named and shamed in chapter 4 for its remarkable inattention to the factor "language" in comparing results across experiments) was never resolved in favor of one or other intermediate unit for speech processing. As section 12.4.4 elaborates, data from the kind of detection tasks that figured in this debate will not necessarily shed light on the normal process of spoken-word recognition. Researchers realized early on that detection tasks were susceptible to effects of the instructions given to subjects, and of the makeup of the experiment as a whole. Thus the same set of target-bearing items could produce different patterns of results depending on whether subjects were listening for a phoneme or a syllable target (Foss and Swinney 1973; McNeill and Lindig 1973; Healy and Cutting 1976). Responses to phoneme targets were faster if the structure of the onset of the target-bearing word (single phoneme, or cluster) matched that of the word with which the target was modeled for subjects (so if subjects heard "Listen for a [b] as in *bowl*," they responded faster to *back* and *best* than to *bleed* or *blank*, but if they heard "Listen for a [b] as in *blue*" their responses were faster to *bleed* and *blank* than to *back* and *best*; Cutler, Butterfield, and Williams 1987).

Direct comparisons often revealed faster responses to syllable than to phoneme targets. However, this difference disappeared if there were foils among the filler no-response trials, such as the word *fattening* appearing in a sequence for which the phoneme target was [v], or the syllable target was *vat* (Norris and Cutler 1988). In comparisons where syllables had been responded to faster, factors in the experiments could thus have made syllable targets effectively easier than phoneme targets. Responses are also affected by the instructions given to the speaker recording the materials and to the experimenter conducting the testing (Goldinger and Azuma 2003): "Produce your phonemes clearly" leads to materials that produce faster phoneme detections, whereas "Produce your syllables clearly" leads to materials that produce faster syllable detections, and experimenters' beliefs about whether phonemes or syllables are responded to faster also induce matching results.

Obligatory conversion of speech input into intermediate representations, in the manner implied by much of the units of perception debate, has given way in current models to the continuous cascade of information across processing levels and the continuous (re)evaluation of lexical candidates. In cascade models, the relation between the prelexical and the lexical processing levels involves no irretrievable commitment to categorical decisions, but rather it is probabilistic, with the weighting of probabilities going up and down as the input alters (see the Shortlist figures in chapter 3). Even in such a framework, note that the phoneme as a participating level of description enjoys a built-in advantage; by definition, phonemes are minimal differences with a lexical consequence, so that in most cases decisions about lexical identity will be based on selections at some point between, effectively, phonemic alternatives. Thus categorical decisions can be viewed as falling out of lexical processing, whenever one word is selected over another word differing from it by one phoneme. That does not mean that such decisions are explicitly made in the course of recognizing the word. Note, too, that attempts to determine which such categories are most "basic" usually favor the phoneme; thus Decoene (1993) used matching tasks borrowed from the literature on prototypicality of semantic categories, and, on finding prototypicality effects for both physical form and category identity of phonemes but only for category identity of syllables, judged phonemes to be perceptually more basic than syllables.

The continuous-processing framework is in fact compatible with a role for categories at all levels. In chapter 4, for instance, where the role of rhythmic categories in speech segmentation was documented, this role was argued to be distinct from classification. Categories of rhythm, such as the foot, the syllable, or the mora, can exercise a necessary effect in segmentation without any need for them to function as intermediate representations in the speech processing chain. The following section illustrates this point for the smallest proposed rhythmic unit, on the grounds that an efficient way to examine the potential contribution of rhythmic categories as units of representation in listening is to look at the smallest one first. If the smallest proposed unit plays no integral role, it is at least very improbable that any larger units will do so.

12.3.1 Case Study: A Rhythmic Category and Its Role in Processing

The smallest proposed unit of rhythmic structure is the mora in Japanese. As explained in chapter 4, the mora is a subsyllabic unit and can be as small as a single segment; it is never larger than a complex onset plus a single vowel (e.g., *Kyo-* of *Kyoto*). The indivisibility or otherwise of this unit was addressed in several ways by Cutler and Otake (2002), starting with the word reconstruction task. If morae are the only units in listening, then any change in a mora should have equal effect in this task. For instance, changing the third mora of the four-mora word *pa-no-ra-ma* (which means the same in Japanese as in English) into *re*, *za*, or *ze* should have equal effect. The three morae *re*, *za*, and *ze* are all equally not the mora *ra*, and the fact that the first two of them overlap with *ra* in one phoneme should be irrelevant. But it was not—listeners came up with *panorama* much more quickly if they were given *panorema* or *panozama* rather than *panozema*. Whatever the position of the mora in the word (initial, medial, or final), it was always the case that if the nonword stimulus differed from the underlying target word in only part of a mora, the target was found more easily than if the difference involved all segments of the mora.

With the same nonwords, a lexical decision task addressed how quickly listeners could decide that the stimuli were indeed not words. The point at which each nonword became distinct from any real word (nonword uniqueness point, or NUP) was determined. The best predictor of "NO" response time in the lexical decision experiment was the overall duration from the NUP to the end of the nonword. This accounted for nearly 12 percent of the variance in RTs. The number of phonemes from the NUP to the nonword end accounted for an additional 2.5 percent of the variance. But the number of morae did not make a significant contribution.

These two results showed that Japanese words are recognized in a continuous manner, not in mora-size chunks. That is to say, spoken-word recognition in Japanese is just like spoken-word recognition in any other language. Puns also yielded evidence that Japanese language users manipulate submoraic structure in words. What do Japanese punsters do? Very much what punsters in English do (as shown, for example, by Lagerquist 1980)—they change as little as possible of the word, so that their listeners can most easily recover the intended word (punning is the skill that is exploited in the word reconstruction task, after all!). About seven-eighths of the analyzed puns changed only a single phoneme (e.g., *yokohaba tasogare* 'twilight in breadth', a reference to the song *Yokohama tasogare* 'twilight in Yokohama'; [m] has become [b] but everything else is unchanged). Only in one-eighth of the puns was more than one phoneme changed.

The same pattern even appeared in goroawase puns, a traditional literary form from the Edo period (a nineteenth-century period renowned for literary and artistic output; in particular, the art of the woodcut). The aim of a goroawase punster is to achieve an elegant contribution to an ongoing conversation that is at the same time a subtle distortion of a name, a well-known quotation from poetry or literature, or a proverb. One of the chief Edo period artists, Utagawa Kuniyoshi, produced two series of woodcuts consisting of goroawase distortions of the names of the coaching stations along the main Tokyo to Kyoto highway. Figure 12.2 shows one of the woodcuts; it is from a series in which all the pictures involve cats performing various actions. The cat in this picture is playing with two pieces of dried fish. The viewer is intended to retrieve *nihon* 'two cylindrical objects' *dashi* 'soup ingredients' and to appreciate this as a play on the name of the first stop from the Tokyo end, namely *Nihonbashi*. The change is in a single phoneme, [b] becoming [d]. In more than two-thirds of Utagawa Kuniyoshi's puns, less than a mora changed. Thus even in this highly literary period, when moraically based poetry flourished (and well before any influence of Western alphabetic orthography on Japanese consciousness), puns typically involved the smallest possible change: just one phoneme.

Puns offer a window onto speakers' knowledge of listening. Speakers do not want puns to be obscure—they want the cleverness of their pun to be appreciated rapidly. The best way to do that is to make the distortion minimal, so that the listener can get from the spoken form to the distorted underlying form without delay. "Minimal" in Japanese is just the same as minimal in English or any other language—Japanese

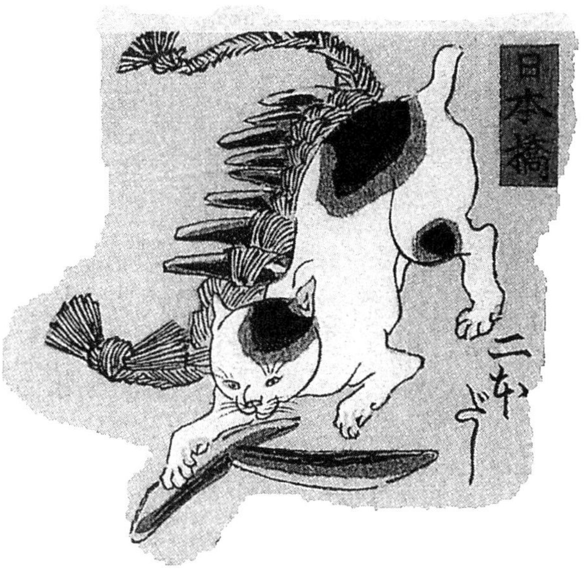

Figure 12.2
A cat with two cylinder-shaped soup ingredients, or *nihon dashi*, being a play on the town name Nihonbashi, by Utagawa Kuniyoshi. Even the puns in classical mora-based Japanese art forms are primarily phoneme based.

puns, just like English puns, mostly involve single-phoneme alterations.[1] The speakers' apprehension of how listeners operate is accurate; the experimental evidence from word reconstruction and lexical decision also indicates continuous processing, with decisions between words being made on whatever quanta of information are available. This is just as true in Japanese, with its rhythmically important mora, as in languages where the active rhythmic units are much larger. The conclusion must be that rhythmic units do not operate as intermediate levels of representation in listening.

12.3.2 Locating the Rhythmic Category in the Cascaded Model

Perhaps the last outpost of the units of perception proposal is to be found in recent arguments about the mora. As described in chapter 4, Japanese exhibits little tolerance for phonological sequences that violate the native moraic constraints. Loanwords from languages that allow more complex syllable structures are adapted by vowel insertion: English *glove* and *glass* become *gurabu* and *gurasu* in Japanese, and a famous U.S. credit card company is known in Japan as *American Ekisupuresu*. Strings that violate Japanese phonological rules are often treated by Japanese listeners in speech perception experiments as if such inserted vowels were there.

For instance, Japanese listeners and French listeners performed simple discrimination tasks with VCCV strings such as *ebzo*, which would violate Japanese phonological rules, versus VCVCV strings (e.g., *ebuzo*, which is legal in Japanese). French listeners could clearly discriminate between *ebzo* and *ebuzo*, but Japanese listeners responded to violating strings as if they were the legal ones (Dupoux, Kakehi, et al. 1999). ERP studies with an oddball paradigm (as described in chapter 6) further showed that French listeners detected a switch from one of these structures to the other (e.g., from *ebuzo* to *ebzo*), but Japanese listeners did not (Dehaene-Lambertz et al. 2000).

For many years now, a wide range of evidence has been accruing from ERP studies that reveals quite early reflections of processes that are not perceptually primary but logically dependent on prior access to some other aspect of the speech signal. These processes include the recognition of lexical status in the native language (Jacobsen et al. 2004), of semantic category membership (Rodríguez-Fornells et al. 2002), of contextual appropriateness (Van Berkum, Brown, and Hagoort 1999; Van Berkum, Hagoort, and Brown 1999), and of the semantic congruity of speaker identity and message (Van Berkum et al. 2008). As pointed out by Rodríguez-Fornells and colleagues, the evidence is most compatible with rapid cascade of processing across levels in speech recognition, so that all levels are effectively operating in parallel with maximum efficiency, uninterrupted by obligatory categorical decisions. Thus the ERP evidence of different phonological processing by French and Japanese listeners does not imply that they have different levels of representation.

As described in the preceding section, if Japanese listeners are computing early moraic representations, they are not using them as minimal differences between words. Likewise, if listeners actually perceptually restored the missing vowels in illegal sequences such as *ebzo*, they should have done the same with the vowels that would have made *gasu* easy to find in sequences such as *gasub* or *gasuch*, or *hamu* in *nyakhamu* (Cutler et al. 2009, discussed in chapter 5); but they did not. Indeed, there is further evidence, from the same team that carried out the French-Japanese comparisons just described, that is consistent with the continuous-processing interpretation; words with a deleted vowel were accepted by Japanese listeners in lexical decision if and only if the vowel required to create a word was the one most often inserted in such environments; that is, *ku* rather than *ka* (Dupoux, Fushimi, et al. 1999). This resembles the finding that the availability of competitors assists detection of, say, *sake* in *nyaksake* in Cutler et al.'s (2009) study; if there is lexical experience of a form, such as [ksa] as a possible pronunciation of *kusa*, then cascaded processing can do something with it.

Further evidence concerning the level of processing at which Japanese listeners insert vowels into consonant sequences comes from phoneme processing in context, as noted in chapter 6. Effects of adjacent phonemes on one another occur, as all researchers agree, at a prelexical level of processing. One such effect is compensation for coarticulation (see chapter 6; see also section 12.4.3). For instance, listeners shift their evaluation of a stop consonant ambiguous between [t] and [k] as a function of whether it was preceded by [s] (which induces more [k] responses) or [ʃ] (more [t]; Mann and Repp 1981). Now consider the Japanese case. Japanese has no coda obstruents, hence no sequences such as [ɪʃta], as Mann and Repp used. But sequences such as [sk] or [st], and also [ʃk] and [ʃt], do indeed arise as surface forms in Japanese, as a result of the devoicing of an intervening vowel. In practice, the necessary environments for compensation for coarticulation thus exist. If the underlying vowel were perceptually restored at the prelexical level, the consonants would then be separated by a vowel and no compensation would be needed. This would mean that English listeners would show compensatory adjustment, but Japanese listeners would not; however, Japanese and English listeners adjust their responses to the second sound in such sequences in the same way (Kingston et al., 2011). This parallel performance suggests that the vowels are absolutely not there for Japanese listeners in any sense that would affect their prelexical processing of the auditory signal.

12.4 Flow of Information in Speech Processing

Given all the evidence that has been summarized here in support of separable prelexical and lexical processing, the relationship between these levels must also be spelled out. If there is one issue that divides psycholinguistics, this is it. In the processing of syntax or of words, in the visual or the auditory mode, in production or in perception, there are those who believe that the operation of lower-level processes is directly affected by the outcome of higher-level processes, and those who do not, and the likelihood is that they will never agree (see, for instance, Norris, McQueen, and Cutler 2000 and the thirty-one largely dissenting commentaries it evoked, or McClelland, Mirman, and Holt 2006, plus McQueen, Norris, and Cutler 2006b).

What is at issue is the processes themselves, and the relationships between them. It is not whether there is influence of higher-level processing at the earliest possible point there could be—of course there is. If there is one lesson to be learned from all the evidence recounted in this book, it is that speech processing is tailored for efficiency, so whatever information comes available will be used. But the question that divides psycholinguists is how higher-level influence is exercised.

Interactionist models allow information from higher processing levels to flow to lower levels and inform processing decisions. This is, literally, top-down information flow. The way in which processing happens at a given level can be changed by the input from higher levels, so that the operation of processes varies from instance to instance, in response to factors quite external to the process in question. In spoken-word processing, the debate has concerned whether prelexical processes are influenced by lexical and sentence-level knowledge; an interactionist might thus claim that the process by which you decide whether you are hearing a [t] or a [k] can be modulated by what the interpretation of preceding words has been (see section 12.4.2). In the area of this book, the principal representative of this genre is TRACE (McClelland and Elman 1986).

In contrast, autonomous models hold that processing at each level should be independent—that is, not subject to such external influence. The flow of information is strictly in the logical order, from the acoustic signal through prelexical processing to lexical processing and so on; thus the flow is bottom-up only. Information cascades, as we have said: it flows continuously from the lower levels to the higher levels. This allows decisions at higher levels to be made on the basis of less-elaborated information arriving from the lower levels, if the higher-level decisions so far seem to warrant it; but there is no reverse flow of information. Lower processing levels maintain their autonomy, so that the operation of processes never varies from instance to instance; the only thing that varies is how much use needs to be made of this processing at higher levels. Thus your decision about whether you are hearing a [t] or a [k] is always the outcome of the same process. This constancy does not rule out the possibility of later effects of context on such a decision; the interpretation of preceding words may cause higher levels not to wait for the process's final decision, or even to override it. Merge (Norris et al. 2000), to be described in section 12.4.4, is a model of this type.

Psychologists prefer to use the term "top-down" strictly in the way just described. The term makes a claim about direction of information flow. It describes an architectural feature of information processing models: that they allow information to flow in a direction contrary to the input's trajectory. In some other research areas a looser usage sometimes prevails, where the term refers to any facilitatory influence of context, regardless of how it may be explained. Here, the term should be read in the psychological sense.

The reason why the failure to agree on the issue of information flow persists is that both types of model are capable of accounting for the empirical evidence. A preference for one type of model over the other is usually dictated by philosophical issues. Thus autonomous modelers prefer to avoid adding components (such as a reverse-direction connection) if these components can be dispensed with. (This principle, "Entities should not be unnecessarily multiplied," is known as Occam's razor, after William of Occam, who introduced it into philosophy.) This is especially so when such components may prove to be powerful and difficult to control, as is the case with reverse-direction information flow. The latter, if not held in check, can lead to hallucination—for instance, activation of a word on the basis of contextual probability, in defiance of there being no bottom-up evidence for it at all.

The interaction versus autonomy issue has stimulated a great deal of spoken-word recognition research, and this section can only skim the surface of the debate. The main body of results has come from explicit phoneme-decision tasks (see sections 12.4.1 and 12.4.2), and as already noted, the question of compensation for phoneme coarticulation (see section 12.4.3) has been the most empirically productive topic of all.

12.4.1 Lexical Effects in Phoneme Restoration and Phoneme Decision

Much exploration of the relation between phonetic and lexical processing has been conducted with these phoneme-level tasks. When listeners hear words in which a phoneme has been fully replaced by a noise, they usually report having heard an intact word with concurrent noise—the "phoneme restoration" phenomenon (Warren 1970). After all, hearing a brief noise (such as a cough) at the same time as an incoming speech signal is a common experience. Samuel (1981a, 1981b) extended the experimental use of phoneme restoration by comparing stimuli in which the noise fully replaced a phoneme with stimuli in which the noise was indeed only overlaid on the speech. Imagine the word *progress* with the first vowel excised and replaced by a cough, or the same word with the vowel there underneath a cough that extends exactly the length of the vowel and effectively masks it.

This comparison tested whether the phoneme restoration effect arises from top-down influence from the lexical level on perceptual judgments about phonemes; if it does, then listeners should hear these replaced and overlaid versions of *progress* as the same. It turned out that the replaced and overlaid versions were indeed hard to discriminate in real words, despite the fact that they were much more discriminable in nonwords (e.g., *crogless*, with the first vowel treated in the same way). Further, discriminability was worse in high-frequency words than in low-frequency words, and it was worse when the distorted word was preceded by the same word undistorted. There was more phoneme restoration in words with more than one completion (e.g., *-egion*) than for words with a unique completion (*-esion*; Samuel 1987). These results were interpreted in terms of top-down influences of lexical content on phonetic decision making; information from the lexicon indicating a probable phoneme made it harder to decide, from minimal acoustic evidence, whether the phoneme was indeed there.

Some early phoneme detection findings, though, suggested that lexical factors did not directly influence phoneme-level responses. For instance, although the frequency of a word before the target was found to affect RT, the frequency of the word bearing the target itself did not (Foss and Blank 1980; Foss and Gernsbacher 1983); so in the four sentences of example (12.1), the target phoneme [b] would be detected faster after *gray* (high frequency) than after *tan* (low frequency) but would not differ on *bucket* (high frequency) versus *buzzard* (low frequency).

(12.1) a. Sitting on the fence was a gray bucket
b. Sitting on the fence was a tan bucket
c. Sitting on the fence was a gray buzzard
d. Sitting on the fence was a tan buzzard

The same was true for lexical status; RTs were slower for targets preceded by a nonword rather than a real word, but they were not affected by whether the target itself was in a nonword or word (Foss and Blank 1980; Foss, Harwood, and Blank 1980). All this suggested that phonemes can be detected before the words they occur in are retrieved; that is, without lexical influence.

However, other findings suggested that lexical processes could affect phoneme detection. For instance, targets on real words produced faster RTs than targets on nonwords (Rubin, Turvey, and Van Gelder 1976), and targets (in initial position) were detected faster on high-frequency than on low-frequency words (as long as subjects expected targets to occur anywhere in a word and not just word initially; Segui and Frauenfelder 1986). In several studies, targets were responded to faster on highly predictable than on less predictable words (Morton and Long 1976; Dell and Newman 1980; Mehler and Segui 1987).

Resolving these apparently inconsistent findings required a model that allowed phoneme detection to occur in different ways or at different levels of processing, with task demands controlling which option prevailed. Cutler, Mehler, et al. (1987) manipulated characteristics of the stimuli and examined what happened to lexical status effects in phoneme detection. The degree of task monotony proved to be a relevant factor: if all items in an experiment (not just those with targets) are CVC monosyllables, for instance, the stimuli tend to be rather monotonous: *duck nace yill moss tip*. . . . Then, subjects shift attention away from the meaning and just concentrate on detecting the target phoneme. Word-nonword RT differences disappeared with such item sets. If the items were made rather less monotonous (just by adding some differently structured filler words: *cooler bupple huss value tip* . . .), subjects tended to attend more to word meaning, and word-nonword differences returned. Manipulating the number of simultaneous tasks that subjects had to do also made higher-level effects on phoneme detection come and go (Eimas, Hornstein, and Payton 1990; Eimas and Nygaard 1992): for instance, lexical effects appeared when there was a concurrent task that oriented attention to the lexical level (e.g., lexical decision) but not when a concurrent task oriented attention to acoustic processing (e.g., judging the relative duration of a tone and a word).

One way to explain all these findings at once is to assume that phoneme detection responses can always be made via more than one route—either prelexically or as a result of access to a lexical entry. In such a model, lexical effects can facilitate detection, but they cannot inhibit it (because a fast lexically based response can perhaps be made before a prelexically based response, but a response slowed by the lexicon will always have been beaten by the prelexically based response). This was consistent with a finding by Frauenfelder, Segui, and Dijkstra (1990) that detection of phonemes in nonwords was not affected by whether the nonwords were wordlike. A top-down model would have predicted that *vocabutary* would activate *vocabulary*, making the [t] in the nonword hard to detect, but this was not so (N.B. this experiment was actually in French). Wurm and Samuel (1997) followed this up with almost the same experiment, but in English, and found that detection in such nonwords (e.g., *vocabutary*, with a [t] target later than the UP of the base word) was actually faster than in matched other nonwords. They attributed this to an effect of attention allocation (which, they argued, might even mask top-down inhibitory influence).

A third study of the same kind involved nonwords that differed from real words in just a single feature of the final phoneme (e.g., *diminis*, *apprentish*, *arsenit*, *deposik*) or in more features (e.g., *automatis*, *academish*, *abolit*, *blemik*; Mirman, McClelland, and Holt 2005). Listeners monitored for these final phonemes; they detected the targets that were one-feature mismatches with real words more slowly than the targets that were further from real words. This was exactly the pattern of inhibition predicted by a top-down model (indeed, Mirman et al. confirmed the prediction in TRACE simulations). Given, say, [k] as target and *deposi-* as input, the lexical activation predicted that the next phoneme would be [t], different from the specified target. The result was inhibition, slowing detection of the target. The closer the predicted and target phonemes in number of features, the more inhibition there was.

All models allow lexical activation in real words to produce prediction of the correct target phoneme (and consequent faster RTs). Top-down models predict that this can also happen with wordlike nonwords. A model that explains the real-word facilitation by invoking more than one detection route does not predict facilitation in nonwords, because responses via the lexical route will only be possible with words. Phoneme detection in sets of nonwords such as *rigament*, *kigament*, and *maffiment* (with target [t] in each case) indeed revealed lexical facilitation (Connine et al. 1997; see chapter 3). Here, *rigament* differs from the real base word (*ligament*) only by one feature of the initial phoneme, *kigament* is a little further away (a multiple-feature difference), and *maffiment* is a control nonword. Detection was faster in the minimally altered nonwords than in the control, and it was faster for a one-feature than for a multiple-feature difference from the real word. The result was replicated in German (Bölte and Coenen 2002; Bölte and Connine 2004). These results, like those of Mirman et al., indicate a lexical influence on phonemes in nonwords. The model with more than one route cannot account for this.

12.4.2 Lexical Effects in Phonemic Categorization

As described in chapter 11 (see section 11.6), phonetic categorization decisions can be caused to shift. One of the factors that can induce such a shift is lexical status, and explorations of its effect have played an important role in the information flow debate.

In Ganong's (1980) original demonstration of the effect of lexical status on phoneme decisions, an ambiguous sound between [d] and [t] was interpreted differently before *-eep* versus *-eek*, because *deep* and *teak* are words but *deek* and *teep* are not. Listeners' categorizations produce more real-word outcomes than nonword outcomes. Was this evidence of top-down lexical influence on phoneme processing? A small research industry sprang up to test this. Lexical effects were found in slower, but not in faster, responses to such word-initial phonemes, which suggested response bias, not top-down influence from the lexicon (Fox 1984; Burton, Baum, and Blumstein 1989), and lexical effects were more likely with stimuli of relatively poor acoustic quality (Burton et al. 1989). The response bias argument led Connine and Clifton (1987) to compare the effect of lexical status on phonemic categorization with the effect of another response bias—namely, a varying monetary payoff. The effects turned out to differ: payoff produced a significant RT difference between consistent and inconsistent responses at the continuum endpoints but not at the category boundary, whereas lexical status produced a significant difference at the boundary but not at the endpoints. A manipulation of sentence context induced an effect at the phoneme boundary similar to the effect induced by lexical status (Borsky, Tuller, and Shapiro 1998).

In word-final position, one might expect that even more lexical influence would be available than in word-initial position. An ambiguous fricative between [s] and [ʃ] was indeed more likely to be judged as [s] after *ki-* (*kiss* is a word but *kish* is not) but as [ʃ] after *fi-* (*fish* is a word but *fiss* is not; McQueen 1991). However, here again the lexical effect seemed more like a decision bias than a top-down effect, because it again only appeared when the stimuli were of relatively poor acoustic quality, and it was certainly not larger than the effect found for word-initial decisions such as in *deep-teep*.

Dissociation between lexical effects and the inferred rate of speech effect supported another case against a top-down interpretation of lexical effects in phonemic categorization. In the inferred rate of speech effect (see chapter 11), decisions about temporally based categories are modulated by relative duration of successive speech components; if speech is fast, for instance, then relatively less duration is needed for a phoneme to sound long. This is part of prelexical processing, and it proves to be unaffected by whether responses are slow and fast. But in this it contrasts with the effects of lexical status; they disappear when subjects are required to respond very quickly (Miller and Dexter 1988), just as do effects of sentence context on phonetic categorization (Miller et al. 1984). The effect of inferred speaking rate on listeners' judgments of the relative goodness of individual exemplars of a category (Miller and Volaitis 1989) is also quite different from the effect of lexical status on such judgments—rate effects change the shape of the goodness judgment curve, altering which exemplars sound best, but lexical status merely affects decisions at the category boundary, without changing the curve shape (Allen and Miller 2001). The lexical effects are thus qualitatively different from other effects at the prelexical level.

Most lexical effects on phonemic categorization concern continua from words to nonwords, but an effect can also be found in continua with two nonword endpoints (Newman, Sawusch, and Luce 1997). A continuum from *gipe* to *kipe* elicited more [k] judgments in the ambiguous region, but on from *gice* to *kice* elicited somewhat more [g] judgments. All four of these endpoints are nonwords, but the *-ipe* pair has a denser lexical neighborhood with [k], whereas the *-ice* pair has a denser lexical neighborhood with [g]—that is, there are more real words in the sets *cap*, *cup*, and *keep* and *guess*, *goose*, and *ghost* than in the sets *gap* and *gape* or *case* and *kiss*. Just as with the lexical effects in phoneme detection, top-down models offer a more natural explanation of this effect than strictly bottom-up models of phonemic categorization do. As for phoneme detection, Newman et al. noted, the advantage for the real-word end of a word-nonword continuum might be explained in terms of categorization decisions via more than one route. But again, such an explanation would only allow responses via the lexical route for words, not for nonwords, however wordlike they were.

12.4.3 Compensation for Coarticulation

Compensation for phoneme coarticulation (see section 6.1 in chapter 6) has been a central issue in the debate about lexical-to-prelexical information flow. As this compensation affects the phonetic interpretation of acoustic information in the input, it ought to occur at a prelexical level. So, if this process itself were subject to lexical influence, then the lexical information would have to be operating top-down; in other words, there would be evidence for feedback from lexical to prelexical processing. To test this hypothesis, Elman and McClelland (1988) appended a single ambiguous consonant between [s] and [ʃ] to the strings *Christma-* (where [s] would give *Christmas*) versus *fooli-* (where [ʃ] would produce *foolish*). These were presented as preceding context for another ambiguous phoneme, between [t] and [k], beginning the syllable *-apes*. The string could therefore be interpreted in its entirety as *Christmas tapes* or *capes*, and *foolish tapes* or *capes*. The crucial data concerned how the [t]-[k] continuum was interpreted; if [t]-[k] decisions were affected by the preferred interpretation of the ambiguous fricative, then it could not be due to acoustic cues in the fricative, because this was always the same, but it could be due to feedback from the lexicon determining phonetic decisions. A shift of [t]-[k] judgments, in the same direction as Mann and Repp (1981) had found with real [s]-[ʃ] preceding context, was indeed observed: the ambiguous stop was judged somewhat more often as [t] after the ambiguous fricative on *fooli-* but somewhat more often as [k] after the ambiguous fricative on *Christma-*. This striking finding launched a string of follow-up studies and gave heart to the proponents of top-down information flow.

However, it was possible to simulate the result in a strictly bottom-up framework. Norris (1993) trained a model to map featural input onto phonemic—or phonemic and lexical—outputs. The model learned that [t] and [k] have different features after [s] versus [ʃ]. It also learned transitional probabilities (TP)—which sequences of sounds are most likely to be encountered. (As chapters 4 and 8 showed, these probabilities are easily learned from speech input, even by very young infants.) With ambiguous input replacing both the fricative and the stop, the model used the preceding phonetic context to identify the fricative, based on the TP. Then it allowed this fricative decision to influence decisions about the stop. The fricative decisions could not have been directly affected by lexical information, because there were no lexical-to-phonetic pathways in the model.

This raised the question of whether the listeners in Elman and McClelland's (1988) experiment could also have been profiting from TP information. After a schwa (as in the final syllable of *Christmas*) an [s] is more likely to occur in English than a [ʃ], whereas after [ɪ] (as in *foolish*), a [ʃ] is more likely than an [s]. Two new sets of materials were constructed by Pitt and McQueen (1998). One set compared *bush* versus *juice*—words with a lexical bias (given that swapping the two fricatives makes two nonwords) but no TP bias to either of the fricatives. This set could test whether a lexically consistent compensation effect would appear with unbiased materials. Another set of materials consisted of nonwords—which, of course, cannot exercise direct lexical influence. In these nonwords, TP induced strong bias in favor of one or the other fricative. Thus *ders* is [s] biased because the lexicon contains many words in which this syllable nucleus precedes [s] (*curse*, *hearse*, *person*, etc.) but few in which it precedes [ʃ] (*exertion*, etc.), whereas the bias in *naish* is the reverse: very many words with [eɪʃ] (*station*, *patient*, *gracious*, etc.), fewer with [eɪs] (*place*, *basin*, etc.). These materials could test whether a TP bias could affect the compensation effect.

Syllables beginning *bu-*, *jui-*, *der-*, and *nai-*, all with the same final [s]-[ʃ]-ambiguous fricative, were used as preceding context for a [t]-[k]-ambiguous stop preceding

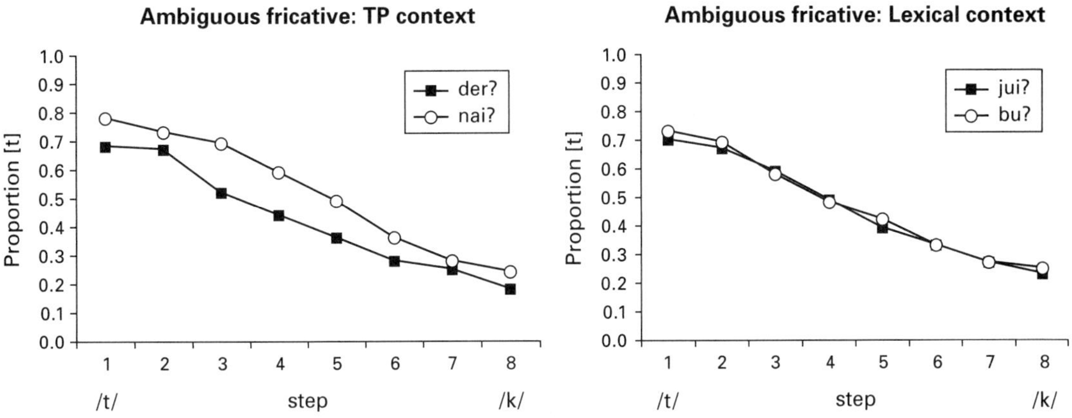

Figure 12.3
Categorizations of an ambiguous sound between [t] and [k] at the beginning of *-apes*, after another ambiguous sound between [s] and [ʃ]. In both cases the decisions about [s] versus [ʃ] were shifted, either by TP (for *ders*, *naish*) or by lexical identity (for *juice*, *bush*). But does this shift for the fricative decision carry over to the decision about the stop consonant that follows? The answer is yes for the TP-induced shifts (left panel), no for the lexically induced shifts (right panel). (Data from Pitt and McQueen 1998.)

-apes, as in Elman and McClelland's study. Listeners had to make decisions about both the fricative and the stop. Figure 12.3 shows the results. When there was TP bias but no lexical bias, compensation for coarticulation did occur: listeners were more likely to report *capes* after *der-*, and *tapes* after *nai-* (left panel of the figure). But when there was lexical bias but no TP bias, no compensation on the [t]-[k] decisions occurred—the *tapes-capes* categorization functions after *bu-* and *jui-* (right panel of the figure) were indistinguishable. Importantly, a lexical effect was indeed observed on the ambiguous fricative: *jui-* produced significantly more [s] judgments, and *bu-* produced significantly more [ʃ] judgments. Listeners were thus more inclined to choose responses making words (*juice* and *bush*) not nonwords (*juish* and *bus*), just as Ganong (1980) and others had found. But these lexically influenced fricative decisions did not in turn influence the stop decisions.

The important finding here is the dissociation between the effects on the fricative and on the following stop. There were indeed lexical effects on how listeners interpreted the fricative. The effects did not, however, influence how listeners interpreted the stop.

Note that Elman and McClelland's (1988) words (*Christmas*, *foolish*) were longer than those in Pitt and McQueen's (1998) study (*bush*, *juice*), and greater length might produce more lexical effect; long pairs such as *distinguish*, *consensus* (preceding *tame*/*came*) indeed elicited stronger compensation effects than short pairs

(Samuel and Pitt 2003). Another study involved short words (*bliss*, *brush*, followed by *tape*/*cape*) in which the TP, the authors computed, should have worked in a direction opposite to lexical effects (Magnuson et al. 2003); lexical compensation effects were found. However, in this experiment there was an initial training phase focused on the lexical stimulus endpoints, and this was crucial, McQueen, Jesse, and Norris (2009) found. If Magnuson et al.'s study was replicated exactly, the same results appeared, but if the training phase was changed, the results in the main experiment changed. A training phase that focused on the nonword endpoints (*blish*, *bruss*) produced a reverse compensation effect in the main experiment (i.e., the ambiguous stop tended to be judged as [t] after *bli*[s/ʃ], but as [k] after *bru*[s/ʃ], although lexical effects would predict the opposite). A training phase in which lexical and nonword endpoints were equally balanced produced no compensation effects at all. Note that in all these cases the actual experimental phases were identical; only the preliminary training varied. There seemed to be strong effects of perceptual learning in this type of experimental situation, but there was no evidence for top-down lexical effects on perception.

12.4.4 The Merge Model

The debate about lexical effects in prelexical processing has not been helped by being so dependent on evidence from tasks that require categorical decisions, such as phoneme categorization or phoneme detection. The picture of speech processing sketched in this book has no natural role for explicit decisions about phonemic identity during processing. Continuous bottom-up cascade of probabilistically weighted information means that prelexical processes do not have to commit irretrievably to categorical decisions. Communication from the prelexical to lexical levels in speech processing is probabilistic, with the weighting of category probabilities going up and down as the input alters.

Nonetheless, sometimes we do need to be able to make explicit decisions about phonemes. Learning new words or the names of people may be one reason. Correcting others' mispronunciations may be another; detecting puns and slips of the tongue yet another.

These abilities require access to a decision mechanism that assesses phoneme identity. But there is no reason to have such a decision mechanism involved in every speech perception operation, where the goal is to understand the speaker's message as rapidly as possible, rather than to judge the identity of the phonemes that make it up. That means, then, that the explicit phonemic-decision tasks are not tapping directly into normal speech processing. This is hardly surprising, given that no laboratory task is fully natural. Lexical tasks may seem a bit closer to natural, in the sense that they call on the level at which selections have to be made in listening, but even these do not map directly onto any aspect of our natural experience with speech. We can easily decide (in lexical decision) whether a spoken form is a word we know—but usually we do not have to do this; we assume it will be so, because people will not say nonwords at us. Why should they? They want to communicate, and they can best do this by using the words we all have in common. The phonemic decision tasks are likewise unnatural. However, like the lexical tasks, they draw on capacities that we must be able to exercise (in learning about new words and so on). The challenge for the psycholinguist is therefore to work out exactly what the evidence from experiments with each of these tasks implies about the structure of the language processing system.

The decision processes in such tasks as phoneme detection or phoneme categorization lead to a phoneme identification as response. But suppose that the normal cascaded speech processing stream involves no explicit phoneme identifications. Then we must attribute the output used for the phonemic decision tasks to a separate decision mechanism, which would also be needed for learning new names, detecting puns, and other such occasional tasks that are not an intrinsic part of recognition. Because we know that phoneme decisions can be affected by lexical factors, the decision mechanism could be one that integrates information from both speech input and lexical structure to arrive at a decision about a particular phoneme. The existence of this separate mechanism would have no implications for the flow of information in spoken-word recognition, which could be, as described, continuous, cascaded, and strictly bottom-up.

Such a model, constructed by Norris et al. (2000), correctly simulated the outcome of many of the experiments described here. The model is called Merge (because it merges prelexical and lexical information in arriving at its decision), and its architecture is sketched in figure 12.4. Using the figure, consider what might be happening in phoneme-detection experiments such as those of Cutler, Mehler, et al. (1987), where the phonemes occurred in CVC items such as *tip*, *bip*, *bid*, and *tid*. Prelexical processing sends a continuous flow of information to the lexicon and at the same time to the phoneme detector. Given that the input in these experiments was unambiguous and not distorted or masked in any way, the activation will be heavily weighted to a single phoneme, with only very weak support offered for similar phonemes. If the target is [t], and the input is *tid*, then the phoneme detector will receive from prelexical processing strong support for [t] and perhaps a little weak residual support for similar consonants (alveolar [d] and [n]; voiceless [k] and [θ]; other stops such as [d], [k], etc.). From the lexicon it will receive only a little weak support in favor of [t] from words beginning *ti-* such as *tick*, *tilt*, or *tingle*. The prelexical support for [t] effectively drives the response. If the input is *tip*, what the phoneme detector receives from the prelexical processor is exactly the same, but

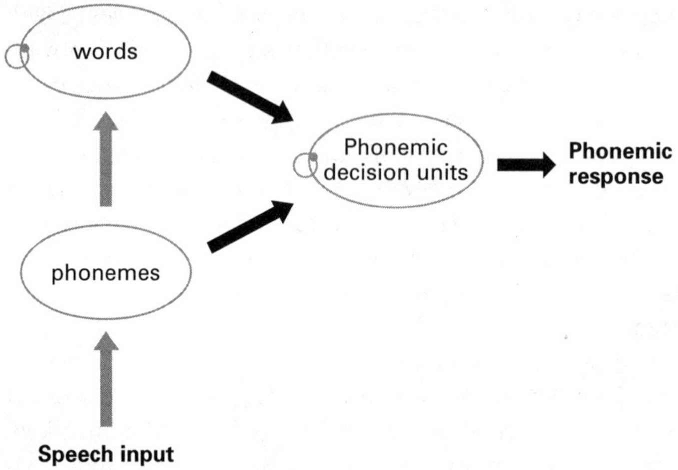

Figure 12.4
The Merge model of phonemic decision making. In normal processing of speech, information flows unidirectionally from the input to the lexicon. Words are matched or mismatched by the input, and the unit of mismatch is, most often, effectively phonemic (e.g., the word is *bit*, not *bid*). However, explicit identification of phonemes is no part of the process. When such explicit identifications are needed (for learning new names, interpreting puns, or taking part in phonemic decision experiments), then a dedicated phonemic decision process can make them, drawing both on information from the speech input and on relevant information from other sources, such as the lexicon.

what it receives from the lexical level is augmented, because activation of *tip* in the lexicon adds support to [t]. The detection response can then be based on a merger of prelexical and lexical support.

However, it does not have to be based on both. The detector can allow one or the other source of information to weigh more heavily, as a function of task demands. Thus in Cutler, Mehler, et al.'s (1987) experiments, as we saw before, a monotonous string of exclusively CVC words and nonwords caused listeners to focus on the prelexical processing alone in making their decisions, whereas a slightly more varied list increased attention to lexical processing and, in turn, increased the contribution of lexical information to phoneme decisions. The monotonous list led to no effects of lexical status on phoneme decisions; the more varied list led to faster responses in, for instance, *tip* than *tid*. In the Merge model, these effects can differ because of changes in how the decision process weights sources of input, without anything in the flow of information from prelexical to lexical processing being influenced.

The Merge model provided an explanation of how lexical effects could show up in nonwords (as in Newman et al.'s [1997] phoneme categorization experiment in which subjects preferred to respond with *kipe* and *gice* rather than *gipe* and *kice*, or Connine et al.'s [1997] phoneme-detection advantage for [t] in the *ligament*-like *rigament*, or Mirman et al.'s [2005] inhibition of [t] in *arsenit*). It is not that what is in the lexicon affects how nonwords are first processed as they are heard; it affects any decision about speech input, including decisions about nonwords. Merge also accounts for all the findings of faster responses to words than to nonwords, as well as for the difficulty of rejecting nonwords in lexical decision when they contain coarticulatory information consistent with a real word (see chapter 3). Likewise, it accounts for the finding of Pitt and Samuel (1995) of greater lexical effects for words with a later rather than early UP (i.e., a greater advantage for [m] detection in *formulate* than in *dormitory* over their respective matched nonwords); as Pitt and Samuel calculated, words with late UP formed part of a larger competitor population. In Merge, decisions about their component phonemes would thus be informed by more input from the lexicon.

12.4.5 Is Feedback Ever Necessary?

Flow of information continues to be one of the most active issues in speech perception modeling. As remarked earlier, the philosophical preferences of the participants play a role; many of us cannot see why a more complicated model, with added directional connectivity, should ever be chosen if a simpler model can account for the same data. Moreover, although it is obviously good to be able to call on higher-level information to resolve resistant lower-level ambiguity, it is hard to see why one should use top-down flow of information to do it. The information that comes top-down will be consistent with whichever word the bottom-up information most strongly supports. But if that word is already most strongly supported, more support changes nothing. The success rate of word recognition, which is presumably the listener's desired bottom line, cannot be improved by adding top-down feedback; only the path to achieving it can be made more complicated.

Where lexical effects on prelexical processing are reported, they are often noticeably weak (see the meta-analysis by Pitt and Samuel 1993, as well as Samuel and Pitt 2003 and McQueen et al. 2009). The evidence cited in support of top-down flow is largely from explicit detection and categorization tasks, often involves effects in nonwords, and often rests on inhibition rather than facilitation; but such tasks do not form part of normal listening, nonwords do not form part of normal speech input, and inhibition offers no positive argument for adding processing complexity. Also extraneous to normal listening, but called on in this debate, is selective adaptation. This term refers to the effect of repeated presentation of a word containing a given phoneme on listeners' later phonetic categorizations: the proportion of response choices for the adapted phoneme is reduced. Selective adaptation can be induced by words in which the adapting phoneme is ambiguous or masked, but its identity is biased by lexical context (Samuel 1997, 2001); just as repeated presentation of *bet* would cause a shift away from [b] in a later categorization task, so did repeated presentation of *alphabet* with the [b] masked by noise. Recall, however, that selective adaptation of phoneme decisions differs, both in its buildup and dissipation, from perceptual learning about phonemes (Bertelson et al. 2003). Repeated presentation of the same sounds over and over again is not part of our usual linguistic experience (unless, perhaps, there is a two-year-old somewhere nearby). Perceptual learning, in contrast, is a natural process for adapting to new talkers, new situations, or language change.

Indeed, the very fact that perceptual learning happens is evidence that change in the input has been detected, and not overridden from the top down. If top-down information could always resolve every case of phonemic uncertainty, then there would be no need to adjust phonemic categorization at the prelexical level, and in consequence there would be no generalization of learning to new words. The lexical influence that results in these adjustments of prelexical processing is an error-correcting signal, resulting from detection of an imperfect match to the lexicon; it is not an automatic flow of lexical information that tells prelexical processing what its output should be. Its benefit is that it tailors future prelexical processing, not that it guides current lexical processing.

A clear case for how top-down flow of information in speech perception could significantly help listeners in their everyday life—and in particular, better equip them for future processing in the way that perceptual learning does—has thus yet to be made. Still, the debate is surely not over. New ideas still appear, and yet more will appear in the future. For instance, the vowel normalization first demonstrated by Ladefoged and Broadbent (1957; see chapter 11) proved to be independent of lexical processing, in that its magnitude is unaffected by whether a context phrase consists of real words (e.g., *toen was hier __ gezegd* 'then was here said') versus nonwords containing the same vowels (*noet fas tier __ ketegd*; Mitterer 2006). The formant values of the vowels here had a constant influence, irrespective of whether words cued their phonemic identity, which indicates that the normalization process was sensitive to the acoustic properties of the vowels only. Likewise, memory traces of distorted words presented for serial recall are unaffected by whether higher-level information is available to cue their identity (Frankish 2008). In this study, the addition of visual information succeeded in making an unclear word sound clear to listeners, but the memory effects were just the same as for words unaccompanied by such disambiguation. Again, the implication was that the laying down of a trace in acoustic memory was impervious to anything but the acoustic information in the speech signal. So far, the bottom line of these studies is the bottom line of this section: there is no evidence that compels the assumption of direct influence of higher-level information on lower-level processes.

12.5 Conclusion: Universal and Language Specific

The major change from the beginning of psycholinguistics (in the 1960s and 1970s) to the present day has been, in my view, the one that has made this book what it is—the shift from a concentration on the universals of linguistic processing alone to a recognition that the universals can be most fruitfully studied through language-specificity, and that language-specificity is central to linguistic processing. This book would have been much thinner had psycholinguistics not made this move.

Changes won't stop happening, and psycholinguistics won't stand still. Many gaps in our knowledge remain. Here are a few areas in which the gaps stand out:

1. How can language-specificity best be incorporated in computational processing models? Should the model be a learning device (like the human infant), or are there principled ways to constrain language-specificity?
2. What is the contribution of individual differences to initial language learning, and to what extent do such differences also characterize adult listening? What are the dimensions of linguistic variation across individuals anyway? Are some aspects of language-specific structure more variable across individuals than others?
3. Where is the first computational model of processing incorporating prosodic structure? (Cutler and Donselaar [2001] could run Shortlist simulations capturing the segmental match and mismatch effects of interword competition in their study, but the suprasegmental effects could not be modeled because Shortlist, like all other models, has no way to represent them.)
4. Why is prosodic structure (almost completely) missing from so many other areas of listening research too, such as nonnative listening? Why do studies of prosodic perception hardly ever involve direct crosslinguistic comparisons?
5. How does language change work, exactly? Individuals change their phoneme production to keep pace with their language community (see chapter 11). But the perceptual flexibility that underlies this also allows adaptation of a phoneme category boundary to be specific to the situation and the speaker, with no implications for perception of other speakers, or in other situations. When does perception induce a shift in production? What is the tipping point? Is an overwhelming majority of input episodes the crucial factor, or is it a majority of different speakers contributing the episodes? In either case, is there a relation to the role of immersion in perceptual learning for an L2?
6. How should we model the joint use of episodic and abstract knowledge in spoken-word recognition? As the present chapter has made clear, neither an abstract-only nor an episodic-only model can account for what we know. But we do not yet understand how the two types of knowledge are used together.
7. What is the best way to make computational models of spoken-word processing more able to deal with real speech? There have been all too few attempts at rap-

12. Choosing the Right Experimental Task

Experimental methods differ in where they tap into the process of speech recognition. Choosing a task for a psycholinguistic purpose means first deciding exactly what the job is—that is, where in the model of speech recognition an effect is predicted, expected, or feared to occur.

Do we predict an effect on speech segmentation? Then we might choose word-spotting. Do we predict an effect on lexical activation? Then eye-tracking or cross-modal priming are the first tasks to look at. That's the first step.

But if we use cross-modal priming, should the primes be fragments? Or whole words? Should they be spoken in sentences or in isolation? With what prime-target relationship—identity or associative? And if we use eye-tracking, should the display be pictures? Or printed words? Or natural scenes? Should the subjects have to do something or just passively listen? Answering all these questions, too, depends on formulating the experimental expectations exactly, as well as on considerations such as whether the language can supply the necessary materials (you cannot do eye-tracking with pictures if there are not enough picturable concepts to fit your requirements; you cannot do lexical decision on monosyllables if every permissible syllable of the language is meaningful). The existing literature is the best guide as to what issues each task can illuminate.

Only ten tasks have been described in these panels in some detail. They are all behavioral tasks that might be used in any psycholinguistic laboratory. More detail about them, and lots of illustrative references, can be found in Grosjean and Frauenfelder 1996. Some less-frequent tasks have appeared at various points in the text (e.g., word identification in noise, in chapters 3 and 10; word reversal, in chapters 4 and 6). Obviously, there are other experimental methods, too. Some require more specialist equipment, such as the various brain imaging methods, or recording of electrophysiological responses in the brain (ERP evidence was cited at various points in the text, from chapter 1 on). Brain methods do not entail any particular behavioral task, although they can all be combined with such a task if need be. The reason for concentrating on the behavioral tasks in these panels was to make clear the logic (and the usefulness) of the laboratory work of psycholinguistics.

If none of the existing tasks seems right, a new task can always be invented. Often when a new task is invented, a resulting publication describes it and argues for it in detail; it is useful to watch out for such publications and imagine what one could use the new task for. (Some examples of this genre are the pause detection task of Mattys and Clark [2002] or the continuous tracking task of Spivey, Grosjean, and Knoblich [2005].)

But the fundamental questions for choosing a task remain: What do I want to understand, and at what level of processing do I expect to find it? And what measure does a task deliver, and how does that measure relate to the question I want to answer?

prochement between engineering models with a real front end and psychological models with a real vocabulary and the ability to simulate human performance (such as Scharenborg et al. 2005). Shortlist B (Norris and McQueen 2008), with its simulations based on probabilities derived from a large speech perception study, is also a step in the right direction. But how best to obtain all the language-specific probability sets needed by such a model?

These questions are not insoluble, and reliable tools are on hand to help solve them. The behavioral techniques used in the research recounted here are, in most cases, pretty well understood (the most useful of them have been described in some detail in individual panels in earlier chapters, and see panel 12 for how to choose between them). Of course, one of the front lines of current progress is our understanding of the brain mechanisms underlying language processing, and a future area of progress should be the genetic underpinnings of language ability. But progress in neuroscience and genetics will not render redundant an understanding of the mental mechanisms and representations involved in all language processing, including listening to speech.

Although the central message of this book is that listening to speech is, from beginning to end, tailored to a specific language, in this ending chapter there has in fact been relatively little language-specificity. This is because the chapter has dealt largely with general issues of architecture—how processes relate to one another, for instance—and these architectural principles are putatively universal. At least, the author of this book cannot imagine what type of linguistic variation would induce language-specific variation in the basic architecture of listening, such as whether top-down information flow is necessary. (As usual, I'd be happy to be proven wrong here—not, of course, because I want to be wrong; I don't—but because overturning basic assumptions pushes us ahead.)

The view of native listening that emerges from the evidence summarized in this book is one characterized by optimal efficiency. The architecture of listening allows information to be exploited as soon as it is available. What the listener wants to extract from incoming speech is the message intended by the speaker. The basic units of a message (of most messages, anyway) are words. Words are the meaningful units stored in memory and contacted by speech signals. Incoming speech continuously modulates the relative likelihood of word candidates, with use being made of whatever acoustic information is relevant, regardless of its level of phonetic or phonological description. At the same time, situation-specific likelihoods (discourse context and utterance context, so far) and overall likelihoods (word frequencies, transition probabilities, grammatical construction frequencies) can be drawn on to sharpen the candidate selection and speed the process of understanding that message.

So far, so universal. But language-specificity lurks at every turn. The words are language specific, so what exactly is stored in lexical memory, and hence what units are activated by speech input, differs a lot across languages. Segmentation is universally required (a spoken language where segmentation would be unnecessary also defies imagination); but language-specific phonological structure is exploited to segment the input into words. This structure includes phoneme sequence constraints; both the permissibility and the probability of such sequences are language specific, but they are incorporated into the processing architecture where they can be used as early as possible. (Recall that Pitt and McQueen [1998] showed that the effects of phonetic transition probabilities are distinct from the effects of lexical status.) And finally, the phonetic repertoire is language specific, so different dimensions of acoustic information in the signal may need to be processed in the first place.

But further, language-specificity is found not only in the acoustic dimensions and the structural elements and their ordering, but in effects of the system as a whole. We have seen that the same phonetic distinctions signaled by the same acoustic cues are apprehended differently as a function of the other members of the phonetic repertoire from which they must be distinguished. Likewise, we have seen that aspects of word structure signaled acoustically in the same way in different languages may be relevant or irrelevant for lexical selection, depending on their patterning in the vocabulary as a whole.

The efficiency of native listening is responsible for this too. For every aspect of speech signals that is used in listening, we can be confident that it is used not because it is there but because it is useful.

The interplay of universal and language specific can be seen in every one of the preceding chapters. What spoken language is like is partly dependent on the structure of human brains and articulators (hence universal) and partly on the structure of individual linguistic systems (hence specific). Spoken-word recognition involves activation of phonological units, with effective competition between them as their relative probability is modulated by the input, and it involves separation of phonological from conceptual representations. This is a sketch of the architecture of all listening, but the precise implementation—how the input modulates probabilities, and the structure of the representations—is determined by what is most efficient for the language in question. Listening to speech in any language involves segmentation, but the cues that listeners use to segment utterances are those that are most efficient for their native language. The Possible Word Constraint is available to infants before they have a vocabulary, but whether it is useful in adult word recognition depends on the probabilities of the language-specific vocabulary. Fine phonetic detail and prosodic structure are always available for use in listening, but how and where they are useful depends on the structure of vocabularies and grammars. Infants learn whatever language is presented in their environment, and what they learn allows them to make their processing as usefully specific as possible, as early as possible. The downside of such early specialization is that nonnative listening is less efficient than native listening, but again, how exactly this discrepancy manifests itself depends on both the native and the nonnative languages. Among the many positive consequences of the early specialization are the robustness and flexibility characteristic of listening—at least, of listening in the native language.

Although the story is far from complete, it is clear that spoken-word recognition research has come far in the few decades of its existence. We not only have a picture of the architecture of listening, and the extent to which this may or may not vary, but we have above all come to realize its most important property: its adaptation to cross-language variation, as a part of its dependence on listening experience. Listening to speech is exquisitely adapted to each listener's speech experience. Listening to this book as a spoken text would have enriched that experience in a way that reading it as a printed text never could!

Phonetic Appendix

Notations between square brackets, in this book, use the International Phonetic Alphabet (IPA), an agreed way of representing the sounds of speech in any and all languages. Here the transcriptions do not distinguish between phonemes (distinctive interword contrasts) and their precise phonetic realizations, which can vary across contexts. Rather, the notations are broad phonetic representations serving both purposes.

The phonetic notation of sounds is based, as can be seen in the charts, on how the sounds are articulated. In this appendix the phonetic terminology that occurs in the text is briefly explained, and the sounds referred to are listed with examples. There are many more speech sounds in the full IPA list, and many more subtle distinctions between sounds. For more detail, see the *Handbook of the International Phonetic Association*, http://www.langsci.ucl.ac.uk/ipa/, or Ladefoged and Maddieson 1996.

How Sounds Are Categorized

1. Vowels

Vowels are categorized by the vocal tract shape created by positioning the tongue as the vocal cords vibrate. There are two principal dimensions: (a) vowel **height**, contrasting *high* (or *close*), where the tongue body is domed high and close to the roof of the mouth, to *low* (or *open*), where the tongue body is lower and there is more open space between tongue and roof of mouth; (b) vowel **backness**, which contrasts *front*, where the highest point of the tongue is nearer the front of the mouth, to *back*, where it is further back. Also relevant is whether the lips are **rounded** as the vowel is spoken. Simple vowels are called monophthongs. Many vowels are diphthongs; that is, two vowels functioning as one for the purposes of phonemic contrast between words.

2. Consonants

Consonants are categorized by (a) the **place** of articulation involved in saying them, whereby in most cases the reference is to what some part of the tongue touches; (b) the **manner** in which the articulation occurs; and (c) for stops and fricatives, whether there is **voicing**, that is, whether the vocal cords are vibrating (*voiced*) or not (*voiceless*).

The **places** of articulation (not all of them relevant to English) are:

bilabial: the lips
dental: the teeth
labiodental: upper teeth and lower lip
alveolar: the ridge at the front of the palate, behind the upper teeth
postalveolar: the back of the alveolar ridge (used when the blade of the tongue touches)
retroflex: the back of the alveolar ridge (used when the curled tongue tip touches)
palatal: hard palate
velar: velum, or soft palate
uvular: uvula
pharyngeal: pharynx
glottal: glottis

And the **manners** of articulation are:

stop (or *plosive*): the airflow through the vocal tract is fully closed off, then released
fricative: there is frication as two articulators in the vocal tract are brought close together
nasal: airflow goes out through the nose instead of the mouth
lateral: incomplete closure, so airflow runs along the sides of the mouth
approximant: two articulators are close, but not close enough to produce frication
affricate: a stop closely followed by a fricative (again two articulations that act as one)
tap, *flap*: brief contact between tongue and (usually) alveolar ridge

Phonetic Symbols

1. Vowels

[æ] as in *pad*
[ɛ] as in *bed*
[ɪ] as in *bid*
[ɒ] as in *pod* (British)
[ʌ] as in *bud*

[i] as in *bead*	
[u] as in *booed*	
[ʊ] as in *put*	
[ə] as in *pedestrian*	
[ɜ] as in *bird* (British)	
[ɔ] as in *bawd*	
[ɑ] as in *dada*	
[o] as in U.S. *bode*, or Dutch *Oktober*	
[oʊ] as in *bode* (British)	diphthong
[aʊ] as in *pout*	diphthong
[ɔɪ] as in *buoyed*	diphthong
[eɪ] as in *paid*	diphthong
[aɪ] as in *bide*	diphthong
[ɛə] as in *bear* (British)	diphthong
[ø] mid front rounded; as in Finnish *näkö*	
[y] high front rounded; as in French *rue*, German *Bücher*, even in English *pew*	
[ɚ] as in *bird* (U.S.)	
[a] as in French *pas*	
[e] as in French *thé*	

2. Consonants

[p] as in *pay*	voiceless bilabial stop
[t] as in *tea*	voiceless alveolar stop
[k] as in *car* or *key*	voiceless velar stop
[b] as in *bee*	voiced bilabial stop
[d] as in *day*	voiced alveolar stop
[g] as in *gay*	voiced velar stop
[s] as in *say*	voiceless alveolar fricative
[f] as in *fee*	voiceless labiodental fricative
[θ] as in *thigh*	voiceless dental fricative
[ʃ] as in *shy*	voiceless postalveolar fricative
[z] as in *zoo*	voiceless alveolar fricative
[v] as in *vie*	voiced labiodental fricative
[ð] as in *they*	voiced dental fricative
[ʒ] as in *measure*	voiced postalveolar fricative
[ʧ] as in *chew*	voiceless postalveolar affricate
[ʤ] as in *jay*	voiced postalveolar affricate
[ç] as in German *Licht*	voiceless palatal fricative

[x] as in Scottish *loch*, (Southern) Dutch *licht* or German *lacht*	voiceless velar fricative
[h] as in *hay*	voiceless glottal fricative
[m] as in *may*	bilabial nasal
[n] as in *knee* or *new*	alveolar nasal
[ŋ] as in *hang*	velar nasal
[ɴ] as in Japanese *san*	uvular nasal
[l] as in *lie*	alveolar lateral approximant
[r] as in *ray* or *wry*	alveolar approximant
[j] as in *you*	palatal approximant
[w] as in *way*	velar approximant
[ɽ] as in Japanese *tempura*	postalveolar flap

A useful machine-readable phonetic alphabet is SAMPA (www.phon.ucl.uk/home/sampa).

Notes

Chapter 1

1. The sound [a] is what the doctor wants to hear (*say aah. . .*). The square bracket notation represents a phonetic symbol; see the Phonetic Appendix for more on this.

2. This does not entail that *mama* is assigned the same meaning in all languages it occurs in. In Pitjatjantjara, *mama* means 'father', and *baba* means 'dog'.

3. The Japanese (but not the English) subjects detected the targets in Japanese *kinshi* or *taoru*, and also English *candy*, more rapidly than the targets in *inori*, *tokage*, or *canopy*. Chapter 4 explains why.

4. The English study (Broersma and Cutler 2011) is described in chapter 9.

Chapter 2

1. This illustration is from a demonstration made and used in lectures for many years by Pim Levelt. Many thanks to him for permission to use it. For him, the chief point of the demonstration is to call attention to the rapidity with which speakers produce so many separate articulatory gestures, expressing the words and propositions of their message. Speech being a communicative undertaking, the demonstration works just as well for the listener's task in extracting the message.

2. Hay and Bauer (2007) explain this correlation with findings from listening, which can be found in chapters 8 and 11: learning phonemic contrasts is easier if there is evidence from different talkers. In a larger population, evidence is likely to be heard from more talkers, so more distinct phonemic categories can be established.

3. This is called Zipf's Law (Zipf 1935). It is one of the many interesting properties of word frequency distributions, which contain a huge majority of very rare members (Baayen 2001). As will become clear, Zipf's Law plays a role in language processing; of course, it holds for all languages.

4. The vowels in the base forms are tense; those in the derived forms are lax.

5. Perhaps it would be interesting to replicate the ALL experiment in a consonant-mutating language such as Welsh.

6. Ferrets don't do too badly, either (Mesgarani et al. 2008).

7. Note that changes in closed-class usage not only occur rarely, but when they do occur they tend to meet strong resistance from members of a language community. Once there were attempts to replace the pairs *he* and *she* and *him* and *her*, with a non-sex-marked pronoun in English; they did not work. In contemporary Dutch, nothing exercises letter writers to the daily papers quite as much as the steady spread of the casual-speech usage *hun hebben*—which is roughly equivalent to saying *them have* instead of *they have* in English. In contrast, most open-class additions and alterations in language pass unmarked by comment.

Chapter 3

1. Connine, Blasko, and Titone (1993) did, however, find priming from nonwords similar to associates of a target, if nonword and associate differed in just a single phonological feature. In their study, *marriage* primed RING, but so, to a reduced extent, did the nonwords *narriage* and *mallage*.

2. Quantity distinctions produce a measurable pronunciation difference. They should not be confused with spelling differences, as in English where there is no pronunciation difference in the [l] of *balance* and *ballad*, or the [i:] of *be* and *bee*.

Chapter 4

1. English orthography, characteristically idiosyncratic, refuses to reflect such exclusions. The letter *h* thus happily turns up in word-final position. But *speech* ends with the affricate [tʃ], *bath* with [θ], and *mynah* rhymes with *China*. No [h] sound occurs anywhere in these.

2. This latter version resembles the prosody production technique called reiterant speech (Larkey 1983), in which an utterance is mimicked with repetitions of a single syllable such as *ma-*. If *mamama* is said in a way that mimics *syllable*, then the first *ma-* is strongest; if *mamama* mimics *detection*, the second *ma-* is strongest, and so on.

3. The renaissance character of the recent ALL literature was at first not obvious to all. Now there are calls to bring together the implicit learning literature about grammar learning and the statistical learning literature about segmentation; see, for example, Perruchet and Pacton 2006.

Chapter 5

1. The principal source of the difference is again that compound words are listed as unitary lemmas in Dutch but as separate words in English; *nail*, *file*, *polish*, *nail file*, and *nail polish* are listed under three one-word lemmas (*nail*, *file*, *polish*) in the English lexicon but five in the Dutch lexicon (*nagel*, *vijl*, *lak*, *nagelvijl*, *nagellak*). Parts of compounds cannot be ruled out by such a PWC operation, given that the residue is obviously always a whole word. As noted in chapter 2, this orthographic convention says nothing about segmentation and competition in listening. Compounds may be processed as units by all listeners, and then *nail* should be considered as an embedding in *nail file* and *nail polish* in English, as it is in the computations for Dutch.

2. Note that the primary meaning of *jumper* in British English has little semantic relation to its original stem, *jump*, just as the alternative English term for the same article of clothing, *sweater*, has little semantic relation to the stem *sweat*.

Chapter 6

1. Neither of these is actually a word in Dutch. Without the [t], *blas* and *blan* are also not words.

Chapter 7

1. Recent evidence from Italian (Sulpizio and McQueen 2011) suggests that Italian listeners may ignore suprasegmental stress cues in words that have default stress patterns, but attend to them when stress marking deviates from the majority pattern. More about this study can be learned from chapter 12.

2. See Pierrehumbert and Beckman 1988 for more detail.

Chapter 8

1. The very large literature on phonetic acquisition cannot be completely covered here; see Eimas, Miller, and Jusczyk 1987 for a review of how the first discoveries illuminated categorization skills, Jusczyk 1997 for a complete review of the field to that date, and Kuhl et al. 2008 and Saffran, Werker, and Werner 2006 for more recent results. The latter in particular describe how phonetic skills depend on developing auditory abilities. A review of infant auditory development can be found in Moore and Linthicum 2007.

Chapter 9

1. "The phoneme and the basic phonological representations of our native language are so tightly coupled to our perception that even when we hear words (or sentences) from a language with quite different phonology, we tend to analyze these words in terms of the phonemic representations of the native language" (Polivanov 1931: 79–80, my translation). Thanks to Segui, Frauenfelder, and Hallé (2001) for bringing this quote to my attention.

2. Best and Tyler (2007) note that yet further L1 to not-L1 mappings are in principle possible, albeit so far unattested.

3. Syllable finally, where the Japanese category cannot occur, Japanese listeners experience little difficulty with the [r]-[l] contrast (Sheldon and Strange 1982).

4. As noted in chapter 2, new concepts only rarely produce a newly created form in the open-class lexicon, like *modem* or *bling*. Far more usually, new concepts are labeled with an old word form, or a combination of old words, given a new meaning: *cell phone*, *crack*, *podcast*, *space shuttle*, *web surfer*. (This process can itself spawn apparently new forms; e.g., *weblog* became *blog*.) Old concepts are also easily labeled with familiar names in an extended meaning, as with *tall* (applied to coffee cup size to mean *small*), *gay*, or *sanitation engineer*. Homophones are clearly the order of the day for lexicons.

5. Many thanks again to Dennis Pasveer for assistance in this task.

Chapter 11

1. This has to be true if only because there is no hard and fast line that defines when two similar linguistic systems are dialects of the same language or separate languages. "A language is a dialect with an army" is the cynical summary of this ineluctable continuity (but this would make British English and Canadian English separate languages, and Canadian English and Quebec French dialects of the same language). Mutual intelligibility, either in speech or in writing, provides no diagnostic either; dialectal pronunciation variants can inhibit understanding (consider a Glaswegian visiting Alabama), and writing systems differ along quite independent dimensions (the distinct Chinese languages do share an orthography, whereas the Serbian and Croatian varieties of Serbo-Croatian do not). Varieties of the same language share most of their syntax, and most of their lexicon, and hence most of their repertoire of phonemic contrasts, but the thresholds cannot be quantified.

2. Note however that several of the cited instances of dialect adaptation involved immersion (Evans and Iverson's [2004] Northern Britishers who had moved south, in comparison to those who had stayed put; Scott and Cutler's [1984] British émigrés in the United States, in comparison to the stay-at-homes). In an immersion situation, the majority of talkers one listens to will require such adaptation. Whether there is a categorical difference between immersion and occasional exposure, or whether the effects of exposure are strictly incremental, has yet to be investigated.

Chapter 12

1. Although a minimal difference between two words is phoneme sized, phonemes can also be more or less similar to one another. Phonemes differing from one another in a single feature are more similar (and more confusable) than phonemes differing on more features. If smaller differences make puns better even below the phoneme level, then *kitchen think* is a better pun on *kitchen sink* than *kitchen pink* or *kitchen wink* would be. But whether a pun works depends on the situation as well as on the pun's sound.

References

Abercrombie, D. (1967). *Elements of general phonetics*. Edinburgh: Edinburgh University Press.

Abrams, R. M., & Gerhardt, K. J. (1996). The fetal sound environment. *Journal of the Acoustical Society of America*, *100*, 2710.

Abrams, R. M., Gerhardt, K. J., Huang, X., Peters, A. J. M., & Langford, R. G. (2000). Musical experiences of the unborn baby. *Journal of Sound and Vibration*, *231*, 253–258.

Ades, A. E. (1976). Adapting the property detectors for speech perception. In R. Wales & E. Walker (Eds.), *New approaches to language mechanisms* (pp. 55–108). Amsterdam: North-Holland.

Ainsworth, W. A., & Cervera, T. (2001). Effects of noise adaptation on the perception of voiced plosives in isolated syllables. In P. Dalsgaard, B. Lindberg & H. Benner (Eds.), *Proceedings of the 7th European Conference on Speech Communication and Technology (EUROSPEECH 2001),* Aalborg (pp. 371–374). Aalborg, Denmark: Center for Personkommunikation, Aalborg University.

Akker, E., & Cutler, A. (2003). Prosodic cues to semantic structure in native and nonnative listening. *Bilingualism: Language and Cognition*, *6*, 81–96.

Al-jasser, F. (2008). The effect of teaching English phonotactics on the lexical segmentation of English as a foreign language. *System*, *36*, 94–106.

Allen, J. S., & Miller, J. L. (2001). Contextual influences on the internal structure of phonetic categories: A distinction between lexical status and speaking rate. *Perception & Psychophysics*, *63*, 798–810.

Allen, J. S., & Miller, J. L. (2004). Listener sensitivity to individual talker differences in voice-onset-time. *Journal of the Acoustical Society of America*, *115*, 3171–3183.

Allen, J. S., Miller, J. L., & DeSteno, D. (2003). Individual talker differences in voice-onset-time. *Journal of the Acoustical Society of America*, *113*, 544–552.

Allopenna, P., Magnuson, J., & Tanenhaus, M. (1998). Tracking the time course of spoken word recognition using eye movements: Evidence for continuous mapping models. *Journal of Memory and Language*, *38*, 419–439.

van Alphen, P. M., & van Berkum, J. J. A. (2010). Is there pain in champagne? Semantic involvement of words within words during sense-making. *Journal of Cognitive Neuroscience*, *22*, 2618–2626.

van Alphen, P., & McQueen, J. M. (2001). The time-limited influence of sentential context on function word identification. *Journal of Experimental Psychology: Human Perception and Performance, 27*, 1057–1071.

van Alphen, P. M., & McQueen, J. M. (2006). The effect of voice onset time differences on lexical access. *Journal of Experimental Psychology: Human Perception and Performance, 32*, 178–196.

van Alphen, P. M., & Smits, R. (2004). Acoustical and perceptual analysis of the voicing distinction in Dutch initial plosives: The role of prevoicing. *Journal of Phonetics, 32*, 455–491.

Altenberg, E. P. (2005). The perception of word boundaries in a second language. *Second Language Research, 21*, 325–358.

Altmann, G., & Carter, D. (1989). Lexical stress and lexical discriminability: Stressed syllables are more informative, but why? *Computer Speech & Language, 3*, 265–275.

Andics, A., McQueen, J. M., Petersson, K. M., Gál, V., Rudas, G., & Vidnyánszky, Z. (2010). Neural mechanisms for voice recognition. *NeuroImage, 52*, 1528–1540.

Andics, A., McQueen, J. M., & van Turennout, M. (2007). Phonetic context influences voice discriminability. In J. Trouvain & W. J. Barry (Eds.), *Proceedings of the 16th International Congress of Phonetic Sciences,* Saarbrücken (pp. 1829–1832). Dudweiler: Pirrot.

Andruski, J. E., Blumstein, S. E., & Burton, M. (1994). The effect of subphonetic differences on lexical access. *Cognition, 52*, 163–187.

Aoyama, K. (2003). Perception of syllable-initial and syllable-final nasals in English by Korean and Japanese speakers. *Second Language Research, 19*, 251–265.

Aoyama, K., Flege, J. E., Guion, S. G., Akahane-Yamada, R., & Yamada, T. (2004). Perceived phonetic dissimilarity and L2 speech learning: The case of Japanese /r/ and English /l/ and /r/. *Journal of Phonetics, 32*, 233–250.

Archibald, J. (1992). Transfer of L1 parameter settings: Some empirical evidence from Polish metrics. *Canadian Journal of Linguistics, 37*, 301–339.

Archibald, J. (1993). *Language learnability and L2 phonology: The acquisition of metrical parameters*. Dordrecht: Kluwer.

Archibald, J. (1997). The acquisition of English stress by speakers of nonaccentual languages: Lexical storage versus computation of stress. *Linguistics, 35*, 167–181.

Archibald, J. (1998). *Second language phonology*. Amsterdam: John Benjamins.

Armitage, S. E., Baldwin, B. A., & Vince, M. A. (1980). The fetal sound environment of sheep. *Science, 208*, 1173–1174.

Aslin, R. N., & Pisoni, D. B. (1980). Effects of early linguistic experience on speech discrimination by infants: A critique of Eilers, Gavin, and Wilson (1979). *Child Development, 51*, 107–112.

Aslin, R. N., Pisoni, D. B., Hennessy, B. L., & Perey, A. J. (1981). Discrimination of voice onset time by human infants: New findings and implications for the effects of early experience. *Child Development, 52*, 1135–1145.

Aslin, R. N., Saffran, J. R., & Newport, E. L. (1998). Computation of conditional probability statistics by 8-month-old infants. *Psychological Science, 9*, 321–324.

Aslin, R. N., Woodward, J. Z., LaMendola, N. P., & Bever, T. G. (1996). Models of word segmentation in fluent maternal speech to infants. In J. L. Morgan & K. Demuth (Eds.), *Signal to syntax: Bootstrapping from speech to grammar in early acquisition* (pp. 117–134). Hillsdale, NJ: Erlbaum.

Au, T. K., Knightly, L. M., Jun, S.-A., & Oh, J. S. (2002). Overhearing a language during childhood. *Psychological Science, 13*, 238–243.

Au, T. K., Oh, J. S., Knightly, L. M., Jun, S.-A., & Romo, L. F. (2008). Salvaging a childhood language. *Journal of Memory and Language, 58*, 998–1011.

Aydelott, J., & Bates, E. (2004). Effects of acoustic distortion and semantic context on lexical access. *Language and Cognitive Processes, 19*, 29–56.

Baayen, R. H. (2001). *Word frequency distributions*. Dordrecht: Kluwer.

Baayen, R. H., Dijkstra, T., & Schreuder, R. (1997). Singulars and plurals in Dutch: Evidence for a parallel dual route model. *Journal of Memory and Language, 37*, 94–117.

Baayen, R. H., McQueen, J. M., Dijkstra, T., & Schreuder, R. (2003). Frequency effects in regular inflectional morphology: Revisiting Dutch plurals. In R. H. Baayen & R. Schreuder (Eds.), *Morphological structure in language processing* (pp. 355–390). Berlin: Mouton de Gruyter.

Baayen, R. H., Piepenbrock, R., & van Rijn, H. (1993). *The CELEX lexical database*. Philadelphia: Linguistic Data Consortium, University of Pennsylvania [CD-ROM].

Baddeley, A. D. (1999). *Essentials of human memory*. Hove: Psychology Press.

Banel, M.-H., & Bacri, N. (1994). On metrical patterns and lexical parsing in French. *Speech Communication, 15*, 115–126.

Banel, M.-H., & Bacri, N. (1997). Reconnaissance de la parole et indices de segmentation metriques et phonotactiques [Cooperation and conflict between metrical cues and phonotactic cues in speech segmentation]. *L'Année Psychologique, 97*, 77–112.

Bard, E. G., & Anderson, A. (1983). The unintelligibility of speech to children. *Journal of Child Language, 10*, 265–292.

Bard, E. G., & Anderson, A. (1994). The unintelligibility of speech to children: Effects of referent availability. *Journal of Child Language, 21*, 623–648.

Bard, E. G., Shillcock, R. C., & Altmann, G. T. M. (1988). The recognition of words after their acoustic offsets in spontaneous speech: Effects of subsequent context. *Perception & Psychophysics, 44*, 395–408.

Bardhan, N. P., Aslin, R. N., & Tanenhaus, M. (2006). Return of the weckud wetch: Rapid adaptation to a new accent. *Journal of the Acoustical Society of America, 119*, 3423 (Abstract).

Barry, W. J., & Russo, M. (2003). Measuring rhythm: Is it separable from speech rate? In A. Mettouchi & G. Ferré (Eds.), *Actes de interfaces prosodiques* (pp. 15–20). Nantes: Université Nantes.

Bashford, J. A., Warren, R. M., & Lenz, P. W. (2006). Polling the effective neighborhoods of spoken words with the verbal transformation effect. *Journal of the Acoustical Society of America, 119*, EL55–EL59.

Bashford, J. A., Warren, R. M., & Lenz, P. W. (2008). Evoking biphone neighborhoods with verbal transformations: Illusory changes demonstrate both lexical competition and inhibition. *Journal of the Acoustical Society of America, 123*, EL32.

Bates, E., Devescovi, A., Hernandez, A., & Pizzamiglio, L. (1996). Gender priming in Italian. *Perception & Psychophysics*, *58*, 992–1004.

Bauer, L. (1985). Tracing phonetic change in the received pronunciation of British English. *Journal of Phonetics*, *13*, 61–81.

Bausenhart, K. M., Rolke, B., & Ulrich, R. (2007). Knowing when to hear aids what to hear. *Quarterly Journal of Experimental Psychology*, *60*, 1610–1615.

Beckman, M. E., & Pierrehumbert, J. B. (1986). Intonational structure in Japanese and English. *Phonology Yearbook*, *3*, 255–309.

Beddor, P. S., Harnsberger, J. D., & Lindemann, S. (2002). Language-specific patterns of vowel-to-vowel coarticulation: Acoustic structures and their perceptual correlates. *Journal of Phonetics*, *30*, 591–627.

Beddor, P. S., & Strange, W. (1982). Cross-language study of perception of the oral-nasal distinction. *Journal of the Acoustical Society of America*, *71*, 1551–1561.

Bell, A. (1978). Syllabic consonants. In J. Greenberg (Ed.), *Universals of human language: Phonology* (Vol. 2, pp. 153–201). Stanford, CA: Stanford University Press.

Bell, A., Brenier, J. M., Gregory, M., Girand, C., & Jurafsky, D. (2009). Predictability effects on durations of content and function words in conversational English. *Journal of Memory and Language*, *60*, 92–111.

Benasich, A. A., & Tallal, P. (2002). Infant discrimination of rapid auditory cues predicts later language impairment. *Behavioural Brain Research*, *136*, 31–49.

Benguerel, A.-P. (1999). Stress-timing vs. syllable-timing vs. mora-timing: The perception of speech rhythm by native speakers of different language. *VARIA, Etudes & travaux*, *3*, 1–18.

Benkí, J. R. (2003). Quantitative evaluation of lexical status, word frequency, and neighborhood density as context effects in spoken word recognition. *Journal of the Acoustical Society of America*, *113*, 1689–1705.

Bent, T., & Bradlow, A. R. (2003). The interlanguage speech intelligibility benefit. *Journal of the Acoustical Society of America*, *114*, 1600–1610.

Bent, T., Bradlow, A. R., & Wright, B. (2006). The influence of linguistic experience on the cognitive processing of pitch in speech and non-speech sounds. *Journal of Experimental Psychology: Human Perception and Performance*, *32*, 97–103.

Berent, I., Balaban, E., & Vaknin-Nusbaum, V. (2011). How linguistic chickens help spot spoken-eggs: Phonological constraints on speech identification. *Frontiers in Psychology, 2*, 182. DOI: 10.3389/fpsyg.2011.00182.

Berkovits, R. (1980). Perception of intonation in native and non-native speakers of English. *Language and Speech*, *23*, 271–280.

van Berkum, J. J. A., van den Brink, D., Tesink, C. M. J. Y., Kos, M., & Hagoort, P. (2008). The neural integration of speaker and message. *Journal of Cognitive Neuroscience*, *20*, 580–591.

van Berkum, J. J. A., Brown, C. M., & Hagoort, P. (1999). Early referential context effects in sentence processing: Evidence from event-related brain potentials. *Journal of Memory and Language*, *41*, 147–182.

van Berkum, J. J. A., Hagoort, P., & Brown, C. M. (1999). Semantic integration in sentences and discourse: Evidence from the N400. *Journal of Cognitive Neuroscience*, *11*, 657–671.

Bernstein Ratner, N. (1984a). Phonological rule usage in mother-child speech. *Journal of Phonetics, 12*, 245–254.

Bernstein Ratner, N. (1984b). Patterns of vowel modification in mother-child speech. *Journal of Child Language, 11*, 557–578.

Bernstein Ratner, N. (1986). Durational cues which mark clause boundaries in mother-child speech. *Journal of Phonetics, 14*, 303–309.

Bertelson, P., Vroomen, J., & de Gelder, B. (2003). Visual recalibration of auditory speech identification: A McGurk after effect. *Psychological Science, 14*, 592–597.

Bertoncini, J., Bijeljac-Babic, R., Blumstein, S. E., & Mehler, J. (1987). Discrimination in neonates of very short CVs. *Journal of the Acoustical Society of America, 82*, 31–37.

Bertoncini, J., Bijeljac-Babic, R., Jusczyk, P. W., Kennedy, L. J., & Mehler, J. (1988). An investigation of young infants' perceptual representations of speech sounds. *Journal of Experimental Psychology: General, 117*, 21–33.

Bertoncini, J., Floccia, C., Nazzi, T., & Mehler, J. (1995). Morae and syllables: Rhythmical basis of speech representations in neonates. *Language and Speech, 38*, 311–329.

Best, C. T. (1994). The emergence of native-language phonological influences in infants: A perceptual assimilation model. In J. C. Goodman & H. C. Nusbaum (Eds.), *The development of speech perception: The transition from speech sounds to spoken words* (pp. 167–224). Cambridge, MA: MIT Press.

Best, C. T. (1995). A direct realist perspective on cross-language speech perception. In W. Strange (Ed.), *Speech perception and linguistic experience: Theoretical and methodological issues in cross-language speech research* (pp. 167–200). Timonium, MD: York Press.

Best, C. T., McRoberts, G. W., & Goodell, E. (2001). Discrimination of non-native consonant contrasts varying in perceptual assimilation to the listener's native phonological system. *Journal of the Acoustical Society of America, 109*, 775–794.

Best, C. T., McRoberts, G. W., & Sithole, N. M. (1988). Examination of perceptual reorganization for nonnative speech contrasts: Zulu click discrimination by English-speaking adults and infants. *Journal of Experimental Psychology: Human Perception and Performance, 14*, 345–360.

Best, C. T., & Tyler, M. D. (2007). Nonnative and second-language speech perception: Commonalities and complementarities. In M. Munro & O.-S. Bohn (Eds.), *Second language speech learning* (pp. 13–34). Amsterdam: John Benjamins.

Bialystok, E., Craik, F. I. M., & Freedman, M. (2007). Bilingualism as a protection against the onset of symptoms of dementia. *Neuropsychologia, 45*, 459–464.

Bialystok, E., Craik, F. I. M., Klein, R., & Viswanathan, M. (2004). Bilingualism, aging, and cognitive control: Evidence from the Simon task. *Psychology and Aging, 19*, 290–303.

Bialystok, E., Craik, F. I. M., & Ryan, J. (2006). Executive control in a modified antisaccade task: Effects of aging and bilingualism. *Journal of Experimental Psychology: Learning, Memory, and Cognition, 32*, 1341–1354.

Bialystok, E., Luk, G., Peets, K. F., & Yang, S. (2010). Receptive vocabulary differences in monolingual and bilingual children. *Bilingualism: Language and Cognition, 13*, 525–531.

Bijeljac-Babic, R., Bertoncini, J., & Mehler, J. (1993). How do four day old infants categorize multisyllabic utterances. *Developmental Psychology, 29*, 711–721.

Birch, S. L., & Garnsey, S. M. (1995). The effect of focus on memory for words in sentences. *Journal of Memory and Language, 34*, 232–267.

Birdsong, D. (1999). *Second language acquisition and the Critical Period Hypothesis*. Mahwah, NJ: Erlbaum.

Birnholz, J. C., & Benacerraf, B. R. (1983). The development of human fetal hearing. *Science, 222*, 516–518.

Black, J. W., & Hast, M. H. (1962). Speech reception with altering signal. *Journal of Speech and Hearing Research, 5*, 70–75.

Blake, J., & de Boysson-Bardies, B. (1992). Patterns in babbling: A cross-linguistic study. *Journal of Child Language, 19*, 51–74.

Blumenfeld, H. K., & Marian, V. (2007). Constraints on parallel activation in bilingual spoken language processing: Examining proficiency and lexical status using eye-tracking. *Language and Cognitive Processes, 22*, 633–660.

Blutner, R., & Sommer, R. (1988). Sentence processing and lexical access: The influence of the focus-identifying task. *Journal of Memory and Language, 27*, 359–367.

Boatman, D., Hall, C., Goldstein, M. H., Lesser, R., & Gordon, B. (1997). Neuroperceptual differences in consonant and vowel discrimination: As revealed by direct cortical electrical interference. *Cortex, 33*, 83–98.

Boatman, D., Lesser, R., Hall, C., & Gordon, B. (1994). Auditory perception of segmental features: A functional-neuroanatomic study. *Journal of Neurolinguistics, 8*, 225–234.

Bock, J. K., & Mazzella, J. R. (1983). Intonational marking of given and new information: Some consequences for comprehension. *Memory & Cognition, 11*, 64–76.

de Boer, B., & Kuhl, P. K. (2003). Investigating the role of infant-directed speech with a computer model. *Acoustics Research Letters Online, 4*, 129–134.

Bohn, O.-S., & Munro, M. J. (2007). *Language experience in second language speech learning: In honor of James Emil Flege*. Amsterdam: John Benjamins.

Bolinger, D. L. (1964). Around the edge of language: Intonation. *Harvard Educational Review, 34*, 282–296.

Bolinger, D. (1978). Intonation across languages. In J. H. Greenberg (Ed.), *Universals of human language: Vol. 2. Phonology* (pp. 471–524). Stanford, CA: Stanford University Press.

Bölte, J., & Coenen, E. (2002). Is phonological information mapped onto semantic information in a one-to-one manner? *Brain and Language, 81*, 384–397.

Bölte, J., & Connine, C. M. (2004). Grammatical gender in spoken word recognition in German. *Perception & Psychophysics, 66*, 1018–1032.

Bonatti, L. L., Peña, M., Nespor, M., & Mehler, J. (2005). Linguistic constraints on statistical computations: The role of consonants and vowels in continuous speech processing. *Psychological Science, 16*, 451–459.

Bonatti, L. L., Peña, M., Nespor, M., & Mehler, J. (2007). On consonants, vowels, chickens, and eggs. *Psychological Science, 18*, 924–925.

Bond, Z. S. (1981). Listening to elliptic speech: Pay attention to stressed vowels. *Journal of Phonetics, 9*, 89–96.

Bond, Z. S. (1999). *Slips of the ear: Errors in the perception of casual conversation*. San Diego, CA: Academic Press.

Bond, Z. S., & Fokes, J. (1991). Identifying foreign languages. In *Proceedings of the 12th International Congress of Phonetic Sciences*, Aix-en-Provence (vol. *2*, pp. 198–201).

Bond, Z. S., & Garnes, S. (1980). Misperceptions of fluent speech. In R. A. Cole (Ed.), *Perception and production of fluent speech* (pp. 115–132). Hillsdale, NJ: Erlbaum.

Bond, Z.S., & Moore, T. J. (1994). A note on the acoustic-phonetic characteristics of inadvertently clear speech. *Speech Communication*, *14*, 325–337.

Bond, Z. S., & Small, L. H. (1983). Voicing, vowel, and stress mispronunciations in continuous speech. *Perception & Psychophysics*, *34*, 470–474.

Bond, Z. S., & Stockmal, V. (2002). Distinguishing samples of spoken Korean from rhythmic and regional competitors. *Language Sciences*, *24*, 175–185.

Bond, Z. S., Stockmal, V., & Muljani, D. (1998). Learning to identify a foreign language. *Language Sciences*, *20*, 353–367.

Borsky, S., Tuller, B., & Shapiro, L. P. (1998). "How to milk a coat": The effects of semantic and acoustic information on phoneme categorization. *Journal of the Acoustical Society of America*, *103*, 2670–2676.

Bortfeld, H., & Morgan, J. L. (1999). Disentangling multiple sources of stress in infant-directed speech. In A. Greenhill, H. Littlefield & C. Tano (Eds.), *Proceedings of the 23rd annual Boston University Conference on Language Development* (pp. 103–111). Somerville, MA: Cascadilla Press.

Bortfeld, H., Morgan, J. L., Golinkoff, R. M., & Rathbun, K. (2005). Mommy and me: Familiar names help launch babies into speech stream segmentation. *Psychological Science*, *4*, 298–304.

Bortfeld, H., Wruck, E., & Boas, D. A. (2007). Assessing infants' cortical response to speech using near-infrared spectroscopy. *NeuroImage*, *34*, 407–415.

Bosch, L., & Sebastián-Gallés, N. (1997). Native-language recognition abilities in 4-month-old infants from monolingual and bilingual environments. *Cognition*, *65*, 33–69.

Bosch, L., & Sebastián-Gallés, N. (2001). Evidence of early language discrimination abilities in infants from bilingual environments. *Infancy*, *2*, 29–49.

Bosch, L., & Sebastián-Gallés, N. (2003). Simultaneous bilingualism and the perception of a language-specific vowel contrast in the first year of life. *Language and Speech*, *46*, 217–243.

de Boysson-Bardies, B., Sagart, L., & Durand, C. (1984). Discernible differences in the babbling of infants according to target language. *Journal of Child Language*, *11*, 1–15.

de Boysson-Bardies, B., & Vihman, M. M. (1991). Adaptation to language: Evidence from babbling and first words in four languages. *Language*, *67*, 297–319.

Bradley, D. C., Sánchez-Casas, R. M., & García-Albea, J. E. (1993). The status of the syllable in the perception of Spanish and English. *Language and Cognitive Processes*, *8*, 197–233.

Bradlow, A. R., & Alexander, J. A. (2007). Semantic and acoustic enhancements for speech-in-noise recognition by native and non-native listeners. *Journal of the Acoustical Society of America*, *121*, 2339–2349.

Bradlow, A. R., & Bent, T. (2002). The clear speech effect for non-native listeners. *Journal of the Acoustical Society of America*, *112*, 272–284.

Bradlow, A. R., & Bent, T. (2008). Perceptual adaptation to non-native speech. *Cognition*, *106*, 707–729.

Bradlow, A. R., Clopper, C., Smiljanic, R., & Walter, M. A. (2010). A perceptual phonetic similarity space for languages: Evidence from five native language listener groups. *Speech Communication*, *52*, 930–994.

Bradlow, A. R., Nygaard, L. C., & Pisoni, D. B. (1999). Effects of talker, rate, and amplitude variation on recognition memory for spoken words. *Perception & Psychophysics*, *61*, 206–219.

Bradlow, A. R., & Pisoni, D. B. (1999). Recognition of spoken words by native and non-native listeners: Talker-, listener-, and item-related factors. *Journal of the Acoustical Society of America*, *106*, 2074–2085.

Bradlow, A. R., Pisoni, D. B., Akahane-Yamada, R., & Tohkura, Y. (1997). Training Japanese listeners to identify English /r/ and /l/: IV. Some effects of perceptual learning on speech production. *Journal of the Acoustical Society of America*, *101*, 2299–2310.

Braine, M. D. S., Brody, R. E., Brooks, P. J., Sudhalter, V., Ross, J. A., Catalano, L., & Fisch, S. M. (1990). Exploring language acquisition in children with a miniature artificial language: Effects of item and pattern frequency, arbitrary subclasses, and correction. *Journal of Memory and Language*, *29*, 591–610.

Braun, B., & Chen, A. (2010). Intonation of "now" in resolving scope ambiguity in English and Dutch. *Journal of Phonetics*, *38*, 431–444.

Braun, B., & Tagliapietra, L. (2010). The role of contrastive intonation contours in the retrieval of contextual alternatives. *Language and Cognitive Processes*, *25*, 1024–1043.

Braun, B., & Tagliapietra, L. (2011). On-line interpretation of intonational meaning in L2. *Language and Cognitive Processes*, *26*, 224–235.

Bregman, A. S. (1990). *Auditory scene analysis: The perceptual organization of sound*. Cambridge, MA: MIT Press.

Brent, M. R. (1996). Advances in the computational study of language acquisition. *Cognition*, *61*, 1–38.

Brent, M. R., & Cartwright, T. A. (1996). Distributional regularity and phonotactic constraints are useful for segmentation. *Cognition*, *61*, 93–125.

Brent, M. R., & Siskind, J. M. (2001). The role of exposure to isolated words in early vocabulary development. *Cognition*, *81*, B33–B44.

Broadbent, D., Ladefoged, P., & Lawrence, W. (1956). Vowel sounds and perceptual constancy. *Nature*, *178*, 815–816.

Broersma, M. (2002). Comprehension of non-native speech: Inaccurate phoneme processing and activation of lexical competitors. In J. H. L. Hansen & B. Pellum (Eds.), *Proceedings of the 7th International Conference on Spoken Language Processing*, Denver (pp. 261–264). Denver: Center for Spoken Language Research, University of Colorado Boulder [CD-ROM].

Broersma, M. (2005). Perception of familiar contrasts in unfamiliar positions. *Journal of the Acoustical Society of America*, *117*, 3890–3901.

Broersma, M. (2008). Flexible cue use in nonnative phonetic categorization. *Journal of the Acoustical Society of America*, *124*, 712–715.

Broersma, M. (2010). Perception of final fricative voicing: Native and nonnative listeners' use of vowel duration. *Journal of the Acoustical Society of America*, *127*, 1636–1644.

Broersma, M., & Cutler, A. (2008). Phantom word recognition in L2. *System*, *36*, 22–34.

Broersma, M., & Cutler, A. (2011). Competition dynamics of second-language listening. *Quarterly Journal of Experimental Psychology*, *64*, 74–95.

Brooks, P. J., Braine, M. D. S., Catalano, L., Brody, R. E., & Sudhalter, V. (1993). Acquisition of gender-like noun subclasses in an artificial language: The contribution of phonological markers to learning. *Journal of Memory and Language*, *32*, 76–95.

Broselow, E., Hurtig, R., & Ringen, C. (1987). The perception of second language prosody. In G. Ioup & S. Weinberger (Eds.), *Interlanguage phonology* (pp. 350–362). Cambridge, MA: Newbury House.

Brouwer, S. (2010). *Processing strongly reduced forms in casual speech*. Ph.D. dissertation, MPI Series in Psycholinguistics 57, Radboud University Nijmegen.

Brouwer, S., Mitterer, H., & Huettig, F. (2010). Shadowing reduced speech and alignment. *Journal of the Acoustical Society of America*, *128*, EL32–EL37.

Brouwer, S., Mitterer, H., & Huettig, F. (2012). Speech reductions change the dynamics of competition during spoken word recognition. *Language and Cognitive Processes*. Advance online publication. doi:10.1080/01690965.2011.555268.

Brouwer, S., Mitterer, H., & Huettig, F. (2013). Discourse context and the recognition of reduced and canonical spoken words. *Applied Psycholinguistics*. doi: 10.1017/S0142716411000853.

Browman, C. P. (1978). Tip of the tongue and slip of the ear: Implications for language processing. *UCLA Working Papers in Phonetics*, *42*, i–149.

Brown, C. (1998). The role of the L1 grammar in the L2 acquisition of segmental structure. *Second Language Research*, *14*, 136–193.

Brown, G. (2008). Selective listening. *System*, *36*, 10–21.

Brown, J. D., & Kondo-Brown, K. (Eds.) (2006). *Perspectives on teaching connected speech to second language speakers*. Honolulu: University of Hawai'i Press.

Bürki-Cohen, J., Grosjean, F., & Miller, J. L. (1989). Base-language effects on word identification in bilingual speech: Evidence from categorical perception experiments. *Language and Speech*, *32*, 355–371.

Burnham, D. K. (1986). Developmental loss of speech perception: Exposure to and experience with a first language. *Applied Psycholinguistics*, *7*, 207–240.

Burnham, D., & Dodd, B. (1998). Familiarity and novelty preferences in infants' auditory-visual speech perception: Problems, factors, and a solution. In C. Rovee-Collier, L. Lipsitt & H. Hayne (Eds.), *Advances in infancy research* (Vol. 12, pp. 170–187). Stamford, CT: Ablex.

Burnham, D., Francis, E., Webster, D., Luksaneeyanawin, S., Attapaiboon, C., Lacerda, F., & Keller, P. (1996). Perception of lexical tone across languages: Evidence for a linguistic mode of processing. In H. T. Bunnell & W. Idsardi (Eds.), *Proceedings of the 4th International Conference on Spoken Language Processing,* Philadelphia (Vol. 1, pp. 2514–2517). Philadelphia: University of Delaware and A. I. duPont Institute.

Burnham, D., & Jones, C. (2002). Categorical perception of lexical tone by tonal and non-tonal language speakers. In C. Bow (Ed.), *Proceedings of the 9th Australian International Conference on Speech Science and Technology*, Melbourne (pp. 515–519). Canberra: Australian Speech Science and Technology Association (ASSTA).

Burnham, D., Kirkwood, K., Luksaneeyanawin, S., & Pansottee, S. (1992). Perception of Central Thai tones and segments by Thai and Australian adults. In *Proceedings of the 3rd International Symposium of Language and Linguistic: Pan-Asiatic Linguistics*, Bangkok (Vol. 1, pp. 546–560). Bangkok: Chulalongkorn University Press.

Burnham, D., Kitamura, C., & Vollmer-Conna, U. (2002). What's new pussycat: On talking to animals and babies. *Science*, *296*, 1435.

Burns, T. C., Yoshida, K. A., Hill, K., & Werker, J. F. (2007). The development of phonetic representation in bilingual and monolingual infants. *Applied Psycholinguistics*, *28*, 455–474.

Burton, M. W., Baum, S. R., & Blumstein, S. E. (1989). Lexical effects on the phonetic categorization of speech: The role of acoustic structure. *Journal of Experimental Psychology: Human Perception and Performance*, *15*, 567–575.

Byers-Heinlein, K., Burns, T. C., & Werker, J. F. (2010). The roots of bilingualism in newborns. *Psychological Science*, *2*, 343–348.

Bynon, T. (1977). *Historical linguistics*. Cambridge: Cambridge University Press.

Cacciari, C., & Tabossi, P. (1988). The comprehension of idioms. *Journal of Memory and Language*, *27*, 668–683.

Cairns, H., & Kamerman, J. (1975). Lexical information processing during sentence comprehension. *Journal of Verbal Learning and Verbal Behavior*, *14*, 170–179.

Cairns, P., Shillcock, R., Chater, N., & Levy, J. (1997). Bootstrapping word boundaries: A bottom-up corpus-based approach to speech segmentation. *Cognitive Psychology*, *33*, 111–153.

Callan, D., Jones, J. A., Callan, A. M., & Akahane-Yamada, R. (2004). Phonetic perceptual identification by native- and second-language speakers differentially activates brain regions involved with acoustic phonetic processing and those involved with articulatory-auditory/orosensory internal models. *NeuroImage*, *22*, 1182–1194.

Caramazza, A., Chialant, D., Capasso, R., & Miceli, G. (2000). Separable processing of consonants and vowels. *Nature*, *403*, 428–430.

Carlson, R., Elenius, K., Granström, B., & Hunnicutt, S. (1985). Phonetic and orthographic properties of the basic vocabulary of five European languages. *STL-Quarterly Progress and Status Report*, *26*, 63–94.

Carlson, R., Hirschberg, J., & Swerts, M. (2005). Cues to upcoming Swedish prosodic boundaries: Subjective judgment studies and acoustic correlates. *Speech Communication*, *46*, 326–333.

Carvalho, C., McQueen, J. M., & Cutler, A. (2002). The Possible Word Constraint (PWC). In J. Bohnemeyer, A. Kelly & R. Abdel Rahman (Eds.), *MPI Annual Report 2002* (p. 21). Nijmegen: MPI for Psycholinguistics.

Chambers, K. E., Onishi, K. H., & Fisher, C. (2003). Infants learn phonotactic regularities from brief auditory experience. *Cognition*, *87*, B69–B77.

Chee, M. W. L., Soon, C. S., & Lee, H. L. (2003). Common and segregated neuronal networks for different languages revealed using functional magnetic resonance adaptation. *Journal of Cognitive Neuroscience*, *15*, 85–97.

Chen, H.-C., & Cutler, A. (1997). Auditory priming in spoken and printed word recognition. In H.-C. Chen (Ed.), *The cognitive processing of Chinese and related Asian languages* (pp. 77–81). Hong Kong: Chinese University Press.

Chen, A., den Os, E., & de Ruiter, J. P. (2007). Pitch accent type matters for online processing of information status: Evidence from natural and synthetic speech. *Linguistic Review*, *24*, 317–344.

Cheour, M., Ceponiene, R., Lehtokovski, A., Luuk, A., Allik, J., Alho, K., & Näätänen, R. (1998). Development of language-specific phoneme representations in the infant brain. *Nature Neuroscience*, *1*, 351–353.

Cheour-Luhtanen, M., Alho, K., Sainio, K., Rinne, T., Reinikainen, K., Pohjavuori, M., Aaltonen, O., Eerola, O., & Näätänen, R. (1996). The ontogenetically earliest discriminative response of the human brain. *Psychophysiology*, *33*, 478–481.

Ching, Y. C. T. (1988). Lexical tone perception by Cantonese deaf children. In I. M. Liu, M. J. Chen & H.-C. Chen (Eds.), *Cognitive aspects of the Chinese language* (Vol. 1, pp. 93–102). Hong Kong: Asian Research Service.

Cho, T. (2004). Prosodically conditioned strengthening and vowel-to-vowel coarticulation in English. *Journal of Phonetics*, *32*, 141–176.

Cho, T., & Keating, P. A. (2001). Articulatory and acoustic studies on domain-initial strengthening in Korean. *Journal of Phonetics*, *29*, 155–190.

Cho, T., & McQueen, J. M. (2005). Prosodic influences on consonant production in Dutch: Effects of prosodic boundaries, phrasal accent and lexical stress. *Journal of Phonetics*, *33*, 121–157.

Cho, T., & McQueen, J. M. (2006). Phonological versus phonetic cues in native and nonnative listening: Korean and Dutch listeners' perception of Dutch and English consonants. *Journal of the Acoustical Society of America*, *119*, 3085–3096.

Cho, T., McQueen, J. M., & Cox, E. A. (2007). Prosodically driven phonetic detail in speech processing: The case of domain-initial strengthening in English. *Journal of Phonetics*, *35*, 210–243.

Christophe, A., Dupoux, E., Bertoncini, J., & Mehler, J. (1994). Do infants perceive word boundaries? An empirical study of the bootstrapping of lexical acquisition. *Journal of the Acoustical Society of America*, *95*, 1570–1580.

Christophe, A., Guasti, T., Nespor, M., Dupoux, E., & van Ooyen, B. (1997). Reflections on phonological bootstrapping: Its role for lexical and syntactic acquisition. *Language and Cognitive Processes*, *12*, 585–612.

Christophe, A., Mehler, J., & Sebastián-Gallés, N. (2001). Perception of prosodic boundary correlates by newborn infants. *Infancy*, *2*, 385–394.

Christophe, A., & Morton, J. (1998). Is Dutch native English? Linguistic analysis by 2-month-olds. *Developmental Science*, *1*, 215–219.

Christophe, A., Peperkamp, S., Pallier, C., Block, E., & Mehler, J. (2004). Phonological phrase boundaries constrain lexical access I. Adult data. *Journal of Memory and Language*, *51*, 523–547.

Church, B. A., & Schacter, D. L. (1994). Perceptual specificity of auditory priming: Implicit memory for voice intonation and fundamental frequency. *Journal of Experimental Psychology: Learning, Memory, and Cognition*, *20*, 521–533.

Cieślicka, A. (2006). Literal salience in on-line processing of idiomatic expressions by second language learners. *Second Language Research*, *22*, 115–144.

Clahsen, H., & Felser, C. (2006). Grammatical processing in language learners. *Applied Psycholinguistics*, *27*, 3–42.

Clark, G. M. (2002). Learning to understand speech with the cochlear implant. In M. Fahle & T. Poggio (Eds.), *Textbook of perceptual learning* (pp. 147–160). Cambridge, MA: MIT Press.

Clarke, C. M., & Garrett, M. F. (2004). Rapid adaptation to foreign-accented English. *Journal of the Acoustical Society of America*, *116*, 3647–3658.

Clarke, C. M., & Luce, P. A. (2005). Perceptual adaptation to speaker characteristics: VOT boundaries in stop voicing categorization. In *Proceedings of the ISCA Workshop on Plasticity in Speech Perception (PSP 2005)* (pp. 23–26). London: University College London [CD-ROM].

Clarke-Davidson, C. M., Luce, P. A., & Sawusch, J. R. (2008). Does perceptual learning in speech reflect changes in phonetic category representation or decision bias? *Perception & Psychophysics*, *70*, 604–618.

Clifton, C., Cutler, A., McQueen, J. M., & van Ooijen, B. (1999). Processing of inflected forms. *Behavioral and Brain Sciences*, *22*, 1018–1019.

Clopper, C. G., & Bradlow, A. R. (2006). Effects of dialect variation on speech intelligibility in noise. *Journal of the Acoustical Society of America*, *119*, 3424.

Clopper, C. G., & Pisoni, D. B. (2004). Some acoustic cues for the perceptual categorization of American English regional dialects. *Journal of Phonetics*, *32*, 111–140.

Clopper, C. G., & Pisoni, D. B. (2006). Effects of region of origin and geographic mobility on perceptual dialect categorization. *Language Variation and Change*, *18*, 193–221.

Cluff, M. S., & Luce, P. A. (1990). Similarity neighborhoods of spoken two-syllable words: Retroactive effects on multiple activation. *Journal of Experimental Psychology: Human Perception and Performance*, *16*, 551–563.

Coenen, E., Zwitserlood, P., & Bölte, J. (2001). Variation and assimilation in German; Consequences for lexical access and representation. *Language and Cognitive Processes*, *16*, 535–564.

Cohen, M. M., & Massaro, D. W. (1995). Perceiving visual and auditory information in consonant-vowel and vowel syllables. In C. Sorin, J. Mariani, H. Meloni & J. Schoentgen (Eds.), *Tribute to Max Wajskop: Levels in speech communication: Relations and interactions* (pp. 25–37). Amsterdam: Elsevier.

Cohen, A., & Starkweather, J. A. (1961). Vocal cues to the identification of language. *American Journal of Psychology*, *74*, 90–93.

Cole, R. A., & Jakimik, J. (1978). Understanding speech: How words are heard. In G. Underwood (Ed.), *Strategies of information processing* (pp. 67–116). London: Academic Press.

Cole, R. A., & Jakimik, J. (1980). How are syllables used to recognize words? *Journal of the Acoustical Society of America*, *67*, 965–970.

Cole, R. A., Jakimik, J., & Cooper, W. E. (1978). Perceptibility of phonetic features in fluent speech. *Journal of the Acoustical Society of America*, *64*, 44–56.

Coleman, J. S. (1999). The nature of vocoids associated with syllabic consonants in Tashlhiyt Berber. In J. J. Ohala, Y. Hasegawa, M. Ohala, D. Granville & A. C. Bailey (Eds.), *Proceedings of the 14th International Congress of Phonetic Sciences*, San Francisco (pp. 735–738). University of California Press.

Collier, R., & 't Hart, J. (1975). The role of intonation in speech perception. In A. Cohen & S. G. Nooteboom (Eds.), *Structure and process in speech perception* (pp. 107–121). Heidelberg: Springer.

Colombo, J., & Bundy, R. S. (1983). Infant response to auditory familiarity and novelty. *Infant Behavior and Development*, *6*, 305–311.

Comrie, B. (1989). *Language universals and linguistic typology* (2nd ed.). Chicago: University of Chicago Press.

Connine, C. M. (2004). It's not what you hear but how often you hear it: On the neglected role of phonological variant frequency in auditory word recognition. *Psychonomic Bulletin & Review*, *11*, 1084–1089.

Connine, C. M., Blasko, D. G., & Titone, D. (1993). Do the beginnings of spoken words have a special status in auditory word recognition? *Journal of Memory and Language*, *32*, 193–210.

Connine, C. M., Blasko, D. G., & Wang, J. (1994). Vertical similarity in spoken word recognition: Perceptual ambiguity, sentence context and individual differences. *Perception & Psychophysics*, *56*, 624–636.

Connine, C. M., & Clifton, C. E. (1987). Interactive use of lexical information in speech perception. *Journal of Experimental Psychology: Human Perception and Performance*, *13*, 291–299.

Connine, C. M., Clifton, C. E., & Cutler, A. (1987). Effects of lexical stress on phonetic categorization. *Phonetica*, *44*, 133–146.

Connine, C. M., Mullennix, J., Shernoff, E., & Yelen, J. (1990). Word familiarity and frequency in visual and auditory word recognition. *Journal of Experimental Psychology: Learning, Memory, and Cognition*, *16*, 1084–1096.

Connine, C. M., Ranbom, L., & Patterson, D. J. (2008). Processing variant forms in spoken word recognition: The role of variant frequency. *Perception & Psychophysics*, *70*, 403–411.

Connine, C. M., Titone, D., Deelman, T., & Blasko, D. (1997). Similarity mapping in spoken word recognition. *Journal of Memory and Language*, *37*, 463–480.

Connine, C. M., Titone, D., & Wang, J. (1993). Auditory word recognition: Extrinsic and intrinsic effects of word frequency. *Journal of Experimental Psychology: Learning, Memory, and Cognition*, *19*, 81–94.

Content, A., Kearns, R. K., & Frauenfelder, U. H. (2001). Boundaries versus onsets in syllabic segmentation. *Journal of Memory and Language*, *45*, 177–199.

Content, A., Meunier, C., Kearns, R. K., & Frauenfelder, U. H. (2001). Sequence detection in pseudowords in French: Where is the syllable effect? *Language and Cognitive Processes*, *16*, 609–636.

Cooper, N., Cutler, A., & Wales, R. (2002). Constraints of lexical stress on lexical access in English: Evidence from native and nonnative listeners. *Language and Speech*, *45*, 207–228.

Cooper, R. M. (1974). The control of eye fixation by the meaning of spoken language: A new methodology for the real-time investigation of speech perception, memory, and language processing. *Cognitive Psychology*, *6*, 84–107.

Cooper, R. P., & Aslin, R. N. (1990). Preference for infant-directed speech in the first month after birth. *Child Development*, *61*, 1584–1595.

de Cornulier, B. (1982). *Théorie du vers*. Paris: Le Seuil.

Costa, A., Cutler, A., & Sebastián-Gallés, N. (1998). Effects of phoneme repertoire on phoneme decision. *Perception & Psychophysics*, *60*, 1022–1031.

Cowan, N. (1991). Recurrent speech patterns as cues to the segmentation of multisyllabic sequences. *Acta Psychologica*, *77*, 121–135.

Cowan, N., & Morse, P. A. (1986). The use of auditory and phonetic memory in vowel discrimination. *Journal of the Acoustical Society of America*, *79*, 500–507.

Cowan, N., Suomi, K., & Morse, P. A. (1982). Echoic storage in infant perception. *Child Development*, *53*, 984–990.

Cristià, A. (2010). Phonetic enhancement of sibilants in infant-directed speech. *Journal of the Acoustical Society of America*, *128*, 424–434.

Crowther, C. S., & Mann, V. (1992). Native language factors affecting use of vocalic cues to final consonant voicing. *Journal of the Acoustical Society of America*, *92*, 711–722.

Crystal, T. H., & House, A. S. (1988). A note on the variability of timing control. *Journal of Speech and Hearing Research*, *31*, 497–502.

Cunillera, T., Toro, J. M., Sebastián-Gallés, N., & Rodríguez-Fornells, A. (2006). The effect of stress and statistical cues on continuous speech segmentation: An event-related brain potential study. *Brain Research*, *1123*, 168–178.

Curtin, S., Mintz, T. H., & Christiansen, M. H. (2005). Stress changes the representational landscape: Evidence from word segmentation. *Cognition*, *96*, 233–262.

Cutler, A. (1976a). Phoneme-monitoring reaction time as a function of preceding intonation contour. *Perception & Psychophysics*, *20*, 55–60.

Cutler, A. (1976b). Beyond parsing and lexical look-up: An enriched description of auditory sentence comprehension. In R. J. Wales & E. C. T. Walker (Eds.), *New approaches to language mechanisms* (pp. 133–149). Amsterdam: North-Holland.

Cutler, A. (1986). *Forbear* is a homophone: Lexical prosody does not constrain lexical access. *Language and Speech*, *29*, 201–220.

Cutler, A. (1990). Exploiting prosodic probabilities in speech segmentation. In G. T. M. Altmann (Ed.), *Cognitive models of speech processing: Psycholinguistic and computational perspectives* (pp. 105–121). Cambridge, MA: MIT Press.

Cutler, A. (1993). Phonological cues to open- and closed-class words in the processing of spoken sentences. *Journal of Psycholinguistic Research*, *22*, 109–131.

Cutler, A. (2005a). Lexical stress. In D. B. Pisoni & R. E. Remez (Eds.), *The handbook of speech perception* (pp. 264–289). Oxford: Blackwell.

Cutler, A. (2005b). The lexical statistics of word recognition problems caused by L2 phonetic confusion. In *Proceedings of the 9th European Conference on Speech Communication and Technology,* Lisbon, Portugal (pp. 413–416). Adelaide, Australia: Causal Productions

Cutler, A. (2009). Greater sensitivity to prosodic goodness in non-native than in native listeners. *Journal of the Acoustical Society of America*, *125*, 3522–3525.

Cutler, A., & Butterfield, S. (1990a). Durational cues to word boundaries in clear speech. *Speech Communication*, *9*, 485–495.

Cutler, A., & Butterfield, S. (1990b). Syllabic lengthening as a word boundary cue. In R. Seidl (Ed.), *Proceedings of the 3rd Australian International Conference on Speech Science and Technology*, Melbourne (pp. 324–328). Canberra: Australian Speech Science and Technology Association.

Cutler, A., & Butterfield, S. (1992). Rhythmic cues to speech segmentation: Evidence from juncture misperception. *Journal of Memory and Language, 31*, 218–236.

Cutler, A., Butterfield, S., & Williams, J. N. (1987). The perceptual integrity of syllabic onsets. *Journal of Memory and Language, 26*, 406–418.

Cutler, A., & Carter, D. M. (1987). The predominance of strong initial syllables in the English vocabulary. *Computer Speech and Language, 2*, 133–142.

Cutler, A., & Chen, H.-C. (1995). Phonological similarity effects in Cantonese word recognition. In K. Elenius & P. Branderus (Eds.), *Proceedings of 13th International Congress of Phonetic Sciences* (Vol. 1, pp. 106–109). Stockholm: KTH and Stockholm University.

Cutler, A., & Chen, H.-C. (1997). Lexical tone in Cantonese spoken-word processing. *Perception & Psychophysics, 59*, 165–179.

Cutler, A., & Clifton, C. (1984). The use of prosodic information in word recognition. In H. Bouma & D. G. Bouwhuis (Eds.), *Attention and performance X: Control of language processes* (pp. 183–196). Hillsdale, NJ: Erlbaum.

Cutler, A., Cooke, M., Garcia Lecumberri, M. L., & Pasveer, D. (2007). L2 consonant identification in noise: Cross-language comparisons. In H. van Hamme & R. van Son (Eds.), *Proceedings of Interspeech 2007*, Antwerp, Belgium (pp. 1585–1588). Adelaide, Australia: Causal Productions [CD-ROM].

Cutler, A., Dahan, D., & van Donselaar, W. (1997). Prosody in the comprehension of spoken language: A literature review. *Language and Speech, 40*, 141–201.

Cutler, A., Demuth, K., & McQueen, J. M. (2002). Universality versus language-specificity in listening to running speech. *Psychological Science, 13*, 258–262.

Cutler, A., & van Donselaar, W. (2001). *Voornaam* is not (really) a homophone: Lexical prosody and lexical access in Dutch. *Language and Speech, 44*, 171–195.

Cutler, A., Eisner, F., McQueen, J. M., & Norris, D. (2010). How abstract phonemic categories are necessary for coping with speaker-related variation. In C. Fougeron, B. Kühnert, M. D'Imperio & N. Vallée (Eds.), *Laboratory phonology 10* (pp. 91–111). Berlin: Mouton de Gruyter.

Cutler, A., & Fodor, J. A. (1979). Semantic focus and sentence comprehension. *Cognition, 7*, 49–59.

Cutler, A., & Foss, D. J. (1977). On the role of sentence stress in sentence processing. *Language and Speech, 20*, 1–10.

Cutler, A., Garcia Lecumberri, M. L., & Cooke, M. (2008). Consonant identification in noise by native and non-native listeners: Effects of local context. *Journal of the Acoustical Society of America, 124*, 1264–1268.

Cutler, A., Hawkins, J. A., & Gilligan, G. (1985). The suffixing preference: A processing explanation. *Linguistics, 23*, 723–758.

Cutler, A., & Koster, M. (2000). Stress and lexical activation in Dutch. In B. Yuan, T. Huang & X. Tang (Eds.), *Proceedings of the 6th International Conference on Spoken Language Processing*, Beijing (Vol. 1, pp. 593–596). Beijing: China Military Friendship Publish.

Cutler, A., McQueen, J., Baayen, H., & Drexler, H. (1994). Words within words in a real-speech corpus. In R. Togneri (Ed.), *Proceedings of the 5th Australian International Conference on Speech Science and Technology*, Perth (Vol. 1, pp. 362–367). Canberra: Australian Speech Science and Technology Association (ASSTA).

Cutler, A., McQueen, J. M., Butterfield, S., & Norris, D. (2008). Prelexically-driven retuning of phoneme boundaries. In J. Fletcher, D. Loakes, R. Goecke, D. Burnham & M. Wagner (Eds.), *Proceedings of Interspeech 2008*, Brisbane (p. 2056). Adelaide, Australia: Causal Productions [CD-ROM].

Cutler, A., McQueen, J. M., Jansonius, M., & Bayerl, S. (2002). The lexical statistics of competitor activation in spoken-word recognition. In C. Bow (Ed.), *Proceedings of the 9th Australian International Conference on Speech Science and Technology,* Melbourne (pp. 40–45). Canberra: Australian Speech Science and Technology Association (ASSTA).

Cutler, A., McQueen, J. M., Norris, D., & Somejuan, A. (2001). The roll of the silly ball. In E. Dupoux (Ed.), *Language, brain, and cognitive development: Essays in honor of Jacques Mehler* (pp. 181–194). Cambridge, MA: MIT Press.

Cutler, A., Mehler, J., Norris, D., & Segui, J. (1983). A language-specific comprehension strategy. *Nature*, *304*, 159–160.

Cutler, A., Mehler, J., Norris, D., & Segui, J. (1986). The syllable's differing role in the segmentation of French and English. *Journal of Memory and Language*, *25*, 385–400.

Cutler, A., Mehler, J., Norris, D. G., & Segui, J. (1987). Phoneme identification and the lexicon. *Cognitive Psychology*, *19*, 141–177.

Cutler, A., Mehler, J., Norris, D., & Segui, J. (1989). Limits on bilingualism. *Nature*, *340*, 229–230.

Cutler, A., Mehler, J., Norris, D., & Segui, J. (1992). The monolingual nature of speech segmentation by bilinguals. *Cognitive Psychology*, *24*, 381–410.

Cutler, A., & Norris, D. (1988). The role of strong syllables in segmentation for lexical access. *Journal of Experimental Psychology: Human Perception and Performance*, *14*, 113–121.

Cutler, A., Norris, D., & Sebastián-Gallés, N. (2004). Phonemic repertoire and similarity within the vocabulary. In S. H. Kin & M. Jin Bae (Eds.), *Proceedings of the 8th International Conference on Spoken Language Processing,* Jeju Island, Korea (Vol. 1, pp. 65–68). Seoul: Sunjin Printing Co. [CD-ROM].

Cutler, A., & Otake, T. (1994). Mora or phoneme? Further evidence for language-specific listening. *Journal of Memory and Language*, *33*, 824–844.

Cutler, A., & Otake, T. (1998). Assimilation of place in Japanese and Dutch. In R. H. Mannell & J. Robert-Ribes (Eds.), *Proceedings of the 5th International Conference on Spoken Language Processing*, Sydney (Vol. 5, pp. 1751–1754). Canberra: Australian Speech Science and Technology Association (ASSTA).

Cutler, A., & Otake, T. (1999). Pitch accent in spoken-word recognition in Japanese. *Journal of the Acoustical Society of America*, *105*, 1877–1888.

Cutler, A., & Otake, T. (2002). Rhythmic categories in spoken-word recognition. *Journal of Memory and Language*, *46*, 296–322.

Cutler, A., & Otake, T. (2004). Pseudo-homophony in non-native listening. Paper presented at the 147th meeting, Acoustical Society of America, New York, May 2004. *Journal of the Acoustical Society of America*, *115*, 2392 (Abstract).

Cutler, A., Otake, T., & McQueen, J. M. (2009). Vowel devoicing and the perception of spoken Japanese words. *Journal of the Acoustical Society of America, 125*, 1693–1703.

Cutler, A., & Pasveer, D. (2006). Explaining cross-linguistic differences in effects of lexical stress on spoken-word recognition. In R. Hoffmann & H. Mixdorff (Eds.), *Proceedings of the 3rd International Conference on Speech Prosody,* Dresden (pp. 237–240). Dresden: TUDpress.

Cutler, A., Sebastián-Gallés, N., Soler Vilageliu, O., & van Ooijen, B. (2000). Constraints of vowels and consonants on lexical selection: Cross-linguistic comparisons. *Memory & Cognition, 28*, 746–755.

Cutler, A., Smits, R., & Cooper, N. (2005). Vowel perception: Effects of non-native language vs. non-native dialect. *Speech Communication, 47*, 32–42.

Cutler, A., Wales, R., Cooper, N., & Janssen, J. (2007). Dutch listeners' use of suprasegmental cues to English stress. In J. Trouvain & W. J. Barry (Eds.), *Proceedings of the 16th International Congress of Phonetic Sciences,* Saarbrücken (pp. 1913–1916). Dudweiler: Pirrot.

Cutler, A., Weber, A., & Otake, T. (2006). Asymmetric mapping from phonetic to lexical representations in second-language listening. *Journal of Phonetics, 34*, 269–284.

Cutler, A., Weber, A., Smits, R., & Cooper, N. (2004). Patterns of English phoneme confusions by native and non-native listeners. *Journal of the Acoustical Society of America, 116*, 3668–3678.

Dahan, D., Magnuson, J. S., & Tanenhaus, M. K. (2001). Time course of frequency effects in spoken-word recognition: Evidence from eye movements. *Cognitive Psychology, 42*, 317–367.

Dahan, D., Magnuson, J. S., Tanenhaus, M. K., & Hogan, E. M. (2001). Subcategorical mismatches and the time course of lexical access: Evidence for lexical competition. *Language and Cognitive Processes, 16*, 507–534.

Dahan, D., Swingley, D., Tanenhaus, M. K., & Magnuson, J. S. (2000). Linguistic gender and spoken-word recognition in French. *Journal of Memory and Language, 42*, 465–480.

Dahan, D., & Tanenhaus, M. K. (2005). Looking at the rope when looking for the snake: Conceptually mediated eye movements during spoken-word recognition. *Psychonomic Bulletin & Review, 12*, 453–459.

Dahan, D., Tanenhaus, M. K., & Chambers, C. G. (2002). Accent and reference resolution in spoken-language comprehension. *Journal of Memory and Language, 47*, 292–314.

Darcy, I., Peperkamp, S., & Dupoux, E. (2007). Bilinguals play by the rules: Perceptual compensation for assimilation in late L2-learners. In J. Cole & J. Hualde (Eds.), *Laboratory Phonology 9* (pp. 411–442). Berlin: Mouton de Gruyter.

Dasher, R., & Bolinger, D. (1982). On pre-accentual lengthening. *Journal of the International Phonetic Association, 12*, 58–69.

Dauer, R. (1987). Phonetic and phonological components of language rhythm. In Ü. Viks (Ed.), *Proceedings of the 11th International Congress of Phonetic Sciences*, Tallinn, Estonia (pp. 447–450). Estonia: Academy of Sciences of the Estonian SSR.

Davis, M. H., Johnsrude, I. S., Hervais-Adelman, A., Taylor, K., & McGettigan, C. (2005). Lexical information drives perceptual learning of distorted speech: Evidence from the comprehension of noise-vocoded sentences. *Journal of Experimental Psychology: General, 134*, 222–241.

Davis, M. H., Marslen-Wilson, W. D., & Gaskell, M. G. (2002). Leading up the lexical garden-path: Segmentation and ambiguity in spoken word recognition. *Journal of Experimental Psychology: Human Perception and Performance, 28*, 218–244.

DeCasper, A. J., & Fifer, W. P. (1980). Of human bonding: Newborns prefer their mothers' voices. *Science*, *208*, 1174–1176.

DeCasper, A. J., Lecanuet, J.-P., Busnel, M.-C., Granier-Deferre, C., & Maugeais, R. (1994). Fetal reactions to recurrent maternal speech. *Infant Behavior and Development*, *17*, 159–164.

DeCasper, A. J., & Prescott, P. A. (1984). Human newborns' perception of male voices: Preference, discrimination and reinforcing value. *Developmental Psychobiology*, *17*, 481–491.

DeCasper, A. J., & Spence, M. J. (1986). Prenatal maternal speech influences newborns' perception of speech sounds. *Infant Behavior and Development*, *9*, 133–150.

Dechovitz, D. (1977). Information conveyed by vowels: A confirmation. *Haskins Laboratory Status Report on Speech Research*, *SR-53*(54), 213–219.

Decoene, S. (1993). Testing the speech unit hypothesis with the primed matching task: Phoneme categories are perceptually basic. *Perception & Psychophysics*, *53*, 601–616.

Deelman, T., & Connine, C. M. (2001). Missing information in spoken word recognition: Nonreleased stop consonants. *Journal of Experimental Psychology: Human Perception and Performance*, *27*, 656–663.

Dehaene-Lambertz, G., Dupoux, E., & Gout, A. (2000). Electrophysiological correlates of phonological processing: A cross-linguistic study. *Journal of Cognitive Neuroscience*, *12*, 635–647.

Dejean de la Bâtie, B., & Bradley, D. C. (1995). Resolving word boundaries in spoken French: Native and non-native strategies. *Applied Psycholinguistics*, *16*, 59–81.

Dell, F., & Elmedlaoui, M. (1985). Syllabic consonants and syllabification in Imdlawn Tashlhiyt Berber. *Journal of African Languages and Linguistics*, *7*, 105–130.

Dell, F., & Elmedlaoui, M. (1988). Syllabic consonants in Berber: Some new evidence. *Journal of African Languages and Linguistics*, *10*, 1–17.

Dell, G. S. (1990). Effects of frequency and vocabulary type on phonological speech errors. *Language and Cognitive Processes*, *5*, 313–349.

Dell, G. S., & Newman, J. E. (1980). Detecting phonemes in fluent speech. *Journal of Verbal Learning and Verbal Behavior*, *19*, 608–623.

Dell, G. S., Reed, K. D., Adams, D. R., & Meyer, A. S. (2000). Speech errors, phonotactic constraints, and implicit learning: A study of the role of experience in language production. *Journal of Experimental Psychology: Learning, Memory, and Cognition*, *26*, 1355–1367.

Demany, L., McKenzie, B., & Vurpillot, E. (1977). Rhythm perception in early infancy. *Nature*, *266*, 718–719.

Deterding, D. (2001). The measurement of rhythm: A comparison of Singapore and British English. *Journal of Phonetics*, *29*, 217–230.

Deutsch, W., & Wijnen, F. (1985). The article's noun and the noun's article: Explorations into the representation and access of linguistic gender in Dutch. *Linguistics*, *23*, 793–810.

Diaz, B., Baus, C., Escera, C., Costa, A., & Sebastián-Gallés, N. (2008). Brain potentials to native phoneme discrimination reveal the origin of individual differences in learning the sounds of a second language. *Proceedings of the National Academy of Sciences of the United States of America*, *105*, 16083–16088.

Diehl, R. L., Elman, J. L., & McCusker, S. B. (1978). Contrast effects on stop consonant identification. *Journal of Experimental Psychology: Human Perception and Performance, 4,* 599–609.

Dietrich, C. (2006). *The acquisition of phonological structure: Distinguishing contrastive from non-contrastive variation.* Ph.D. dissertation, MPI Series in Psycholinguistics 40, Radboud University Nijmegen.

Dietrich, C., Swingley, D., & Werker, J. (2007). Native language governs interpretation of salient speech sound differences at 18 months. *Proceedings of the National Academy of Sciences of the United States of America, 104,* 16027–16031.

Dogil, G. & Williams, B. (1999). The phonetic manifestation of word stress in Lithuanian, Polish and German. In H. van der Hulst (Ed.), *Word prosodic systems in the languages of Europe* (pp. 273–334). Berlin: Mouton de Gruyter.

van Donselaar, W., Koster, M., & Cutler, A. (2005). Exploring the role of lexical stress in lexical recognition. *Quarterly Journal of Experimental Psychology, 58A,* 251–273.

van Donselaar, W., Kuijpers, C. T. L., & Cutler, A. (1999). Facilitatory effects of vowel epenthesis on word processing in Dutch. *Journal of Memory and Language, 41,* 59–77.

Dumay, N., Frauenfelder, U. H., & Content, A. (2002). The role of the syllable in lexical segmentation in French: Word-spotting data. *Brain and Language, 81,* 144–161.

Dumay, N., & Gaskell, M. G. (2007). Sleep-associated changes in the mental representation of spoken words. *Psychological Science, 18,* 35–39.

Dupoux, E., Fushimi, T., Kakehi, K., & Mehler, J. (1999). Prelexical locus of an illusory vowel effect in Japanese. In K. Erdőhegyi, G. Németh, & G. Olaszy (Eds.), *Proceedings of EUROSPEECH'99,* Budapest, Hungary (pp. 1675–1678). Budapest: Technical University of Budapest, Department of Telecommunications & Telematics.

Dupoux, E., & Green, K. (1997). Perceptual adjustment to highly compressed speech: Effects of talker and rate changes. *Journal of Experimental Psychology: Human Perception and Performance, 23,* 914–927.

Dupoux, E., Kakehi, K., Hirose, Y., Pallier, C., & Mehler, J. (1999). Epenthetic vowels in Japanese: A perceptual illusion? *Journal of Experimental Psychology: Human Perception and Performance, 25,* 1568–1578.

Dupoux, E., & Mehler, J. (1990). Monitoring the lexicon with normal and compressed speech: Frequency effects and the prelexical code. *Journal of Memory and Language, 29,* 316–335.

Dupoux, E., Pallier, C., Sebastián-Gallés, N., & Mehler, J. (1997). A destressing "deafness" in French? *Journal of Memory and Language, 36,* 406–421.

Dupoux, E., Peperkamp, S., & Sebastián-Gallés, N. (2001). A robust method to study stress "deafness". *Journal of the Acoustical Society of America, 110,* 1606–1618.

Efremova, I. B., Fintoft, K., & Ormestad, H. (1963). Intelligibility of tonic accent. *Phonetica, 10,* 203–212.

Eilers, R. E., Wilson, W. R., & Moore, J. M. (1977). Developmental changes in speech discrimination in infants. *Journal of Speech and Hearing Research, 20,* 766–780.

Eimas, P. D., & Corbit, J. D. (1973). Selective adaptation of linguistic feature detectors. *Cognitive Psychology, 4,* 99–109.

Eimas, P. D., Hornstein, S. B. M., & Payton, P. (1990). Attention and the role of dual codes in phoneme monitoring. *Journal of Memory and Language*, *29*, 160–180.

Eimas, P. D., Miller, J. L., & Jusczyk, P. W. (1987). On infant speech perception and the acquisition of language. In S. Harnad (Ed.), *Categorical perception: The groundwork of cognition* (pp. 161–195). Cambridge: Cambridge University Press.

Eimas, P. D., & Nygaard, L. C. (1992). Contextual coherence and attention in phoneme monitoring. *Journal of Memory and Language*, *31*, 375–395.

Eimas, P. D., Siqueland, E. R., Jusczyk, P., & Vigorito, J. (1971). Speech perception in infants. *Science*, *171*, 303–306.

Eisner, F., & McQueen, J. M. (2005). The specificity of perceptual learning in speech processing. *Perception & Psychophysics*, *67*, 224–238.

Eisner, F., & McQueen, J. M. (2006). Perceptual learning in speech: Stability over time. *Journal of the Acoustical Society of America*, *119*, 1950–1953.

El Aissati, A., McQueen, J. M., & Cutler, A. (2012). Finding words in a language that allows words without vowels. *Cognition*. doi: 0.1016/j.cognition.2012.03.006

Ellis, R. (1994). *The study of second language acquisition*. Oxford: Oxford University Press.

Ellis, L., & Hardcastle, W. J. (2002). Categorical and gradient properties of assimilation in alveolar to velar sequences: Evidence from EPG and EMA data. *Journal of Phonetics*, *30*, 373–396.

Elman, J. L., & McClelland, J. L. (1988). Cognitive penetration of the mechanisms of perception: Compensation for coarticulation of lexically restored phonemes. *Journal of Memory and Language*, *27*, 143–165.

Emmorey, K. D. (1989). Auditory morphological priming in the lexicon. *Language and Cognitive Processes*, *4*, 73–92.

Emmorey, K. D. (2002). *Language, cognition, and the brain: Insights from sign language research*. Mahwah, NJ: Erlbaum.

Ernestus, M., & Baayen, R. H. (2003). Predicting the unpredictable: Interpreting neutralized segments in Dutch. *Language*, *79*, 5–38.

Ernestus, M., & Baayen, R. H. (2006). The functionality of incomplete neutralization in Dutch: The case of past-tense formation. In L. M. Goldstein, D. H. Whalen & C. T. Best (Eds.), *Laboratory Phonology 8* (pp. 27–49). Berlin: Mouton de Gruyter.

Ernestus, M., & Baayen, H. (2007). Paradigmatic effects in auditory word recognition: The case of alternating voice in Dutch. *Language and Cognitive Processes*, *22*, 1–24.

Ernestus, M., Baayen, H., & Schreuder, R. (2002). The recognition of reduced word forms. *Brain and Language*, *81*, 162–173.

Ernestus, M., Lahey, M., Verhees, F., & Baayen, R. H. (2006). Lexical frequency and voice assimilation. *Journal of the Acoustical Society of America*, *120*, 1040–1051.

Ernestus, M., & Mak, W. M. (2004). Distinctive phonological features differ in relevance for both spoken and written word recognition. *Journal of Brain and Language*, *90*, 378–392.

Escudero, P., & Boersma, P. (2004). Bridging the gap between L2 speech perception research and phonological theory. *Studies in Second Language Acquisition*, *26*, 551–585.

Escudero, P., Hayes-Harb, R., & Mitterer, H. (2008). Novel second-language words and asymmetric lexical access. *Journal of Phonetics*, *36*, 345–360.

Evans, B. G., & Iverson, P. (2004). Vowel normalization for accent: An investigation of best exemplar locations in northern and southern British English sentences. *Journal of the Acoustical Society of America, 115*, 352–361.

Evans, B. G., & Iverson, P. (2005). Plasticity in speech production and perception: A study of accent change in young adults. In *Proceedings of the ISCA Workshop on Plasticity in Speech Perception (PSP 2005)*. London: University College London [CD-ROM].

Evans, N., & Levinson, S. C. (2009). The myth of language universals: Language diversity and its importance for cognitive science. *Behavioral and Brain Sciences, 32*, 429–492.

Fear, B. D., Cutler, A., & Butterfield, S. (1995). The strong/weak syllable distinction in English. *Journal of the Acoustical Society of America, 97*, 1893–1904.

Fenn, K. M., Nusbaum, H. C., & Margoliash, D. (2003). Consolidation during sleep of perceptual learning of spoken language. *Nature, 425*, 614–616.

Fennell, C. T., & Werker, J. F. (2003). Early word learners' ability to access phonetic detail in well-known words. *Language and Speech, 46*, 245–264.

Fenson, L., Dale, P., Reznick, J. S., Bates, E., Thal, D., & Pethick, S. J. (1994). *Variability in early communicative development*. Monographs of the Society for Research in Child Development, 59, 1–173.

Fenson, L., Bates, E., Dale, P., Goodman, J., Reznick, J. S., & Thal, D. (2000). Measuring variability in early child language: Don't shoot the messenger. *Child Development, 71*, 323–328.

Fernald, A. (1985). Four-month-old infants prefer to listen to motherese. *Infant Behavior and Development, 8*, 181–195.

Fernald, A., & Kuhl, P. (1987). Acoustic determinants of infant preference for motherese speech. *Infant Behavior and Development, 10*, 279–293.

Fernald, A., & Simon, T. (1984). Expanded intonation contours in mothers' speech to newborns. *Developmental Psychology, 20*, 104–113.

Fernald, A., Taeschner, T., Dunn, J., Papousek, M., de Boysson-Bardies, B., & Fukui, I. (1989). A cross-language study of prosodic modifications in mothers' and fathers' speech to preverbal infants. *Journal of Child Language, 16*, 477–501.

Fernald, A., Zangl, R., Portillo, A. L., & Marchman, V. A. (2008). Looking while listening: Using eye movements to monitor spoken language comprehension by infants and young children. In I. A. Sekerina, E. M. Fernández & H. Clahsen (Eds.), *Developmental psycholinguistics: On-line methods in children's language processing* (pp. 97–135). Amsterdam: John Benjamins.

Fernandes, T., Ventura, P., & Kolinsky, R. (2007). Statistical information and coarticulation as cues to word boundaries: A matter of signal quality. *Perception & Psychophysics, 69*, 856–864.

Field, J. (2005). Intelligibility and the listener: The role of lexical. stress. *TESOL Quarterly, 39*, 399–423.

Field, J. (2008). Revising segmentation hypotheses in first and second language listening. *System, 36*, 35–51.

Flege, J. E. (1984). The detection of French accent by American listeners. *Journal of the Acoustical Society of America, 76*, 692–707.

Flege, J. E. (1989). Chinese subjects' perception of the word-final English /t/-/d/ contrast: Performance before and after training. *Journal of the Acoustical Society of America, 86*, 1684–1697.

Flege, J. E. (1995). Second language speech learning: Theory, findings, and problems. In W. Strange (Ed.), *Speech perception and linguistic experience: Issues in cross-language research* (pp. 233–277). Timonium, MD: York Press.

Flege, J. E. (1999). Age of learning and second language speech. In D. Birdsong (Ed.), *Second language acquisition and the Critical Period Hypothesis* (pp. 101–132). Hillsdale, NJ: Erlbaum.

Flege, J. E. (2003). Assessing constraints on second-language segmental production and perception. In N. Schiller & A. Meyer (Eds.), *Phonetics and phonology in language comprehension and production: differences and similarities* (pp. 319–355). Berlin: Mouton de Gruyter.

Flege, J. E., & Eefting, W. (1987). Cross-language switching in stop consonant perception and production by Dutch speakers of English. *Speech Communication*, *6*, 185–202.

Flege, J. E., & Hillenbrand, J. (1986). Differential use of temporal cues to the /s/-/z/ contrast by native and non-native speakers of English. *Journal of the Acoustical Society of America*, *79*, 508–517.

Flege, J. E., MacKay, I. R. A., & Meador, D. (1999). Native Italian speakers' perception and production of English vowels. *Journal of the Acoustical Society of America*, *106*, 2973–2987.

Flege, J. E., Munro, M. J., & Fox, R. A. (1994). Auditory and categorical effects on cross-language vowel perception. *Journal of the Acoustical Society of America*, *95*, 3623–3641.

Flege, J. E., Takagi, N., & Mann, V. (1996). Lexical familiarity and English-language experience affect Japanese adults' perception of /ɹ/ and /l/. *Journal of the Acoustical Society of America*, *99*, 1161–1173.

Flege, J. E., & Wang, C. (1989). Native-language phonotactic constraints affect how well Chinese subjects perceive the word-final /t/-/d/ contrast. *Journal of Phonetics*, *17*, 299–315.

Flemming, L., Wang, Y., Caprihan, A., Eiselt, M., Haueisen, J., & Okada, Y. (2005). Evaluation of the distortion of EEG signals caused by a hole in the skull mimicking the fontanel in the skull of human neonates. *Clinical Neurophysiology*, *116*, 1141–1152.

Fletcher, J. (1991). Rhythm and final lengthening in French. *Journal of Phonetics*, *19*, 193–212.

Fok, C. Y.-Y. (1974). A perceptual study of tones in Cantonese. *Centre of Asian Studies: Occasional Papers and Monographs* (No. 18). Hong Kong: Centre of Asian Studies, University of Hong Kong.

Fónagy, I. (1966). Electrophysiological and acoustic correlates of stress and stress perception. *Journal of Speech and Hearing Research*, *9*, 231–244.

Foss, D. J. (1970). Some effects of ambiguity upon sentence comprehension. *Journal of Verbal Learning and Verbal Behavior*, *9*, 699–706.

Foss, D. J., & Blank, M. A. (1980). Identifying the speech codes. *Cognitive Psychology*, *12*, 1–31.

Foss, D. J., & Gernsbacher, M. A. (1983). Cracking the dual code: Toward a unitary model of phonetic identification. *Journal of Verbal Learning and Verbal Behavior*, *22*, 609–632.

Foss, D. J., Harwood, D. A., & Blank, M. A. (1980). Deciphering decoding decisions: Data and devices. In R. A. Cole (Ed.), *Perception and production of fluent speech* (pp. 165–199). Hillsdale, NJ: Erlbaum.

Foss, D. J., & Jenkins, C. M. (1973). Some effects of context on the comprehension of ambiguous sentences. *Journal of Verbal Learning and Verbal Behavior*, *12*, 577–589.

Foss, D. J., & Swinney, D. A. (1973). On the psychological reality of the phoneme: Perception, identification, and consciousness. *Journal of Verbal Learning and Verbal Behavior, 12*, 246–257.

Fougeron, C., & Steriade, D. (1997). Does deletion of French SCHWA lead to neutralization of lexical distinctions? In G. Kokkinakis, N. Fakotakis & E. Dermatas (Eds.), *Proceedings of the 5th European Conference on Speech Communication and Technology (EUROSPEECH'97)*, Rhodes (pp. 943–946). Patras, Greece: WCL, University of Patras.

Foulkes, P., & Docherty, G. J. (1999). *Urban voices: Accent studies in the British Isles*. London: Arnold.

Fournier, R., Verhoeven, J., Swerts, M., & Gussenhoven, C. (2006). Perceiving word prosodic contrasts as a function of sentence prosody in two Dutch Limburgian dialects. *Journal of Phonetics, 34*, 29–48.

Fowler, C. A. (1988). Differential shortening of repeated content words produced in various communicative contexts. *Language and Speech, 31*, 307–319.

Fowler, C. A., & Housum, J. (1987). Talkers' signaling of "new" and "old" words in speech and listeners' perception and use of the distinction. *Journal of Memory and Language, 26*, 489–504.

Fox, R. A. (1984). Effect of lexical status on phonetic categorization. *Journal of Experimental Psychology: Human Perception and Performance, 10*, 526–540.

Fox, R. A., & Unkefer, J. (1985). The effect of lexical status on the perception of tone. *Journal of Chinese Linguistics, 13*, 69–90.

Frankish, C. (2008). Precategorical acoustic storage and the perception of speech. *Journal of Memory and Language, 58*, 815–836.

Frauenfelder, U. H., Segui, J., & Dijkstra, T. (1990). Lexical effects in phonemic processing: Facilitatory or inhibitory? *Journal of Experimental Psychology: Human Perception and Performance, 16*, 77–91.

Frazier, L., Carlson, K., & Clifton, C., Jr. (2006). Prosodic phrasing is central to language comprehension. *Trends in Cognitive Sciences, 10*, 244–249.

Freedman, D. (1992). *Frequency effects in auditory word recognition using the word-spotting task*. M.Sc. thesis, University of Cambridge.

Friederici, A. D. (1985). Levels of processing and vocabulary types: Evidence from on-line comprehension in normals and agrammatics. *Cognition, 19*, 133–166.

Friederici, A. D., Friedrich, M., & Christophe, A. (2007). Brain responses in 4-month-old infants are already language specific. *Current Biology, 17*, 1208–1211.

Friederici, A. D., & Thierry, G. (2008). *Early language development: Bridging brain and behaviour*. Amsterdam: John Benjamins.

Friederici, A. D., & Wessels, J. M. I. (1993). Phonotactic knowledge of word boundaries and its use in infant speech perception. *Perception & Psychophysics, 54*, 287–295.

Friedrich, C. K. (2002). *Prosody and spoken word recognition—Behavioral and ERP correlates*. Ph.D. dissertation, University of Leipzig.

Friedrich, C. K., Kotz, S. A., Friederici, A. D., & Gunter, T. C. (2004). ERPs reflect lexical identification in word fragment priming. *Journal of Cognitive Neuroscience, 16*, 541–552.

Friedrich, C. K., Kotz, S. A., & Gunter, T. C. (2001). Event-related evidence of word fragment priming: New correlate for language processing? *Psychophysiology*, *38*, S42 (Abstract).

Friedrich, C. K., Schild, U., & Röder, B. (2009). Electrophysiological indices of word fragment priming allow characterizing neural stages of speech recognition. *Biological Psychology*, *80*, 105–113.

Friedrich, M., & Friederici, A. D. (2006). Early N400 development and later language acquisition. *Psychophysiology*, *43*, 1–12.

Frith, U. (1980). Unexpected spelling problems. In U. Frith (Ed.), *Cognitive processes in spelling* (pp. 495–515). London: Academic Press.

Fu, Q.-J., & Galvin, J. J., III. (2007). Perceptual learning and auditory training in cochlear implant recipients. *Trends in Amplification*, *11*, 193–205.

Gandour, J. (1983). Tone perception in Far Eastern languages. *Journal of Phonetics*, *11*, 149–175.

Gandour, J., Wong, D., Lowe, M., Dzemidzic, M., Satthamnuwong, N., Tong, Y., & Li, X. (2002). A cross-linguistic fMRI study of spectral and temporal cues underlying phonological processing. *Journal of Cognitive Neuroscience*, *14*, 1076–1087.

Ganong, W. F. (1980). Phonetic categorization in auditory word perception. *Journal of Experimental Psychology: Human Perception and Performance*, *6*, 110–125.

Garcia Lecumberri, M. L., & Cooke, M. (2006). Effect of masker type on native and non-native consonant perception in noise. *Journal of the Acoustical Society of America*, *119*, 2445–2454.

Garcia Lecumberri, M. L., Cooke, M., & Cutler, A. (2010). Non-native speech perception in adverse conditions: A review. *Speech Communication*, *52*, 864–886.

Garnica, O. K. (1977). Some prosodic and paralinguistic features of speech to young children. In C. E. Snow & C. A. Ferguson (Eds.), *Talking to children: Language input and acquisition* (pp. 63–68). Cambridge: Cambridge University Press.

Gaskell, M. G., & Dumay, N. (2003). Lexical competition and the acquisition of novel words. *Cognition*, *89*, 105–132.

Gaskell, M. G., & Marslen-Wilson, W. D. (1996). Phonological variation and inference in lexical access. *Journal of Experimental Psychology: Human Perception and Performance*, *22*, 144–156.

Gaskell, M. G., & Marslen-Wilson, W. D. (1997). Integrating form and meaning: A distributed model of speech perception. *Language and Cognitive Processes*, *12*, 613–656.

Gaskell, M. G., & Marslen-Wilson, W. D. (1998). Mechanisms of phonological inference in speech perception. *Journal of Experimental Psychology: Human Perception and Performance*, *24*, 380–396.

Gaskell, M. G., Spinelli, E., & Meunier, F. (2002). Perception of resyllabification in French. *Memory & Cognition*, *30*, 798–810.

Gat, I. B., & Keith, R. W. (1978). An effect of linguistic experience: Auditory word discrimination by native and non-native speakers of English. *Audiology*, *17*, 339–345.

Gerhardt, K. J., Abrams, R. M., & Oliver, C. C. (1990). Sound environment of the fetal sheep. *American Journal of Obstetrics and Gynecology*, *162*, 282–287.

Gervain, J., Mehler, J., Werker, J. F., Nelson, C. A., Csibra, G., Lloyd-Fox, S., Shukla, M., & Aslin, R. N. (2011). Near-infrared spectroscopy: A report from the McDonnell infant methodology consortium. *Developmental Cognitive Neuroscience*, *1*, 22–46.

Gilbert, C. D., Sigman, M., & Crist, R. E. (2001). The neural basis of perceptual learning. *Neuron*, *31*, 681–697.

Gleitman, L., & Wanner, E. (1982). Language acquisition: The state of the state of the art. In E. Wanner & L. Gleitman (Eds.), *Language acquisition: The state of the art* (pp. 3–48). Cambridge: Cambridge University Press.

Godfrey, J., Holliman, E., & McDaniel, J. (1992). SWITCHBOARD: Telephone speech corpus for research and development. *Proceedings of the IEEE, ICASSP-92*, *1*, 517–520.

Goedemans, R. (2010). A typology of stress patterns. In H. van der Hulst, R. Goedemans & E. van Zanten (Eds.), *A survey of word accentual patterns in the languages of the world* (pp. 647–668). Berlin: Mouton de Gruyter.

Goggin, J. P., Thompson, C. P., Strube, G., & Simental, L. R. (1991). The role of language familiarity in voice identification. *Memory & Cognition*, *19*, 448–458.

Goldinger, S. D. (1996). Words and voices: Episodic traces in spoken word identification and recognition memory. *Journal of Experimental Psychology: Learning, Memory, and Cognition*, *22*, 1166–1183.

Goldinger, S. D. (1998). Echoes of echoes? An episodic theory of lexical access. *Psychological Review*, *105*, 251–279.

Goldinger, S. D., & Azuma, T. (2003). Puzzle-solving science: The quixotic quest for units in speech perception. *Journal of Phonetics*, *31*, 305–320.

Goldinger, S. D., Luce, P. A., & Pisoni, D. B. (1989). Priming lexical neighbors of spoken words: Effects of competition and inhibition. *Journal of Memory and Language*, *28*, 501–518.

Goldinger, S. D., Pisoni, D. B., & Logan, J. S. (1991). On the nature of talker variability effects on recall of spoken word lists. *Journal of Experimental Psychology: Learning, Memory, and Cognition*, *17*, 152–162.

Goldsmith, J. (1995). Phonological theory. In J. Goldsmith (Ed.), *The handbook of phonological theory*. Oxford: Blackwell.

Goldstein, H. (1983). Word recognition in a foreign language: A study of speech perception. *Journal of Psycholinguistic Research*, *12*, 417–427.

Goldstein, A. G., Knight, P., Bailis, K., & Conover, J. (1981). Recognition memory for accented and unaccented voices. *Bulletin of the Psychonomic Society*, *17*, 217–220.

Goldstein, M. H., & Schwade, J. A. (2008). Social feedback to infants' babbling facilitates rapid phonological learning. *Psychological Science*, *19*, 515–523.

Golestani, N., Molko, N., Dehaene, S., Le Bihan, D., & Pallier, C. (2007). Brain structure predicts the learning of foreign speech sounds. *Cerebral Cortex*, *17*, 575–582.

Golestani, N., & Pallier, C. (2007). Anatomical correlates of foreign speech sound production. *Cerebral Cortex*, *17*, 929–934.

Golestani, N., Paus, T., & Zatorre, R. J. (2002). Anatomical correlates of learning novel speech sounds. *Neuron*, *35*, 997–1010.

Golestani, N., & Zatorre, R. J. (2004). Learning new sounds of speech: Reallocation of neural substrates. *NeuroImage*, *21*, 494–506.

Gómez, R. L. (2002). Variability and detection of invariant structure. *Psychological Science*, *13*, 431–436.

Goodman, J. C., & Huttenlocher, J. (1988). Do we know how people identify spoken words? *Journal of Memory and Language*, *27*, 684–698.

Goslin, J., & Frauenfelder, U. H. (2008). Vowel aperture and syllable segmentation in French. *Language and Speech*, *51*, 199–222.

Gottfried, T. L., & Beddor, P. S. (1988). Perception of temporal and spectral information in French vowels. *Language and Speech*, *31*, 57–75.

Gottfried, T. L., & Suiter, T. L. (1997). Effect of linguistic experience on the identification of Mandarin Chinese vowels and tones. *Journal of Phonetics*, *25*, 207–231.

Goto, H. (1971). Auditory perception by normal Japanese adults of the sounds "l" and "r". *Neuropsychologia*, *9*, 317–323.

Goudbeek, M., Cutler, A., & Smits, R. (2008). Supervised and unsupervised learning of multidimensionally varying non-native speech categories. *Speech Communication*, *50*, 109–125.

Goudbeek, M., Smits, R., & Swingley, D. (2009). Supervised and unsupervised learning of multidimensional auditory categories. *Journal of Experimental Psychology: Human Perception and Performance*, *35*, 1913–1933.

Gow, D. W. Jr. (2001). Assimilation and anticipation in continuous spoken word recognition. *Journal of Memory and Language*, *45*, 133–159.

Gow, D. W. Jr. (2002). Does English coronal place assimilation create lexical ambiguity? *Journal of Experimental Psychology: Human Perception and Performance*, *28*, 163–179.

Gow, D. W. Jr., & Gordon, P. C. (1995). Lexical and prelexical influences on word segmentation: Evidence from priming. *Journal of Experimental Psychology: Human Perception and Performance*, *21*, 344–359.

Gow, D. W. Jr., & Hussami, P. (1999). Acoustic modification in English place assimilation. *Journal of the Acoustical Society of America*, *106*, 2243 (Abstract).

Gow, D. W. Jr., & Im, A. M. (2004). A cross-linguistic examination of assimilation context effects. *Journal of Memory and Language*, *51*, 279–296.

Goyet, L., De Schonen, S., & Nazzi, T. (2010). Words and syllables in fluent speech segmentation by French-learning infants: An ERP study. *Brain Research*, *1332*, 75–89.

Grabe, E. (2002). Variation adds to prosodic typology. In B. Bel & I. Marlin (Eds.), *Proceedings of the 1st International Conference on Speech Prosody,* Aix-en-Provence (pp. 127–132). Aix-en-Provence: Laboratoire Parole et Langage, Université de Provence.

Grabe, E., & Low, E. L. (2002). Durational variability in speech and the rhythm class hypothesis. In C. Gussenhoven & N. Warner (Eds.), *Laboratory phonology 7* (pp. 515–546). Berlin: Mouton de Gruyter.

Grabe, E., Post, B., & Watson, I. (1999). The acquisition of rhythm in English and French. In J. J. Ohala, Y. Hasegawa, M. Ohala, D. Granville & A. C. Bailey (Eds.), *Proceedings of the 14th International Congress of Phonetic Sciences*, San Francisco (pp. 1201–1204). University of California Press.

Grabe, E., Rosner, B. S., García-Albea, J. E., & Zhou, X. (2003). Perception of English intonation by English, Spanish and Chinese listeners. *Language and Speech*, *46*, 375–401.

Graf Estes, K., Evans, J. L., Alibali, M. W., & Saffran, J. R. (2007). Can infants map meaning to newly segmented words? Statistical segmentation and word learning. *Psychological Science*, *18*, 254–260.

Grainger, J., Van Kang, M. N., & Segui, J. (2001). Cross-modal repetition priming of heterographic homophones. *Memory & Cognition*, *29*, 53–61.

Green, T. R. G. (1979). The necessity of syntax markers: Two experiments with artificial languages. *Journal of Verbal Learning and Verbal Behavior*, *18*, 481–496.

Greenberg, J. H. (Ed.), (1963). *Universals of language*. Cambridge, MA: MIT Press.

Greenspan, S. L. (1986). Semantic flexibility and referential specificity of concrete nouns. *Journal of Memory and Language*, *25*, 539–557.

Grieser, D. L., & Kuhl, P. K. (1988). Maternal speech to infants in a tonal language: Support for universal prosodic features in motherese. *Developmental Psychology*, *24*, 14–20.

Griffiths, S. K., Brown, W. S., Jr., Gerhardt, K. J., Abrams, R. M., & Morris, R. J. (1994). The perception of speech sounds recorded within the uterus of a pregnant sheep. *Journal of the Acoustical Society of America*, *96*, 2055–2063.

Grosjean, F. (1980). Spoken word recognition processes and the gating paradigm. *Perception & Psychophysics*, *28*, 267–283.

Grosjean, F. (1985). The recognition of words after their acoustic offset: Evidence and implications. *Perception & Psychophysics*, *38*, 299–310.

Grosjean, F. (1988). Exploring the recognition of guest words in bilingual speech. *Language and Cognitive Processes*, *3*, 233–274.

Grosjean, F. (1989). Neurolinguists, beware! The bilingual is not two monolinguals in one person. *Brain and Language*, *36*, 3–15.

Grosjean, F. (1997). Processing mixed language: Issues, findings, and models. In A. M. de Groot & J. Kroll (Eds.), *Tutorials in bilingualism: Psycholinguistic perspectives* (pp. 225–254). Mahwah, NJ: Erlbaum.

Grosjean, F., Dommergues, J.-Y., Cornu, E., Guillelmon, D., & Besson, C. (1994). The gender-marking effect in spoken word recognition. *Perception & Psychophysics*, *56*, 590–598.

Grosjean, F., & Frauenfelder, U. (Eds.), (1996). Spoken word recognition paradigms. *Special Issue of Language and Cognitive Processes*, *11*.

Grosjean, F., & Gee, J. P. (1987). Prosodic structure and spoken word recognition. *Cognition*, *25*, 135–155.

Grosjean, F., & Hirt, C. (1996). Using prosody to predict the end of sentences in English and French: Normal and brain-damaged subjects. *Language and Cognitive Processes*, *11*, 107–134.

Grosjean, F., & Itzler, J. (1984). Can semantic constraint reduce the role of word frequency during spoken-word recognition? *Bulletin of the Psychonomic Society*, *22*, 180–182.

Guion, S. G., Harada, T., & Clark, J. J. (2004). Early and late Spanish-English bilinguals' acquisition of English word stress patterns. *Bilingualism: Language and Cognition*, *7*, 207–226.

Gussenhoven, C. (1983). *On the grammar and semantics of sentence accents*. Dordrecht: Foris.

Gussenhoven, C., & Broeders, A. (1997). *English pronunciation for student teachers* (2nd ed.). Groningen: Wolters-Noordhoff.

Gussenhoven, C., & Chen, A. (2000). Universal and language-specific effects in the perception of question intonation. In B. Yuan, T. Huang & X. Tang (Eds.), *Proceedings of the 6th International Conference on Spoken Language Processing,* Beijing (Vol. 1, pp. 91–94). Beijing: China Military Friendship Publish.

Hagoort, P. (2005). Broca's complex as the unification space for language. In A. Cutler (Ed.), *Twenty-first century psycholinguistics: Four cornerstones* (pp. 157–173). Mahwah, NJ: Erlbaum.

Hahne, A., & Friederici, A. (2001). Processing a second language: Late learners' comprehension mechanisms as revealed by event-related brain potentials. *Bilingualism: Language and Cognition, 4*, 123–141.

Hallé, P. A., & Best, C. T. (2007). Dental-to-velar perceptual assimilation: A cross-linguistic study of the perception of dental stop+/l/ clusters. *Journal of the Acoustical Society of America, 121*, 2899–2914.

Hallé, P. A., & de Boysson-Bardies, B. (1994). Emergence of an early lexicon. *Infant Behavior and Development, 17*, 119–129.

Hallé, P. A., & de Boysson-Bardies, B. (1996). The format of representation of recognized words in infants' early receptive lexicons. *Infant Behavior and Development, 19*, 463–481.

Hallé, P. A., de Boysson-Bardies, B., & Vihman, M. M. (1991). Beginnings of prosodic organization: Intonation and duration patterns of disyllables produced by Japanese and French infants. *Language and Speech, 34*, 299–318.

Hallé, P. A., Chéreau, C., & Segui, J. (2000). Where is the /b/ in "absurde" [apsyrd]? It is in French listeners' minds. *Journal of Memory and Language, 43*, 618–639.

Hallé, P. A., Segui, J., Frauenfelder, U., & Meunier, C. (1998). Processing of illegal consonant clusters: A case of perceptual assimilation? *Journal of Experimental Psychology: Human Perception and Performance, 24*, 592–608.

Hankamer, J. (1989). Morphological parsing and the lexicon. In W. D. Marslen-Wilson (Ed.), *Lexical representation and process* (pp. 392–408). Cambridge, MA: MIT Press.

Hanson, V. L., Shankweiler, D., & Fischer, F. W. (1983). Determinants of spelling ability in deaf and hearing adults: Access to linguistic structure. *Cognition, 14*, 323–344.

Hanulíková, A., McQueen, J. M., & Mitterer, H. (2010). Possible words and fixed stress in the segmentation of Slovak speech. *Quarterly Journal of Experimental Psychology, 63*, 555–579.

Hanulíková, A., Mitterer, H., & McQueen, J. M. (2011). Effects of first and second language on segmentation of non-native speech. *Bilingualism: Language and Cognition, 14*, 506–521.

Hardcastle, W. J., & Hewlett, N. (1999). *Coarticulation: Theory, data, and techniques*. Cambridge: Cambridge University Press.

Harley, B., Howard, J., & Hart, D. (1995). Second language processing at different ages: Do younger learners pay more attention to prosodic cues to sentence structure? *Language Learning, 45*, 43–71.

Harrington, J. (2006). An acoustic analysis of "happy-tensing" in the Queen's Christmas broadcasts. *Journal of Phonetics, 34*, 439–457.

Harrington, J., & Cassidy, S. (1994). Dynamic and target theories of vowel classification: Evidence from monophthongs and diphthongs in Australian English. *Language and Speech*, *37*, 357–373.

Harrington, J., Palethorpe, S., & Watson, C. (2000a). Does the Queen speak the Queen's English? *Nature*, *408*, 927–928.

Harrington, J., Palethorpe, S., & Watson, C. (2000b). Monophthongal vowel changes in received pronunciation: An acoustic analysis of the Queen's Christmas broadcasts. *Journal of the International Phonetic Association*, *30*, 63–78.

Harrington, J., Palethorpe, S., & Watson, C. (2005). Deepening or lessening the divide between diphthongs? An analysis of the Queen's annual Christmas Broadcasts. In W. J. Hardcastle & J. M. Beck (Eds.), *A figure of speech: A festschrift for John Laver* (pp. 227–262). Mahwah, NJ: Erlbaum.

Harrington, J., Watson, G., & Cooper, M. (1989). Word boundary detection in broad class and phoneme strings. *Computer Speech and Language*, *3*, 367–382.

Harris, K. S. (1958). Cues for the discrimination of American English fricatives in spoken syllables. *Language and Speech*, *1*, 1–17.

Hart, B. (1991). Input frequency and children's first words. *First Language*, *11*, 289–300.

Haveman, A. (1997). *The open/closed-class distinction in spoken-word recognition*. Ph.D. dissertation, MPI Series in Psycholinguistics 4, University of Nijmegen.

Hawkins, J. A., & Gilligan, G. (1988). Prefixing and suffixing universals in relation to basic word order. *Lingua*, *74*, 219–259.

Hawkins, S., & Nguyen, N. (2003). Effects on word recognition of syllable-onset cues to syllable-coda voicing. In J. K. Local, R. A. Ogden & R. A. M. Temple (Eds.), *Papers in laboratory phonology VI* (pp. 38–57). Cambridge: Cambridge University Press.

Hawkins, S., & Nguyen, N. (2004). Influence of syllable-coda voicing on the acoustic properties of syllable-onset /l/ in English. *Journal of Phonetics*, *32*, 199–231.

Hawkins, S., & Warren, P. (1994). Phonetic influences on the intelligibility of conversational speech. *Journal of Phonetics*, *22*, 493–511.

Hay, J., & Bauer, L. (2007). Phoneme inventory size and population size. *Language*, *83*, 388–400.

Hay, J., Jannedy, S., & Mendoza-Denton, N. (1999). Oprah and /ay/: Lexical frequency, referee design, and style. In J. J. Ohala, Y. Hasegawa, M. Ohala, D. Granville & A. C. Bailey (Eds.), *Proceedings of the 14th International Congress of Phonetic Sciences,* San Francisco (pp. 1389–1392). University of California Press.

Hay, J., Warren, P., & Drager, K. (2006). Factors influencing speech perception in the context of a merger-in-progress. *Journal of Phonetics*, *34*, 458–484.

Hay, J. F., Sato, M., Coren, A. E., Moran, C. L., & Diehl, R. L. (2006). Enhanced contrast for vowels in utterance focus: A cross-language study. *Journal of the Acoustical Society of America*, *119*, 3022–3033.

Hayes, J. R., & Clark, H. H. (1970). Experiments on the segmentation of an artificial speech analogue. In J. R. Hayes (Ed.), *Cognition and the development of language* (pp. 221–234). New York: Wiley.

Hayes-Harb, R. (2005). Optimal L2 speech perception: Native speakers of English and Japanese consonant length contrasts. *Journal of Language and Linguistics*, *4*, 1–29.

Hayes-Harb, R. (2007). Lexical and statistical evidence in the acquisition of second language phonemes. *Second Language Research*, *23*, 1–31.

Hayes-Harb, R., & Masuda, K. (2008). Development of the ability to lexically encode novel L2 phonemic contrasts. *Second Language Research*, *24*, 5–33.

Hazan, V., & Simpson, A. (1998). The effect of cue-enhancement on the intelligibility of nonsense word and sentence materials presented in noise. *Speech Communication*, *24*, 211–226.

Hazan, V., & Simpson, A. (2000). The effect of cue-enhancement on consonant intelligibility in noise: Speaker and listener effects. *Language and Speech*, *43*, 273–294.

Healy, A. F., & Cutting, J. E. (1976). Units of speech perception: Phoneme and syllable. *Journal of Verbal Learning and Verbal Behavior*, *15*, 73–83.

Heath, S. B. (1983). *Ways with words: Language, life, and work in communities and classrooms*. Cambridge: Cambridge University Press.

Henderson, A. I. (1980). Juncture pause and intonation fall and the perceptual segmentation of speech. In H. W. Dechert & M. Raupach (Eds.), *Temporal variables in speech: Studies in honour of Frieda Goldman-Eisler* (pp. 199–207). The Hague: Mouton.

Hernandez, T. M., Aldridge, M. A., & Bower, T. G. R. (2000). Structural and experiential factors in newborns' preference for speech sounds. *Developmental Science*, *3*, 46–49.

Herron, D., & Bates, E. (1997). Sentential and acoustic factors in the recognition of open- and closed-class words. *Journal of Memory and Language*, *37*, 217–239.

Hervais-Adelman, A., Davis, M. H., Johnsrude, I. S., & Carlyon, R. P. (2008). Perceptual learning of noise vocoded words: Effects of feedback and lexicality. *Journal of Experimental Psychology: Human Perception and Performance*, *34*, 460–474.

van Heuven, V. J. (1985). Perception of stress pattern and word recognition: Recognition of Dutch words with incorrect stress position. *Journal of the Acoustical Society of America*, *78*, S21 (Abstract).

van Heuven, V. J. (1988). Effects of stress and accent on the human recognition of word fragments in spoken context: Gating and shadowing. In W. A. Ainsworth & J. N. Holmes (Eds.), *Proceedings of Speech '88, 7th FASE symposium* (pp. 811–818). Edinburgh: Institute of Acoustics.

van Heuven, V. J., & Hagman, P. (1988). Lexical statistics and spoken word recognition in Dutch. In P. Coopmans & A. Hulk (Eds.), *Linguistics in the Netherlands 1988* (pp. 59–68). Dordrecht: Foris.

Hillenbrand, J. M., Clark, M. J., & Houde, R. A. (2000). Some effects of duration on vowel recognition. *Journal of the Acoustical Society of America*, *108*, 3013–3022.

Hillenbrand, J., Getty, L. A., Clark, M. J., & Wheeler, K. (1995). Acoustic characteristics of American English vowels. *Journal of the Acoustical Society of America*, *97*, 3099–3111.

Himmelmann, N. P., & Ladd, D. R. (2008). Prosodic description: An introduction for fieldworkers. *Language Documentation and Conservation*, *2*, 244–274.

Hintzman, D. L. (1986). "Schema abstraction" in a multiple-trace memory model. *Psychological Review*, *93*, 411–428.

Hirata, Y. (2004). Training native English speakers to perceive Japanese length contrasts in word versus sentence contexts. *Journal of the Acoustical Society of America, 116*, 2384–2394.

Hirsh-Pasek, K., Kemler Nelson, D. G., Jusczyk, P. W., Cassidy, K. W., Druss, B., & Kennedy, L. J. (1987). Clauses are perceptual units for young infants. *Cognition, 26*, 269–286.

Hockema, S. A. (2006). Finding words in speech: An investigation of American English. *Language Learning and Development, 2*, 119–146.

Hodgson, P., & Miller, J. L. (1996). Internal structure of phonetic categories: Evidence for within-category trading relations. *Journal of the Acoustical Society of America, 100*, 565–576.

Hoen, M., Meunier, F., Grataloup, C.-L., Pellegrino, F., Grimault, N., Perrin, F., Perrot, X., & Collet, L. (2007). Phonetic and lexical interferences in informational masking during speech-in-speech comprehension. *Speech Communication, 12*, 905–916.

Höhle, B., & Weissenborn, J. (2003). German-learning infants' ability to detect unstressed closed-class elements in continuous speech. *Developmental Science, 6*, 122–127.

Houston, D. M., Jusczyk, P. W., Kuijpers, C., Coolen, R., & Cutler, A. (2000). Cross-language word segmentation by 9-month-olds. *Psychonomic Bulletin & Review, 7*, 504–509.

Houston, D. M., Santelmann, L. M., & Jusczyk, P. W. (2004). English-learning infants' segmentation of trisyllabic words from fluent speech. *Language and Cognitive Processes, 19*, 97–136.

Houston-Price, C., & Nakai, S. (2004). Distinguishing novelty and familiarity effects in infant preference procedures. *Infant and Child Development, 13*, 341–348.

Howes, D. (1957). On the relation between intelligibility and frequency of occurrence of English words. *Journal of the Acoustical Society of America, 29*, 296–305.

Huettig, F., & McQueen, J. M. (2007). The tug of war between phonological, semantic and shape information in language-mediated visual search. *Journal of Memory and Language, 57*, 460–482.

Huttenlocher, D. P., & Zue, V. W. (1984). A model of lexical access from partial phonetic information. In *Proceedings of the IEEE, International Conference on Acoustics, Speech, and Signal Processing (ICASSP-84), 9*, 391–394.

Imai, S., Walley, A. C., & Flege, J. E. (2005). Lexical frequency and neighborhood density effects on the recognition of native and Spanish-accented words by native English and Spanish listeners. *Journal of the Acoustical Society of America, 117*, 896–907.

International Phonetic Association. (1999). *Handbook of the International Phonetic Association*. Cambridge: Cambridge University Press.

Isenberg, D., Walker, E. C. T., & Ryder, J. M. (1980). A top-down effect on the identification of function words. *Journal of the Acoustical Society of America, 68*, S48 (Abstract).

Ito, K., & Speer, S. R. (2008). Anticipatory effect of intonation: Eye movements during instructed visual search. *Journal of Memory and Language, 58*, 541–573.

Iverson, P., Kuhl, P. K., Akahane-Yamada, R., Diesch, E., Tohkura, Y., Ketterman, A., & Siebert, C. (2003). A perceptual interference account of acquisition difficulties for non-native phonemes. *Cognition, 87*, B47–B57.

Jacobsen, T., Horváth, J., Schröger, E., Lattner, S., Widmann, A., & Winkler, I. (2004). Pre-attentive auditory processing of lexicality. *Brain and Language, 88*, 54–67.

Jamieson, D. G., & Morosan, D. E. (1986). Training non-native speech contrasts in adults: Acquisition of the English /ð/-/θ / contrast by francophones. *Perception & Psychophysics*, *40*, 205–215.

Janse, E., Nooteboom, S., & Quené, H. (2007). Coping with gradient forms of /t/-deletion and lexical ambiguity in spoken word recognition. *Language and Cognitive Processes*, *22*, 161–200.

Jescheniak, J. D., & Levelt, W. J. M. (1994). Word frequency effects in speech production: Retrieval of syntactic information and of phonological form. *Journal of Experimental Psychology: Learning, Memory, and Cognition*, *20*, 824–843.

Jesse, A., & McQueen, J. M. (2011). Positional effects in the lexical retuning of speech perception. *Psychonomic Bulletin & Review*, *18*, 943–950.

Jia, G., Strange, W., Wu, Y., Collado, J., & Guan, Q. (2006). Perception and production of English vowels by Mandarin speakers: Age-related differences vary with amount of L2 exposure. *Journal of the Acoustical Society of America*, *119*, 1118–1130.

Jiang, J., Chen, M., & Alwan, A. (2006). On the perception of voicing in syllable-initial plosives in noise. *Journal of the Acoustical Society of America*, *119*, 1092–1105.

Johnson, E. K. (2005a). Grammatical gender and early word recognition in Dutch. In A. Brugos, M. R. Clark-Cotton & S. Ha (Eds.), *Proceedings of the 29th annual Boston University Conference on Language Development* (Vol. 1, pp. 320–330). Somerville, MA: Cascadilla Press.

Johnson, E. K. (2005b). English-learning infants' representations of word-forms with iambic stress. *Infancy*, *7*, 95–105.

Johnson, E. K. (2008). Infants use prosodically conditioned acoustic-phonetic cues to extract words from speech. *Journal of the Acoustical Society of America*, *123*, EL144–EL148.

Johnson, E. K., & Jusczyk, P. W. (2001). Word segmentation by 8-month-olds: When speech cues count more than statistics. *Journal of Memory and Language*, *44*, 548–567.

Johnson, E. K., Jusczyk, P. W., Cutler, A., & Norris, D. (2003). Lexical viability constraints on speech segmentation by infants. *Cognitive Psychology*, *46*, 65–97.

Johnson, E. K., & Seidl, A. H. (2009). At 11 months, prosody still outranks statistics. *Developmental Science*, *12*, 131–141.

Johnson, E. K., & Tyler, M. D. (2010). Testing the limits of statistical learning for word segmentation. *Developmental Science*, *13*, 339–345.

Johnson, E. K., Westrek, W., Nazzi, T., & Cutler, A. (2011). Infant ability to tell voices apart rests on language experience. *Developmental Science*, *14*, 1002–1011.

Johnson, K. (1990). The role of perceived speaker identity in F0 normalization of vowels. *Journal of the Acoustical Society of America*, *88*, 642–654.

Johnson, K. (1997). Speech perception without speaker normalization: An exemplar model. In K. Johnson & J. Mullennix (Eds.), *Talker variability in speech processing* (pp. 145–166). San Diego, CA: Academic Press.

Jongenburger, W. (1996). *The role of lexical stress during spoken-word processing*. Ph.D. dissertation, University of Leiden. The Hague: Holland Academic Graphics.

Jongman, A., Wade, T., & Sereno, J. (2003). On improving the perception of foreign-accented speech In M. J. Solé, D. Recasens & J. Romero (Eds.), *Proceedings of the 15th International Congress of Phonetic Sciences*, Barcelona (pp. 1561–1564). Barcelona: Universitat Autonomá de Barcelona.

Ju, M., & Luce, P. A. (2004). Falling on sensitive ears: Constraints on bilingual lexical activation. *Psychological Science*, *15*, 314–318.

Junge, C., Cutler, A., & Hagoort, P. (2010). Ability to segment words from speech as a precursor of later language development: Insights from electrophysiological responses in the infant brain. In M. Burgess, J. Davey, C. Don & T. McMinn (Eds.), *Proceedings of the 20th International Congress on Acoustics*, Sydney (ICA 2010) (pp. 3727–3732). Sydney, Australia: Australian Acoustical Society, NSW Division.

Junge, C., Hagoort, P., Kooijman, V., & Cutler, A. (2010). Brain potentials for word segmentation at seven months predict later language development. In K. Franich, K. M. Iserman & L. L. Keil (Eds.), *Proceedings of the 34th annual Boston University Conference on Language Development* (Vol. 1, pp. 209–220). Somerville, MA: Cascadilla Press.

Junge, C., Kooijman, V., Hagoort, P., & Cutler, A. (2012). Rapid recognition at 10 months as a predictor of language development. *Developmental Science*. doi:10.1111/j.14677687.2012.1144.x

Jurafsky, D., Bell, A., & Girard, C. (2002). The role of the lemma in form variation. In C. Gussenhoven & N. Warner (Eds.), *Laboratory phonology 7* (pp. 3–34). Berlin: Mouton de Gruyter.

Jusczyk, P. W. (1997). *The discovery of spoken language*. Cambridge, MA: MIT Press.

Jusczyk, P. W., & Aslin, R. N. (1995). Infants' detection of the sound patterns of words in fluent speech. *Cognitive Psychology*, *29*, 1–23.

Jusczyk, P. W., Cutler, A., & Redanz, N. (1993). Infants' preference for the predominant stress patterns of English words. *Child Development*, *64*, 675–687.

Jusczyk, P. W., Friederici, A. D., Wessels, J. M., Svenkerud, V. Y., & Jusczyk, A. M. (1993). Infants' sensitivity to the sound patterns of native language words. *Journal of Memory and Language*, *32*, 402–420.

Jusczyk, P. W., Hirsh-Pasek, K., Kemler Nelson, D. G., Kennedy, L. J., Woodward, A., & Piwoz, J. (1992). Perception of acoustic correlates of major phrasal units by young infants. *Cognitive Psychology*, *24*, 252–293.

Jusczyk, P. W., & Hohne, E. A. (1997). Infants' memory for spoken words. *Science*, *277*, 1984–1986.

Jusczyk, P. W., Hohne, E. A., & Bauman, A. (1999). Infants' sensitivity to allophonic cues for word segmentation. *Perception & Psychophysics*, *61*, 1465–1476.

Jusczyk, P. W., Houston, D., & Newsome, M. (1999). The beginnings of word segmentation in English-learning infants. *Cognitive Psychology*, *39*, 159–207.

Jusczyk, P. W., Luce, P. A., & Charles-Luce, J. (1994). Infants' sensitivity to phonotactic patterns in the native language. *Journal of Memory and Language*, *33*, 630–645.

Jusczyk, P. W., & Thompson, E. (1978). Perception of a phonetic contrast in multisyllabic utterances by 2-month-old infants. *Perception & Psychophysics*, *23*, 105–109.

Kabak, B., Maniwa, K., & Kazanina, N. (2010). Listeners use vowel harmony and word-final stress to spot nonsense words: A study of Turkish and French. *Laboratory Phonology*, *1*, 207–224.

Kahn, D. (1976). *Syllable-based generalizations in English phonology*. Ph.D. dissertation, MIT, Cambridge, MA.

Kakehi, K., Kato, K., & Kashino, M. (1996). Phoneme/syllable perception and the temporal structure of speech. In T. Otake & A. Cutler (Eds.), *Phonological structure and language processing: Cross-linguistic studies* (pp. 125–143). Berlin: Mouton de Gruyter.

Kalikow, D. N., Stevens, K. N., & Elliott, L. L. (1977). Development of a test of speech intelligibility in noise using sentence materials with controlled word predictability. *Journal of the Acoustical Society of America*, *61*, 1337–1351.

Keane, E. (2006). Rhythmic characteristics of colloquial and formal Tamil. *Language and Speech*, *49*, 299–332.

Kearns, R. K. (1994). *Prelexical speech processing by mono- and bilinguals*. Ph.D. dissertation, University of Cambridge.

Kearns, R. K., Norris, D., & Cutler, A. (2002). Syllable processing in English. In J. H. L. Hansen, & B. Pellum (Eds.), *Proceedings of the 7th International Conference on Spoken Language Processing*, Denver (pp. 1657–1660). Denver: Center for Spoken Language Research, University of Colorado Boulder [CD-ROM].

Keating, P., Cho, T., Fougeron, C., & Hsu, C. (2003). Domain-initial strengthening in four languages. In J. Local, R. Ogden, & R. Temple (Eds.) *Phonetic interpretation: Papers in laboratory phonology 6* (pp. 145–163). Cambridge: Cambridge University Press.

Keidel, J. L., Jenison, R. L., Kluender, K. R., & Seidenberg, M. S. (2007). Does grammar constrain statistical learning? Commentary on Bonatti, Peña, Nespor, and Mehler (2005). *Psychological Science*, *18*, 922–923.

Kempley, S., & Morton, J. (1982). The effects of priming with regularly and irregularly related words in auditory word recognition. *British Journal of Psychology*, *73*, 441–454.

Kemps, R., Ernestus, M., Schreuder, R., & Baayen, H. (2004). Processing reduced word forms: The suffix restoration effect. *Brain and Language*, *90*, 117–127.

Kemps, R. J., Ernestus, M., Schreuder, R., & Baayen, H. (2005). Prosodic cues for morphological complexity: The case of Dutch plural nouns. *Memory & Cognition*, *33*, 430–446.

Kemps, R. J., Wurm, L. H., Ernestus, M., Schreuder, R., & Baayen, H. (2005). Prosodic cues for morphological complexity in Dutch and English. *Language and Cognitive Processes*, *20*, 43–73.

Kim, J., Davis, C., & Cutler, A. (2008). Perceptual tests of rhythmic similarity: II. Syllable rhythm. *Language and Speech*, *51*, 342–358.

Kim, K. H. S., Relkin, N. R., Lee, K. M., & Hirsch, J. (1997). Distinct cortical areas associated with native and second languages. *Nature*, *388*, 171–174.

Kingston, J., Kawahara, S., Mash, D., & Chambless, D. (2011). Auditory contrast versus compensation for coarticulation: Data from Japanese and English listeners. *Language and Speech*, *54*, 499–525.

Kirby, J. (2010). Dialect experience in Vietnamese tone perception. *Journal of the Acoustical Society of America*, *127*, 3749–3757.

Kirchhoff, K., & Schimmel, S. (2005). Statistical properties of infant-directed versus adult-directed speech: Insights from speech recognition. *Journal of the Acoustical Society of America*, *117*, 2224–2237.

Kisilevsky, B. S., Hains, S. M. J., Lee, K., Xie, X., Huang, H., Ye, H. H., Zhang, K., & Wang, Z. (2003). Effects of experience on fetal voice recognition. *Psychological Science*, *14*, 220–224.

Kitamura, C., & Burnham, D. (1998). The infant's response to maternal vocal affect. In C. Rovee-Collier, L. Lipsitt, & H. Hayne (Eds.), *Advances in infancy research* (Vol. 12, pp. 221–236). Stamford: Ablex.

Kitamura, C., & Burnham, D. (2003). Pitch and communicative intent in mothers' speech: Adjustments for age and sex in the first year. *Infancy*, *4*, 85–110.

Kitamura, C., Thanavishuth, C., Burnham, D., & Luksaneeyanawin, S. (2002). Universality and specificity in infant-directed speech: Pitch modifications as a function of infant age and sex in a tonal and non-tonal language. *Infant Behavior and Development*, *24*, 372–392.

Kluender, K. R., Diehl, R. L., & Killeen, P. R. (1987). Japanese quail can learn phonetic categories. *Science*, *237*, 1195–1197.

Kolinsky, R., Morais, J., & Cluytens, M. (1995). Intermediate representations in spoken word recognition: Evidence from word illusions. *Journal of Memory and Language*, *34*, 19–40.

Kooijman, V. (2007). *Continuous-speech segmentation at the beginning of language acquisition: Electrophysiological evidence*. Ph.D. dissertation, MPI Series in Psycholinguistics 44, Radboud University Nijmegen.

Kooijman, V., Hagoort, P., & Cutler, A. (2005). Electrophysiological evidence for prelinguistic infants' word recognition in continuous speech. *Brain Research: Cognitive Brain Research*, *24*, 109–116.

Kooijman, V., Hagoort, P., & Cutler, A. (2009). Prosodic structure in early word segmentation: ERP evidence from Dutch ten-month-olds. *Infancy*, *14*, 591–612.

Korman, M. (1984). Adaptive aspects of maternal vocalizations in differing contexts at ten weeks. *First Language*, *5*, 158–159 (Abstract).

Koster, C. J. (1987). *Word recognition in foreign and native language*. Dordrecht: Foris.

Koster, M., & Cutler, A. (1997). Segmental and suprasegmental contributions to spoken-word recognition in Dutch. In G. Kokkinakis, N. Fakotakis & E. Dermatas (Eds.), *Proceedings of the 5th European Conference on Speech Communication and Technology* (*EUROSPEECH'97*), Rhodes (pp. 2167–2170). Patras, Greece: WCL, University of Patras.

Köster, O., & Schiller, N. O. (1997). Different influences of the native language of a listener on speaker recognition. *Forensic Linguistics*, *4*, 18–28.

Kovács, Á. M. (2009). Early bilingualism enhances mechanisms of false-belief reasoning. *Developmental Science*, *12*, 48–54.

Kovács, Á. M., & Mehler, J. (2009). Cognitive gains in 7-month-old bilingual infants. *Proceedings of the National Academy of Sciences of the United States of America*, *106*, 6556–6560.

Kraljic, T., Brennan, S. E., & Samuel, A. G. (2008). Accommodating variation: Dialects, idiolects, and speech processing. *Cognition*, *107*, 51–81.

Kraljic, T., & Samuel, A. G. (2005). Perceptual learning for speech: Is there a return to normal? *Cognitive Psychology*, *51*, 141–178.

Kraljic, T., & Samuel, A. G. (2006). Generalization in perceptual learning for speech. *Psychonomic Bulletin & Review*, *13*, 262–268.

Kraljic, T., & Samuel, A. G. (2007). Perceptual adjustments to multiple speakers. *Journal of Memory and Language*, *56*, 1–15.

Kraljic, T., Samuel, A. G., & Brennan, S. E. (2008). First impressions and last resorts: How listeners adjust to speaker variability. *Psychological Science*, *19*, 332–338.

Krumhansl, C. L., & Jusczyk, P. W. (1990). Infants' perception of phrase structure in music. *Psychological Science*, *1*, 70–73.

Kubozono, H. (2002). Temporal neutralization in Japanese. In C. Gussenhoven & N. Warner (Eds.), *Laboratory phonology 7* (pp. 171–201). Berlin: Mouton de Gruyter.

van Kuijk, D., & Boves, L. (1999). Acoustic characteristics of lexical stress in continuous telephone speech. *Speech Communication*, *27*, 95–111.

Kuijpers, C., Coolen, R., Houston, D., & Cutler, A. (1998). Using the head-turning technique to explore cross-linguistic performance differences. In C. Rovee-Collier, L. Lipsitt & H. Hayne (Eds.), *Advances in infancy research* (Vol. 12, pp. 205–220). Stamford: Ablex.

Kuijpers, C., & van Donselaar, W. (1998). The influence of rhythmic context on schwa epenthesis and schwa deletion. *Language and Speech*, *41*, 87–108.

Kuijpers, C., van Donselaar, W., & Cutler, A. (1996). Phonological variation: Epenthesis and deletion of schwa in Dutch. In H. T. Bunnell & W. Idsardi (Eds.), *Proceedings of the 4th International Conference on Spoken Language Processing, Philadelphia* (Vol. 1, pp. 94–97). Philadelphia: University of Delaware and A. I. duPont Institute.

Kuijpers, C., van Donselaar, W., & Cutler, A. (2002). Perceptual effects of assimilation-induced violation of final devoicing in Dutch. In J. H. L. Hansen & B. Pellum (Eds.), *Proceedings of the 7th International Conference on Spoken Language Processing*, Denver (pp. 1661–1664). Denver: Center for Spoken Language Research, University of Colorado Boulder [CD-ROM].

Kuhl, P. K. (1979). Speech perception in early infancy: Perceptual constancy for spectrally dissimilar vowel categories. *Journal of the Acoustical Society of America*, *66*, 1668–1679.

Kuhl, P. K. (1991). Human adults and human infants show a "perceptual magnet effect" for the prototypes of speech categories, monkeys do not. *Perception & Psychophysics*, *50*, 93–107.

Kuhl, P. K., Andruski, J. E., Chistovich, I. A., Chistovich, L. A., Kozhevnikova, E. V., Ryskina, V. L., Stolyarova, E. I., Sundberg, U., & Lacerda, F. (1997). Cross-language analysis of phonetic units in language addressed to infants. *Science*, *277*, 684–686.

Kuhl, P. K., Conboy, B. T., Coffey-Corina, S., Padden, D., Rivera-Gaxiola, M., & Nelson, T. (2008). Phonetic learning as a pathway to language: New data and Native Language Magnet Theory-expanded (NLM-e). *Philosophical Transactions of the Royal Society B*, *363*, 979–1000.

Kuhl, P. K., & Iverson, P. (1995). Linguistic experience and the "perceptual magnet effect." In W. Strange (Ed.), *Speech perception and linguistic experience: Issues in cross-language research* (pp. 121–154). Baltimore: York Press.

Kuhl, P. K., & Miller, J. L. (1978). Speech perception by the chinchilla: Identification functions for synthetic VOT stimuli. *Journal of the Acoustical Society of America*, *63*, 905–917.

Kuhl, P. K., Stevens, E., Hayashi, A., Deguchi, T., Kiritani, S., & Iverson, P. (2006). Infants show a facilitation effect for native language phonetic perception between 6 and 12 months. *Developmental Science*, *9*, 13–21.

Kuhl, P., Williams, K. A., Lacerda, F., Stevens, K. N., & Lindblom, B. (1992). Linguistic experience alters phonetic perception in infants by 6 months of age. *Science*, *255*, 606–608.

Kuzla, C., Cho, T., & Ernestus, M. (2007). Prosodic strengthening of German fricatives in duration and assimilatory devoicing. *Journal of Phonetics*, *35*, 301–320.

Kuzla, C., & Ernestus, M. (2011). Prosodic conditioning of phonetic detail in German plosives. *Journal of Phonetics*, *39*, 143–155.

Kuzla, C., Ernestus, M., & Mitterer, H. (2010). Compensation for assimilatory devoicing and prosodic structure in German fricative perception. In C. Fougeron, B. Kühnert, M. D'Imperio & N. Vallée (Eds.), *Laboratory phonology 10* (pp. 731–757). Berlin: Mouton de Gruyter.

Labov, W., Karen, M., & Miller, C. (1991). Near-mergers and the suspension of phonemic contrast. *Language Variation and Change*, *3*, 33–74.

Lacerda, F. (1995). The perceptual-magnet effect: An emergent consequence of exemplar-based phonetic memory. In K. Elenius & P. Branderus (Eds.), *Proceedings of 13th International Congress of Phonetic Sciences*, Stockholm (Vol. 2, pp. 140–147). Stockholm: KTH and Stockholm University.

Ladd, D. R. Jr. (1981). On intonational universals. In T. Myers, J. Laver & J. Anderson (Eds.), *The cognitive representation of speech* (pp. 389–397). Amsterdam: North Holland.

Ladd, D. R. (2008). *Intonational phonology* (2nd ed.). Cambridge: Cambridge University Press.

Ladd, D. R., & Morton, R. (1997). The perception of intonational emphasis: Continuous or categorical? *Journal of Phonetics*, *25*, 313–342.

Ladefoged, P. (1989). A note on "Information conveyed by vowels." *Journal of the Acoustical Society of America*, *85*, 2223–2224.

Ladefoged, P., & Disner, S. (2012). *Vowels and consonants* (3rd ed.). Blackwell.

Ladefoged, P., & Broadbent, D. (1957). Information conveyed by vowels. *Journal of the Acoustical Society of America*, *29*, 98–104.

Ladefoged, P., & Maddieson, I. (1996). *The sounds of the world's languages*. Oxford: Blackwell.

Lagerquist, L. M. (1980). Linguistic evidence from paranomasia. In *Papers from the 16th Regional Meeting, Chicago Linguistic Society* (pp. 185–191). Chicago: Chicago Linguistic Society.

Lahiri, A., & Marslen-Wilson, W. D. (1991). The mental representation of lexical form: A phonological approach to the recognition lexicon. *Cognition*, *38*, 245–294.

Lahiri, A., & Marslen-Wilson, W. D. (1992). Lexical processing and phonological representation. In G. J. Docherty & D. R. Ladd (Eds.), *Papers in laboratory phonology 2: Gesture segment prosody* (pp. 229–254). Cambridge: Cambridge University Press.

Lane, H., & Tranel, B. (1971). The Lombard sign and the role of hearing in speech. *Journal of Speech and Hearing Research*, *14*, 677–709.

Larkey, L. S. (1983). Reiterant speech: An acoustic and perceptual validation. *Journal of the Acoustical Society of America*, *73*, 1337–1345.

Larson-Hall, J. (2004). Predicting perceptual success with segments: A test of Japanese speakers of Russian. *Second Language Research*, *20*, 33–76.

Laver, J. (1994). *Principles of phonetics*. Cambridge: Cambridge University Press.

Leach, L., & Samuel, A. G. (2007). Lexical configuration and lexical engagement: When adults learn new words. *Cognitive Psychology*, *55*, 306–353.

Lecanuet, J. P., Granier-Deferre, C., Jacquet, A.-Y., & DeCasper, A. J. (2000). Fetal discrimination of low-pitched musical notes. *Developmental Psychobiology*, *36*, 29–39.

Lee, C.-Y. (2009). Identifying isolated, multispeaker Mandarin tones from brief acoustic input: A perceptual and acoustic study. *Journal of the Acoustical Society of America, 125*, 1125–1137.

Lee, C.-Y., Tao, L., & Bond, Z. S. (2008). Identification of acoustically modified Mandarin tones by native listeners. *Journal of Phonetics, 36*, 537–563.

Lee, C.-Y., Tao, L., & Bond, Z. S. (2010). Identification of multi-speaker Mandarin tones in noise by native and non-native listeners. *Speech Communication, 52*, 900–910.

Lee, Y.-S., Vakoch, D. A., & Wurm, L. H. (1996). Tone perception in Cantonese and Mandarin: A cross-linguistic comparison. *Journal of Psycholinguistic Research, 25*, 527–542.

Leech, G. (1993). 100 million words of English. *English Today, 33*, 9, 9–15.

Lehiste, I. (1960). An acoustic-phonetic study of internal open juncture. *Phonetica, 5*(suppl.), 5–54.

Lehiste, I., & Peterson, G. E. (1959). Vowel amplitude and phonemic stress in American English. *Journal of the Acoustical Society of America, 31*, 428–435.

Lehnert-LeHouillier, H. (2010). A cross-linguistic investigation of cues to vowel length perception. *Journal of Phonetics, 38*, 472–482.

Levelt, W. J. M., Roelofs, A., & Meyer, A. S. (1999). A theory of lexical access in speech production. *Behavioral and Brain Sciences, 22*, 1–38.

Levitt, A. G., & Utman, J. G. A. (1992). From babbling towards the sound systems of English and French: A longitudinal two-case study. *Journal of Child Language, 19*, 19–49.

Levitt, A. G., & Wang, Q. (1991). Evidence for language-specific rhythmic influences in the reduplicative babbling of French and English learning infants. *Language and Speech, 34*, 235–249.

van Leyden, K., & van Heuven, V. J. (1996). Lexical stress and spoken word recognition: Dutch vs. English. In C. Cremers & M. den Dikken (Eds.), *Linguistics in the Netherlands 1996* (pp. 159–170). Amsterdam: John Benjamins.

Liberman, A. M., Delattre, P. C., & Cooper, F. S. (1952). The role of selected stimulus variables in the perception of unvoiced stop consonants. *American Journal of Psychology, 65*, 497–516.

Liberman, A. M., Delattre, P. C., Cooper, F. S., & Gerstman, L. J. (1954). The role of consonant-vowel transitions in the perception of the stop and nasal consonants. *Psychological Monographs, 68*, 1–13.

Lieberman, P. (1963). Some effects of semantic and grammatical context on the production and perception of speech. *Language and Speech, 6*, 172–187.

van Linden, S., & Vroomen, J. (2007). Recalibration of phonetic categories by lipread speech versus lexical information. *Journal of Experimental Psychology: Human Perception and Performance, 33*, 1483–1494.

Lisker, L., & Abramson, A. S. (1964). A cross-language study of voicing in initial stops: Acoustical measurements. *Word, 20*, 384–422.

Lisker, L., & Abramson, A. S. (1967). Some effects of context on voice onset time in English stops. *Language and Speech, 10*, 1–28.

Liu, H.-M., Kuhl, P. K., & Tsao, F.-M. (2003). An association between mothers' speech clarity and infants' speech discrimination skills. *Developmental Science, 6*, F1–F10.

Lively, S. E., Logan, J. S., & Pisoni, D. B. (1993). Training Japanese listeners to identify English /r/ and /l/. II: The role of phonetic environment and talker variability in learning new perceptual categories. *Journal of the Acoustical Society of America*, *94*, 1242–1255.

Lively, S. E., Pisoni, D. B., Yamada, R. A., Tohkura, Y., & Yamada, T. (1994). Training Japanese listeners to identify English /r/ and /l/. III: Long-term retention of new phonetic categories. *Journal of the Acoustical Society of America*, *96*, 2076–2087.

LoCasto, P., & Connine, C. M. (2002). Rule-governed missing information in spoken word recognition: Schwa vowel deletion. *Perception & Psychophysics*, *64*, 208–219.

Loebach, J. L., & Pisoni, D. (2008). Perceptual learning of spectrally degraded speech and environmental sounds. *Journal of the Acoustical Society of America*, *123*, 1126–1139.

Logan, J. S., Lively, S. E., & Pisoni, D. B. (1991). Training Japanese listeners to identify English /r/ and /l/: A first report. *Journal of the Acoustical Society of America*, *89*, 874–886.

Lorch, M., & Meara, P. (1989). How people listen to languages they don't know. *Language Sciences*, *11*, 343–353.

Low, E. L., Grabe, E., & Nolan, F. (2000). Quantitative characterization of speech rhythm: Syllable-timing in Singapore English. *Language and Speech*, *43*, 377–401.

Lotz, J., Abramson, A. S., Gerstman, L. J., Ingemann, F., & Nemser, W. J. (1960). The perception of English stops by speakers of English, Spanish, Hungarian, and Thai: A tape-cutting experiment. *Language and Speech*, *3*, 71–77.

Loukina, A., Kochanski, G., Rosner, B., Keane, E., & Shih, C. (2011). Rhythm measures and dimensions of durational variation in speech. *Journal of the Acoustical Society of America*, *129*, 3258–3270.

Love, T., Maas, E., & Swinney, D. (2003). The influence of language exposure on lexical and syntactic language processing. *Journal of Experimental Psychology*, *50*, 204–216.

Lucas, M. (1987). Frequency effects on the processing of ambiguous words in sentence contexts. *Language and Speech*, *30*, 25–46.

Luce, P. A. (1986). A computational analysis of uniqueness points in auditory word recognition. *Perception & Psychophysics*, *39*, 155–158.

Luce, P. A., Goldinger, S. D., Auer, E. T., Jr., & Vitevitch, M. S. (2000). Phonetic priming, neighborhood activation, and PARSYN. *Perception & Psychophysics*, *62*, 615–625.

Luce, P. A., & Lyons, E. A. (1998). Specificity of memory representations for spoken words. *Memory & Cognition*, *26*, 708–715.

Luce, P. A., & McLennan, C. T. (2005). Spoken word recognition: The challenge of variation. In D. B. Pisoni & R. E. Remez (Eds.), *Handbook of speech perception* (pp. 591–609). Malden, MA: Blackwell.

Luce, P. A., & Pisoni, D. B. (1998). Recognizing spoken words: The neighborhood activation model. *Ear and Hearing*, *19*, 1–36.

Luce, P. A., Pisoni, D. B., & Goldinger, S. D. (1990). Similarity neighborhoods of spoken words. In G. T. M. Altmann (Ed.), *Cognitive models of speech processing: Psycholinguistic and computational perspectives* (pp. 122–147). Cambridge, MA: MIT Press.

van der Lugt, A. H. (1999). *From speech to words*. Ph.D. dissertation, MPI Series in Psycholinguistics 13, University of Nijmegen.

van der Lugt, A. H. (2001). The use of sequential probabilities in the segmentation of speech. *Perception & Psychophysics, 63*, 811–823.

MacDonald, M. C., Just, M. A., & Carpenter, P. A. (1992). Working memory constraints on the processing of syntactic ambiguity. *Cognitive Psychology, 24*, 56–98.

Mack, M. (1988). Sentence processing by non-native speakers of English: Evidence from the perception of natural and computer-generated anomalous L2 sentences. *Journal of Neurolinguistics, 3*, 293–316.

MacKain, K. S., Best, C. T., & Strange, W. (1981). Categorical perception of English /r/ and /l/ by Japanese bilinguals. *Applied Psycholinguistics, 2*, 369–390.

Maddieson, I. (1984). *Patterns of sounds*. Cambridge: Cambridge University Press.

Magen, H. S. (1998). The perception of foreign-accented speech. *Journal of Phonetics, 26*, 381–400.

Magnuson, J. S., Dixon, J. A., Tanenhaus, M. K., & Aslin, R. N. (2007). The dynamics of lexical competition during spoken word recognition. *Cognitive Science, 31*, 133–156.

Magnuson, J. S., McMurray, B., Tanenhaus, M. K., & Aslin, R. N. (2003). Lexical effects on compensation for coarticulation: The ghost of Christmash past. *Cognitive Science, 27*, 285–298.

Makárova, V. (2001). Perceptual correlates of sentence-type intonation in Russian and Japanese. *Journal of Phonetics, 29*, 137–154.

Mandel, D. R., Jusczyk, P. W., & Pisoni, D. B. (1995). Infants' recognition of the sound patterns of their own names. *Psychological Science, 6*, 314–317.

Mani, N., Coleman, J., & Plunkett, K. (2008). Phonological specificity of vocalic features at 18-months. *Language and Speech, 51*, 3–21.

Mani, N., & Plunkett, K. (2007). Phonological specificity of consonants and vowels in early lexical representations. *Journal of Memory and Language, 57*, 252–272.

Mann, V. A. (1980). Influence of preceding liquid on stop-consonant perception. *Perception & Psychophysics, 28*, 407–412.

Mann, V. A., & Repp, B. H. (1980). Influence of vocalic context on the perception of [ʃ]-[s] distinction. *Perception & Psychophysics, 28*, 213–228.

Mann, V. A., & Repp, B. H. (1981). Influence of preceding fricative on stop consonant perception. *Journal of the Acoustical Society of America, 69*, 548–558.

Manuel, S. (1999). Cross-language studies: Relating language-particular coarticulation patterns to other language-particular facts. In W. J. Hardcastle & N. Hewlett (Eds.), *Coarticulation: Theory, data, and technique* (pp. 179–198). Cambridge: Cambridge University Press.

Manuel, S. Y., Shattuck-Hufnagel, S., Huffman, M., Stevens, K. N., Carlson, R., & Hunnicutt, S. (1992). Studies of vowel and consonant reduction. In J. J. Ohala, T. M. Nearey, B. L. Derwing, M. M. Hodge & G. E. Wiebe (Eds.), *Proceedings of the International Conference on Spoken Language Processing '92 (ICSLP)*, Banff, Alberta (pp. 943–946). Edmonton: University of Alberta, Canada.

Marian, V., Blumenfeld, H., & Boukrina, O. (2008). Sensitivity to phonological similarity within and across languages. *Journal of Psycholinguistic Research, 37*, 141–170.

Marian, V., & Spivey, M. (1999). Activation of Russian and English cohorts during bilingual spoken word recognition. In M. Hahn & S. C. Stoness (Eds.), *Proceedings of the 21st annual Conference of the Cognitive Science Society*, Vancouver (pp. 349–354). Mahwah, NJ: Erlbaum.

Marslen-Wilson, W. D. (1980). Speech understanding as a psychological process. In J. C. Simon (Ed.), *Spoken language generation and understanding* (pp. 39–67). Dordrecht: Reidel.

Marslen-Wilson, W. D. (1984). Function and process in spoken word recognition. In H. Bouma & D. G. Bouwhuis (Eds.), *Attention and performance X* (pp. 125–150). Hillsdale, NJ: Erlbaum.

Marslen-Wilson, W. D. (1990). Activation, competition, and frequency in lexical access. In G. T. M. Altmann (Ed.), *Cognitive models of speech processing: Psycholinguistic and computational perspectives* (pp. 148–172). Cambridge, MA: MIT Press.

Marslen-Wilson, W. D. (2001). Access to lexical representations: Cross-linguistic issues. *Language and Cognitive Processes*, *16*, 699–708.

Marslen-Wilson, W. D. (2006). Morphology and language processing. In K. Brown (Ed.), *Encyclopedia of language and linguistics* (pp. 295–300). Oxford: Elsevier.

Marslen-Wilson, W. D., Tyler, L. K., Waksler, R., & Older, L. (1994). Morphology and meaning in the English mental lexicon. *Psychological Review*, *101*, 3–33.

Marslen-Wilson, W. D., & Warren, P. (1994). Levels of perceptual representation and process in lexical access: Words, phonemes, and features. *Psychological Review*, *101*, 653–675.

Marslen-Wilson, W. D., & Welsh, A. (1978). Processing interactions and lexical access during word recognition in continuous speech. *Cognitive Psychology*, *10*, 29–63.

Marslen-Wilson, W. D., & Zhou, X. (1999). Abstractness, allomorphy, and lexical architecture. *Language and Cognitive Processes*, *14*, 321–352.

Marslen-Wilson, W. D., & Zwitserlood, P. (1989). Accessing spoken words: The importance of word onsets. *Journal of Experimental Psychology: Human Perception and Performance*, *15*, 576–585.

Martin, C., Mullennix, J., Pisoni, D., & Summers, W. (1989). Effects of talker variability on recall of spoken word lists. *Journal of Experimental Psychology: Learning, Memory, and Cognition*, *15*, 676–684.

Mason, H. M. (1946). Understandability of speech in noise as affected by region of origin of speaker and listener. *Speech Monographs*, *13*, 54–58.

Massaro, D. W., & Cohen, M. M. (1983). Phonological context in speech perception. *Perception & Psychophysics*, *34*, 338–348.

Matter, J. F. (1986). *A la recherche des frontières perdues: Etude sur la perception de la parole en français*. Ph.D. dissertation, University of Utrecht. Amsterdam: De Werelt.

Matthei, E. H., & Kean, M. L. (1989). Postaccess processes in the open vs. closed class distinction. *Brain and Language*, *36*, 163–180.

Mattys, S. L. (2000). The perception of primary and secondary stress in English. *Perception & Psychophysics*, *62*, 253–265.

Mattys, S. L. (2004). Stress versus coarticulation: Toward an integrated approach to explicit speech segmentation. *Journal of Experimental Psychology: Human Perception and Performance*, *30*, 397–408.

Mattys, S. L., Brooks, J., & Cooke, M. (2009). Recognizing speech under a processing load: Dissociating energetic from informational factors. *Cognitive Psychology*, *59*, 203–243.

Mattys, S. L., Carroll, L. M., Li, C. K. W., & Chan, S. L. Y. (2010). Effects of energetic and informational masking on speech segmentation by native and non-native speakers. *Speech Communication*, *52*, 887–899.

Mattys, S. L., & Clark, J. H. (2002). Lexical activity in speech processing: Evidence from pause detection. *Journal of Memory and Language*, *47*, 343–359.

Mattys, S. L., & Jusczyk, P. W. (2001). Phonotactic cues for segmentation of fluent speech by infants. *Cognition*, *78*, 91–121.

Mattys, S. L., & Samuel, A. G. (1997). How lexical stress affects speech segmentation and interactivity: Evidence from the migration paradigm. *Journal of Memory and Language*, *36*, 87–116.

Mattys, S. L., & Samuel, A. G. (2000). Implications of stress pattern differences in spoken word recognition. *Journal of Memory and Language*, *42*, 571–596.

Mattys, S. L., White, L., & Melhorn, J. F. (2005). Integration of multiple speech segmentation cues: A hierarchical framework. *Journal of Experimental Psychology: General*, *134*, 477–500.

Mauth, K. (2002). *Morphology in speech comprehension*. Ph.D. dissertation, MPI Series in Psycholinguistics 20, University of Nijmegen.

Mayberry, R. I., Lock, E., & Kazmi, H. (2002). Linguistic ability and early language exposure. *Nature*, *417*, 38.

Maye, J., Aslin, R. N., & Tanenhaus, M. K. (2008). The Weckud Wetch of the Wast: Lexical adaptation to a novel accent. *Cognitive Science*, *32*, 543–562.

Maye, J., Weiss, D. J., & Aslin, R. N. (2008). Statistical phonetic learning in infants: Facilitation and feature generalization. *Developmental Science*, *11*, 122–134.

Maye, J., Werker, J. F., & Gerken, L. (2002). Infant sensitivity to distributional information can affect phonetic discrimination. *Cognition*, *82*, B101–B111.

Mayo, L. H., Florentine, M., & Buus, S. (1997). Age of second-language acquisition and perception of speech in noise. *Journal of Speech, Language, and Hearing Research*, *40*, 686–693.

Mazoyer, B. M., Tzourio, N., Frak, V., Syrota, A., Murayama, N., Levrier, O., Salamon, G., Dehaene, S., Cohen, L., & Mehler, J. (1993). The cortical representation of speech. *Journal of Cognitive Neuroscience*, *5*, 467–479.

McAllister, J. (1991). The processing of lexically stressed syllables in read and spontaneous speech. *Language and Speech*, *34*, 1–26.

McCann, D. R. (1976). The structure of the Korean Sijo. *Harvard Journal of Asiatic Studies*, *36*, 114–134.

McCandliss, B. D., Fiez, J. A., Protopapas, A., Conway, M., & McClelland, J. L. (2002). Success and failure in teaching the [r]-[l] contrast to Japanese adults: Tests of a Hebbian model of plasticity and stabilization in spoken language perception. *Cognitive, Affective & Behavioral Neuroscience*, *2*, 89–108.

McCarthy, J. J., & Prince, A. S. (1995). Prosodic morphology. In J. Goldsmith (Ed.), *Handbook of phonology* (pp. 318–366). Oxford: Blackwell.

McClelland, J. L., & Elman, J. L. (1986). The TRACE model of speech perception. *Cognitive Psychology*, *18*, 1–86.

McClelland, J. L., Mirman, D., & Holt, L. L. (2006). Are there interactive processes in speech perception? *Trends in Cognitive Sciences*, *10*, 363–369.

McGurk, H., & McDonald, J. (1976). Hearing lips and seeing voices. *Nature*, *264*, 746–748.

McLaughlin, J., Osterhout, L., & Kim, A. (2004). Neural correlates of second-language word learning: Minimal instruction produces rapid change. *Nature Neuroscience*, *7*, 703–704.

McLennan, C. T., & Luce, P. A. (2005). Examining the time course of indexical specificity effects in spoken word recognition. *Journal of Experimental Psychology: Learning, Memory, and Cognition*, *31*, 306–321.

McLennan, C. T., Luce, P. A., & Charles-Luce, J. (2003). Representation of lexical form. *Journal of Experimental Psychology: Learning, Memory, and Cognition*, *29*, 539–553.

McMurray, B., Aslin, R., Tanenhaus, M., Spivey, M., & Subik, D. (2008). Gradient sensitivity to within-category variation in words and syllables. *Journal of Experimental Psychology: Human Perception and Performance*, *34*, 1609–1631.

McMurray, B., Tanenhaus, M. K., & Aslin, R. N. (2002). Gradient effects of within-category phonetic variation on lexical access. *Cognition*, *86*, B33–B42.

McMurray, B., Tanenhaus, M. K., & Aslin, R. N. (2009). Within-category VOT affects recovery from "lexical" garden paths: Evidence against phoneme-level inhibition. *Journal of Memory and Language*, *60*, 65–91.

McNeill, D., & Lindig, K. (1973). The perceptual reality of phonemes, syllables, words and sentences. *Journal of Verbal Learning and Verbal Behavior*, *12*, 419–430.

McQueen, J. M. (1991). The influence of the lexicon on phonetic categorization: Stimulus quality in word-final ambiguity. *Journal of Experimental Psychology: Human Perception and Performance*, *17*, 433–443.

McQueen, J. M. (1993). Rhyme decisions to spoken words and nonwords. *Memory & Cognition*, *21*, 210–222.

McQueen, J. M. (1998). Segmentation of continuous speech using phonotactics. *Journal of Memory and Language*, *39*, 21–46.

McQueen, J. M., & Cutler, A. (1992). Words within words: Lexical statistics and lexical access. In J. J. Ohala, T. M. Nearey, B. L. Derwing, M. M. Hodge & G. E. Wiebe (Eds.), *Proceedings of the International Conference on Spoken Language Processing '92 (ICSLP)*, Banff, Alberta (Vol. 1, pp. 221–224). Edmonton: University of Alberta, Canada.

McQueen, J. M., & Cutler, A. (1998). Spotting (different types of) words in (different types of) context. In R. A. Mannell & J. Robert-Ribes (Eds.), *Proceedings of the 5th International Conference on Spoken Language Processing,* Sydney (Vol. 6, pp. 2791–2794). Canberra: Australian Speech Science and Technology Association (ASSTA).

McQueen, J. M., Cutler, A., Briscoe, T., & Norris, D. (1995). Models of continuous speech recognition and the contents of the vocabulary. *Language and Cognitive Processes*, *10*, 309–331.

McQueen, J. M., Cutler, A., & Norris, D. (2006). Phonological abstraction in the mental lexicon. *Cognitive Science*, *30*, 1113–1126.

McQueen, J. M., Jesse, A., & Norris, D. (2009). No lexical-prelexical feedback during speech perception or: Is it time to stop playing those Christmas tapes? *Journal of Memory and Language*, *61*, 1–18.

McQueen, J. M., Norris, D., & Cutler, A. (1994). Competition in spoken word recognition: Spotting words in other words. *Journal of Experimental Psychology: Learning, Memory, and Cognition*, *20*, 621–638.

McQueen, J. M., Norris, D., & Cutler, A. (1999). Lexical influence in phonetic decision making: Evidence from subcategorical mismatches. *Journal of Experimental Psychology: Human Perception and Performance*, *25*, 1363–1389.

McQueen, J. M., Norris, D., & Cutler, A. (2006a). The dynamic nature of speech perception. *Language and Speech*, *49*, 101–112.

McQueen, J. M., Norris, D., & Cutler, A. (2006b). Are there really interactive processes in speech perception? *Trends in Cognitive Sciences*, *10*, 533.

McQueen, J. M., Otake, T., & Cutler, A. (2001). Rhythmic cues and possible-word constraints in Japanese speech segmentation. *Journal of Memory and Language*, *45*, 103–132.

McQueen, J. M., & Pitt, M. A. (1996). Transitional probability and phoneme monitoring. In *Proceedings of the 4th International Conference on Spoken Language Processing*, Philadelphia (Vol. 4, pp. 2502–2505). Philadelphia: University of Delaware and A. I. duPont Institute.

McQueen, J. M., Tyler, M., & Cutler, A. (2013). Lexical retuning of children's speech perception: Evidence for knowledge about words' component sounds. *Language Learning and Development*. doi: 10.1080/15475441.2011.641887

McQueen, J. M., & Viebahn, M. (2007). Tracking recognition of spoken words by tracking looks to printed words. *Quarterly Journal of Experimental Psychology*, *60*, 661–671.

McRae, K., Spivey-Knowlton, M. J., & Tanenhaus, M. K. (1998). Modeling the influence of thematic fit (and other constraints) in on-line sentence comprehension. *Journal of Memory and Language*, *38*, 283–312.

Meador, D., Flege, J. E., & MacKay, I. R. (2000). Factors affecting the recognition of words in a second language. *Bilingualism: Language and Cognition*, *3*, 55–67.

Mechelli, A., Crinion, J. T., Noppeney, U., O'Doherty, J., Ashburner, J., Frackowiak, R. S., & Price, C. J. (2004). Structural plasticity in the bilingual brain. *Nature*, *431*, 757.

Mehler, J., Dommergues, J.-Y., Frauenfelder, U., & Segui, J. (1981). The syllable's role in speech segmentation. *Journal of Verbal Learning and Verbal Behavior*, *20*, 298–305.

Mehler, J., Jusczyk, P., Lambertz, G., Halsted, N., Bertoncini, J., & Amiel-Tison, C. (1988). A precursor of language acquisition in young infants. *Cognition*, *29*, 143–178.

Mehler, J., & Segui, J. (1987). English and French speech processing: Some psycholinguistic investigations. In M. E. H. Schouten (Ed.), *The psychophysics of speech perception* (pp. 405–418). Netherlands: Nijhoff.

Mehler, J., Segui, J., & Carey, P. (1978). Tails of words: Monitoring ambiguity. *Journal of Verbal Learning and Verbal Behavior*, *1*, 29–37.

Mehta, G., & Cutler, A. (1988). Detection of target phonemes in spontaneous and read speech. *Language and Speech*, *31*, 135–156.

Mesgarani, N., David, S. V., Fritz, J. B., & Shamma, S. A. (2008). Phoneme representation and classification in primary auditory cortex. *Journal of the Acoustical Society of America*, *123*, 899–909.

Meunier, F., & Segui, J. (2002). Cross-modal morphological priming in French. *Brain and Language*, *83*, 89–102.

Meunier, F., Seigneuric, A., & Spinelli, E. (2008). The morpheme gender effect. *Journal of Memory and Language*, *58*, 88–99.

Meyer, A. S., Roelofs, A., & Levelt, W. J. M. (2003). Word length effects in object naming: The role of a response criterion. *Journal of Memory and Language*, *48*, 131–147.

Miller, M. (1984). On the perception of rhythm. *Journal of Phonetics*, *12*, 75–83.

Miller, J. L., & Dexter, E. R. (1988). Effects of speaking rate and lexical status on phonetic perception. *Journal of Experimental Psychology: Human Perception and Performance, 14*, 369–378.

Miller, J. L., Green, K., & Schermer, T. M. (1984). A distinction between the effects of sentential speaking rate and semantic congruity on word identification. *Perception & Psychophysics, 36*, 329–337.

Miller, J. L., & Grosjean, F. (1997). Dialect effects in vowel perception: The role of temporal information in French. *Language and Speech, 40*, 277–288.

Miller, J. L., & Liberman, A. M. (1979). Some effects of later-occurring information on the perception of stop consonant and semivowel. *Perception & Psychophysics, 25*, 457–465.

Miller, J. L., & Volaitis, L. E. (1989). Effect of speaking rate on the perceptual structure of a phonetic category. *Perception & Psychophysics, 46*, 505–512.

Mills, D. L., Prat, C., Zangl, R., Stager, C. L., Neville, H. J., & Werker, J. F. (2004). Language experience and the organization of brain activity to phonetically similar words: ERP evidence from 14- and 20-month-olds. *Journal of Cognitive Neuroscience, 16*, 1452–1464.

Minematsu, N., & Hirose, K. (1995). Role of prosodic features in the human process of perceiving spoken words and sentences in Japanese. *Journal of the Acoustical Society of Japan, 16*, 311–320.

Mirman, D., Magnuson, J. S., Graf Estes, K., & Dixon, J. A. (2008). The link between statistical segmentation and word learning in adults. *Cognition, 108*, 271–280.

Mirman, D., McClelland, J. L., & Holt, L. L. (2005). Computational and behavioral investigations of lexically induced delays in phoneme recognition. *Journal of Memory and Language, 52*, 424–443.

Mitterer, H. (2006). On the causes of compensation for coarticulation: Evidence for phonological mediation. *Perception & Psychophysics, 68*, 1227–1240.

Mitterer, H., & Blomert, L. (2003). Coping with phonological assimilation in speech perception: Evidence for early compensation. *Perception & Psychophysics, 65*, 956–969.

Mitterer, H., Chen, Y., & Zhou, X. (2011). Phonological abstraction in processing lexical-tone variation: Evidence from a learning paradigm. *Cognitive Science, 35*, 184–197.

Mitterer, H., Csépe, V., & Blomert, L. (2006). The role of perceptual integration in the perception of assimilated word forms. *Quarterly Journal of Experimental Psychology, 59*, 1305–1334.

Mitterer, H., Csépe, V., Honbolygo, F., & Blomert, L. (2006). The recognition of phonologically assimilated words does not depend on specific language experience. *Cognitive Science, 30*, 451–479.

Mitterer, H., & Ernestus, M. (2006). Listeners recover /t/s that speakers reduce: Evidence from /t/-lenition in Dutch. *Journal of Phonetics, 34*, 73–103.

Mitterer, H., & McQueen, J. M. (2009a). Processing reduced word-forms in speech perception using probabilistic knowledge about speech production. *Journal of Experimental Psychology: Human Perception and Performance, 35*, 244–263.

Mitterer, H., & McQueen, J. M. (2009b). Foreign subtitles help but native-language subtitles harm foreign speech perception. *PLoS ONE, 4*, e7785.

Mitterer, H., & de Ruiter, J. P. (2008). Recalibrating color categories using world knowledge. *Psychological Science, 19*, 629–634.

Miyawaki, K., Strange, W., Verbrugge, R., Liberman, A. M., Jenkins, J. J., & Fujimura, O. (1975). An effect of linguistic experience: The discrimination of [r] and [l] by native speakers of Japanese and English. *Perception & Psychophysics, 18*, 331–340.

Molfese, D., Freeman, R., & Palermo, D. (1975). The ontogeny of brain lateralization for speech and non-speech stimuli. *Brain and Language, 2*, 356–368.

Molfese, D., & Molfese, V. (1985). Electrophysiological indices of auditory discrimination in newborn infants: The bases for predicting later language development? *Infant Behavior and Development, 8*, 197–211.

Molfese, D., & Molfese, V. (1997). Discrimination of language skills at five years of age using event related potentials recorded at birth. *Developmental Neuropsychology, 13*, 133–156.

Monaghan, P., & Shillcock, R. (2003). Connectionist modelling of the separable processing of consonants and vowels. *Brain and Language, 86*, 83–98.

Moon, C., Bever, B. T., & Fifer, W. P. (1992). Canonical and noncanonical syllable discrimination by 2-day-old infants. *Journal of Child Language, 19*, 1–17.

Moon, C., Cooper, R. P., & Fifer, W. P. (1993). Two-day-olds prefer their native language. *Infant Behavior and Development, 16*, 495–500.

Moon, C., & Fifer, W. P. (1990). Syllables as signals for 2-day-old infants. *Infant Behavior and Development, 13*, 377–390.

Moore, J. K., & Linthicum, F. H. Jr. (2007). The human auditory system: A timeline of development. *International Journal of Audiology, 46*, 460–478.

Morais, J., Cary, L., Alegria, J., & Bertelson, P. (1979). Does awareness of speech as a sequence of phones arise spontaneously? *Cognition, 7*, 323–331.

Morgan, J. L. (1996). A rhythmic bias in preverbal speech segmentation. *Journal of Memory and Language, 35*, 666–688.

Morgan, J. L., & Demuth, K. (1996). Signal to syntax: An overview. In J. L. Morgan & K. Demuth (Eds.), *Signal to syntax: Bootstrapping from speech to grammar in early acquisition* (pp. 1–22). Mahwah, NJ: Erlbaum.

Morgan, J. L., Meier, R. P., & Newport, E. L. (1987). Structural packaging in the input to language learning: Contributions of prosodic and morphological marking of phrases to the acquisition of language. *Cognitive Psychology, 19*, 498–550.

Morton, J. (1969). Interaction of information in word perception. *Psychological Review, 76*, 165–178.

Morton, J. (1970). A functional model for memory. In D. A. Norman (Ed.), *Models of human memory* (pp. 203–254). New York: Academic Press.

Morton, J., & Long, J. (1976). Effect of word transitional probability on phoneme identification. *Journal of Verbal Learning and Verbal Behavior, 15*, 43–51.

Mrzljak, L., Uylings, H. B., van Eden, C. G., & Judas, M. (1990). Neuronal development in human prefrontal cortex in prenatal and postnatal stages. *Progress in Brain Research, 85*, 185–222.

Mueller, J. L. (2005). Electrophysiological correlates of second language processing. *Second Language Research, 21*, 152–174.

Mueller, J. L., Bahlmann, J., & Friederici, A. D. (2008). The role of pause cues in language learning: The emergence of event-related potentials related to sequence processing. *Journal of Cognitive Neuroscience*, *20*, 892–905.

Mullennix, J. W., Pisoni, D. B., & Martin, C. S. (1989). Some effects of talker variability on spoken word recognition. *Journal of the Acoustical Society of America*, *85*, 365–378.

Munro, M. J. (1998). The effects of noise on the intelligibility of foreign-accented speech. *Studies in Second Language Acquisition*, *20*, 139–154.

Munro, M. J., & Derwing, T. M. (1995). Foreign accent, comprehensibility and intelligibility in the speech of second language learners. *Language Learning*, *45*, 73–97.

Murty, L., Otake, T., & Cutler, A. (2007). Perceptual tests of rhythmic similarity: I. Mora rhythm. *Language and Speech*, *50*, 77–99.

Nábělek, A. K., & Donahue, A. M. (1984). Perception of consonants in reverberation by native and non-native listeners. *Journal of the Acoustical Society of America*, *75*, 632–634.

Narayan, C. R., Werker, J. F., & Beddor, P. S. (2010). The interaction between acoustic salience and language experience in developmental speech perception: Evidence from nasal place discrimination. *Developmental Science*, *13*, 407–420.

Nazzi, T., Bertoncini, J., & Mehler, J. (1998). Language discrimination by newborns: Toward an understanding of the role of rhythm. *Journal of Experimental Psychology: Human Perception and Performance*, *24*, 756–766.

Nazzi, T., Iakimova, G., Bertoncini, J., Frédonie, S., & Alcantara, C. (2006). Early segmentation of fluent speech by infants acquiring French: Emerging evidence for crosslinguistic differences. *Journal of Memory and Language*, *54*, 283–299.

Nazzi, T., Jusczyk, P. W., & Johnson, E. K. (2000). Language discrimination by English-learning 5-month-olds: Effects of rhythm and familiarity. *Journal of Memory and Language*, *43*, 1–19.

Nazzi, T., Kemler Nelson, D. G., Jusczyk, P. W., & Jusczyk, A. M. (2000). Six-month-olds' detection of clauses embedded in continuous speech: Effects of prosodic well-formedness. *Infancy*, *1*, 123–147.

Nespor, M., & Vogel, I. (1983). Prosodic structure above the word. In A. Cutler & D. R. Ladd (Eds.), *Prosody: Models and measurements* (pp. 123–140). Heidelberg: Springer.

Newman, R., Bernstein Ratner, N., Jusczyk, A. M., Jusczyk, P. W., & Dow, K. A. (2006). Infants' early ability to segment the conversational speech signal predicts later language development: A retrospective analysis. *Developmental Psychology*, *42*, 643–655.

Newman, R. S., Clouse, S. A., & Burnham, J. L. (2001). The perceptual consequences of within-talker variability in fricative production. *Journal of the Acoustical Society of America*, *109*, 1181–1196.

Newman, R. S., Sawusch, J. R., & Luce, P. A. (1997). Lexical neighborhood effects in phonetic processing. *Journal of Experimental Psychology: Human Perception and Performance*, *23*, 873–889.

Newman, R. S., Sawusch, J. R., & Wunnenberg, T. (2011). Cues and cue interactions in segmenting words in fluent speech. *Journal of Memory and Language*, *64*, 460–476.

Newport, E. L., & Aslin, R. N. (2004). Learning at a distance I. Statistical learning of non-adjacent dependencies. *Cognitive Psychology*, *48*, 127–162.

Nguyen-Hoan, M., & Taft, M. (2010). The impact of a subordinate L1 on L2 auditory processing in adult bilinguals. *Bilingualism: Language and Cognition*, *13*, 217–230.

Nishinuma, Y. (1994). How do the French perceive tonal accent in Japanese? Experimental evidence. In *Proceedings of the 3rd International Conference on Spoken Language Processing*, Yokohama (pp. 1739–1742). Tokyo: The Acoustical Society of Japan.

Nishinuma, Y., Arai, M., & Ayusawa, T. (1996). Perception of tonal accent by Americans learning Japanese. In H. T. Bunnell & W. Idsardi (Eds.), *Proceedings of the 4th International Conference on Spoken Language Processing*, Philadelphia (Vol. 1, pp. 646–649). Philadelphia: University of Delaware and A. I. duPont Institute.

Nooteboom, S. G. (1981). Lexical retrieval from fragments of spoken words: Beginnings vs. endings. *Journal of Phonetics*, *9*, 407–424.

Nooteboom, S. G., & Doodeman, G. J. N. (1980). Production and perception of vowel length in spoken sentences. *Journal of the Acoustical Society of America*, *67*, 276–287.

Nooteboom, S. G., & Kruyt, J. G. (1987). Accents, focus distribution, and the perceived distribution of given and new information: An experiment. *Journal of the Acoustical Society of America*, *82*, 1512–1524.

Nooteboom, S. G., & Truin, P. G. M. (1980). Word recognition from fragments of spoken words by native and non-native listeners. *IPO Annual Progress Report*, *15*, 42–47.

Nooteboom, S. G., & van der Vlugt, M. J. (1988). A search for a word-beginning superiority effect. *Journal of the Acoustical Society of America*, *84*, 2018–2032.

Norris, D. (1993). Bottom-up connectionist models of "interaction." In G. T. M. Altmann & R. Shillcock (Eds.), *Cognitive models of speech processing: The second Sperlonga meeting* (pp. 211–234). Hillsdale, NJ: Erlbaum.

Norris, D. (1994). Shortlist: A connectionist model of continuous speech recognition. *Cognition*, *52*, 189–234.

Norris, D. (2005). How do computational models help us develop better theories? In A. Cutler (Ed.), *Twenty-first century psycholinguistics: Four cornerstones* (pp. 331–346). Hillsdale, NJ: Erlbaum.

Norris, D., Butterfield, S., McQueen, J. M., & Cutler, A. (2006). Lexically guided retuning of letter perception. *Quarterly Journal of Experimental Psychology*, *59*, 1505–1515.

Norris, D., & Cutler, A. (1988). The relative accessibility of phonemes and syllables. *Perception & Psychophysics*, *43*, 541–550.

Norris, D., Cutler, A., McQueen, J. M., & Butterfield, S. (2006). Phonological and conceptual activation in speech comprehension. *Cognitive Psychology*, *53*, 146–193.

Norris, D., & McQueen, J. M. (2008). Shortlist B: A Bayesian model of continuous speech recognition. *Psychological Review*, *115*, 357–395.

Norris, D., McQueen, J. M., & Cutler, A. (1995). Competition and segmentation in spoken word recognition. *Journal of Experimental Psychology: Learning, Memory, and Cognition*, *21*, 1209–1228.

Norris, D., McQueen, J. M., & Cutler, A. (2000). Merging information in speech recognition: Feedback is never necessary. *Behavioral and Brain Sciences*, *23*, 299–325.

Norris, D., McQueen, J. M., & Cutler, A. (2003). Perceptual learning in speech. *Cognitive Psychology*, *47*, 204–238.

Norris, D., McQueen, J. M., Cutler, A., & Butterfield, S. (1997). The possible-word constraint in the segmentation of continuous speech. *Cognitive Psychology*, *34*, 191–243.

Norris, D., McQueen, J. M., Cutler, A., Butterfield, S., & Kearns, R. (2001). Language-universal constraints on speech segmentation. *Language and Cognitive Processes*, *16*, 637–660.

Nosofsky, R. M. (1988). Exemplar-based accounts of relations between classification, recognition, and typicality. *Journal of Experimental Psychology: Learning, Memory, and Cognition*, *14*, 700–708.

Nosofsky, R. M. (1991). Tests of an exemplar model for relating perceptual classification and recognition memory. *Journal of Experimental Psychology: Human Perception and Performance*, *17*, 3–27.

Nygaard, L. C. (2005). Perceptural integration of linguistic and nonlinguistic properties of speech. In D. B. Pisoni & R. E. Remez (Eds.), *Handbook of speech perception* (pp. 390–413). Oxford: Blackwell.

Nygaard, L. C., Burt, S. A., & Queen, J. S. (2000). Surface form typicality and asymmetric transfer in episodic memory for spoken words. *Journal of Experimental Psychology: Learning, Memory, and Cognition*, *26*, 1228–1244.

Nygaard, L. C., & Pisoni, D. B. (1998). Talker-specific learning in speech perception. *Perception & Psychophysics*, *60*, 355–376.

Nygaard, L. C., Sommers, M. S., & Pisoni, D. B. (1994). Speech perception as a talker-contingent process. *Psychological Science*, *5*, 42–46.

Nygaard, L. C., Sommers, M. S., & Pisoni, D. B. (1995). Effects of stimulus variability on perception and representation of spoken words in memory. *Perception & Psychophysics*, *57*, 989–1001.

Oh, J. S., Jun, S.-A. J., Knightly, L. M., & Au, T. K. (2003). Holding on to childhood language memory. *Cognition*, *86*, B53–B64.

Ohala, J. J., & Gilbert, J. B. (1981). Listeners' ability to identify languages by their prosody. In P. Léon & M. Rossi (Eds.), *Problèmes de prosodie, II: Expérimentations, modèles et fonctions* (pp. 123–131). Ottawa: Didier.

Onifer, W., & Swinney, D. A. (1981). Accessing lexical ambiguities during sentence comprehension: Effects of frequency of meaning and contextual bias. *Memory & Cognition*, *9*, 225–236.

Onishi, K. H., Chambers, K. E., & Fisher, C. (2002). Learning phonotactic constraints from brief auditory exposure. *Cognition*, *83*, B13–B23.

Onnis, L., Monaghan, P., Christiansen, M. H., & Chater, N. (2004). Variability is the spice of learning, and a crucial ingredient for detecting and generalizing in nonadjacent dependencies. In K. Forbus, D. Gentner & T. Regier (Eds.), *Proceedings of the 26th Annual Meeting Cognitive Science Society*, Chicago (pp. 1047–1052). Austin, TX: Cognitive Science Society.

Onnis, L., Monaghan, P., Richmond, K., & Chater, N. (2005). Phonology impacts segmentation in speech processing. *Journal of Memory and Language*, *53*, 225–237.

van Ooijen, B. (1996). Vowel mutability and lexical selection in English: Evidence from a word reconstruction task. *Memory & Cognition*, *24*, 573–583.

van Ooijen, B., Cutler, A., & Norris, D. (1991). Detection times for vowels versus consonants. In *Proceedings of the 2nd European Conference on Speech Communication and Technology (EUROSPEECH '91),* Genova, Italy (Vol. 3, pp. 1451–1454).

van Ooijen, B., Bertoncini, J., Sansavini, A., & Mehler, J. (1997). Do weak syllables count for newborns? *Journal of the Acoustical Society of America, 102,* 3735–3741.

Oostdijk, N. (2000). The Spoken Dutch Corpus Project. *ELRA Newsletter, 5,* 4–8.

van Oostendorp, M. (2008). Hoe de slot-*r* verdween uit het Nederlands. *Onze Taal, 2/3,* 53–55.

Orsolini, M., & Marslen-Wilson, W. D. (1997). Universals in morphological representation: Evidence from Italian. *Language and Cognitive Processes, 12,* 1–47.

Osser, H., & Peng, F. (1964). A cross-cultural study of speech rate. *Language and Speech, 7,* 120–125.

Otake, T., & Cutler, A. (1999). Perception of suprasegmental structure in a non-native dialect. *Journal of Phonetics, 27,* 229–253.

Otake, T., Hatano, G., Cutler, A., & Mehler, J. (1993). Mora or syllable? Speech segmentation in Japanese. *Journal of Memory and Language, 32,* 358–378.

Otake, T., Hatano, G., & Yoneyama, K. (1996). Speech segmentation by Japanese listeners. In T. Otake & A. Cutler (Eds.), *Phonological structure and language processing: Cross-linguistic studies* (pp. 183–201). Berlin: Mouton de Gruyter.

Otake, T., McQueen, J. M., & Cutler, A. (2010). Competition in the perception of spoken Japanese words. In T. Kobayashi, K. Hirose, & S. Nakamura (Eds.), *Proceedings of the 11th annual Conference of the International Speech Communication Association* (INTERSPEECH 2010), Makuhari (pp. 114–117). Tokyo: Tokyo Institute of Technology.

Pallier, C. (1997). The Possible Word Constraint and language-specific word structure. In K. Drozd & J. van de Weijer (Eds.), *MPI Annual Report 1997* (p. 8). Nijmegen: MPI for Psycholinguistics.

Pallier, C., Colomé, A., & Sebastián-Gallés, N. (2001). The influence of native-language phonology on lexical access: Exemplar-based vs. abstract lexical entries. *Psychological Science, 12,* 445–449.

Pallier, C., Dehaene, S., Poline, J., LeBihan, D., Argenti, A., Dupoux, E., Mehler, J. (2003). Brain imaging of language plasticity in adopted adults: Can a second language replace the first? *Cerebral Cortex, 13,* 155–161.

Pallier, C., Sebastián-Gallés, N., Felguera, T., Christophe, A., & Mehler, J. (1993). Attentional allocation within the syllabic structure of spoken words. *Journal of Memory and Language, 32,* 373–389.

Palmeri, T. J., Goldinger, S. D., & Pisoni, D. B. (1993). Episodic encoding of voice attributes and recognition memory for spoken words. *Journal of Experimental Psychology: Learning, Memory, and Cognition, 19,* 309–328.

Papousek, M., & Hwang, S.-F. C. (1991). Tone and intonation in Mandarin babytalk to presyllabic infants: Comparison with registers of adult conversation and foreign language instruction. *Applied Psycholinguistics, 12,* 481–504.

Parikh, G., & Loizou, P. (2005). The influence of noise on vowel and consonant cues. *Journal of the Acoustical Society of America, 118,* 3874–3888.

Pater, J., Stager, C., & Werker, J. (2004). The perceptual acquisition of phonological contrasts. *Language, 80*, 384–402.

Pegg, J. E., & Werker, J. F. (1997). Adult and infant perception of two English phones. *Journal of the Acoustical Society of America, 102*, 3742–3753.

Pegg, J. E., Werker, J. F., & McLeod, P. J. (1992). Preference for infant-directed over adult-directed speech: Evidence from 7-week-old infants. *Infant Behavior and Development, 15*, 325–345.

Pelucchi, B., Hay, J. F., & Saffran, J. R. (2009). Statistical learning in a natural language by 8-month-old infants. *Child Development, 80*, 674–685.

Peña, M., Bonatti, L. L., Nespor, M., & Mehler, J. (2002). Signal-driven computations in speech processing. *Science, 298*, 604–607.

Peña, M., Maki, A., Kovacic, D., Dehaene-Lambertz, G., Koizumi, H., Bouquet, F., & Mehler, J. (2003). Sounds and silence: An optical topography study of language recognition at birth. *Proceedings of the National Academy of Sciences of the United States of America, 100*, 11702–11705.

Pennington, M. C., & Ellis, N. C. (2000). Cantonese speakers' memory for English sentences with prosodic cues. *Modern Language Journal, 84*, 372–389.

Peperkamp, S., & Dupoux, E. (2002). A typological study of stress "deafness". In C. Gussenhoven & N. L. Warner (Eds.), *Papers in laboratory phonology VII* (pp. 203–240). Berlin: Mouton de Gruyter.

Peperkamp, S., Le Calvez, R., Nadal, J.-P., & Dupoux, E. (2006). The acquisition of allophonic rules: Statistical learning with linguistic constraints. *Cognition, 101*, B31–B41.

Peperkamp, S., Vendelin, I., & Dupoux, E. (2010). Perception of predictable stress: A cross-linguistic investigation. *Journal of Phonetics, 38*, 422–430.

Perdue, C. (1993). *Adult language acquisition: Cross-linguistic perspectives* (Vol. 1 and 2). Cambridge: Cambridge University Press.

Peretz, I., Lussier, I., & Béland, R. (1996). The roles of phonological and orthographic code in word stem completion. In T. Otake & A. Cutler (Eds.), *Phonological structure and language processing: Cross-linguistic studies* (pp. 217–226). Berlin: Mouton de Gruyter.

Perrachione, T. K., Pierrehumbert, J. B., & Wong, P. C. M. (2009). Differential neural contributions to native- and foreign-language talker identification. *Journal of Experimental Psychology: Human Perception and Performance, 35*, 1950–1960.

Perrachione, T. K., & Wong, P. C. M. (2007). Learning to recognize speakers of a non-native language: Implications for the functional organization of human auditory cortex. *Neuropsychologia, 45*, 1899–1910.

Perruchet, P., & Pacton, S. (2006). Implicit learning and statistical learning: One phenomenon, two approaches. *Trends in Cognitive Sciences, 10*, 233–238.

Perruchet, P., Peereman, R., & Tyler, M. D. (2006). Do we need algebraic-like computations? A reply to Bonatti, Peña, Nespor, and Mehler (2006). *Journal of Experimental Psychology: General, 135*, 322–326.

Perruchet, P., Tyler, M. D., Galland, N., & Peereman, R. (2004). Learning nonadjacent dependencies: No need for algebraic-like computations. *Journal of Experimental Psychology: General, 133*, 573–583.

Peterson, G. E., & Barney, H. L. (1952). Control methods used in a study of the vowels. *Journal of the Acoustical Society of America, 24*, 175–184.

Pfitzinger, H. R. (1999). Local speech rate perception in German speech. In J. J. Ohala, Y. Hasegawa, M. Ohala, D. Granville & A. C. Bailey (Eds.), *Proceedings of the 14th International Congress of Phonetic Sciences*, San Francisco (pp. 893–896). University of California Press.

Pfitzinger, H. R., & Tamashima, M. (2006). Comparing perceptual local speech rate of German and Japanese speech. In R. Hoffmann & H. Mixdorff (Eds.), *Proceedings of the 3rd International Conference on Speech Prosody*, Dresden (Vol. 1, pp. 105–108). Dresden: TUDpress.

Pickett, E. R., Blumstein, S. E., & Burton, M. W. (1999). Effects of speaking rate on the singleton/geminate consonant contrast in Italian. *Phonetica, 56*, 135–157.

Pierrehumbert, J. (2001). Exemplar dynamics: Word frequency, lenition, and contrast. In J. Bybee & P. Hopper (Eds.), *Frequency effects and the emergence of lexical structure* (pp. 137–157). Amsterdam: John Benjamins.

Pierrehumbert, J. (2002). Word-specific phonetics. In C. Gussenhoven & N. Warner (Eds.), *Laboratory phonology 7* (pp. 101–140). Berlin: Mouton de Gruyter.

Pierrehumbert, J., & Beckman, M. E. (1988). *Japanese tone structure*. Linguistic Inquiry Monographs, 15. Cambridge, MA: MIT Press.

Pierrehumbert, J., & Talkin, D. (1992). Lenition of /h/ and glottal stop. In G. Doherty & D. R. Ladd (Eds.), *Papers in laboratory phonology II* (pp. 90–117). Cambridge: Cambridge University Press.

Pierson, L. L., Gerhardt, K. J., Abrams, R. M., & Huang, X. (1997). Effects of intense noise exposure on the auditory brain-stem response and inner ear histology of fetal sheep. *Journal of the Acoustical Society of America, 102*, 3110.

de Pijper, J. R., & Sanderman, A. A. (1994). On the perceptual strength of prosodic boundaries and its relation to suprasegmental cues. *Journal of the Acoustical Society of America, 96*, 2037–2047.

Pike, K. L. (1945). *The intonation of American English*. Ann Arbor: University of Michigan.

Pilon, R. (1981). Segmentation of speech in a foreign language. *Journal of Psycholinguistic Research, 10*, 113–122.

Pisoni, D. B. (1973). Auditory and phonetic memory codes in the discrimination of consonants and vowels. *Perception & Psychophysics, 13*, 253–260.

Pitt, M. A. (2009). How are pronunciation variants of spoken words recognized? A test of generalization to newly learned words. *Journal of Memory and Language, 61*, 19–36.

Pitt, M. A., & McQueen, J. M. (1998). Is compensation for coarticulation mediated by the lexicon? *Journal of Memory and Language, 39*, 347–370.

Pitt, M. A., & Samuel, A. G. (1993). An empirical and meta-analytic evaluation of the phoneme identification task. *Journal of Experimental Psychology: Human Perception and Performance, 19*, 699–725.

Pitt, M. A., & Samuel, A. G. (1995). Lexical and sublexical feedback in auditory word recognition. *Cognitive Psychology, 29*, 149–188.

Pluymaekers, M., Ernestus, M., & Baayen, R. H. (2005). Lexical frequency and acoustic reduction in spoken Dutch. *Journal of the Acoustical Society of America, 118*, 2561–2569.

Polivanov, E. (1931). La perception des sons d'une langue étrangère. *Travaux du Cercle Linguistique de Prague, 4*, 79–96.

Polka, L. (1991). Cross-language speech perception in adults: Phonemic, phonetic, and acoustic contributions. *Journal of the Acoustical Society of America, 89*, 2961–2977.

Polka, L. (1992). Characterizing the influence of native language experience on adult speech perception. *Perception & Psychophysics, 52*, 37–52.

Polka, L., Colantonio, C., & Sundara, M. (2001). A cross-language comparison of /d—ð/ perception: Evidence for a new developmental pattern. *Journal of the Acoustical Society of America, 109*, 2190–2200.

Polka, L., & Werker, J. F. (1994). Developmental changes in perception of nonnative vowel contrasts. *Journal of Experimental Psychology: Human Perception and Performance, 20*, 421–435.

Pollack, I., Rubenstein, H., & Decker, L. (1959). Intelligibility of known and unknown message sets. *Journal of the Acoustical Society of America, 31*, 273–279.

Port, R. F., & O'Dell, M. L. (1985). Neutralization of syllable-final voicing in German. *Journal of Phonetics, 13*, 455–471.

Quené, H. (1992). Durational cues for word segmentation in Dutch. *Journal of Phonetics, 20*, 331–350.

Quené, H., & Koster, M. L. (1998). Metrical segmentation in Dutch: Vowel quality or stress? *Language and Speech, 41*, 185–202.

Querleu, D., Renard, X., Versyp, F., Paris-Delrue, L., & Crépin, G. (1988). Fetal hearing. *European Journal of Obstetrics and Reproductive Biology, 29*, 191–212.

Racine, I., & Grosjean, F. (2000). Influence de l'effacement du schwa sur la reconnaissance des mots en parole continue [The effect of schwa deletion on word recognition in continuous speech]. *L'Année Psychologique, 100*, 393–417.

Ramus, F. (2002). Acoustic correlates of linguistic rhythm: Perspectives. In B. Bel & I. Marlin (Eds.), *Proceedings of the 1st International Conference on Speech Prosody*, Aix-en-Provence (pp. 115–120). Aix-en-Provence: Laboratoire Parole et Langage, Université de Provence.

Ramus, F., & Mehler, J. (1999). Language identification with suprasegmental cues: A study based on speech resynthesis. *Journal of the Acoustical Society of America, 105*, 512–521.

Ramus, F., Nespor, M., & Mehler, J. (1999). Correlates of linguistic rhythm in the speech signal. *Cognition, 73*, 265–292.

Ranbom, L. J., & Connine, C. M. (2007). Lexical representation of phonological variation in spoken word recognition. *Journal of Memory and Language, 57*, 273–298.

Reber, A. S. (1967). Implicit learning of artificial grammars. *Journal of Verbal Learning and Verbal Behavior, 6*, 855–863.

Reid, A. A., & Marslen-Wilson, W. D. (2003). Lexical representation of morphologically complex words: Evidence from Polish. In R. H. Baayen & R. Schreuder (Eds.), *Morphological structure in language processing* (pp. 287–336). Berlin: Mouton de Gruyter.

Reinisch, E., Jesse, A., & McQueen, J. M. (2010). Early use of phonetic information in spoken word recognition: Lexical stress drives eye movements immediately. *Quarterly Journal of Experimental Psychology, 63*, 772–783.

Reinisch, E., Jesse, A., & McQueen, J. M. (2011). Speaking rate affects the perception of duration as a suprasegmental lexical-stress cue. *Language and Speech, 54*, 147–165.

Remez, R. E., Rubin, P. E., Pisoni, D. B., & Carrell, T. D. (1981). Speech perception without traditional speech cues. *Science, 212*, 947–950.

Repp, B. H. (1983). Bidirectional contrast effects in the perception of VC–CV sequences. *Perception & Psychophysics, 33*, 147–155.

Repp, B. H. (1988). Integration and segregation in speech perception. *Language and Speech, 31*, 239–271.

Repp, B. H., & Liberman, A. M. (1987). Phonetic category boundaries are flexible. In S. R. Harnad (Ed.), *Categorical perception* (pp. 89–112). Cambridge: Cambridge University Press.

Repp, B. H., & Lin, H.-B. (1990). Integration of segmental and tonal information in speech perception: A cross-linguistic study. *Journal of Phonetics, 18*, 481–495.

Reznick, J. S., & Goldfield, B. A. (1992). Rapid change in lexical development in comprehension and production. *Developmental Psychology, 28*, 406–413.

Rhebergen, K. S., Versfeld, N. J., & Dreschler, W. A. (2005). Release from informational masking by time reversal of native and non-native interfering speech. *Journal of the Acoustical Society of America, 118*, 1274–1277.

Richards, D. S., Frentzen, B., Gerhardt, K. J., McCann, M. E., & Abrams, R. M. (1992). Sound levels in the human uterus. *Obstetrics and Gynecology, 80*, 186–190.

Rigault, A. (1970). L'accent dans deux langues à accent fixe: Le français et le tchèque [Stress in two fixed-stress languages: French and Czech]. *Studia Phonetica, 3*, 1–12.

Rivera-Gaxiola, M., Csibra, G., Johnson, M. H., & Karmiloff-Smith, A. (2000). Electrophysiological correlates of cross-linguistic speech perception in native English speakers. *Behavioural Brain Research, 111*, 13–23.

Rivera-Gaxiola, M., Klarman, L., Garcia-Sierra, A., & Kuhl, P. K. (2005). Neural patterns to speech and vocabulary growth in American infants. *Neuroreport, 16*, 495–498.

Rivera-Gaxiola, M., Silva-Pereyra, J., & Kuhl, P. K. (2005). Brain potentials to native and non-native speech contrasts in 7- and 11-month-old American infants. *Developmental Science, 8*, 162–172.

Roach, P. (1982). On the distinction between "stress-timed" and "syllable-timed" languages. In D. Crystal (Ed.), *Linguistic controversies: Essays in linguistic theory and practice in honour of F. R. Palmer* (pp. 73–79). London: Arnold.

Roach, P. (1998). Some languages are spoken more quickly than others. In L. Bauer & P. Trudgill (Eds.), *Language myths* (pp. 150–159). London: Penguin.

Roach, P., Knowles, G., Varadi, T., & Arnfield, S. (1993). MARSEC: A machine-readable Spoken English Corpus. *Journal of the International Phonetic Association, 23*, 47–53.

Roberts, M., & Summerfield, Q. (1981). Audiovisual presentation demonstrates that selective adaptation in speech perception is purely auditory. *Perception & Psychophysics, 30*, 309–314.

Roder, B. J., Bushnell, E. W., & Sasseville, A. M. (2000). Infants' preferences for familiarity and novelty during the course of visual processing. *Infancy*, *1*, 491–507.

Rodríguez-Fornells, A., Schmitt, B. M., Kutas, M., & Münte, T. F. (2002). Electrophysiological estimates of the time course of semantic and phonological encoding during listening and naming. *Neuropsychologia*, *40*, 778–787.

Rogers, C. L., Lister, J. J., Febo, D. M., Besing, J. M., & Abrams, H. B. (2006). Effects of bilingualism, noise and reverberation on speech perception by listeners with normal hearing. *Applied Psycholinguistics*, *27*, 465–485.

Rolke, B., & Hofmann, P. (2007). Temporal uncertainty degrades perceptual processing. *Psychonomic Bulletin & Review*, *14*, 522–526.

de Rooij, J. J. (1975). Prosody and the perception of syntactic boundaries. *IPO Annual Progress Report*, *10*, 36–39.

Rost, G. C., & McMurray, B. (2009). Speaker variability augments phonological processing in early word learning. *Developmental Science*, *12*, 339–349.

Rubin, P., Turvey, M. T., & van Gelder, P. (1976). Initial phonemes are detected faster in spoken words than in nonwords. *Perception & Psychophysics*, *19*, 394–398.

Rugg, M. D. (1985). The effect of semantic priming and word repetition on event-related potentials. *Psychophysiology*, *22*, 642–647.

Rüschemeyer, S.-A., Nojack, A., & Limbach, M. (2008). A mouse with a roof? effects of phonological neighbors on processing of words in sentences in a non-native language. *Brain and Language*, *104*, 132–144.

Russell, A., Penny, L., & Pemberton, C. (1995). Speaking fundamental frequency changes over time in women: A longitudinal study. *Journal of Speech and Hearing Research*, *38*, 101–109.

Saffran, J. R., Aslin, R. N., & Newport, E. L. (1996). Statistical learning by 8-month-old infants. *Science*, *274*, 1926–1928.

Saffran, J. R., Johnson, E. K., Aslin, R. N., & Newport, E. L. (1999). Statistical learning of tone sequences by human infants and adults. *Cognition*, *70*, 27–52.

Saffran, J. R., Newport, E. L., & Aslin, R. N. (1996). Word segmentation: The role of distributional cues. *Journal of Memory and Language*, *35*, 606–621.

Saffran, J., & Thiessen, E. (2005). Learning how to learn: The acquisition of stress-based word segmentation strategies by infants. In *Proceedings of the ISCA Workshop on Plasticity in Speech Perception (PSP 2005)*, London (pp. 248–251). London: University College London [CD-ROM].

Saffran, J. R., Werker, J., & Werner, L. (2006). The infant's auditory world: Hearing, speech, and the beginnings of language. In R. Siegler & D. Kuhn (Eds.), *Handbook of child development* (pp. 58–108). New York: Wiley.

Salasoo, A., & Pisoni, D. B. (1985). Interaction of knowledge sources in spoken word identification. *Journal of Memory and Language*, *24*, 210–231.

Salverda, A. P., Dahan, D., & McQueen, J. M. (2003). The role of prosodic boundaries in the resolution of lexical embedding in speech comprehension. *Cognition*, *90*, 51–89.

Salverda, A. P., Dahan, D., Tanenhaus, M. K., Crosswhite, K., Masharov, M., & McDonough, J. (2007). Effects of prosodically modulated sub-phonetic variation on lexical competition. *Cognition*, *105*, 466–476.

Sambeth, A., Ruohio, K., Alku, P., Fellman, V., & Huotilainen, M. (2008). Sleeping newborns extract prosody from continuous speech. *Clinical Neurophysiology*, *119*, 332–341.

Samuel, A. G. (1981a). Phonemic restoration: Insights from a new methodology. *Journal of Experimental Psychology: General*, *110*, 474–494.

Samuel, A. G. (1981b). The role of bottom-up confirmation in the phonemic restoration illusion. *Journal of Experimental Psychology: Human Perception and Performance*, *7*, 1124–1131.

Samuel, A. G. (1987). Lexical uniqueness effects on phonemic restoration. *Journal of Memory and Language*, *26*, 36–56.

Samuel, A. G. (1997). Lexical activation produces potent phonemic percepts. *Cognitive Psychology*, *32*, 97–127.

Samuel, A. G. (2001). Some empirical tests of Merge's architecture. *Language and Cognitive Processes*, *16*, 709–714.

Samuel, A. G., & Pitt, M. A. (2003). Lexical activation (and other factors) can mediate compensation for coarticulation. *Journal of Memory and Language*, *48*, 416–434.

Sanders, L. D., & Neville, H. J. (2003a). An ERP study of continuous speech processing. I Segmentation, semantics, and syntax in native speakers. *Cognitive Brain Research*, *15*, 228–240.

Sanders, L. D., & Neville, H. J. (2003b). An ERP study of continuous speech processing. II. Segmentation, semantics, and syntax in non-native speakers. *Cognitive Brain Research*, *15*, 214–227.

Sanders, L. D., Neville, H. J., & Woldorff, M. G. (2002). Speech segmentation by native and non-native speakers: The use of lexical, syntactic, and stress-pattern cues. *Journal of Speech, Language, and Hearing Research*, *45*, 519–530.

Sanders, L. D., Newport, E. L., & Neville, H. J. (2002). Segmenting nonsense: An event-related potential index of perceived onsets in continuous speech. *Nature Neuroscience*, *5*, 700–703.

Sankoff, G., & Blondeau, H. (2007). Language change across the lifespan: /r/ in Montreal French. *Language*, *83*, 560–588.

Sato, Y., Sogabe, Y., & Mazuka, R. (2010). Discrimination of phonemic vowel length by Japanese infants. *Developmental Psychology*, *46*, 106–119.

Savin, H. B. (1963). Word frequency effect and errors in the perception of speech. *Journal of the Acoustical Society of America*, *35*, 200–206.

Savin, H. B., & Bever, T. G. (1970). The nonperceptual reality of the phoneme. *Journal of Verbal Learning and Verbal Behavior*, *9*, 295–302.

Sawusch, J. R., & Nusbaum, H. C. (1979). Contextual effects in vowel perception. I: Anchor-induced contrast effects. *Perception & Psychophysics*, *25*, 292–302.

Sawusch, J. R., & Jusczyk, P. W. (1981). Adaptation and contrast in the perception of voicing. *Journal of Experimental Psychology: Human Perception and Performance*, *7*, 408–421.

Schacter, D. L., & Church, B. A. (1992). Auditory priming: Implicit and explicit memory for words and voices. *Journal of Experimental Psychology: Learning, Memory, and Cognition*, *18*, 915–930.

Schafer, G. (2005). Infants can learn decontextualized words before their first birthday. *Child Development*, *76*, 87–96.

Scharenborg, O., Norris, D., ten Bosch, L., & McQueen, J. M. (2005). How should a speech recognizer work? *Cognitive Science*, *29*, 867–918.

Schenkein, J. (1980). A taxonomy for repeating action sequences in natural conversation. In B. Butterworth (Ed.), *Language production* (Vol. 1, pp. 21–47). London: Academic Press.

Schieffelin, B. B. (1985). The acquisition of Kaluli. In D. I. Slobin (Ed.), *The cross-linguistic study of language acquisition* (Vol. 1, pp. 525–593). Hillsdale, NJ: Erlbaum.

Schieffelin, B. B., & Ochs, E. (1983). A cultural perspective on the transition from prelinguistic to linguistic communication. In R. M. Golinkoff (Ed.), *The transition from prelinguistic to linguistic communication* (pp. 115–131). Hillsdale, NJ: Erlbaum.

Schiller, N. O., & Köster, O. (1996). Evaluation of a foreign speaker in forensic phonetics: A report. *Forensic Linguistics*, *3*, 176–185.

Schiller, N. O., Köster, O., & Duckworth, M. (1997). The effect of removing linguistic information upon identifying speakers of a foreign language. *Forensic Linguistics*, *4*, 1–17.

Schiller, N. O., Meyer, A. S., & Levelt, W. J. M. (1997). The syllabic structure of spoken words: Evidence from the syllabification of intervocalic consonants. *Language and Speech*, *40*, 103–140.

Schirmer, A., Tang, S.-L., Penney, T. B., Gunter, T. C., & Chen, H.-C. (2005). Brain responses to segmentally and tonally induced semantic violations in Cantonese. *Journal of Cognitive Neuroscience*, *17*, 1–12.

Schreuder, R., & Baayen, R. H. (1994). Prefix stripping re-revisited. *Journal of Memory and Language*, *33*, 357–375.

Schulpen, B., Dijkstra, A., Schriefers, H. J., & Hasper, M. (2003). Recognition of interlingual homophones in bilingual auditory word recognition. *Journal of Experimental Psychology: Human Perception and Performance*, *29*, 1155–1178.

Schwab, S., & Grosjean, F. (2004). La perception du débit en langue seconde [The perception of speech rate in a second language]. *Phonetica*, *61*, 84–94.

Scobbie, J. M. (2005). Interspeaker variation as the long term outcome of dialectally varied input: Speech production evidence for fine-grained plasticity. In *Proceedings of the ISCA Workshop on Plasticity in Speech Perception (PSP 2005)*, London (pp. 56–59). London: University College London [CD-ROM].

Scott, D. R., & Cutler, A. (1984). Segmental phonology and the perception of syntactic structure. *Journal of Verbal Learning and Verbal Behavior*, *23*, 450–466.

Sebastián-Gallés, N., & Bosch, L. (2002). Building phonotactic knowledge in bilinguals: Role of early exposure. *Journal of Experimental Psychology: Human Perception and Performance*, *28*, 974–989.

Sebastián-Gallés, N., & Bosch, L. (2009). Developmental shift in the discrimination of vowel contrasts in bilingual infants: Is the distributional account all there is to it? *Developmental Science*, *12*, 874–887.

Sebastián-Gallés, N., Dupoux, E., Segui, J., & Mehler, J. (1992). Contrasting syllabic effects in Catalan and Spanish. *Journal of Memory and Language*, *31*, 18–32.

Sebastián-Gallés, N., Echeverría, S., & Bosch, L. (2005). The influence of initial exposure on lexical representation: Comparing early and simultaneous bilinguals. *Journal of Memory and Language*, *52*, 240–255.

Sebastián-Gallés, N., Martí, M. A., Carreiras, M., & Cuetos, F. (2000). *LEXESP: Léxico informatizado del español*. Barcelona: Edicions Universitat de Barcelona.

Sebastián-Gallés, N., Rodríguez-Fornells, A., de Diego-Balaguer, R., & Díaz, B. (2006). First- and second-language phonological representations in the mental lexicon. *Journal of Cognitive Neuroscience*, *18*, 1277–1291.

Sebastián-Gallés, N., & Soto-Faraco, S. (1999). Online processing of native and non-native phonemic contrasts in early bilinguals. *Cognition*, *72*, 111–123.

Sedivy, J., Tanenhaus, M., Eberhard, K., Spivey-Knowlton, M., & Carlson, G. (1995). Using intonationally-marked presuppositional information in on-line language processing: Evidence from eye movements to a visual model. In J. D. Moore & J. F. Lehman (Eds.), *Proceedings of the 17th annual Conference of the Cognitive Science Society*, Pittsburgh (pp. 375–380). Mahwah, NJ: Erlbaum.

Segui, J., & Frauenfelder, U. (1986). The effect of lexical constraints upon speech perception. In F. Klix & H. Hagendorf (Eds.), *Human memory and cognitive capabilities: Mechanisms and performances* (pp. 795–808). Amsterdam: North-Holland.

Segui, J., Frauenfelder, U., & Hallé, P. (2001). Phonotactic constraints shape speech perception: Implications for sublexical and lexical processing. In E. Dupoux (Ed.), *Language, brain, and cognitive development: Essays in honor of Jacques Mehler* (pp. 195–208). Cambridge, MA: MIT Press.

Segui, J., Frauenfelder, U., & Mehler, J. (1981). Phoneme monitoring, syllable monitoring and lexical access. *British Journal of Psychology*, *72*, 471–477.

Seidl, A., & Johnson, E. K. (2006). Infant word segmentation revisited: Edge alignment facilitates target extraction. *Developmental Science*, *9*, 565–573.

Seidl, A., & Johnson, E. K. (2008). Boundary alignment enables 11-month-olds to segment vowel initial words from speech. *Journal of Child Language*, *35*, 1–24.

Sekiguchi, T. (2006). Effects of lexical prosody and word familiarity on lexical access of spoken Japanese words. *Journal of Psycholinguistic Research*, *35*, 369–384.

Sekiguchi, T., & Nakajima, Y. (1999). The use of lexical prosody for lexical access of the Japanese language. *Journal of Psycholinguistic Research*, *28*, 439–454.

Selfridge, O. G. (1959). Pandemonium: A paradigm for learning. In D. V. Blake & A. M. Uttley (Eds.), *Proceedings of the Symposium on Mechanisation of Thought Processes* (pp. 511–529). London: HMSO.

Shady, M. E. (1996). *Infants' sensitivity to function morphemes*. Ph.D. dissertation, State University of New York, Buffalo.

Shafer, V. L., Shucard, D. W., Shucard, J. L., & Gerken, L. (1998). An electrophysiological study of infants' sensitivity to the sound patterns of English speech. *Journal of Speech, Language, and Hearing Research*, *41*, 874–886.

Shannon, R. V., Zeng, F.-G., Kamath, V., Wygonski, J., & Ekelid, M. (1995). Speech recognition with primarily temporal cues. *Science*, *270*, 303–304.

Sharp, D. J., Scott, S. K., Cutler, A., & Wise, R. J. S. (2005). Lexical retrieval constrained by sound structure: The role of the left inferior frontal gyrus. *Brain and Language*, *92*, 309–319.

Shattuck-Hufnagel, S., & Turk, A. E. (1996). A prosody tutorial for investigators of auditory sentence processing. *Journal of Psycholinguistic Research*, *25*, 193–247.

Shatzman, K. B., & McQueen, J. M. (2006a). Segment duration as a cue to word boundaries in spoken-word recognition. *Perception & Psychophysics*, *68*, 1–16.

Shatzman, K. B., & McQueen, J. M. (2006b). Prosodic knowledge affects the recognition of newly acquired words. *Psychological Science*, *17*, 372–377.

Sheldon, A., & Strange, W. (1982). The acquisition of /r/ and /l/ by Japanese learners of English: Evidence that speech production can precede speech perception. *Applied Psycholinguistics*, *3*, 243–261.

Shen, X. S. (1989). Toward a register approach in teaching Mandarin tones. *Journal of Chinese Language Teachers Association*, *24*, 27–47.

Shi, R., Cutler, A., Werker, J., & Cruickshank, M. (2006). Frequency and form as determinants of functor sensitivity in English acquiring infants. *Journal of the Acoustical Society of America*, *119*, EL61–EL67.

Shi, R., Marquis, A., & Gauthier, B. (2006). Segmentation and representation of function words in preverbal French-learning infants. In D. Bamman, T. Magnitskaia & C. Zaller (Eds.), *Proceedings of the 30th annual Boston University Conference on Language Development* (Vol. 2, pp. 549–560). Somerville, MA: Cascadilla Press.

Shi, R., Morgan, J. L., & Allopenna, P. (1998). Phonological and acoustic bases for earliest grammatical category assignment: A cross-linguistic perspective. *Journal of Child Language*, *25*, 169–201.

Shi, R., & Werker, J. F. (2001). Six-month old infants' preference for lexical words. *Psychological Science*, *12*, 70–75.

Shi, R., & Werker, J. F. (2003). The basis of preference for lexical words in 6-month-old infants. *Developmental Science*, *6*, 484–488.

Shi, R., Werker, J. F., & Cutler, A. (2006). Recognition and representation of function words in English-learning infants. *Infancy*, *10*, 187–198.

Shi, R., Werker, J. F., & Morgan, J. L. (1999). Newborn infants' sensitivity to perceptual cues to lexical and grammatical words. *Cognition*, *72*, B11–B21.

Shields, J. L., McHugh, A., & Martin, J. G. (1974). Reaction time to phoneme targets as a function of rhythmic cues in continuous speech. *Journal of Experimental Psychology*, *102*, 250–255.

Shillcock, R. (1990). Lexical hypotheses in continuous speech. In G. T. M. Altmann (Ed.), *Cognitive models of speech processing* (pp. 24–49). Cambridge, MA: MIT Press.

Shillcock, R. C., & Bard, E. G. (1993). Modularity and the processing of closed-class words. In G. T. M. Altmann & R. Shillcock (Eds.), *Cognitive models of speech processing: The second Sperlonga meeting* (pp. 163–185). Hillsdale, NJ: Erlbaum.

Shockey, L., & Bond, Z. S. (1980). Phonological processes in speech addressed to children. *Phonetica*, *37*, 267–274.

Shoemaker, E. M. (2010). Nativelike attainment in L2 listening: The segmentation of spoken French. In K. Dziubalska-Kolaczyk, M. Wrembel, & M. Kul (Eds.), *Proceedings of the 6th International Symposium on the Acquisition of Second Language Speech, New Sounds 2010*, Poznan. Poznan: Adama Mickiewicz University.

Sholicar, J. R., & Fallside, F. (1988). A prosodically and lexically constrained approach to continuous speech recognition. In M. Wagner (Ed.), *Proceedings of the 2nd Australian*

International Conference on Speech Science and Technology, Sydney (pp.106–111). Canberra: Australian Speech Science and Technology Association (ASSTA).

Simon, J. R., & Wolf, J. D. (1963). Choice reaction times as a function of angular stimulus-response correspondence and age. *Ergonomics*, *6*, 99–105.

Simpson, S. A., & Cooke, M. (2005). Consonant identification in N-talker babble is a non-monotonic function of N. *Journal of the Acoustical Society of America*, *118*, 2775–2778.

Singh, L. (2008). Influences of high and low variability on infant word recognition. *Cognition*, *106*, 833–870.

Singh, L., Morgan, J. L., & Best, C. T. (2002). Infants' listening preferences: Baby talk or happy talk? *Infancy*, *3*, 365–394.

Sjerps, M. J., & McQueen, J. M. (2010). The bounds on flexibility in speech perception. *Journal of Experimental Psychology: Human Perception and Performance*, *36*, 195–211.

Skoruppa, K., Cristià, A., Peperkamp, S., & Seidl, A. (2011). English-learning infants' perception of word stress patterns. *Journal of the Acoustical Society of America*, *130*, EL50-EL55.

Skoruppa, K., Pons, F., Christophe, A., Bosch, L., Dupoux, E., Sebastián-Gallés, N., Alves Limissuri, R., & Peperkamp, S. (2009). Language-specific stress perception by 9-month-old French and Spanish infants. *Developmental Science*, *12*, 914–919.

Slobin, D. I. (1982). Universal and particular in the acquisition of language. In E. Wanner & L. R. Gleitman (Eds.), *Language acquisition: The state of the art* (pp. 128–172). Cambridge: Cambridge University Press.

Slowiaczek, L. M. (1990). Effects of lexical stress in auditory word recognition. *Language and Speech*, *33*, 47–68.

Slowiaczek, L. M. (1991). Stress and context in auditory word recognition. *Journal of Psycholinguistic Research*, *20*, 465–481.

Slowiaczek, L. M., & Dinnsen, D. A. (1985). On the neutralizing status of Polish word-final devoicing. *Journal of Phonetics*, *13*, 325–341.

Slowiaczek, L. M., Nusbaum, H. C., & Pisoni, D. B. (1987). Phonological priming in auditory word recognition. *Journal of Experimental Psychology: Learning, Memory, and Cognition*, *13*, 64–75.

Slowiaczek, L. M., Soltano, E. G., & Bernstein, H. L. (2006). Lexical and metrical stress in word recognition: Lexical or pre-lexical influences? *Journal of Psycholinguistic Research*, *35*, 491–512.

Slowiaczek, L. M., & Szymanska, H. J. (1989). Perception of word-final devoicing in Polish. *Journal of Phonetics*, *17*, 205–212.

Small, L. H., & Squibb, K. D. (1989). Stressed vowel perception in word recognition. *Perceptual and Motor Skills*, *68*, 179–185.

Small, L. H., Simon, S. D., & Goldberg, J. S. (1988). Lexical stress and lexical access: Homographs versus nonhomographs. *Perception & Psychophysics*, *44*, 272–280.

Smits, R. (2001). Hierarchical categorization of coarticulated phonemes: A theoretical analysis. *Perception & Psychophysics*, *63*, 1109–1139.

Smits, R., Warner, N., McQueen, J. M., & Cutler, A. (2003). Unfolding of phonetic information over time: A database of Dutch diphone perception. *Journal of the Acoustical Society of America*, *113*, 563–574.

Snijders, T., Kooijman, V., Cutler, A., & Hagoort, P. (2007). Neurophysiological evidence of delayed segmentation in a foreign language. *Brain Research, 1178*, 106–113.

Snoeren, N., Hallé, P., & Segui, J. (2006). A voice for the voiceless: Production and perception of assimilated stops in French. *Journal of Phonetics, 34*, 241–268.

Snoeren, N., Segui, J., & Hallé, P. (2008). Perceptual processing of partially and fully assimilated words in French. *Journal of Experimental Psychology: Human Perception and Performance, 34*, 193–204.

Soderstrom, M., Seidl, A., Nelson, D. G., & Jusczyk, P. W. (2003). The prosodic bootstrapping of phrases: Evidence from prelinguistic infants. *Journal of Memory and Language, 49*, 249–267.

Sommers, M. S. (2005). Age-related changes in spoken word recognition. In D. Pisoni & R. Remez (Eds.), *The handbook of speech perception* (pp. 469–493). Malden, MA: Blackwell.

van Son, R. J. J. H., & Pols, L. C. W. (1995). The influence of local context on the identification of vowels and consonants. In J. M. Pardo (Ed.), *Proceedings of EUROSPEECH'95*, Madrid (pp. 967–970). Madrid: Universidad Politecnica.

Sorace, A. (1993). Incomplete vs. divergent representations of unaccusativity in non-native grammars of Italian. *Second Language Research, 9*, 22–48.

Soto-Faraco, S., Sebastián-Gallés, N., & Cutler, A. (2001). Segmental and suprasegmental mismatch in lexical access. *Journal of Memory and Language, 45*, 412–432.

Spence, M. J., & DeCasper, A. J. (1987). Prenatal experience with low-frequency maternal voice sounds influences neonatal perception of maternal voice samples. *Infant Behavior and Development, 10*, 133–142.

Spinelli, E., Cutler, A., & McQueen, J. M. (2002). Resolution of liaison for lexical access in French. *Revue Française de Linguistique Appliquée, 7*, 83–96.

Spinelli, E., McQueen, J. M., & Cutler, A. (2003). Processing resyllabified words in French. *Journal of Memory and Language, 48*, 233–254.

Spinelli, E., & Gros-Balthazard, F. (2007). Phonotactic constraints help to overcome effects of schwa deletion in French. *Cognition, 104*, 397–406.

Spinelli, E., & Racine, I. (2008). How do prereader and reader children process schwa deletion? Paper presented at the 49th annual meeting, Psychonomic Society, Chicago. *Abstracts of the Psychonomic Society, 13*, 58.

Spivey, M. J., Grosjean, M. J., & Knoblich, G. (2005). Continuous attraction toward phonological competitors. *Proceedings of the National Academy of Sciences of the United States of America, 102*, 10393–10398.

Spivey, M., & Marian, V. (1999). Cross talk between native and second languages: Partial activation of an irrelevant lexicon. *Psychological Science, 10*, 281–284.

Stager, C. L., & Werker, J. F. (1997). Infants listen for more phonetic detail in speech perception than in word-learning tasks. *Nature, 388*, 381–382.

Stankler, J. (1991). *Phonological distinctions as morphological signals*. M.Phil. thesis. University of Cambridge.

Stanners, R. F., Neiser, J. J., Hernon, W. P., & Hall, R. (1979). Memory representation for morphologically related words. *Journal of Verbal Learning and Verbal Behavior, 18*, 399–412.

Stanners, R. F., Neiser, J. J., & Painton, S. (1979). Memory representation for prefixed words. *Journal of Verbal Learning and Verbal Behavior*, *18*, 733–743.

Stern, D. N., Spieker, S., Barnett, R. K., & MacKain, K. (1983). The prosody of maternal speech: Infant age and context related changes. *Journal of Child Language*, *10*, 1–15.

Stevens, K. N., Liberman, A. M., Studdert-Kennedy, M., & Öhman, S. (1969). Crosslanguage study of vowel perception. *Language and Speech*, *12*, 1–23.

Stockmal, V., Markus, D., & Bond, Z. S. (2005). Measures of native and non-native rhythm in a quantity language. *Language and Speech*, *48*, 55–63.

Stockmal, V., Moates, D. R., & Bond, Z. S. (2000). Same talker, different language. *Applied Psycholinguistics*, *21*, 383–393.

Stockmal, V., Muljani, D., & Bond, Z. S. (1996). Perceptual features of unknown foreign languages as revealed by multi-dimensional scaling. In H. T. Bunnell & W. Idsardi (Eds.), *Proceedings of the 4th International Conference on Spoken Language Processing*, Philadelphia (pp. 1748–1751). Philadelphia: University of Delaware and A. I. duPont Institute.

Strange, W. (1989). Dynamic specification of coarticulated vowels spoken in sentence context. *Journal of the Acoustical Society of America*, *85*, 2135–2153.

Strange, W. (1995). *Speech perception and linguistic experience: Issues in cross-language speech research*. Timonium, MD: York Press.

Strange, W., & Dittmann, S. (1984). Effects of discrimination training on the perception of /r-l/ by Japanese adults learning English. *Perception & Psychophysics*, *36*, 131–145.

Strange, W., Jenkins, J. J., & Johnson, T. L. (1983). Dynamic specification of coarticulated vowels. *Journal of the Acoustical Society of America*, *74*, 695–705.

Streeter, L. A. (1976). Language perception of 2-month-old infants shows effects of both innate mechanisms and experience. *Nature*, *259*, 39–41.

Streeter, L. A., & Nigro, G. N. (1979). The role of medial consonant transitions in word perception. *Journal of the Acoustical Society of America*, *65*, 1533–1541.

Sullivan, J. W., & Horowitz, F. D. (1983). The effects of intonation on infant attention: The role of the rising intonation contour. *Journal of Child Language, 10*, 521–534.

Sulpizio, S., & McQueen, J. M. (2011). Italians use abstract knowledge about lexical stress during spoken-word recognition. *Journal of Memory and Language*, *66*, 177–193.

Sumner, M., & Samuel, A. G. (2005). Perception and representation of regular variation: The case of final /t/. *Journal of Memory and Language*, *52*, 322–338.

Sundara, M., Polka, L., & Molnar, M. (2008). Development of coronal stop perception: Bilingual infants keep pace with their monolingual peers. *Cognition*, *108*, 232–242.

Sundberg, U., & Lacerda, F. (1999). Voice Onset Time in speech to infants and adults. *Phonetica*, *56*, 186–199.

Suomi, K., McQueen, J. M., & Cutler, A. (1997). Vowel harmony and speech segmentation in Finnish. *Journal of Memory and Language*, *36*, 422–444.

Suomi, K., Toivanen, J., & Ylitalo, R. (2003). Durational and tonal correlates of accent in Finnish. *Journal of Phonetics*, *31*, 113–138.

Suomi, K., & Ylitalo, R. (2004). On durational correlates of word stress in Finnish. *Journal of Phonetics*, *32*, 35–63.

Svartvik, J., & Quirk, R. (1980). *A corpus of English conversation*. Lund: CWK Gleerup.

Swerts, M., Krahmer, E., & Avesani, C. (2002). Prosodic marking of information status in Dutch and Italian: A comparative analysis. *Journal of Phonetics*, *30*, 629–654.

Swingley, D. (1995). Segmentation of speech in a foreign language. In H. Hendriks, J. M. McQueen & S. Aal (Eds.), *MPI Annual Report 1995* (p. 12). Nijmegen: MPI for Psycholinguistics.

Swingley, D. (2003). Phonetic detail in the developing lexicon. *Language and Speech*, *46*, 265–294.

Swingley, D. (2005a). 11-month-olds' knowledge of how familiar words sound. *Developmental Science*, *8*, 432–443.

Swingley, D. (2005b). Statistical clustering and the contents of the infant vocabulary. *Cognitive Psychology*, *50*, 86–132.

Swingley, D. (2007). Lexical exposure and word-form encoding in 1.5-year-olds. *Developmental Psychology*, *43*, 454–464.

Swingley, D., & Aslin, R. N. (2000). Spoken word recognition and lexical representation in very young children. *Cognition*, *76*, 147–166.

Swingley, D., & Aslin, R. N. (2002). Lexical neighborhoods and the word-form representations of 14-month-olds. *Psychological Science*, *13*, 480–484.

Swingley, D., & Aslin, R. N. (2007). Lexical competition in young children's word learning. *Cognitive Psychology*, *54*, 99–132.

Swingley, D., Pinto, J. P., & Fernald, A. (1999). Continuous processing in word recognition at 24 months. *Cognition*, *71*, 73–108.

Swinney, D. A. (1979). Lexical access during sentence comprehension: (Re)consideration of context effects. *Journal of Verbal Learning and Verbal Behavior*, *18*, 645–659.

Swinney, D. A. (1981). Lexical processing during sentence comprehension: Effects of higher order constraints and implications for representation. In T. Myers, J. Laver & J. Anderson (Eds.), *The cognitive representation of speech* (pp. 201–209). Amsterdam: North-Holland.

Swinney, D. A., & Hakes, D. (1976). Effects of prior context upon lexical access during sentence comprehension. *Journal of Verbal Learning and Verbal Behavior*, *15*, 681–689.

Swinney, D. A., Onifer, W., Prather, P., & Hirshkowitz, M. (1979). Semantic facilitation across sensory modalities in the processing of individual words and sentences. *Memory & Cognition*, *7*, 159–165.

Swinney, D. A., & Prather, P. (1980). Phoneme identification in a phoneme-monitoring experiment: The variable role of uncertainty about vowel contexts. *Perception & Psychophysics*, *27*, 104–110.

Swinney, D. A., Zurif, E. B., & Cutler, A. (1980). Effects of sentential stress and word class upon comprehension in Broca's aphasics. *Brain and Language*, *10*, 132–144.

Tabossi, P. (1988a). Effects of context on the immediate interpretation of unambiguous nouns. *Journal of Experimental Psychology: Learning, Memory, and Cognition*, *14*, 153–162.

Tabossi, P. (1988b). Accessing lexical ambiguity in different types of sentential contexts. *Journal of Memory and Language*, *27*, 324–340.

Tabossi, P., Burani, C., & Scott, D. (1995). Word identification in fluent speech. *Journal of Memory and Language*, *34*, 440–467.

Tabossi, P., Collina, S., Mazzetti, M., & Zoppello, M. (2000). Syllables in the processing of spoken Italian. *Journal of Experimental Psychology: Human Perception and Performance*, *26*, 758–775.

Tabossi, P., Colombo, L., & Job, R. (1987). Accessing lexical ambiguity: Effects of context and dominance. *Psychological Research*, *49*, 161–167.

Taft, M. (1984). Exploring the mental lexicon. *Australian Journal of Psychology*, *36*, 35–46.

Taft, M. (1986). Lexical access codes in visual and auditory word recognition. *Language and Cognitive Processes*, *1*, 297–308.

Taft, M., & Chen, H.-C. (1992). Judging homophony in Chinese: The influence of tones. In H.-C. Chen & O. J. L. Tzeng (Eds.), *Language processing in Chinese* (pp. 151–172). Amsterdam: North-Holland.

Taft, M., & Hambly, G. (1986). Exploring the cohort model of spoken word recognition. *Cognition*, *22*, 259–282.

Tagliapietra, L., Fanari, R., De Candia, C., & Tabossi, P. (2009). Phonotactic regularities in the segmentation of spoken Italian. *Quarterly Journal of Experimental Psychology*, *62*, 392–415.

Tagliapietra, L., & McQueen, J. M. (2010). What and where in speech recognition: Geminates and singletons in spoken Italian. *Journal of Memory and Language*, *63*, 306–323.

Takagi, N. (1995). Signal detection modeling of Japanese listeners' /r/-/l/ labeling behavior in a one-interval identification task. *Journal of the Acoustical Society of America*, *97*, 563–574.

Tamminen, J., & Gaskell, M. G. (2008). Newly learned spoken words show long-term lexical competition effects. *Quarterly Journal of Experimental Psychology*, *61*, 361–371.

Tanenhaus, M. K., Magnuson, J. S., Dahan, D., & Chambers, C. (2000). Eye movements and lexical access in spoken language comprehension: Evaluating a linking hypothesis between fixations and linguistic processing. *Journal of Psycholinguistic Research*, *29*, 557–580.

Tanenhaus, M. K., Spivey-Knowlton, M. J., Eberhard, K. M., & Sedivy, J. C. (1995). Integration of visual and linguistic information in spoken language comprehension. *Science*, *268*, 1632–1634.

Tauroza, S., & Allison, D. (1990). Speech rates in British English. *Applied Linguistics*, *11*, 90–105.

Terken, J., & Nooteboom, S. (1987). Opposite effects of accentuation and deaccentuation on verification latencies for given and new information. *Language and Cognitive Processes*, *2*, 145–163.

Theodore, R. M., & Miller, J. L. (2010). Characteristics of listener sensitivity to talker-specific phonetic detail. *Journal of the Acoustical Society of America*, *128*, 2090–2099.

Thierry, G., Vihman, M., & Roberts, M. (2003). Familiar words capture the attention of 11-month-olds in less than 250 ms. *NeuroReport*, *14*, 2307–2310.

Thiessen, E. D. (2007). The effect of distributional information on children's use of phonemic contrasts. *Journal of Memory and Language*, *56*, 16–34.

Thiessen, E. D., Hill, E. A., & Saffran, J. R. (2005). Infant-directed speech facilitates word segmentation. *Infancy*, *7*, 53–71.

Thiessen, E. D., & Saffran, J. R. (2003). When cues collide: Use of stress and statistical cues to word boundaries by 7- to 9-month-old infants. *Developmental Psychology*, *39*, 706–716.

Thiessen, E. D., & Saffran, J. R. (2004). Spectral tilt as a cue to word segmentation in infancy and adulthood. *Perception & Psychophysics*, *66*, 779–791.

Thompson, C. P. (1987). A language effect in voice identification. *Applied Cognitive Psychology*, *1*, 121–131.

Thompson-Schill, S. L. (2005). Dissecting the language organ: A new look at the role of Broca's area in language processing. In A. Cutler (Ed.), *Twenty-first century psycholinguistics: Four cornerstones* (pp. 173–189). Hillsdale, NJ: Erlbaum.

Thompson-Schill, S. L., D'Esposito, M., Aguirre, G. K., & Farah, M. J. (1997). Role of left inferior prefrontal cortex in retrieval of semantic knowledge: A reevaluation. *Proceedings of the National Academy of Sciences of the United States of America*, *94*, 14792–14797.

Tincoff, R., & Jusczyk, P. W. (1999). Some beginnings of word comprehension in 6-month-olds. *Psychological Science*, *10*, 172–175.

Titone, D. A., & Connine, C. M. (1994). Comprehension of idiomatic expressions: Effects of predictability and literality. *Journal of Experimental Psychology: Learning, Memory, and Cognition*, *20*, 1126–1138.

Toro, J. M., Nespor, M., Mehler, J., & Bonatti, L. L. (2008). Finding words and rules in a speech stream: Functional differences between vowels and consonants. *Psychological Science*, *19*, 137–144.

Toro, J. M., Shukla, M., Nespor, M., & Endress, A. D. (2008). The quest for generalizations over consonants: Asymmetries between consonants and vowels are not the by-product of acoustic differences. *Perception & Psychophysics*, *70*, 1515–1525.

Toro, J. M., Sinnett, S., & Soto-Faraco, S. (2005). Speech segmentation by statistical learning depends on attention. *Cognition*, *97*, B25–B34.

Toro-Soto, J. M., Rodríguez-Fornells, A., & Sebastián-Gallés, N. (2007). Stress placement and word segmentation by Spanish speakers. *Psicológica*, *28*, 167–176.

Trainor, L. J., Austin, C. M., & Desjardins, R. N. (2000). Is infant-directed speech prosody a result of the vocal expression of emotion? *Psychological Science*, *11*, 188–195.

Trehub, S. E. (1976). The discrimination of foreign speech contrasts by infants and adults. *Child Development*, *47*, 466–472.

Trehub, S. E., & Henderson, J. L. (1996). Temporal resolution in infancy and subsequent language development. *Journal of Speech and Hearing Research*, *39*, 1315–1320.

Treiman, R., & Danis, C. (1988). Syllabification of intervocalic consonants. *Journal of Memory and Language*, *27*, 87–104.

Treiman, R., Salasoo, A., Slowiaczek, L. M., & Pisoni, D. B. (1982). Effects of syllable structure on adults' phoneme monitoring performance. *Research on Speech Perception Progress Report No. 8*. Bloomington: Indiana University, Speech Research Laboratory.

Tremblay, A. (2008). Is second language lexical access prosodically constrained? Processing of word stress by French Canadian second language learners of English. *Applied Psycholinguistics*, *29*, 553–584.

Trouvain, J., & Gut, U. (Eds.), (2007). *Non-native prosody: Phonetic description and teaching practice*. Berlin: Mouton de Gruyter.

Trubetzkoy, N. (1939). *Grundzüge der Phonologie*. Travaux du Cercle Linguistique de Prague 7.

Tsang, K. K., & Hoosain, R. (1979). Segmental phonemes and tonal phonemes in comprehension of Cantonese. *Psychologia*, *22*, 222–224.

Tsao, F.-M., Liu, H.-M., & Kuhl, P. K. (2004). Speech perception in infancy predicts language development in the second year of life: A longitudinal study. *Child Development*, *75*, 1067–1084.

Tseng, C.-Y. (1990). *An acoustic phonetic study on tones in Mandarin Chinese.* Taipei: Academia Sinica.

Tsushima, T., Takizawa, O., Sasaki, M., Shiraki, S., Nishi, K., Kohno, M., Menyuk, P., & Best, C. (1994). Discrimination of English /r-l/ and /w-y/ by Japanese infants at 6–12 months: Language-specific developmental changes in speech perception abilities. In *Proceedings of the 3rd International Conference on Spoken Language Processing,* Yokohama (pp. 1695–1698). Tokyo, Japan: The Acoustical Society of Japan.

Tuaycharoen, P. (1978). The babbling of a Thai baby: Echoes and responses to the sounds made by adults. In N. Waterson & C. E. Snow (Eds.), *The development of communication* (pp. 111–125). Chichester: Wiley.

Tuinman, A. (2011). *Processing casual speech in native and non-native language.* Ph.D. dissertation, MPI Series in Psycholinguistics 60, Radboud University Nijmegen.

Tuinman, A., Mitterer, H., & Cutler, A. (2011a). Perception of intrusive /r/ in English by native, cross-language and cross-dialect listeners. *Journal of the Acoustical Society of America, 130,* 1643–1652.

Tuinman, A., Mitterer, H., & Cutler, A. (2011b). The efficiency of cross-dialectal word recognition. In *Proceedings of the 12th annual Conference of the International Speech Communication Association (INTERSPEECH 2011)*. Florence, Italy. Adelaide, Australia: Causal Productions [CD-ROM].

Tuinman, A., Mitterer, H., & Cutler, A. (2012). Resolving ambiguity in familiar and unfamiliar casual speech. *Journal of Memory and Language*. doi: 10.1016/j.jml.2012.02.001.

Tyler, L. K. (1984). The structure of the initial cohort: Evidence from gating. *Perception & Psychophysics*, *36*, 417–427.

Tyler, L. K., Marslen-Wilson, W., Rentoul, J., & Hanney, P. (1988). Continuous and discontinuous access in spoken word-recognition: The role of derivational prefixes. *Journal of Memory and Language*, *27*, 368–381.

Tyler, L. K., & Wessels, J. (1983). Quantifying contextual contributions to word-recognition processes. *Perception & Psychophysics*, *34*, 409–420.

Tyler, M. D. (2006). French listeners can use stress to segment words in an artificial language. In P. Warren & C. I. Watson (Eds.), *Proceedings of the 11th Australasian International Conference on Speech Science and Technology,* Auckland, NZ (pp. 222–227).Canberra: Australasian Speech Science and Technology Association Inc. (ASSTA).

Tyler, M. D., & Cutler, A. (2009). Cross-language differences in cue use for speech segmentation. *Journal of the Acoustical Society of America*, *126*, 367–376.

Uchanski, R. M., & Braida, L. D. (1998). Effects of token variability on our ability to distinguish between vowels. *Perception & Psychophysics*, *60*, 533–543.

Utman, J. A., Blumstein, S. E., & Burton, M. W. (2000). Effects of subphonetic and syllable structure variation on word recognition. *Perception & Psychophysics*, *62*, 1297–1311.

Utman, J. A., Blumstein, S. E., & Sullivan, K. (2001). Mapping from sound to meaning: Reduced lexical activation in Broca's aphasics. *Brain and Language*, *79*, 444–472.

Vaissière, J. (1983). Language-independent prosodic features. In A. Cutler & D. R. Ladd (Eds.), *Prosody: Models and measurements* (pp. 53–66). Berlin: Springer.

Valian, V., & Coulson, S. (1988). Anchor points in language learning: the role of marker frequency. *Journal of Memory and Language*, *27*, 71–86.

Valian, V., & Levitt, A. (1996). Prosody and adults' learning of syntactic structure. *Journal of Memory and Language*, *35*, 497–516.

Vallabha, G. K., McClelland, J. L., Pons, F., Werker, J. F., & Amano, S. (2007). Unsupervised learning of vowel categories from infant-directed speech. *Proceedings of the National Academy of Sciences of the United States of America*, *104*, 13273–13278.

Vallduví, E. (1992). *The informational component*. New York: Garland.

Van Engen, K. J., & Bradlow, A. R. (2007). Sentence recognition in native- and foreign-language multi-talker background noise. *Journal of the Acoustical Society of America*, *121*, 519–526.

Van Lancker, D., & Canter, G. J. (1981). Idiomatic versus literal interpretations of ditropically ambiguous sentences. *Journal of Speech and Hearing Research*, *24*, 64–69.

Vanlancker-Sidtis, D. (2003). Auditory recognition of idioms by native and nonnative speakers of English: It takes one to know one. *Applied Psycholinguistics*, *24*, 45–57.

Van Summers, W., Pisoni, D. B., Bernacki, R. H., Pedlow, R. I., & Stokes, M. A. (1988). Effects of noise on speech production: Acoustic and perceptual analysis. *Journal of the Acoustical Society of America*, *84*, 917–928.

Van de Ven, M. (2011). *The role of acoustic detail and context in the comprehension of reduced pronunciation variants*. Ph.D. dissertation, MPI Series in Psycholinguistics 65, Radboud University Nijmegen.

Venditti, J. J., Jun, S.-A., & Beckman, M. E. (1996). Prosodic cues to syntactic and other linguistic structures in Japanese, Korean, and English. In J. Morgan & K. Demuth (Eds.), *Signal to syntax: Bootstrapping from speech to grammar in early acquisition* (pp. 287–311). Mahwah, NJ: Erlbaum.

Ventureyra, V. A., Pallier, C., & Yoo, H.-Y. (2004). The loss of first language phonetic perception in adopted Koreans. *Journal of Neurolinguistics*, *17*, 79–91.

Vihman, M. M., Nakai, S., DePaolis, R. A., & Hallé, P. (2004). The role of accentual pattern in early lexical representation. *Journal of Memory and Language*, *50*, 336–353.

Vitevitch, M. S. (2002). Influence of onset density on spoken-word recognition. *Journal of Experimental Psychology: Human Perception and Performance*, *28*, 270–278.

Vitevitch, M. S. (2003a). Change deafness: The inability to detect changes between two voices. *Journal of Experimental Psychology: Human Perception and Performance*, *29*, 333–342.

Vitevitch, M. S. (2003b). The influence of sublexical and lexical representations on the processing of spoken words in English. *Clinical Linguistics & Phonetics*, *17*, 487–499.

Vitevitch, M. S. (2007). The spread of the phonological neighborhood influences spoken word recognition. *Memory & Cognition*, *35*, 166–175.

Vitevitch, M. S., & Luce, P. A. (1998). When words compete: Levels of processing in perception of spoken words. *Psychological Science*, *9*, 325–329.

Vitevitch, M. S., & Luce, P. A. (1999). Probabilistic phonotactics and neighborhood activation in spoken word recognition. *Journal of Memory and Language*, *40*, 374–408.

Vitevitch, M. S., & Rodríguez, E. (2005). Neighborhood density effects in spoken word recognition in Spanish. *Journal of Multilingual Communication Disorders*, *3*, 64–73.

Vitevitch, M. S., Stamer, M. K., & Sereno, J. A. (2008). Word length and lexical competition: Longer is the same as shorter. *Language and Speech*, *51*, 361–383.

Volaitis, L. E., & Miller, J. L. (1992). Phonetic prototypes: Influence of place of articulation and speaking rate on the internal structure of voicing categories. *Journal of the Acoustical Society of America*, *92*, 723–735.

Vroomen, J., & de Gelder, B. (1995). Metrical segmentation and lexical inhibition in spoken word recognition. *Journal of Experimental Psychology: Human Perception and Performance*, *21*, 98–108.

Vroomen, J., & de Gelder, B. (1997). Activation of embedded words in spoken word recognition. *Journal of Experimental Psychology: Human Perception and Performance*, *23*, 710–720.

Vroomen, J., & de Gelder, B. (1999). Lexical access of resyllabified words: Evidence from phoneme monitoring. *Memory & Cognition*, *27*, 413–421.

Vroomen, J., van Linden, S., de Gelder, B., & Bertelson, P. (2007). Visual recalibration and selective adaptation in auditory—visual speech perception: Contrasting build-up courses. *Neuropsychologia*, *45*, 572–577.

Vroomen, J., van Linden, B., Keetels, M., de Gelder, B., & Bertelson, P. (2004). Selective adaptation and recalibration of auditory speech by lipread information: dissipation. *Speech Communication*, *44*, 55–61.

Vroomen, J., Tuomainen, J., & de Gelder, B. (1998). The roles of word stress and vowel harmony in speech segmentation. *Journal of Memory and Language*, *38*, 133–149.

Vroomen, J., van Zon, M., & de Gelder, B. (1996). Cues to speech segmentation: Evidence from juncture misperceptions and word spotting. *Memory & Cognition*, *24*, 744–755.

Wagner, A. (2008). *Phoneme inventories and patterns of speech sound perception*. Ph.D. dissertation, MPI Series in Psycholingvistics 49, Radboud University Nijmegen.

Wagner, A., & Ernestus, M. (2008). Identification of phonemes: Differences between phoneme classes and the effect of class size. *Phonetica*, *65*, 106–127.

Wagner, A., Ernestus, M., & Cutler, A. (2006). Formant transitions in fricative identification: The role of native fricative inventory. *Journal of the Acoustical Society of America*, *120*, 2267–2277.

Wagner, M., & Watson, D. G. (2010). Experimental and theoretical advances in prosody: A review. *Language and Cognitive Processes*, *25*, 905–945.

Wakefield, J. A., Jr., Doughtie, E. B., & Yom, B.-H. L. (1974). The identification of structural components of an unknown language. *Journal of Psycholinguistic Research*, *3*, 261–269.

Wang, Y., Spence, M., Jongman, A., & Sereno, J. (1999). Training American listeners to perceive Mandarin tones. *Journal of the Acoustical Society of America*, *106*, 3649–3658.

Ward, C. D., & Cooper, R. P. (1999). A lack of evidence in 4-month-old human infants for paternal voice preference. *Developmental Psychobiology*, *35*, 49–59.

Warner, N., Jongman, A., Cutler, A., & Mücke, D. (2001). The phonological status of Dutch epenthetic schwa. *Phonology*, *18*, 387–420.

Warner, N., Jongman, A., Sereno, J., & Kemps, R. (2004). Incomplete neutralization and other sub-phonemic durational differences in production and perception: Evidence from Dutch. *Journal of Phonetics*, *32*, 251–276.

Warner, N., Kim, J., Davis, C., & Cutler, A. (2005). Use of complex phonological patterns in processing: Evidence from Korean. *Journal of Linguistics*, *41*, 353–387.

Warner, N., Smits, R., McQueen, J. M., & Cutler, A. (2005). Phonological and statistical effects on timing of speech perception: Insights from a database of Dutch diphone perception. *Speech Communication*, *46*, 53–72.

Warner, N., & Weber, A. (2001). Perception of epenthetic stops. *Journal of Phonetics*, *29*, 53–87.

Warren, R. M. (1961). Illusory changes of distinct speech upon repetition—the verbal transformation effect. *British Journal of Psychology*, *52*, 249–258.

Warren, R. M. (1970). Perceptual restoration of missing speech sounds. *Science*, *167*, 392–393.

Warren, P., Rae, M., & Hay, J. (2003). Word recognition and sound merger: The case of the front-centering diphthongs in NZ English. In M. J. Solé, D. Recasens & J. Romero (Eds.), *Proceedings of the 15th International Congress of Phonetic Sciences*, Barcelona, Spain (pp. 2989–2992). Adelaide, Australia: Causal Productions [CD-ROM].

Watanabe, K. (1988). Sentence stress perception by Japanese students. *Journal of Phonetics*, *16*, 181–186.

Watson, D. G., Tanenhaus, M., & Gunlogson, C. (2008). Interpreting pitch accents in on-line comprehension: H* vs. L+H*. *Cognitive Science*, *32*, 1232–1244.

Wauquier-Gravelines, S. (1994). Segmentation lexicale en français parlé [Lexical segmentation in spoken French]. In *Proceedings of the XXèmes Journées d'Etude sur la Parole,* Trégastel (pp. 517–522). Lannion: Groupement TSS et France Télécom CNET/LAA.

Weber, A. (2001). Help or hindrance: How violation of different assimilation rules affects spoken-language processing. *Language and Speech*, *44*, 95–118.

Weber, A. (2002). Assimilation violation and spoken-language processing: A supplementary report. *Language and Speech*, *45*, 37–46.

Weber, A., & Cutler, A. (2004). Lexical competition in non-native spoken-word recognition. *Journal of Memory and Language*, *50*, 1–25.

Weber, A., & Cutler, A. (2006). First-language phonotactics in second-language listening. *Journal of the Acoustical Society of America*, *119*, 597–607.

Weber, C., Hahne, A., Friedrich, M., & Friederici, A. D. (2004). Discrimination of word stress in early infant perception: Electrophysiological evidence. *Cognitive Brain Research*, *18*, 149–161.

Weber-Fox, C. M., & Neville, H. J. (1996). Maturational constraints on functional specializations for language processing: ERP and behavioral evidence in bilingual speakers. *Journal of Cognitive Neuroscience*, *8*, 231–256.

van de Weijer, J. (1999). *Language input for word discovery*. Ph.D. dissertation, MPI Series in Psycholinguistics 9, University of Nijmegen.

van de Weijer, J. (2001a). Vowels in infant- and adult-directed speech. In A. Karlsson & J. van de Weijer (Eds.), *Lund Working Papers 49—Proceedings of Fonetik 2001* (pp. 172–175). Lund: Lund University Libraries.

van de Weijer, J. (2001b). *The importance of single-word utterances for early word recognition.* In *Proceedings of Early Language Acquisition (ELA2001).* Lyon, France.

van de Weijer, J. (2003). Consonant variation within words. In D. Archer, P. Rayson, A. Wilson & T. McEnery (Eds.), *Proceedings of the Corpus Linguistics 2003 Conference: University Centre for Computer Corpus Research on Language Technical Papers*, Lancaster (Vol. 16, pp. 184–190). Lancaster: Lancaster University.

van de Weijer, J. (2005). Listeners' sensitivity to consonant variation within words. *Lund Working Papers, 51*, 225–239.

Weikum, W. M., Vouloumanos, A., Navarra, J., Soto-Faraco, S., Sebastián-Gallés, N., & Werker, J. F. (2007). Visual language discrimination in infancy. *Science, 316*, 1159.

Wells, J. C. (1982). *Accents of English.* Cambridge: Cambridge University Press.

Werker, J. F. (1986). The effect of multilingualism on phonetic perceptual flexibility. *Applied Psycholinguistics, 7*, 141–156.

Werker, J. F. (1995). Exploring developmental changes in cross-language speech perception. In L. R. Gleitman & M. Liberman (Eds.) *An invitation to cognitive science: Language.* (pp. 87–106). Cambridge, MA: MIT Press.

Werker, J. F., Fennell, C. T., Corcoran, K. M., & Stager, C. L. (2002). Infants' ability to learn phonetically similar words: Effects of age and vocabulary size. *Infancy, 3*, 1–30.

Werker, J. F., Gilbert, J. H., Humphrey, K., & Tees, R. C. (1981). Developmental aspects of cross-language speech perception. *Child Development, 52*, 349–355.

Werker, J. F., & Lalonde, C. E. (1988). Cross-language speech perception: Initial capabilities and developmental change. *Developmental Psychology, 24*, 672–683.

Werker, J. F., & McLeod, P. J. (1989). Infant preference for both male and female infant-directed talk: A developmental study of attentional and affective responsiveness. *Canadian Journal of Psychology, 43*, 230–246.

Werker, J. F., Pegg, J. E., & McLeod, P. J. (1994). A cross-language investigation of infant preference for infant-directed communication. *Infant Behavior and Development, 17*, 323–333.

Werker, J. F., & Polka, L. (1993). Developmental changes in speech perception: New challenges and new directions. *Journal of Phonetics, 21*, 83–101.

Werker, J. F., Pons, F., Dietrich, C., Kajikawa, S., Fais, L., & Amano, S. (2007). Infant-directed speech supports phonetic category learning in English and Japanese. *Cognition, 103*, 147–162.

Werker, J. F., & Tees, R. C. (1984a). Cross-language speech perception: Evidence for perceptual reorganization during the first year of life. *Infant Behavior and Development, 7*, 49–63.

Werker, J. F., & Tees, R. C. (1984b). Phonemic and phonetic factors in adult cross-language speech perception. *Journal of the Acoustical Society of America, 75*, 1866–1878.

Whalen, D. H. (1984). Subcategorical phonetic mismatches slow phonetic judgments. *Perception & Psychophysics, 35*, 49–64.

Whalen, D. H., Levitt, A. G., & Wang, Q. (1991). Intonational differences between the reduplicative babbling of French- and English-learning infants. *Journal of Child Language, 18*, 501–516.

White, K. S., & Morgan, J. L. (2008). Sub-segmental detail in early lexical representations. *Journal of Memory and Language, 59*, 114–132.

Whitney, P., McKay, T., Kellas, G., & Emerson, W. A. Jr. (1985). Semantic activation of noun concepts in context. *Journal of Experimental Psychology: Learning, Memory, and Cognition, 11*, 126–135.

van Wijngaarden, S. J., Steeneken, H. J. M., & Houtgast, T. (2002). Quantifying the intelligibility of speech in noise for non-native listeners. *Journal of the Acoustical Society of America, 111*, 1906–1916.

Williams, J. N. (1988). Constraints upon semantic activation during sentence comprehension. *Language and Cognitive Processes, 3*, 165–206.

Wilson, C. (2006). Learning phonology with substantive bias: An experimental and computational study of velar palatalization. *Cognitive Science, 30*, 945–982.

Wingfield, A., Goodglass, H., & Lindfield, K. C. (1997). Word recognition from acoustic onsets and acoustic offsets: Effects of cohort size and syllabic stress. *Applied Psycholinguistics, 18*, 85–100.

Winkler, I., Kushnerenko, E., Horváth, J., Čeponienė, R., Fellman, V., Huotilainen, M., Näätänen, R., & Sussman, E. (2003). Newborn infants can organize the auditory world. *Proceedings of the National Academy of Sciences of the United States of America, 100*, 11812–11815.

Winters, S. J., Levi, S. V., & Pisoni, D. B. (2008). Identification and discrimination of bilingual talkers across languages. *Journal of the Acoustical Society of America, 123*, 4524–4538.

Wong, P. C. M., & Perrachione, T. K. (2007). Learning pitch patterns in lexical identification by native English-speaking adults. *Applied Psycholinguistics, 28*, 565–585.

Wong, P. C. M., Skoe, E., Russo, N. M., Dees, T., & Kraus, N. (2007). Musical experience shapes human brainstem encoding of linguistic pitch patterns. *Nature Neuroscience, 10*, 420–422.

Woodrow, H. (1909). A quantitative study of rhythm: The effect of variations in intensity, rate, and duration. *Archives de Psychologie, 14*, 1–66.

Woutersen, M., de Bot, K., & Weltens, B. (1995). The bilingual lexicon: Modality effects in processing. *Journal of Psycholinguistic Research, 24*, 289–298.

Wright, R. (2003). Factors of lexical competition in vowel articulation. In J. Local, R. Ogden & R. Temple (Eds.), *Phonetic interpretation: Papers in laboratory phonology 6* (pp. 75–87). Cambridge: Cambridge University Press.

Wright, S., & Kerswill, P. (1989). Electropalatography in the analysis of connected speech processes. *Clinical Linguistics & Phonetics, 3*, 49–57.

Wurm, L. H. (1997). Auditory processing of prefixed English words is both continuous and decompositional. *Journal of Memory and Language, 37*, 438–461.

Wurm, L. H. (2000). Auditory processing of polymorphemic pseudowords. *Journal of Memory and Language, 42*, 255–271.

Wurm, L. H., & Aycock, J. (2003). Recognition of spoken prefixed words: The role of early conditional root uniqueness points. In R. H. Baayen & R. Schreuder (Eds.), *Morphological structure in language processing* (pp. 259–286). Berlin: Mouton de Gruyter.

Wurm, L. H., & Ross, S. E. (2001). Conditional root uniqueness points: Psychological validity and perceptual consequences. *Journal of Memory and Language*, *45*, 39–57.

Wurm, L. H., & Samuel, A. G. (1997). Lexical inhibition and attentional allocation during speech perception: Evidence from phoneme monitoring. *Journal of Memory and Language*, *36*, 165–187.

Yaeger-Dror, M. (1994). Phonetic evidence for sound change in Quebec French. In P. Keating (Ed.), *Phonological structure and phonetic form—Papers in laboratory phonology 3* (pp. 267–292). Cambridge: Cambridge University Press.

Yamada, R. A. (1995). Age and acquisition of second language speech sounds: Perception of American English /ɹ/ and /l/ by native speakers of Japanese. In W. Strange (Ed.), *Speech perception and linguistic experience: Issues in cross-language research* (pp. 305–320). Baltimore: York Press.

Ye, Y., & Connine, C. M. (1999). Processing spoken Chinese: The role of tone information. *Language and Cognitive Processes*, *14*, 609–630.

Yip, M. C. W. (2000). Spoken word recognition of Chinese homophones: The role of context and tone neighbors. *Psychologia*, *43*, 135–143.

Yip, M. C. W. (2001). Phonological priming in Cantonese spoken-word processing. *Psychologia*, *44*, 223–229.

Yip, M. C. W. (2004a). Possible-word constraints in Cantonese speech segmentation. *Journal of Psycholinguistic Research*, *33*, 165–173.

Yip, M. C. W. (2004b). Interference effects of possible-word constraints (PWC) in Cantonese speech segmentation. *Psychologia*, *47*, 169–177.

Ylinen, S., Shestakova, A., Alku, P., & Huotilainen, M. (2005). The perception of phonological quantity based on durational cues by native speakers, second-language users and nonspeakers of Finnish. *Language and Speech*, *48*, 313–338.

Yoon, Y. B., & Derwing, B. L. (1995). Syllable saliency in the perception of Korean words. In K. Elenius & P. Branderus (Eds.), *Proceedings of 13th International Congress of Phonetic Sciences, Stockholm* (Vol. 2, pp. 602–605). Stockholm: KTH and Stockholm University.

Yoon, Y. B., & Derwing, B. L. (2001). A language without a rhyme: Syllable structure experiments in Korean. *Canadian Journal of Linguistics*, *46*, 187–237.

Zamuner, T. S. (2006). Sensitivity to word-final phonotactics in 9- to 16-month-old infants. *Infancy*, *10*, 77–95.

Zipf, G. K. (1935). *The psychobiology of language: An introduction to dynamic philology*. Cambridge, MA: MIT Press.

Zipf, G. K. (1949). *Human behaviour and the principle of least effort*. Reading, MA: Addison-Wesley.

Zhou, X., & Marslen-Wilson, W. (1994). Words, morphemes and syllables in the Chinese mental lexicon. *Language and Cognitive Processes*, *9*, 393–422.

Zhou, X., & Marslen-Wilson, W. (1995). Morphological structure in the Chinese mental lexicon. *Language and Cognitive Processes*, *10*, 545–600.

van Zon, M. (1997). *Speech processing in Dutch: A cross-linguistic approach.* Ph.D. dissertation, Tilburg University.

Zwicky, A. (1979). Classical malapropisms. *Language Sciences, 1,* 339–348.

Zwitserlood, P. (1989). The locus of the effects of sentential-semantic context in spoken-word processing. *Cognition, 32,* 25–64.

Zwitserlood, P. (1996). Form priming. *Language and Cognitive Processes, 11,* 589–596.

Zwitserlood, P., & Schriefers, H. (1995). Effects of sensory information and processing time in spoken-word recognition. *Language and Cognitive Processes, 10,* 121–136.

Name Index

Subject Index